The Government Contracts Reference Book

The Government Contracts Reference Book

A Comprehensive Guide to the Language of Procurement

Ralph C. Nash, Jr.
Steven L. Schooner

Joan Nelson Phillips, Editor in Chief

The George Washington University
WASHINGTON DC

© Copyright 1992 by The George Washington University

This publication is designed to provide accurate and authoritative information in regard to the subject matter covered. It is sold with the understanding that the publisher is not engaged in rendering legal, accounting, or other professional service. If legal advice or other expert assistance is required, the services of a competent professional person should be sought.

—From the *Declaration of Principles* jointly adopted by a Committee of the American Bar Association and a Committee of Publishers and Associations.

This book does not represent an official position of the U.S. Department of Justice or any other U.S. Government agency.

Library of Congress Cataloging in Publication Data

Nash, Ralph C.
    The government contracts reference book : a comprehensive guide to the language of procurement / Ralph C. Nash, Jr., Steven L. Schooner : Joan Nelson Phillips, editor in chief.
        p. cm.
    Includes bibliographical references.
    ISBN 0-935165-19-3
    1. Public contracts—United States—Encyclopedias. 2. Contracts. Letting of—United States—Encyclopedias. 3. Government purchasing—Law and legislation—United States—Encyclopedias. I. Schooner, Steven L. II. Phillips, Joan Nelson. III. Title.
KF846.4.N37 1992
346.73'023'03—dc20
[347.3062303]   92-8925
                                        CIP

About the Authors

Ralph C. Nash, Jr., is a widely recognized author and lecturer in the Government contracts field. A Professor of Law at the National Law Center of The George Washington University, he founded the University's Government Contracts Program in 1960 and served as its Director from 1960 to 1966 and from 1979 to 1984. In addition to teaching, he does consulting work for Government agencies, private corporations, and law firms. He is active in the Public Contracts Section of the American Bar Association, is a member of the Procurement Round Table, and is a Fellow and serves on the Board of Advisors of the National Contract Management Association. Professor Nash is the author of *Government Contract Changes* and the coauthor of several texts, including *Formation of Government Contracts*, *Administration of Government Contracts*, *Cost Reimbursement Contracting*, *Patents and Technical Data*, and *Construction Contracting*. He received an A.B. from Princeton University and a J.D. from The George Washington University.

Steven L. Schooner practices Government contract law in the Commercial Litigation Branch of the Department of Justice. Previously, he practiced with private law firms and served as a Commissioner at the Armed Services Board of Contract Appeals. He received his B.A. from Rice University, J.D. from the College of William and Mary, and LL.M. from The George Washington University. He is a Certified Professional Contracts Manager, an Associate Editor of the American Bar Association's *Public Contract Law Journal*, and the author or coauthor of articles published in the *Public Contract Law Journal*, the *Construction Lawyer*, and other professional publications.

Contents

Preface

The Government Contracts Reference Book began to take shape in 1989, when Steve Schooner saw the need for a dictionary-style work that all manner of practitioners in the Government contracts field could consult for accessible, concise, definitive, information. Steve drafted the original plans for such a work and laid the foundation. He combed the regulations and other authoritative sources for terms and definitions. He then put the framework in place, augmenting rudimentary definitions with summary, explanatory, and illustrative discussions and with references to additional information sources.

At Ralph Nash's hand, the work reached its present dimensions and took on a distinctive style. Through his collaboration, beginning in 1990, the number of entries and the size of the manuscript grew dramatically, and the book's scope and format were refined. Each entry was given a "nutshell" definition, followed by statements of significance or function in the Government procurement context. Many more sources of useful information were identified. Individual entries and sets of related entries became, in effect, mini-tutorials on their subject matter.

The book's design and construction benefited from the labors of many individuals. Bill Greene added NASA-specific terms, nuances, and references. Ed Lovett did the same from a DoE perspective. J. Jones and LeRoy Ward expanded and enhanced the ADP-related entries. Jim Nagle contributed legal and construction-related entries. Each of these five also suggested many useful improvements to the work as a whole. Richard Loeb and Matthew Blum of OFPP's Cost Accounting Standards Board reviewed and refined the cost-related coverage, and Bob Centola suggested improvements in the coverage on Federal

ix

appropriations. In addition, Mark Flanigan's and Don Vogler's considerable efforts in the early editorial stages enhanced both content and readability.

Many skilled and devoted craftspeople contributed to this work. Bill Reilly performed a comprehensive language edit of the manuscript and contributed substantive additions to many of the entries. Barbara Barnes undertook copy editing as well as the tedious but crucial work of bringing uniformity to the book's mass of references and cross-references. Patty Tobin, supported by her staff at the Government Contracts Program library, tirelessly tracked down information, supplied and checked citations, and offered helpful suggestions. Leslie Dimond did the cover and book design, and Claudia Jao lent her touch to the pages. Carol Martin's and Midge Easter's word processing and proofreading skills lightened the editorial load, as did Margaret Shirley's eye and ear.

Finally, credit must go to Ed Phelps. His initial enthusiasm for the concept, and his forbearance throughout, have provided the underpinning for the effort.

Each facet of the work on this book has served to reveal further work needed: entries yet to be added, statements to be clarified, information to be updated, cross-references to be included. Even as we go forward with this first printing, we are planning the additions, renovations, and improvements to be made in future editions. In that effort, we welcome any contributions from you, our readers.

Joan Nelson Phillips
Editor in Chief

How to Use This Reference Book

To Find the Term You're Looking For

Alphabetization

This book uses the letter-by-letter mode of alphabetizing used in most dictionaries and encyclopedias. Multiple-word terms are treated as single words. For example,

CONTRACT INSURANCE/PENSION REVIEW

follows **CONTRACTING OUT** as though it were spelled

CONTRACTINSURANCEPENSIONREVIEW

without spacing or punctuation. Similarly, **FORM, FIT, AND FUNCTION DATA** follows **FORMAL SOURCE SELECTION**, as spaces and commas are disregarded.

Terms containing numbers are alphabeticized by treating the numbers as words. **8(a) PROGRAM** is alphabetized as **EIGHTAPROGRAM**, for example, and **A-76 POLICY** as **ASEVENTYSIXPOLICY**.

Acronyms and Abbreviations

Because many terms in Government contracting have acronyms or abbreviations, and because these shortened forms are often as familiar as the full terms, common-use acronyms and abbreviations have been included in the book's entry titles:

COST-PLUS-FIXED FEE (CPFF) CONTRACT

QUALIFIED PRODUCTS LIST (QPL)

Virtually all entry titles, however, are terms spelled out in full (**RE-QUEST FOR PROPOSALS (RFP)** as opposed to **RFP**, for example). If you want to look up an acronym or abbreviation but don't know what it stands for, you can find the full term in *Acronyms and Abbreviations Used in This Reference Book*, which begins on page 429. You can also refer to this listing if you need to look up one of the handful of acronyms (FAR, DoD, DoE, GSA, NASA, and a few others) that have been used in the text without full-term introduction in order to save space.

To Locate Additional Information

Cross-References

In order to gain a better understanding of one term, it will sometimes be helpful to refer to the book's entry on another term. The book's cross-referencing system has therefore been designed to guide you to entries that provide additional detail, discuss closely related concepts, or define terminology that must be read with a precise meaning. To save space and preserve readability, most such cross-references are made internally by using SMALL CAPITALS to highlight the appropriate words within the body of the original entry:

> The contractor is generally entitled to a time extension if there is an EXCUSABLE DELAY and to additional compensation if there is a COMPENSABLE DELAY.

To enable the cross-reference to be made within syntax, certain letters or inconsequential words are sometimes added to the exact entry title, in lowercase:

> The term is generally used with regard to LETTER CONTRACTs.

> A common law rule providing that an ACCEPTANCE OF an OFFER becomes effective (creates a binding contract) when . . .

Alternatively, a "see" or "see also" reference may be used:

> . . . it was held that the measure for determining the amount of an EQUITABLE ADJUSTMENT is reasonable cost (see REASONABLENESS OF COST) . . .

> See also CERTIFICATION OF CLAIM.

Note that, when a term is fully defined at another entry, a *blind* entry is provided:

> **PETTY CASH**   See IMPREST FUND.

Much of the value of this book lies in the cross-referencing structure, which will enable you to get a basic but sound introduction to many subject areas by studying sets of related terms.

References to Other Sources

Many of the entries in *The Government Contracts Reference Book* will lead you to pertinent information to be found in various other documents.

Most entries cite other documents (frequently the Federal Acquisition Regulation (FAR)) as the source for the capsule definitions provided or for other statements made. In such cases, the source document is cited immediately following the definition or statement derived from it:

> **CONTRACTING** Purchasing, renting, leasing, or otherwise obtaining supplies or services from non-Federal sources. FAR 2.101.

Note that, taking care to preserve the original meaning, we have edited or paraphrased these excerpts when necessary to conform them to this book's editorial style, enhance their readability, or present in them information derived from several sentences or paragraphs of the source document.

In addition to the FAR, regulations cited in this book include the Department of Defense FAR Supplement (DFARS), the Department of Energy Acquisition Regulation (DEAR), the National Aeronautics and Space Administration (NASA) FAR Supplement (NFS), and the Federal Information Resources Management Regulation (FIRMR). References to these regulations are current as of December 1991; in some cases, proposed changes pending at that time are noted. Readers are encouraged to refer to fully up-to-date copies of the regulations themselves, both to read the excerpted information in context and to determine whether it has been affected by post-1991 revision.

Many of the book's entries treat or cite procurement-related statutes. In most cases, reference is made to the current (1991) version of the U.S. Code. Pertinent court and board of contract appeals decisions are referenced as well, following *A Uniform System of Citation* ("Blue Book") style.

Some 50 texts are cited in this reference book. They appear in the entries in roman (regular) typeface, often with "see" (or "see also") references to signal that they provide useful information beyond that synopsized in this book:

See The U.S. Government Manual.

See Cibinic and Nash, Administration of Government Contracts 817–72.

To save space, these citations are limited to the following elements, as applicable: author(s); volume number; title; chapter, section, or page. Complete bibliographic information can be found in the listing *Texts Cited in This Reference Book*, beginning on page 439.

Scores of articles from more than 20 different periodicals are cited as well. These citations give the author's (authors') last name(s), article title (in italics), applicable volume/issue/page data, periodical name, and date:

> Martell and Featherstun, *Convenience Termination: More Selected Problems*, 91-13 Briefing Papers (Dec. 1991)

> Vogel, *Impossibility of Performance—A Closer Look*, 9 Pub. Cont. L.J. 110 (1977)

To find the full name of the periodical as well as information about the publisher, refer to the listing *Periodicals Cited in This Reference Book*, which begins on page 443.

In addition to texts and periodicals, many other types of documents are referenced in this book. These are documents issued by both Government and private industry, and they take a number of forms: pamphlet, booklet, study report, manual, and so forth. Their titles are italicized, and information on obtaining them is provided, in the entries in which they appear.

A

ABSTRACT OF BIDS See ABSTRACT OF OFFERS.

ABSTRACT OF OFFERS The record of all bids received on an unclassified, sealed-bid procurement. FAR 14.403 requires the BID OPENING officer to personally and publicly open all BIDs received and have them recorded on Standard Form (SF) 1409, Abstract of Offers, FAR 53.301-1409, or SF 1410, Abstract of Offers—Construction, FAR 53.301-1410. The bid opening officer must complete the abstract and certify its accuracy as soon after bid opening as possible. Because they are available for public inspection, abstracts will not contain information about failure to meet minimum standards of RESPONSIBILITY, apparent collusion of bidders, or other matters properly exempt from public disclosure. When bid items are too numerous to warrant complete recording, abstract entries for individual bids may be limited to item numbers and corresponding prices.

ACCELERATED PERFORMANCE See ACCELERATION.

ACCELERATED PROCEDURE A procedure for the accelerated disposition of appeals before the agency BOARDs OF CONTRACT APPEALS (BCAs) that is required by the CONTRACT DISPUTES ACT (CDA) OF 1978 at 41 U.S.C. 607(f). This procedure is sometimes referred to as the "Rule 12.3 procedure" because it is implemented by Uniform Rule 12.3 (see UNIFORM RULES). The accelerated procedure applies to claims of $50,000 or less, and the contractor alone may elect it. The Government is powerless to stop the contractor from electing the procedure in appropriate circumstances. Uniform Rule 12.1(c) explains that the contractor must make the election to proceed pursuant to Rule 12.3 within 60 days of receipt of the notice of docketing "unless such period is extended by the Board for good cause." The BCA has 180 days

1

after the election to issue a decision on the appeal. For claims of $10,000 or less, a contractor may elect an alternate expedited procedure (see EXPEDITED PROCEDURES). Neither procedure is available if the contractor appeals the decision of the contracting officer to the CLAIMS COURT (Cl. Ct.). See *Report of the Federal Contract Claims and Remedies Committee on Ways of Expediting Appeals Before the Boards of Contract Appeals*, 16 Pub. Cont. L.J. 161 (1986).

ACCELERATION   The speeding up of the work to complete performance earlier than otherwise anticipated. If a contractor accelerates on its own initiative to ensure completion within the contract schedule, the additional costs of that acceleration are not recoverable from the Government. In addition, the Schedules for Construction Contracts clause in FAR 52.236-15 permits the contracting officer to order acceleration without compensation if the contractor has fallen behind schedule. Compensable acceleration occurs when the Government orders accelerated performance that is not required to meet the current contract schedule. This generally occurs constructively (as a type of CONSTRUCTIVE CHANGE) when the Government requires the contractor to meet the current contract schedule in the face of an EXCUSABLE DELAY. Such a delay entitles the contractor to a schedule extension, and an order to meet the original schedule is equivalent to an order to complete the work in advance of schedule. A constructive acceleration thus typically entails an excusable delay, Government knowledge of the delay, some Government statement or act construed as an acceleration order, notice by the contractor that the order is a constructive change, and incurring of additional costs of accelerated effort. See Cibinic and Nash, Administration of Government Contracts 339–40.

ACCEPTANCE OF OFFER   The formal act of the recipient of an OFFER, typically the Government, that results in a legally binding contract. The standard forms for issuing solicitations—Standard Form (SF) 33, Solicitation, Offer, and Award, FAR 53.301-33; SF 1442, Solicitation, Offer, and Award (Construction, Alteration, or Repair), FAR 53.301-1442—contain a block for the signature of the CONTRACTING OFFICER (CO) signifying acceptance. Acceptance is also made by sending a NOTICE OF AWARD. Acceptance is generally binding at the time of transmission of the acceptance document (the MAILBOX RULE). See Cibinic and Nash, Formation of Government Contracts 162–77.

ACCEPTANCE OF WORK The act of an authorized representative of the Government by which the Government, for itself or as an agent of another, (1) assumes ownership of existing identified supplies tendered or (2) approves specific services rendered as partial or complete performance of a contract. FAR 46.101. Acceptance of supplies or services is the responsibility of the contracting officer. FAR 46.502. Acceptance constitutes acknowledgment that the supplies or services conform to applicable contract quality and quantity requirements. Acceptance may take place before delivery, at the time of delivery, or after delivery, depending on the terms and conditions of the contract. Neither supplies nor services are ordinarily accepted before completion of Government contract QUALITY ASSURANCE (QA) actions. Acceptance is usually evidenced by execution of an acceptance certificate on an inspection and receiving report (see MATERIAL INSPECTION AND RECEIVING REPORT (MIRR)) or commercial shipping document/packing list. FAR 46.501. Acceptance has unusual legal significance in Government contracting because the Inspection of Supplies—Fixed-Price clause in FAR 52.246-2 and the Inspection of Construction clause in FAR 52.246-12 make acceptance "conclusive" on the Government except for LATENT DEFECTs, FRAUD, GROSS MISTAKEs AMOUNTING TO FRAUD, and any right of the Government under warranties (see WARRANTY). See Hedlund, *The Relationship of Government Contract Warranties to Inspection and Acceptance*, 29 A.F. L. Rev. 103 (1988); Cibinic and Nash, Administration of Government Contracts 621–66; Bednar, chap. 10, Construction Contracting 815–24.

ACCESSORY ITEM An item that facilitates or enhances the operation of PLANT EQUIPMENT but is not essential for its operation. FAR 45.501. With regard to management of GOVERNMENT PROPERTY in the possession of contractors, FAR 45.505-5 requires that a contractor maintain the property record of accessory items as part of the record of the associated plant equipment.

ACCORD AND SATISFACTION A method of resolving an issue whereby the parties agree (enter into an executory "accord") to (1) give and accept something ("satisfaction") in settlement of the issue and (2) perform the agreement. If the performance is not rendered, the other party has the election to pursue its rights under the original contract. If the performance is rendered, the new contract discharges the original contract. Restatement (Second) of Contracts § 279. Accord and satisfaction is normally accomplished by execution of a bilateral MODIFICATION and payment by the Government in accordance with the modification. See Cibinic and Nash, Administration of Government Contracts 928–33.

ACCOUNTING CLASSIFICATION REFERENCE NUMBER (ACRN) A two-position control code used in all contracts assigned for contract administration to DLA's DEFENSE CONTRACT MANAGEMENT COMMAND (DCMC) or to the plant cognizance representatives of the military departments and agencies. It provides a method of relating the long-line accounting classification citation number to detailed line-item scheduled information. DFARS 204.7107. The ACRN may be any combination of a discrete two-position alphanumeric code assigned to each accounting classification within each contract (except that the letters "I" and "O" are not used). The code is shown as a detached prefix to the long-line accounting classification number, usually in the Accounting and Appropriation Data block of the contract. DFARS 204.7107(d).

ACCUMULATING COSTS Collecting cost data in an organized manner, such as through a system of accounts. FAR 31.001. Cost Accounting Standard 401, FAR 30.401, requires that a contractor's practices in estimating costs in order to price a proposal be consistent with the COST ACCOUNTING PRACTICEs the contractor uses in accumulating contract costs, and that, conversely, the contractor's practices in accumulating actual contract costs be consistent with practices used in pricing the related proposal.

ACCURATE, COMPLETE, AND CURRENT The standard that COST OR PRICING DATA must meet when submitted in accordance with the TRUTH IN NEGOTIATIONS ACT (TINA). When the data are required, contractors must certify as soon as practicable after reaching agreement, that, to the best of their knowledge and belief, the data submitted to the contracting officer meet the standard as of the date the contractor and the Government agreed on a price. FAR 15.804-4. If, before agreement on price, the contracting officer learns that any cost or pricing data submitted are inaccurate, incomplete, or noncurrent (see DEFECTIVE COST OR PRICING DATA), the contracting officer should bring the information to the attention of the contractor so that the data can be corrected, completed, or made current. After contract award, the Government is entitled to a price adjustment, including profit or fee, of any "significant" amount by which the price was increased because the data were inaccurate, incomplete, or noncurrent. FAR 15.804-7. See the Price Reduction for Defective Cost or Pricing Data clause at FAR 52.215-22. And see Cibinic and Nash, Administration of Government Contracts 97–99.

ACQUISITION Acquiring by contract, with appropriated funds, supplies or services (including construction) by and for the use of the Federal Government through purchase or lease, whether the supplies or services are already in existence or must be created, developed, demonstrated, and evaluated. FAR 2.101. Acquisition begins at the point when agency needs are established and includes description of the agency's requirements, solicitation and selection of sources, award of contracts, contract financing, contract performance, contract administration, and those technical and management functions directly related to the process of fulfilling agency needs by contract. The procurement statutes generally use the synonymous term PROCUREMENT. However, "acquisition" is generally used in the FAR to describe this activity. See Cibinic and Nash, Administration of Government Contracts 13–22.

ACQUISITION FORECASTING Public announcement of annual contract opportunities pursuant to the Business Opportunity Development Reform Act of 1988, 15 U.S.C. 631 *et seq*. NASA defines "contract opportunity" as planned new contract awards exceeding $25,000, and, as required by statute, issues a publicly available forecast and semiannual update of expected contract opportunities for the fiscal year. Opportunities for small business concerns, particularly those owned by socially and economically disadvantaged individuals, are included. NFS Subpart 18-7.72.

ACQUISITION INSTRUMENT IDENTIFICATION A system for identifying numbers to be assigned to NASA contracts and related instruments. NFS Subpart 18-4.71. The basic number will remain unchanged throughout the life of the instrument. It consists of 11 alphanumeric characters. A five-position "prefix" begins with "NAS" (except for certain reimbursable contracts, which use "DEN") and ends with a two-position identifier of the installation responsible for the contract. A hyphen is inserted after the prefix and is followed by a six-position set of serial numbers assigned by each installation, without regard to fiscal year or type of contract. (As an exception, "(F)" appears in the final position for facilities contracts.) The two-position installation identifier used in the contract number prefix is also used as the initial two positions of solicitation numbers, but the rest of the solicitation identifying numbers are installation-unique. Purchase orders, including blanket purchase orders, use a simplified identification system. NFS 18-4.7103. See also PROCUREMENT INSTRUMENT IDENTIFI-CATION (PII) NUMBERS.

ACQUISITION LIFE CYCLE See ACQUISITION PROCESS.

ACQUISITION PLAN A plan addressing all technical, business, management and other significant considerations that will control an acquisition. It summarizes ACQUISITION PLANNING delibera-tions and must identify milestones for decisions in the acquisition process. FAR 7.105 contains detailed guidance on the contents of written acquisition plans. See Cibinic and Nash, Formation of Government Contracts 320–22.

ACQUISITION PLANNING The process by which the efforts of all personnel responsible for an acquisition are coordinated and integrated through a comprehensive plan for fulfilling the agency need in a timely manner and at a reasonable cost. Acquisition planning includes developing the overall strategy for managing the acquisition. FAR 7.101. This planning process is conducted pursuant to the statutory requirement in 10 U.S.C. 2305(a)(1)(A)(ii) and 41 U.S.C. 253a(a)(1)(B) that agencies conduct "advance procurement planning." Its purpose is to ensure that FULL AND OPEN COMPETITION is obtained to the greatest extent feasible. FAR Part 7 prescribes policies and procedures for (1) developing ACQUISITION PLANs, (2) determining whether to use commercial or Government resources for acquisition of supplies or services, and (3) deciding whether it is more economical to lease equipment than to purchase it. Some agencies prescribe extensive additions and/or modifications to the FAR guidance (DFARS Subpart 207.1; NFS Subpart 18-7.1). See Cibinic and Nash, Formation of Government Contracts 319–37.

ACQUISITION PROCESS A basic framework for managing a DoD system ACQUISITION PROGRAM, from identification of a mission need for the SYSTEM to be acquired through production, imple-mentation, and improvement of that system. DoD Directive 5000.2, *Defense Acquisition Management Policies and Proce-dures*, 23 Feb. 1991, parts 2 and 3, delineates the five phases of the process, each preceded by a milestone or other decision point, during which the system goes through research, development, test and evaluation, and production. These phases are: (1) concept exploration, (2) demonstration and validation, (3) development, (4) production and deployment, and (5) operations support.

ACQUISITION PROGRAM A directed effort (1) aimed at providing a new or improved capability to meet a validated need and (2) funded through a procurement appropriation or a research, development, test, and evaluation (RDT&E) appropriation. An acquisition program may include development, procurement, and modification of systems, subsystems, equipment, and components. It may also involve supporting equipment, systems, projects, and studies. Postak, Glossary of Terms, in Subcontracts—Government and Industry Issues.

ACQUISITION SAVINGS Savings resulting from the application of a VALUE ENGINEERING CHANGE PROPOSAL (VECP) to contracts awarded by the same contracting office or its successor for essentially the same unit. FAR 48.001. Acquisition savings include: (1) INSTANT CONTRACT SAVINGS, (2) CONCURRENT CONTRACT SAVINGS, and (3) FUTURE CONTRACT SAVINGS. See Cibinic and Nash, Administration of Government Contracts 308–11.

ACQUISITION STRATEGY The conceptual framework for conducting a MAJOR SYSTEM acquisition. The term encompasses the broad concepts and objectives that direct and control the overall development, production, and deployment of a system. OMB Circular No. A-109, *Major System Acquisitions*, 5 Apr. 1976, establishes the requirements for developing an acquisition strategy. Such a strategy must be written, must be tailored to the particular needs of the system acquisition program, and must set forth an overall plan for satisfying the mission need in the most effective, economical, and timely manner. The contents of a written acquisition strategy are the same as those of an ACQUISITION PLAN, subject to any requirements peculiar to the major system acquisition. FAR 34.004.

ACQUISITION STREAMLINING Effort of a procuring agency that results in more efficient and more effective use of resources to design, develop, produce, or deploy quality systems. FAR 7.101. The objective of acquisition streamlining is to reduce the time and cost required for acquiring systems and to improve the quality of those systems by ensuring that solicitations and contracts contain only those necessary specifications, standards, and related documents that have been tailored (see TAILORING) for application at the most appropriate time in the acquisition cycle. FAR 10.002. See Nash, *Acquisition Streamlining: Revamping the Competitive Negotiation Process*, 4 N&CR ¶ 38 (June 1990); *Defense Management: Efforts to Streamline Acquisition Management Structure*, GAO/NSIAD-91-15 (Dec. 1990). Streamlining techniques are being tested by DoD (see DoD Directive 5000.2, *Defense Acquisition Management Policies and Procedures*, 23 Feb. 1991, part 10C) and NASA.

ACTUAL CASH VALUE The cost of replacing damaged property with other property of like kind and quality in the physical condition of the property immediately before the damage. FAR 31.001. Cost Accounting Standard 416, FAR 30.416, states that in measuring actual losses to be covered by a contractor's SELF-INSURANCE program, the amount of loss must be measured, in part, by the actual cash value of the property destroyed. FAR 30.416-50(a)(2).

ACTUAL COST An amount determined on the basis of incurred costs as distinguished from forecasted costs. FAR 30.301, 31.001. Actual costs include STANDARD COSTs properly adjusted for applicable variances. They are those costs sustained in fact, on the basis of costs incurred, as distinguished from projected or estimated costs. Armed Services Pricing Manual (ASPM) vol. 1, app. B. The actual cost history of producing the same or a similar product is a fact taken into account when COST ANALYSIS is performed. Actual costs can also be used, as a general rule, when EQUITABLE ADJUSTMENTs can be determined after the work has been performed. See HISTORICAL COST.

ACTUARIAL ASSUMPTION A prediction of future conditions affecting PENSION PLAN costs (such as mortality rate, employee turnover, compensation levels, pension fund earnings, and changes in values of pension funds assets). FAR 31.001. Cost Accounting Standard 412, FAR 30.412, provides that, in accounting for pension costs and allocating them to COST OBJECTIVEs, actuarial assumptions must be separately identified and take into account past as well as anticipated experience. It also states that their validity may be evaluated on an aggregate basis. FAR 30.412(b)(2).

ACTUARIAL COST METHOD A technique that uses actuarial assumptions to measure the present value of future pension benefits and pension fund administrative expenses, and that assigns the cost of such benefits and expenses to COST ACCOUNTING PERIODs. FAR 31.001. Under Cost Accounting Standard 412, FAR 30.412, an actuarial cost method used in determining and measuring component costs of a defined-benefit PENSION PLAN must measure separately (1) the normal cost of the cost accounting period, (2) a part of any unfunded ACTUARIAL LIABILITY, (3) an interest equivalent on the unamortized portion of such liability, and (4) an adjustment for any ACTUARIAL GAIN AND LOSS. FAR 30.412-40. Alternatively, such a cost method must meet the four requirements for any other projected-benefit cost method set forth at 30.412-50(b)(2).

ACTUARIAL GAIN AND LOSS The effect on PENSION PLAN costs resulting from differences between ACTUARIAL ASSUMPTIONs and actual experience. FAR 31.001. Cost Accounting Standard 413, FAR 30.413, provides guidance on adjusting pension costs by measuring actuarial gains and losses and assigning them to COST ACCOUNTING PERIODs. It requires that actuarial gains and losses (1) be calculated annually and assigned to the cost accounting period for which the actual valuation is made and to subsequent periods and (2) identified separately from unfunded actuarial liabilities. It permits them to be amortized through subsequent pension contributions or offset by gains and losses in subsequent cost accounting periods. FAR 30.413-40(a), -50(a), -50(b)(2)(iii).

ACTUARIAL LIABILITY Pension costs attributable, under the ACTUARIAL COST METHOD in use, to the years preceding the date of a particular actuarial valuation. FAR 31.001. As of such date, the actuarial liability represents the excess of the present value of the future benefits and administrative expenses over the present value of future contributions, for the normal cost for all PENSION PLAN participants and beneficiaries. The excess of the actuarial liability over the value of the assets of a pension plan is the unfunded actuarial liability. Pension plan costs applicable to prior years that were specifically unallowable (see ALLOWABLE COST) under then-existing Government contracts must be separately identified and excluded from unfunded actuarial liability. FAR 30.412-50(a)(2).

ADDENDUM An alteration of a solicitation issued by the contracting agency to all potential offerors prior to the time for receipt of bids or proposals. This term is no longer used; the FAR uses the term AMENDMENT.

ADEQUATE COMPETITION The level of competition required in competitive negotiated procurements (see NEGOTIATION) prior to the COMPETITION IN CONTRACTING ACT (CICA) in order to justify AWARD ON INITIAL PROPOSALS. In general, this was a sufficient amount of competition to ensure that the award price was a FAIR AND REASONABLE PRICE. The term is no longer used in Federal procurement, but the concept of a sufficient amount of competition to ensure fair and reasonable prices is still found in FAR 13.106, dealing with the SET-ASIDE of SMALL PURCHASEs for small business.

ADEQUATE EVIDENCE Information sufficient to support the reasonable belief that a particular act or omission has occurred, for purposes of SUSPENSION of a contractor. FAR 9.403. FAR 9.407-1(b) requires agency officials to consider the amount of evidence, its credibility, whether there is corroboration of important allegations, and what inferences can reasonably be drawn. See Cibinic and Nash, Formation of Government Contracts 264–65.

ADEQUATE PRICE COMPETITION The degree of competition that permits the contracting officer to waive the requirement for COST OR PRICING DATA under the TRUTH IN NEGOTIATIONS ACT (TINA). FAR 15.804-3(b) provides that price competition exists when (1) offers are solicited, (2) two or more responsible (see RESPONSIBILITY) offerors that can satisfy the Government's requirements submit priced offers responsive to the solicitation's expressed requirements, and (3) these offerors compete independently for a contract to be awarded to the responsible offeror submitting the lowest evaluated price. If price competition exists, it is presumed to be adequate unless (1) one or more known and qualified offerors has been unreasonably denied an opportunity to compete, (2) the low offeror has such a decided advantage that it is practically immune from competition, or (3) the lowest price is determined to be unreasonable. A price is based on adequate price competition if it results directly from price competition, or if PRICE ANALYSIS alone clearly demonstrates that the price is reasonable in comparison with current or recent prices for the same (or substantially the same) items purchased in comparable quantities and under comparable terms and conditions, under contracts that resulted from adequate price competition. See Cibinic and Nash, Formation of Government Contracts 870–71.

ADJUSTMENT   An alteration of the contract price to reflect some changed circumstances in the performance of the contract. See EQUITABLE ADJUSTMENT and PRICE ADJUSTMENT.

ADMINISTRATIVE CHANGE   A unilateral contract CHANGE, in writing, that does not affect the substantive rights of the parties (for example, a change in the paying office or the appropriation data). FAR 43.101. See also MODIFICATION.

ADMINISTRATIVE CONTRACTING OFFICER (ACO)   A CONTRACTING OFFICER (CO) who is administering contracts. FAR 2.101. (Formal ACO designations are not made by all agencies.) An administrative contracting officer does most of his or her work after the PROCURING CONTRACTING OFFICER (PCO) has awarded the contract but generally does not have the authority to enter into MODIFICATIONs. An ACO functions at and through a contract administration office and performs contract administration functions involving, among other things, contractors' employee compensation structures and insurance plans, postaward orientation, forward pricing rate agreements, advance agreements, allowable costs, disputes, Cost Accounting Standards (CAS), progress payments, cost overruns, modifications, traffic management, tax exemption and duty-free entry certificates, labor relations, quality assurance, safety requirements, property administration, engineering surveillance, acceptance and rejection of waivers and deviations, value engineering programs, contractor purchasing system review, consent to subcontracts, and monitoring of small business subcontracting plan compliance. FAR 42.302. See Cibinic and Nash, Administration of Government Contracts 27–28.

ADMINISTRATIVE DISPUTE RESOLUTION ACT A 1990 act, 5 U.S.C. 581–593, that requires all Federal agencies to adopt a policy addressing the use of ALTERNATIVE DISPUTE RESOLUTION (ADR) procedures, in lieu of litigation, to settle claims and disputes. One such procedure, ARBITRATION, is allowed, for the first time, in situations in which all parties agree to its use. The act also amends the CONTRACT DISPUTES ACT (CDA) OF 1978 to authorize contracting officers to use ADR until 1 Oct. 1995. See Cibinic and Nash, *The Administrative Dispute Resolution Act: Making a Mountain out of a Molehill*, 5 N&CR ¶ 34 (June 1991); Parrette, *The Contract Disputes Act and the Administrative Dispute Resolution Act: A Richness of Remedies, Finally Ready for Trial*, 20 Pub. Cont. L.J. 293 (1991).

ADMINISTRATIVE JUDGE A member of a BOARD OF CONTRACT APPEALS (BCA) functioning under the CONTRACT DISPUTES ACT (CDA) OF 1978. 41 U.S.C. 607(b)(1). The term was created by the BCAs and is synonymous with the statutory term "member of an agency board." Commonly confused with the title "administrative law judge" (see Keyes, Government Contracts under the Federal Acquisition Regulation 528) the position of administrative judge was created by the Contract Disputes Act under Title 41, not by the Administrative Procedure Act under Title 5. Unlike administrative law judges, the BCAs' administrative judges are contract law specialists with 5 years or more of public contract law experience and are not subject to reassignment by the Office of Personnel Management (OPM). The Commerce Clearing House *Board of Contract Appeals Decisions* includes a looseleaf binder containing brief biographies of the various administrative judges (Commerce Clearing House, 4025 West Peterson Avenue, Chicago, IL 60646).

ADVANCE ACQUISITION An exception to the full funding policy which allows acquisition of long-lead-time items (advanced long-lead acquisition) or economic order quantities (see ECONOMIC ORDER QUANTITY (EOQ)) in a FISCAL YEAR (FY) previous to that in which the related end item is to be acquired. FAR 17.101. Advance acquisitions may include materials, parts, and components as well as costs associated with the further processing of those materials, parts, and components. DoD is authorized to make use of this technique in multiyear procurements by 10 U.S.C. 2306(h)(4).

ADVANCE AGREEMENT An agreement as to the allowability of costs, negotiated by a contracting officer and a contractor before the costs are incurred. See ALLOWABLE COST. FAR 31.109 provides guidance on the negotiation of such agreements and suggests their use to avoid possible subsequent DISALLOWANCE or DISPUTE based on unreasonableness or nonallocability (see REASONABLENESS OF COST and ALLOCABLE COST) of "special or unusual costs." Advance agreements may be negotiated either before or during a contract. The advance agreement must be (1) in writing, (2) executed by both contracting parties, and (3) incorporated into applicable current and future contracts. It must contain a statement of its applicability and duration. Advance agreements may be negotiated with a particular contractor for a single contract, for a group of contracts, or for all contracts with a contracting office, an agency, or several agencies. See also FAR Subpart 42.10 and DFARS Subpart 242.10, which discuss the negotiation of advance agreements for INDEPENDENT RESEARCH AND DEVELOPMENT (IR&D) costs and BID AND PROPOSAL (B&P) COSTS.

ADVANCE PAYMENT   An advance of money made by the Government to a contractor before, in anticipation of, and applicable to performance under a contract or contracts. Armed Services Pricing Manual (ASPM) vol. 1, app. B. Agencies may authorize advance payments in negotiated and sealed-bid contracts if appropriate under the civilian or defense procurement acts (41 U.S.C. 255 and 10 U.S.C. 2307, respectively) or under Pub. L. 85-804, 50 U.S.C. 1431-1435, which provides for EXTRAORDINARY CONTRACTUAL ACTION. FAR 32.401. Agencies should authorize advance payments sparingly, as they are the least preferred method of contract FINANCING. FAR 32.106. However, advance payments may be appropriate for R&D with educational institutions and for the management and operation of Government-owned plants. FAR 31.403. For advance payments to be authorized, the statutes provide that (1) the contractor must give adequate security, (2) the payments must not exceed the unpaid contract price, and (3) the agency head or a designee must determine that advance payment is in the public interest or facilitates the national defense. FAR 32.402-411 contains detailed guidance on these requirements. When advance payments are used, the Advance Payments clause in FAR 52.232-12 is required. FAR 32.412. See Cibinic and Nash, Administration of Government Contracts 885–87.

ADVANCE PROCUREMENT PLANNING   See ACQUISITION PLANNING.

ADVERTISED PROCUREMENT The preferred form of procurement before the passage of the COMPETITION IN CONTRACTING ACT (CICA). This term was synonymous with FORMAL ADVERTISING and is now called SEALED BIDDING. See Shnitzer, Government Contract Bidding 3-6 and 3-7.

ADVERTISEMENT Any single message prepared for placement in communications media, regardless of the number of placements. FAR 5.501. FAR Subpart 5.5 provides guidance on the use of paid advertisements as a means of informing potential offerors of contracting opportunities with the Government. FAR 31.205-1 places strict limitations on the allowability of the advertising costs incurred by contractors. NASA does not permit the use of paid advertisements for procurement purposes. NFS 18-5.502. See ALLOWABLE COST and RECRUITMENT COSTS.

ADVERTISING MATERIAL Material designed to acquaint the Government with a prospective contractor's present products or potential capabilities, or to determine the Government's interest in buying these products. FAR 15.501. FAR 15.503(b) provides that such materials are not UNSOLICITED PROPOSALs.

ADVISORY AND ASSISTANCE SERVICES Services acquired to support or improve agency policy development, decision making, management, and administration, or to support or improve the operation of management systems. FAR 37.201. Acquisition of advisory and assistance services is a legitimate way to improve Government services and operations. Such services may be used at all organizational levels to help managers achieve maximum effectiveness or economy in their operations. FAR 37.202. Advisory and assistance services may take the form of information, advice, opinions, alternatives, conclusions, recommendations, training, or direct assistance. FAR 37.203. Such services are treated in OMB Circular No. A-120 (revised), *Guidelines for the Use of Advisory and Assistance Services*, 4 Jan. 1988; OFPP Policy Letter 89-1, *Conflict of Interest Policies Applicable to Consultants*; and DoD Directive 4205.2, *DoD Contracted Advisory and Assistance Services (CAAS)*, 27 Jan. 1986. To implement OFPP Letter 89-1, FAR 9.507-1(c) requires the inclusion of the Organizational Conflicts of Interest Certificate—Advisory and Assistance Services provision in solicitations for advisory and assistance services when the contract amount is expected to exceed $25,000. DFARS Subpart 237.270 authorizes the award of master agreements under which orders may be placed for specific advisory and assistance services.

AEROSPACE INDUSTRIES ASSOCIATION OF AMERICA (AIA) A nonprofit trade association representing the nation's manufacturers of commercial, military, and business aircraft, helicopters, aircraft engines, missiles, spacecraft, and related components and equipment. AIA's professional staff works through councils and committees made up of volunteers from member companies who develop policy on significant issues and present industry's point of view. AIA speaks for industry on such issues as procurement policy, legislative affairs, civil aviation, environmental concerns, technology development, and internationalization of the industry. (AIA, 1250 Eye Street, N.W., Washington, DC 20005; (202) 371–8400.)

AFFILIATES Associated business concerns or individuals if, directly or indirectly, (a) either one controls or can control the other or (b) a third party controls or can control both. FAR 2.101. In determining whether a company qualifies as a SMALL BUSINESS CONCERN, the sales and employees of an affiliate are combined with the sales and employees of the company being evaluated. FAR 19.101 contains a detailed definition of this term when it is used to determine the SIZE STATUS of a firm. Purchases from affiliates are MAKE ITEMs rather than BUY ITEMs. Affiliates are also subject to DEBARMENT or SUSPENSION. FAR Subpart 9.4. See Cibinic and Nash, Formation of Government Contracts 268–70.

AFFILIATION See AFFILIATES.

AFFIRMATIVE ACTION A contractual requirement under the Equal Opportunity clause, FAR 52.222-26, to take positive steps to ensure that a contractor's workforce is composed of members of minority groups commensurate with their representation in the local area. Detailed requirements are set forth in Department of Labor regulations at 41 CFR 60-2. Generally, a contractor must (1) make a utilization analysis of its workforce, (2) determine that there is underutilization of minority groups that are not employed in representative percentages, (3) establish a set of "goals and timetables" to reach representative percentages, and (4) adopt policies for recruitment and training that will assist in achieving the goals. Prime contractors performing contracts in excess of

$500,000 must also take affirmative action to subcontract with LABOR SURPLUS AREA (LSA) CONCERNs. FAR 20.301, 52.220-3. See Cibinic and Nash, Formation of Government Contracts 984–86.

AFFIRMATIVE ACTION PROGRAM   A contractor's program that complies with Department of Labor regulations in 41 CFR 60-1 and 60-4 to ensure EQUAL EMPLOYMENT OPPORTUNITY (EEO) to minorities and women. FAR 22.801. Under such program a contractor must use best efforts to bring its employment of minorities and women to a level commensurate with the number of minorities and women in the community through AFFIRMATIVE ACTION. Such efforts include establishing employment goals, adopting a timetable for reaching such goals, and recruiting and training minorities and women. See Cibinic and Nash, Formation of Government Contracts 986–88.

AGENCY   Any executive department, military department or defense agency, or other agency or independent establishment of the executive branch. FAR 9.403. This term has a variety of meanings depending on the context in which it is used. See Cibinic and Nash, Formation of Government Contracts 2–4, for a discussion of the term. See FAR 24.101 for a slightly different definition of the term.

AGENCY HEAD   See HEAD OF THE AGENCY.

AGENCY-PECULIAR PROPERTY   Government-owned personal property that is peculiar to the mission of one agency. FAR 45.301. DFARS 245.301 defines the term as used in DoD; NFS 18-45.501, as used by NASA. Agency-peculiar material excludes Government material, SPECIAL TEST EQUIPMENT, SPECIAL TOOLING, and FACILITIES.

AGENCY PROCUREMENT REQUEST (APR)   A request by a Federal agency for the GENERAL SERVICES ADMINISTRATION (GSA) to (1) acquire FEDERAL INFORMATION PROCESSING (FIP) RESOURCES for the agency or (2) provide a DELEGATION OF PROCUREMENT AUTHORITY (DPA) to the agency to acquire these items. FIRMR 201-4.001. An agency submits an APR if the conditions of its contemplated procurement are not covered by a regulatory delegation (FIRMR 201-20.305-1) or by a specific agency delegation (FIRMR 201-20.305-2). See FIRMR Bulletin C-5, *Dele-*

gation of Procurement Authority for a Specific Acquisition, for procedures agencies must follow and the information that must be included in an APR.

AGENCY RECORD A document in the possession of a Government agency that is subject to the provisions of the FREEDOM OF INFORMATION ACT (FOIA). The act contains no definition of "agency record," but the term has been interpreted broadly in litigation. See Nash and Rawicz, Patents and Technical Data 531–48.

AGREEMENT A written instrument of understanding, negotiated between an agency or contracting activity and a contractor, containing contract clauses that will apply to future contracts. See FAR Subpart 16.7. The two types of agreements described in the FAR are BASIC AGREEMENTs (BAs) and BASIC ORDERING AGREE-MENTs (BOAs). Agreements are not contracts that are legally binding on the parties because the Government makes no promise to purchase any supplies or services. However, agreements facilitate the making of future contracts because they spell out all standard terms and conditions of such future contracts.

AIR FREIGHT FORWARDER An indirect air carrier that is responsible for the transportation of property from the point of receipt to the point of destination, and utilizes for the whole or any part of such transportation the services of a direct air carrier or its agent, or of another air freight forwarder. FAR 47.401. These contracts are subject to the requirements of the FLY AMERICAN ACT when they move property that is financed by the Government. See FAR 47.404.

ALL-DISPUTES CLAUSE A DISPUTEs clause that gives the BOARDs OF CONTRACT APPEALS (BCAs) jurisdiction to hear all disputes "RELATING TO THE CONTRACT." The current Disputes clause in FAR 52.233-1 is an all-disputes clause. The adoption of such a clause was one of the major innovations included in the CONTRACT DISPUTES ACT (CDA) OF 1978. Its main benefit is that it precludes the contractor from having to file CLAIMs on one contract in both the agency BCA and the court (called FRAGMEN-TATION OF REMEDIES).

ALLOCABLE COST A cost that is assignable or chargeable to one or more COST OBJECTIVEs in accordance with the relative benefits received or other equitable relationships defined or agreed upon by contractual parties. Armed Services Pricing Manual (ASPM) vol. 1, app. B. FAR 31.201-4 provides that a cost is allocable to a Government contract if it (1) is incurred specifically for the contract, (2) benefits both the contract and other work, and can be distributed in reasonable proportion to the benefits received, or (3) is necessary to the overall operation of the business, although a direct relationship to any particular cost objective cannot be shown. See Cibinic, *Confusion Between Allocability and Allowability*, 5 N&CR ¶ 14 (Mar. 1991).

ALLOCATION OF COST   The assignment of an item of cost, or a group of items of cost, to one or more COST OBJECTIVEs; the term includes both direct assignment of cost and the reassignment of a share from an INDIRECT COST POOL. FAR 31.001. Substantial guidance on the proper allocation of costs is contained in the COST ACCOUNTING STANDARDS (CAS) in FAR Part 30 (which have been proposed for recodification at 48 CFR Chapter 99, to be published also in a supplementary chapter of the FAR; see 56 Fed. Reg. 26968 (12 June 1991)). See ALLOCABLE COST.

ALLOCATION OF FUNDS   In DoD, the process by which the Assistant Secretary of Defense (Comptroller) subdivides APPORTIONMENTs among the Secretaries of the military departments, by which the Secretaries further subdivide the funds among their heads of operating agencies, and by which the heads of operating agencies in turn subdivide (suballocate) the funds among their subordinate commanders. Hill, The Dollars and Sense of Government Contract Funding 54–55.

ALLOCATION OF WORK   The assignment of work to a source without following the normal competitive processes.   FAR Subpart 8.7 requires the allocation of certain specified work to workshops for the BLIND AND OTHER SEVERELY HANDICAPPED.

ALLOTMENT   In DoD, the process by which commanders, Major Commanders, or Special Operating Agencies distribute their allocated funds (see ALLOCATION OF FUNDS) to themselves, to installation commanders, or to other subordinate organizations. This process may continue into as many suballotments as necessary.   Hill, The Dollars and Sense of Government Contract Funding 55.

ALLOWABLE COST A cost that the Government will permit to be recovered (reimbursed by the Government) for the performance of a contract. FAR 31.201-2 provides that the factors to be considered in determining whether a cost is allowable include (1) reasonableness (see REASONABLENESS OF COST), (2) allocability (see ALLOCABLE COST), (3) standards promulgated by the COST ACCOUNTING STANDARDS (CAS) BOARD, (4) GENERALLY ACCEPTED ACCOUNTING PRINCIPLES (GAAP) and practices appropriate to the particular circumstances, (5) the terms of the contract, and (6) any limitations set forth in FAR Subpart 31.2. FAR 31.205 contains detailed guidance on the allowability of 51 categories of "selected costs." Costs, including directly associated costs, that are expressly unallowable must be identified and excluded from any billing, claim, or proposal applicable to a Government contract. FAR 31.201-6. See 10 U.S.C. 2324 for special rules and sanctions that apply to allowable costs under defense contracts. And see Cibinic, *Confusion Between Allocability and Allowability*, 5 N&CR ¶ 14 (Mar. 1991).

ALTERNATIVE DISPUTE RESOLUTION (ADR) Any procedure that is used, in lieu of litigation, to resolve issues in controversy, including but not limited to, settlement negotiations, conciliation, facilitation, mediation, fact finding, MINITRIALs, and ARBITRATION. FAR 33.201. Such techniques are now recognized and encouraged by the Administrative Dispute Resolution Act, 5 U.S.C. 581–593, as implemented by FAR Subpart 33.2. The techniques are intended to resolve DISPUTEs without the time, expense, and cost of formal litigation, whether before a court or an agency BOARD OF CONTRACT APPEALS (BCA). ADR is sometimes called "alternate" dispute resolution. It includes any alternative to full-scale litigation, whether mandatory or voluntary, binding or nonbinding, structured or unstructured. ADR is often conducted with the understanding that the record of the proceeding will be kept confidential and that—if the selected method's conclusions are not acceptable to either party—the normal litigation process may be begun or resumed. See Arnavas and Duffy, *Alternative Dispute Resolution*, 88-8 Briefing Papers (July 1988); Administrative Conference of the United States, Sourcebook: Federal Agency Use of Alternative Means of Dispute Resolution (compilation of articles, papers, and agency examples); Cibinic and Nash, *The Alternative Dispute Resolution Act: Making a Mountain out of a Molehill*, 5 N&CR ¶ 34 (June 1991).

ALTERNATIVE SOURCE SELECTION PROCEDURES Procedures, used by a Government agency to solicit COMPETITIVE PROPOSALS, that do not conform to the detailed requirements of FAR Subpart 15.6. FAR 15.613 permits agencies to adopt such procedures. See the DoD "Four Step" procedure in DFARS 215.613, the NASA procedure in NFS 18-15.613, and the DoE procedure in DEAR 915.613. Generally, these procedures provide for limited discussion with offerors prior to SOURCE SELECTION and NEGOTIATION with the winning contractor after selection.

AMBIGUITY Contract language that is capable of being understood to have more than one meaning. The test for determining whether the language is ambiguous is whether reasonable persons would find the contract subject to more than one interpretation. A PATENT ambiguity is obvious, since it arises from defective, obscure, or senseless language. In contrast, a LATENT ambiguity arises from language that appears clear and intelligible but that—because of some extrinsic fact or extraneous evidence—requires interpretation or a choice between two or more possible meanings. Black's Law Dictionary. See also CONTRA PROFERENTEM. Contractors frequently receive EQUITABLE ADJUSTMENTs for latent ambiguities, but they are held to a DUTY TO SEEK CLARIFICATION of patent ambiguities. See Cibinic and Nash, Administration of Government Contracts, chap. 2, for complete guidance on the process of contract interpretation. See Gottleib, *Latent & Patent Conditions*, 27 Cont. Mgmt. 20 (Aug. 1987); Nash, *Ambiguities: They Can't Be Proved by Subsequent Clarification of the Language*, 5 N&CR ¶ 25 (May 1991).

AMENDMENT An alteration to a solicitation. FAR 14.208, 15.410. The FAR distinguishes between amendments and modifications: amendments alter solicitations and modifications alter contracts. Amendments must be issued on Standard Form 30, Amendment of Solicitation/Modification of Contract, FAR 53.301-30. FAR 14.208(a), 15.410(a). Failure to acknowledge receipt of an amendment to an INVITATION FOR BIDS (IFB) can result in a bid being nonresponsive. FAR 14.208. Detailed instructions on the proper response upon receipt of an amendment are set forth in the solicitation provisions Amendments to Invitations for Bids in FAR 52.214-3 and Amendments to Solicitations in FAR 52.215-8. In normal legal terminology an amendment is a formal legal document altering a contract by mutual agreement (hence signed by both parties). FAR 43.103 discusses such documents using the terms "bilateral modification" (see MODIFICATION) and SUPPLE-MENTAL AGREEMENT. See Cibinic and Nash, Formation of Government Contracts 365–69.

AMENDMENT WITHOUT CONSIDERATION   A contract alteration that benefits the contractor but contains no consideration to the Government. Authority to make such alterations is conferred by Pub. L. 85-804, 50 U.S.C. 1431–1435, as implemented by Executive Order 10789, 14 Nov. 1958, as amended. Procedures for use of this authority are set forth in FAR Part 50, EXTRAORDINARY CONTRACTUAL ACTION.

AMERICAN INSTITUTE OF ARCHITECTS (AIA)   A national professional society, founded in 1857, whose members are licensed architects, graduate architects, and retired architects. AIA promotes design excellence and fosters professionalism and accountability through professional development programs and achievement awards. It also maintains a 30,000-volume library and publishes reference books and standard documents on legal, contract, and accounting forms. The organization maintains a Government Affairs department. (AIA, 1735 New York Avenue, N.W., Washington, DC 20006; (202) 626–7300.)

AMERICAN SOCIETY OF CIVIL ENGINEERS (ASCE)   A national professional society of engineers founded in 1852. ASCE supports research, offers continuing education courses and technical specialty conferences, and presents achievement awards. It also offers bibliographic information retrieval services. (ASCE, 345 E. 47th Street, New York, NY 10017; (212) 705–7496.)

AMERICAN SUBCONTRACTORS ASSOCIATION (ASA)   A national trade association, founded in 1966, whose members are construction subcontractors of trades and specialties such as foundations, concrete, masonry, steel, mechanical, drywall, electrical, painting, plastering, roofing, and acoustical. ASA works with other segments of the construction industry to promote ethical practices, beneficial legislation, and business education. It maintains a Government Relations committee. (ASA, 1004 Duke Street, Alexandria, VA 22314; (703) 684–3450.)

AMORTIZATION   An accounting procedure that gradually reduces the cost value of a limited life or intangible asset through periodic charges to income. Barron's Finance and Investment Handbook.

When the purchase method of accounting for a BUSINESS COMBI-NATION is used, allowable amortization is limited to the amounts that would have been allowed had the combination not taken place. FAR 31.205-52. In measuring and allocating the COST OF CAPITAL COMMITTED TO FACILITIES in accordance with Cost Accounting Standard 414, FAR 30.414, contractors must take into account INTANGIBLE CAPITAL ASSETS subject to amortization.

ANNOUNCEMENT OF OPPORTUNITY (AO) A NASA BROAD AGENCY ANNOUNCEMENT (BAA) generally used to solicit proposals for on-board flight experiments. Special proposal preparation, evaluation, and selection regulations are found in NFS Subpart 18-70.1, NASA Acquisition of Investigations System. The regulations are also available as an offprint, NHB 8030.6, Guidelines for the Acquisition of Investigations. AOs are publicized in the same manner as other solicitations and also through a mailing list maintained by the Office of Space Science and Applications, Code S, at NASA Headquarters.

ANNUAL APPROPRIATION See APPROPRIATION.

ANNUAL FUNDING The current congressional practice of including in authorizations and appropriations authority and funds to cover the needs of an agency for only one FISCAL YEAR (FY) at a time. FAR 17.101. This practice is used, with rare exceptions, for all types of APPROPRIATIONs. It can lead to inefficient procurement on a year-to-year basis but can be overcome by the use of OPTIONs or MULTIYEAR CONTRACTING. See Principles of Federal Appropriations Law (2d ed.), chap.2.

ANNUAL RECEIPTS The annual average gross revenue of a concern. In some instances, the qualification of a company as a SMALL BUSINESS CONCERN is determined by its annual receipts. For companies in business over 3 years, the amount is determined by averaging the receipts for the last 3 fiscal years. For a company in business for less than 3 complete fiscal years, total receipts for the period it has been in business are divided by the number of weeks including fractions of a week that it has been in business, and multiplied by 52. FAR 19.101 contains a detailed definition of the types of revenues that are included in annual receipts. See also STANDARD INDUSTRIAL CLASSIFICATION (SIC).

ANSWER In a contract DISPUTE, a formal pleading presented to a court by the DEFENDANT, or to a BOARD OF CONTRACT APPEALS (BCA) by the RESPONDENT, in response to a COMPLAINT filed by the PLAINTIFF, or appellant (see APPELLANT BEFORE BOARD OF CONTRACT APPEALS and APPELLANT BEFORE FEDERAL CIRCUIT COURT OF APPEALS). This statement is normally filed by the Government because the plaintiff, or appellant, is normally the contractor.

ANTICIPATORY REPUDIATION Statements or acts of a contractor before an actual BREACH OF CONTRACT that indicate that the contractor does not intend or is unable to complete, or continue to perform under, the contract. Black's Law Dictionary. Anticipatory repudiation is sometimes called "anticipatory breach." Because the contractor has a duty to proceed under the contract, the contractor may, by statements, actions, or refusal to provide adequate assurance of performance, manifest intention not to perform. Generally in this case the Government need not wait for the performance period to run in order to terminate the contract for default (see TERMINATION FOR DEFAULT). See Cibinic and Nash, Administration of Government Contracts 717–24; Cibinic, *Anticipatory Repudiation: We're Out of Here*, 5 N&CR ¶ 15 (Mar. 1991); U.C.C. 2-610, 2-611.

ANTI-DEFICIENCY ACT A statute prohibiting Government agencies from obligating the Government, by contract or otherwise, in excess of or in advance of appropriations, unless authorized by some specific statute. Codified at 31 U.S.C. 1341–1351 since 1982, the act prevents Government employees from involving the Government in expenditures or liabilities beyond those contemplated and authorized by Congress. As a result, the Government uses clauses such as the Limitation of Cost clause at FAR 52.232-20 to limit its liability in COST-REIMBURSEMENT CONTRACTs. Government officers and employees can be fined or imprisoned for violating the act. The act's salient features include (1) prohibitions against authorizing or incurring obligations or expenditures in excess of amounts apportioned by the OFFICE OF MANAGEMENT AND BUDGET (OMB) or permitted by agency regulations and (2) establishment of procedures for determining responsibility for violations and for reporting them to the Congress and, through OMB, to the President. Jones, Glossary: Defense Acquisition Acronyms and Terms. See Principles of Federal Appropriations Law (2d ed.), chap. 6, part C; Cibinic and Nash,

Formation of Government Contracts 31, 38; Cibinic, *The Anti-Deficiency Act and Implied Warranty of Specifications: Strange Bedfellows*, 3 N&CR ¶ 8 (Jan. 1989).

ANTI-KICKBACK ACT OF 1986 An act, 41 U.S.C. 51–58, to deter subcontractors from making payments and contractors from accepting payments for the purpose of improperly obtaining or rewarding favorable treatment. FAR 3.502-2. The act prohibits any person from providing KICKBACKs, soliciting kickbacks, or including the amount of the kickback in the contract price. It imposes criminal penalties for engaging in these prohibited practices, provides for recovery of civil penalties by the United States, requires the reporting of suspected violations, and calls for the inclusion of contract provisions regarding the act. FAR 3.502-2. The act is implemented through the use of the Anti-Kickback Procedures clause in FAR 52.203-7. See Arnavas, *The New Anti-Kickback Act*, 87-9 Briefing Papers (Aug. 1987). See also COPELAND ANTI-KICKBACK ACT.

ANTI-LOBBYING ACT A 1919 act, 18 U.S.C. 1913, providing that no money appropriated by Congress may be used to pay for any personal service, advertisement, communication, or other device intended or designed to influence a member of Congress to favor or oppose any legislation or APPROPRIATION. The act does not prohibit requests, through proper official channels, for legislation and appropriations deemed necessary for the efficient conduct of the public business. The act includes criminal fines and imprisonment as penalties for violations. Another act, known as the BYRD AMENDMENT and passed in 1989, prohibits the use of appropriated funds to influence Government personnel (in both the legislative and executive branches). This act, implemented in FAR Subpart 3.8, requires certifications and disclosures on contracts exceeding $100,000. See also LOBBYING COSTS.

ANTITRUST VIOLATION A violation of a U.S. law intended to ensure that markets operate competitively. 10 U.S.C. 2305(b)(5) and 41 U.S.C. 253(B)(e) require that such violations be reported to the Attorney General. Any agreement or mutual understanding among competing firms that restrains the natural operation of market forces is suspect. FAR 3.303. See Kovacic, The Antitrust Government Contracts Handbook; Nash, *Antitrust Violations in Government Contracting*, 3 N&CR ¶ 66 (Sep. 1989); Eger, *Con-*

tractor Team Arrangements under the Antitrust Laws, 17 Pub. Cont. L.J. 595 (1988).

APPARENT AUTHORITY Obvious, evident, or manifest authority that a reasonably prudent person, using diligence and discretion, would, in view of a principal's conduct, naturally suppose the principal's agent to possess. Black's Law Dictionary. The Federal Government is not bound by unauthorized agents with apparent authority; only properly designated CONTRACTING OFFI-CERs (COs), or their representatives acting within the limits of their designated authority, can obligate the Government. Therefore, anyone dealing with the Government should ascertain whether a person who purports to act for the Government has the authority to do so, and not rely on a mere appearance of authority. See Cibinic and Nash, Formation of Government Contracts 63–89.

APPEAL FILE A file containing all documents pertaining to a DIS-PUTE, which Uniform Rule 4 (see UNIFORM RULES) requires the contracting officer to assemble. This file is frequently called the "Rule 4 file." It represents one of the more significant differences between appeals before a BOARD OF CONTRACT APPEALS (BCA) and litigation before the U.S. CLAIMS COURT (Cl. Ct). The Rule 4 procedure, applying only to BCA appeals, is intended to make all pertinent documents immediately available to the contractor and the BCA. The rule gives the contractor an opportunity to supplement this appeal file. Rule 4 requires and encourages both parties to present relevant documents in support of their respective cases and facilitates the production of documents as an aid to further discovery. It operates as an automatic, first-round discovery order without eliminating customary discovery proceedings; documents contained in the appeal file are considered, without further action by the parties, as part of the record upon which the BCA will render its decision. See Federal Bar Association, Manual for Practice Before the Boards of Contract Appeals III-11. In PRO-TESTs before the GENERAL SERVICES ADMINISTRATION BOARD OF CONTRACT APPEALS (GSBCA), an appeal file is called a *protest* file, containing the same information as discussed here.

APPEAL FROM A CONTRACTING OFFICER'S DECISION
The document that a contractor must file before a BOARD OF CON-TRACT APPEALS (BCA) to obtain review of a DECISION OF THE CON-TRACTING OFFICER. Contractors must file their appeals with the agency BCA and furnish a copy to the contracting officer within

90 days of receiving a contracting officer's decision. 41 U.S.C. 606; FAR 33.211. The notice of appeal should include (1) a statement of intent to appeal, (2) reference to a contract and the agency involved so that the BCA can identify the DISPUTE, and (3) signature by an authorized representative. GENERAL SERVICES ADMINISTRATION BOARD OF CONTRACT APPEALS (GSBCA) Rule 5 directs the contractor to include also "a brief account of the circumstances giving rise to the appeal." The contractor may begin an appeal on the basis of DEEMED DENIAL jurisdiction; if the contracting officer fails to render a decision within 60 days of a CLAIM, the CONTRACT DISPUTES ACT (CDA) OF 1978 deems that the contracting officer has denied the claim, and the contractor may appeal. 41 U.S.C. 605(c)(5). In lieu of appealing to the BCA, the contractor may bring a DIRECT ACCESS suit within 12 months in the CLAIMS COURT (Cl. Ct.). See Cibinic and Nash, Administration of Government Contracts 1001–13. See also COMPLAINT.

APPEAL FROM THE RULING OF A COURT OR BOARD A document, filed by either the contractor or the Government, requesting the COURT OF APPEALS FOR THE FEDERAL CIRCUIT (CAFC or Fed. Cir.) to review a decision of a BOARD OF CONTRACT APPEALS (BCA) or of the U.S. CLAIMS COURT (Cl. Ct.). A BCA's decision is final unless either the HEAD OF THE AGENCY (with prior approval of the Attorney General) or a contractor appeals the decision within 120 days after receipt of a copy. 41 U.S.C. 607. Appeals from rulings of the U.S. Claims Court must be made within 60 days. 28 U.S.C. 2521, 2107. It should be noted that, under the EQUAL ACCESS TO JUSTICE ACT (EAJA), 5 U.S.C. 504, the Government cannot appeal a BCA's award of ATTORNEY'S FEES.

APPELLANT BEFORE BOARD OF CONTRACT APPEALS The contractor that files an APPEAL FROM A CONTRACTING OFFICER'S DECISION before a BOARD OF CONTRACT APPEALS (BCA). Since all appeals are from a DECISION OF THE CONTRACTING OFFICER, regardless of whether the DISPUTE arises from a contractor or a Government CLAIM, the contractor is always the appellant. The Government thus becomes the RESPONDENT. In spite of the use of these titles, the Board conducts a DE NOVO review of the dispute. The contractor, or appellant, may be represented before the BCA by an attorney, by a corporate officer, or, in some instances, by himself or herself. See, for example, ARMED SERVICES BOARD OF CONTRACT APPEALS (ASBCA) Rule 26. Sole-proprietor contractors can handle their own appeals, partnerships can be represented by a partner, and corporations can be represented by a corporate officer. Of course, any of these types of contractors may retain an attorney, provided that the attorney has been admitted to practice in a State's highest court.

APPELLANT BEFORE FEDERAL CIRCUIT COURT OF APPEALS The party bringing an appeal before the U.S. COURT OF APPEALS FOR THE FEDERAL CIRCUIT (CAFC or Fed. Cir.), the court authorized by the CONTRACT DISPUTES ACT (CDA) OF 1978 to review the decisions of the BOARDs OF CONTRACT APPEALS (BCAs) or the CLAIMS COURT (Cl. Ct.). The appellant must have been one of the litigants in the forum from which the appeal is taken. If the appellant is the Government, it will be represented by the Justice Department, even if agency counsel represented it before the Board or the Claims Court.

APPLIED RESEARCH Effort that (1) normally follows BASIC RESEARCH but may not be severable from it, (2) attempts to determine and exploit the potential of scientific discoveries or improvements in technology, materials, processes, methods, devices or techniques, and (3) attempts to advance the state of the art. FAR 35.001. Applied research does not include DEVELOP-MENT—those efforts whose principal aim is design, development, or test of specific items or services to be considered for sale.

APPORTIONMENT A distribution made by the OFFICE OF MAN-AGEMENT AND BUDGET (OMB) of amounts available for OBLIGA-TION in an APPROPRIATION or fund account. Apportionments divide amounts available for obligation by specific time periods (usually quarters), activities, projects, or objects, or by a combina-tion of these. The amounts so apportioned limit the amount of obligations that may be incurred. Apportionment prevents the need for deficiency or supplemental appropriations and ensures that there is no need for drastic curtailment of the activity for which the appropriation is made. That is, apportionment should prevent an agency from spending its entire appropriation before the end of the FISCAL YEAR (FY) and requiring Congress to grant an additional appropriation or else allow activity to grind to a halt. Principles of Federal Appropriations Law (2d ed.), chap. 6, part C.

APPROPRIATED FUNDS Funds made available by Congress for specified purposes, including formation of contracts. See APPRO-PRIATION.

APPROPRIATION An authorization by act of Congress permitting Federal agencies to incur OBLIGATIONs and to make payments out of the Treasury for specified purposes. Appropriation acts make funds available for obligation for one FISCAL YEAR (FY) (annual appropriations), for a specified number of years (multiyear appropriations), or for an unlimited period (no-year appropriations). General appropriations are for broad categories of work (such as R&D, procurement, operation and maintenance) while specific appropriations are for specific projects (most frequently construction projects). Contractors are limited by the amounts in a specific appropriation but not by those in a general appropriation. See 31 U.S.C. 1301 *et seq.*; Principles of Federal Appropriations Law (2d ed.), chap. 2. An appropriation bill is a measure before a legislative body to authorize the expenditure of public moneys and to stipulate the amount, manner, and purpose of the various items of expenditure. Black's Law Dictionary.

APPROVAL A contracting officer's written notification to a contractor that the Government agrees with a proposed course of conduct. FAR 9.301 defines this term as it relates to the acceptance of test results when the contract requires FIRST ARTICLE TESTING.

APPROVED PURCHASING SYSTEM A contractor's purchasing system that has been reviewed and approved in accordance with the CONTRACTOR PURCHASING SYSTEM REVIEW (CPSR). FAR 44.101. A contractor with an approved purchasing system is required to get far less prior consent of the contracting officer for subcontracts that it issues during contract performance. See FAR 44.201.

APPROVING AUTHORITY An agency official or contract adjustment board authorized to approve EXTRAORDINARY CONTRACTUAL ACTIONs under Pub. L. 85-804, 50 U.S.C. 1431–1435, and Executive Order 10789, 14 Nov. 1958, as amended. FAR 50.001.

ARBITRATION A private dispute resolution technique whereby parties voluntarily refer disputes to an impartial third party (an arbitrator or panel of arbitrators, typically made up of experts in the field) for a decision based on the presentation of evidence and arguments. Arbitration typically proves more expeditious and less expensive than litigation. In binding arbitration, the parties agree in advance to be bound by the arbitrator's determination and award. Nonbinding arbitration differs in that the parties may consider the determination a recommendation rather than a final judgment. Arbitration, binding and nonbinding, has frequently been used between contractors and subcontractors. The Government, however, was not permitted to use binding arbitration (31 U.S.C. 3702(a); 8 Comp. Gen. 96 (1928)) until 1991, when such use was authorized by the ADMINISTRATIVE DISPUTE RESOLUTION ACT (with the proviso that the HEAD OF THE AGENCY be permitted to vacate any arbitration award). 5 U.S.C. 590(c). See Behre, *Arbitration: A Permissible or Desirable Method for Resolving Disputes Involving Federal Acquisition and Assistance Contracts?* 16 Pub. Cont. L.J. 66 (1986); Bednar, chap. 14, Construction Contracting 1021–72. See also ALTERNATIVE DISPUTE RESOLUTION (ADR).

ARCHITECT-ENGINEER (A-E) CONTRACT A Government contract for ARCHITECT-ENGINEER (A-E) SERVICES. Such contracts are entered into using special source selection procedures as required by the BROOKS ACT (ARCHITECT-ENGINEER PROCURE-MENTS). See FAR Subpart 36.6. These procedures are conducted in two phases. In the first phase, the agency prepares a "final selection list" of firms, in order of preference, that are considered the most highly qualified to perform the services based on all relevant criteria except the fee to be paid for the services. In the second phase, the contracting officer negotiates the contract with the most preferred firm on the selection list. If a satisfactory contract cannot be negotiated with this firm, the contracting officer is then permitted to negotiate with the next most preferred firm. See Ness and Medill-Jones, *A-E Government Contracts*, 88-11 Constr. Briefings (Oct. 1988); Braude, chap. 15, Construction Contracting.

ARCHITECT-ENGINEER (A-E) SERVICES Services in the field of architect-engineering, including (1) professional services of an architectural or engineering nature that are associated with research, development, design, construction, alteration, or repair of real property and are required by law to be performed by a registered, licensed, or certified architect or engineer; (2) such other professional services, as determined by the contracting officer, that logically or justifiably require performance by a registered or licensed architect or engineer; and (3) incidental services that members of the architectural or engineering professions or those in their employ may logically or justifiably perform in conjunction with professional architect-engineer services. FAR 36.102. These services must be acquired under the procedures set forth in the BROOKS ACT (ARCHITECT-ENGINEER PROCUREMENTS). See Braude, chap. 15, Construction Contracting; Ness and Medill-Jones, *A-E Government Contracts*, 88-11 Constr. Briefings (Oct. 1988). See also ARCHITECT-ENGINEER (A-E) CONTRACT.

AREAWIDE CONTRACT A master contract for UTILITY SERVICEs entered into between the GENERAL SERVICES ADMINISTRATION (GSA) and a utility service supplier, under the authority of 40 U.S.C. 481, to cover the utility service to all Federal agencies from that supplier for a period not to exceed 10 years. FAR 8.301. Federal agencies, including DoD, are covered when an authorization attached to the areawide contract is completed and accepted by the supplier and executed by the agency and the supplier. FAR 8.304-2. See FAR Subpart 8.3 for procedures to be followed in contracting for utility services.

"ARISING UNDER THE CONTRACT" Falling within the scope of a contract clause and therefore providing a remedy (usually an EQUITABLE ADJUSTMENT) for some event that occurred during contract performance. Prior to the enactment of the CONTRACT DISPUTES ACT (CDA) OF 1978, BOARDs OF CONTRACT APPEALS (BCAs) had jurisdiction only over DISPUTEs that were found to arise under the contract. Other cases were required to be resolved by the Court of Claims. The Contract Disputes Act abolished this rule by granting the BCAs jurisdiction over all disputes "RELATING TO THE CONTRACT." "Arising under the contract" still has significance, however, because the standard Disputes clause in FAR 52.233-1 provides that the contractor has a DUTY TO PROCEED only with regard to claims that meet the "arising under" test.

ARMED SERVICES BOARD OF CONTRACT APPEALS (ASBCA) DoD's BOARD OF CONTRACT APPEALS (BCA). As the largest BCA, the ASBCA employs 37 ADMINISTRATIVE JUDGEs (most agency BCAs consist of the minimum required 3 administrative judges) and maintains a pending docket of approximately 2,400 active appeals. Whereas most BCAs include one administrative judge who serves as the Board's chair and another who serves as vice chair, the ASBCA, because of its size, has three vice chairs. The ASBCA resolves disputes involving DoD, Department of State, Agency for International Development, Department of Health and Human Services, and other agencies. Although the ASBCA's offices are located in Falls Church, Virginia, the Board's administrative judges travel across the country and around the world to give contractors the opportunity to litigate their disputes. See Williams, *A Brief Look at the Armed Services Board of Contract Appeals*, 22 Pub. Cont. Newsl. 3 (Fall 1986); Nash, *The Armed Services Board of Contract Appeals: A Status Report* 1 N&CR ¶ 31 (Apr. 1987); Dingman, *Primary Jurisdiction and the Armed Services BCA*, 10 Geo. Mason U. L. Rev. 473 (Spring 1988).

ARMED SERVICES PRICING MANUAL (ASPM) A two-volume manual, based on the policies and procedures of the FAR and the DFARS, containing instructional material covering the entire range of CONTRACT PRICING. It uses detailed discussions and examples to illustrate the application of pricing policies to pricing problems, but it is not directive in nature. The first volume deals with contract pricing in general, whereas the second focuses specifically on PRICE ANALYSIS. The ASPM contains a topical index, appendices, a list of acronyms, and a short glossary. It is used for training in classrooms and on the job and also as a reference handbook. Copies may be purchased in looseleaf from the U.S. Government Printing Office, Washington DC 20402, or in reduced-size paperback form from Commerce Clearing House, Inc., 4025 West Peterson Avenue, Chicago, IL 60646.

ARMED SERVICES PROCUREMENT ACT (ASPA) The statute governing the procurement procedures followed by DoD, the NATIONAL AERONAUTICS AND SPACE ADMINISTRATION (NASA), and the Coast Guard. It was originally enacted in 1947 and is now codified at 10 U.S.C. 2301-2330. It has been modified numerous times, with the most sweeping changes enacted in the COMPETITION IN CONTRACTING ACT (CICA) in 1984. See Cibinic and Nash, Formation of Government Contracts 2–5. NASA derives its procurement authority from ASPA, but that does not modify its civilian agency role as established by the Space Act, 42 U.S.C. 2452.

ARMED SERVICES PROCUREMENT REGULATION (ASPR) The original regulation issued under the ARMED SERVICES PROCUREMENT ACT (ASPA) to promulgate the procedures to be followed by DoD. During its existence the ASPR was a top-level regulation that was by far the most complete procurement regulation in the Federal Government. It was in effect from 1948 to 1984, when it was renamed the DEFENSE ACQUISITION REGULATION (DAR). In 1984, the DAR was replaced by the current FEDERAL ACQUISITION REGULATIONS (FAR) SYSTEM combining defense and civilian agency regulations. Many of the DAR/ASPR clauses, provisions, and textual explanations survived the merger and were incorporated in simplified form into the FAR; many of those that failed to survive can now be found in the DEPARTMENT OF DEFENSE FAR SUPPLEMENT (DFARS).

ARMS EXPORT CONTROL ACT (AECA) A 1990 act, 22 U.S.C. 2751 *et seq.*, setting forth the U.S. policy of facilitating the common defense by controlling the export of products and technology through the requirement for mandatory licensing of exports, to friendly countries only, of data, research, development, production, procurement, and LOGISTICS support. The AECA provides for FOREIGN MILITARY SALES (FMS) for purposes including internal security, legitimate self-defense, maintenance or restoration of international peace and security, and participation in regional or collective arrangements.

AS-BUILT DRAWINGS See RECORD DRAWINGS.

A-76 POLICY The policy of the executive branch, first promulgated by the Bureau of the Budget in 1955, that the Government should generally rely on the private sector for commercially available goods and services. Detailed guidance on determining whether commercial activities should be performed under contract with commercial sources or in-house using Government facilities and personnel is contained in OMB Circular No. A-76 (revised), *Performance of Commercial Activities*, 16 Aug. 1983, most recently amended 28 Feb. 1991; its Supplement, containing the Cost Comparison Handbook; and FAR Subpart 7.3. The policy recognizes that some functions are inherently governmental and must be performed by Government personnel; it also states that the Government should contract out if certain criteria are met and should give appropriate consideration to relative cost in deciding between Government performance and performance under contract. OMB Circular No. A-76 and the FAR provide that in comparing the costs of Government and contractor performance, agencies must base the contractor's cost of performance on firm offers. See Perfilio, *Contracting Out: A Road Map*, 30 A.F. L. Rev. 69 (1988); Catania, *Contracting Out: Management and Labor at*

War under Section 7106 of the Civil Service Reform Act, 16 Pub. Cont. L.J. 287 (1986).

ASIAN-PACIFIC AMERICANS U.S. citizens whose origins are in Japan, China, the Philippines, Vietnam, Korea, Samoa, Guam, the United States Trust Territory of the Pacific Islands, the Northern Mariana Islands, Laos, Kampuchea (Cambodia), Taiwan, Burma, Thailand, Malaysia, Indonesia, Singapore, Brunei, Republic of the Marshall Islands, or the Federated States of Micronesia. FAR 19.001(b)(2). These persons are presumed to be socially and economically disadvantaged for the purpose of determining the ownership of a SMALL DISADVANTAGED BUSINESS CONCERN (SDBC). See FAR 52.219-2, 52.219-8.

AS-PLANNED DRAWINGS Drawings that show how a CONSTRUCTION contractor or subcontractor plans to perform the work under contract. Such drawings are updated as changes, delays, and other eventualities occur during performance and thus eventually take the form of "as-built" or RECORD DRAWINGS. They are often used, in conjunction with record drawings, to prove DELAY.

ASSEMBLY The piecing or bringing together of various interdependent or interrelated parts or components so as to make an operable whole or unit. FAR 22.601. Under the WALSH-HEALEY PUBLIC CONTRACTS ACT a company that performs assembly qualifies as a MANUFACTURER. The same result occurs under the BUY AMERICAN ACT as it applies to supplies.

ASSET An amount recorded on a contractor's BALANCE SHEET representing the value of property owned by or debts owed to the contractor. Assets may be cash, near-cash (accounts receivable, temporary investments, notes receivable), or nonmonetary. Nonmonetary assets consumed in the creation of goods and services have limited lives, while others, such as land, have unlimited lives. "Capital assets" are long-term assets that are not bought or sold in the normal course of business. Such assets may be further classified as TANGIBLE CAPITAL ASSETs and INTANGIBLE CAPITAL ASSETs.

ASSET ACCOUNTABILITY UNIT A TANGIBLE CAPITAL ASSET which is a component of plant and equipment that is capitalized (see CAPITALIZATION) when acquired or whose replacement is capitalized when the unit is removed, transferred, sold, abandoned, demolished, or otherwise disposed of. FAR 30.301. A contractor's capitalization policy must provide for identification of asset accountability units to the maximum extent practical. FAR 30.404-40(b)(2).

ASSIGNMENT OF CLAIMS   A contractor's transfer or making over to a bank, trust company, or other financing institution, as security for a loan to the contractor, of the contractor's right to be paid by the Government for contract performance. FAR 32.801. Under the Assignment of Claims Act, 31 U.S.C. 3727a, a contractor may assign moneys due—or to become due—under a contract, if (1) the contract specifies payments aggregating $1,000 or more; (2) the assignment is made to a bank, trust company, or other financing institution, including any Federal lending agency; (3) the contract does not prohibit the assignment; (4) the assignment covers all unpaid amounts payable under the contract, is made only to one party, and is not subject to further assignment; and (5) the assignee sends a written notice of the assignment to the contracting officer, to the SURETY on any bond applicable to the contract, and to the disbursing officer designated in the contract to make payment. FAR 32.802. See Vickery and Paalborg, *Assignment of Claims Act*, 87-3 Briefing Papers (Feb. 1987).

ASSIGNMENT OF CONTRACT   Transfer of the rights and obligations under a contract to another party. 31 U.S.C. 3727 and 41 U.S.C. 15 prohibit contractors from assigning contracts; however, assignment of contracts may be made with the consent of the contracting officer. *Tuftco Corp. v. United States*, 222 Ct. Cl. 277, 614 F.2d 740 (1980). Such assignments are called NOVATIONs in FAR Subpart 42.12, which contains procedures for entering into such agreements. See Nash and Cibinic, II Federal Procurement Law 1958–70; Mullin, *Novation Agreements in Response to Merger and Consolidation in the Aerospace Industry*, 29 A.F. L. Rev. 69 (1988); Victorino, Shirk, and Kennedy, *Acquisitions & Mergers*, 85-9 Briefing Papers (Sep. 1985).

ASSIGNMENT OF COST TO COST ACCOUNTING PERIODS   A method or technique used in determining the amount of cost to be assigned to individual COST ACCOUNTING PERIODs. FAR 30.302-1. Examples of COST ACCOUNTING PRACTICEs that involve the assignment of cost to cost accounting periods are requirements for the use of specified accrual basis accounting or cash basis accounting for a cost element.

ASSISTANCE SERVICES   See ADVISORY AND ASSISTANCE SERVICES.

ASSIST AUDIT   An audit performed by one audit office at the request of another. The assist audit is usually an adjunct to or an integral part of an audit being performed by the requesting audit office. Armed Services Pricing Manual (ASPM) vol. 1, app. B. The DEFENSE CONTRACT AUDIT AGENCY (DCAA) Contract Audit Manual explains that the prime contractor is primarily responsible for awarding subcontracts, monitoring their performance, and paying each subcontractor for the work accomplished under the subcontracts' terms. Accordingly, the prime contractor is also responsible for audits of its subcontractors. However, it is DCAA's policy to perform assist audits of incurred costs whenever such audits are determined to be of potential benefit to the Government and necessary to ensure adequate and effective review of a contractor's operations or cost representations. DCAA Contract Audit Manual (CAM) 6-801.1.

ASSOCIATED GENERAL CONTRACTORS OF AMERICA (AGC)   A national trade association, founded in 1918, whose members include general contractors, subcontractors, industry suppliers, and service firms. AGC conducts seminars and conferences, provides tax services, compiles statistics on job accidents, and bestows safety and outstanding achievement awards. It maintains 65 committees, including liaison committees with Federal agencies, and it publishes manuals, studies, and model contract documents. (AGC, 1957 E Street, N.W., Washington, DC 20006; (202) 393-2040.)

ATTORNEY'S FEES   Compensation, at an hourly rate, fixed rate, or contingent fee, for the performance of professional services. Most attorney's fees in Government contract litigation are paid at an hourly rate for time reasonably expended. In Government contracts, contractors generally cannot recover their attorney's fees for litigation against the Government. Under the EQUAL ACCESS TO JUSTICE ACT (EAJA), 5 U.S.C. 504, 28 U.S.C. 2412, however, small contractors can recover their attorney's fees and expenses in litigation before the CLAIMS COURT (Cl. Ct.) and the BOARDs OF CONTRACT APPEALS (BCAs) under the CONTRACT DISPUTES ACT (CDA) OF 1978. Recovery is permitted if (1) the small contractor becomes the PREVAILING PARTY, (2) the Government's position is not SUBSTANTIALLY JUSTIFIED, and (3) no special circumstances make an award unjust. See Kinlin, *Equal Access To Justice Act*, 16 Pub. Cont. L.J. 266 (1986). Costs related to legal proceedings are unallowable if the proceedings result in a criminal conviction, imposition of a monetary penalty, debarment or suspension, or voiding of the contract. FAR 31.205-47. See Kinlin, A Current Guide to Recovery under the Equal Access to Justice Act; Connelly and Schooner, *Recovery of Costs for Defense Against the Government's Charge of Illegality*, 16 Pub. Cont. L.J. 94 (1986).

AUCTION A buying or selling technique whereby open bidding is continued until no competitor is willing to submit a better bid. FAR 15.610(e)(2) prohibits the contracting officer and other Government personnel from engaging in auction techniques, such as (1) indicating to an offeror a cost or price that it must meet to obtain further consideration, (2) advising an offeror of its price standing relative to another offeror (however, it *is* permissible to inform an offeror that its cost or price is considered by the Government to be too high or unrealistic), and (3) otherwise furnishing information about other offerors' prices. See Feldman, *Traversing the Tightrope Between Meaningful Discussions and Improper Practices in Negotiated Federal Acquisitions: Technical Transfusion, Technical Leveling, and Auction Techniques*, 17 Pub. Cont. L.J. 211, 246 (1987); Cibinic and Nash, Formation of Government Contracts 613, 628.

AUDIT The systematic examination of records and other documents and the securing of evidence—by confirmation, physical inspection, or otherwise—for one or more of the following purposes: determining the propriety or legality of proposed or consummated transactions; ascertaining whether all transactions have been recorded and are reflected accurately in accounts; determining the existence of recorded assets and the inclusiveness of recorded liabilities; determining the accuracy of financial or statistical statements or reports and the fairness of the facts they present; determining the degree of compliance with established policies and procedures of financial transactions and business management; and appraising an accounting system and making recommendations concerning it. Armed Services Pricing Manual (ASPM) vol. 1, app. B. Contract audit is an integral part of procurement by NEGOTIATION. Its purpose is to assist in achieving prudent contracting by having Government AUDITORs provide Government procurement personnel with financial information and advice on contractual matters and the effectiveness, efficiency, and economy of the contractor's operations. DCAA Contract Audit Manual (CAM) 1-104.2. On cost-reimbursement contracts, audit ensures that a contractor has incurred all costs claimed for reimbursement. In conducting a contract audit before award of a contract or negotiation of a claim, the auditor must examine or develop sufficient evidence to support a valid opinion of the extent to which costs or estimates contained in a contractor's CLAIM or PROPOSAL are (1) reasonable as to nature and amount, (2) allocable, (3) measurable by the application of duly promulgated COST ACCOUNTING STANDARDS (CAS) and generally accepted accounting principles and practices appropriate to the particular circumstances, and (4) in accordance with applicable cost limitations or exclusions as stated in the contract or in the FAR. Although the detection of fraud or similar unlawful activity is not a primary function of contract audit, the auditor must constantly be alert to situations or transactions that may indicate such activity. DCAA Contract Audit Manual (CAM) 1-104. Cibinic, *Audit of Contractors' Records: "Everything I've Got Belongs to You,"* 5 N&CR ¶ 5 (Jan. 1991); Cibinic, *Keeping Audit Reports Away from the Auditee: What You Don't Know Can Hurt You,* 4 N&CR ¶ 21 (Apr. 1990).

AUDITOR   A person conducting AUDIT activities. Broad authority to audit Government programs is vested in the Comptroller General of the United States (see GENERAL ACCOUNTING OFFICE (GAO)). The Comptroller General also has authority under the EXAMINATION OF RECORDS CLAUSE to audit Government contractors. Most contract audit is performed by agency auditors, who are generally assigned to the agency INSPECTOR GENERAL (IG), except in DoD where they are assigned to the DEFENSE CONTRACT AUDIT AGENCY (DCAA). Auditors perform work for other agencies through cross-servicing arrangements. See FAR Subpart 42.1. And see Cibinic, *Role of the Auditor: Any Room Left for the Contracting Officer?* 1 N&CR ¶ 66 (Aug. 1987); Cibinic, *Auditor Interviews of Contractor Employees: Wolf in Sheep's Clothing,* 1 N&CR ¶ 92 (Dec. 1987); Cibinic, *Auditor Interviews of Contractor Employees: Dropped From Estimating System Regulations,* 2 N&CR ¶ 28 (May 1988).

AUTHORIZATION   Legal authority to carry out a program. Statutes granting authorization are initiated in the legislative committees of Congress having cognizance over the agency.

involved. Generally, they are a prerequisite to an APPROPRIATION for that program or agency. The purpose of the authorization process is to ensure that the legislative committees have reviewed and approved the current programs of their respective agencies before the appropriations committees make the final decisions on the amount of funds that should be provided to carry out agency missions. See Cibinic and Nash, Formation of Government Contracts 32–43.

AUTHORIZATION AND CONSENT   Authorization by the Government for a contractor to use an invention that has been patented but to which the Government has no rights. Under 28 U.S.C. 1498(a), when such authorization and consent has been granted, the owner of the patent can only sue the Government in the CLAIMS COURT (Cl. Ct.) (it cannot sue the contractor for damages or obtain an injunction against the contractor to block use of the patent). The Government grants such authorization and consent in order to further the progress of work on its contracts—to obtain the performance of the work in the most effective manner without the need to create new technology. FAR 27.201-2 provides for the use of two different Authorization and Consent clauses. The clause in FAR 52.227-1 is used in supply and service contracts (including CONSTRUCTION contracts) and gives authorization and consent to use all patents necessary to perform the specified work or required to be used by the contracting officer. The Alternate I clause in FAR 52.227-1 is used in RESEARCH AND DEVELOPMENT (R&D) contracts and gives blanket authorization and consent to use any invention.

AUTHORIZED REPRESENTATIVE   An employee of a CONTRACTING ACTIVITY with the authority to perform CONTRACT ADMINISTRATION activities. Both FAR 2.101 and the Definitions clause in FAR 52.202-1 state that authorized representatives are CONTRACTING OFFICERs (COs). However, it is generally recognized that they do not have the authority to enter into agreements or MODIFICATIONs that alter the terms of existing contracts. When authorized representatives act within the scope of their authority, the Government agency runs the risk that it will be bound by their actions under the doctrine of IMPLIED AUTHORITY. See Cibinic and Nash, Administration of Government Contracts 28–47; Reifel and Bastianelli, *Contracting Officer Authority*, 86-4 Briefing Papers (Mar. 1986); Tepfer, *Authority and the Contracting Officer's Representatives*, 24 A.F. L. Rev. 1 (1984).

AUTOMATIC DATA PROCESSING EQUIPMENT (ADPE)
Defined by the BROOKS ACT (AUTOMATIC DATA PROCESSING
PROCUREMENTS) as any equipment or interconnected systems or
subsystems of equipment used in the automatic acquisition,
storage, manipulation, management, movement, control, display,
switching interchange, transmission, or reception of data or
information by a Federal agency or under a contract with a Federal
agency. These systems include computers, ancillary equipment,
software, and related services. 40 U.S.C. 759(a)(2). The FEDERAL
INFORMATION RESOURCES MANAGEMENT REGULATION (FIRMR), as
of Amendment 1, Oct. 1990, adopts the term FEDERAL INFORMA-
TION PROCESSING (FIP) RESOURCES in place of the term ADPE, to
minimize confusion between the statutory definition of ADPE and
the popular meaning of the term. FIRMR 201-4.001; FIRMR
Bulletin A-1, *Federal Information Resources Management
Regulation (FIRMR) Applicability.*

**AUTOMATIC DATA PROCESSING EQUIPMENT/DATA
SYSTEM (ADPE/DS)** A specific automated system maintained
by the GENERAL SERVICES ADMINISTRATION (GSA) to provide an
inventory of the Federal Government's computer systems.
FIRMR 201-4.001. Agencies must periodically survey their
FEDERAL INFORMATION PROCESSING (FIP) RESOURCES and submit
an inventory to GSA. Complete surveys must be conducted at
least once every 3 years and any year in which a sampling shows
significant discrepancies. FIRMR 201-21.203. Procedures for
making reports and submissions are contained in the *GSA
ADPE/DS Reporting Procedures and Users Manual.* See FIRMR
201-21.201.

AUTOMATIC DATA PROCESSING FUND See INFORMATION
TECHNOLOGY FUND (ITF).

AUTOMATIC DATA PROCESSING RESOURCES See FEDERAL
INFORMATION PROCESSING (FIP) RESOURCES.

AUTOMATIC STAY A mechanism by which contract AWARD is
withheld or further performance of a contract is suspended when
a disappointed bidder or offeror files a timely PROTEST with the
COMPTROLLER GENERAL (COMP. GEN.). This authority derives
from the COMPETITION IN CONTRACTING ACT (CICA). 31 U.S.C.
3553(c) and (d); FAR 33.104; 4 CFR 21.4. When an agency is
notified that a protest has been filed prior to contract award, the

agency is required by law not to make award before the protest is resolved, unless the HEAD OF THE CONTRACTING ACTIVITY decides that urgent and compelling circumstances significantly affecting the interests of the United States will not permit waiting for the decision. Similarly, when an agency is notified of a protest within 10 days after award has been made, the law requires the agency to direct the contractor to suspend performance until the protest is resolved. Because little more than a postage stamp and a letter of protest is required to stop the procurement process, the stay is often referred to as the "twenty-nine-cent injunction." See Dempsey and Fioravanti, *The Automatic Suspension Provision for GAO Bid Protests: When 10 Days May Not Be 10 Days*, 30 Cont. Mgmt. 9 (Mar. 1990). A similar provision permits the GENERAL SERVICES ADMINISTRATION BOARD OF CONTRACT APPEALS (GSBCA) to stay award or suspend performance by withdrawing an agency's DELEGATION OF PROCUREMENT AUTHORITY (DPA) when a disappointed offeror files a protest concerning a solicitation for FEDERAL INFORMATION PROCESSING (FIP) RESOURCES.

AUTOMATIC SUSPENSION See AUTOMATIC STAY.

AUXILIARY ITEM An item without which the basic unit of PLANT EQUIPMENT cannot operate. FAR 45.501. FAR 45.505-5 requires that records of such items be maintained as a part of the record of the associated item of plant equipment.

AVOIDANCE OF CONTRACT The withdrawal by one party from a contract or contract modification without performance because of a defect in the process of entering into the contract or contract modification. The most common grounds for avoidance are ECONOMIC DURESS, FRAUD, illegality, MUTUAL MISTAKE, and UNCONSCIONABILITY.

AWARD The notification by the Government that it will contract with a private party. The award of a contract is usually made by ACCEPTANCE OF an OFFER that has been made by an offeror. In procurements by SEALED BIDDING, the contracting officer makes a contract award by written notice, within the time for acceptance specified in the bid or the extension, to the responsible bidder whose bid, conforming to the SOLICITATION, is the most advantageous to the Government, considering only price and the price-related factors included in the solicitation. FAR 14.407-1. In procurements by NEGOTIATION, the contracting officer awards a contract with reasonable promptness to the successful offeror (the source whose BEST AND FINAL OFFER (BAFO) is most advantageous to the Government, considering price and other factors included in the solicitation) by transmitting a written notice of the award to that offeror. FAR 15.1002. Award is frequently made by signing one of the standard forms provided by the FAR. See Standard Form (SF) 26, Award/Contract, FAR 53.301-26; SF 33, Solicitation, Offer and Award, FAR 53.301-33. It can also be made by issuing a NOTICE OF AWARD.

AWARD FEE The FEE that the contractor receives above the BASE FEE in a COST-PLUS-AWARD FEE (CPAF) CONTRACT. The total amount of fee available to be awarded is set forth in the original contract and should be an amount that is sufficient to provide motivation for excellence in such areas as quality, timeliness, technical ingenuity, and cost-effective management. FAR 16.305. The amount of the award fee that is actually paid is determined by the Government's evaluation of the contractor's performance in terms of criteria stated in the contract. This determination is made unilaterally by the Government and is not subject to the DISPUTEs clause. FAR 16.404-2. The award fee is usually paid in increments of 3, 4, or 6 months based on the contractor's performance during that period. DFARS 216.404-2 and NFS 18-16.405-70(b) permit the award fee feature to be used in appropriate circumstances in fixed-price contracts as well. Cibinic and Nash, Formation of Government Contracts 775–90.

AWARD ON INITIAL PROPOSALS Award of a competitively negotiated contract (see NEGOTIATION) on the basis of the initial proposals received, without conducting DISCUSSION with the OFFERORs in the COMPETITIVE RANGE. Under the COMPETITION IN CONTRACTING ACT (CICA) such award could be made only if it could be clearly demonstrated from the existence of FULL AND OPEN COMPETITION or accurate prior cost experience that it would result in "the lowest overall cost to the Government." Because this standard prevented award on initial proposals unless the selected proposal contained the lowest cost to the Government offered by any contractor submitting a technically acceptable proposal, it was changed in 1990 by amendment of the ARMED SERVICES PROCUREMENT ACT (ASPA) at 10 U.S.C. 2305(b)(4). The change permits award on initial proposals whenever the contracting officer determines that discussions are not necessary and the solicitation contains a clause stating that the agency intends to award without discussions. See Nash and Cibinic, *Postscript: Award Without Discussions*, 5 N&CR ¶ 1 (Jan. 1991). The prior standard is still applicable to agencies subject to the FEDERAL PROPERTY AND ADMINISTRATIVE SERVICES ACT (FPASA) OF 1949. See FAR 15.610(a) for the two different standards for award on initial proposals and FAR 52.215-16 for the clauses that are prescribed to permit use of this procedure. And see Cibinic, *Award on Initial Proposals: Love at First Sight*, 1 N&CR ¶ 81 (Nov. 1987).

AWARD WITHOUT DISCUSSIONS   See AWARD ON INITIAL PROPOSALS.

B

BACK PAY Payment to employees of previously earned compensation. Back pay may result from a negotiated settlement, order, or court decree that resolves a violation of Federal labor laws or the Civil Rights Act of 1964. It falls into two categories: payment of additional compensation to employees for work performed for which they were underpaid, and payment resulting from such violations as improper discharge or discrimination. Back pay resulting from underpaid work is compensation for the work performed and is an ALLOWABLE COST; all other back pay resulting from violation of Federal labor laws or the Civil Rights Act is unallowable. FAR 31.205-6(h). See Walterscheid, *Back Pay as a Remedy under Executive Order 11246: A Study in Administrative Activism*, 18 Pub. Cont. L.J. 559 (1989).

BAD DEBTS Losses arising from uncollectible accounts receivable due from customers. FAR 31.205-3 makes such losses, whether actual or estimated, UNALLOWABLE COSTs.

BALANCE OF PAYMENTS PROGRAM A nonstatutory program giving preference to American products over foreign products. See FAR Subpart 25.3. The program applies to acquisitions of work to be performed outside of the United States. It provides that, unless one of nine exceptions applies, the foreign offer must be increased for evaluation purposes by a factor of 50 percent (excluding duty). FAR 25.302. See Stamps, *The Department of Defense Balance of Payments Program: A Brief History and Critique*, 18 Pub. Cont. L.J. 528 (1989).

BALANCE SHEET A financial statement of a contractor setting forth its ASSETs, liabilities, and net worth. Contracting officers review prospective contractors' financial statements, including balance sheets, to determine if they have, or are able to obtain, adequate financial resources to perform the contract (see RESPONSIBILITY).

"BASED ON" PRICE A price that is comparable to a previous price that was an ESTABLISHED CATALOG OR MARKET PRICE or a price established through ADEQUATE PRICE COMPETITION. When a "based on" price is submitted in a negotiated procurement, the contracting officer need not obtain COST OR PRICING DATA. FAR 15.804-3. A price is "based on" the established catalog or market price of a COMMERCIAL PRODUCT sold in substantial quantities to the general public if the item being purchased is sufficiently similar to the commercial item to permit any price difference to be identified and justified without resort to COST ANALYSIS. FAR 15.804-3(c)(6). A price is "based on" adequate price competition if it results directly from such competition, or if PRICE ANALYSIS alone clearly demonstrates that it is reasonable in comparison with current or recent prices for the same or substantially the same items purchased in comparable quantities, and under comparable terms and conditions, under contracts that resulted from adequate price competition. FAR 15.804(b)(3). See also DFARS 215.804-3(b)(3) for examples of a price "based on" adequate price competition.

BASE FEE A fixed dollar amount established at the inception of a COST-PLUS-AWARD FEE (CPAF) CONTRACT as the amount of profit the contractor will receive under the contract, regardless of the quality of performance. In addition to this base fee, the contractor receives an AWARD FEE in an amount that reflects the Government's periodic judgmental evaluation of contractor performance. The base fee is established, administered, and paid like a fixed fee under a COST-PLUS-FIXED FEE (CPFF) CONTRACT.

BASIC AGREEMENT A written instrument of understanding (not a CONTRACT) negotiated between a procuring activity and a contractor. FAR 16.702. It sets forth the contract clauses that will apply to future procurements. Basic agreements are used to expedite future procurements when there is a likelihood that a substantial number of future contracts will be issued. Basic agreements must be revised annually to incorporate contract clauses that are currently applicable.

BASIC ORDERING AGREEMENT (BOA) A written instrument of understanding (not a CONTRACT) negotiated between a procuring activity and a contractor. FAR 16.703. A BOA contains (1) terms and clauses that will apply to any future orders placed during the BOA's term, (2) a description, as specific as practicable, of supplies or services to be provided, and (3) methods for pricing, issuing, and delivering future orders. BOAs may be used to expedite contracting for supplies or services when specific items, quantities, and prices are not known but a substantial number of requirements are anticipated. They are frequently issued to multiple contractors and may not be used to avoid the requirements for competition. FAR 16.703(d). See Raleigh, *The Basic Ordering Agreement: Basically*, 22 Cont. Mgmt. 12 (Dec. 1982).

BASIC RESEARCH Research that is directed toward increase of knowledge in science. FAR 35.001, 31.205-18. The primary aim of basic research is a fuller knowledge or understanding of the subject under study, rather than any practical application thereof. It is the first stage of the RESEARCH AND DEVELOPMENT (R&D) process and is followed by APPLIED RESEARCH.

BENCHMARK Test or tests conducted on computer hardware, software, or telecommunications equipment to determine (1) that the configuration performs in accordance with vendor-published PERFORMANCE SPECIFICATIONS; (2) that the configuration satisfies certain functional requirements that cannot be measured in terms of performance and/or design criteria; (3) the estimated annual costs to an agency for teleprocessing services; and (4) the size system that must be purchased (e.g., how many components are needed to process the anticipated workload). The term has been broadly interpreted to include evaluation exercises of varying degrees of complexity. In general, there are two types of benchmarks: operational capability demonstrations (OCDs) and live test demonstrations (LTDs), the latter being the more rigorous. See CAPABILITY VALIDATION. And see FIRMR Bulletin C-4, *Performance and Capability Validation of FIP Systems*, and FIRMR 201-20.304.

BEST AND FINAL OFFER (BAFO) An offer submitted to the Government in a competitive negotiated procurement (see NEGOTIATION) after written or oral DISCUSSIONs have been conducted. FAR 15.611. The contracting officer issues to all offerors still within the COMPETITIVE RANGE a request for BAFOs. The request includes (1) notice that discussions are concluded, (2) notice that the offeror has the opportunity to submit a BAFO, (3) a common cutoff date and time allowing a reasonable opportunity for submission of BAFOs, and (4) notice of the ramifications of late submission. Once the contracting officer receives the BAFOs, the contracting officer may not reopen discussions unless it is clearly in the Government's interest to do so. If the contracting officer does reopen discussions, the contracting officer must issue an additional request for BAFOs to all offerors still within the competitive range. Following evaluation of the BAFOs, the contracting officer selects the source whose offer is most advantageous to the Government, considering price and the other factors included in the solicitation. FAR 15.611. See Cibinic and Nash, Formation of Government Contracts 637–44; Nash and Cibinic, *Limiting Multiple Best and Finals: Cure or Disease?* 2 N&CR ¶ 60 (Oct. 1988); Feldman, *Traversing the Tightrope Between Meaningful Discussions and Improper Practices in Negotiated Federal Acquisitions: Technical Transfusion, Technical Leveling, and Auction Techniques*, 17 Pub. Cont. L.J. 211, 246 (1987).

BEST EFFORTS   A contractual obligation to *attempt* to meet a goal—as, for example, under the LIMITATION OF COST (LOC) CLAUSE, which requires contractors to use their best efforts to perform the work within the estimated cost of the contract. In contracts exceeding the $25,000 small purchase limitation, under the Utilization of Women-Owned Small Businesses clause at FAR 52.219-13, contractors must agree to use their "best efforts" to give women-owned small businesses the maximum practicable opportunity to participate in subcontracts that is consistent with efficient performance of the contract. FAR 19.902. But this obligation differs from that created by AFFIRMATIVE ACTION POLICIES. For instance, the standard applied to contractors with regard to creating LABOR SURPLUS AREA (LSA) subcontracting opportunities distinguishes between (1) contracts exceeding the small purchase limitation that do not exceed $500,000, under which contractors must use their best efforts, and (2) contracts exceeding $500,000, under which contractors must take affirmative action. FAR 20.301; Utilization of Labor Surplus Area Concerns clause, FAR 52.220-3.

BID   An OFFER submitted to the Government in response to an INVITATION FOR BIDS (IFB). BIDDERs must be given a reasonable time (generally at least 30 days) to prepare and submit bids, consistent with the needs of the Government. FAR 14.202-1.

Bids must conform in all material respects to the IFB in order to be responsive (see RESPONSIVENESS) and thus eligible for award. See Shnitzer, Government Contract Bidding.

BID AND PROPOSAL (B&P) COSTS   Costs incurred by a contractor in preparing, submitting, and supporting BIDs and PROPOSALs (whether or not solicited) on potential contracts. B&P costs do not include the costs of efforts sponsored by a grant or cooperative agreement or required in contract performance. FAR 31.205-18. Generally discussed in conjunction with INDEPENDENT RESEARCH AND DEVELOPMENT (IR&D) costs, B&P costs receive extensive treatment as a "selected cost" under FAR 31.205-18 and under Cost Accounting Standard 420, FAR 30.420. Instructions for negotiating advance agreements for IR&D/B&P costs are given in FAR Subpart 42.10. See Shnitzer, *Bid or Proposal & Protest Costs under CICA*, 88-12 Briefing Papers (Nov. 1988); Victorino and Briggerman, *The IR&D/B&P/Selling Costs Dilemma*, 87–10 Briefing Papers (Sep. 1987). Recovery of bid or proposal costs represents a potential monetary remedy for a successful protester before the GENERAL ACCOUNTING OFFICE (GAO) or before the GENERAL SERVICES ADMINISTRATION BOARD OF CONTRACT APPEALS (GSBCA). 31 U.S.C. 3554(c)(1)(B); 40 U.S.C. 759(h)(5)(C)(ii). If the protester prevails in the protest action and had a substantial chance for award of the contract but does not receive the award, the protester may recover the costs of preparing the bid or proposal. Typically, however, the protest forums will not award bid or proposal costs if the successful protester gains the opportunity to compete for the procurement. See Cibinic and Nash, Formation of Government Contracts 1043–44.

BID BOND   A BOND that serves as a BID GUARANTEE. Such bonds are used frequently in public construction projects and sometimes, but rarely, in nonconstruction contracts. See Shnitzer, Government Contract Bidding, chaps. 7 and 14; Patin, chap. 17, Construction Contracting 1209–22; Cibinic, *Bid Bonds and Bid Guarantees: Is the Tail Wagging the Dog?* 2 N&CR ¶ 16 (Mar. 1988).

BIDDER   One who submits a BID. While this term technically refers only to an OFFEROR on a sealed bid procurement (see SEALED BIDDING), it is frequently used to refer to any offeror on a Government procurement—whether sealed bid, competitive negotiation, or otherwise.   See Schnitzer, Government Contract Bidding, chap. 3.

BIDDERS' CONFERENCE See PRE-BID CONFERENCE and PREPROPOSAL CONFERENCE.

BIDDERS MAILING LIST See SOLICITATION MAILING LIST.

BIDDING TIME The time allowed prospective BIDDERs to prepare and submit their bids—the time, that is, between SOLICITATION issuance and BID OPENING. All INVITATIONS FOR BIDS (IFBs) must allow a reasonable bidding time, consistent with the needs of the Government; bidding time of at least 30 calendar days must be provided when synopsis in the COMMERCE BUSINESS DAILY (CBD) is required by the Small Business Act, 15 U.S.C. 631, and the Office of Federal Procurement Policy Act, 41 U.S.C. 401 *et seq.* If bidding time were unduly limited, some potential sources might be precluded from bidding, and others might be forced to raise their bids by including amounts to cover contingencies. Thus, to avoid unduly restricting competition or paying higher than necessary prices, consideration must be given to the following factors in establishing a reasonable bidding time: (1) the degree of urgency, (2) the complexity of the requirement, (3) the anticipated extent of subcontracting, (4) whether a PRESOLICITATION NOTICE was issued, (5) the geographic distribution of bidders, and (6) normal mailing time for both IFBs and bids. FAR 14.202-1; FAR 36.303(a) (construction contracts). See Schnitzer, Government Contract Bidding, chap. 5.

BID GUARANTEE A form of security assuring that the BIDDER (1) will not withdraw a BID within the period specified for acceptance and (2) will execute a written contract and furnish required BONDs, including any necessary coinsurance or reinsurance agreements, within the time specified in the bid. FAR 28.001. FAR 28.101-1(a) permits the use of bid guarantees *only* when a PERFORMANCE BOND or a PAYMENT BOND is required. Such guarantees must be in an amount adequate to protect the Government from loss and must be at least 20 percent of the bid price but not more than $3 million. FAR 28.101-2. See Cibinic, *Bid Bonds and Bid Guarantees: Is the Tail Wagging the Dog?* 2 N&CR ¶ 16 (Mar. 1988).

BID OPENING   The public opening of BIDs submitted to the Government in a sealed bid procurement (see SEALED BIDDING). The INVITATION FOR BIDS (IFB) specifies an exact date and time for opening of bids. When the set time arrives, the bid opening officer informs those present of that fact and then (1) personally and publicly opens all bids received before the set time, (2) if practical, reads the bids aloud to the persons present, and (3) has the bids recorded. FAR 14.402-1. However, the general public may not have access to the opening of classified bids (see CLASSIFIED ACQUISITION). FAR 14.402-2. Bid openings may be postponed if the contracting officer has reason to believe that the bids of an important segment of bidders have been delayed for causes beyond the bidders' control, or in the case of an emergency or unanticipated event that interrupts normal governmental processes. FAR 14.402-3. Bids are recorded on an ABSTRACT OF OFFERS. See Schnitzer, Government Contract Bidding, chap. 18.

BID PROTEST   See PROTEST.

BID SAMPLE   A sample to be furnished by a BIDDER to show the characteristics of the product offered in a bid. FAR 14.202-4. Such a sample may be required only when the product has characteristics that cannot be described adequately in the SPECIFI-CATION or PURCHASE DESCRIPTION. Bid samples are used only to determine the RESPONSIVENESS of the bid, not to determine a bidder's ability to produce the required items. The use of bid samples is appropriate for products that must be suitable from the standpoint of balance, facility of use, general "feel," color, pattern, or other characteristic that cannot be described adequately in the specification. A standard solicitation provision to be used when bid samples are required is provided in FAR 52.214-20.

BIFURCATION OF ENTITLEMENT AND QUANTUM   A distinction between the *right* to recover additional compensation under a contract and the *amount* of compensation to be recovered; the separation of issues of entitlement (referring to whether a party prevails) and quantum (referring to the amount a party recovers) in the hearing of a DISPUTE before a BOARD OF CONTRACT APPEALS (BCA). (The CLAIMS COURT (Cl. Ct.) does not follow this procedure.) BCAs generally prefer to hear only entitlement issues, assuming that, in most cases, the parties will be able to successful-ly negotiate quantum if the contractor is held to be entitled to compensation. The facts relating to entitlement are often simple, whereas the quantum issues are complex; if the contractor fails to establish a right to recover, the BCA and the parties need not invest time and energy in calculating how much the contractor will *not* recover. Thus, prehearing instructions often explain that quantum will not be heard unless the BCA has expressly agreed to hear it, full cost schedule and supporting information have been furnished, and the Government has had an opportunity to conduct an audit. When a contractor's claim to entitlement is sustained, the BCA remands the negotiation of quantum to the contracting officer and closes the file. If the parties fail to agree, the contractor must request a DECISION OF THE CONTRACTING OFFICER (CO) on quantum. Upon receipt of this decision, or after sufficient time passes for DEEMED DENIAL jurisdiction, the contractor can file a new notice of appeal with the BCA. See *B&A Electric Co.*, ASBCA 28649(R), 30721(R), 87-2 BCA ¶ 19,879; Nash, *Bifurcation: A Good Appeals Board Procedure That Is in Jeopardy*, 4 N&CR ¶ 71 (Dec. 1990).

BILATERAL CONTRACT A contract in which parties exchange promises to perform reciprocal obligations in the future. Except for SMALL PURCHASEs, virtually all Government contracts are bilateral contracts. Bilateral contracts are contrasted with unilateral contracts, in which one party makes a promise in exchange for the performance of the other party.

BILATERAL MODIFICATION See MODIFICATION.

BILLING RATE An INDIRECT COST rate established temporarily for interim reimbursement of incurred indirect costs and adjusted as necessary pending establishment of a FINAL INDIRECT COST RATE. FAR 42.701. The contracting officer establishes a billing rate on the basis of information resulting from recent review, previous audits or experience, or similar reliable data or experience of other contracting activities. Once established, billing rates may be prospectively or retroactively revised by mutual agreement of the contracting officer or auditor and the contractor, at either party's request, to prevent substantial overpayment or underpayment. The elements of indirect cost and the base used in computing billing rates must not be construed as determining either the indirect costs to be distributed or the bases for distribution in the final settlement. FAR 42.704.

BILL OF LADING A document evidencing receipt of goods for shipment, issued by a person engaged in the business of transporting or forwarding goods (including airbills). U.C.C. 1-201(6)). A bill of lading is a contract between the transportation firm and the party shipping the goods. In Government contracting this form of contract can be used by the Government (a Government bill of lading) or a contractor (a commercial bill of lading). Guidance on the use of bills of lading is found in FAR Part 47. FAR 9.403 provides that firms shipping goods for the Government on either Government or commercial bills of lading are contractors subject to DEBARMENT and SUSPENSION.

BILL OF MATERIALS A report by a supplier which specifies the quantities of various materials required to produce a designated quantity of supplies of a particular kind. DFARS 210.001. A bill of materials is a descriptive and quantitative listing of materials, supplies, parts, and components required to produce a designated complete end item of material or assembly or subassembly. It may also show estimated costs or fixed prices. Armed Services Pricing Manual (ASPM) vol. 1, app. B. A bill of materials is required only if the contracting officer determines that such a bill is necessary to develop materials or component requirements for production and maintenance programs, for INDUSTRIAL MOBILIZATION purposes, or for other specified purposes. DFARS 210.070.

BLANKET PURCHASE AGREEMENT (BPA) A simplified method of filling the Government's anticipated repetitive needs for supplies or services by establishing "charge accounts" with qualified sources of supply. FAR 13.201. BPAs are designed to reduce administrative costs in accomplishing SMALL PURCHASEs by eliminating the need for individual purchase documents. BPAs must contain the following terms and conditions: (1) a description of the arrangement; (2) the extent of obligation; (3) pricing; (4) a purchase limitation; (5) notice of individuals authorized to purchase under the BPA, and dollar limitations by title of position and name; (6) delivery tickets; and (7) invoices. FAR 13.203-1. Individual purchases under BPAs may not exceed the dollar limitation for small purchases, and the existence of a BPA does not justify sole-source purchasing (see SOLE SOURCE). FAR 13.204.

BLIND AND OTHER SEVERELY HANDICAPPED *Blind*—An individual or class of individuals whose central visual acuity does not exceed 20/200 in the better eye with correcting lenses; or, where the acuity is better than that, it is accompanied by a limit to the field of vision in the better eye that subtends an angle of no greater than 20 degrees at its largest diameter. *Other severely handicapped*—An individual or class of individuals with a physical or mental disability that constitutes a substantial handicap to employment and is of such a nature as to prevent the individual from currently engaging in normal competitive employment. 41 U.S.C. 46b. The Javits-Wagner-O'Day Act, 41 U.S.C. 46–48c, requires Government entities to purchase certain supplies and services from workshops for the blind and other severely handicapped ("sheltered workshops"), if the supplies or services are available when required. FAR Subpart 8.7 prescribes policies and procedures for implementing the act and the rules of the Committee for Purchase from the Blind and Other Severely Handicapped.

BOARD OF CONTRACT APPEALS (BCA) An administrative board established in a procuring agency to hear and decide DISPUTEs under the CONTRACT DISPUTES ACT (CDA) OF 1978. There are presently 12 BCAs. The CDA established the BCAs at 41 U.S.C. 607(a) and defined their jurisdiction over Federal contract performance disputes at 41 U.S.C. 607(d). The BCAs resolve disputes, as distinguished from PROTEST actions, between the Federal Government and contractors. However, BCAs have on occasion been granted jurisdiction by specific statute or agency delegation to process protests as well; the primary example is the GENERAL SERVICES ADMINISTRATION BOARD OF CONTRACT APPEALS (GSBCA), which, pursuant to the COMPETITION IN CONTRACTING ACT (CICA) and the BROOKS ACT (AUTOMATIC DATA PROCESSING PROCUREMENTS), handles protests relating to FEDERAL INFORMATION PROCESSING (FIP) RESOURCES. The ARMED SERVICES BOARD OF CONTRACT APPEALS (ASBCA) is the largest BCA with 37 ADMINISTRATIVE JUDGEs. The second largest, the GSBCA, has 12 administrative judges. Most of the 12 BCAs consist of the minimum required 3 administrative judges. See also APPEAL FROM A CONTRACTING OFFICER'S DECISION and APPEAL FROM THE RULING OF A COURT OR BOARD. And see Anthony, *Court or Board: A Contractor's Alternatives*, 31 Fed. B. News & J. 115.

BOILERPLATE Standard contract language that is used by a party on all contracts of a certain type. In Government procurement this term is generally used to describe the GENERAL PROVISIONS that are included in contracts pursuant to FAR Part 52.

BONA FIDE AGENCY An established commercial or selling agency, maintained by a contractor for the purpose of securing business, that neither exerts nor proposes to exert improper influence to solicit or obtain Government contracts nor holds itself out as being able to obtain any Government contract or contracts through improper influence. FAR 3.401. Payments to such an agency are not improper under the contract provisions barring CONTINGENT FEEs. See Cibinic and Nash, Formation of Government Contracts 131–32.

BONA FIDE EMPLOYEE A person, employed by a contractor and subject to the contractor's supervision and control as to time, place, and manner of performance, who neither exerts nor proposes to exert improper influence to solicit or obtain Government contracts nor holds out as being able to obtain any Government contract or contracts through improper influence. FAR 3.401. Payments to such employees are not improper under the contract provisions barring CONTINGENT FEEs. See Cibinic and Nash, Formation of Government Contracts 131–32.

BOND A written instrument executed by an offeror or contractor (the principal) and a second party (the SURETY or sureties) to ensure fulfillment of the principal's obligations to a third party (the obligee or the Government) identified in the bond. If the principal's obligations are not met, the bond ensures payment, to the extent stipulated, of any loss sustained by the obligee. Types of bonds discussed in the FAR include (1) ADVANCE PAYMENT bonds, which secure fulfillment of the contractor's obligations under an advance payment provision; (2) BID BONDs, a form of BID GUARANTEE ensuring that the bidder will not withdraw a bid within the period specified and will execute a written contract within the time specified in the bid; (3) PERFORMANCE BONDs, which secure performance and fulfillment of the contractor's obligations under the contract; (4) PAYMENT BONDs, which ensure payments as required by law to all persons supplying labor or material in the prosecution of the work required by the contract; and (5) PATENT INFRINGEMENT bonds, which secure fulfillment of the contractor's obligations under a patent provision. FAR 28.001. Mentioned but not discussed in the FAR are fidelity bonds, used for ensuring the faithful performance of employees to their employers and their employers' clients (e.g., to cover losses by theft or embezzlement). See Patin, chap. 17, Construction Contracting 1209–1320; Cibinic, *Bid Bonds and Bid Guarantees: Is the Tail Wagging the Dog?* 2 N&CR ¶ 16 (Mar. 1988).

BONDING COSTS The costs incurred by a contractor when the Government requires assurance against financial loss to itself or others stemming from an act or default of the contractor, or when the contractor requires similar assurance. Included are the costs of such BONDs as bid, performance, payment, advance payment, patent infringement, and fidelity bonds. Costs of bonding required by the terms of the contract are ALLOWABLE COSTs. FAR 31.205-4. Costs of bonding required by the contractor in the general conduct of its business are allowable to the extent that (1) such bonding is in accordance with sound business practice and (2) the rates and premiums are reasonable under the circumstances.

BONUS A payment of extra compensation to an employee. FAR 31.205-6(f) specifies when the costs of such payments by contractors may be treated as ALLOWABLE COSTs.

BORROWER The recipient of a loan. FAR 32.301 defines the term narrowly to include only a contractor, subcontractor (at any tier), or other supplier who receives a GUARANTEED LOAN.

BRAND-NAME-OR-EQUAL DESCRIPTION A PURCHASE DESCRIPTION that identifies a product by its brand name and model or part number or other appropriate nomenclature by which it is offered for sale and permits offers on products essentially equal to the specified brand-name product. FAR 10.001. ("Brand-name product" is directly defined by NFS 18-10.001.) A brand-name-or-equal description is generally the minimum acceptable description in Government contracting; prospective contractors must be allowed to offer products other than those named by brand if those other products will meet the needs of the Government in essentially the same manner. FAR 10.004(b). Traditionally, this type of purchase description was required to set forth those salient physical, functional, or other characteristics of the brand-name product that were deemed essential in meeting the Government's needs. However, the FAR contains no such requirement; it leaves this issue to agency policy. See DFARS 210.004(b)(3), requiring the inclusion of salient characteristics in

DoD procurements using this type of purchase description. See Cibinic and Nash, Formation of Government Contracts 413–14.

BREACH OF CONTRACT   Failure, without legal excuse, to perform any promise that forms the whole or part of a contract. Breach can be found of both express promises in a contract and IMPLIED PROMISEs that are inherent in the transaction. "Breach" also means the unequivocal, distinct, and absolute refusal to perform under the agreement. It may also entail the prevention or hindrance by a party to the contract of any occurrence or performance required under the contract for the creation or continuance of a right in favor of the other party or for the discharge of a duty by that party. Constructive breach, which entails the concept of REPUDIATION, takes place when a party disables itself from performance by some act or declares, before the time of performance comes, that it does not intend to perform. Black's Law Dictionary. Traditionally, in Government contract law, breach of contract by the Government meant the Government's failure to perform one of its contractual obligations that was not redressable under a contract clause (thus not a CONSTRUCTIVE CHANGE). Prior to the CONTRACT DISPUTES ACT (CDA) OF 1978, appeals boards could not award damages for such breaches of contract. However, under the act they now have the authority to award such damages. See Braude, chap. 15, Construction Contracting 1086–1101.

BREAKOUT   A Government decision to procure a component or part directly from its manufacturer rather than from a systems contractor. DFARS Appendix D contains guidance on breakout during the manufacturing process (invfolving furnishing the components to the systems contractor as GOVERNMENT-FUR-NISHED MATERIAL (GFM)); DFARS Appendix E addresses breakout during the procurement of replenishment parts. The purpose of breakout is to acquire the components or parts at a reduced price by avoiding the need to pay a systems contractor's overhead and profit. See Payson and Hernaez, *Systems Breakout: An Alternative Acquisition Strategy*, 29 Cont. Mgmt. 8 (Aug. 1989); Young, *Breakout—The Mystery Unveiled*, 19 NCMJ 33 (1985). Breakout is also loosely used to mean obtaining additional competition, especially from small businesses. See BREAKOUT ADVOCATE.

BREAKOUT ADVOCATE   An employee of a CONTRACTING ACTIVITY specifically assigned the task of seeking opportunities to reduce Government expenditures by using BREAKOUT. 10

U.S.C. 2452 requires the Secretary of Defense to have breakout advocates. See also 15 U.S.C. 644. These advocates are frequently called Breakout Procurement Center Representatives when they participate in the activities of the SMALL BUSINESS ADMINISTRATION (SBA) Procurement Center Representatives (PCRs). PCRs are advocates for increasing SMALL BUSINESS CONCERN participation in Federal procurement through traditional SET-ASIDEs. Breakout PCRs (BPCRs) further that objective by advocating COMPETITION; they identify items being procured on a sole-source basis (see SOLE SOURCE) and then identify and overcome factors that prevent competitive procurement of those items. In other words, BPCRs break the item out for competition and encourage small business concerns to participate in future competitive procurements for those items. BPCRs assert that small business concerns can provide breakout items at prices substantially lower than the sole-source price being paid to the prime contractor for a major system.

BRIBERY The crime of offering, giving, receiving, or soliciting any thing of value to influence action as an official or in discharge of a public duty. 18 U.S.C. 201 proscribes such behavior on the part of "any officer or employee or person acting for or on behalf of the United States, or any department or agency or branch of government thereof, . . . in any official function." Giving or receiving gifts DURING THE CONDUCT OF A PROCUREMENT is also proscribed by the PROCUREMENT INTEGRITY provisions of 41 U.S.C. 423. See Cibinic and Nash, Formation of Government Contracts 112–15.

BROAD AGENCY ANNOUNCEMENT (BAA) An announcement by a procuring agency of areas of RESEARCH interest, including criteria for selecting proposals and soliciting the participation of all offerors capable of satisfying the agency's needs. FAR 6.102(d)(2). Under 10 U.S.C. 2302(2) and 41 U.S.C. 259(b), the solicitation of research proposals by BAAs is one of the COMPETITIVE PROCEDURES meeting the statutory requirement for FULL AND OPEN COMPETITION. However, BAAs may be used only when meaningful proposals with varying scientific or technical approaches can reasonably be expected. BAAs should (1) describe the agency's research interest, (2) describe the criteria for selecting the proposals, their relative importance, and the method of evaluation, (3) specify the period of time during which proposals will be accepted, and (4) contain instructions for the preparation and submission of proposals. Proposals are evaluated by peer or scientific review. The primary bases for award are technical excellence, importance to agency programs, and fund availability. FAR 35.016. Contracts are awarded until the agency has utilized its research funds in the area of interest. See Cibinic and Nash, Formation of Government Contracts 678–88; Bolos, *Innovative Procurement Concepts—The Broad Agency Announcement*, 31 Cont. Mgmt. 4 (Feb. 1991). See also RESEARCH AND DEVELOPMENT (R&D).

BROOKS ACT (ARCHITECT-ENGINEER PROCUREMENTS)
A 1972 act, Pub. L. 92-582 as amended, 40 U.S.C. 541 *et seq.*, requiring the use of special procedures to procure ARCHITECT-ENGINEER (A-E) SERVICES. The procedures to be followed are set forth in FAR Subpart 36.6. They call for the selection of A-Es based on qualifications (as stated in Standard Form (SF) 254, Architect-Engineer and Related Services Questionnaire, FAR 53.301-254, or in SF 255, Architect-Engineer and Related Services Questionnaire for Specific Project, FAR 53.301-255, and assessed during discussions) without evaluation of the proposed price for the work to be accomplished. Contract negotiations must be conducted with the highest-ranked offeror and award must be made to that firm unless a reasonable price cannot be agreed upon. See Cibinic and Nash, Formation of Government Contracts 672–78.

BROOKS ACT (AUTOMATIC DATA PROCESSING PROCUREMENTS)
A 1965 act, Pub. L. 89-306 as amended, 40 U.S.C. 759, requiring the use of special procedures to procure FEDERAL INFORMATION PROCESSING (FIP) RESOURCES. Under the Brooks Act, the GENERAL SERVICES ADMINISTRATION (GSA) has exclusive authority to procure FIP resources (ADPE) for Government agencies, but it may delegate to agencies, by means of DELEGATIONs OF PROCUREMENT AUTHORITY (DPAs), procurement authority to lease, purchase, or maintain FIP resources. GSA may also transfer FIP resources between Federal agencies and create equipment pools and data processing centers. Through subsequent amendments to the Brooks Act, including the COMPETITION IN CONTRACTING ACT (CICA), jurisdiction over PROTESTs regarding FIP resources procurements lies with the GENERAL SERVICES ADMINISTRATION BOARD OF CONTRACT APPEALS (GSBCA). 40 U.S.C. 759(f). Implementing regulations can be found in the FEDERAL INFORMATION RESOURCES MANAGEMENT REGULATION (FIRMR), 41 CFR 201, and the Rules of the General Services Board

of Contract Appeals (see UNIFORM RULES). See Tolle, *A Review of the First Year of ADP Protests at the GSBCA*, 16 Pub. Cont. L.J. 120 (1986).

BUDGET AUTHORITY Authority provided by law to enter into obligations that will result in immediate or future outlays involving Government funds. 2 U.S.C. 622(2). Budget authority is that authority required to enter into a binding OBLIGATION in accordance with the ANTI-DEFICIENCY ACT. Budget authority is conferred in two ways: (1) the enactment of an APPROPRIATION act or (2) the enactment of a statute conferring CONTRACTING AUTHORITY.

BUILDING CONSTRUCTION activity as distinguished from manufacturing, the furnishing of materials, or servicing and maintenance work. FAR 22.401. The term refers to work on buildings, structures, and improvements of all types, such as bridges, dams, plants, highways, parkways, streets, subways, tunnels, sewers, mains, power lines, pumping stations, heavy generators, railways, airports, terminals, docks, piers, wharves, ways, lighthouses, buoys, jetties, breakwaters, levees, canals, dredging, shoring, rehabilitation and reactivation of plants, scaffolding, drilling, blasting, excavating, clearing, and landscaping. The manufacture or furnishing of materials, articles, supplies, or equipment is not "building" unless conducted in connection with, and at the site of, construction activity as described above. Contracting for building-type work is subject to the DAVIS-BACON ACT and the procedures in FAR Part 36. See Patin, chap. 18, Construction Contracting 1395–1439.

BULK FUNDING A system whereby a contracting officer receives authorization from a fiscal and accounting officer to obligate funds on purchase documents, against a specified lump sum of funds reserved for the purpose, for a specified period of time, rather than obtaining individual obligational authority on each purchase document. FAR 13.101. FAR 13.401(c) requires agencies to use bulk funding to the maximum extent practicable to increase the efficiency of SMALL PURCHASE PROCEDURES.

BURDEN An INDIRECT COST.

BUREAU OF STANDARDS See NATIONAL INSTITUTE OF STANDARDS AND TECHNOLOGY (NIST).

BUSINESS COMBINATION The legal bringing together under common control of a corporation and one or more incorporated or unincorporated firms, generally into a single organization. The single organization carries on the activities of the previously separate, independent enterprises. There are two basic approaches to obtaining control over assets owned and used by other firms. The acquiring firm may buy the desired assets and thereby obtain title to their use directly, or it may obtain an ownership interest in the common stock of another company, enabling the acquiring firm to exercise indirect control over the other firm's assets. The two basic approaches can be adopted in various forms, as follows: (1) acquisition of assets, (2) acquisition of stock, (3) statutory merger, (4) statutory consolidation. There are two methods of accounting for a business combination: the purchase method and the pooling-of-interest method. DCAA Contract Audit Manual (CAM) 7-1700. FAR 31.205-52 limits the allowability of AMORTIZATION, cost of money (see COST OF MONEY FACTORS (CMF)), and DEPRECIATION when the purchase method is used. FAR Subpart 42.12 contains procedures for recognizing business combinations by processing CHANGE OF NAME AGREEMENTs or NOVATIONs.

BUSINESS UNIT Any part of an organization, or an entire business organization, that is not divided into SEGMENTs. FAR 31.001. To ensure consistency and efficiency, a single OVERHEAD RATE must be established for all contracts held by a contractor business unit. FAR 42.703. Cost Accounting Standard 410, FAR 30.410, provides criteria for the process of allocating a business unit's GENERAL AND ADMINISTRATIVE EXPENSE (G&A) to its final COST OBJECTIVES.

BUY AMERICAN ACT An act, 41 U.S.C. 10a–10d, originally enacted in 1933, which generally requires that, in purchasing supplies and CONSTRUCTION MATERIALS for public use, only DOMESTIC END PRODUCTs may be procured, unless the items (1) are for use outside the United States, (2) would be unreasonable in cost, or (3) are not mined, produced, or manufactured domestically in sufficient and reasonably available commercial quantities of satisfactory quality. Also exempt are items purchased for commissary resale, or items for which the head of the agency determines that domestic preference would be inconsistent with the public interest. FAR 25.102(a). The FAR contains separate regulations for supplies (Subpart 25.1) and construction materials

(Subpart 25.2). With regard to supplies, it provides a preference evaluation system for domestic end products over foreign end products as defined in FAR 25.101. Foreign offers are evaluated by including duty, whether or not actually paid, and adding 6 percent to the total (or 12 percent if the domestic offeror is a SMALL BUSINESS CONCERN or a LABOR SURPLUS AREA (LSA) CONCERN). When they exceed these margins, domestic prices are deemed unreasonable, and competing foreign offers may be accepted. FAR 25.105. FAR 25.108 lists approximately 100 articles, materials, and supplies excepted from application of the Buy American Act. See Kenney and Duberstein, *Domestic Preference Provisions*, 89-3 Briefing Papers (Feb. 1989); Golub and Fenske, *U.S. Government Procurement: Opportunities and Obstacles for Foreign Contractors*, 20 Geo. Wash. J. Int'l L. & Econ. 567 (1987).

BUY INDIAN ACT An act, 25 U.S.C. 47, authorizing the Secretary of the Interior to SET ASIDE procurements for Indian owned and controlled enterprises. In 1976, the Bureau of Indian Affairs (BIA) formally adopted the policy that purchases and contracts be made with qualified Indian contractors to the maximum practicable extent. Buy Indian procurements are conducted in much the same way as other procurements are, the primary difference being that only Indian owned or controlled enterprises are eligible for award.

BUYING-IN Submitting an offer below anticipated costs in the expectation of increasing the contract amount after award (for example, through unnecessary or excessively priced contract modifications) or receiving follow-on contracts at artificially high prices to recover losses incurred on the buy-in contract. FAR 3.501-1. Buying-in may decrease competition or result in poor contract performance. The Government should minimize the opportunity for buying-in. It can seek a price commitment covering as much of the program as is practical by using (a) MULTIYEAR CONTRACTING or (b) priced OPTIONs for additional quantities that, together with the firm contract quantity, equal the program requirements. Or it can employ other safeguards, such as amortizing nonrecurring costs or determining that the offered price is unreasonable. When a buy-in is suspected, the contracting officer generally has the discretion to award a contract at the "buy-in" price but is directed to take appropriate action to ensure that buying-in losses are not recovered by the contractor through contract modifications or follow-on contracts. FAR 3.501-2. See Cibinic and Nash, Formation of Government Contracts 150, 465, 860; Virdin and Gallatin, *Buying In*, 84-3 Briefing Papers (Mar. 1984).

BUY ITEM An item or work effort to be produced or performed by a SUBCONTRACTOR. FAR 15.701. Such items are reviewed by the contracting officer when FAR 15.703 requires review of a contractor's MAKE-OR-BUY PROGRAM. See also MAKE ITEM.

BYRD AMENDMENT A provision in the Department of the Interior Appropriations Act for FY 1990, Pub. L. 101-121, 31 U.S.C. 1352, that imposes lobbying restrictions on all Government contractors. These restrictions, which became effective in Dec. 1989, prohibit recipients of Federal funds (that is, recipients of contracts, grants, loans, or cooperative agreements) from using those funds to pay persons to attempt to influence members of Congress or their staffs or members of the executive branch in connection with the award, extension, or modification of a contract, grant, or other funding instrument. The provisions, which flow down to subcontracts exceeding $100,000 regardless of tier, carry civil penalties of $10,000 to $100,000. This act is implemented by FAR Subpart 3.8, which requires the use of the solicitation provision Certification and Disclosure Regarding Payments to Influence Certain Federal Transactions (FAR 52.203-11) in all solicitations for contracts exceeding $100,000.

C

CANCELLATION CEILING The maximum amount that the Government is obligated to pay a contractor when there is a CANCELLATION OF a MULTIYEAR CONTRACT. FAR 17.101. Under 10 U.S.C. 2306(h)(2)(B), both RECURRING COSTS and NONRECURRING COSTS may be included in this ceiling. However, FAR 17.101 provides that, normally, only nonrecurring costs will be included. The amount that is actually paid to the contractor upon settlement for unrecovered costs (which cannot exceed the ceiling) is referred to as the cancellation charge.

CANCELLATION OF CONTRACT Notification to a contractor that the Government considers the contract null and void and will not be bound by its terms. Cancellation is generally proper only when the contractor has violated a criminal statute or committed some other gross impropriety. *United States v. Mississippi Valley Generating Co.*, 364 U.S. 520 (1961). Cancellation for BRIBERY, gratuities (see GRATUITY), or CONFLICT OF INTEREST is permitted by 18 U.S.C. 218. See FAR Subpart 3.7.

CANCELLATION OF MULTIYEAR CONTRACT Notification to a contractor that the Government will not make funds available for contract performance for any future year of a multiyear contract, or failure to notify the contractor that funds are available for performance of the succeeding program-year requirement. FAR 17.101. Such cancellation permits the contractor to recover costs in accordance with the Cancellation of Items clause in FAR 52.217-2, up to the amount of the CANCELLATION CEILING. See Cibinic and Nash, Formation of Government Contracts 820–35.

CANCELLATION OF SOLICITATION Notification to potential offerors, before AWARD, that a procurement will be permanently or temporarily stopped. Cancellation of an INVITATION FOR BIDS

62

(IFB) involves a loss of time, effort, and money spent by the Government and bidders. Therefore, IFBs should not be cancelled unless cancellation is clearly in the public interest (for instance, when the supplies or services are no longer required or when amendments to the IFB would be of such magnitude that a new IFB is desirable). FAR 14.209. When an IFB is cancelled, bids that have been received must be returned unopened to the bidders, and a notice of cancellation must be sent to all prospective bidders to which IFBs were issued. Preservation of the integrity of the SEALED BIDDING system dictates that, after bids have been opened, award must be made to the *responsible* bidder (see RESPONSIBILITY) that submitted the lowest *responsive* bid (see RESPONSIVENESS), unless there is a compelling reason to reject all bids and cancel the invitation. Therefore cancellation of IFBs after bid opening is to be avoided even more than cancellation before bid opening. FAR 14.404-1. With regard to competitive proposals solicited in contracting by NEGOTIATION, the contracting officer is to cancel the original REQUEST FOR PROPOSALS (RFP) and issue a new one, regardless of the stage of the acquisition, if a change is so substantial that it warrants complete revision of the RFP. FAR 15.606. See Ginsburg and Patin, chap. 2, Construction Contracting 169–80.

CAPABILITY VALIDATION Technical verification of the ability of a proposed ADP system configuration or replacement component, or the features or functions of its software, to satisfy functional requirements. The intent of the capability validation is to ensure that the proposed FEDERAL INFORMATION PROCESSING (FIP) RESOURCEs can provide the functions required by the Government. FIP performance requirements are not implied or measured in the validation. Examples of capability validation include operational capability demonstrations (OCDs), verification of conformance with information processing standards, expert examination of the technical literature supplied with the offer, contacts with other users of the proposed resource, and vendor certification of conformance with the functional requirements. FIRMR 201-4.001; FIRMR 201-20.304. See FIRMR Bulletin C-4, *Performance and Capability Validation of FIP Systems*. See also BENCHMARK.

CAPITALIZATION Setting up expenditures as ASSETs rather than treating them as current expenses. General accounting practices require contractors to capitalize the costs of tangible assets when they exceed predetermined amounts. Cost Accounting Standard 404, FAR 30.404, sets forth principles governing such capitalization. Once assets are capitalized, their cost is charged to contracts through DEPRECIATION.

CARDINAL CHANGE A CHANGE that is beyond the SCOPE OF THE CONTRACT and thus cannot be ordered by the contracting officer under the contract's Changes clause. Cardinal changes are BREACHes OF CONTRACT. In determining whether a change is beyond the scope of the contract and therefore a cardinal change, courts and boards compare the total work performed by the contractor with the work called for by the original contract. Work lies within the scope of contract if it can fairly and reasonably be regarded as within the contemplation of the parties when the contract was entered into or if it is essentially the same work that the parties bargained for when the contract was awarded. See Cibinic and Nash, Administration of Government Contracts 286–96; Nash, chap. 6, Construction Contracting 504–06.

CARGO PREFERENCE ACTS Acts giving preference to U.S.-owned vessels in the shipment of work under Government contracts. See FAR Subpart 47.5. The Cargo Preference Act of 1904, 10 U.S.C. 2631, requires that DoD use only U.S.-FLAG VESSELs for ocean transportation of supplies for the Army, Navy, Air Force, or Marine Corps, unless those vessels are not available at fair and reasonable rates. Under the Cargo Preference Act of 1954, 46 U.S.C. 1241(b), Government agencies acquiring supplies that require ocean transportation must ensure that at least 50 percent of the gross tonnage of the supplies is transported in privately owned U.S.-flag commercial vessels, to the extent that such vessels are available at fair and reasonable rates. The Cargo Preference Act of 1954 may be temporarily waived when the Congress, the President, or the Secretary of Defense declares the existence of an emergency that justifies a temporary waiver. 10 U.S.C. 2306(f). When this act is applicable, the clause at FAR 52.247-64 is used. See Cibinic, *Transportation of Supplies: Up with American Bottoms*, 4 N&CR ¶ 34 (May 1990); Cibinic, *Postscript: Cargo Preference*, 5 N&CR ¶ 29 (May 1991); Cibinic, *Correction: Cargo Preference*, 5 N&CR ¶ 64 (Nov. 1991).

CARIBBEAN BASIN COUNTRY END PRODUCT A product produced or manufactured in a country designated by the President as a beneficiary under the CARIBBEAN BASIN ECONOMIC

RECOVERY ACT. Such an end product must be an article (1) that is wholly the growth, product, or manufacture of a Caribbean Basin country or (2) that, in the case of an article consisting in whole or in part of materials from another country or instrumentality, has been substantially transformed in a Caribbean Basin country into a new and different article of commerce with a name, character, or use distinct from that of the article or articles from which it was transformed. The term does not, however, embrace products excluded from duty-free treatment for Caribbean countries under 19 U.S.C. 2703(b) (certain textiles, footwear, luggage, leather products, tuna, petroleum, watches, and watch parts). FAR 25.401. See Kenney and Duberstein, *Domestic Preference Provisions*, 89-3 Briefing Papers (Feb. 1989).

CARIBBEAN BASIN ECONOMIC RECOVERY ACT A 1983 act, 19 U.S.C. 2701 *et seq.*, making certain countries eligible for the TRADE AGREEMENTS ACT OF 1979 exceptions to the BUY AMERICAN ACT. These countries are in addition to those designated in the Trade Agreements Act itself. FAR 25.401 makes 22 countries, which the President designated as beneficiaries under the act, eligible for this preference. The list currently includes Antigua and Barbuda, Aruba, Bahamas, Barbados, Belize, British Virgin Islands, Costa Rica, Dominica, Dominican Republic, El Salvador, Grenada, Guatemala, Honduras, Jamaica, Monserrat, Netherlands Antilles, Panama, St. Christopher-Nevis, St. Lucia, St. Vincent and the Grenadines, Tobago, and Trinidad. The U.S. Trade Representative has determined that these countries provide appropriate reciprocal, competitive Government procurement opportunities for U.S. products and suppliers. The FAR contains a list of products excluded from duty-free treatment for Caribbean countries, such as (1) certain textiles and apparel, (2) leather wearing apparel (footwear, gloves, luggage), (3) tuna (in airtight containers), (4) petroleum goods, and (5) watches and watch parts. FAR 25.401. See Kenney and Duberstein, *Domestic Preference Provisions*, 89-3 Briefing Papers (Feb. 1989).

CARRIER (TELECOMMUNICATIONS) A common carrier, foreign carrier, or noncommon carrier engaged in providing TELECOMMUNICATIONS SERVICES. "Common carrier" means any entity engaged in the business of providing telecommunications services that are regulated by the Federal Communications Commission or other governmental body. "Noncommon carrier" means any entity other than a common carrier offering telecommunications facilities, services, or equipment for lease. "Foreign carrier" means any person, partnership, association, joint-stock company, trust, governmental body, or corporation not subject to regulation by a U.S. governmental body and not doing business as a citizen of the United States, providing telecommunications services outside the territorial limits of the United States. DFARS 239.7401. DFARS Subpart 239.75 states DoD policy on acquiring telecommunications services from common, noncommon, and foreign carriers.

CARRIER (TRANSPORTATION) A common carrier or a contract carrier. FAR 47.001. "Common carrier" means an entity holding itself out to the general public to provide transportation for compensation; "contract carrier" means an entity providing transportation for compensation under continuing agreement with one party or a number of parties. FAR 47.001. Guidance on contracts for transportation is contained in FAR Subpart 47.2.

CAS-COVERED CONTRACT Any negotiated contract or subcontract in which a COST ACCOUNTING STANDARDS (CAS) clause is required to be included. FAR 30.301. Such contracts are subject to either full or modified coverage of the Cost Accounting Standards requirements in accordance with the rules in FAR 30.201-2, which provide 15 exemptions from those requirements.

CATALOG OR MARKET PRICE See ESTABLISHED CATALOG OR MARKET PRICE.

CATEGORY OF MATERIAL A particular kind of goods, comprised of identical or interchangeable units, acquired or produced by a contractor, that are intended to be sold, or consumed, or used in the performance of either direct or indirect functions. FAR 30.301. Under Cost Accounting Standard 411, FAR 30.411, contracts must adjust the purchase price of a category of material by extra charges incurred, or discounts and credits earned, when accounting for the acquisition costs of material.

CEILING PRICE A price established by the parties that will be the maximum price that the Government will pay regardless of the cost of performance. Ceiling prices are included in all FIXED-PRICE INCENTIVE (FPI) CONTRACTs and FIXED-PRICE REDETERMINA-TION—RETROACTIVE (FPRR) CONTRACTs (FAR 16.206) and may be used in FIXED-PRICE REDETERMINATION—PROSPECTIVE (FPRP)

CONTRACTs (FAR 16.205). They are also included in COST-REIMBURSEMENT CONTRACTs on occasion. Ceiling prices are subject to revision under all contract clauses calling for EQUITABLE ADJUSTMENT or PRICE ADJUSTMENT.

CERTIFICATE OF APPOINTMENT See WARRANT.

CERTIFICATE OF COMMERCIAL PRICING See COMMERCIAL PRICING CERTIFICATE.

CERTIFICATE OF COMPETENCY (COC) Certification, by the SMALL BUSINESS ADMINISTRATION (SBA) under the Small Business Act, 15 U.S.C. 637(b)(7), that a SMALL BUSINESS CONCERN meets the standard of RESPONSIBILITY with regard to performing a particular Government contract. The issuance of a COC overrides a determination of nonresponsibility made by a contracting officer. When a contracting officer determines that a small business concern is nonresponsible, the concern must be given the opportunity to refer the matter to the SBA, which will decide whether or not to issue a COC. See FAR Subpart 19.6. Application for a COC consists of two forms to be completed by the small business contractor: SBA Form 74, Application for Certificate of Competency, and SBA Form 355, Application for Small Business Size Determination. See Efron and Muchmore, *Certificates of Competency*, 87-11 Briefing Papers (Oct. 1987).

CERTIFICATE OF CONFORMANCE A certification of a contractor that contractual supplies or services are of the quality specified and conform in all respects to the contract requirements. FAR 52.246-15. This certificate may be required of contractors and is used as a substitute for full inspection by the Government. FAR 46.504.

CERTIFICATE OF CURRENT COST OR PRICING DATA Certification by a successful offeror on a negotiated procurement that the COST OR PRICING DATA submitted to the Government was, to the best of its knowledge and belief, ACCURATE, COMPLETE, AND CURRENT as of the date when price agreement was reached. This certification includes the cost or pricing data supporting any ADVANCE AGREEMENTs and FORWARD PRICING RATE AGREEMENTs (FPRAs) between the offeror and the Government that are part of the proposal. FAR 15.804-4 contains a copy of the certificate and requires that it be submitted as soon as practicable after price agreement is reached. See Pettit and Meagher, *Certification*, 87-7 Briefing Papers (June 1987).

CERTIFICATION   A signed representation that certain facts are accurate. A certification can entail either (1) an explicit representation of fact requiring the inclusion of data and signature by the contractor ("The contractor hereby certifies that . . ." or "This is to certify that . . .") or (2) a deemed representation of a particular fact without execution of a specific certification document or use of specific certification language. The Government uses certifications in such matters as contractor status; truth of a matter; origin of a component; compliance with specifications; compliance with applicable laws; accuracy, currency, and completeness of cost or pricing data (see CERTIFIED COST OR PRICING DATA); and good faith, accuracy, and completeness in reflecting the amount owed with regard to claims, past contractual performance, and other matters. See Allen and Davis, *Government Contract Certifications*, 28 Cont. Mgmt. 5 (June 1988); Pettit and Meagher, *Certification*, 87-7 Briefing Papers (June 1987); Lovitky, *Frequently Encountered Problems with Certification of Claims under the Contract Disputes Act*, 16 Pub. Cont. L.J. 511 (1987).

CERTIFICATION OF CLAIM   A certification by a contractor under the CONTRACT DISPUTES ACT (CDA) that (1) a claim is made in good faith, (2) the supporting data are accurate and complete to the best of the certifier's knowledge and belief, and (3) the amount requested accurately reflects the contract adjustment for which the contractor believes the Government is liable. This certification is required by 41 U.S.C. 605(c)(1) for all claims over $50,000. FAR 33.207 requires that this certification be signed by (1) a senior company official in charge at the contractor plant or location involved or (2) an officer or general partner of the contractor having overall responsibility for the conduct of the contractor's affairs. These requirements have been strictly enforced by the courts and BOARDs OF CONTRACT APPEALS (BCAs). See Ivey, *Claim Certification*, 91-11 Briefing Papers (Oct. 1991); Cibinic and Nash, *Contractor Certification of Claims: Looking for "Mr./Ms. Right,"* 5 N&CR ¶ 27 (May 1991); Nash, *The Contract Disputes Act: A Prescription for Wheelspinning*, 4 N&CR ¶ 29 (May 1990).

CERTIFIED COST OR PRICING DATA   COST OR PRICING DATA submitted by an offeror on a negotiated procurement as required by the TRUTH IN NEGOTIATIONS ACT (TINA). The act requires such submission, unless an exemption applies, for negotiated procurement actions (see NEGOTIATION) expected to exceed $100,000, or, for DoD, NASA, and the Coast Guard, for contracts awarded after 5 Dec. 1990 expected to exceed $500,000. FAR 15.804-2. Exempt are actions whose prices are (1) based on ADEQUATE PRICE COMPETITION, (2) based on ESTABLISHED CATALOG OR MARKET PRICE of COMMERCIAL PRODUCTs sold in substantial quantities to the general public, or (3) set by law or regulation. FAR 15.804-3. Requests for exemption are submitted on Standard Form 1412, Claim for Exemption from Submission of Certified Cost or Pricing Data, FAR 53.301-1412. When the data are submitted, they are either appended to Standard Form 1411, CONTRACT PRICING PROPOSAL COVER SHEET, FAR 53.301-1411, or specifically identified by the contractor. See FAR 15.804-6. After price agreement is reached on a contract that requires submission of certified cost or pricing data, the contractor must submit a CERTIFICATE OF CURRENT COST OR PRICING DATA. See also DEFECTIVE COST OR PRICING DATA.

CERTIFIED PROFESSIONAL CONTRACTS MANAGER (CPCM) An individual who has attained certain levels of education, experience, and knowledge pertaining to contracts management. To be eligible, candidates must have 2 years of relevant procurement or contracting experience, hold a bachelor's degree, and have taken two procurement and contracting classes, one legal class, one financial management class, and four procurement-related classes. Candidates must pass a two-part, 6-hour written examination administered by the NATIONAL CONTRACT MANAGEMENT ASSOCIATION (NCMA). The first part includes two required questions and a number of general questions, whereas the second part concentrates on specific areas of contracts management: legal, finance, economics, and accounting; production; contracting; logistics of management; commercial purchasing; and State and local government procurement. Many NCMA chapters have created study groups to help candidates prepare for the examination. CPCM recertification is required every 5 years. See 27 Cont. Mgmt. (Special Education Issue, Nov. 1987).

CHANGE Any alteration to a contract permitted by a contract clause. Most changes are issued under the Changes clause of a contract. Contract changes may be bilateral, signed by both the contractor and the contracting officer, or unilateral, signed only by the contracting officer. A bilateral change is issued by a bilateral MODIFICATION and is often referred to as a supplemental agreement. A UNILATERAL CHANGE is issued by a unilateral modification and is generally called a CHANGE ORDER. FAR 43.103. See also CONSTRUCTIVE CHANGE. And see Nash, Government Contract Changes; Cibinic and Nash, Administration of Government Contracts, chap. 4.

CHANGED CONDITIONS See DIFFERING SITE CONDITIONS.

CHANGE-OF-NAME AGREEMENT A legal instrument executed by the contractor and the Government that recognizes the legal change of name of the contractor without disturbing the original contractual rights and obligations of the parties. FAR 42.1201. FAR 42.1205 contains guidance on when such an agreement should be used and provides a model agreement. See also NOVATION.

CHANGE ORDER A written order signed by the contracting officer, directing the contractor to make a CHANGE without the contractor's consent, as authorized by the contract's Changes clause. FAR 43.101. Generally, Government contracts contain one of the Changes clauses in FAR 52.243-1 through -6 permitting the contracting officer to make unilateral changes, in designated areas, within the general SCOPE OF THE CONTRACT. These changes are accomplished by issuing written orders on Standard Form 30, Amendment of Solicitation/Modification of Contract, FAR 53.301-30. Change orders must be issued by the contracting officer, except when authority to issue such orders is delegated to an administrative contracting officer. FAR 43.202. Upon receipt of a change order, the contractor must continue performance of the contract as changed, except that, in cost-reimbursement or incrementally funded contracts, the contractor is not obligated to continue performance or incur costs beyond the established funding limits. FAR 43.201 and 52.243-1 through -6. See Nash, Government Contract Changes, chap. 7.

CHANGE TO COST ACCOUNTING PRACTICE Any alteration in a COST ACCOUNTING PRACTICE, whether or not the practice is covered by a DISCLOSURE STATEMENT, but excluding the following: (1) the initial adoption of a cost accounting practice when a cost is first incurred or a function is first created, (2) the partial or total elimination of a cost or the cost of a function, or (3) the revision of a cost accounting practice for a cost that previously had been immaterial. FAR 30.302-2. FAR 30.302-3 contains illustrations of changes that meet this definition and FAR 30.302-4 describes changes that do not. The Cost Accounting Standards clause in FAR 52.230-3 requires that the parties negotiate an EQUITABLE ADJUSTMENT if the price is affected by a change to the contractor's cost accounting practice. See Davis, *Changes in Cost Accounting Practice* (thesis for The George Washington University National Law Center's Government Contracts Program, 1989).

CHRISTIAN DOCTRINE   A legal rule providing that clauses required by regulation to be included in Government contracts will be read into a contract whether or not physically included in the contract, unless a proper DEVIATION from the regulations has been obtained. The doctrine derives from the case of *G. L. Christian & Assoc. v. United States*, 160 Ct. Cl. 1, 312 F.2d 418, 160 Ct. Cl. 58, 320 F.2d 345, *cert. denied*, 375 U.S. 954 (1963), 170 Ct. Cl. 902, *cert. denied*, 382 U.S. 821 (1965), in which it was held that the termination for convenience clause applied even though it had been omitted from the contract, since the procurement regulations required its inclusion. The Christian doctrine should not, however, be read to mean that *all* procurement regulations have the force and effect of law; it applies only to those regulations that implement fundamental procurement policy. See Nash and Cibinic, *Mandatory Clauses: The Regulations Override the Contract*, 4 N&CR ¶ 13 (Feb. 1990).

CIVIL DEFENSE COSTS   Costs incurred by a contractor in planning for, and protecting life and property against, the possible effects of enemy attack. FAR 31.205-5. Costs of civil defense measures (including costs in excess of normal plant protection costs, first aid training and supplies, fire fighting training and equipment, posting of additional exit notices and directions, and other approved civil defense measures) undertaken on the contractor's premises pursuant to suggestions or requirements of civil defense authorities are allowable (see ALLOWABLE COST) when allocated to all work of the contractor. Costs of capital ASSETs acquired for civil defense purposes are allowable through depreciation. Contributions to local civil defense funds and projects are unallowable.

CIVILIAN AGENCY ACQUISITION COUNCIL (CAAC)   The Government body that, with the DEFENSE ACQUISITION REGULATO-

RY COUNCIL (DAR COUNCIL), prepares and issues revisions to the FAR through coordinated action. FAR 1.201-1. Each council maintains cognizance over specified portions of the FAR and is responsible for (1) agreeing with the other council on all revisions, (2) submitting to the FAR Secretariat information required for publishing a Federal Register notice soliciting comments, (3) considering all comments received, (4) arranging for public meetings, (5) preparing any final revision in the appropriate FAR format and language, and (6) submitting any final revision to the FAR Secretariat for publication in the Federal Register and printing. Members of the CAAC (1) represent their agencies on a full-time basis, (2) are selected for their superior qualifications in terms of acquisition experience and demonstrated professional expertise, and (3) are funded by their respective agencies. The Chairperson of the CAAC is the representative of the Administrator of General Services; the other members represent the Departments of Agriculture, Commerce, Energy, Health and Human Services, the Interior, Labor, State, Transportation, the Treasury, and Veterans Affairs as well as the Environmental Protection Agency and the Small Business Administration.

CLAIM A written demand or assertion by one of the contracting parties seeking, as a matter of right, the payment of money, the adjustment or interpretation of contract terms, or other relief arising under, or relating to, the contract. FAR 33.201. A claim *arising under* a contract is a claim that can be resolved under a contract CLAUSE providing for relief sought by the claimant; a claim *relating to* a contract is one for which no specific contract clause provides such relief. However, a written demand or assertion by the contractor seeking the payment of money exceeding $50,000 is subject to the CERTIFICATION OF CLAIM requirement of the CONTRACT DISPUTES ACT (CDA) OF 1978 and FAR 33.207. A voucher, invoice, or other routine request for payment that is not in DISPUTE when submitted is not a claim. See Nash, *The Contract Disputes Act: No Claim, No Jurisdiction*, 5 N&CR ¶ 66 (Dec. 1991); Cibinic, *What's a "Claim": Is Prior Disagreement Necessary?* 2 N&CR ¶ 25 (May 1988); Hoover, *Recognizing Government Contractors' Claims and Contracting Officers' Final Decisions*, 29 A.F. L. Rev. 85 (1988); Nash, chap. 6, Construction Contracting 531–56; Patin and Ginsburg, chap. 16, Construction Contracting 1186–1207.

CLAIMS COURT (Cl. Ct.) A court of the United States established especially to hear and decide legal claims against the Government. Its basic jurisdiction is conferred by 28 U.S.C. 1491, but it has a variety of additional jurisdictional statutes. Under the CONTRACT DISPUTES ACT (CDA) OF 1978, 41 U.S.C. 601–613, as amended, this court shares concurrent jurisdiction with the BOARDs OF CONTRACT APPEALS (BCAs) over Government contract DISPUTEs (each contractor appealing a DECISION OF THE CONTRACTING OFFICER must elect either the agency BCA or the Claims Court). The other jurisdiction of the Claims Court most relevant to Government procurement concerns PROTESTs (preaward only), 28 U.S.C. 1491(a)(3), disputes concerning fraud or forfeiture, 41 U.S.C. 604 and 28 U.S.C. 1491, and patent and copyright disputes, 28 U.S.C. 1498. The Federal Courts Improvement Act of 1982 created the Claims Court from the Trial Division of the Court of Claims. See White, *The New Government Contract Courts*, 83-11 Briefing Papers (Nov. 1983); Anthony and Smith, *The Federal Courts Improvement Act of 1982: Its Impact on the Resolution of Federal Contract Disputes*, 13 Pub. Cont. L.J. 201 (1983); England, *Constitutionality of Article I Court Adjudication of Contract Disputes Act Claims*, 16 Pub. Cont. L.J. 338 (1987); Sumison, *Injunctive Relief in the United States Claims Court: Does a Bid Protestor Have Standing?* 16 Pub. Cont. L.J. 530 (1987).

CLARIFICATION A Government communication with an offeror on a competitively negotiated procurement (see NEGOTIATION) for the sole purpose of eliminating minor irregularities, informalities, or apparent CLERICAL MISTAKEs in a proposal. FAR 15.601. Clarification is accomplished by explanation or substantiation, either in response to Government inquiry or as initiated by the offeror. Unlike DISCUSSION, clarification does not give the offeror an opportunity to revise or modify its proposal, except to the extent that correction of apparent clerical mistakes results in a revision. FAR 15.607 requires the contracting officer to examine all proposals for minor informalities or irregularities and apparent clerical mistakes, and to communicate with the offerors to clarify these matters. If the communication prejudices the interest of other offerors, however, the contracting officer must enter into discussions with all other offerors in the COMPETITIVE RANGE before making award. FAR 15.607. The term "clarification" is also used to describe an inquiry by a contractor regarding ambiguous specifications; see DUTY TO SEEK CLARIFICATION.

CLASSIFIED ACQUISITION An ACQUISITION that consists of one or more contracts in which offerors are required to have access to CLASSIFIED INFORMATION in order to properly submit an OFFER or QUOTATION, to understand the performance requirements of a CLASSIFIED CONTRACT under the acquisition, or to perform the contract. FAR 4.401. FAR Subpart 4.4 provides guidance on such acquisitions.

CLASSIFIED CONTRACT   Any contract whose performance requires, or will require, access to CLASSIFIED INFORMATION by the contractor or its employees. A contract may be a classified contract even though the contract document is not classified. FAR 4.401. Such contracts may be awarded only to contractors who have complied with the security requirements of the Department of Defense.

CLASSIFIED INFORMATION   Any information or material, regardless of its physical form or characteristics, that is owned by, produced by or for, or under the control of the U.S. Government; is determined pursuant to Executive Order 12356, 6 Apr. 1982, to require protection against unauthorized disclosure; and is so designated. FAR 4.401. Such information is classified Confidential, Secret, or Top Secret. National Security Act, 50 U.S.C. 401 *et seq.* See DEAR 904.401; Executive Order 12333, 4 Dec. 1981.

CLAUSE   A term or condition used in CONTRACTs—or in both SOLICITATIONs and contracts—and applying after contract award, or both before and after award. FAR 52.101. A term used only in solicitations is called a PROVISION. FAR Subpart 52.2 sets forth the texts of all standard FAR clauses (as does DFARS Subpart 252.2 for DFARS clauses), each in its own separate subsection. The subpart is arranged by subject matter in the same order as, and keyed to, the parts of the FAR. All FAR clause numbers begin with "52.2." The next two digits correspond to the number of the FAR part in which the clause is prescribed. The number is completed by a hyphen and a sequential number assigned within each section of FAR Subpart 52.2. The FAR clause number will be followed by the clause's title and—in contracts—by its effective date (e.g., 52.203-3, Gratuities (APR 1984)). FAR Subpart 52.1 contains instructions for using clauses, and FAR Subpart 52.3 contains an extensive PROVISION AND CLAUSE MATRIX. See Farrell and Pankowski, *FAR Contract Clauses— First Impressions*, 24 Cont. Mgmt. 21 (Feb. 1984).

CLAUSE MATRIX See PROVISION AND CLAUSE MATRIX.

CLERICAL MISTAKE A mistake of a contractor that is apparent on the face of a bid or proposal. Such mistakes are routinely corrected by contracting officers in accordance with the procedures set forth in FAR 14.406-2 and FAR 15.607. Examples of such mistakes are obvious misplacement of decimal points, incorrect discounts, reversal of prices and misdesignation of units. Other mistakes in bids or proposals alleged before contract award are dealt with under more elaborate procedures in accordance with FAR 14.406 or FAR 15.607. See Cibinic and Nash, Formation of Government Contracts 489–500, 614–16.

CLOSEOUT The process of settling all outstanding contractual issues to ensure that each party has met all of its obligations, and documenting the contract file accordingly. The primary objectives of contract closeout are (1) to identify and resolve, before memories fade, any uncompleted obligations or pending liabilities on the part of either the Government or the contractor and (2) to ensure that contract-related decisions and actions have been properly documented. FAR 4.804 provides instructions for the closeout of contract files.

CODE OF ETHICS A written code, adopted by a Government contractor, setting forth the basic ethical rules that the contractor follows. DoD has strongly encouraged its contractors to adopt such codes to ensure that they conduct themselves only with the highest degree of integrity (see PROCUREMENT INTEGRITY) and honesty. Thus, DFARS 203.7001 states that contractor systems of management controls should provide for a written code of business ethics. A code of ethics serves as a mechanism by which questionable activities can be brought to the attention of management and places the contractor's corporate seal on compliance with Government antifraud initiatives. The code of ethics gains effectiveness if (1) the policy is communicated to employees in writing, (2) employees certify that they have read the code and understood it, and (3) individuals found violating the code are disciplined. See Seyfarth et al., The Government Contract Compliance Handbook 2-2; Mur, *Ethics in Government Contracting: Putting Your House in Order*, 20 NCMJ 15 (1987) (see appendices for sample codes, including the Grumman Code of Business Conduct).

CODE OF FEDERAL REGULATIONS (CFR) A Government codification of the general and permanent rules published in the FEDERAL REGISTER by the executive departments and agencies of the Federal Government. The Code is divided into 50 titles, each representing a broad area subject to Federal regulation. Each title is subdivided into chapters, which usually bear the name of the issuing agency. Each chapter is further subdivided into parts covering specific regulatory areas. For example, Title 41, Public Contracts and Property Management, Subtitle E, Federal Information Resources Management Regulations System, Chapter 201, contains the Federal Information Resources Management Regulation (FIRMR). Title 48 contains the Federal Acquisition Regulations System (Chapter 1 contains the FAR, Chapter 2 contains the DFARS, and following chapters include other supplemental regulations). The CFR is published annually and is available from the U.S. Government Printing Office, Washington, DC 20402.

COLLATERAL COSTS Agency costs of operation, maintenance logistic support, or GOVERNMENT-FURNISHED PROPERTY. FAR 48.001. If these costs are reduced as a result of a VALUE ENGINEERING CHANGE PROPOSAL (VECP), the contractor is entitled to a share of the resulting COLLATERAL SAVINGS.

COLLATERAL SAVINGS Measurable net reductions in the agency's overall projected COLLATERAL COSTS, resulting from a VALUE ENGINEERING CHANGE PROPOSAL (VECP). Such savings are exclusive of ACQUISITION SAVINGS; they result without regard to changes in the acquisition cost. FAR 48.104-2 and the Value Engineering clauses in FAR 52.248-1, -2, and -3 provide that such savings are calculated solely by the CONTRACTING OFFICER (CO) and may not exceed $100,000 or the contract price or cost, whichever is greater. See Cibinic and Nash, Administration of Government Contracts 310–11.

COLLUSIVE BIDDING A fraudulent agreement between OFFERORs to eliminate competition or restrain trade. FAR 3.301(a). Generally, such bidding involves exchanging information before bidding or agreeing which offeror will submit the low bid. Collusive bidding is a violation of the antitrust laws that must be reported to the Attorney General by the procuring agency. FAR 3.303. See Cibinic and Nash, Formation of Government Contracts 143–49; Coate, *Techniques for Protecting Against Collusion in Sealed Bid Markets*, 30 Antitrust Bull. 897 (Winter 1985).

COMMERCE BUSINESS DAILY (CBD) A daily publication of the Department of Commerce listing U.S. Government solicitations, contract awards, subcontracting leads, sales of surplus property, and foreign business opportunities. 15 U.S.C. 637(e) and 41 U.S.C. 416 require that agencies publish a SYNOPSIS of proposed contract actions in the CBD at least 15 days before issuing an invitation for bids or request for proposals. See FAR Subpart 5.2. The primary purposes of the CBD notice are to improve small business access to acquisition information and to enhance competition by publicizing contracting and subcontracting opportunities. Subscriptions to the CBD are available from the U.S. Government Printing Office, Washington, DC 20402. Extensive discussion of the preparation and transmittal of CBD notices can be found at FAR 5.207.

COMMERCIAL BILL OF LADING See BILL OF LADING.

COMMERCIAL IMPRACTICABILITY See IMPRACTICABILITY OF PERFORMANCE.

COMMERCIAL ITEM DESCRIPTION (CID) A type of PURCHASE DESCRIPTION used by Government agencies in procuring COMMERCIAL PRODUCTs and COMMERCIAL-TYPE PRODUCTs. A CID is prepared by the requiring agency through selective application and tailoring of a document or documents prepared by private industry. FAR 10.002 states that CIDs are to be preferred over other types of Government specifications and standards.

COMMERCIALITY Selling or trading an item to the public in the course of normal business operations. Commerciality is one of two conditions that must be met if an item is to be considered as having an ESTABLISHED CATALOG OR MARKET PRICE, which would exempt the item from the requirement that CERTIFIED COST OR PRICING DATA be submitted to the contracting officer. (The other condition is that the item be sold in substantial quantities to the general public.) See FAR 15.804-3(c)(3). Items (which may be either supplies or services) meet the condition of commerciality if they are of a class or kind (1) regularly used for other than Government purposes and (2) sold or traded in the course of conducting normal business operations. (The "substantial quantities" condition is met when the quantities regularly sold to other than affiliates of the seller for end use by other than Government agencies are sufficient to constitute a real commercial market.)

COMMERCIAL PRICING CERTIFICATE A certification by an offeror that the prices offered are no higher than prices charged to other customers within the last 60 days. Such a certificate is required by 41 U.S.C. 253e when certain items sold to the public are bought by Government agencies. The standard certificate is set forth in FAR 52.215-32, and the procedures governing its use are contained in FAR 15.813. These regulations also contain exemptions from the use of the certificate.

COMMERCIAL PRODUCT A product—such as an item, material, component, subsystem, or system—that is regularly used for other-than-Government purposes and that is sold or traded to the general public in the course of normal business operations at prices based on ESTABLISHED CATALOG OR MARKET PRICEs. FAR 11.001. FAR Part 11 contains guidance on the purchase of commercial products. There is a strong congressional preference for the purchase of commercial products rather than the development of new items. See 10 U.S.C. 2325 requiring the purchase of NONDEVELOPMENTAL ITEMs (NDIs) to the maximum extent practicable and 41 U.S.C. 424 establishing an Advocate for the Acquisition of Commercial Products in the Office of Federal Procurement Policy. See Kirby and Ursini, *Commercial Products Procurement*, 91-3 Briefing Papers (Feb. 1991); Nash, *Buying Commercial Products: Can the Government Benefit by Adopting Commercial Practices?* 4 N&CR ¶ 30 (May 1990).

COMMERCIAL-TYPE PRODUCT A commercial product (1) modified to meet some Government-peculiar physical requirement or addition or (2) otherwise identified differently from its normal commercial counterparts. FAR 11.001. Such products fall within the guidance for the acquisition of COMMERCIAL PRODUCTs.

COMMISSION ON GOVERNMENT PROCUREMENT (COGP) Commission that studied Federal procurement and recommended to Congress methods to promote the economy, efficiency, and effectiveness of procurement by the executive branch. Created by Pub. L. 91-129 in 1969, the Commission, made up of 12 members (2 congressmen, 2 senators, the Comptroller General, 2 executive branch officials, and 5 non-Government persons) submitted its findings and recommendations in 1972. The Commission's four-volume report included a Blueprint for Action that outlined an integrated system for the Federal procurement process, addressing policy control, the statutory framework, the work force, funding, contracting officer authority, contract administration and audit, disputes and protests, and the uses of commercial products and services. See the Procurement Round Table Report *Reforming Federal Procurement: What the Commission on Government Procurement Recommended and What Has Happened*, 31 Cont. Mgmt. 16 (Feb. 1991).

COMMON CARRIER   See CARRIER (TELECOMMUNICATIONS) and CARRIER (TRANSPORTATION).

COMMUNICATIONS SECURITY (COMSEC) The communications security systems, services, and concepts that constitute protective measures taken to deny unauthorized persons information derived from telecommunications of the U.S. Government related to national security and to ensure the authenticity of any such communications. FIRMR 201-4.001. GSA operates and maintains COMSEC systems and services to meet the requirements of the agencies. Agencies must consider using these systems and services to meet their requirements. FIRMR 201-24.203-2; FIRMR Bulletin C-19, *Information System Security (INFOSEC)*.

COMPARABILITY The condition that exists when an offered price can be compared with some other price in the process of PRICE ANALYSIS. This condition, necessary for effective price comparison, exists when all price-related differences have been identified and accounted for so that the prices being compared are based on relatively equal assumptions. A practical definition of "comparable" is "having enough similar characteristics or qualities to make comparison useful." When engaged in price analysis, the Government has two choices if it cannot establish comparability: it can disregard the data, or it can discount them. See Armed Services Pricing Manual (ASPM) vol. 2, chap. 15.

COMPATIBILITY-LIMITED REQUIREMENT   A type of SPECIFICATION used in acquiring FEDERAL INFORMATION PROCESSING (FIP) RESOURCES. It limits offerors to only those firms capable of offering hardware or software compatible with (i.e., capable of working with) the Government's existing configuration. Use of this type of specification must be supported by a statement that (1) the agency has technical or operational requirements for compatibility when adding resources to, or replacing a portion of, an installed base of resources, and the agency determines that replacing additional portions of the installed base to avoid compatibility-limited requirements is not advantageous to the Government; or (2) the agency determines that the risk and impact of a conversion failure on agency critical mission needs would be so great that acquiring noncompatible resources is not a feasible alternative. FIRMR 201-20.103-4.

COMPENSABLE DELAY A DELAY, incurred by a contractor in contract performance, for which the Government is required to give compensation. There are two standard clauses providing for such compensation: (1) the Suspension of Work clause in FAR 52.212-12, which must be used in all fixed-price construction and architect-engineer contracts and (2) the Government Delay of Work clause in FAR 52.212-15, which must be used in all fixed-price supply contracts except those for commercial items. These clauses give a price adjustment (excluding profit) when an unreasonable delay is caused by an act (or failure to act) of the contracting officer in the administration of the contract. If a clause of this nature is not included in the contract, the contractor may obtain compensation for a delay caused by the Government under a BREACH OF CONTRACT theory. See Cibinic and Nash, Administration of Government Contracts 450–78; McGovern, *Compensating Contractors for Delay Related Costs*, 24 Cont. Mgmt. 12 (Oct. 1984).

COMPENSATED PERSONAL ABSENCE The cost of vacations, sick leave, holidays, and other compensated absences of employees from work. Cost Accounting Standard 408, FAR 30.408, requires that such costs be assigned to the accounting period in which the entitlement was earned and provides guidance on the interpretation of this requirement. FAR 31.205-6(m) provides that such costs incurred by a contractor are allowable (see ALLOWABLE COST) to the extent that they are reasonable.

COMPENSATION FOR PERSONAL SERVICES All remuneration paid by a contractor currently or accrued, in whatever form and whether paid immediately or deferred, for services rendered by employees to the contractor during the period of contract performance (except with regard to severance pay costs and pension costs). FAR 31.205-6. Such compensation is generally an allowable cost subject to the detailed guidance in FAR 31.205-6. Compensation for personal services includes, but is not limited to, salaries; wages; directors' and executive committee members' fees; bonuses (including stock bonuses); incentive awards; employee stock options, stock appreciation rights, and stock ownership plans; employee insurance; fringe benefits; contributions to pension, annuity, and management-employee incentive compensation plans; and allowances for off-site pay, incentive pay, location allowances, hardship pay, severance pay, and cost-of-living differentials. See Petit and Victorino, *Personal Compensation Costs*, 84-6 Briefing Papers (June 1984).

COMPETING CONTRACTOR Any entity that is, or is reasonably likely to become, a competitor for or recipient of a contract or subcontract under any procurement of property or services or any person acting on behalf of such an entity. 41 U.S.C. 423(n)(2). Competing contractors are subject to many of the provisions governing PROCUREMENT INTEGRITY. FAR 3.104-4(b) contains additional guidance on the meaning of "competing contractor."

COMPETITION The effort of sellers of products or services to secure the business of the buyer by proposing the most attractive contract terms. In Government procurement, competition involves the attempt by more than one offeror to obtain a contract, with the winner being selected on the basis of criteria established in a SOLICITATION issued by the purchasing activity. The COMPETITION IN CONTRACTING ACT (CICA) of 1984 established FULL AND OPEN COMPETITION as the primary goal of Government procurement. FAR Part 6 sets forth the competition requirements that derive from this act. When the Government obtains ADEQUATE PRICE COMPETITION in a negotiated procurement, the contracting officer may waive the requirement for the submission of CERTIFIED COST OR PRICING DATA. See Cibinic and Nash, Formation of Government Contracts 287–386.

COMPETITION ADVOCATE An employee of a CONTRACTING ACTIVITY specifically assigned the task of challenging barriers to competition and promoting FULL AND OPEN COMPETITION. 41 U.S.C. 404 requires that each executive agency and each contracting activity appoint a competition advocate. Such advocates are generally high-ranking employees reporting directly to the heads of their agency or activity. 41 U.S.C. 405 requires that they report to Congress on the success of their efforts. FAR 6.501 requires that they must be in a position other than that of the agency SENIOR PROCUREMENT EXECUTIVE, must not be assigned any duties inconsistent with those of competition advocate, and must be provided with necessary staff or assistance. Competition advocates are charged with (1) promoting full and open competition and challenging barriers to it; (2) reviewing contracting operations to identify (a) opportunities and actions necessary to achieve full and open competition and (b) the conditions that unnecessarily restrict it; (3) preparing annual reports; (4) recommending goals and plans for increasing competition; and (5) recommending a system of personal and organizational accountability—one that motivates individuals to promote competition and recognizes those who do. FAR 6.502. Cibinic and Nash, Formation of Government Contracts 311.

COMPETITION IN CONTRACTING ACT (CICA) A 1984 act, 41 U.S.C. 251 *et seq.* and 10 U.S.C. 2304 *et seq.*, that amended the two basic procurement statutes (the ARMED SERVICES PROCUREMENT ACT (ASPA) and the FEDERAL PROPERTY AND ADMINISTRATION SERVICES ACT (FPASA) OF 1949) to enhance competition, granted statutory authorization for the GAO's PROTEST function, created protest jurisdiction for Federal information processing (FIP) resources procurements at the General Services Administration Board of Contract Appeals (GSBCA), and revised protest procedures. CICA was the first major revision to the procurement statutes since the 1940s. It introduced the phrase FULL AND OPEN COMPETITION, replaced the familiar non-negotiated procurement label "formal advertising" with "sealed bidding," and placed the COMPETITIVE PROPOSALS (competitive NEGOTIATION) method on a par with SEALED BIDDING. Recognizing that negotiation could be as competitive as sealed bidding, CICA did away with the requirement to execute a DETERMINATION AND FINDINGS (D&F) to justify use of negotiation instead of formal advertising. Instead, it established a requirement to execute a justification—and obtain approval of it—for any procurement in which full and open competition would not be obtained. See FAR Parts 6, 14, 15, and 33; Callahan and Vest, *The Competition in Contracting Act—A Marketing Tool*, 20 NCMJ 67 (1987); Cohen, *The Competition in Contracting Act*, 14 Pub. Cont. L.J. 1 (1983).

COMPETITIVE ADVANTAGE An advantage of one competitor over another. Normally, the Government is not concerned with competitive advantages held by one competitor in the procurement process because many advantages are inherent in a free economy. For example, a competitor may have an advantage because of its superior design capabilities, its geographic location (resulting in lower transportation costs), its lower taxes (because its State has low tax rates), or its more productive employees. However, it is the policy of the Government to attempt to overcome UNFAIR COMPETITIVE ADVANTAGEs. The Government also attempts to compensate for the advantage gained by manufacturing materials and products in a foreign country; see BUY AMERICAN ACT.

COMPETITIVE ALTERNATIVE SOURCE See DUAL SOURCE.

COMPETITIVE NEGOTIATION See COMPETITIVE PROPOSALS.

COMPETITIVE PROCEDURES Contracting procedures that meet the statutory requirement for FULL AND OPEN COMPETITION in Government procurement. 10 U.S.C. 2304(a)(2) and 41 U.S.C. 253(a)(2) cite two major types of competitive procedures: SEALED BIDDING and COMPETITIVE PROPOSALS. 10 U.S.C. 2302(2) and 41 U.S.C. 259(b) list five additional types of competitive procedures: (1) BROOKS ACT (ARCHITECT-ENGINEER PROCUREMENTS) procedures, (2) BROAD AGENCY ANNOUNCEMENT (BAA), (3) MULTIPLE-AWARD SCHEDULE (MAS) contracting, (4) procurements under 15 U.S.C. 644 (small business SET-ASIDE), and (5) SMALL BUSINESS INNOVATIVE RESEARCH contracting.

COMPETITIVE PROPOSALS A procedure used in negotiated procurement (see NEGOTIATION) that (1) is initiated by a REQUEST FOR PROPOSALS (RFP) setting out the Government's requirements and the criteria for evaluation of offers, (2) contemplates the submission of timely proposals by the maximum number of known qualified offerors, (3) usually provides for discussion or negotiation with those offerors found to be within the COMPETITIVE RANGE, and (4) concludes with the award of a contract to the offeror whose offer is most advantageous to the Government, considering price and the other factors included in the solicitation. Guidance on this procedure is contained in FAR Parts 6 and 15. This procedure is one of the major COMPETITIVE PROCEDURES that meets the requirement for FULL AND OPEN COMPETITION.

COMPETITIVE RANGE The range of proposals that have a reasonable chance of being selected for contract award under a COMPETITIVE PROPOSALS procurement. FAR 15.609 requires that this range be determined by the contracting officer on the basis of price or cost and other factors stated in the solicitation. Unless there is an AWARD ON INITIAL PROPOSALS, the contracting officer must conduct written or oral DISCUSSIONs with all responsible offerors (see RESPONSIBILITY) who submit proposals within the competitive range. FAR 15.609(a) provides that when there is doubt as to whether a proposal is in the competitive range, the proposal should be included. Following written or oral discussions, a proposal may be dropped from the competitive range if it no longer has a reasonable chance of being selected for award. BEST AND FINAL OFFERs (BAFOs) are obtained from those offerors whose proposals remain in the competitive range following written or oral discussions. FAR 15.611. See Cibinic and Nash, Formation of Government Contracts 596–609.

COMPLAINT In a contract DISPUTE, a written statement in which the PLAINTIFF before the U.S. CLAIMS COURT (Cl. Ct.) or the APPELLANT BEFORE a BOARD OF CONTRACT APPEALS gives a direct statement of each of its claims, the bases for these claims, and the dollar amount claimed to the extent known.

COMPLETION BOND See PERFORMANCE BOND.

COMPTROLLER GENERAL (COMP. GEN.) The officer of the Government, appointed by the President of the United States to serve a 15-year term, who heads the GENERAL ACCOUNTING OFFICE (GAO). Title 31 of the United States Code requires the Comptroller General to investigate all matters relating to the receipt, disbursement, and application of public funds. The Comp. Gen. and the GAO also have the power to examine the records of contractors doing business with the Government (see EXAMINATION OF RECORDS CLAUSE), evaluate and assess the results of Government programs (and typically issue reports), and evaluate and issue recommendations on protests pursuant to the COMPETITION IN CONTRACTING ACT (CICA). FAR 33.104. See also Hordell, *Everyone Has Heard of the United States General Accounting Office—But What Does It Do?* 36 Fed. B. News & J. 328 (1989).

COMPUTER PROGRAM A series of instructions or statements in a form acceptable to a computer, designed to cause the computer to execute an operation or operations. DFARS 227.401. Computer programs include operating systems, assemblers, compilers, interpreters, data management systems, utility programs, sort–merge programs, and ADPE maintenance/diagnostic programs, as well as applications programs such as payroll, inventory control, and engineering analysis programs. Computer programs may be either machine-dependent or machine-independent and may be general-purpose in nature or designed to satisfy the requirements of a particular user. Computer programs are one type of COMPUTER SOFTWARE.

COMPUTER SOFTWARE Computer programs, procedures, rules, or routines specifically designed to make use of and extend the capabilities of AUTOMATIC DATA PROCESSING EQUIPMENT (ADPE). It includes operating systems, assemblers, compilers, interpreters, data base management systems, utility programs, sort–merge programs, maintenance–diagnostic programs, firmware, and applications programs. For the purpose of procurement policy, computer software is an element of FEDERAL INFORMATION PROCESSING (FIP) RESOURCES subject to the statutes and regulations governing such resources. The FIRMR distinguishes "application software," which means a series of instructions that cause the computer to execute an operation, and "common-use software," which means software that deals with applications common to many agencies and usable with minor reprogramming by many agencies. FIRMR 201-4.001. When used in the FAR policy that allocates the rights of the contracting parties to software prepared or delivered under Government contracts, the term includes COMPUTER PROGRAMs, computer data bases, and COMPUTER SOFTWARE DOCUMENTATION. FAR 27.401. However, under DFARS 227.401, which governs rights in software acquired by DoD, the term includes only computer programs and computer data bases, not documentation. In general, both the FAR and the DFARS regulations permit the contractor to claim RESTRICTED RIGHTS to software that is DEVELOPED AT PRIVATE EXPENSE. See Nash, *Rights in Computer Software: Something Worth Fighting For*, 4 N&CR ¶ 16 (Mar. 1990); Davis, *Acquisition of Rights in Computer Software by the Department of Defense*, 17 Pub. Cont. L.J. 77 (1987); Samuelson, *Understanding the Implications of Selling Rights in Software to the Defense Department: A Journey through the Regulatory Maze*, 13 Rutgers Computer Tech. L.J. 33 (1987).

COMPUTER SOFTWARE DOCUMENTATION Recorded information, including computer listings and printouts, that (1) documents the design or details of computer software, (2) explains the capabilities of the software, (3) provides data for testing the software, or (4) provides operating instructions. See DFARS 227.401, which states that such documentation must be in human-readable form (as distinguished from machine-readable). Under 10 U.S.C. 2320 and DFARS Subpart Part 227.4, this type of documentation is TECHNICAL DATA for the purposes of allocating the rights of the contracting parties to the information; under FAR Subpart 27.4, it is COMPUTER SOFTWARE for purposes of allocating rights. Under FIRMR 201-4.001, it is "application software" (see COMPUTER SOFTWARE) for purposes of procurement policy. See Samuelson, *Understanding the Implications of Selling Rights in Software to the Defense Department: A Journey Through the Regulatory Maze*, 13 Rutgers Computer Tech. L.J. 33 (1987).

CONCEPT EXPLORATION   The process, conducted at the beginning of a MAJOR SYSTEM ACQUISITION, of refining the proposed concept and reducing the concept's technical uncertainties. FAR 34.005-3. This is designated as "Phase 0" of the DoD acquisition process.   See Part 3 of DoD Instruction 5000.2, *Defense Acquisition Management Policies and Procedures*, 23 Feb. 1991. The process has also been called "concept formulation." Agencies have generally awarded two or more firm-fixed-price contracts to competing contractors to perform this task.

CONCEPTUAL DESIGN   The initial stage of a contract for ARCHITECT-ENGINEER (A-E) SERVICES.   In contracts with DoE, conceptual design requires the A-E to provide preliminary studies to (1) develop a project scope that satisfies a program need or statutory requirements; (2) validate feasibility and attainable performance levels; (3) identify and quantify risks; (4) develop a reliable budget estimate and a realistic performance schedule; (5) develop project criteria and design parameters for all engineering disciplines; (6) identify applicable codes and standards, quality assurance requirements, environmental studies, construction materials, space allowances, energy conservation features, health and safety safeguards, security requirements, and any other features or requirements necessary to describe the project. DEAR 936.605(c)(1). See also TITLE I, TITLE II, TITLE III SERVICES.

CONCERN   Any business entity organized for profit (even if its ownership is in the hands of a nonprofit entity) that has a place of business located in the United States and that makes a significant contribution to the U.S. economy through payment of taxes and/or use of American products, material and/or labor, etc. "Concern" includes but is not limited to an individual, partnership, corporation, joint venture, association, or cooperative. FAR 19.001. This term is used in the FAR Part 19 guidance on determining whether potential contractors are eligible for the benefits of the SMALL BUSINESS ACT.

CONCURRENT CONTRACT SAVINGS Net reductions in the prices of other contracts that are definitized (see DEFINITIZATION) and ongoing at the time a VALUE ENGINEERING CHANGE PROPOSAL (VECP) is accepted. The term is also used in the context of situations in which contractors or prospective contractors have some bias relating to a procurement or would gain a competitive advantage from a procurement; see ORGANIZATIONAL CONFLICT OF INTEREST (OCI). FAR 3.601 prohibits contracting officers from knowingly awarding contracts to Government employees or to business concerns owned or controlled by Government employees. This policy seeks to avoid any conflict of interest that might arise between the employees' interests and their Government duties and any appearance of favoritism or preferential treatment. See Sutton, *Conflicts of Interest in the Acquisition Process*, 29 A.F. L. Rev. 165 (1988). See also PROCUREMENT INTEGRITY.

CONFIGURATION MANAGEMENT A procedure for applying technical and administrative direction and surveillance to identify and document the functional and physical characteristics of an item or SYSTEM, control any changes to those characteristics, and record and report the change process and implementation status. The goal of configuration management is to ensure that continuous changes to a product do not result in unacceptable cost growth. The configuration management process must be carefully tailored to the capacity, size, scope, nature, complexity, and phase of the life cycle of the system involved. Postak, Glossary of Terms, in Subcontracts—Government and Industry Issues. In DoD configuration management, procedures are contained in Military Standard 480B, 15 July 1988 (major systems), and Military Standard 481B, 15 July 1988 (other items). See Collins et al., *Configuration Management and Complex Weapon Systems: Challenges in the Competitive Environment*, 27 Cont. Mgmt. 20 (Sep. 1987).

CONFLICT OF INTEREST A clash between the public interest and the private pecuniary interest of the individual concerned. Black's Law Dictionary. The term is typically used in regard to public officials and their relationship to matters of private interest or private gain; see PERSONAL CONFLICT OF INTEREST. It is also used in regard to persons who have left Government employment; see REVOLVING DOOR. The term also identifies those situations in which contractors or prospective contractors have some bias relating to a procurement or would gain a competitive advantage from a procurement; see ORGANIZATIONAL CONFLICT OF INTEREST (OCI). With regard to Government procurement, FAR 3.601 prohibits contracting officers from knowingly awarding contracts to Government employees or to business concerns owned or controlled by Government employees. This policy seeks to avoid any conflict of interest that might arise between the employees' interest and their Government duties, and any appearance of favoritism or preferential treatment. See Sutton, *Conflicts of Interest in the Acquisition Process*, 29 A.F. L. Rev. 165 (1988). See also PROCUREMENT INTEGRITY.

CONSEQUENTIAL DAMAGES Those losses, injuries, or damages that do not flow directly and immediately from the act of a party but flow instead from some of the consequences or results of that party's act. Consequential damages resulting from a seller's BREACH OF CONTRACT, for example, include (1) any loss resulting from general or particular requirements and needs that the seller at the time of contracting had reason to know of and that could not reasonably be prevented by COVER or otherwise and (2) any injury to persons or property proximately resulting from any breach of warranty. Black's Law Dictionary; U.C.C. 2-715(2). Contractors generally cannot recover consequential damages from the Government, and FAR Subpart 46.8 provides that it is the policy of the Government to relieve contractors from liability for Government property that is damaged after acceptance of items delivered on contracts. See the Limitation of Liability clauses in FAR 52.246-23 through -25.

CONSIDERATION The inducement to a contract: the cause, motive, price, or impelling influence that leads a party to enter a contract. Black's Law Dictionary. A binding contract requires an offer, acceptance of the offer, and consideration. Consideration generally requires two elements: (1) something must be given that the law regards as of sufficient legal value for the purpose—either a benefit to the seller or a detriment to the buyer, and (2) the something (benefit or detriment of legal value) must be dealt with by the parties as the agreed-upon price or exchange for the promise—there must be a "bargained-for exchange." The requirement for consideration does not require that what is relied upon for consideration be equivalent in value to the promise; the consideration need only have "some value." Murray on Contracts § 55.

CONSISTENCY IN ALLOCATING COSTS The allocation of each type of contract cost on the same basis. Cost Accounting Standard 402, FAR 30.402, requires such consistency and gives detailed guidance on the interpretation of this rule. See COST ACCOUNTING STANDARDS (CAS).

CONSISTENCY IN ESTIMATING, ACCUMULATING, AND REPORTING COSTS The treating of comparable transactions in the same manner for cost accounting purposes whether a contractor is estimating costs or accumulating and reporting costs. Cost Accounting Standard 401, FAR 30.401, requires such consistency and gives detailed guidance on the interpretation of this rule. See COST ACCOUNTING STANDARDS (CAS).

CONSOLIDATED LIST OF DEBARRED, SUSPENDED, AND INELIGIBLE CONTRACTORS See PARTIES EXCLUDED FROM PROCUREMENT PROGRAMS.

CONSOLIDATED LOCAL TELECOMMUNICATIONS SERVICE The local communications service provided by GSA to all Federal agencies located in a building, complex, or geographical area. FIRMR 201-4.001. The FIRMR requires agencies to use available consolidated local telecommunications service to meet their local telecommunications requirements or request an exception to the mandatory use of these services for unique requirements. FIRMR 201-24.102.

CONSTRUCTION Construction, alteration, or repair (including dredging, excavating, and painting) of buildings, structures, or other REAL PROPERTY. FAR 36.102. For purposes of the FAR definition, the terms "buildings, structures, or other real property" include but are not limited to improvements of all types, such as improvements to bridges, dams, plants, highways, parkways, streets, subways, tunnels, sewers, mains, power lines, cemeteries, pumping stations, railways, airport facilities, terminals, docks, piers, wharves, ways, lighthouses, buoys, jetties, breakwaters, levees, canals, and channels. Construction does not include the manufacture, production, furnishing, construction, alteration, repair, processing, or assembling of vessels, aircraft, or other kinds of PERSONAL PROPERTY. FAR Part 36 contains guidance on the procedures to be followed in buying construction, and FAR Subpart 22.4 covers the procedures required by the DAVIS-BACON ACT. The FAR contains special clauses for construction contracts. See the PROVISION AND CLAUSE MATRIX in FAR Subpart 52.3. And see Cibinic and Nash, Formation of Government Contracts 16–17; Bednar et al., chaps. 1–18, Construction Contracting.

CONSTRUCTION ACTIVITY An activity at any organizational level of the Department of Defense that (1) is responsible for the architectural, engineering, and related technical aspects of the planning, design, and CONSTRUCTION of facilities and (2) receives its technical guidance from the Army Office of the Chief of Engineers, Naval Facilities Engineering Command, or Air Force Directorate of Civil Engineering. DFARS 236.102.

CONSTRUCTION, ALTERATION, OR REPAIR See CONSTRUCTION.

CONSTRUCTION MANAGEMENT A method of acquiring CONSTRUCTION in which the Government contracts with a construction manager to assist in project design and construction. During the design phase the construction manager monitors the design for constructability and conformance with the project budget. During construction the construction manager acts as the agent of the Government in assisting in the award of contracts for elements of the project and acting as a GENERAL CONTRACTOR to coordinate the construction process. See Nash, chap. 1, Construction Contracting 5–7.

CONSTRUCTION MANAGEMENT ASSOCIATION OF AMERICA (CMAA) A national trade association, founded in 1918, that encourages the growth of construction management as a professional service and promotes ethical standards. CMAA presents seminars, forums, and awards, and it publishes a Standards of Practice manual and model contract documents. The organization also provides telephone referral services on technical and legal issues. (CMAA, 12355 Sunrise Valley Drive, Suite 640, Reston, VA 22091; (703) 391–1200.)

CONSTRUCTION MATERIALS Articles, materials, and supplies brought to the construction site for incorporation into the building or work. FAR 25.201. Under the provisions of the BUY AMERI-

CAN ACT, such materials must be of domestic origin unless their cost is unreasonable or they are not reasonably available in commercial quantities. FAR 25.202.

CONSTRUCTIVE CHANGE An oral or written act or omission by the contracting officer or other authorized Government official that is construed as having the same effect as a written CHANGE ORDER. A constructive change consists of two elements: a change element, which calls for examination of the actual performance to see whether it went beyond the minimum standards demanded by the contract; and an order element, in which the Government's representative, by word or deed, requires the contractor to perform work that is not a necessary part of its contract. Claims for constructive changes are the primary means used by contractors to obtain additional compensation for performing fixed-price contracts. Included are claims concerning CONTRACT INTERPRE-TATION, defective specifications (see IMPLIED WARRANTY OF SPECIFICATIONS), nondisclosure of information (see SUPERIOR KNOWLEDGE), IMPRACTICABILITY OF PERFORMANCE, breach of the DUTY TO COOPERATE, and ACCELERATION. See Nash, Government Contract Changes, chaps. 10–15.

CONSULTANTS See INDIVIDUAL EXPERTS AND CONSULTANTS and PROFESSIONAL AND CONSULTANT SERVICES.

CONTINGENCY A possible future event or condition arising from presently known or unknown causes, the cost outcome of which is indeterminable at the present time. Armed Services Pricing Manual (ASPM) vol. 1, app. B. Costs of allowances for contingencies are generally considered UNALLOWABLE COSTs for historical costing purposes because historical costing deals with costs incurred and recorded on the contractor's books. FAR 31.205-7. However, in some cases (for example, contract terminations), a contingency factor applicable to a past period may be recognized in the interest of expediting settlement. In connection with estimates of future costs, contingencies fall into two categories: (1) those that may arise from presently known and existing conditions, the effects of which are foreseeable within reasonable limits of accuracy (for example, anticipated costs of rejects and defective work) and (2) those that may arise from presently known or unknown conditions, the effects of which cannot be anticipated so precisely (the results of pending litigation, for example). In negotiating contract prices, contracting officers generally are willing to include the first category but attempt to exclude the second category from the price.

CONTINGENT FEE Any commission, percentage, brokerage, or other fee that is contingent upon the success that a person or concern has in securing a Government contract. FAR 3.401. Such fees are prohibited by 10 U.S.C. 2306(b) and 41 U.S.C. 254(a). Contractors' arrangements to pay contingent fees for soliciting or obtaining Government contracts have long been considered contrary to public policy because such arrangements may lead to attempted or actual exercise of improper influence (which is *any* influence that induces or tends to induce a Government employee or officer to give consideration or to act regarding a Government contract on any basis other than the merits of the matter). Negotiated solicitations and contracts must contain a warranty by the contractor against contingent fees.   See FAR 52.203-4, Contingent Fee Representation and Agreement; FAR 52.203-5, Covenant Against Contingent Fees; Standard Form 119, Statement of Contingent or Other Fees, FAR 53.301-119. As an exception to the warranty, contingent fee arrangements between a contractor and a BONA FIDE EMPLOYEE or a BONA FIDE AGENCY are permitted. For breach of the contractor's warranty, the Government may annul the contract or recover the full amount of the contingent fee. FAR 3.402. FAR 31.205-33(a) also precludes the allowability of the cost of consultants when they are contingent on the recovery of costs.

CONTRACT An agreement, enforceable by law, between two or more competent parties, to do or not do something not prohibited by law, for a legal CONSIDERATION. FAR 2.101 defines a contract as a mutually binding legal relationship that obligates the seller to furnish supplies or services (including construction) and the buyer to pay for them.   Such a contract is a procurement contract as distinguished from a contract for employment or for sale of property. The definition encompasses all types of commitments that obligate the Government to an expenditure of appropriated funds and that, except as otherwise authorized, are in writing. The FAR states that, in addition to the standard bilateral instruments, Government procurement contracts take the form of awards and NOTICEs OF AWARDs; job orders or task letters issued under BASIC ORDERING AGREEMENTs; LETTER CONTRACTs; orders, such as PURCHASE ORDERs, under which the contract becomes effective upon written acceptance or actual performance; bilateral contract modifications (see MODIFICATIONS); and other written instruments. 31 U.S.C. 6301 *et seq.* distinguishes between contracts, GRANTs and COOPERATIVE AGREEMENTs and contains guidance as to when each type of instrument should be used. In this sense, procurement contracts are those instruments governed by the FEDERAL ACQUISITION REGULATION (FAR).

CONTRACT ADMINISTRATION   Any administrative activity undertaken by either the Government or the contractor during the time from contract AWARD to contract CLOSEOUT. More specifically, the term refers to steps taken by the Government representatives responsible for ensuring Government and contractor compliance with the terms and conditions of the contract. Such steps include routine tasks such as monitoring contractor progress, reviewing invoices, processing payments, inspecting deliverables, and closing out the contract file; they also include problem-solving activities that are necessitated by unforeseeable circumstances—changes, problems, and disagreements—that arise following contract award. FAR Part 42 contains general guidance on these activities, including a long list of functions that are generally considered to be part of the contract administration process. See Cibinic and Nash, Administration of Government Contracts, chap. 1.

CONTRACT ADMINISTRATION OFFICE   An office within a contracting activity that performs assigned postaward functions related to CONTRACT ADMINISTRATION and also handles certain assigned preaward functions. FAR 2.101.

CONTRACT AUDIT MANUAL   See DCAA CONTRACT AUDIT MANUAL (CAM).

CONTRACT AWARD   See AWARD.

CONTRACT CARRIER   See CARRIER (TRANSPORTATION).

CONTRACT CLAUSE   See CLAUSE.

CONTRACT COST PRINCIPLES   See COST PRINCIPLES.

CONTRACT DATA REQUIREMENTS LIST (CDRL)   A list of all technical data to be delivered on a contract with DoD, prepared using DD Form 1423, DFARS 253.303-1423. The purpose of this list is to identify, in a single document, all technical data ordered under a contract in order to permit the management of such data. DFARS 227.405-70(a) requires that the Data Requirements clause in DFARS 252.227-7031 be included in all R&D and supply contracts over $25,000. This clause provides that only data items included on DD Form 1423 (and data called for by standard clauses) must be delivered under the contract. The purpose of this requirement is to force procuring activities in DoD to list technical data items on DD Form 1423 rather than include them in the numerous specifications and drawings that may be part of the contract documents. See Nash and Rawicz, Patents and Technical Data, chap. 6.

CONTRACT DISPUTES ACT (CDA) OF 1978 An act, Pub. L. 95-563, 41 U.S.C. 601–613, 10 U.S.C. 2324, that establishes the procedures to be used by contractors and contracting officers in resolving DISPUTEs arising out of and relating to contracts. The act contains detailed provisions for handling contract CLAIMs by and against the Government, including (1) certification of contractor claims of $50,000 or more (see CERTIFICATION OF CLAIM); (2) contractor and Government claims as the subject of a DECISION OF THE CONTRACTING OFFICER; (3) APPEAL FROM A CONTRACTING OFFICER'S DECISION to a BOARD OF CONTRACT APPEALS (BCA) within 90 days or to the U.S. CLAIMS COURT (Cl. Ct.) within 12 months of becoming final; (4) appeals from either the BCAs or the Claims Court to the COURT OF APPEALS FOR THE FEDERAL CIRCUIT (CAFC or Fed. Cir.); (5) establishment of the BCAs and ADMINISTRATIVE JUDGEs (members of BCAs); (6) SMALL CLAIMS PROCEDUREs and ACCELERATED PROCEDUREs before the BCAs; (7) payment of INTEREST on claims to contractors; (8) BCA subpoena power; (9) penalties for submission of fraudulent claims; and (10) payment of claims. The act is implemented by FAR Subpart 33.2 and the Disputes clause at FAR 52.233-1. See Dover and Pollack, *Invoking the Contract Disputes Act: Potential Pitfalls*, 90-8 Briefing Papers (July 1990); Bednar, chap. 13, Construction Contracting 960–77, 1009–18.

CONTRACTED ADVISORY AND ASSISTANCE SERVICES (CAAS) See ADVISORY AND ASSISTANCE SERVICES.

CONTRACT FINANCING See FINANCING.

CONTRACT FINANCING PAYMENT See FINANCING PAYMENT.

CONTRACTING Purchasing, renting, leasing, or otherwise obtaining supplies or services from non-Federal sources. FAR 2.101.
Contracting includes description (but not determination) of supplies and services required, selection and solicitation of sources,
preparation and award of contracts, and all phases of contract
administration. It does not include making GRANTs or COOPERA-
TIVE AGREEMENTs. Contracting is a subset of ACQUISITION or
PROCUREMENT.

CONTRACTING ACTIVITY An element of an agency so designated by the agency head and delegated broad authority for
acquisition functions. FAR 2.101. In NASA regulations, the term
is synonymous with "NASA Headquarters," "Installation," "Field
Installation." NFS 18-2.101. DoD contracting activities are listed
at DFARS 202.101.

CONTRACT AUTHORITY A form of BUDGET AUTHORITY under
which contracts or other obligations may be entered into in
advance of an APPROPRIATION or in excess of amounts otherwise
available in a revolving fund. Legislation providing new contracting authority must also provide that it will be effective for any
FISCAL YEAR only to such extent or in such amounts as provided
in appropriations acts. 31 U.S.C. 1351(a). When an agency has
contracting authority, it may enter into contracts without an appropriation without violating the ANTI-DEFICIENCY ACT.   Since
contracting authority itself is not an appropriation—it provides
authority to enter into binding contracts rather than the funds to
make payments under them—a contractor cannot be paid until the
obligation is funded by a subsequent appropriation or by the use
of a revolving fund. See Principles of Federal Appropriations Law
(2d ed.), chap. 2. See Cibinic and Nash, Formation of Government Contracts 31–106.

CONTRACTING METHODS See METHODS OF PROCUREMENT.

CONTRACTING OFFICE An office that awards or executes a
CONTRACT for supplies or services and performs postaward functions not assigned to a CONTRACT ADMINISTRATION OFFICE. FAR
2.101.

CONTRACTING OFFICER (CO) An employee of the Government with the authority to legally bind the Government by signing
a contractual instrument. FAR 2.101 defines a contracting officer

as a person with the authority to enter into, administer, and/or terminate contracts and make related DETERMINATIONs AND FINDINGS (D&Fs). It then states: "The term includes certain AUTHORIZED REPRESENTATIVEs of the contracting officer acting within the limits of their authority as delegated by the contracting officer." There are three types of contracting officers, each with different responsibilities in contract procurement, management, and execution. A purchasing or PROCURING CONTRACTING OFFICER (PCO) has authority to enter into a contract, an ADMINIS-TRATIVE CONTRACTING OFFICER (ACO) administers the perfor-mance of the contract, and a TERMINATION CONTRACTING OFFICER (TCO) is responsible for contract termination. Each must make determinations and findings related to his or her area of contract management. FAR 1.602-1. Contracting officers are responsible for ensuring performance of all necessary actions for effective contracting, ensuring compliance with the terms of the contract, and safeguarding the interest of the Government in its contractual relationships. FAR 1.602.2. Contracting officers are appointed in writing, on a Standard Form 1402, Certificate of Appointment (see WARRANT). FAR 53.301-1402. In selecting contracting officers, the appointing official must consider the complexity and dollar value of the acquisitions to be assigned and the candidates' training, education, business acumen, judgment, character, and reputation. FAR 1.603-2. See Bednar and Jones, The DOD Contracting Officer; Reifel and Bastianelli, *Contracting Officer Authority*, 86-4 Briefing Papers (Mar. 1986).

CONTRACTING OFFICER REPRESENTATIVE (COR) An employee of a CONTRACTING ACTIVITY designated by a CON-TRACTING OFFICER (CO) to perform certain CONTRACT ADMINIS-TRATION activities. A COR is an AUTHORIZED REPRESENTATIVE of a contracting officer within the scope of his or her authority but is rarely given the authority to enter into contractual agreements or AMENDMENTs. Not all agencies use the term COR, but some of their regulations contain guidance on the functions of such employees. See GSARS Subpart 542.2 and AFARS Subpart 42.90. And see Cibinic and Nash, Administration of Government Contracts 28–47; Reifel and Bastianelli, *Contracting Officer Authority*, 86-4 Briefing Papers (Mar. 1986).

CONTRACTING OFFICER'S DECISION See DECISION OF THE CONTRACTING OFFICER.

CONTRACTING OFFICER TECHNICAL REPRESENTATIVE (COTR) A technical employee of a CONTRACTING ACTIVITY designated by a CONTRACTING OFFICER (CO) to perform CONTRACT ADMINISTRATION activities in regard to technical issues. A COTR is an AUTHORIZED REPRESENTATIVE of a contracting officer but is rarely given the authority to enter into contractual agreements or AMENDMENTs. Frequently the authority of COTRs is delineated by TECHNICAL DIRECTION clauses. Not all of the agencies use the term COTR, but some of their regulations contain guidance on the functions of such employees. See, for example, NFS 18-42.270, 18-53.303-1634. And see Reifel and Bastianelli, *Contracting Officer Authority*, 86-4 Briefing Papers (Mar. 1986).

CONTRACTING OUT See A-76 POLICY.

CONTRACT INSURANCE/PENSION REVIEW (CIPR) An in-depth evaluation of a contractor's insurance program, pension plans, other deferred compensation plans, and related policies, procedures, practices, and costs. The Defense Logistics Agency (DLA) is the designated DoD executive agency for CIPRs. DFARS 242.7301. ADMINISTRATIVE CONTRACTING OFFICERs (ACOs) are responsible for determining the reasonableness of Government contractors' insurance/pension costs. Insurance/pension specialists assigned to certain DLA defense contract administration services regions conduct CIPRs to help ACOs make these determinations. A CIPR should be the only formal review of a contractor's insurance/pension program, except for (1) periodic tests of the system performed by contract administration personnel and by the DEFENSE CONTRACT AUDIT AGENCY (DCAA) or (2) any special reviews the ACO may initiate. If any organization believes that additional reviews of the contractor's insurance/pension program should be performed, that request should be conveyed to the ACO. DFARS 242.7301. See also INSURANCE and PENSION PLAN.

CONTRACT INTERPRETATION The process of determining what the parties agreed to in their bargain. Contract interpretation involves determining the meaning of words, supplying missing terms and filling in gaps, resolving ambiguities, and, at times, finding that the parties must perform in a manner that appears contrary to the words of the contractual document. The basic objective of contract interpretation is to determine the intent of the parties. Various rules of interpretation define contract terms, determine ORDER OF PRECEDENCE among the various parts of the contract, or seek to read the contract as a whole, interpreting it so as to (1) avoid rendering its terms meaningless, (2) avoid conflict, and (3) fulfill the principal purpose of the parties. Cibinic and Nash, Administration of Government Contracts, chap. 2.

CONTRACT LINE ITEM See LINE ITEM.

CONTRACT MODIFICATION See MODIFICATION.

CONTRACT NUMBER A number assigned by a contracting agency to identify a procurement action and provide the most efficient point of reference in correspondence dealing with the action. In DoD contracting actions, uniform PROCUREMENT INSTRUMENT IDENTIFICATION (PII) NUMBERS are assigned to all contracts and related instruments. DFARS 204.7000. NASA has a uniform ACQUISITION INSTRUMENT IDENTIFICATION system covering solicitations and contracts. NFS Subpart 18-4.71.

CONTRACTOR Usually used to denote a party that enters into a CONTRACT with the Government. However, the term may be applied to any individual or other legal entity that directly or indirectly (e.g., through an affiliate) submits offers for or receives a Government contract, that may reasonably be expected to submit offers for or receive a Government contract, or that conducts business (or may reasonably be expected to conduct business) with the Government as an agent or representative of another contractor. ("Government contract," as used here, includes a contract for carriage under Government or commercial bills of lading, or a subcontract under a Government contract.) FAR 9.403. With regard to subcontracting, "contractor" (i.e., PRIME CONTRACTOR) means the total contractor organization or a separate entity of it (such as an affiliate, division, or plant) that performs its own purchasing. FAR 44.101. Both the prime contractor and any SUBCONTRACTOR are defined as contractors for the purposes of equal employment opportunity (FAR 22.801) and Service Contract Act (FAR 22.1001) compliance.

CONTRACTOR-ACQUIRED PROPERTY Property acquired or otherwise provided by a contractor for performing a contract and to which the Government has title. FAR 45.101. Contractor-acquired property is treated as GOVERNMENT PROPERTY for the purpose of management and control under the provisions of FAR Subpart 45.5.

CONTRACTOR COST DATA REPORTING (CCDR) A system through which contractors report projected and actual costs and related data to DoD for selected procurements, typically MAJOR SYSTEM ACQUISITION programs. The CCDR provides the procuring activity with an "independent cost estimate" of all of the activity's major acquisitions as well as the means to compare a system with other related systems. Grskovich, *What is C/SCSC?—In English, Please!* 23 NCMJ 25 (1990). See DoD Instruction 5000.2, *Defense Acquisition Management Policies and Procedures*, 23 Feb. 1991, part 11D; DD Form 1921, Cost Data Summary Report, DFARS 253.303-1921. See also COST/ SCHEDULE CONTROL SYSTEMS CRITERIA (C/SCSC) and WORK BREAKDOWN STRUCTURE (WBS).

CONTRACTOR INVENTORY See INVENTORY.

CONTRACTOR PURCHASING SYSTEM REVIEW (CPSR)
The complete evaluation by the Government of a contractor's purchasing of material and services, subcontracting, and subcontract management, from development of the requirement through completion of subcontract performance. FAR 44.101. The objective of a CPSR is to evaluate the efficiency and effectiveness with which the contractor spends Government funds and complies with Government policy when subcontracting. The review provides the administrative contracting officer (ACO) with a basis for granting, withholding, or withdrawing approval of the contractor's purchasing system. FAR 44.301. Contractors are subject to a CPSR if their expected sales to the Government under other than sealed bidding procedures are expected to exceed $10 million during the next 12 months. FAR 44.302. The review specifically focuses on (1) the degree of price competition obtained; (2) pricing policies and techniques; (3) methods of evaluating subcontractors' responsibility; (4) treatment accorded affiliates; (5) policies and procedures regarding labor surplus area concerns and small business concerns; (6) planning, award, and postaward management of major subcontract programs; (7) compliance with Cost Accounting Standards in awarding subcontracts; (8) appropriateness of types of contracts used; and (9) management control systems to administer progress payments to subcon-tractors. FAR 44.303. See DFARS Subpart 244.3 and Appendix C; Prokopy,

Contractor Purchasing System Review: What Is It? 28 Cont. Mgmt. 20 (Oct. 1988).

CONTRACTOR RISK ASSESSMENT GUIDE (CRAG) A DoD initiative providing for reduced oversight of contractors that meet certain specified standards of internal audit and control. The purpose is to launch a cooperative effort by DoD and private industry to (1) encourage contractors to develop more effective internal control systems and (2) improve the effectiveness and efficiency of DoD oversight. CRAG is a voluntary endeavor, under which a contractor can seek administrative contracting officer review and approval of its program. Two guides available through industry associations, *DoD Contractor Risk Assessment Guide* (Oct. 1988) and *DoD Contractor Risk Assessment Guide Program* (Nov. 1988), identify control objectives for the five areas that the Government considers of highest risk in relation to cost or pricing: indirect cost submissions, labor charging, MATERIAL MANAGEMENT AND ACCOUNTING SYSTEMs (MMASs), estimating systems, and purchasing. See also SELF-GOVERNANCE. And see Carren and Seal, *The Challenges of CRAG*, 89-6 CP&AR 3 (June 1989); Menestrina, *CRAG: Just Another Four-Letter Word?* 29 Cont. Mgmt. 8 (Apr. 1989); *DoD Unveils Contractor Risk Assessment Guide Program to Reduce Oversight*, 50 Fed. Cont. Rep. 913, 933 (5 Dec. 1988).

CONTRACTOR TEAM ARRANGEMENT See TEAM ARRANGEMENT.

CONTRACTOR VERSUS GOVERNMENT PERFORMANCE See A-76 POLICY.

CONTRACTOR WEIGHTED AVERAGE SHARE (CWAS) A DoD system, used in the late 1960s and 1970s, for reduced Government oversight when a contractor's business was predominantly commercial or competitive fixed-priced work. DoD considered it desirable (1) to measure the cost–risk motivation imposed on individual contractors (as evidenced by the nature and type of the contracts) and (2) whenever practicable, to eliminate administrative controls and overhead audits on those contractors that attained a verifiable "weighted average share" or risk that met a prescribed threshold. The CWAS concept was based on the premise that, with good management and proper motivation to be cost-conscious, industry would control costs much more effectively than could detailed review, control, and overhead audit by Government personnel. ASPR 3-1001. DoD eliminated the program in 1983.

CONTRACT PRICING The function that gathers, assimilates, evaluates, and, in establishing objectives, brings to bear all the skills and techniques needed to shape a specific PRICING ARRANGEMENT. Those skills and techniques include PRICE ANALYSIS, COST ANALYSIS, and use of accounting and technical evaluations and systems analysis techniques to facilitate the negotiation of realistic pricing arrangements. Armed Services Pricing Manual (ASPM) vol. 1, chap. 1.

CONTRACT PRICING PROPOSAL COVER SHEET A document (Standard Form 1411) prescribed by FAR 15.804-6(b) for contractors' use in submitting pricing proposals for negotiated procurements. This form is to be prepared in accordance with the instructions and formats of FAR Table 15-2 (see FAR 15.804-6), and must be used by contractors when submitting COST OR PRICING DATA to the Government. FAR Table 15-2 includes extensive discussion of the form and the required attachments: a cost element breakdown for each proposed LINE ITEM, supporting breakdowns for each cost element, and summary total amounts covering all line items when more than one line item is proposed. Standard Form 1411 must also include breakdowns for the following basic elements of cost, if applicable: materials, subcontracted items, standard commercial items, interorganizational transfers, raw materials, purchased parts, direct labor, indirect costs, other costs, royalties, and facilities capital cost of money. The form includes a certification that the data reflect the contractor's "best estimate," and such certification has been used against contractors in criminal prosecutions.

CONTRACT SCOPE See SCOPE OF THE CONTRACT.

CONTRACT SPECIALIST An employee of a CONTRACTING ACTIVITY in the GS 1102 personnel series. This series also includes procurement analysts, contract negotiators, cost/price analysts, and contract administrators. This series of employees forms the pool that is the main source of CONTRACTING OFFICERs (COs).

CONTRACT TYPE See TYPE OF CONTRACT.

CONTRACTUAL RELIEF See EXTRAORDINARY CONTRACTUAL ACTION.

CONTRACT WORK HOURS AND SAFETY STANDARDS ACT (CWHSSA) A 1962 act, 40 U.S.C. 327–333, that regulates the wages and working conditions of LABORERS OR MECHANICS performing work under certain Government contracts. The act requires that at least time-and-a-half overtime be paid to any such laborer or mechanic who works more than 8 hours in a day or 40 hours in a week. Any contractor or subcontractor who violates these requirements is liable to the employee for unpaid wages and to the Government for liquidated damages of $10 for each calendar day in violation. FAR Subpart 22.3 implements the CWHSSA requirements.

CONTRA PROFERENTEM (kon'tra prō-fe-ren'tem) A rule of contract interpretation meaning "against the party who proffers or puts forward a thing." The rule is applied to construe ambiguous provisions or clauses (see AMBIGUITY) most strongly against the party who selected the language or drafted the clause or provision. Black's Law Dictionary. In most cases, the rule applies against the Government; as the customary drafter, the Government bears the responsibility for using language that permits only one reasonable interpretation. The rule is not applied against the Government, however, if the contractor has failed to meet its DUTY TO SEEK CLARIFICATION. See Beran, *Specifications: The Duty Trilogy—Government and Contractor Responsibilities, Part One—The Drafter's Duty to Convey Unambiguous Information and the Other's Duty to Seek Clarification*, 27 Cont. Mgmt. 4 (Aug. 1987), 12 (Sept. 1987), and 11 (Oct. 1987); Flynn, *The Rule* Contra Proferentem *in the Government Contract Interpretation Process*, 11 Pub. Cont. L.J. 2 (1980). The rule also does not apply when the contract language is drafted jointly by both parties.

CONTRIBUTION See DONATION.

CONTROLLED MATERIALS The various shapes and forms of steel, copper, aluminum, and nickel alloys specified in Schedule II, and defined in Schedule III, of the DEFENSE PRIORITIES AND ALLOCATION SYSTEM (DPAS). FAR 12.301. The use of these materials on defense contracts is given priority by their designation as RATED ORDERs in contracts and subcontracts. See FAR Subpart 12.3.

CONVENIENCE TERMINATION See TERMINATION FOR CONVENIENCE.

COOPERATIVE AGREEMENT A legal instrument used principally for transferring money, property, or services to a State or local government or to another recipient in order to accomplish a public purpose of support or stimulation where substantial involvement is expected between the Government agency and the recipient. 31 U.S.C. 6305. See Riley, III Federal Contracts, Grants and Assistance 85. A cooperative agreement is frequently similar to a COST-SHARING CONTRACT. However, a cost-sharing contract is subject to the FEDERAL ACQUISITION REGULATION (FAR), whereas a cooperative agreement is not. Thus, agencies entering into cooperative agreements generally have substantial freedom to structure the terms and conditions of the agreement. Regulatory guidance is issued by agencies in the form of assistance regulations, in cooperation with the OFFICE OF MANAGEMENT AND BUDGET (OMB). However, statutes enabling specific programs, as well as certain other regulations, may contain requirements for cooperative agreements that differ from the usual assistance regulations or even resemble ACQUISITION approaches. For example, the Cooperative Agreement with Canada is a MEMORANDUM OF UNDERSTANDING (MOU) that does not fall within the scope of 31 U.S.C. 6305. Brown, *A Federal Agency's Authority to Use a Cooperative Agreement for a Particular Project*, 18 Pub. Cont. L.J. 188 (1988).

COOPERATIVE RESEARCH AND DEVELOPMENT AGREEMENT (CRADA) Agreement between a Government laboratory or Government-owned, contractor-operated laboratory and a private organization to jointly conduct RESEARCH AND DEVELOPMENT (R&D) work. Such an agreement permits companies' R&D personnel to work alongside Government scientists to combine the resources of the private sector, State and local governments, universities, or consortia with those of the Federal Government. CRADAs are authorized by 15 U.S.C. 3701 *et seq.* They are a means of FEDERAL TECHNOLOGY TRANSFER whereby the Government may share its research resources but may not use appropriated funds to conduct joint research projects. See Duncombe, *Federal Technology Transfer: A Look at the Benefits and Pitfalls of One of the Country's Best Kept Secrets*, 37 Fed. B. News & J. 608 (1990).

COPELAND ANTI-KICKBACK ACT A 1934 act, 18 U.S.C. 874, 40 U.S.C. 276c, that contains provisions to prevent KICKBACKs by construction workers to contractors or subcontractors on projects financed in whole or in part by the Government. This act is implemented by FAR 22.403-2 and the clause at FAR 52.222-10.

COPYRIGHT The exclusive rights of an author in works (literary, musical, dramatic, choreographic, pictorial, graphic, sculptural, audiovisual or sound recordings) that he or she has created. The key rights are (1) reproduction, (2) preparation of derivative works, (3) distribution by sale or leasing, (4) performance, or (5) public display. Title 17 of the United States Code governs these rights. Authors obtain the rights at the time the work is first created (without regard to publication) and may register their works in the Copyright Office of the Library of Congress. Copyright has become an important facet of Government contracting because most SOFTWARE is copyrighted by its creators.

CORPORATE ADMINISTRATIVE CONTRACTING OFFICER (CACO) An ADMINISTRATIVE CONTRACTING OFFICER (ACO) assigned to a corporation that has more than one location with resident ACOs. CACOs deal with corporate management and perform Government review and approval of corporate-wide policies, procedures, and activities in order to ensure uniform treatment. FAR 42.601. Typical CACO functions include (1) determining final INDIRECT COST rates for COST-REIMBURSEMENT CONTRACTs, (2) establishing ADVANCE AGREEMENTs or recommendations on corporate/home office expense allocations, and (3) administering COST ACCOUNTING STANDARDS (CAS) applicable to corporate-level and corporate-directed accounting practices. FAR 42.603.

COST The sum or equivalent expended, paid, or charged for something. Black's Law Dictionary. The Government recognizes only ALLOWABLE COSTs in computing the costs that it will reimburse under COST-REIMBURSEMENT CONTRACTs and in pricing actions under FIXED-PRICE CONTRACTs.

COST ACCOUNTING PERIOD The period of time used to accumulate and report costs. Cost Accounting Standard 406, FAR 30.406, requires that a contractor's FISCAL YEAR (FY) be used as the cost accounting period unless certain exceptions apply. The major impact of the cost accounting period is that it is used to determine a contractor's INDIRECT COST rates. The same cost accounting period must be used for accumulating costs in an indirect cost pool and for establishing an allocation base. See ALLOCATION OF COST.

COST ACCOUNTING PRACTICE Any disclosed or established accounting method or technique that is used for (1) measuring cost (defining the components of cost, determining the basis for cost measurement, and establishing criteria for the use of alternative cost management techniques); (2) determining the amount of cost to be assigned to individual COST ACCOUNTING PERIODs; and (3) allocating costs to COST OBJECTIVEs, both directly and indirectly. FAR 30.302-1. The determination of the amount paid or a change in the amount paid for a unit of goods and services is not a cost accounting practice. Cost Accounting Standard 402, FAR 30.402, requires that contractors follow consistent cost accounting practices.

COST ACCOUNTING STANDARDS (CAS) A series of accounting standards originally issued by the COST ACCOUNTING STANDARDS (CAS) BOARD under Pub. L. 91-379, 50 U.S.C. app. 2168, to achieve uniformity and consistency in measuring, assigning, and allocating costs to contracts with the Federal Government. The 19 standards that were issued between 1970 to 1980 are now incorporated in FAR Subpart 30.4. Under Pub. L. 91-379, certain national defense contractors and subcontractors awarded negotiated contracts have been required to comply with the standards, disclosing in writing and consistently following the COST ACCOUNTING PRACTICEs the standards describe. (For cost accounting standard purposes, all NASA contracts are considered to be "national defense" contracts. NFS 18-30.101.) Certain nondefense contractors have also been required to comply with the standards, as a matter of policy. FAR 30.101. However, under Pub. L. 100-679, 41 U.S.C. 422, which reestablished the CAS Board after its abolishment in 1980, the standards promulgated by the new Board apply to civilian contracts as well as defense contracts. The standards do not apply to sealed bid contracts or small business concerns. FAR 30.000. Each of the 19 standards consists of 6 parts: purpose, fundamental requirement, technique for application, illustration, interpretation, and exemption. The standards deal with consistency in estimating, accumulating, and reporting costs (CAS 401); consistency in allocating costs incurred for the same purpose (CAS 402); allocation of home office expenses (CAS 403); capitalization of tangible assets (CAS 404); accounting for unallowable costs (CAS 405); selection of cost accounting periods (CAS 406); use of standard costs for direct material and direct labor (CAS 407); accounting for costs of compensated personal absence (CAS 408); depreciation of tangible capital assets (CAS 409); allocation of business unit general and administrative expenses to final cost objectives (CAS 410); accounting for acquisition costs of material (CAS 411); composition and measurement of pension cost (CAS 412); adjustment and allocation of pension cost (CAS 413); cost of money as an element of the cost of facilities capital (CAS 414); accounting for the cost of deferred compensation (CAS 415); accounting for insurance costs (CAS 416); cost of money as an element of the cost of capital assets under construction (CAS 417); allocation of direct and indirect costs (CAS 418); and accounting for independent R&D and bid and proposal costs (CAS 420). FAR 30.401 through 30.418 and FAR 30.420. See Gallagher and Chadick, *Cost Accounting Standards: New Developments*, 89-6 Briefing Papers (May 1989).

COST ACCOUNTING STANDARDS (CAS) BOARD The governmental entity with the exclusive authority to make, promulgate, amend, and rescind COST ACCOUNTING STANDARDS (CAS) and interpretations of them. The CAS Board was originally established in 1970 by Pub. L. 91-379, 50 U.S.C. app. 2168. That Board, which promulgated the current 19 standards, was part of the legislative branch and was chaired by the Comptroller General. Its jurisdiction was limited to national defense contracts, and it was abolished in 1980 after Congress failed to provide an appropriation. Section 5 of Pub. L. 100-679, 41 U.S.C. 422, the Office of Federal Procurement Policy Act Amendments of 1988, reestablished the CAS Board as an independent board within the Office of Management and Budget's OFFICE OF FEDERAL PROCUREMENT POLICY (OFPP). By law, the Board consists of five members. The Administrator of OFPP chairs the Board. The other four members, each experienced in Government contract cost accounting, are as follows: (1) two representatives of the Federal Government, one representing DoD and the other representing GSA; and (2) two individuals from the private sector (both appointed by the Administrator of OFPP), one representing industry and one who is particularly knowledgeable about cost accounting problems and systems. 41 U.S.C. 422(a). Rules and regulations promulgated by the CAS Board are presently incorporated into FAR Part 30. They have been proposed for recodification at 48 CFR Chapter 99, to be published in a supplementary chapter of the FAR; see 56 Fed. Reg. 26968 (12 June 1991). See Lemmer and Hildebrandt, *The New CAS Board: Whose Wish Has Come True?* 31 Cont. Mgmt. 22 (Dec. 1991); Cibinic, *The Reincarnation of the Cost Accounting Standards Board*, 2 N&CR ¶ 74 (Dec. 1988); Cibinic, *Postscript: Cost Accounting Standards Board*, 3 N&CR ¶ 85 (Dec. 1989); Cibinic, *Cost Accounting Standards Board*, 3 N&CR ¶ 50 (July 1989).

COST ANALYSIS Review and evaluation of (1) the separate cost elements and proposed profit contained in an offeror's or contractor's COST OR PRICING DATA and (2) the judgmental factors applied in projecting the estimated costs, for the purpose of forming an opinion on the degree to which the proposed costs represent what the cost of the contract should be, assuming reasonable economy and efficiency. FAR 15.801. Cost analysis is used to establish the basis for negotiating contract prices when PRICE COMPETITION is inadequate or lacking altogether and when PRICE ANALYSIS, by itself, does not ensure price reasonableness (see FAIR AND REASONABLE PRICE). Armed Services Pricing Manual (ASPM) vol. 1, app. B. The contracting officer uses the following techniques and procedures, as appropriate, to perform cost analysis: (1) verification of cost or pricing data and evaluation of cost elements; (2) evaluation of the effect of current practices on future costs; (3) comparison of costs proposed for individual cost elements with previously incurred actual costs, previous cost estimates, independent Government estimates, and forecasts; (4) verification of compliance with the FAR COST PRINCIPLES and applicable COST ACCOUNTING STANDARDS (CAS); (5) identification of any cost or pricing data needed to make the proposal ACCURATE, COMPLETE, AND CURRENT; and (6) analysis of the results of MAKE-OR-BUY PROGRAM reviews. FAR 15.805.3. The contracting officer should also perform cost analysis in selecting and negotiating a contract type in the absence of effective price competition and when price analysis is insufficient. FAR 16.104(c). See Cibinic and Braude, chap. 9, Construction Contracting 717–84.

COST CONTRACT A COST-REIMBURSEMENT CONTRACT in which the contractor receives no fee. FAR 16.302. Such a contract may be appropriate for RESEARCH AND DEVELOPMENT (R&D) work, particularly with nonprofit educational institutions or other nonprofit organizations, and for FACILITIES CONTRACTs.

COST INCURRED See INCURRED COST.

COST INPUT The cost, except GENERAL AND ADMINISTRATIVE (G&A) EXPENSEs, that for contract costing purposes is allocable (see ALLOCABLE COST) to the production of goods and services during a COST ACCOUNTING PERIOD. FAR 31.001.

COST OBJECTIVE A function, organizational subdivision, contract, or other work unit for which cost data are desired and for which provision is made to accumulate and measure the cost of processes, products, jobs, capitalized projects, and so forth. FAR 31.001. A final cost objective is a cost objective that has allocated to it both DIRECT COSTs and INDIRECT COSTs and, in the contractor's accumulation system, is one of the final accumulation points.

COST OF CAPITAL COMMITTED TO FACILITIES An imputed cost of the capital a contractor has committed to its FACILITIES, determined by applying a cost of money rate to facilities capital. FAR 31.001. Also called "facilities capital cost of money." This cost is computed in accordance with Cost Accounting Standard 414, FAR 30.414. The computation derives the cost by multiplying the net book value of facilities allocated to a contract by the Treasury Interest Rate. The amount is imputed because it does not depend on whether a contractor has obtained the facilities by borrowed capital or equity financing. FAR 31.205-10 provides that such cost is allowable (see ALLOWABLE COST) when it is "specifically identified or proposed in cost proposals." NFS Subpart 18-30.70 governs facilities capital employed for facilities by NASA. See also COST OF MONEY AS A COST OF CAPITAL ASSETS UNDER CONSTRUCTION and COST OF MONEY FACTORS (CMF).

COST OF MONEY AS A COST OF CAPITAL ASSETS UNDER CONSTRUCTION An imputed cost of the capital a contractor has used to construct, fabricate, or develop new FACILITIES. FAR 30.417-40. This cost is computed in accordance with Cost Accounting Standard 417, FAR 30.417. It is added to the capitalized acquisition cost of the facilities when they are placed on the contractor's BALANCE SHEET as an ASSET.

COST OF MONEY FACTORS (CMF) Factors developed by overhead pools at contractors' business units, using Form CASB CMF (FAR 30.414, app. A, Facilities Capital Cost of Money Factors Computation), to measure a contractor's COST OF CAPITAL COMMITTED TO FACILITIES. Three elements are required: (1) business unit facilities capital data (the net book value for each cost accounting period), (2) overhead allocation bases (the same as the bases used to compute the proposed overhead rates), and (3) the TREASURY INTEREST RATE. Cost of money factors are also used to develop the "facilities capital employed" base used in prenegotiation profit objectives under the DoD WEIGHTED GUIDELINES METHOD. DFARS 215.970. Actual cost of money factors are required when it is necessary to determine final allowable costs for cost settlement or repricing in accordance with Cost Accounting Standard 414, Cost of Money as an Element of the Cost of Facilities Capital, and with FAR 31.205-10. See DFARS 230.7003.

COST OR PRICING DATA All facts that, as of the date of agreement on the price of a contract (or the price of a contract modification), a prudent buyer or seller would reasonably expect to affect price negotiations significantly. The term does not include facts that are judgmental, but does include the factual information from which a judgment was derived. 10 U.S.C. 2306a(g). A more elaborate definition is included in FAR 15.801. It states that these data do not reflect on the accuracy of the contractor's judgment (see FACT and JUDGMENT IN PRICING) about estimated future costs or projections, but they do include the data upon which the contractor bases that judgment. It further states that cost or pricing data are all facts that can reasonably be expected to contribute to the soundness of estimates of future costs and to the validity of determinations of costs already incurred. They include such factors as vendor quotations, nonrecurring costs, information on changes in production methods and changes in production or purchasing volume, data supporting projections of business prospects and objectives and related operations costs, unit-cost trends such as those associated with labor efficiency, make-or-buy decisions, estimated resources needed to attain business goals, and information on management decisions that could have a significant bearing on costs. See Lovitky, *Cost and Pricing Data Defined: An Analysis of the Scope of Contractor Disclosure Requirements Pursuant to the Truth in Negotiations Act*, 20 NCMJ 79 (1987). See also CERTIFIED COST OR PRICING DATA.

COST OVERRUN The excess of ALLOWABLE COSTs incurred by a contractor on a COST-REIMBURSEMENT CONTRACT over the ESTIMATED COST of the contract. Under the LIMITATION OF COST (LOC) CLAUSE contractors are not obligated to incur such overruns and the Government is not obligated to reimburse such costs. This term is also used, on occasion, to refer to the incurrence of more costs than predicted in the performance of FIXED-PRICE CON-TRACTs. See Cost Accounting Standard 405, FAR 30.405-40, which requires that unallowable cost overruns be allocated to the contract on which they were incurred rather than to some other account.

COST-PLUS-A-PERCENTAGE-OF-COST (CPPC) CONTRACT A type of contract containing some element that obligates the Government to pay the contractor an amount (in the form of either profit or cost) undetermined at the time the contract was made and to be incurred in the future, based on a percentage of future costs. *Muschany v. United States*, 324 U.S. 49, 61–62 (1944). A cost-plus-a-percentage-of-cost system of contracting is prohibited by 10 U.S.C. 2306(a) and 41 U.S.C. 254(b). This prohibition can apply to either a COST-REIMBURSEMENT CONTRACT or a FIXED-PRICE CONTRACT if either contains any element that permits a payment to increase if the contractor incurs greater costs. The purpose of the prohibition is to prevent contracts that motivate a contractor to increase its profits by increasing costs of perfor-mance. See Cibinic and Nash, Formation of Government Con-tracts 708–15.

COST-PLUS-AWARD FEE (CPAF) CONTRACT A COST-REIMBURSEMENT CONTRACT that provides for a fee consisting of (1) a BASE FEE (which may be zero) fixed at inception of the contract and (2) an AWARD FEE, based upon a periodic judgmental evaluation by the Government, sufficient to provide motivation for excellence in such areas as quality, timeliness, technical ingenuity, and cost-effective management during contract performance. FAR 16.305. The contractor may earn the award amount in whole or in part. The determination of the award fee is made unilaterally by the Government and is not subject to the DISPUTEs clause. FAR 16.404-2. CPAF contracts have been widely used to contract for services. One of their major features is that they require the Government to give contractors regular evaluations of their performance (usually every 3 to 6 months). See Cibinic and Nash, Formation of Government Contracts 775–90; Kannan, *Challeng-*

ing Award Fee Determinations under Federal Government Contracts, 20 Pub. Cont. L.J. 197 (1991).

COST-PLUS-FIXED FEE (CPFF) CONTRACT A COST-REIM-BURSEMENT CONTRACT that provides for payment to the contractor of a negotiated FEE (profit) that is fixed at the inception of the contract. FAR 16.306(a). This fixed fee does not vary with actual cost but may be adjusted as a result of changes in the work to be performed under the contract. The CPFF type of contract permits contracting for efforts that might otherwise present too great a risk to contractors, but it gives the contractor less incentive to control costs than does a FIXED-PRICE CONTRACT. FAR 16.306(b) limits its use to those situations where the Government has not established reasonably firm objectives (such as contracts for research). There are two forms of CPFF contracts: (1) the completion form, in which the work is described by stating a definite goal or target and an end product (frequently a report) and (2) the term form, in which the contract calls for a stated level of effort (usually hours or days of specified classes of labor) over a given period of time. FAR 16.306(d).

COST-PLUS-INCENTIVE FEE (CPIF) CONTRACT A COST-REIMBURSEMENT CONTRACT that provides for the initially negotiated TARGET FEE to be adjusted later by a formula based on the relationship of total ALLOWABLE COSTs to total TARGET COSTs. FAR 16.304. This contract type specifies a target cost, a target fee, a MINIMUM FEE, a MAXIMUM FEE, and a fee adjustment formula. After contract performance, the fee payable to the contractor is determined in accordance with the formula. FAR 16.404-1. To encourage the contractor to manage the contract effectively, the formula provides, within limits, for increases in fee above target fee when total allowable costs are less than target costs, and decreases in fee below target fee when total allowable costs exceed target costs. When the total allowable cost is greater or less than the range of costs (the RANGE OF INCENTIVE EFFEC-TIVENESS (RIE)) within which the fee adjustment formula operates, the contractor is paid total allowable costs plus the minimum or maximum fee. See the Incentive Fee clause at FAR 52.216-10. And see Cibinic and Nash, Formation of Government Contracts 746–59.

COST PRINCIPLES The rules promulgated by the Government in FAR Part 31 that define which costs are allowable (see ALLOW-

ABLE COST) by the Government in the negotiation and administration of Government contracts. This part of the FAR contains contract cost principles and procedures for (1) the pricing of contracts, subcontracts, and contract modifications whenever cost analysis is performed and (2) the determination, negotiation, or allowance of costs when required by a contract clause. These principles are made a part of all COST-REIMBURSEMENT CONTRACTs by incorporation by reference in the Allowable Cost and Payment clause at FAR 52.2.16-7.

COST-REALISM ANALYSIS Review of an offeror's proposal to determine if the costs proposed are realistic for the work to be performed, reflect a clear understanding of the requirements, and are consistent with the offeror's technical proposal. DFARS 215.801. See also FAR 35.008(e). The primary purpose of cost-realism analysis in COST-REIMBURSEMENT CONTRACTs is to adjust an offeror's cost estimate to reflect the probable cost of performance in accordance with FAR 15.605(d) and thereby prevent offerors from gaining an advantage over competitors by proposing unrealistically low estimated costs. See Nash, *Cost Realism Analysis in Cost Reimbursement Contracts: What Are the Rules of the Game?* 5 N&CR ¶ 40 (July 1991); Cibinic, *Cost Realism Analysis in Negotiated Fixed Price Contracts: Confusion at the GAO or a New Limitation on Buy-ins?* 4 N&CR ¶ 61 (Oct. 1990).

COST-REIMBURSEMENT CONTRACT A contract that provides for payment to the contractor of allowable incurred costs to the extent provided in the contract. FAR 16.301-1. Cost-reimbursement contracts are distinguished from FIXED-PRICE CONTRACTs, under which payment is made to the contractor on the basis of pre-established prices. Cost-reimbursement contracts are suitable for use only when the uncertainties involved in contract performance do not permit costs to be estimated with sufficient accuracy to use any type of fixed-price contract. FAR 16.301-2. They may be used only when (1) the contractor's accounting system is adequate for determining applicable costs, (2) Government surveillance during performance will provide reasonable assurance that efficient methods and effective cost controls are used, and (3) a determination is made that a cost-reimbursement contract is likely to be less costly than any other type or that obtaining the needed supplies or services without the use of a cost-reimbursement contract is impracticable. FAR 16.301-3. In order to avoid violation of the ANTI-DEFICIENCY ACT, all cost-reimbursement contracts must contain the LIMITATION OF COST (LOC) CLAUSE. This clause limits the Government's obligation by stipulating that it will pay only the contract's ESTIMATED COST or TARGET COST (plus any prescribed FEE). Cost-reimbursement pricing arrangements include COST CONTRACTs, COST-SHARING CONTRACTs, COST-PLUS-INCENTIVE FEE (CPIF) CONTRACTs, COST-PLUS-AWARD FEE (CPAF) CONTRACTs, and COST-PLUS-FIXED FEE (CPFF) CONTRACTs. COST-PLUS-A-PERCENTAGE-OF-COST (CPPC) CONTRACTs are prohibited. See Cibinic and Nash, Cost Reimbursement Contracting.

COST RISK An assessment of possible monetary loss or gain in light of the work to be done under a contract. It is one of the elements to be considered in negotiating a FAIR AND REASONABLE PRICE, as well as in determining the TYPE OF CONTRACT to be used. See FAR 16.104. Cost risk is assessed in order that the contractor can be compensated commensurately with the extent of risk assumed. Factors included in a cost risk assessment are the reliability of the contractor's proposed costs, the extent of contingency factors included in the proposed costs, the relative firmness or uncertainty of the estimated costs for major components, subcontracts, etc., and the contractor's prior profit experience with the same or similar supplies or systems. DCAA Contract Audit Manual (CAM) 9-903.2.

COST/SCHEDULE CONTROL SYSTEM A management system requiring the contract to establish a WORK BREAKDOWN STRUCTURE (WBS) for all of the work to be performed on the contract and to record performance and costs for each element of that structure. The purpose of such systems is to track the contractor's performance at a level of detail that will provide early information if a contractor is not performing on schedule or at the predicted costs. Guidance on such systems is contained in DoD Instruction 5000.2, *Defense Acquisition Management Policies and Procedures*, 10 June 1977, part 11B.

COST/SCHEDULE CONTROL SYSTEMS CRITERIA (C/SCSC) A set of 35 criteria that specify the minimum requirements a contractor's management control system must satisfy in order to meet the COST/SCHEDULE CONTROL SYSTEM requirement in certain contracts with DoD. Typically, the criteria apply to major system acquisition programs and subcontracts within those programs. The criteria are broken down into five groups: organization

(5 criteria), planning and budgeting (11 criteria), accounting (7 criteria), analysis (6 criteria), and revisions and access to data (6 criteria). C/SCSC basically entails four steps: establishing a baseline with the development of a WORK BREAKDOWN STRUC-TURE (WBS) and an applicable budget down to the lowest work element possible, managing the base line, measuring performance as the work is accomplished, and assessing what is left to be accomplished from the plan and making a projection of the estimate to complete the work. These steps should produce a reliable estimate of the TOTAL COST of a given contract. See Grskovich, *What is C/SCSC?—In English, Please!* 23 NCMJ 25 (1990); DoD Instruction 5000.2, *Defense Acquisition Management Policies and Procedures*, 10 June 1977, part 11B. See also COST/SCHEDULE STATUS REPORT (C/SSR).

COST/SCHEDULE STATUS REPORT (C/SSR) A report submitted by a contractor that provides summarized cost and schedule performance status for use by the PROGRAM MANAGER (PM) in decision making. The C/SSR is intended to provide the PM with a clear description of the contract cost and schedule status at a given point in time. If the Government desires the contractor to submit these reports, the requirement for submission must be included in the solicitation document and the contract as a CONTRACT DATA REQUIREMENTS LIST (CDRL) requirement on DD Form 1423 (DFARS 253.303-1423). See Dominic, *Understanding the C/SSR*, 30 Cont. Mgmt. 8 (Nov. 1990).

COST-SHARING CONTRACT An explicit arrangement under which the contractor bears some of the burden of reasonable, allocable, and allowable contract cost. FAR 35.001. A cost-sharing contract is a COST-REIMBURSEMENT CONTRACT under which the contractor receives no FEE and is reimbursed only for an agreed-upon portion of its ALLOWABLE COSTs. Such a contract may be used only when the contractor agrees to absorb a portion of the costs in the expectation of substantial compensating benefits. FAR 16.303. Cost-sharing arrangements may call for the contractor to participate in the costs of the contract by accepting INDIRECT COST rates lower than the anticipated actual rates. In such cases, a negotiated indirect cost rate ceiling may be incorporated into the contract for prospective application. FAR 42.707. Another common form of cost sharing is the award of a FIXED-PRICE CONTRACT at less than the contractor's estimated costs of performance.

COST UNDERRUN The incurrence of costs less than those in the contract's TARGET COST (in a FIXED-PRICE INCENTIVE (FPI) CONTRACT or a COST-PLUS-INCENTIVE FEE (CPIF) CONTRACT), ESTIMATED COST (in any other COST-REIMBURSEMENT CONTRACT), or a redeterminable price (in a FIXED-PRICE REDETERMINATION—PROSPECTIVE (FPRP) CONTRACT or FIXED-PRICE REDETERMINATION—RETROACTIVE (FPRR) CONTRACT). An underrun is caused by the contractor's actual costs being under target or under anticipated contract cost, but not for reasons such as quantity changes, engineering changes, or economic changes. Armed Services Pricing Manual (ASPM) vol. 1, app. B. See also DCAA Contract Audit Manual (CAM) 3-S102.1.

COURSE OF DEALING See PRIOR COURSE OF DEALING.

COURT OF APPEALS FOR THE FEDERAL CIRCUIT (CAFC or Fed. Cir.) The appellate (reviewing) court for both the U.S. CLAIMS COURT (Cl. Ct.) and the various agency BOARDs OF CONTRACT APPEALS (BCAs). 28 U.S.C. 1295(a)(3), (a)(10); 41 U.S.C. 607(g). To the extent that the Supreme Court rarely considers decisions regarding Government contract disputes, the Court of Appeals for the Federal Circuit typically provides the last opportunity for their review. The Federal Courts Improvement Act of 1982 created the Court of Appeals for the Federal Circuit from the appellate division of the Court of Claims and the Court of Customs and Patent Appeals. See Latham, Government Contract Disputes, chap. 18; Shea and Schaengold, *A Guide to the Court of Appeals for the Federal Circuit*, 90-13 Briefing Papers (Dec. 1990); White, *The New Government Contract Courts*, 83-11 Briefing Papers (Nov. 1983); Anthony and Smith, *The Federal Courts Improvement Act of 1982: Its Impact on the Resolution of Federal Contract Disputes*, 13 Pub. Cont. L.J. 201 (1983).

COVER The common law right of a buyer, after BREACH OF CONTRACT by the seller, to purchase goods in substitution for those due from the seller if such purchase is made in good faith and without unreasonable delay. The buyer may then recover as DAMAGES the difference between the cost of such cover and the contract price, plus any incidental and CONSEQUENTIAL DAMAGES but less expenses saved. U.C.C. 2-712(1), (2).

CRITICAL ISSUE An aspect of a SYSTEM's capability—operational, technical, or other—that must be questioned before the system's overall suitability can be known. This aspect is of primary importance in reaching a decision to allow the system to advance to the next phase of DEVELOPMENT. Jones, Glossary: Defense Acquisition Acronyms and Terms.

CRITICAL ITEM A subsystem, component, material, or other item whose nonavailability when required could seriously jeopardize the successful completion of program requirements. A critical item is also an item that could have an adverse impact on cost, schedule, quality, or technical performance. Postak, Glossary of Terms, in Subcontracts—Government and Industry Issues.

CRITICAL PATH METHOD (CPM) A scheduling technique used by contractors to plan, coordinate, and control work activities so as to complete contract work as quickly and economically as possible. CPM has become an accepted means of substantiating delay CLAIMs before the courts and boards of contract appeals. The "critical path" represents the longest chain of interrelated activities in the project schedule diagram. A delay in completing an item on this critical path delays the entire project. Proving delay typically entails comparing AS-PLANNED DRAWINGS or CPM diagrams with RECORD (as-built) DRAWINGS or CPM diagrams. See Margulies, chap. 8, Construction Contracting 662–67; Wickwire, et al., *Use of Critical Path Method Techniques in Contract Claims: Issues and Developments 1974 to 1988*, 18 Pub. Cont. L.J. 338 (1989). And see the Schedules for Construction Contracts clause in FAR 52.236-15, which requires construction contractors to provide a schedule of anticipated performance to the contracting officer shortly after award of the contract.

CURE NOTICE A delinquency notice that must be issued by the Government prior to TERMINATION FOR DEFAULT of a supply or service contract before the contract's delivery date. See paragraph (a)(2) of the Default (Fixed-Price Supply and Service) clause in FAR 52.249-8. FAR 49.607(a) contains a suggested form of the notice. FAR 49.402-3 contains the procedures that must be followed by contracting officers in determining whether to terminate for default. FAR 49.402-3(d) provides that, if the time remaining does not permit a "cure" period of 10 days or more, the cure notice should not be issued. Failure to issue a cure notice when required will result in an invalid termination for default, with the result that the termination will be converted to a TERMINATION FOR CONVENIENCE. See also SHOW CAUSE NOTICE.

CUSTODIAL RECORDS Written memoranda of any kind, such as requisitions, issue hand receipts, tool checks, and stock record books, used to control items from tool cribs, tool rooms, and stockrooms. FAR 45.501. FAR 45.505-3(c) requires that the contractor maintain such records of tool crib items, guard force items, protective clothing, and other items issued to employees when these items are GOVERNMENT-FURNISHED MATERIAL (GFM) or material to which the Government has title.

CUSTOMARY PROGRESS PAYMENT A PROGRESS PAYMENT made under general FAR guidance, using the customary progress payment rate (which is adjusted from time to time in accordance with economic conditions and currently is 85 percent for large businesses and 90 percent for small businesses), the cost base, and the frequency of payment established in the Progress Payments clause in FAR 52.232-16, and either the ordinary liquidation method (see FAR 32.503-8) or the alternate method (see FAR 32.503-9). Any other progress payment based on cost is considered an UNUSUAL PROGRESS PAYMENT.

D

DAMAGES Pecuniary compensation or indemnity, which may be recovered in a judicial or quasijudicial forum (e.g., the CLAIMS COURT (Cl. Ct.) or the BOARDs OF CONTRACT APPEALS (BCAs)) by one who suffers loss, detriment, or injury through BREACH OF CONTRACT by the act, omission, or negligence of another. Compensatory damages compensate the injured party for the injury sustained and for nothing more. CONSEQUENTIAL DAMAGES do not flow directly and immediately from the act of the other party but, rather, from the consequences or results of the act. Punitive or exemplary damages represent an amount over and above that required to compensate the injured party for the wrong done; they are intended to punish or make an example of the wrongdoer. Black's Law Dictionary. Damages are infrequently awarded in Government contracts because of the large number of contract clauses giving EQUITABLE ADJUSTMENTs and PRICE ADJUSTMENTs.

DATA Recorded information, regardless of form or the media on which it may be recorded. FAR 27.401. The term includes TECHNICAL DATA and COMPUTER SOFTWARE. The term does not include information incidental to contract administration, such as financial, administrative, cost, pricing, or management information. DFARS 227.401 contains a similar, but much shorter, definition. When this type of information is created by contractors in the performance of contracts, it is subject to LIMITED RIGHTS, RESTRICTED RIGHTS, UNLIMITED RIGHTS, or GOVERNMENT-PURPOSE LICENSE RIGHTS (GPLR) as specified in contract clauses.

DATA ITEM DESCRIPTION (DID) A description of a TECHNICAL DATA item to be provided under a contract with DoD. The form used for this description is DD Form 1664, DFARS 253.303-1664. DIDs are listed on the CONTRACT DATA REQUIREMENTS LIST

118

(CDRL) that is incorporated into contracts. See Nash and Rawicz, Patents and Technical Data, chap. 6.

DATA PROCESSING EQUIPMENT   See AUTOMATIC DATA PROCESSING EQUIPMENT (ADPE).

DAVIS-BACON ACT   An act, 40 U.S.C. 276a, passed in 1931, requiring payment of not less than prevailing wage rates to workers on Federal or federally funded CONSTRUCTION projects of over $2,000. FAR 22.403-1. Prevailing wage rates, set by the Department of Labor, are the wages paid to the majority of the LABORERS OR MECHANICS falling within the same specific classifications on similar projects in the area during the period in question. If the same wage is not paid to a majority of those employed in the classification, the prevailing wage is the average of the wages paid, weighted by the total number of employees in the classification. FAR 22.404. Wage determinations are published in the Federal Register and in the Government Printing Office document *General Wage Determinations Issued under the Davis-Bacon and Related Acts.* See Stephenson, chap. 3, Construction Contracting 225–30; Schooner, *The Davis-Bacon Act: Controversial Implementation of the 50% Rule,* 5 Constr. Law. (No. 3) 9 and 10 Employee Rel. L.J. 702.

DCAA CONTRACT AUDIT MANUAL (CAM)   A publication of the DEFENSE CONTRACT AUDIT AGENCY (DCAA) (sometimes referred to as the Defense Contract Audit Manual, or DCAM) containing detailed guidance on auditing policies and procedures followed by DCAA auditors. The manual is instructive rather than directive in nature, and its contents apply to the audit of all types of contracts. The manual is available from the U.S. Government Printing Office, Washington, DC 20402.

DEBARMENT   Action taken by a debarring official—the HEAD OF THE AGENCY, or a designee authorized by the agency head to impose debarment—to exclude a contractor from Government contracting and Government-approved subcontracting for a reasonable, specified period. FAR 9.403. FAR Subpart 9.4 contains the policies and procedures governing debarment of contractors. When a contractor is proposed for debarment, it is excluded from the award of contracts by being placed on the list of PARTIES EXCLUDED FROM PROCUREMENT PROGRAMS. FAR 9.404. Causes for debarment include (1) conviction of or civil judgment for (a) commission of a FRAUD or criminal offense related to obtaining or performing a public contract, (b) ANTITRUST VIOLATION, (c) commission of embezzlement, theft, forgery, BRIBERY, making false statements, or the like, or (d) commission of any other offense indicating a lack of business integrity or business honesty that seriously and directly affects the contractor's present RESPON-SIBILITY; (2) violation of the terms of a Government contract so serious as to justify debarment, such as (a) willful failure to perform or (b) a history of failure to perform or unsatisfactory performance; (3) violations of the Drug-Free Workplace Act of 1988 (see DRUG-FREE WORKPLACE); and (4) any other cause of so serious or compelling a nature that it affects the present responsi-bility of a Government contractor or subcontractor. FAR 9.406-2. Remedial measures and mitigating factors for contracting officers to consider in making debarment decisions are set forth at FAR 9.406-1(a). See Toomey et al., *Debarment & Suspension/Edition III*, 89-4 Briefing Papers (Mar. 1989); Nadler, *Suspension and Debarment of Government Contractors: The Current Climate*, 22 NCMJ 9 (1989); Norton, *The Questionable Constitutionality of the Suspension and Debarment Provisions of the Federal Acquisition Regulations: What Does Due Process Require?* 18 Pub. Cont. L.J. 633 (1989).

DEBARRING OFFICIAL An agency head or a designee authorized by the agency head to impose DEBARMENT. FAR 9.403.

DEBRIEFING Explanation by a procuring agency of why an offeror did not win a competition for a negotiated contract (see NEGOTIA-TION). FAR 15.1003 requires that when a contract is awarded on a basis other than price and price-related factors alone, an unsuccessful offeror, upon written request, must be debriefed and furnished the basis for the selection decision and contract award. Debriefing information includes the Government's evaluation of the significant weak or deficient factors in the offeror's proposal but not point-by-point comparisons with other offerors' proposals. The debriefing does not reveal the relative merits or technical standing of competitors or the evaluation scoring, nor does it reveal information not releasable under the FREEDOM OF INFORMA-TION ACT (FOIA), such as trade secrets, privileged or confidential manufacturing processes and techniques, or privileged or confi-dential commercial and financial information. The contracting officer must include a written summary of the debriefing in the contract file. See Cibinic, *Debriefing: Tell It Like It Is*, 4 N&CR ¶ 43 (July 1990).

DEBT COLLECTION ACT A 1982 act, 51 U.S.C. 5514, prescribing procedures for the collection of debts owed to the United States. The Debt Collection Act is part of a complex of statutes and regulations making up the process by means of which the Government collects debts. The complex also includes the FEDERAL CLAIMS COLLECTION ACT of 1966, the CONTRACT DISPUTES ACT (CDA) OF 1978, and the Federal Claims Collection Standards. Of particular note are the procedures agencies must follow in undertaking debt collection through administrative SETOFF. The Government must give the debtor written notice of the type and amount of the CLAIM and an opportunity to (1) inspect and copy the agency's records relating to the claim, (2) request agency review of the agency's decision related to the claim, and (3) enter into a written agreement with the Government to repay the claim. The Debt Collection Act is partially implemented in FAR Subpart 32.6. See Cibinic and Nash, Administration of Government Contracts 913–15; Thrasher, *Application of the Debt Collection Act of 1982 to Government Contracts*, 29 A.F. L. Rev. 133 (1988).

DECISION OF THE CONTRACTING OFFICER A written document signed by a CONTRACTING OFFICER (CO) ruling on a CLAIM by or against the Government. Under the CONTRACT DISPUTES ACT (CDA) OF 1978, all claims by a contractor against the Government relating to a contract must also be in writing and must be submitted to the contracting officer for a decision. All claims by the Government against a contractor relating to a contract must also be the subject of a decision by the contracting officer. A decision describes the claim, references pertinent contract terms, states areas of factual agreement and disagreement, states the reasons for the decision reached, and informs the contractor of its rights to challenge the decision through an APPEAL FROM A CONTRACTING OFFICER'S DECISION. 41 U.S.C. 605(a). Contracting officers' decisions, often called "final decisions," must inform the contractor that it may either appeal the decision to a BOARD OF CONTRACT APPEALS (BCA) within 90 days or bring an action directly in the U.S. CLAIMS COURT (Cl. Ct.) within 12 months. If the contracting officer fails to render a decision, the BCAs and Claims Court may deem the claim denied (see DEEMED DENIAL) 60 days after its submission. Procedures for issuing decisions are contained in FAR 33.211 and the Disputes clause at FAR 52.233-1.

DECREMENT A reduction or price reduction. A decrement factor may represent a percentage by which a subcontractor reduces its contract price if, for example, the prime contractor purchases more than a specified amount of supplies. Subcontractors may also use a decrement to compensate for the amount of profit generated in an INTERORGANIZATIONAL TRANSFER. See *Grumman Aerospace Corp.*, ASBCA 35188, 35189, 90-2 BCA ¶ 22,842. The DCAA Contract Audit Manual (CAM) directs auditors to review the methodologies used by contractors in arriving at subcontractor price reductions, to ensure that the data used for decrements was reasonably accurate, current, and representative. The manual explains that information concerning patterns of reductions from quotes to actual prices paid may be useful in evaluating a cost estimate. DCAA Contract Audit Manual (CAM) 9-404.6.

DECREMENT FACTOR See DECREMENT.

DEEMED DENIAL A legal rule under the CONTRACT DISPUTES ACT (CDA) OF 1978 permitting a contractor to appeal (see APPEAL FROM THE CONTRACTING OFFICER'S DECISION) the failure of a contracting officer to issue a decision (see DECISION OF THE CONTRACTING OFFICER). 41 U.S.C. 605(c)(5). If the contractor submits a CLAIM, and the contracting officer fails to render a decision within 60 days of receiving the claim (or within a reasonable time if the claim is for over $50,000), the act provides that this failure will be deemed a decision of the contracting officer to deny the claim and will authorize the commencement of an appeal or suit on the claim. This "deemed denial" jurisdiction confers upon the contractor all rights that flow from receipt of a contracting officer's decision. Although the Contracts Disputes Act provides a statute of limitations for appeals (90 days to an agency BOARD OF CONTRACT APPEALS (BCA) or 1 year to the CLAIMS COURT (Cl. Ct.)) when the contractor has received a decision of the contracting officer, no similar provision exists when the contracting officer fails to render a decision on a valid claim and thereby prompts "deemed denial" jurisdiction. See *Pathman Constr. Co. v. United States*, 817 F.2d 1573 (Fed. Cir. 1987). Thus, the contractor will not lose any appeal rights if it takes no action when a contracting officer fails to render a decision.

DE FACTO DEBARMENT   A refusal of the Government to deal with a contractor that is construed by a court to constitute a DEBARMENT, even though formal debarment procedures are not used.   Generally, de facto debarment has been found in cases where a Government agency refuses to award one or more contracts on the basis that the OFFEROR does not meet the requisite standards of RESPONSIBILITY.   See *Old Dominion Dairy Prod., Inc. v. Secretary of Defense*, 631 F.2d 953 (D.C. Cir. 1980), where de facto debarment was found because of lack of integrity.   The court held the contractor was entitled to the DUE PROCESS OF LAW accorded by the debarment procedures to protect its constitutional liberty interest.   De facto debarments will also be found when an agency declares an offeror nonresponsible on repeated occasions without instituting formal debarment procedures.   See Cibinic and Nash, Formation of Government Contracts 246–50.

DEFAULT   The omission or failure to perform a legal or contractual duty, to observe a promise or discharge an obligation, or to perform an agreement.   Black's Law Dictionary.   The Government follows standard procedures in cases where a contractor is found to be in default in the performance of a contract.   See TERMINATION FOR DEFAULT.   And see Williamson and Medill-Jones, *Government Damages for Default*, 89-7 Briefing Papers (June 1989).

DEFAULT TERMINATION   See TERMINATION FOR DEFAULT.

DEFECT   The absence of something that is necessary for completeness or perfection, or a deficiency in something essential to a thing's intended, proper use.   A product is defective if it is not fit for the ordinary purposes for which it is sold and used.   A LATENT DEFECT is a defect that is not apparent to the buyer by reasonable observation or inspection.   A PATENT DEFECT, in contrast, means a defect that is apparent to the buyer on normal INSPECTION.   Black's Law Dictionary.   A defect is of concern in the context of both contract formation and contract performance.   Defective Government SPECIFICATIONs or plans may result in a contractor's entitlement to a price increase.   Defective performance by a contractor may result in the Government's rejection of a contractor's supplies or services or in a contract's TERMINATION FOR DEFAULT.

DEFECTIVE COST OR PRICING DATA   COST OR PRICING DATA subsequently found to have been inaccurate, incomplete, or noncurrent. Under the TRUTH IN NEGOTIATIONS ACT (TINA), the Government is entitled to an adjustment of the negotiated price, including profit or fee, to exclude any significant sum by which the price was increased because of the defective data, provided the Government had relied upon the data. See FAR 15.804-7 for guidance on the computation of the adjustment. The Government's entitlement to a reduction in price is ensured by the inclusion in the contract of one of the clauses prescribed in FAR 15.804-8, such as Price Reduction for Defective Cost or Pricing Data in FAR 52.215-22 and Price Reduction for Defective Cost or Pricing Data—Modifications in FAR 52.215-23. These clauses give the Government the right to a price adjustment for defects in cost or pricing data submitted by the contractor or by a prospective or actual subcontractor.

DEFECTIVE PRICING See DEFECTIVE COST OR PRICING DATA.

DEFECTIVE SPECIFICATIONS   See IMPLIED WARRANTY OF SPECIFICATIONS.

DEFENDANT The party against whom a suit is filed in court. In the U.S. CLAIMS COURT (Cl. Ct.) the Government is always the defendant even though the suit may be based on a Government CLAIM under the CONTRACT DISPUTES ACT (CDA) OF 1978. In such cases the contractor is referred to as the PLAINTIFF. If such cases are appealed to a BOARD OF CONTRACT APPEALS (BCA), the contractor is referred to as the appellant (see APPELLANT BEFORE BOARD OF CONTRACT APPEALS) and the Government is called the RESPONDENT.

DEFENSE ACQUISITION BOARD (DAB)   The senior DoD acquisition review board that controls the continuation of major acquisition programs. This board is chaired by the Defense Acquisition Executive (DAE); the Vice Chairman of the Joint Chiefs of Staff serves as the vice chair. The DAB assists the DAE with milestone and program reviews, policy formation, and acquisition resource recommendations. It is the primary forum in which DoD components provide advice and assistance concerning acquisition matters to the Secretary of Defense. The DAB is supported by 10 acquisition committees that assist in program review and policy formation. It is established by DoD Instruction 5000.49, 11 *Defense Acquisition Board*, 11 Sep. 1989, and operates under procedures set forth in part 13 of DoD Instruction

5000.2, *Defense Acquisition Management Policies and Procedures*, 23 Feb. 1991.

DEFENSE ACQUISITION CIRCULARS (DACs) Government publications that revise, amend, and supplement the DEFENSE FAR SUPPLEMENT (DFARS). DACs are approved and issued by the DEFENSE ACQUISITION REGULATORY COUNCIL (DAR COUNCIL)— in most cases, after a period of public notice and comment that begins with publication in the FEDERAL REGISTER. See DFARS 201.304. DACs are numbered sequentially by edition (for example, 91-1, 91-2).

DEFENSE ACQUISITION REGULATION (DAR) The regulation that controlled DoD procurement from 1949 until early 1984, known until 1978 as the Armed Services Procurement Regulation (ASPR). In 1984, the DAR and the Federal Procurement Regulations (FPR) were replaced by the current regulatory system, based on the FEDERAL ACQUISITION REGULATION (FAR). Many of the DAR/ASPR clauses, provisions, and textual explanations survived and were incorporated in the FAR in simplified form. Many of the DAR/ASPR remnants that were not incorporated in the FAR were retained in the DEPARTMENT OF DEFENSE FAR SUPPLEMENT (DFARS). The DFARS, DAR, and ASPR applied or now apply specifically to procurements involving the Office of the Secretary of Defense; the Departments of the Army, Navy, and Air Force; the Defense Logistics Agency (DLA); and other defense agencies.

DEFENSE ACQUISITION REGULATORY COUNCIL (DAR COUNCIL) The organization in DoD with the responsibility for issuing procurement regulations. The DAR Council and the CIVILIAN AGENCY ACQUISITION COUNCIL (CAAC) prepare and issue revisions to the FEDERAL ACQUISITION REGULATION (FAR) through coordinated action. See FAR 1.201-1. The DAR Council also maintains the DEPARTMENT OF DEFENSE FAR SUPPLEMENT (DFARS). See DFARS 201.201-1. Each council maintains cognizance over specified portions of the FAR and is responsible for (1) agreeing on all revisions with the other council, (2) submitting to the FAR SECRETARIAT information required for publishing a Federal Register notice soliciting comments, (3) considering all comments received, (4) arranging for public meetings, (5) preparing any final revision in the appropriate FAR format and language, and (6) submitting any final revision to the FAR Secretariat for publication in the Federal Register and for printing and distribution. The

Director of the DAR Council represents the Secretary of Defense. The Council's membership includes representatives of the military departments, the Defense Logistics Agency (DLA), and NASA. See DoD Directive 5000.35, *Defense Acquisition Regulatory System*, 8 Mar. 1978.

DEFENSE CONTRACT ADMINISTRATION SERVICE (DCAS)
An organization within the Defense Logistics Agency (DLA) that performed CONTRACT ADMINISTRATION on assigned contracts at contractor plants. It has been renamed the DEFENSE CONTRACT MANAGEMENT COMMAND (DCMC).

DEFENSE CONTRACT AUDIT AGENCY (DCAA)
A DoD organization that has the responsibility of performing contract audit services for the department. The DCAA was established by DoD Directive 5105.36, *Defense Contract Audit Agency*, 8 June 1978, to perform all contract auditing for DoD and to provide all DoD procurement and contract administration activities with accounting and financial advisory services in connection with negotiating, administering, and settling contracts and subcontracts. DCAA also furnishes contract audit services to other Government agencies. DCAA Contract Audit Manual (CAM) 1-102. DCAA is a separate DoD agency under the direction, authority, and control of the Assistant Secretary of Defense (Comptroller). CAM 1-103.

DEFENSE CONTRACT AUDIT MANUAL (DCAM)
See DCAA CONTRACT AUDIT MANUAL (CAM).

DEFENSE CONTRACT MANAGEMENT COMMAND (DCMC)
An organization within the Defense Logistics Agency (DLA) that performs CONTRACT ADMINISTRATION services for all parts of DoD and other agencies. It was established under Defense Management Review recommendation DMR 916, effective Feb. 1990, to replace Defense Contract Administrative Services (DCAS), and it performs the services described at FAR 42.302 and DFARS 242.302. Contract administration services include all actions accomplished in or near a contractor's plant for the Government's benefit that are (1) necessary to the performance of a contract or (2) in support of the buying offices, system and project managers, and other organizations.

DEFENSE CONTRACTOR   Any party that enters into a contract with the United States to produce material or perform services for the national defense. FAR 30.301. A defense contractor is an employer that, under a contract with the United States or any other contract that the President, Secretary of the Army, Secretary of the Air Force, Secretary of the Navy, or Secretary of Transportation certifies to be necessary to the national defense, either (1) produces, maintains, or stores arms, armaments, ammunition, implements of war, munitions, machinery, tools, clothing, food, fuel, or other articles or supplies (or parts or ingredients of articles or supplies) or (2) constructs, reconstructs, repairs, or installs a building, plant, structure, or facility. 41 U.S.C. 50.

DEFENSE PRIORITIES AND ALLOCATIONS SYSTEM (DPAS)   A system controlling the usage of critical materials and facilities to ensure that they would be used for national defense in the event of an emergency. See FAR Subpart 12.3. Certain contracts and orders are accorded preferential treatment by being designated as RATED ORDERs under the Defense Priorities and Allocations System regulation, which guides the Department of Commerce's Office of Industrial Resource Administration (OIRA) in developing, coordinating, and administering a system of priorities and allocations with respect to industrial resources, pursuant to Title I of the Defense Production Act of 1950, 50 U.S.C. app. 2061 *et seq.* The DPAS legislation provides that programs that maximize domestic energy supplies are eligible for priorities and allocations support. Rated orders placed in support of authorized energy programs are equivalent to orders placed in support of authorized defense programs under the DPAS; they receive the same preferential treatment throughout the industrial supply chain. DEAR 912.302(d). The Federal Emergency Management Agency (FEMA) authorizes certain national defense programs for priorities and allocations support. 15 CFR 700.

DEFENSE PRODUCTION POOL   A pool of SMALL BUSINESS CONCERNs that have joined together to submit offers on one or more defense production contracts; that have entered into an agreement governing their organization, relationship, and procedures; and that have gained appropriate approvals. FAR 9.701. FAR 9.702 provides that Government agencies must treat such pools as they treat any other Government contractor.

DEFENSE RESEARCH AND DEVELOPMENT POOL A pool
of SMALL BUSINESS CONCERNs that have joined together to submit
offers on one or more defense RESEARCH AND DEVELOPMENT
(R&D) contracts; that have entered into an agreement governing
their organization, relationship, and procedures; and that have
gained appropriate approvals. FAR 9.701. FAR 9.702 provides
that Government agencies must treat such pools as they treat any
other Government contractor.

DEFENSE SYSTEMS MANAGEMENT COLLEGE (DSMC) A
joint Military Service and Office of the Secretary of Defense
professional institution that operates under the direction of a
policy guidance council chaired by the Under Secretary of
Defense (Acquisition) to support acquisition management and
fulfill education and training requirements. The DSMC's mission
entails conducting advanced courses of study in managing the
acquisition of defense systems; conducting research and special
studies in defense acquisition management; assembling and
disseminating information about new policies, methods, and
practices in defense acquisition management; and providing
oversight for DoD's education and training program for the
acquisition work force. DSMC, Program Manager's Notebook.

DEFERRED COMPENSATION An award an employer makes to
compensate an employee for services rendered one or more COST
ACCOUNTING PERIODs before the date when the employee receives
the compensation. FAR 31.001. This definition does not include
the amount of year-end accruals for salaries, wages, or bonuses
that are to be paid within a reasonable period of time after the end
of a cost accounting period. The costs of such compensation are
generally considered to be ALLOWABLE COSTs pursuant to FAR
31.205-6(k), if the costs are accounted for in accordance with Cost
Accounting Standard 415, FAR 30.415.

DEFICIENCY Any part of a proposal that fails to satisfy the
Government's requirements. FAR 15.601. FAR 15.610 requires
that CONTRACTING OFFICERs (COs) disclose deficiencies to offerors
within the COMPETITIVE RANGE on competitive negotiated
procurements during written or oral DISCUSSIONs, unless such
disclosure would involve (1) TECHNICAL TRANSFUSION, (2)
TECHNICAL LEVELING, or (3) AUCTION.

DEFINITE-QUANTITY CONTRACT A type of contract providing for delivery of a definite quantity of specific supplies or services for a fixed period, with deliveries at designated locations to be scheduled upon order. FAR 16.502. Definite-quantity contracts are one of the three types of INDEFINITE-DELIVERY CONTRACTs. They may be used when it can be determined in advance that (1) a definite quantity of supplies or services will be required during the contract period and (2) the supplies or services are regularly available or will be available after a short lead-time. By buying a stated quantity for delivery on a deferred basis, the Government seeks to induce contractors to submit low prices and to reduce its costs of maintaining high levels of inventory.

DEFINITIZATION Agreement between a Government agency and a contractor on definitive terms, specifications, and price to replace an UNDEFINITIZED CONTRACTUAL ACTION. DFARS 217.7401. 10 U.S.C. 2326 places strict requirements on the definitization of such actions. This term is generally used with regard to LETTER CONTRACTs.

DELAY An event that slows the performance of the work by a Government contractor. In Government contracts, the contractor generally bears the RISK of both time and cost for delays caused by the contractor or within the contractor's control. However, the contractor is generally entitled to a time extension if there is an EXCUSABLE DELAY and to additional compensation if there is a COMPENSABLE DELAY. See Cibinic and Nash, Administration of Government Contracts, chap. 6; Margulies, chap. 8, Construction Contracting 617–79.

DELEGATION OF CONTRACTING OFFICER AUTHORITY The granting of authority to act as a CONTRACTING OFFICER (CO) for an EXECUTIVE AGENCY. FAR 1.603 requires that each agency establish a system for the selection, appointment, and termination of appointment of contracting officers. Agency procedures for delegating contracting officer authority are found in each agency FAR Supplement. Each contracting officer with delegated authority is given a WARRANT using the Certificate of Appointment in Standard Form 1402, FAR 53.301-1402.

DELEGATION OF PROCUREMENT AUTHORITY (DPA) The granting of authority by the GENERAL SERVICES ADMINISTRATION (GSA) to an agency to procure FEDERAL INFORMATION PROCESSING

(FIP) RESOURCES, or ADPE. Such delegation is necessary under the BROOKS ACT (AUTOMATIC DATA PROCESSING EQUIPMENT) because GSA has the sole authority to procure ADPE. The Administrator of GSA, however, may delegate the authority to lease, purchase, or maintain ADPE to an agency senior official who has sufficient experience, resources, and ability to carry out procurements fairly and effectively. See 40 U.S.C. 759. Agencies may also procure ADPE under blanket regulatory DPAs, specific agency or agency-component blanket DPAs, or specific acquisition DPAs (in which the agency submits an AGENCY PROCUREMENT REQUEST (APR) to GSA). FIRMR 201-23.103 through 106. Government agencies must comply with the provisions of the Government-wide ADP sharing program before contracting for commercial ADP services or support services.

DELINQUENCY NOTICE A notice from the contracting officer to a contractor, asserting that contract performance is delinquent and requesting that the contractor provide information as to the delinquency. FAR 49.607 discusses two types of delinquency notices: (1) CURE NOTICEs and (2) SHOW CAUSE NOTICEs.

DELIVERY ORDER An order for supplies or services placed against an established contract or with Government sources of supply. FAR 13.101. FAR 13.505-1 provides that such orders may be issued using Optional Form (OF) 347, Order for Supplies or Services, or OF 348, Order for Supplies or Services Schedule—Continuation, which are set forth at FAR 53.302-347 and -348.

DELIVERY OR PERFORMANCE SCHEDULE The contract provision setting forth the time of delivery or performance. This provision is included in the UNIFORM CONTRACT FORMAT, in Section F. FAR 14.201-1 and FAR 15.406-1. FAR 12.101 requires that contracting officers ensure that delivery schedules are realistic and meet the requirements of the acquisition. Schedules that are unreasonably tight tend to restrict competition, are inconsistent with small business policies, and may result in higher contract prices. When establishing contract delivery schedules for supply or service contracts, the contracting officer must consider factors such as urgency of the need, production time, market conditions, transportation time, industry practices, capabilities of small business concerns, administrative time for obtaining and evaluating offers and awarding contracts, time for contractors to comply with any conditions precedent to contract performance, and time for the Government to perform its obligations under the contract.   Scheduling the completion date for construction contracts requires consideration of the nature and complexity of the project, construction seasons involved, required completion date, availability of materials and equipment, capacity of the contractor to perform, and advisability of multiple completion dates. FAR 12.102.

DE NOVO Considering a matter without regard to prior procedures. When a contractor files an APPEAL FROM A CONTRACTING OFFICER'S DECISION under the CONTRACT DISPUTES ACT (CDA) OF 1978, the BOARD OF CONTRACT APPEALS (BCA) or the CLAIMS COURT (Cl. Ct.) will rehear the case completely and decide it on the basis of the evidence heard.   Thus, the prior decision of the contracting officer is not binding on the BCA or Claims Court in any way, and the proceeding before the BCA or Claims Court is in the nature of a new trial, not a review of the record made by the contracting officer.

DEPARTMENT OF DEFENSE (DoD) The Office of the Secretary of Defense (OSD), the military departments, and the defense agencies constitute DoD. The "military departments" include the Departments of the Army, the Navy, and the Air Force (the Marine Corps. is a part of the Department of the Navy).   The "defense agencies" are the Defense Advanced Research Projects Agency, the Defense Commissary Agency, the Defense Information Systems Agency, the Defense Intelligence Agency, the Defense Investigative Service, the Defense Logistics Agency, the Defense Mapping Agency, the Defense Nuclear Agency, the National Security Agency, the On-Site Inspection Agency, the Strategic Defense Initiative Organization, and the United States Special Operations Command. DFARS 202.101. DoD contracts fall under the coverage of the FEDERAL ACQUISITION REGULATION (FAR) and the DEPARTMENT OF DEFENSE FAR SUPPLEMENT (DFARS), as well as lower-level supplementary regulations for the independent Departments. Before the FAR went into effect in 1984, DoD contracts were governed by the DEFENSE ACQUISITION REGULATION (DAR) and its predecessor, the ARMED SERVICES PROCUREMENT REGULATION (ASPR). See the U.S. Government Manual.

DEPARTMENT OF DEFENSE DIRECTIVES SYSTEM   A single, uniform system governing the coordination, publication, dissemination, implementation, and biennial review of issuances maintained within DoD. The system includes (1) DoD Directives (DoDDs), which publish Secretary of Defense decisions on policies, plans, programs, charters, delegations of authority, or other major actions; (2) DoD Instructions (DoDIs), which provide supplementary guidance to implement Secretary of Defense decisions; (3) DoD publications, which implement or supplement DoDDs and DoDIs by providing uniform procedures for management or operational systems and by disseminating administrative information (these publications include handbooks and manuals, designated by the suffixes "H" and "M," respectively); and (4) DoD transmittals, which change or cancel DoD issuances. When directive-type memoranda of continuing application issued by principal staff assistants cannot, because of time constraints, be published in the DoD Directives System at the time of signature, they are to be reissued as DoD issuances within 90 days. Directive-type memoranda of a one-time nature are not issued in the DoD Directives System. DoD Directive 5025.1, *Department of Defense Directives System*, 23 Dec. 1988, and DoD Directive 5025.1-M, *Department of Defense Directives System Procedures*, Dec. 1990. Although all procurement regulations are required to be included in the FAR and the DFARS, the DoD Directives System contains a significant amount of information bearing directly on the procurement process. Instructions for obtaining documents in the DoD Directives System are available from the DoD Directives Division, Room 286, The Pentagon, Washington, DC 20301-1155; (703) 697-4111.

DEPARTMENT OF DEFENSE FAR SUPPLEMENT (DFARS)
The procurement regulation applicable to DoD that implements and supplements the FEDERAL ACQUISITION REGULATION (FAR). It applies specifically to procurements involving the Office of the Secretary of Defense; the Departments of the Army, Navy, and Air Force; and the Defense Logistics Agency (DLA) and other defense agencies. The FAR and the DFARS contain guidance and direction to DoD contracting personnel as to (1) which provisions, clauses, cost principles, and Cost Accounting Standards are authorized for DoD contracts and (2) what other procedures and actions must be followed in awarding and administering DoD contracts. The DFARS is not a stand-alone document; it must be read in conjunction with the FAR. The DFARS is amended through the use of DEFENSE ACQUISITION CIRCULARS (DACs), which are issued by the DEFENSE ACQUISITION REGULATORY

COUNCIL (DAR COUNCIL) and resemble FEDERAL ACQUISITION CIRCULARS (FACs). DFARS 201.304. Implementing coverage in the DFARS is numbered in the same way as the FAR material it implements, with the addition of a "2" or "20" prefix (the DFARS is Chapter 2 of Title 48). Thus the DFARS parts corresponding to FAR Parts 1 through 53 are Parts 201 through 253, the DFARS coverage paralleling FAR Subpart 52.1 is Subpart 252.1, and DFARS 201.101 implements FAR 1.101.   Supplementary coverage, for which there is no parallel in the FAR, is distinguished by using numbers 70 and above (e.g., Part 270, Subpart 245.73).   Supplementary numbering is used only when the DFARS text cannot be integrated intelligibly with counterpart text in the FAR. DFARS 201.303. The DFARS can be purchased in paperback from Commerce Clearing House, Inc., 4025 West Peterson Avenue, Chicago, IL 60646, or as part of the looseleaf-bound subscription edition of the FEDERAL ACQUISITION REGULATIONS (FAR) SYSTEM available from the U.S. Government Printing Office, Washington DC 20402.

DEPARTMENT OF ENERGY (DoE) U.S. Government agency established by the Department of Energy Organization Act, 42 U.S.C. 7131, effective 1 Oct. 1977, pursuant to Executive Order 12009 of 13 Sep. 1977. The act consolidated the major Federal energy functions into one Cabinet-level department, transferring to DoE all the responsibilities of several components of the Department of the Interior, including the Energy Research and Development Administration and the Federal Energy Administration. See the U.S. Government Manual.

DEPARTMENT OF ENERGY ACQUISITION REGULATION (DEAR) The DoE regulation that implements and supplements the FEDERAL ACQUISITION REGULATION (FAR). The DEAR is not a stand-alone document but must be read in conjunction with the FAR. DEAR 901.101. It is divided into the same parts, subparts, sections, subsections, and paragraphs as the FAR. The implementing passages of the DEAR are numbered the same as the FAR to the extent possible, except that they are preceded with a "9" or a "90" because the DEAR is Chapter 9 of Title 48 of the CODE OF FEDERAL REGULATIONS (CFR). DEAR 901.104-2. The DEAR is revised by Acquisition Letters issued by the DoE SENIOR PROCUREMENT EXECUTIVE.   DEAR 901.301-70.   The DEAR is available from the U.S. Government Printing Office, Washington

DC 20402, as part of the looseleaf-bound subscription edition of the FEDERAL ACQUISITION REGULATIONS (FAR) SYSTEM.

DEPRECIATION A charge to current operations that systematically and logically distributes the cost of a TANGIBLE CAPITAL ASSET, less estimated RESIDUAL VALUE, over the estimated useful life of the asset. FAR 31.205-11(a). Depreciation does not involve a process of valuation but is based on the acquisition cost of the ASSET. Useful life, as distinguished from physical life, is the prospective period of economic usefulness in a particular contractor's operations. Cost Accounting Standard 409, FAR 30.409, provides guidance on the computation of depreciation and generally requires that the costs be distributed equally over the years of use of the asset. FAR 31.205-11 provides that depreciation is an ALLOWABLE COST.

DESCRIPTIVE LITERATURE Information such as cuts, illustrations, drawings, and brochures showing the characteristics or construction of a product or explaining its operation. FAR 14.202-5(a). When required by the Descriptive Literature solicitation provision in FAR 52.214-21, descriptive literature is furnished by bidders as part of their bids to describe the products offered. The term includes only information required to determine acceptability of the product. Descriptive literature excludes other information, such as that furnished in connection with the qualifications of a bidder or for use in operating or maintaining equipment. FAR 14.202-5(b) states that the Government should not require bidders to furnish descriptive literature unless the contracting office needs it to determine before award whether the products offered meet the SPECIFICATION and to establish exactly what the bidder proposes to furnish. However, requiring descriptive literature is a means that contracting officers use to determine whether bidders actually intend to meet the contract SPECIFICATIONs and to identify bids that are not responsive (see RESPONSIVENESS).

DESIGNATED BILLING OFFICE The office (or person) designated in the contract as the point to which the contractor submits invoices and contract financing requests. FAR 32.902. This office can be the Government disbursing office, the contract administration office, the office accepting the supplies delivered or services performed, the contract audit office, or even a non-Government agent. In some cases, more than one office may be designated to receive invoices and contract financing requests. When payments are subject to the PROMPT PAYMENT ACT (PPA), they must be made within 30 days of the date a proper INVOICE is received in the designated billing office. FAR 32.905(a).

DESIGNATED PAYMENT OFFICE The place designated in the contract to make invoice payments or contract financing payments. Normally, this will be the Government disbursing office. FAR 32.902. See also DISBURSING OFFICER (DO).

DESIGNATED SENIOR OFFICIAL The senior official designated by executive agencies subject to the PAPERWORK REDUCTION ACT OF 1980 as responsible for carrying out the agency's Information Resources Management (IRM) functions (see 44 U.S.C. 3506). For Federal agencies not subject to the Paperwork Reduction Act, the designated senior official is the senior IRM official designated by the agency head as responsible for acquisitions of FEDERAL INFORMATION PROCESSING (FIP) RESOURCES) made under a DELEGATION OF PROCUREMENT AUTHORITY (DPA).

DESIGN/BUILD A method of construction contracting that combines the architectural, engineering, and construction services required for a project into a single agreement. Under such an agreement, the owner contracts with a single entity; the contractor providing the end product is responsible for both design and construction. That contractor is responsible for any deficiencies or defects in the design, except to the extent that such responsibility is specifically waived or limited by the contract. This format is widely used in the industrial sector. It is sometimes called "turnkey" construction because, at least in theory, the owner presents its requirements to a design/build organization and, at some later date, the designer/builder simply hands over the keys of the building to the owner. See Nash, chap. 1, Construction Contracting 7–9.

DESIGN SPECIFICATIONS SPECIFICATIONs that set forth precise measurements, tolerances, materials, in-process and finished-product tests, quality control measures, inspection requirements, and other specific information. The Government uses design specifications in solicitations when the technical requirements are definite and can be communicated clearly to potential offerors. Design specifications permit the Government to award solely on the basis of price and price-related factors, since no flexibility is allowed and all responsive bids are therefore design-identical. Design specifications increase the Government's liability for claims that arise during contract performance regarding design defects, since the Government generally assumes responsibility for the correctness and adequacy of design specifications (see IMPLIED WARRANTY OF SPECIFICATIONS). Consequently, FAR 10.002 requires that FUNCTIONAL SPECIFICATIONS and PERFORMANCE SPECIFICATIONS be used instead of design specifications whenever practicable. See Cibinic and Nash, Formation of Government Contracts 340; Nash, chap. 1, Construction Contracting 21–23.

DESIGN-TO-COST A management concept in accordance with which (1) rigorous cost goals are established during the development of a system (see ACQUISITION PROCESS) and (2) control of costs (acquisition, operating, and support) is achieved by practical tradeoffs between operational capability, performance, costs, and schedule. Cost, as a key design parameter, is addressed on a continuing basis and as an inherent part of the development and production process. Design-to-cost parameters for operation and support are selected and then expressed in dollars or other measurable factors. Firm goals and thresholds are established before FULL-SCALE DEVELOPMENT begins. Jones, Glossary: Defense Acquisition Acronyms and Terms. Procuring agencies are to consider design-to-cost in the ACQUISITION PLANNING process, as appropriate. FAR 7.105. DoD Directive 5000.2, *Defense Acquisition Management Policies and Procedures*, 23 Feb. 1991, part 6K, contains policies and procedures establishing cost as a design constraint early in the acquisition process.

DETERMINATION AND FINDINGS (D&F) A written approval by an authorized official that is required by statute or regulation as a prerequisite to certain contracting actions. FAR 1.701. The determination is a conclusion or decision supported by the findings. The findings, which are statements of fact or rationale essential to support the determination, must cover each requirement of the statute or regulation. FAR 1.704 requires that D&Fs set forth enough facts and circumstances to clearly and convincingly justify the specific determination made. As a minimum, a D&F must include (1) identification of the agency and the contracting activity, and of the document as a D&F; (2) a description of the contracting action; (3) citation of the appropriate statute and/or regulation; (4) findings that detail the particular circumstances, facts, or reasoning essential to support the determination;

(5) a determination based on the findings; (6) the expiration date of the D&F, if required; and (7) the date and signature of the official authorized to sign the D&F. Further requirements may apply in a given situation; for example, FAR 14.406-4 lists specific types of statements that a D&F must contain in documenting the contracting officer's handling of a mistake in bid that the contractor discovers and asks to correct following contract award.

DEVELOPED The condition that applies to an item, component, or process when it exists and is workable. This condition is part of the determination of intellectual property rights in FAR Subpart 27.4 and DFARS Subpart 227.4. DFARS 227.401 provides that to meet the test of being developed, an item or component must have been constructed or the process practiced. Workability is generally established when the item, component, or process has been analyzed or tested sufficiently to demonstrate to reasonable people skilled in the applicable art that there is a high probability that it will operate as intended. Whether, how much, and what type of analysis or testing is required to establish workability depends on the nature of the item, component, or process, and the state of the art. To be considered "developed," the item, component, or process need not be at the stage when it could be offered for sale or sold on the commercial market, nor must the item, component, or process be actually reduced to practice within the meaning of Title 35 of the United States Code. See DeVecchio, *The Bell Helicopter Textron Decision: Expanding the Government's Rights in Technical Data*, 16 Pub. Cont. L.J. 1 (1986).

DEVELOPED AT PRIVATE EXPENSE A condition of an item, component, or process wherein no part of the cost of development was paid for by the Government. This term is used, without definition, in the policy on rights to TECHNICAL DATA in FAR Subpart 27.4. It is generally believed that private expense includes all costs not charged as DIRECT COSTs to a contract.

DEVELOPED EXCLUSIVELY AT PRIVATE EXPENSE A condition of an item, component, or process wherein no part of the cost of development was paid for by the Government and the development was not required for the performance of a Government contract or subcontract. DFARS 227.401. 10 U.S.C. 2320(a)(2)(B) provides that, with certain exceptions, TECHNICAL DATA pertaining to items processed or developed exclusively at private expense may be submitted to the Government with markings prohibiting their disclosure. INDEPENDENT RESEARCH AND DEVELOPMENT (IR&D) costs and BID AND PROPOSAL (B&P) COSTS as defined in FAR 31.205-18, whether or not included in a formal IR&D program, are considered to be private expenses. All other indirect costs of development are considered Government-funded when development was required for the performance of a Government contract or subcontract.

DEVELOPMENT   The systematic use, under whatever name, of scientific and technical knowledge in the design, development, testing, or evaluation of a potential new product or service (or of an improvement in an existing product or service), for the purpose of meeting specific performance requirements or objectives. FAR 35.001. Development includes the functions of design engineering, prototyping, and engineering testing. It generally follows APPLIED RESEARCH in the RESEARCH AND DEVELOPMENT (R&D) process. In the context of INDEPENDENT RESEARCH AND DEVELOPMENT (IR&D), FAR 31.205-18 provides that development excludes (1) subcontracted technical effort for the sole purpose of developing an additional source for an existing product, and (2) development effort for manufacturing or production of materials, systems, processes, methods, equipment, tools, and techniques not intended for sale. DFARS 235.001 breaks development into several categories: exploratory development, advanced development, engineering development, and operational system development.

DEVIATION   Noncompliance with a mandatory procurement regulation. FAR Subpart 1.4 sets forth the procedures to be used in obtaining the authority to deviate from the FAR. FAR 1.401 provides that deviation means any one or combination of the following: (1) issuance or use of a policy, procedure, PROVISION, CLAUSE, method, or practice of conducting acquisition actions of any kind, at any stage of the acquisition process, that is inconsistent with the FAR; (2) omission of any provision or clause when the FAR requires its use; (3) use of any provision or clause with modified or alternate language not authorized by the FAR; (4) use of a provision or clause prescribed by the FAR on a "substantially as follows" or "substantially the same as" basis if such use is inconsistent with the intent, principle, or substance of the prescription or coverage on the subject matter in the FAR; (5) authorization of lesser or greater limitations on the use of any provision, clause, policy, or procedure prescribed by the FAR; and (6) issuance of any policy or procedure that governs the contracting process or otherwise controls contracting relationships that is not incorporated into agency acquisition regulations in accordance with the rules set forth in FAR Subpart 1.3. FAR 52.107 requires contracting officers to use the Authorized Deviation clauses in FAR 52.252-5 and -6 to notify offerors and contractors when a solicitation or contract contains clauses that deviate from the FAR. See DFARS Subpart 201.4 for DoD's policy on deviations. Mandatory clauses that are omitted from a contract without a proper deviation are read into the contract following the CHRISTIAN DOCTRINE.

DIFFERING SITE CONDITIONS Conditions at the site of the CONSTRUCTION work for which an EQUITABLE ADJUSTMENT is given under the Differing Site Conditions clause in FAR 52.236-2. This clause provides that differing site conditions are (1) subsurface or LATENT (not discoverable by ordinary inspection) physical conditions at a construction site that differ materially from the conditions indicated in the contract (commonly referred to as "Type I" differing site conditions) or (2) unknown physical conditions at the site, of an unusual nature, that differ materially from conditions ordinarily encountered and generally recognized as inhering in work of the kind provided for in the contract (commonly referred to as "Type II" differing site conditions). See McClure, *Differing Site Conditions: Evaluating the Material Difference*, 15 Pub. Cont. L.J. 138 (1984). The clause serves to take some of the risk out of bidding. For example, bidders do not have to take their own soil borings or consider how large a contingency allowance should be added to the bid price to cover the risk of unanticipated, unfavorable subsurface conditions. The Government benefits from more accurate bidding, without inflation for potentially nonexistent risks, and pays for difficult subsurface work only when such work is found to be necessary but could not reasonably have been anticipated. See Cibinic and Nash, Administration of Government Contracts, chap. 5; Braude, chap. 7, Construction Contracting.

DIRECT ACCESS Litigation of a contract DISPUTE before the U.S. CLAIMS COURT (Cl. Ct.). Under the CONTRACT DISPUTES ACT (CDA) OF 1978, the contractor, upon receipt of a DECISION OF THE CONTRACTING OFFICER, may, within 90 days, elect to file an appeal with a BOARD OF CONTRACT APPEALS (BCA). In the alternative, the contractor, within 12 months, may bring an action directly in the Claims Court—thus obtaining "direct access" to the court without first going to a BCA. FAR 33.211 mandates that contracting officers explain this election to contractors when rendering a decision on a CLAIM. Whereas litigation before the BCAs is referred to as an "appeal," Claims Court litigation is referred to as a "direct access suit." Prior to enactment of the Contract Disputes Act, contractors could obtain direct access to the court only when a BCA had no jurisdiction; that is, only when the claim was not considered "ARISING UNDER THE CONTRACT". There is no direct access for appeal of a TERMINATION FOR DEFAULT when no monetary claim is asserted. *Overall Roofing and Construction, Inc. v. United States*, 929 F.2d 687 (Fed. Cir. 1991). See Nash, *Postscript III: No Jurisdiction in Claims Court over Default Termination Claims*, 5 N&CR ¶ 33 (June 1991).

DIRECT COST Any cost specifically identified with a particular final COST OBJECTIVE. FAR 31.202. The term is not necessarily limited to items incorporated in the end product as material or labor. Armed Services Pricing Manual (ASPM) vol. 1, app. B. FAR 31.202(a) provides that no final cost objective may have any cost allocated to it (see ALLOCATION OF COST) as a direct cost if other costs incurred for the same purpose in like circumstances have been included in any INDIRECT COST POOL to be allocated to that or any other final cost objective. Costs identified specifically with the contract are direct costs of the contract and are to be charged directly to the contract. All costs specifically identified with other final cost objectives are direct costs of those cost objectives and are not to be charged to the contract directly or indirectly. FAR 31.202(b) provides that for practical reasons, direct costs of minor dollar amounts may be treated as indirect costs if the accounting treatment is consistently applied and the results achieved are substantially the same as treating them as direct costs.

DIRECTIVE A written communication that initiates or governs action, conduct, or procedure. FIRMR 201-2.001. Directives are often issued as circulars, notices, regulations, orders, or handbooks; they include materials usually issued to multiple addresses in multiple copies for insertion in policy, administrative, or operations manuals. News releases, program announcements, catalogs, price lists, training materials, and correspondence are not included. "Directives management" means the effective and efficient development, distribution, maintenance, and use of directives. "External directive" means officially prescribed guidance such as rules, notices, and regulations issued to a primary audience outside the originating agency. "Internal directive" means officially prescribed intra-agency policy or procedure, delegation of authority, or assignment of responsibility. See also DEPARTMENT OF DEFENSE DIRECTIVES SYSTEM.

DIRECT LABOR Labor specifically identified with a particular final COST OBJECTIVE. Manufacturing direct labor includes fabrication, assembly, inspection, and testing of the end product. Engineering direct labor consists of reliability, quality assurance, test, design, and other engineering work readily identified with the end product. Jones, Glossary: Defense Acquisition Acronyms and Terms. Direct labor should be distinguished from indirect labor, which is labor assigned to an INDIRECT COST pool because it is identified with two or more cost objectives but not specifically allocable to any final cost objective.

DIRECT LICENSE A LICENSE to use TECHNICAL DATA granted by the owner of the rights in that data directly to the party that will use the data. Direct licenses are permitted by DFARS 227.403-70(c)(4), but the regulation gives no guidance on their use. They have an advantage over GOVERNMENT-PURPOSE LICENSE RIGHTS (GPLR) in that they establish a direct contractual relationship between the owner of the proprietary right and the user, without interjecting the Government agency between the two parties. DFARS 217.7503(c)(1) states that contracting officers should consider direct licensing as a means of obtaining competition for replenishment parts.

DISALLOWANCE The refusal of the Government to recognize a cost as an ALLOWABLE COST. FAR Subpart 42.8 prescribes policies and procedures for (1) issuing notices of intent to disallow costs and (2) disallowing costs already incurred during the course of performance. DoD has a form for this purpose: DCAA Form 1, Notice of Contract Costs Suspended and/or Disallowed. DFARS 242.803. FAR 42.801 provides that at any time during the performance of a COST-REIMBURSEMENT CONTRACT, FIXED-PRICE INCENTIVE (FPI) CONTRACT, FIXED-PRICE REDETERMINA-TION—PROSPECTIVE (RPRP) CONTRACT, or FIXED-PRICE REDETER-MINATION—RETROACTIVE (FPRR) CONTRACT, the contracting officer responsible for administering the contract may issue the contractor a written notice of intent to disallow specified costs incurred or planned for incurrence. The purpose of the notice is to (1) inform the contractor of this intent as early as practicable and (2) provide for timely resolution of any resulting disagreement. See the Notice of Intent to Disallow Costs clause in FAR 52.242-1. FAR 42.803 provides that under cost-reimbursement contracts, costs can be disallowed after incurrence and deducted from current payments. If a contractor disagrees with a post-incurrence disallowance, the contractor may request discussions with the contracting officer or file a CLAIM under the Disputes clause at FAR 52.233-1.

DISBURSING OFFICER (DO) A Government officer or employee designated to pay out monies and render accounts in accordance with laws and regulations governing the disbursement of public funds. The disbursing officer must (1) disburse monies only upon, and in strict accordance with, vouchers duly certified by the head of the agency or by an officer or employee duly authorized in writing to certify them; (2) examine vouchers as necessary to ascertain whether they are in proper form, duly certified and approved, and correctly computed on the basis of the facts certified; and (3) be held accountable accordingly, except that accountability for the correctness of the computations of certified vouchers lies with the certifying officer and not the disbursing officer. Principles of Federal Appropriations Law (2d ed.), chap. 9, part B. See also 31 U.S.C. 3322(a) and 3325(a).

DISCLAIMER See EXCULPATORY CLAUSE.

DISCLOSURE STATEMENT A written description of a contractor's cost accounting practices and procedures that is filed with the cognizant administrative contracting officer, with a copy to the cognizant contract auditor. FAR 30.202-1 and -5. A disclosure statement, on Form CASB-DS-1, must be submitted by any business unit entering into a negotiated national defense contract or subcontract of $10 million or more, with certain exceptions applying mostly to contracts with prices that are, or are based on, (1) ESTABLISHED CATALOG OR MARKET PRICES of commercial items sold in substantial quantities to the general public or (2) prices set by law or regulation. (Submission may also be required in certain other circumstances.) The presumed or anticipated presence of a competitive environment does not create an exemption from the requirement to submit a disclosure statement. FAR 30.201. Armed Services Pricing Manual (ASPM) vol. 1, app. B.

DISCOUNT FOR PROMPT PAYMENT An invoice payment reduction voluntarily offered by the contractor, in conjunction with the clause at FAR 52.232-8, Discounts for Prompt Payment, if payment is made by the Government prior to the due date. FAR 32.902. The due date is calculated from the date of the contractor's invoice. Prompt payment discounts may be taken only when payment is made within the contractor-specified discount period. FAR 32.903. See also PROMPT PAYMENT ACT (PPA).

DISCREPANCIES INCIDENT TO SHIPMENT All discrepancies incident to shipment of GOVERNMENT PROPERTY to or from a contractor's facility; differences between the property purported to have been shipped and the property actually received. FAR 45.501. Such discrepancies include loss, damage, destruction, improper status and condition coding, errors in identity or classification, and improper consignment. FAR 45.502-2 requires a contractor to provide a statement of such discrepancy to the PROPERTY ADMINISTRATOR.

DISCRETION A power or right, conferred upon Government officers by law, to act officially in certain circumstances according to the dictates of their own judgment and conscience, uncontrolled by the judgment or conscience of others. Black's Law Dictionary. To perform the actions necessary for effective contracting, ensuring compliance with the terms of contracts and safeguarding the interests of the United States in its contractual relationships, contracting officers are allowed wide latitude to exercise discretion and business judgment. FAR Subpart 1.6. Situations in which contracting officers are called upon to exercise discretion include determining which PROPOSALs are in the COMPETITIVE RANGE (FAR 15.609), selecting the appropriate TYPE OF CONTRACT (FAR 16.104), deciding and settling CLAIMs (FAR 33.210), and determining when TERMINATION FOR DEFAULT or TERMINATION FOR CONVENIENCE is in the best interest of the Government (FAR Part 49).

DISCUSSION Any oral or written communication between the Government and an OFFEROR (other than communication made for the purpose of minor CLARIFICATION) in the COMPETITIVE PROPOSALS process, whether or not initiated by the Government, that (1) involves information essential for determining the acceptability of a proposal or (2) gives the offeror an opportunity to revise or modify its proposal. FAR 15.601. Once a discussion with any offeror has occurred, the contracting officer may not make an AWARD but must conduct written or oral discussions with all responsible offerors (see RESPONSIBILITY) that submit proposals within the COMPETITIVE RANGE. The context and extent of discussions are matters for the contracting officer's judgment, but the contracting officer should advise the offerors of DEFICIENCIES, resolve uncertainties, and request correction of suspected MISTAKES. The contracting officer must not engage in TECHNICAL LEVELING, TECHNICAL TRANSFUSION, or AUCTION techniques. FAR 15.610. See Cibinic and Nash, Formation of Government Contracts 609–37; Shnitzer, *Discussions in Negotiated Procurements*, 91-4 Briefing Papers (Mar. 1991); Feldman, *Traversing the Tightrope Between Meaningful Discussions and Improper Practices in Negotiated Federal Acquisitions: Technical Transfusion, Technical Leveling, and Auction Techniques*, 17 Pub. Cont. L.J. 211, 246 (1987).

DISMISSAL WAGES See SEVERANCE PAY.

DISPUTE A disagreement between the contractor and the contracting officer regarding the rights of the parties under a contract. Under the CONTRACT DISPUTES ACT (CDA) OF 1978, 41 U.S.C. 601–613, contractors are permitted to submit CLAIMs (demands for a sum certain) against the Government. Conversely, the Government may make claims against contractors. A dispute originates when a claim is denied by the party against which it is made. Disputes are classified as "ARISING UNDER THE CONTRACT" or "RELATING TO THE CONTRACT". Before litigation is initiated before a BOARD OF CONTRACT APPEALS (BCA) or the U.S. CLAIMS COURT (Cl. Ct.), the dispute must become the subject of a DECISION OF THE CONTRACTING OFFICER. In certain situations, the contracting officer's failure to act will be deemed a decision to deny the claim, and thus will create a dispute (see DEEMED DENIAL). FAR Subpart 33.2 provides guidance to contracting officers on the handling of disputes. A dispute should be distinguished from a PROTEST: a dispute arises between a contractor and the Government during or after the performance of a contract, whereas a protest involves an offeror or prospective contractor and contests the award of the contract or the conduct of the solicitation process itself. See Cibinic and Nash, Administration of Government Contracts, chap. 12; Bednar, chap. 13, Construction Contracting.

DISQUALIFICATION Exclusion of an offeror from a procurement because of an impropriety in the competitive process. Offerors have been disqualified by contracting officers or by the GENERAL SERVICES ADMINISTRATION BOARD OF CONTRACT APPEALS (GSBCA) or the GENERAL ACCOUNTING OFFICE (GAO) because of a CONFLICT OF INTEREST, improper obtaining of information, or MISREPRESENTATION. See Nash, *Disqualification of Offerors: A New Form of Exclusion from the Procurement Process*, 5 N&CR ¶ 17 (Mar. 1991).

DOCUMENTATION See COMPUTER SOFTWARE DOCUMENTATION.

DoD See DEPARTMENT OF DEFENSE (DoD).

DoD FAR SUPPLEMENT (DFARS) See DEPARTMENT OF DEFENSE FAR SUPPLEMENT (DFARS).

DoE See DEPARTMENT OF ENERGY (DoE).

DOMESTIC CONSTRUCTION MATERIAL Material that is given preference under the BUY AMERICAN ACT because it is either (1) unmanufactured CONSTRUCTION material mined or produced in the United States or (2) construction material manufactured in the United States, if the cost of its components mined, produced, or manufactured in the United States exceeds 50 percent of the cost of all its components. FAR 25.201. The cost of each component includes cost of transportation to the place of incorporation into the construction material and any applicable duty (whether or not a duty-free entry certificate is issued). Components of foreign origin are treated as domestic if they are of the same class or kind for which it has been determined that the material is not mined, produced, or manufactured in the United States in sufficient and reasonably available commercial quantities of a satisfactory quality. See Ginsburg and Patin, chap. 2, Construction Contracting 116–20.

DOMESTIC END PRODUCT A product that is given preference under the BUY AMERICAN ACT because it is either (1) an unmanufactured end product mined or produced in the United States or (2) an end product manufactured in the United States, if the cost of its components mined, produced, or manufactured in the United States exceeds 50 percent of the cost of all its components. FAR 25.101. The cost of each component includes cost of transportation to the place of incorporation into the end product and any applicable duty (whether or not a duty-free certificate is issued). Components of foreign origin are treated as domestic if they are of the same class or kind for which it has been determined either (1) that domestic preference would be inconsistent with the public interest or (2) that they are not mined, produced, or manufactured in the United States in sufficient and reasonably available commercial quantities of a satisfactory quality. Components of Canadian origin are treated as domestic by NASA and DoD. FAR 25.103 and NFS 18-25.103. A narrower definition of domestic end product is used in implementing NASA's domestic preference legislation. NFS Subpart 18-25.71.

DOMESTIC PREFERENCE   See BALANCE OF PAYMENTS PROGRAM; BUY AMERICAN ACT; CARGO PREFERENCE ACTS; CARIBBEAN BASIN ECONOMIC RECOVERY ACT; DOMESTIC END PRODUCT; TRADE AGREEMENTS ACT OF 1979.

DONATION   A gift of cash, property, or services to a charitable organization. FAR 31.205-8 provides that the costs of such gifts are UNALLOWABLE COSTs.

DRUG-FREE WORKPLACE   A site for the performance of work under a specific contract, at which employees of the contractor are prohibited from engaging in the unlawful manufacturing, distribution, dispensing, possession, or use of a controlled substance. FAR 23.503. FAR Subpart 23.5 implements the Drug-Free Workplace Act of 1988, 41 U.S.C. 701 *et seq.*, and applies to domestic Government contracts of $25,000 or more. To be considered a responsible source (see RESPONSIBILITY), contractors must certify that they will provide a drug-free workplace, pursuant to the Certification Regarding a Drug-Free Workplace solicitation provision in FAR 52.223-5. Compliance with the certification entails, among other things, posting notices to employees, establishing drug-free awareness programs, requiring notification by employees of related convictions, and making a good-faith effort to maintain a drug-free workplace. Failure to comply may result in suspension of payments, TERMINATION FOR DEFAULT, or SUSPENSION or DEBARMENT of the contractor. See the Drug-Free Workplace clause in FAR 52.223-6; Arnavas and Ganther, *The Drug-Free Workplace*, 89-9 Briefing Papers (Aug. 1989).

DRY BULK CARRIER A vessel used primarily for carrying shipload lots of homogeneous, unmarked, nonliquid cargoes such as grain, coal, cement, and lumber. FAR 47.501. This term is used in connection with implementing the policies of the CARGO PREFERENCE ACTS and the Merchant Marine Act of 1936, which give preference to U.S.-FLAG VESSELs when ocean transportation of supplies is required. See the Preference for Privately Owned U.S.-Flag Commercial Vessels clause in FAR 52.247-64, which requires contractors to compute shipments in such vessels separately in determining whether they have met the requirement that at least 50 percent of the gross tonnage shipped be in U.S.-flag vessels.

DRY CARGO LINER A vessel used for the carriage of heterogeneous marked cargoes in parcel lots. However, any cargo may be carried in these vessels, including cargoes of dry bulk items or, when carried in deep tanks, bulk liquids such as petroleum and vegetable oils. FAR 47.501. This term is used in connection with implementing the policies of the CARGO PREFERENCE ACTS and the Merchant Marine Act of 1936, which give preference to U.S.-FLAG VESSELs when ocean transportation of supplies is required. See the Preference for Privately Owned U.S.-Flag Commercial Vessels clause in FAR 52.247-64, which requires contractors to compute shipments in such vessels separately in determining whether they have met the requirement that at least 50 percent of the gross tonnage shipped be in U.S.-flag vessels.

DUAL SOURCE The existence of two or more sources for the same product or service. 10 U.S.C. 2438 encourages DoD to plan its programs so that it has "competitive alternative sources" for major programs and major subsystems under major programs, from the beginning of full-scale development through the end of the procurement. DFARS 215.804-3(b) provides that COST OR PRICING DATA need not be obtained because ADEQUATE PRICE COMPETITION normally exists in dual source programs where award is split in a range of 0 to 100 percent between two or more offerors who are individually capable of producing the full quantity.

DUE PROCESS OF LAW A constitutional guarantee, found in the Fifth and Fourteenth Amendments, of fundamentally fair treatment by a government. *Substantive* due process requires that no person be arbitrarily denied life, liberty, or property by government action. *Procedural* due process includes notice by the Government and an opportunity to be heard by the government prior to the infringement of a liberty or property interest by the government. Procedural requirements increase with the importance of the interest taken. Black's Law Dictionary. In Government contracting, the issue of due process arises whenever a contractor claims that it has been denied a liberty or property right without proper procedures. Such claims may arise in DEBARMENT and SUSPENSION actions, TERMINATION FOR DEFAULT, and nonresponsibility (see RESPONSIBILITY) determinations. See, for example, *Old Dominion Dairy Products, Inc. v. Secretary of Defense*, 631 F.2d 953 (D.C. Cir. 1980), in which the court found that a liberty interest was infringed without due process in a nonresponsibility determination. For a discussion of this case, see Nash, *Integrity-Based Nonresponsibility Determinations: Why Keep the CO in the Dark?* 1 N&CR ¶ 45 (June 1987) and Nash, *Postscript: The Due Process Requirement in Responsibility Determinations*, 4 N&CR ¶ 7 (Jan. 1990).

DURESS A condition in which one party is induced by a wrongful act or threat of another to enter into a contract under circumstances depriving the first party of the exercise of its free will. Like "undue influence," duress includes conduct that overpowers a party's will and coerces or constrains performance of an act that otherwise would not have been performed. Black's Law Dictionary. Duress is also known as business compulsion. The elements of duress in Government contracting are (1) threat of economic harm that is improper as a violation of the contracting officer's DUTY OF GOOD FAITH AND FAIR DEALING and (2) a showing that the contractor's will was overborne (i.e., that the contractor accepted contract terms because circumstances permitted no alternative). See Cibinic and Nash, Administration of Government Contracts 939–42; Williston on Contracts § 1617; Nash, *Hard Bargaining or Duress: Walking a Narrow Line*, 3 N&CR ¶ 34 (Apr. 1989). Theoretically, duress, UNCONSCIONABILITY, and undue influence may differ, but all are aimed at unconscionable conduct by one party that may permit the other party to avoid a contract (see AVOIDANCE OF CONTRACT). See Murray on Contracts § 93; Harley, *Economic Duress and Unconscionability: How Fair Must the Government Be?* 18 Pub. Cont. L.J. 76 (1988).

DURING THE CONDUCT OF A PROCUREMENT The period beginning with the development, preparation, and issuance of a

SOLICITATION and ending with the AWARD, MODIFICATION, or extension of a contract for the procurement of property and services. FAR 3.104-4. The term includes evaluation of OFFERs, SOURCE SELECTION, and conduct of NEGOTIATIONs. It defines the period during which the PROCUREMENT INTEGRITY rules apply. Each award or each modification constitutes a separate procurement action—that is, a separate period during which the prohibitions and requirements regarding procurement integrity apply. See FAR 3.104-7 and 41 U.S.C. 423. Some agencies have promulgated additional guidance on the determination of the beginning date of this period.

DUTY OF GOOD FAITH AND FAIR DEALING An implied obligation of all contracting parties during the performance and enforcement of a contract. Restatement (Second) of Contracts § 205. "Good faith" is defined at U.C.C. 1-201 as "honesty in fact in the conduct or transaction concerned." When this implied duty is discussed in the context of a Government contract dispute, it is usually in reference to the Government's DUTY TO COOPERATE. See Nash, *The Duty of Good Faith and Fair Dealing: An Emerging Concept?* 3 N&CR ¶ 78 (Nov. 1989).

DUTY OF VERIFICATION The contracting officer's obligation, when a MISTAKE in a BID or PROPOSAL is suspected, to call the mistake or the affected portion of the offer to the offeror's attention, ask for CLARIFICATION, and allow the offeror to either correct the offer before award is made or withdraw it altogether. FAR 14.406 discusses the procedures to be followed for bids, FAR 15.607(c) and 610(c)(4) the procedures for proposals. Requests for verification must inform the offeror of the facts that led the contracting officer to suspect a mistake. If the contracting officer fails to seek verification, the Government may be subject to claims for price adjustment or the contractor may use a claimed mistake as a basis for avoiding performance obligations. See Cibinic and Nash, Formation of Government Contracts 484–88, 595–96.

DUTY TO COOPERATE An implied duty of a contracting party to cooperate with the other party to facilitate the performance of the contract. This duty is most frequently used to hold the Government liable for a CONSTRUCTIVE CHANGE when the Government does not assist the contractor. See Nash, Government Contract Changes, chap. 12. Under Restatement (Second) of Contracts §

205, this duty is defined as one aspect of the DUTY OF GOOD FAITH AND FAIR DEALING. See Cibinic and Nash, Administration of Government Contracts 221–25.

DUTY TO DISCLOSE INFORMATION See SUPERIOR KNOWLEDGE.

DUTY TO INQUIRE See DUTY TO SEEK CLARIFICATION.

DUTY TO PROCEED The obligation of a Government contractor to continue to prosecute work under a Government contract or risk TERMINATION FOR DEFAULT (see FAILURE TO MAKE PROGRESS). The Disputes clause in FAR 52.233-1 states that the contractor "shall proceed diligently with performance of this contract, pending final resolution of any request for relief, claim, appeal, or action "ARISING UNDER THE CONTRACT", and comply with any decision of the Contracting Officer." Alternate I to that clause, used in MAJOR SYSTEM contracts, requires the contractor to proceed in the face of disputes arising under the contract or "RELATING TO THE CONTRACT". With regard to a CHANGE ORDER, the contractor must, except under cost or fund limitations, continue performance of the contract as changed. The Changes—Fixed-Price clause in FAR 52.243-1 (for supply and services contracts) states: "Failure to agree to any adjustment shall be a dispute under the Disputes clause. However, nothing in this clause shall excuse the Contractor from proceeding with the contract as changed." See also the Commencement, Prosecution, and Completion of Work clause in FAR 52.212-3. Exceptions to the duty to proceed are BREACH OF CONTRACT by the Government, CARDINAL CHANGE, and IMPRACTICABILITY. However, it is uncertain whether these exceptions apply to the Alternate I clause. See Nash, Government Contract Changes, chap. 6; Cibinic and Nash, Administration of Government Contracts 702–17.

DUTY TO SEEK CLARIFICATION The duty of an offeror to request the guidance of the contracting officer when a patent AMBIGUITY, obvious omission, or drastic conflict is found in the contract language. The offeror's/contractor's failure to seek clarification in such circumstances is a valid Government defense to a CLAIM for EQUITABLE ADJUSTMENT because of ambiguous specifications. See Cibinic and Nash, Administration of Government Contracts 170–77.

E

EARNED VALUE A technique developed by cost accountants to help management keep better track of project status. Recognizing that cost data alone—or schedule data alone—can lead to distorted perceptions of performance, the technique is based on (1) the budgeted cost of work scheduled (BCWS), (2) the budgeted cost of work performed (BCWP), and (3) the actual cost of work performed (ACWP). BCWS states what a particular task will cost. ACWP provides the actual cost of work performed. BCWP, also called earned value, combines planned and actual elements and evaluates actual performance in terms of the original plan. See DCAA Contract Audit Manual (CAM) 11-205.

ECONOMICALLY DISADVANTAGED INDIVIDUALS SOCIALLY DISADVANTAGED INDIVIDUALS whose ability to compete in the free enterprise system is impaired due to diminished opportunities to obtain capital and credit as compared with others in the same line of business who are not socially disadvantaged. FAR 19.001. Individuals who certify that they are members of named groups (Black Americans, Hispanic Americans, NATIVE AMERICANS, ASIAN-PACIFIC AMERICANS, SUBCONTINENT-ASIAN AMERICANS) are to be considered both socially and economically disadvantaged. FAR 19.001. Businesses owned by such individuals are given special preferences in Government procurement. See SMALL DISADVANTAGED BUSINESS CONCERN (SDBC).

ECONOMIC DURESS See DURESS.

ECONOMIC ORDER QUANTITY (EOQ) A quantity of SUPPLIES that will result in a TOTAL COST and unit cost most advantageous to the Government, where practicable, and does not exceed the quantity reasonably expected to be required by the agency. 10

151

U.S.C. 2384a and 41 U.S.C. 253f require agencies to procure economic order quantities and to include a provision in solicitations inviting offerors to state an opinion on whether the quantity of supplies being procured is economically advantageous to the Government. This requirement is implemented by FAR Subpart 7.2, and the Economic Purchase Quantity—Supplies solicitation provision is set forth in FAR 52.207-4. Economic order quantities can also be procured in advance of the procurement of multiyear items under the advance acquisition procedures used in MULTI-YEAR CONTRACTING. See FAR 17.101.

ECONOMIC PLANNING COSTS Costs of generalized long-range management planning that addresses the future overall development of the contractor's business and may take into account the eventual possibility of economic dislocations or fundamental alterations in those markets in which the contractor currently does business. FAR 31.205-12. Economic planning costs do not include ORGANIZATION COSTS or reorganization costs. Economic planning costs are allowable (see ALLOWABLE COST) as indirect costs to be properly allocated. RESEARCH AND DEVELOPMENT (R&D) costs and engineering costs designed to lead to new products for sale to the general public are not allowable under this cost principle.

ECONOMIC PRICE ADJUSTMENT (EPA) See FIXED-PRICE CONTRACT WITH ECONOMIC PRICE ADJUSTMENT (EPA).

ECONOMIES OF SCALE Reductions in the unit cost of an end product that result from the production of additional units. Economies of scale stem from increased specialization of labor as the volume of output increases, decreased unit costs of materials resulting from volume discounts, better utilization of management, acquisition of more efficient equipment, and greater use of by-products. Jones, Glossary: Defense Acquisition Acronyms and Terms. Because the costs of contract administration are reduced, the Government may also realize economies of scale when purchasing increased quantities from one contractor.

ECONOMY ACT See INTERAGENCY ACQUISITION.

EDUCATION COSTS Costs of providing education for employees. FAR 31.205-44 specifies that such costs incurred by contractors are ALLOWABLE COSTs with some limitations. See also TRAINING COSTS.

EICHLEAY FORMULA   The prevalent method for calculating extended and unabsorbed HOME OFFICE overhead on CONSTRUC-TION contracts. In *Eichleay Corp.*, ASBCA 5183, 60-2 BCA ¶ 2688, *mot. for reconsid.*, 61-1 BCA ¶ 2894, the ASBCA found the formula a "realistic method of allocation of continuing home office expenses." Application of the formula entails a three-step process. First, the ratio of contract billings to total billings for the actual contract period is multiplied by the total overhead for the contract period, to arrive at the overhead, or INDIRECT COST, allocable to the contract. Next, the allocable overhead is divided by the number of days of actual performance to determine the daily contract overhead. Finally, the daily contract overhead is multiplied by the number of days of delay to arrive at the amount claimed for unabsorbed overhead. See Cibinic and Braude, chap. 9, Construction Contracting 751–64; Nash, *The "Eichleay" Formula: Does It Spell Relief?* 5 N&CR ¶ 62 (Nov. 1991).

8(a) PROGRAM   A program, established by section 8(a) of the SMALL BUSINESS ACT, 15 U.S.C. 637(a), authorizing the SMALL BUSINESS ADMINISTRATION (SBA) to enter into contracts with procuring agencies and award subcontracts for performing those contracts to firms eligible for program participation. SBA's subcontractors, which must be SMALL DISADVANTAGED BUSINESS CONCERNs (SDBCs), are referred to as "8(a) contractors." FAR 19.000 and 19.801. The program has been in operation since the late 1960s but has met with mixed success. In 1988 Congress sought to make small disadvantaged businesses more competitive and to curb abuse of the 8(a) program. Those reforms, found in Pub. L. 100-656, 15 U.S.C. 631, (1) require competition among 8(a) firms for manufacturing contracts exceeding $5 million; (2) require such competition for service contracts and nonmanufactur-ing contracts exceeding $3 million; (3) require SBA to establish business activity targets for businesses that have been in the program for 5 years; (4) authorize contracting officers to assess "liquidated damages" against prime contractors that fail to meet small disadvantaged business subcontracting goals; and (5) prohibit SBA employees from holding stock in 8(a) firms for 2 years after leaving SBA. See Magnotti, *Politics and the SBA's 8(a) Program*, 28 Cont. Mgmt. 8 (June 1988).

ELECTRONICS INDUSTRIES ASSOCIATION (EIA) A national trade organization representing the entire spectrum of electronics manufacturers in the United States. Founded in 1924 as the Radio Manufacturers Association, the EIA is organized along product lines, with groups and divisions providing specialized attention to issues facing the electronics industries. EIA departments provide services in marketing statistics, engineering standards, legislative and regulatory information, and public affairs. (EIA, 2001 Eye Street, N.W., Washington, DC 20006; (202) 457–4900.)

EMERGING SMALL BUSINESS A SMALL BUSINESS CONCERN whose size is not greater than 50 percent of the numerical size standard for small businesses in the STANDARD INDUSTRIAL CLASSIFICATION (SIC) code assigned to a contracting opportunity. FAR 19.1002. SMALL PURCHASEs are SET ASIDE for emerging small businesses (see FAR 13.105), and the progress of these firms is being measured as part of the SMALL BUSINESS COMPETI- TIVENESS DEMONSTRATION PROGRAM. This program, during calendar years 1989 through 1992, is intended to (1) show the competitive capabilities of small business on certain classes of unrestricted Government contracts and (2) target for expansion small business set-asides in industries that historically demonstrate low small business involvement. FAR Subpart 19.10, DFARS Subpart 219.10.

EMPLOYEE STOCK OWNERSHIP PLAN (ESOP) An individu- al stock bonus plan designed specifically to invest in the stock of the employer company. FAR 31.205-(6)(j)(8) specifies when the costs of such plans are ALLOWABLE COSTs.

ENGINEERING CHANGE PROPOSAL (ECP) A proposal initiated by either party to make CHANGEs to the drawings or specifications of a contract. Under the DoD CONFIGURATION MANAGEMENT system prescribed in Military Standards 480B and 481B, both 15 July 1988, contractors must prepare ECPs using DD Forms 1692 or 1693. Both DoD and NASA prescribe an Engineering Change Proposals clause (DFARS 252.243-7000; NFS 18-52.243-70) that permits the CONTRACTING OFFICER (CO) to require the contractor to prepare an ECP documenting the effect of a change being initiated by the Government.

ENTERTAINMENT Amusement, diversion, and social activity such as meals, outings, sporting events, and theater performances. FAR

31.205-14 specifies that the costs of entertainment incurred by contractors are UNALLOWABLE COSTs. See also GRATUITY.

ENTITLEMENT/QUANTUM See BIFURCATION OF ENTITLEMENT AND QUANTUM.

ENTITY OF THE GOVERNMENT Any entity of the legislative or judicial branch, any executive agency, military department, Government corporation, or independent establishment, the U.S. Postal Service, or any NONAPPROPRIATED-FUND INSTRUMENTALI- TY (NAFI) of the Armed Forces. FAR 8.701. Such entities must purchase supplies and services from "workshops" for the BLIND AND OTHER SEVERELY HANDICAPPED under the procedures of FAR Subpart 8.7.

EQUAL ACCESS TO JUSTICE ACT (EAJA) An act, 5 U.S.C. 504 and 28 U.S.C. 2412, permitting small contractors to recover attorneys' fees and expenses in litigation against the Government. Under what is called the "American Rule," the parties bear their own litigation expenses, and this rule applies generally when contractors litigate contract disputes. The EAJA is an exception to this rule. It permits small contractors to recover if the contrac- tor prevails in the adjudication (see PREVAILING PARTY), the Government's position is not SUBSTANTIALLY JUSTIFIED, and no special circumstances make an award unjust. The remedies provided by the BOARDs OF CONTRACT APPEALS (BCAs) are addressed in 5 U.S.C. 504, whereas the remedies given by courts, including the CLAIMS COURT (Cl. Ct.), are covered by 28 U.S.C. 2412. See Kinlin, A Current Guide to Recovery under the Equal Access to Justice Act; Nash, *Equal Access to Justice Act: A Statute That Is Working Well*, 2 N&CR ¶ 20 (Apr. 1988); Nash, *Postscript: Equal Access to Justice Act*, 5 N&CR ¶ 61 (Nov. 1991); Tobin and Stiffler, *Recovering Legal Fees under EAJA/Edition II*, 91-7 Briefing Papers (June 1991).

EQUAL EMPLOYMENT OPPORTUNITY (EEO) The treatment of employees and applicants for employment that must be accorded by contractors during the performance of their contracts. The basic requirements are set forth in Executive Order 11246, 24 Sep. 1965, as amended. See FAR Subpart 22.8 and the Equal Opportunity clause in FAR 52.222-26. During performance of Government contracts, contractors must (1) not discriminate against any employee or applicant for employment because of race, color, religion, sex, or national origin; (2) take AFFIRMATIVE ACTION to ensure that applicants are employed, and that employees are treated during employment, without regard to their race, color, religion, sex, or national origin; (3) post in conspicuous places available to employees and applicants for employment the notices to be provided by the contracting officer that explain equal opportunity; (4) state that all qualified applicants will receive consideration for employment without regard to race, color, religion, sex, or national origin; (5) send, to each labor union or representative of workers with which it has a collective bargaining agreement or other contract or understanding, the notice to be provided by the contracting officer advising the labor union or workers' representative of the contractor's commitments; and (6) comply with Executive Order 11246 and the rules, regulations, and orders of the Secretary of Labor. See Cibinic and Nash, Formation of Government Contracts 983–90; Seymour, *A Point of View: Why Executive Order 11246 Should Be Preserved*, 11 Employee Rel. L.J. 568 (1986).

EQUITABLE ADJUSTMENT   A fair price adjustment under a contract clause for changed work, including an adjustment in profit, a change in the delivery schedule, if appropriate, and a change in any other affected terms of the contract. Equitable adjustments can result in price increases for the contractor for increased work, or price reductions for the Government for reduced work. The major contract clause that calls for equitable adjustments is the Changes clause, FAR 52.243-1 through -5. However, the term is a standard contract term that is used in many other clauses. Equitable adjustments are distinguished from DAMAGES, which are given in the absence of a contract clause calling for an equitable adjustment. The basic formula for an equitable adjustment is an estimate of the difference between (1) what it would have reasonably cost to perform the work as originally required and (2) what it will reasonably cost to perform the work as changed. See Nash, Government Contract Changes, chaps. 16–19; Cibinic and Nash, Administration of Government Contracts 108–09.

ESCALATION   See FIXED-PRICE CONTRACT WITH ECONOMIC PRICE ADJUSTMENT (EPA).

ESTABLISHED CATALOG OR MARKET PRICE   A price that establishes an exemption from the requirements for submission of

CERTIFIED COST OR PRICING DATA by an offeror on a negotiated procurement (see NEGOTIATION). Under 10 U.S.C. 2306a(b) and 41 U.S.C. 254(d)(5), such an exemption applies if the prices are, or are based on, established catalog prices or established market prices of commercial items sold in substantial quantities to the general public (see COMMERCIALITY). See FAR 15.804-3(c). To receive the exemption, the offeror must claim it on Standard Form 1412, Claim for Exemption from Submission of Certified Cost or Pricing Data, FAR 53.301-1412. An established catalog price is a price included in a catalog, price list, schedule, or other form that (1) is regularly maintained by a manufacturer or vendor, (2) is published or made available for inspection by customers, and (3) states prices at which sales are currently or were last made to a significant number of buyers constituting the general public. An established market price is a current price, established in the usual and ordinary course of trade between buyers and sellers free to bargain, that can be substantiated from sources independent of the manufacturer or vendor. See Armed Services Pricing Manual (ASPM) vol. 1, app. B. The contracting officer may require certified cost or pricing data despite the existence of an established catalog or market price if he or she makes a written finding that the price is unreasonable and the finding is approved at a level above the contracting officer. FAR 15.804-3(c)(8).

ESTABLISHED MARKET PRICE See ESTABLISHED CATALOG OR MARKET PRICE.

ESTIMATED COST The statement of the anticipated cost of performance of a COST-PLUS FIXED FEE (CPFF) CONTRACT, COST-PLUS-AWARD FEE (CPAF) CONTRACT, or COST CONTRACT. This estimated cost is adjusted for CHANGEs or COST OVERRUNs but, in accordance with the LIMITATION OF COST (LOC) CLAUSE, is a firm limitation on compensation to the contractor until such adjustment is made by a contract MODIFICATION. The estimated cost is negotiated in accordance with the procedures in FAR Subpart 15.8 or established competitively in accordance with those in FAR Subpart 15.6.

ESTIMATING SYSTEM The system used by a contractor to estimate the cost of performance of work under a contract or contract modification. The accuracy and reliability of proposals are increased through the use of an acceptable estimating system. FAR 15.811. The Cost Estimating System Requirements clause at DFARS 252.215-7002 defines "estimating system" as contractor policies, procedures, and practices for generating cost estimates and other data included in proposals submitted to customers in the expectation of receiving contract awards. DFARS 215.811-70 states that, to be considered adequate, a contractor's estimating system must be established, maintained, reliable, and consistently applied, and must produce verifiable, supportable, and documented cost estimates.

ESTOPPEL A legal doctrine preventing a party from asserting a right to the detriment of the other party, when the first party has acted or made statements contrary to the right asserted and the other party has reasonably relied on such conduct. The Supreme Court has strictly limited the use of estoppel against the Government, *Schweiker v. Hansen*, 450 U.S. 785 (1981), but Government contractors are still permitted to use the doctrine when the action or statement relied on is taken by an officer of the Government with the authority to bind the Government. See Cibinic and Nash, Administration of Government Contracts 55–61; Nash, *Equitable Estoppel of the Government: An Argument That Is Hanging by a Thread*, 5 N&CR ¶ 7 (Feb. 1991). The most common form of estoppel against the Government occurs when the Government fails within a reasonable period to terminate a contractor for default because of a late delivery and the contractor continues to work in reliance on the Government's actions. In this situation it is often held that the Government has effectively waived the delivery date and may be estopped from terminating the contract for failure to deliver. *DeVito v. United States*, 188 Ct. Cl. 979, 413 F.2d 1147 (1969); Carberry and Johnstone, *Waiver of the Government's Right to Terminate for Default in Government Contracts*, 17 Pub. Cont. L.J. 470, 478 (1988).

ETHICS Action or conduct that meets accepted standards of behavior. In the field of Government contracting, Government employees are required to meet specified STANDARDS OF CONDUCT in the performance of their duties. Government contractors and offerors for Government contracts are also required to have a satisfactory record of integrity and business ethics. FAR 9.104-1. See Nash, *Ethics*, 4 N&CR ¶ 73 (Dec. 1990); Johnson and Alonge, *Ethics in Government Procurement/Edition II*, 87-8 Briefing Papers (July 1987).

EVALUATION See PROPOSAL EVALUATION.

EVALUATION CRITERIA See EVALUATION FACTORS.

EVALUATION FACTORS The factors used by the Government in a COMPETITIVE PROPOSALS procurement to determine the winning contractor. See FAR 15.605. 10 U.S.C. 2305(a)(2)(A) and 41 U.S.C. 253a(b)(1) require that the Government's solicitation (the REQUEST FOR PROPOSALS (RFP)) clearly state the factors that will be considered in evaluating proposals and selecting a source, and must also state their relative importance. Evaluation factors should be tailored to each acquisition and should include only the factors that will affect the SOURCE SELECTION decision. The evaluation factors that apply to an acquisition and the relative importance of those factors are within the broad discretion of agency acquisition officials. However, price or cost to the Government must be included as an evaluation factor in every source selection. FAR 15.605(b) states that quality (in terms of technical excellence, management, capability, personnel qualifications, prior experience, past performance, and schedule compliance) must also be addressed, but some agencies ignore this requirement when they believe that the source selection should be based solely on price. See Cibinic et al., Source Selection; Nash, *Competitive Negotiation vs. Sealed Bidding: Some Limitations on Agency Discretion*, 5 N&CR ¶ 68 (Dec. 1991); Nash, *Source Selection: Variety of Agency Guidance*, 3 N&CR ¶ 60 (Aug. 1989); Nash, *Source Selection: The "Solicitation-Evaluation-Decision" Linkage*, 1 N&CR ¶ 56 (July 1987).

EXAMINATION OF RECORDS The examination by the COMPTROLLER GENERAL (COMP. GEN.) or the GENERAL ACCOUNTING OFFICE (GAO) of a contractor's books, documents, papers, or other records that directly pertain to transactions under the contract. 10 U.S.C. 2313(b) and (c) and 41 U.S.C. 254(c) require such examination in all negotiated contracts exceeding $10,000, with the exception of SMALL PURCHASE contracts, contracts to obtain utility services at established rates, and contracts with foreign contractors for which the agency head authorized omission. This authority may be exercised until 3 years after final payment or for any shorter period specified for a particular type of record in FAR Subpart 4.7, Contractor Records Retention. It also continues until any claim, appeal, or litigation, or any GAO exception to a contractor's costs or expenses, is disposed of. Guidance on this policy is found in FAR 15.106-1, and the standard Examination of Records clause is set forth in FAR 52.215-1.

EXCESS COSTS OF REPROCUREMENT Costs incurred by the Government in excess of the contract price of a contract that has been terminated for default (see TERMINATION FOR DEFAULT). The standard Default clauses, FAR 52.249-8 through -10, provide that these costs may be recovered from the defaulted contractor if the Government repurchases the supplies or services or completes the work at a price exceeding the price under the terminated contract. FAR 49.402-6 requires the contracting officer, after the default termination, to repurchase against the account of the contractor as soon as practicable and, after payment for the work to complete the contract, make a written demand on the terminated contractor for the total amount of the excess. For the defaulted contractor to be charged for the excess costs of reprocurement (1) the reprocured supplies, services, or work must be the same as or similar to the original; (2) the Government must actually incur the costs; and (3) the Government must reasonably minimize the excess costs (e.g., by obtaining maximum feasible competition). See Cibinic and Nash, Administration of Government Contracts 760–98; Williamson and Medill-Jones, *Government Damages for Default*, 89-7 Briefing Papers (June 1989).

EXCESS FEDERAL INFORMATION PROCESSING (FIP) EQUIPMENT Any Federal information processing (FIP) equipment (see FEDERAL INFORMATION PROCESSING (FIP) RESOURCES) controlled by a Federal agency but no longer required for its needs. FIRMR 201-4.001. Government-owned FIP equipment that is no longer needed for the purpose for which it was acquired is either: (1) reassigned within the agency, (2) declared excess to the agency's needs and made available for interagency screening and transfer, (3) exchanged or sold as part of a transaction to acquire replacement equipment, (4) declared excess and transferred to an agency outside of the GSA EXCESS FEDERAL INFORMATION PROCESSING (FIP) EQUIPMENT PROGRAM, or (5) declared surplus and made available for donation. FIRMR 201-23.001. Agencies must contact GSA if they wish to include their excess capacity of FIP resources in the FIRMR bulletins describing sharing opportunities. FIRMR 201-21.403.

EXCESS FEDERAL INFORMATION PROCESSING (FIP) EQUIPMENT PROGRAM A GSA program designed to help Federal agencies quickly and easily locate up-to-date used equipment for reuse and dispose of equipment that is no longer needed. The program does not cover leased equipment. See

FIRMR Bulletin C-2, *Disposition and Reuse of Federal Information Processing Equipment.*

EXCESS FOREIGN CURRENCY Currencies of certain countries in amounts determined by the Secretary of the Treasury to be excess to the Government's normal requirements. FAR 25.304. These countries are identified in bulletins issued by the OFFICE OF MANAGEMENT AND BUDGET (OMB) and distributed through agency procedures on an expedited basis. Additional information may be obtained from the Department of the Treasury, Office of the Assistant Secretary for International Affairs, Office of Development Policy. Acquisitions of foreign end products, services, or construction paid for in excess or near-excess foreign currencies are an exception to the BALANCE OF PAYMENTS PROGRAM restrictions. Excess and near-excess foreign currencies are to be used whenever feasible in payment of contracts over $1 million performed wholly or partly in any of the listed countries. In some cases, award may be made to an offeror willing to accept payment, in whole or in part, in excess or near-excess foreign currency, even though the offer, when compared with offers in U.S. dollars, is not the lowest received. Price differentials may be funded from excess or near-excess foreign currencies available without charge to agency appropriations, subject to OMB Circular No. A-20 (revised), *Systems of Control over the Use of Foreign Currencies,* 21 May 1966.

EXCESS PERSONAL PROPERTY Any personal property under the control of a Federal agency that the agency head or a designee determines is not required for its needs and for the discharge of its responsibilities. FAR 8.101. FAR 8.102 provides that it is the policy of the Government to use such property in preference to procuring new property and that such policy also applies to cost-reimbursement contractors. Such property is under the control of the GENERAL SERVICES ADMINISTRATION (GSA). See FAR 8.103.

EXCISE TAX A tax on the sale or use of a particular supply or service, levied by the Federal Government and by State and local governments. FAR 31.205-41 specifies the rules governing whether such taxes paid by contractors are ALLOWABLE COSTs. Contractors are frequently not subject to such taxes imposed by the Federal Government. See FAR Subpart 29.2. Contractors bear the risk of determining which excise taxes apply to their contracts but are given price adjustments for changes in such taxes under the Federal, State, and Local Taxes clause in FAR 52.229-3. See STATE AND LOCAL TAXES.

EXCULPATORY CLAUSE A contract clause stating that one of the contracting parties is not liable upon the occurrence of some specified event. These clauses are most frequently used by the Government in an attempt to relieve itself of liability for defective specifications (see IMPLIED WARRANTY OF SPECIFICATIONS). Such clauses are not against public policy but are carefully scrutinized by the courts and BOARDs OF CONTRACT APPEALS (BCAs) to ensure that they are applicable to the specific problem that has been encountered by the contractor. See Cibinic and Nash, Administration of Government Contracts 253–68; Passar, *Government Use of Disclaimers and Exculpatory Clauses in Procurement Contracts* (thesis for The George Washington University National Law Center's Government Contracts Program, 1988).

EXCUSABLE DELAY A delay in the performance of a contract that is caused by an event that is beyond the control and without the fault or negligence of the contractor or its subcontractors at any tier. The TERMINATION FOR DEFAULT clauses indicate that a contractor will not be held liable if its failure to perform a contract arises from such delays. The identified excusable delays in the Default clauses for supply and service contracts in FAR 52.249-8 and -9 and in the Excusable Delays clause at 52.249-10 include (1) acts of God or of the public enemy, (2) acts of the Government in either its sovereign or its contractual capacity, (3) fires, (4) floods, (5) epidemics, (6) quarantine restrictions, (7) strikes, (8) freight embargoes, and (9) unusually severe weather. The fixed-price construction Default clause in FAR 52.249-10 adds as excusable delays the following: (1) acts of another contractor in the performance of a contract with the Government and (2) delays of subcontractors or suppliers at any tier, arising from unforeseeable causes beyond the control and without the fault or negligence of the contractor and its subcontractors or suppliers. See Cibinic and Nash, Administration of Government Contracts 410–50; Nash, *Excusable Delays: Labor Shortages and Loss of Key Employees*, 1 N&CR ¶ 48 (June 1987).

EXECUTIVE AGENCY Instrumentality of the Federal Government bound by the FEDERAL ACQUISITION REGULATION (FAR). Executive agencies include the executive departments (Departments of State, the Treasury, Defense, Justice, the Interior, Agriculture,

Commerce, Labor, Health and Human Services, Housing and Urban Development, Transportation, Energy, Education, and Veterans Affairs), 5 U.S.C. 101; the military departments (Departments of the Army, Navy, and Air Force), 5 U.S.C. 102; any independent establishment, 5 U.S.C. 104(1); and any wholly owned Government corporation within the meaning of 31 U.S.C. 9101 (such as the Export-Import Bank of the United States, the Federal Crop Insurance Corporation, FEDERAL PRISON INDUSTRIES, INC., the Federal Savings and Loan Insurance Corporation, and the Pension Benefit Guaranty Corporation). FAR 2.101. See Cibinic and Nash, Formation of Government Contracts 6–9.

EXECUTORY ACCORD See ACCORD AND SATISFACTION.

EXPEDITED PROCEDURES Procedures used by the BOARDs OF CONTRACT APPEALS (BCAs) for the expedited disposition of any APPEAL FROM A CONTRACTING OFFICER'S DECISION, if the amount in dispute is $10,000 or less. FAR 33.211(a)(3)(v). These "small claims (expedited)" procedures are required by 41 U.S.C. 608(a) and are often referred to as Rule 12.2 procedures because they are discussed in Uniform Rule 12.2 (see UNIFORM RULES). They apply at the sole election of the contractor. Uniform Rule 12.1(c) explains that the contractor must elect to proceed pursuant to Rule 12 within 60 days of receipt of the notice of docketing "unless such period is extended by the BCA for good cause." The Government is not only unable to choose the expedited procedure should it so desire, but it is also, for the most part, powerless to stop the contractor from electing it in appropriate circumstances. Under the expedited procedure, appeals may be decided by a single member of the agency BCA, with such concurrences as may be required by rule or regulation. Appeals must be resolved, whenever possible, within 120 days after the contractor elects to use the procedure. A decision against either party reached under the procedure is final and conclusive and may be set aside only in cases of fraud. Administrative determinations and final decisions under expedited procedures have no value as precedent for future cases.

EXPENSING OF COSTS The charging of the full cost to current accounts, as compared with CAPITALIZATION.

EXPERIENCE CURVE See LEARNING CURVE.

EXPERTS See INDIVIDUAL EXPERTS AND CONSULTANTS.

EXPRESSLY UNALLOWABLE COST A particular item or type of cost that, under the express provisions of an applicable law, regulation, or contract, is specifically named and stated to be an UNALLOWABLE COST. FAR 31.001. FAR 31.201-6 requires that contractors identify such costs and exclude them from any billing, claim, or proposal submitted to the Government. 10 U.S.C. 2324 calls for penalties to be assessed against defense contractors when it is established by clear and convincing evidence that this requirement was not complied with in the submission of proposals for the settlement of INDIRECT COSTs. See Cibinic and Nash, Cost Reimbursement Contracting, chap. 5.

EXTENDED OVERHEAD See UNABSORBED OVERHEAD.

EXTRAORDINARY CONTRACTUAL ACTION An action taken to enter into or amend a contract without CONSIDERATION pursuant to the authority of Pub. L. 85-804, 50 U.S.C. 1431-1435, as amended by Pub. L. 93-155. FAR Part 50 discusses extraordinary contractual actions and prescribes policies and procedures for the Government to use to enter into, amend, or modify contracts in order to facilitate the national defense. This power is used to give contractors additional compensation, without regard to their legal entitlement, when an actual or threatened loss under a defense contract, however caused, will impair the productive ability of a contractor whose continued performance on any defense contract or whose continued operation as a source of supply is found to be essential to the national defense. In such cases, the contract may be amended without consideration, but only to the extent necessary to avoid impairing the contractor's productive ability. An amendment without consideration may also be appropriate when a contractor suffers a loss because of Government action, in which case the contract may be adjusted in the interest of fairness. FAR 50.302-1. Contracts may also be amended or modified to correct mistakes or formalize informal commitments. FAR 50.102(c) notes that certain kinds of contractual relief formerly available only under Pub. L. 85-804 (such as rescission or reformation for mutual mistake) are now available under the authority of the CONTRACT DISPUTES ACT (CDA) OF 1978; it also provides that this authority should be relied on in preference to Pub. L. 85-804. Providing indemnification to contractors is another significant use of this authority. The clause at FAR 52.250-1, Indemnification under Pub. L. 85-804, is inserted in a contract whenever the approving authority determines that the contractor must be indemnified against unusually hazardous or nuclear risks. FAR 50.403-3. See Larson, *Pub. L. 85-804: Who Pays When Private Industry Works?* 27 Cont. Mgmt. 8 (Oct. 1987).

EXTRAORDINARY CONTRACTUAL RELIEF See EXTRAORDINARY CONTRACTUAL ACTION.

F

FACILITIES Property used for production, maintenance, research, development, or testing. FAR 45.301. The term includes PLANT EQUIPMENT and REAL PROPERTY but not MATERIAL, SPECIAL TEST EQUIPMENT, SPECIAL TOOLING, or AGENCY-PECULIAR PROPERTY. When used in a FACILITIES CONTRACT, the term includes all property provided under the contract. FAR 45.301. FAR 45.302 specifies that it is the policy of the Government that contractors provide all facilities needed to perform contracts. However, it then lists a number of situations in which the Government may provide facilities. It further specifies that when a Government agency has made the decision to provide facilities, preference is given to existing Government-owned facilities over new facilities.

FACILITIES CAPITAL The net book value of TANGIBLE CAPITAL ASSETS and of those INTANGIBLE CAPITAL ASSETS that are subject to AMORTIZATION. FAR 31.001. This amount is one of the key elements in the computation of the COST OF CAPITAL COMMITTED TO FACILITIES.

FACILITIES CAPITAL COST OF MONEY (FCCM) See COST OF CAPITAL COMMITTED TO FACILITIES.

FACILITIES CONTRACT A contract under which the Government provides FACILITIES to a contractor or subcontractor for use in performing one or more related contracts for supplies or services. FAR 45.301. Facilities contracts may take any of the following forms: (1) facilities acquisition contracts for the acquisition, construction, and installation of facilities; (2) facilities use contracts for the use, maintenance, accountability, and disposition of facilities; or (3) consolidated facilities contracts for both facilities acquisition and use. Facilities contracts are COST CONTRACTs; the contractor receives no FEE. FAR 45.302-3

166

specifies that facilities may be provided as part of another contract when that contract is (1) a supply contract calling for facilities with a value of no more than $100,000, (2) a CONSTRUCTION contract, (3) a SERVICE CONTRACT connected with a GOVERN-MENT-OWNED, CONTRACTOR-OPERATED PLANT (GOCO), or (4) a contract for work on a Government-operated installation.

FACSIMILE (FAX) Electronic equipment that communicates and reproduces both printed and handwritten material. FACSIMILE BIDs OR PROPOSALs are now accepted by many agencies but may not be considered unless permitted by the solicitation. FAR 14.301(c).

FACSIMILE BID OR PROPOSAL A bid or proposal, or a modification or withdrawal thereof, that is transmitted to and received by the Government by facsimile. Such bids or proposals may be permitted by Government agencies. FAR 14.202-7, 15.402(j). If they are permitted, the solicitation must contain the Facsimile Bids clause in FAR 52.214-31 or the Facsimile Proposals clause in FAR 52.215-18. Guidance to contracting officers on when to permit facsimile proposals is set forth in FAR 15.02(i). See Williamson, *Facsimile Bids and Proposals: A New Option for Contracting*, 19 Pub. Cont. L.J. 689 (1990).

FACT An event that has occurred. Under the TRUTH IN NEGOTIA-TIONS ACT (TINA), the COST OR PRICING DATA that a contractor must submit to the Government includes all facts that a prudent buyer or seller would reasonably expect to significantly affect price negotiations. In this regard, facts are distinguished from judgments. A fact is objectively verifiable by audit or technical evaluation, but a judgment is subjective and cannot be verified except in hindsight. While vendor quotations, nonrecurring costs, information on changes in production methods, data supporting projections of business prospects, unit-cost trends, and the like are considered facts, a pure estimate of the cost of future contract performance based on these facts is considered a judgment. In the application of the Truth in Negotiations Act, it has proved to be very difficult to drawn a firm line between facts and judgments. See Lovitky, *Cost and Pricing Data Defined: An Analysis of the Scope of Contractor Disclosure Requirements Pursuant to the Truth in Negotiations Act*, 20 NCMJ 79 (1987); Lovitky, *Understanding Causation and Determining the Price Adjustment in Defective Pricing Cases*, 17 Pub. Cont. L.J. 407 (1988).

FAILURE TO MAKE PROGRESS A failure of a contractor to perform the work required by a Government supply or service contract in a manner that provides reasonable assurance to the Government that the contract schedule will be met. The Default (Fixed-Price Supply and Service) clause in FAR 52.249-8 provides that the Government may terminate the contract for default before the completion date if the contractor's failure to make progress is such that the performance of the contract is endangered. Terminations based on failure to make progress require that the contracting officer give the contractor notice and an opportunity to cure the failure (a minimum of 10 days) before the Government exercises its right to terminate the contract for default. This type of TERMINATION FOR DEFAULT is distinguished from terminations based on failure to deliver supplies or perform services within the time specified in the contract, which require no CURE NOTICE. See FAR 49.402-3.

FAILURE TO PROSECUTE THE WORK Failure of a contractor to perform the work, or any part thereof, under a construction contract with sufficient diligence to ensure completion within the contract schedule. The Default (Fixed-Price Construction) clause in FAR 52.249-10 provides that the Government may terminate the contract for default before the completion date if the contractor fails to prosecute the work. No CURE NOTICE is required for this type of TERMINATION FOR DEFAULT, but a SHOW CAUSE NOTICE is usually issued prior to termination.

FAIR AND REASONABLE PRICE A fair and reasonable price is one that is fair to both parties, considering the agreed-upon conditions, promised quality, and timeliness of contract performance. Although generally a fair and reasonable price is a function of the law of supply and demand, there are statutory, regulatory, and judgmental limits on the concept. Armed Services Pricing Manual (ASPM) vol. 1, app. B. FAR 15.802(b) requires contracting officers to ensure that supplies and services are purchased under negotiated contracts at fair and reasonable prices. FAR 15.803(c) provides that price negotiation is the means to be used by contracting officers to arrive at this result, while FAR 15.805-2 suggests the use of PRICE ANALYSIS to determine whether the price is fair and reasonable. FAR 14.407-2 requires contracting officers to ensure that sealed bid contracts are awarded at "reasonable" prices. It also suggests that price analysis be used to determine whether the offered price is reasonable.

FAIR LABOR STANDARDS ACT (FLSA) A 1938 act, 29 U.S.C. 206, commonly known as the "Federal Wage and Hour Law." FLSA establishes minimum wage and maximum hour standards but provides that, if an employee is entitled under State law to higher wages or better hours than those mandated by the FLSA, the State law controls. The FLSA applies to industry generally rather than to Government contractors specifically. Federal agencies must encourage contractors to enforce FLSA requirements when applicable. FAR 22.1002-4. See Stephenson, chap. 3, Construction Contracting 219–22.

FAIR MARKET PRICE The price at which bona fide sales have been consummated for assets of like type, quality, and quantity in a particular market at the time of acquisition. Black's Law Dictionary. The expectation that awards will be made at fair market prices is one of the conditions that must be met in order to SET ASIDE an acquisition or class of acquisitions for exclusive small business participation. FAR 19.502-2(a). In DoD, the expectation that award will be made at not more than 10 percent above fair market price is one of the expectations that must be met in order to for an acquisition to be set aside for HISTORICALLY BLACK COLLEGES AND UNIVERSITIES (HBCUs) and MINORITY INSTITUTIONs (MIs). DFARS 226.7003-1.

FAIR MARKET VALUE The price at which supplies would change hands between a willing buyer and a willing seller, with neither buyer nor seller under any compulsion to buy or sell and both having reasonable knowledge of the relevant facts. Black's Law Dictionary. The term arises in discussions of REASONABLENESS OF COST. In *Bruce Constr. Corp. v. United States*, 163 Ct. Cl. 97, 324 F.2d 516 (1963), in reference to the amount of an EQUITABLE ADJUSTMENT, it was held that HISTORICAL COST, rather than fair market value, is the proper measure of cost reasonableness. However, 10 U.S.C. 2324(j) and FAR 31.201-3(a) state that contractors have the burden of proving that the costs they incurred were reasonable—that, among other things, they reflect fair market value.

FALSE CLAIMS ACT An act giving the Government remedies against parties that process false claims. It was originally passed at the time of the Civil War and has now been divided into two sections: the Civil False Claims Act, 31 U.S.C. 3729, and the Criminal False Claims Act, 18 U.S.C. 287. These acts are commonly used to address fraudulent conduct by contractors. To establish a violation of either statute, the Government must prove that (1) the contractor made or presented a CLAIM to the Government, (2) the claim was asserted against the Government, (3) the claim was false, fictitious, or fraudulent, and (4) the contractor knew that the claim was false, fictitious, or fraudulent when presenting it. The primary differences between the civil statute and the criminal statute are the level of intent required, the standard of proof the Government must meet, and the penalties the Government can inflict. Contractors can be found liable for both criminal and civil penalties. In addition, Congress has enacted a *qui tam* statute (see QUI TAM PROCEEDINGS) authorizing private individuals to bring actions for violations of the Civil False Claims Act. See Seyfarth et al., The Government Contract Compliance Handbook 1-4 through 1-6; Waldman, *The 1986 Amendments to the False Claims Act: Retroactive or Prospective?* 18 Pub. Cont. L.J. 470 (1989). See also PROGRAM FRAUD CIVIL REMEDIES ACT.

FALSE STATEMENTS ACT An act, 18 U.S.C. 1001, that prohibits any person, in any matter under the Government's jurisdiction, from "knowingly and willfully" falsifying, concealing, or covering up a material fact, or making a false, fictitious, or fraudulent statement. Considerably broader in scope than the FALSE CLAIMS ACT, the False Statements Act has been held to cover all false statements that might support fraudulent claims or that might pervert or corrupt the authorized functions of a Government agency to which the statements were made. It covers oral as well as written statements and unsworn as well as sworn statements. It also covers the omission of information on a certified statement when the information should have been included. The act applies to matters that involve a Government agency's activity even though the false statement is not made to the Government. The courts have required that a statement must be material to fall within the scope of the act; that is, that it must have a natural tendency to influence or be capable of influencing the actions of a Federal agency. Cibinic and Nash, Administration of Government Contracts 92–94.

FAR See FEDERAL ACQUISITION REGULATION (FAR).

FAR SECRETARIAT The Government organization, housed in the GENERAL SERVICES ADMINISTRATION (GSA), that maintains, prints, publishes, and distributes the FEDERAL ACQUISITION REGULATION

(FAR). Along with the DEFENSE ACQUISITION REGULATORY COUNCIL (DAR COUNCIL) staff, the FAR Secretariat provides the DAR Council and the CIVILIAN AGENCY ACQUISITION COUNCIL (CAAC) with centralized services for keeping a synopsis of current FAR cases (proposed FAR changes) and their status, assigning FAR case numbers, maintaining official case files, assisting parties interested in reviewing the files on completed cases, and performing miscellaneous administrative tasks pertaining to the maintenance of the FAR. FAR 1.201-2.

FAST PAYMENT PROCEDURE A payment procedure that allows payment to a contractor, under limited conditions (such as individual orders not exceeding $25,000, unless the agency authorizes exceptions), before the Government verifies that supplies have been received and accepted. See FAR Subpart 13.3. When the Government intends to use the procedure, the procuring agency will include the Fast Payment Procedure clause in FAR 52.213-1 in the solicitation and contract. Under the procedure, payment may be made on the basis of the contractor's submission of an invoice constituting a representation that (1) the supplies have been delivered to a post office, common carrier (see CARRIER (TRANSPORTATION)), or point of first receipt by the Government and (2) the contractor agrees to replace, repair, or correct supplies not received at destination, damaged in transit, or not conforming to purchase agreements. FAR 13.302(c) provides that title to supplies vests in the Government upon delivery to a post office or common carrier for mailing or shipment, or upon receipt by the Government if the shipment is by means other than Postal Service or common carrier.

FAST-TRACK CONSTRUCTION Method of CONSTRUCTION contracting under which the contractor begins building as soon as the foundation plans are ready and a foundation permit has been issued, despite the fact that the architect-engineer has not finished designing the project. Throughout performance, the architect-engineer must keep ahead of the contractor's progress in order to supply the necessary plans and drawings before each stage of the construction is reached. See Nash, chap. 1, Construction Contracting 7.

FEDERAL ACQUISITION CIRCULARS (FACs) Publications of the Government that revise, amend, and update the FEDERAL ACQUISITION REGULATION (FAR). Revisions to the FAR are prepared and issued through the coordinated action of the DE-FENSE ACQUISITION REGULATORY COUNCIL (DAR COUNCIL) and the CIVILIAN AGENCY ACQUISITION COUNCIL (CAAC). Each council maintains cognizance over specified portions of the FAR and is responsible for agreeing with the other council on revisions. Revisions to the FAR are submitted to the FAR SECRETARIAT and pass through a period of public notice and comment begun by publication in the FEDERAL REGISTER. See FAR Subpart 1.2. FACs were numbered sequentially (84-1 through 84-60) from the original promulgation of the FAR in 1984 until the issuance of the 1990 version of the FAR. They are now numbered sequentially beginning with 90-1 and will continue to be so numbered until a new edition is issued, when the sequence will begin again.

FEDERAL ACQUISITION INSTITUTE (FAI) A research and management facility dedicated to promoting Government-wide career management programs for a professional procurement work force. Originally an organization within the OFFICE OF FEDERAL PROCUREMENT POLICY (OFPP), FAI was transferred to the GENERAL SERVICES ADMINISTRATION (GSA) in Jan. 1984. OFPP retains a "policy oversight role," however. FAI activities include coordinating FEDERAL PROCUREMENT DATA SYSTEM (FPDS) changes with GSA's procurement activities, representing GSA on the OFPP FPDS Policy Committee, establishing and maintaining a contracting officer warrant program, and helping Federal agencies develop policies, standards, criteria, and requirements designed to attract, select, motivate, and retain a more productive, better qualified professional work force.

FEDERAL ACQUISITION REGULATION (FAR) The primary document in the FEDERAL ACQUISITION REGULATIONS (FAR) SYSTEM, containing uniform policies and procedures that govern the ACQUISITION activity of all Federal agencies. The FAR is prepared, issued, and maintained jointly by the Secretary of Defense, the Administrator of General Services, and the NASA Administrator. FAR 1.102. It is published in the daily issue of the FEDERAL REGISTER, in cumulative form in Title 48 of the CODE OF FEDERAL REGULATIONS (CFR), in separate looseleaf form available through the U.S. Government Printing Office, Washington, DC 20402, and in commercial versions (current paperback, looseleaf service (part of the Government Contracts Reporter subscription service), or floppy disk) published by Commerce Clearing House, Inc., 4025 West Peterson Avenue, Chicago, IL 60646. Changes to the FAR are made through FEDERAL ACQUISITION CIRCULARS (FACs). The FAR has 53 parts, which are grouped in 7 subchapters: General—Acquisition Planning, Contracting Methods—Contract Types, Socioeconomic Programs, General Requirements—Special Categories, Contract Management, Clauses, and Forms.

FEDERAL ACQUISITION REGULATIONS (FAR) SYSTEM

The system of regulations that governs the acquisition by contract of supplies and services needed by Federal agencies. The system consists of the FEDERAL ACQUISITION REGULATION (FAR), the primary document, and supplementary regulations issued by individual agencies. Such supplements (for example, the DEPARTMENT OF DEFENSE FAR SUPPLEMENT (DFARS) and the NASA FAR SUPPLEMENT (NFS)) contain regulations limited (in theory, at least) to those needed to (1) implement FAR policies and procedures within the agency or (2) supplement the FAR to satisfy agency-specific needs. Implementation (agency treatment expanding on FAR material) is numbered parallel to the FAR. Supplementation (agency-peculiar material with no FAR counterpart) is given numbers of 70 and up. The FAR System does not include purely internal agency guidance. The documents making up the FAR System are available from Commerce Clearing House, Inc., 4025 West Peterson Avenue, Chicago, IL 60646 as part of the Government Contracts Reporter subscription service. See Cibinic and Nash, Formation of Government Contracts 9–30; Malloy, *FAR Revisited*, 25 Cont. Mgmt. 27 (Jan. 1985).

FEDERAL ACQUISITION REGULATORY (FAR) COUNCIL

The Government organization, established by 41 U.S.C. 421, that is charged with assisting in the direction and coordination of Government-wide procurement policy and regulatory activities. It is made up of the Administrator of the OFFICE OF FEDERAL PROCUREMENT POLICY (OFPP), the Secretary of Defense, and the Administrators of GSA and NASA. DoD, GSA, and NASA are represented, through delegation, by their officials in charge of acquisition policy. The Council, in a very broad sense, manages, coordinates, controls, and monitors maintenance of, and issuance of and changes in, the FEDERAL ACQUISITION REGULATION (FAR). The OFPP Administrator, in conjunction with the FAR Council, ensures that procurement regulations promulgated by an executive agency are consistent with the FAR and are limited to (1) regulations essential to implement Government-wide policies and procedures within the agency and (2) additional policies and procedures required to satisfy the agency's specific and unique needs.

FEDERAL CIRCUIT COURT See COURT OF APPEALS FOR THE FEDERAL CIRCUIT (CAFC or Fed. Cir.).

FEDERAL CLAIMS COLLECTION ACT An act, 31 U.S.C. chap. 37, subchap. II, that provides the basic legal framework for agency collection of debts owed to the United States, with oversight by the GENERAL ACCOUNTING OFFICE (GAO) and the Department of Justice. The act authorizes compromise, suspension, or termination of collection action in limited circumstances—with the U.S. ATtorney General's approval for debts exceeding $100,000 (this threshold was raised from $20,000 in 1990 by the ADMINISTRATIVE DISPUTE RESOLUTION ACT). The act is implemented by the Federal Claims Collection Standards, issued jointly by the GAO and the Department of Justice, 4 CFR Chapter 2. Agency collection action should be aggressive and timely with effective follow-up, using all reasonable means of collection consistent with good business practice and the debtor's ability to pay. Principles of Federal Appropriations Law (2d ed.), chap. 13. Most claims collection is performed by accounting officials of Government agencies. However, procedures for collecting claims on contracts are set forth in FAR Subpart 32.6.

FEDERAL COURTS IMPROVEMENT ACT (FCIA) A 1982 act, 28 U.S.C. 171 *et seq.*, 1494–1497, 1499–1503, that reorganized the courts dealing with Government procurement by eliminating the Court of Claims and creating the U.S. CLAIMS COURT (Cl. Ct.) and the U.S. COURT OF APPEALS FOR THE FEDERAL CIRCUIT (CAFC or Fed. Cir.). The act also conferred new jurisdiction on the Claims Court to hear preaward protests. See 28 U.S.C. 1491(a)(3). See Hrabik, *Federal Courts Improvement Act*, 24 Duq. L. Rev. 945 (1986); Anthony and Smith, *The Federal Courts Improvement Act of 1982: Its Impact on the Resolution of Federal Contract Disputes*, 13 Pub. Cont. L.J. 201 (1983); White, *The New Government Contract Courts*, 83-11 Briefing Papers (Nov. 1983).

FEDERAL INFORMATION PROCESSING (FIP) RESOURCES AUTOMATIC DATA PROCESSING EQUIPMENT (ADPE) as defined in Pub. L. 99-500, the BROOKS ACT (AUTOMATIC DATA PROCESSING PROCUREMENTS), at 40 U.S.C. 759(a)(2); any equipment or interconnected system or subsystem of equipment used in the automatic acquisition, storage, manipulation, management, movement, control, display, switching, interchange, transmission, or reception of data by a Federal agency or under a contract with a Federal agency, if the contract either requires use of such equipment or requires a service performed or a product produced making significant use of such equipment. The term includes equipment, maintenance, software, services, support services, systems, and related supplies. FIRMR 201-4.001. Specific examples of what the term includes and excludes can be found in FIRMR Bulletin A-1. All FIP resources must be acquired in accordance with the procedures established by the Brooks Act. Protests involving FIP resources procurements may be brought before the GENERAL SERVICES ADMINISTRATION BOARD OF CONTRACT APPEALS (GSBCA). 40 U.S.C. 759(f). See Webber, *Bid Protests and Agency Discretion: Where and Why Do the GSBCA and GAO Part Company?* 18 Pub. Cont. L.J. 1 (1988); Tolle, *A Review of The First Year of ADP Bid Protests at the GSBCA*, 16 Pub. Cont. L.J. 120 (1986).

FEDERAL INFORMATION PROCESSING STANDARDS PUBLICATIONS (FIPS PUBS) Official Government publications relating to standards adopted and issued under the provisions of section 111(f)(2) of the Federal Property and Administrative Services Act of 1949, 40 U.S.C. 759(e), and Executive Order 11717, 9 May 1973. FIPS PUBS, issued by the National Institute of Standards and Technology (NIST), fall into two general categories: standards and guidelines. Standards are mandatory, whereas guidelines are informational documents. FIRMR 201-20.303. See Gabig, *A Primer on Federal Information Systems Acquisitions: First Part of a Two-Part Article*, 17 Pub. Cont. L.J. 31, 37 (1987).

FEDERAL INFORMATION RESOURCES MANAGEMENT REGULATION (FIRMR) The regulation setting forth uniform management, acquisition, and use policies and procedures pertaining to the INFORMATION RESOURCES MANAGEMENT (IRM) activities of Federal agencies and those of Government contractors as directed by agencies. FIRMR 201-1. FIRMR Subchapter D establishes unique regulatory coverage on the acquisition of FEDERAL INFORMATION PROCESSING (FIP) RESOURCES by contracting. The FIRMR system consists of the FIRMR, the primary document, and the agency regulations that implement or supplement it. The FIRMR contains the Government-wide regulations governing the management, acquisition, and use of FIP resources and records covered by the BROOKS ACT (AUTOMATIC DATA PROCESSING PROCUREMENTS). It is prepared, issued, and maintained by the GENERAL SERVICES ADMINISTRATION (GSA). Looseleaf copies are available by annual subscription from the U.S. Government Printing Office, Washington, DC 20402.

FEDERAL LABORATORY CONSORTIUM FOR TECHNOLO-GY TRANSFER (FLC) The organization that carries out the formal mission of promoting and strengthening technology transfer across the Federal research system under 15 U.S.C. 3701 *et seq.* Membership is mandatory for most Federal laboratories. The FLC was created in 1971 to facilitate technology transfer between DoD and the State and local governments. In 1974, the FLC was expanded to include other Federal agencies on a voluntary basis. See Duncombe, *Federal Technology Transfer: A Look at the Benefits and Pitfalls of One of the Country's Best Kept Secrets*, 37 Fed. B. News & J. 608 (1990).

FEDERALLY FUNDED RESEARCH AND DEVELOPMENT CENTER (FFRDC) A center—operated, managed, and/or administered by either a university or a consortium of universities, another not-for-profit organization, or an industrial firm as an autonomous firm or as an identifiable separate operating unit of a parent organization—that enables agencies to use private sector resources to accomplish RESEARCH AND DEVELOPMENT (R&D) tasks that are integral to agency missions and operations. FAR 35.017. The Government may enter into contracts with FFRDCs to facilitate long-term relationships and establish the FFRDC's mission, but FFRDCs may not compete with non-FFRDCs on agency-issued REQUESTs FOR PROPOSALS (RFPs) for work other than operation of the FFRDC. FAR 35.017-1. The National Science Foundation (NSF) maintains a master list of FFRDCs. FAR 35.017-6.

FEDERAL NORM Fundamental principles in law and regulation that should be reflected in contractor purchases even though such purchases are not Federal purchases. DEAR 970.7103(b). In stating policy for purchases by MANAGEMENT AND OPERATING (M&O) CONTRACTors, DoE identifies several such principles, including competition in subcontracting and purchase of a fair proportion of supplies and services from SMALL BUSINESS

CONCERNs, SMALL DISADVANTAGED BUSINESS CONCERNs (SDBCs), LABOR SURPLUS AREA (LSA) CONCERNs, and WOMEN-OWNED SMALL BUSINESSES. See DEAR 970.7103(c).

FEDERAL PRISON INDUSTRIES, INC. A self-supporting, wholly owned Government corporation of the District of Columbia (also referred to as UNICOR). FAR 8.601. Through the sale of its products and services to Government agencies, Federal Prison Industries provides training and employment for prisoners confined in Federal penal and correctional institutions. 18 U.S.C. 4121–4128. FAR 8.602 requires agencies to purchase supplies listed in the Schedule of Products Made in Federal Penal and Correctional Institutions at prices not to exceed current market prices, and encourages agencies to use Federal Prison Industries facilities to the maximum extent practicable in purchasing supplies and services not listed on the schedule. Federal Prison Industries diversifies its products and services to prevent private industry from experiencing unfair competition from prison workshops or activities. FAR 8.601(c).

FEDERAL PROCUREMENT DATA SYSTEM (FPDS) A system for collecting and compiling data on Federal procurements. The FPDS provides a comprehensive mechanism for assembling, organizing, and presenting contract placement data for the Federal Government. FAR 4.602. Federal agencies report data to the Federal Procurement Data Center (FPDC), which collects, processes, and disseminates official statistical data on Federal contracting. The data provide (1) a basis for recurring and special reports to the executive and legislative branches and the general public, (2) a means of measuring and assessing the effect of Federal contracting on the nation's economy and the extent to which small business concerns are sharing in Federal contracts, and (3) information for other policy and management control purposes. The data are collected and reported on Standard Form (SF) 279, Federal Procurement Data System (FPDS)—Individual Contract Action Report (Over $10,000), FAR 53.301-279; and SF 281, Federal Procurement Data System (FPDS)—Summary of Contract Actions of $10,000 or Less, FAR 53.301-281.

FEDERAL PROCUREMENT REGULATIONS (FPR) The Federal regulation that set forth uniform policies and procedures applicable to Federal agencies, other than DoD and NASA, in the procurement of supplies and nonpersonal services, including

construction. The FPR was superseded by the FEDERAL ACQUISI-
TION REGULATION (FAR) in 1984. The FPR was prescribed by the
Administrator of General Services under the FEDERAL PROPERTY
AND ADMINISTRATIVE SERVICES ACT (FPASA) OF 1949.

**FEDERAL PROPERTY AND ADMINISTRATIVE SERVICES
ACT (FPASA) OF 1949** The act, 40 U.S.C. 471 *et seq.* and 41
U.S.C. 251 *et seq.*, containing policies and procedures for the use
and disposal of GOVERNMENT PROPERTY by all agencies and for
the procurement of supplies and services, including construction,
by almost all Federal agencies except DoD, NASA and the Coast
Guard. See 41 U.S.C. 252 for a description of the agencies
covered. This act is one of the two major acts prescribing
procurement policies and procedures—the other being the ARMED
SERVICES PROCUREMENT ACT (ASPA). Both acts were significantly
amended in 1984 by the COMPETITION IN CONTRACTING ACT
(CICA). See Cibinic and Nash, Formation of Government Contracts 5–9.

**FEDERAL PROPERTY MANAGEMENT REGULATION
(FPMR)** The regulation that guides and governs the Federal
agencies in their management of property and records. The FPMR
is codified as Chapter 101 of Title 41 of the Code of Federal
Regulations. It is issued by GSA.

FEDERAL REGISTER A daily publication of the Office of the
Federal Register, established in 1935 by the Federal Register Act,
44 U.S.C. 15, as part of a central publications system for promul-
gating the detailed regulations issued by Federal agencies. The
Federal Register is the medium for notifying the public of official
agency actions. Agencies' regulatory documents are filed with the
Office of the Federal Register, placed on public inspection,
published in the Federal Register, and then permanently codified
(numerically arranged) in the CODE OF FEDERAL REGULATIONS
(CFR). Publication in the Federal Register gives a regulation the
force of law. In 1948 the Administrative Procedure Act, 5 U.S.C.
551 *et seq.*, introduced the requirement that the public have an
opportunity to comment on most proposed regulations (excluding
procurement regulations). It stated that, absent good cause, no
regulation would become final less than 30 days from its publication in the Federal Register. It also provided for publication in the
Federal Register of agency statements of organization and
procedural rules. Proposed procurement regulations are required

to be published in the Federal Register by 41 U.S.C. 418b. See the Office of the Federal Register publication *The Federal Register: What It Is and How to Use It* (available from the U.S. Government Printing Office, Washington, DC 20402), which provides comprehensive information on how to obtain Federal Register documents.

FEDERAL SOFTWARE EXCHANGE PROGRAM (FSEP) A GSA program, administered by the Department of Commerce's National Technical Information Service through the Federal Software Exchange Center (FSEC), that promotes and administers the sharing of Government-developed computer programs and related documentation. FIRMR 201-24.201. FSEP is a "mandatory for consideration" GSA program. Before contracting for common-use software (software that deals with applications common to many agencies), agencies must contact the FSEC or review the FSEP exchange catalog to determine whether software available from other agencies would be the most advantageous alternative for meeting the requirement. FIRMR 201-24.201(b). See FIRMR Bulletin C-12, *Federal Software Exchange Program.*

FEDERAL SPECIFICATIONS AND STANDARDS SPECIFICA-TIONs and STANDARDs issued or controlled by GSA and listed in the *GSA Index of Federal Specifications, Standards and Commercial Item Descriptions* (issued annually by GSA and available from the U.S. Government Printing Office, Washington, DC 20402). FAR 10.001. FAR 10.006(a) requires that such specifications and standards be used by all agencies when procuring the covered supplies and services. FAR 10.007 sets forth the procedures for obtaining DEVIATIONs from this requirement.

FEDERAL SUPPLY SCHEDULES (FSS) A series of schedules, compiled by GSA, of commonly used supplies and services available to Government agencies (and some cost-reimbursement contractors) at specified prices. Some schedules designate "mandatory use" agencies, which are required to order from the schedule. Other agencies may use the schedules at their option. Contracting officers, using competitive procedures, award INDEFINITE-DELIVERY CONTRACTs to commercial firms, requiring those firms to provide, under "schedule," specified supplies and services at stated prices for given periods of time. This process permits contracting officers outside GSA to acquire items covered by such schedules without engaging in the time-consuming process of issuing invitations for bids or requests for proposals. The schedules, often referred to as GSA schedules, allow ordering offices to issue delivery orders directly to listed contractors, receive direct shipments, make payment directly to contractors, and administer the orders. Both SINGLE-AWARD SCHEDULEs and MULTIPLE-AWARD SCHEDULEs (MASs) are established. See FAR Subpart 8.4 and Part 38, and the FPMR at 41 CFR Chapter 101, Subchapter E, Part 101-26. GSA can authorize other agencies to award schedule contracts and publish schedules; the Department of Veterans Affairs, for example, awards schedule contracts for medical and nonperishable subsistence items. FAR 38.101(e). See Cibinic and Nash, Formation of Government Contracts 688–95.

FEDERAL TECHNOLOGY TRANSFER The process of shifting federally generated technology and technical know-how to State and local governments or the private sector for development and commercialization. The term "technology transfer" is used to describe the process by which technology or know-how developed for a particular purpose by one organization can be transferred to another organization for use in another area. The goals of Federal technology transfer are economic growth through commercialization of new products or processes and improvement of existing techniques. Companies interested in a particular technology can contact a State technology transfer program, the OFFICE OF RESEARCH AND TECHNOLOGY APPLICATION (ORTA) of a local laboratory, the FEDERAL LABORATORY CONSORTIUM FOR TECHNOLOGY TRANSFER (FLC), or the NATIONAL INSTITUTE OF STANDARDS AND TECHNOLOGY (NIST) in Washington, D.C. The party contacted will try to identify a knowledgeable source within the Federal network. Types of assistance available include technical assistance, access to nonclassified work, use of Federal laboratory facilities or equipment, access to Federal patented inventions for licensing, participation in COOPERATIVE RESEARCH AND DEVELOPMENT AGREEMENTS (CRADAs), and access to information, databases, and publications. See Sweenes, *Government Inventions; Utilizing the Federal Technology Transfer Act of 1986*, 20 Pub. Cont. L.J. 365 (1991); Duncombe, *Federal Technology Transfer: A Look at the Benefits and Pitfalls of One of the Country's Best Kept Secrets*, 37 Fed. B. News & J. 608 (1990).

FEDERAL TELECOMMUNICATIONS STANDARDS (FED-STDS) Official Federal publications relating to standards originally adopted and issued under the provisions of 40 U.S.C. 487. FED-STDS are developed under delegation from GSA by the National Communications System, an interagency organization assigned national security and emergency preparedness telecommunications responsibilities. FED-STDS include the categories in the Federal Supply Class (FSC) of "Telecommunications" that were not redefined as AUTOMATIC DATA PROCESSING EQUIPMENT (ADPE) by the PAPERWORK REDUCTION REAUTHORIZATION ACT OF 1986.

FEDERAL TELECOMMUNICATIONS SYSTEM (FTS)   The umbrella of local and long-distance telecommunications services (including FTS 2000 long-distance services) provided, operated, managed, or maintained by GSA for the common use of all Federal agencies and other authorized users. FIRMR 201-4.001. Agencies must use FTS as the first source of supply for a telecommunications requirement unless the requirement falls outside the scope of FTS or the agency has an exception to the use of FTS services. FIRMR 201-20.305-1.

FEDERAL TORT CLAIMS ACT (FTCA)   An act, 28 U.S.C. 1346(b), 2401–2402, 2671–2672, 2674–2680, permitting persons injured by negligent conduct of the Government to sue for damages in U.S. District Courts. Prior to suit, 28 U.S.C. 2675(a) requires that the injured person file for administrative relief with the agency involved. Thereafter, if relief is not granted, suit in court is permitted. 28 U.S.C. 2680(a) precludes recovery if the Government action is the result of a discretionary act. Recovery under the FTCA is limited to actual damages; punitive damages are barred by 28 U.S.C. 2674. See also TORT.

FEE   The amount paid to the contractor beyond costs under a COST-REIMBURSEMENT CONTRACT. In Government contracting "fee" is the term of art for PROFIT the Government agrees to pay on a cost-reimbursement contract. ("Profit" is used when the contract is a fixed-price type.) In most instances, fee reflects a variety of factors, including RISK. The FIXED FEE on COST-PLUS-FIXED FEE (CPFF) CONTRACTs may not exceed certain statutory limitations. See FAR 15.903(d). The fee may be fixed at the outset of performance, as in a cost-plus-fixed fee contract, or it may vary within a contractually specified minimum–maximum range (see RANGE OF INCENTIVE EFFECTIVENESS (RIE)), as in a COST-PLUS-

INCENTIVE FEE (CPIF) CONTRACT. Armed Services Pricing Manual (ASPM) vol. 1, app. B.

FEE FOR PROFESSIONAL SERVICES The amount paid to a member of a profession for the performance of services. Used in this sense, the "fee" is the PRICE to be paid under a contract for PROFESSIONAL AND CONSULTANT SERVICES when the work is satisfactorily performed. 10 U.S.C. 2306(d) and 41 U.S.C. 254(b) provide that the fee paid for ARCHITECT-ENGINEER (A-E) SERVICES may not exceed 6 percent of the estimated cost of construction of the work designed by the A-E. See FAR 15.903(d)(1)(ii). Neither the statutes nor the procurement regulations limits the fees paid to other professionals.

FIELD PRICING SUPPORT A review and evaluation of the contractor's or subcontractor's PROPOSAL by any or all field pricing support personnel. FAR 15.801. Such personnel may include plant representatives, ADMINISTRATIVE CONTRACTING OFFICERS (ACOs), contract auditors, price analysts, QUALITY ASSURANCE personnel, engineers, legal personnel, and SMALL AND DISADVANTAGED BUSINESS UTILIZATION SPECIALISTs (SADBUSs). FAR 15.805-5(a) requires the use of field pricing support on all negotiated procurements (see NEGOTIATION) in excess of $500,000 requiring COST OR PRICING DATA unless the contracting officer determines that sufficient data is available or agency procedures permit otherwise. See DFARS 215.805-5. In initiating a request for field pricing support, the contracting officer prescribes the extent of the support needed, states the specific areas for which input is required, includes the information necessary to perform the review, and assigns a realistic deadline for receipt of a report. FAR 15.805-5(c).

FINAL COST OBJECTIVE See COST OBJECTIVE.

FINAL DECISION See DECISION OF THE CONTRACTING OFFICER.

FINAL INDIRECT COST RATE A percentage or dollar factor, agreed to by the COST-REIMBURSEMENT CONTRACTor and the Government, expressing the ratio of INDIRECT COST incurred during a prior period to direct labor cost, manufacturing cost, or another appropriate base for the same period. For commercial contractors this rate is established after the close of the contractor's FISCAL YEAR (FY) to which it applies. In the case of cost-reimbursement R&D contracts with educational institutions, the final indirect cost rate may be predetermined; that is, it may be established for a future period on the basis of cost experience with similar contracts, together with supporting data. FAR 42.701. FAR 42.703 requires that a single agency must establish indirect cost rate for each business unit of a contractor. This provides (1) uniformity of approach when more than one contract or agency is involved, (2) economy of administration, and (3) timely settlement under cost-reimbursement contracts. FAR 42.702. The FAR requires that final indirect cost rates be established on the basis of either a contracting officer's or an auditor's determination procedure. FAR 42.705.

FINAL PAYMENT The last payment the Government makes on a contract when the parties believe all obligations under the contract have been closed out. The Government makes final payment upon completion and acceptance of all work required under a contract, once the disbursing officer receives a properly executed and duly certified voucher or invoice showing the total amount agreed upon, less amounts previously paid. The contract may require the contractor to give a RELEASE of CLAIMs and liabilities before the Government makes final payment. The various Changes clauses in FAR 52.243-1 *et seq.*, the Suspension of Work clause, FAR 52.212-12, and the Government Delay of Work clause, FAR 52.212-15, expressly bar claims not asserted by the contractor before final payment. Whether final payment has occurred for the purposes of these clauses depends on the totality of the facts and circumstances of a particular case. See Cibinic and Nash, Administration of Government Contracts 923–25; Nash, *Releases Accompanying Final Payment: Don't Give Up the Farm*, 1 N&CR ¶ 76 (Oct. 1987).

FINANCIAL ACCOUNTING STANDARDS BOARD (FASB) A private organization that establishes standards of financial accounting and reporting. Those standards govern the preparation of financial reports and provide for the guidance and education of the public, including issuers, auditors, and users of financial information. The Board follows certain precepts in conducting its activities: objectivity in decision making, careful weighing of the views of its constituents, promulgation of standards only when expected benefits exceed perceived costs, introduction of changes in ways that least disrupt the continuity of reporting practice, and review of the effects of past decisions. (FASB, High Ridge Park, P.O. Box 3821, Stamford, CT 06906.)

FINANCIAL INABILITY A contractor's incapacity to perform for economic reasons: the contractor cannot buy materials, pay its work force, keep its plant open, or prevent foreclosure. Such inability is generally the responsibility of the contractor, but it may be excusable if caused by an event outside the control of the contractor and may even be compensable if the Government caused it. Financial inability is distinguished from "financial difficulty" (which means economic hardship, but not to the level of incapacity) and from "commercial impracticability" (see IMPRACTICABILITY OF PERFORMANCE). If financial inability is excusable, it may be raised as a defense against TERMINATION FOR DEFAULT or as an excuse for failing to continue performance. Nagle, *Financial Inability in Government Contracts*, 17 Pub. Cont. L.J. 320 (1987).

FINANCING The obtaining by a contractor of the money necessary for performance of a contract. FAR Part 32 governs contract financing. FAR 32.106 states the following order of preference for obtaining financing: (1) equity capital, (2) private financing on reasonable terms, (3) CUSTOMARY PROGRESS PAYMENTs, (4) GUARANTEED LOANs, (5) UNUSUAL PROGRESS PAYMENTs, and (6) ADVANCE PAYMENTs. FAR 32.104 states that Government financing should be provided only to the extent actually needed for prompt and efficient performance, considering the availability of private financing. FAR 32.107, however, provides that if a contractor or offeror meets the RESPONSIBILITY standards prescribed for prospective contractors, the contracting officer may not treat the contractor's need for financial assistance as a handicap for a contract award. The PROMPT PAYMENT ACT (PPA) does not apply to FINANCING PAYMENTs. See Chierichella et al., *Financing Government Contracts*, 86-7 Briefing Papers (June 1986).

FINANCING INSTITUTION An institution dealing in money—as distinguished from other commodities—as the primary function of its business activity. A financing institution may be an individual or a partnership as well as a corporate organization, but it may not be a SURETY, a trust, or an ordinary corporation that incidentally provides financing to its suppliers or to others with whom it deals. The ASSIGNMENT OF CLAIMS Act permits the assignment of contract proceeds to a bank, trust company, or other financing institution. See FAR Subpart 32.8; Principles of Federal Appropriations Law (2d ed.), chap. 12.

FINANCING PAYMENT A Government disbursement of monies to a contractor under a contract clause or other authorization before acceptance of supplies or services by the Government. FAR 32.902. Such payments are not subject to the PROMPT PAYMENT ACT (PPA). Financing payments include (1) ADVANCE PAYMENTs; (2) PROGRESS PAYMENTs based on costs under the Progress Payments clause at FAR 52.232-16; (3) progress payments based on a percentage or stage of completion, other than those made under the Payments under Fixed-Price Construction Contracts clause at FAR 52.232-5 or the Payments under Fixed-Price Architect-Engineer Contracts clause at FAR 52.232-10; and (4) interim payments on cost-reimbursement contracts. Financing payments do not include invoice payments or payments for partial deliveries. FAR 32.902. Generally, the due date for the designated payment office to make financing payments is the 30th day after the designated billing office has received a proper request. FAR 32.906. No interest penalty is paid to a contractor as a result of delayed contract financing payments. FAR 32.907-2. See OMB Circular No. A-125, *Prompt Payment*, 19 Aug. 1982.

FINE A payment required to be made as a result of misconduct. FAR 31.205-15 makes fines UNALLOWABLE COSTs. Fines are generally specified as criminal sanctions under Title 18 of the United States Code.

FIRM-FIXED-PRICE (FFP) CONTRACT A type of contract providing for a price that is not subject to adjustment on the basis of the contractor's cost experience in performing the contract. FAR 16.202-1. FFP contracts are generally subject to adjustment in accordance with contract clauses providing for EQUITABLE ADJUSTMENTs or PRICE ADJUSTMENTs. They place upon the contractor maximum RISK and full responsibility for all costs and resulting profit or loss. They provide maximum incentive for the contractor to control costs and perform effectively and impose a minimum administrative burden upon the contracting parties. FAR 16.103(b) provides that firm fixed-price contracts are the preferred type of contract when the risk involved is minimal or can be predicted with an acceptable degree of certainty. An FFP LEVEL-OF-EFFORT CONTRACT may be used for investigation or study in a specific R&D area. FAR 16.207. See Cibinic and Nash, Formation of Government Contracts 716.

FIRMR   See FEDERAL INFORMATION RESOURCES MANAGEMENT REGULATION (FIRMR).

FIRMWARE   Any automatic data processing hardware-oriented programming at the basic logic level of the computer that is used for machine control, error recovery, mathematical functions, applications programs, engineering analysis programs, and the like. Agencies must conduct conversion studies to determine the costs of converting from current FEDERAL INFORMATION PROCESSING (FIP) RESOURCES to replacement resources. In determining conversion costs agencies may consider the costs of firmware required solely to permit the continued use of application software (see COMPUTER SOFTWARE). FIRMR 201-20.203-4; FIRMR Bulletin C-14, *Conversion of Federal Information Process (FIP) Resources*.

FIRST ARTICLE TESTING   Testing and evaluating first articles for conformance with specified contract requirements before or in the initial stage of production. FAR 9.301. The first articles may be preproduction models or prototypes, initial production samples, test samples, first lots, pilot lots, or pilot models. The procedures governing first article testing are set forth in FAR Subpart 9.3. First article testing and approval ensures that the contractor can furnish a product that conforms to all contract requirements for acceptance. Contracts imposing a first article testing requirement upon the contractor will contain the First Article Approval—Contractor Testing clause at FAR 52.209-3 or the First Article Approval—Government Testing clause at FAR 52.209-4. Failure to deliver or gain approval of first articles may result in TERMINATION FOR DEFAULT. See Cibinic and Nash, Administration of Government Contracts 598.

FISCAL YEAR (FY)   *For contractors*—the accounting period for which annual financial statements are regularly prepared, generally a period of 12 months, 52 weeks, or 53 weeks. FAR 31.001. Cost Accounting Standard 406, FAR 30.406, provides criteria for selecting the time periods to be used as COST ACCOUNTING PERIODs for contract cost estimating, accumulating, and reporting. The standard is intended to reduce the effects of variations in the flow of costs within each cost accounting period; enhance objectivity, consistency, and verifiability; and promote uniformity and comparability in contract cost measurements. *For the Government*—the period running from 1 Oct. through 30 Sep. Thus, the period running from 1 Oct. 1990 through 30 Sep. 1991 is designated FY 91. Generally, APPROPRIATIONs are made for each fiscal year.

FIXED-CEILING-PRICE CONTRACT See FIXED-PRICE REDETERMINATION—RETROACTIVE (FPRR) CONTRACT.

FIXED COSTS Costs of an enterprise that cannot be varied with the amount of work performed. Fixed costs are generally compared to VARIABLE COSTS when analyzing INDIRECT COSTs of a contractor. If the fixed costs comprise a large part of such indirect costs, the contractor's OVERHEAD RATEs can be expected to increase significantly if the amount of work performed declines.

FIXED FEE The FEE agreed upon for the performance of a COST-PLUS-FIXED FEE (CPFF) CONTRACT. 10 U.S.C. 2306(d) and 41 U.S.C. 254(b) provide that fixed fees may not exceed 10 percent of the ESTIMATED COST except in the case of contracts for experimental, developmental, or research work, where the limitation is 15 percent. Fixed fees are negotiated in accordance with FAR Subpart 15.9 as supplemented by agency FAR supplements.

FIXED-PRICE CONTRACT A type of contract providing for a firm pricing arrangement established by the parties at the time of contracting. The policies on the use of this type of contract are set forth in FAR Subpart 16.2. Whereas a FIRM-FIXED-PRICE (FFP) CONTRACT is not subject to adjustment on the basis of the contractor's cost experience in performing the contract, other types of fixed-price contracts are subject to price adjustment on the basis of (1) economic conditions or (2) the contractor's performance of the contract. These types are FIXED-PRICE CONTRACTs WITH ECONOMIC PRICE ADJUSTMENT, FIXED-PRICE INCENTIVE (FPI) CONTRACTs, FIXED-PRICE REDETERMINATION—PROSPECTIVE (FPRP) CONTRACTs, and FIXED-PRICE REDETERMINATION—RETROACTIVE (FPRR) CONTRACTs. See Cibinic and Nash, Formation of Government Contracts 715–36.

FIXED-PRICE CONTRACT WITH ECONOMIC PRICE ADJUSTMENT A type of contract providing for upward or downward revision of the stated contract price upon the occurrence of a specified contingency. FAR 16.203-1. Adjustments may reflect increases or decreases in established prices for specific items, in the contractor's actual costs of labor or material, or in specific indexes of labor or material costs.   FAR 16.203-2 provides that a fixed-price contract with economic price adjustment may be used when (1) there is serious doubt that market or labor conditions will remain stable during an extended period of contract performance and (2) contingencies (see CONTINGENCY) that would otherwise be included in the contract price can be identified and covered separately in the contract. FAR 14.407-4 provides that when the Government proposes inclusion of an economic price adjustment clause in the invitation for bids (IFB), bids will be evaluated on the basis of the quoted prices without adding any amount for price adjustment. However, if no such clause is included in the IFB, the FAR provides that bids proposing economic price adjustment must be rejected unless they propose a ceiling price—in which case they will be evaluated at the ceiling.   Economic price adjustment is sometimes called "escalation"; that is a misnomer, however, because the price can be lowered as well as raised. See Cibinic and Nash, Formation of Government Contracts 717–33.

FIXED-PRICE INCENTIVE (FPI) CONTRACT   A type of contract that provides for adjusting PROFIT and establishing the final contract price by a formula based on the relationship of final negotiated TOTAL COST to total TARGET COST. FAR 16.403. The final price is subject to a CEILING PRICE negotiated at the outset. There are two forms of fixed-price incentive contracts: firm target and successive target. FAR 16.403-1 provides that a firm target is appropriate when the parties can negotiate at the outset a firm target cost, a TARGET PROFIT, a profit adjustment formula, and a ceiling price that will both give the contractor a fair and reasonable incentive and ensure that the contractor assumes an appropriate share of the RISK. FAR 16.403-2 provides that successive targets are appropriate when available cost or pricing information is not sufficient to permit the negotiation of a realistic firm target cost and profit before award. Standard clauses are provided for these types of contracts: the Incentive Price Revision—Firm Target clause in FAR 52.216-16 and the Incentive Price Revision—Successive Targets clause in FAR 52.216-17. See Cibinic and Nash, Formation of Government Contracts 759–66.

FIXED-PRICE LEVEL-OF-EFFORT CONTRACT   A FIRM-FIXED-PRICE (FFP) CONTRACT requiring the contractor to provide a specified level of effort over a stated period of time, on work that can be stated only in general terms, and requiring the Government to pay the contractor a fixed dollar amount. FAR 16.207-1. Such a contract is suitable for investigation or study in a specific research and development area. The product of the contract is usually a report showing the results achieved through application of the required level of effort. Payment, however, is based on the effort expended rather than the results achieved. FAR 16.207-2. Fixed-price level-of-effort contracts may be used only when (1) the work required cannot otherwise be clearly defined; (2) the required level of effort is identified and agreed upon in advance; (3) there is a reasonable assurance that the intended result cannot be achieved by expending less than the stipulated effort; and (4) the contract price is $100,000 or less (unless higher-level approval is obtained). FAR 16.207-3. See Cibinic and Nash, Formation of Government Contracts 797.

FIXED-PRICE REDETERMINATION—PROSPECTIVE (FPRP) CONTRACT   A type of contract that contains a firm fixed price for an initial period of contract delivery or performance and provides for the negotiation of a new firm fixed price for subsequent contract work. The contract specifies the time or times when new prices will be negotiated. FPRP contracts may be used to acquire production or services in quantity in cases when it is possible to negotiation a firm fixed price for an initial period but not for the entire amount of goods or services needed. The initial period should be as long as possible and the subsequent period should be at least 12 months long. FAR 16.205-2. An FPRP contract may be used only when (1) a FIRM FIXED PRICE (FFP) CONTRACT is not feasible and a FIXED-PRICE INCENTIVE (FPI) CONTRACT would not be more appropriate, (2) the contractor's accounting system will permit price redetermination, (3) the prospective pricing periods can be made to conform with operation of the contractor's accounting system, and (4) there is reasonable assurance that price redetermination will take place promptly at the specified times. FAR 16.205-3.

FIXED-PRICE REDETERMINATION—RETROACTIVE (FPRR) CONTRACT   A type of contract under which a CEILING PRICE is negotiated before contract performance and a final fixed price within that ceiling is determined, based on an assessment of the contractor's performance and its actual audited costs, after the work is completed. Because FPRR contracts provide no positive incentive for the contractor to control costs (other than the ceiling price, which may contain a sizable margin for error and uncertainty), FAR 16.206-2 limits their use. They may be used only for research and development estimated at $100,000 or less when a FIRM-FIXED-PRICE (FFP) CONTRACT cannot be negotiated and the dollar amount involved and short performance period make any other fixed-price contract type impracticable. FAR 16.206.3 further narrows the conditions for use to situations in which the contractor's accounting system is adequate for price redetermination, there is reasonable assurance that price redetermination will take place promptly as specified, and the head of the contracting activity or a higher-level official grants approval in writing.

FLOW-DOWN CLAUSES Clauses prescribed by the Government that a PRIME CONTRACTOR incorporates into SUBCONTRACTs. These clauses "flow down" rights and responsibilities of the prime contractor to the subcontractor. Mandatory flow-down clauses are those prime contract clauses that specifically require the inclusion of their text in all subcontracts entered into in support of the prime contract. Other clauses, although not mandatory, should be flowed down to ensure that the subcontractor will provide adequate assistance or cooperation to enable the prime contractor to meet its contractual requirements with the Government. Failure to flow down certain clauses may expose the prime contractor to financial risk if the Government takes certain actions under the prime contract and the subcontract does not obligate the subcontractor to respond in accordance with those actions. See Hoe et al., *Flow Down Clauses in Subcontracts*, 85-5 Briefing Papers (May 1985).

FLY AMERICA ACT An act, section 5 of the International Air Transportation Fair Competitive Practices Act of 1974, 49 U.S.C. 1517, requiring Federal employees and their dependents, consultants, contractors, grantees, and others to use U.S.-flag air carriers for U.S. Government-financed international air travel and transportation of their personal effects or property, to the extent that service by these carriers is available. FAR 47.402. "International air transportation" means transportation by air between a place in the United States and a place outside the United States, or between two places both of which are outside the United States. FAR 47.401.

F.O.B. An abbreviation for "free on board." FAR 47.001. This term is used with the designation of a physical point to determine the responsibility and basis for payment of freight charges and, unless otherwise agreed, the point at which TITLE for supplies passes to the buyer or consignee. The policies on designation of contracts as F.O.B. ORIGIN or F.O.B. DESTINATION are set forth in FAR Subpart 47.3. Contract clauses providing a variety of payment and evaluation arrangements for transportation costs are set forth in FAR 52.247-29 through 52.247-59. See U.C.C. 2-319.

F.O.B. DESTINATION Free on board at destination, or where the seller or consignor delivers the supplies on the seller's or consignor's conveyance to a specified delivery point. FAR 47.001. In this case, unless the contract provides otherwise, the cost of shipping and the risk of loss are borne by the seller or consignor. Guidance on the use of this technique is set forth in FAR 47.303. Various clauses are provided for this type of arrangement in FAR 52.247-34, -35, -43, -44 and -48.

F.O.B. ORIGIN Free on board at the place of origin, or where the seller or consignor places the supplies on the conveyance by which they are to be transported. FAR 47.001. Unless the contract provides otherwise, the cost of shipping and the risk of loss are borne by the buyer or consignee. Guidance on the use of this technique is set forth in FAR 47.303. Various clauses are provided for this type of arrangement in FAR 52.247-29 through -33 and -45 through -47.

FOLLOWER COMPANY See LEADER-COMPANY CONTRACTING.

FORBEARANCE The postponement of the decision to terminate for default (see TERMINATION FOR DEFAULT) while the contracting officer is investigating the reasons for the contractor's failure to meet the contract requirements. With regard to the Government's WAIVER of its right to terminate a contract for late delivery, the contracting officer has a reasonable period of forbearance to investigate the facts and determine what course of action best serves the Government's interests. During the forbearance period, the Government may terminate at any time, without prior notice. The facts and circumstances of each case determine the length of time constituting a reasonable forbearance period; no clear demarcation exists between reasonable forbearance and waiver. Once the forbearance period expires, the Government waives its right to a termination for default and must reestablish a delivery schedule if it wishes to terminate. See Cibinic and Nash, Administration of Government Contracts 728; Carberry and Johnstone, *Waiver of the Government's Right to Terminate for Default in Government Defense Contracts*, 17 Pub. Cont. L.J. 470, 482 (1988).

FORCE MAJEURE (fôrs´ mä-zhur´) A term derived from insurance law, meaning superior or irresistible force, such as lightning, earthquakes, storms, flood, sunstroke, and freezing. Force majeure is at times thought of as an "act of God"—one occasioned exclusively by violence of nature without the interference of any human agency. Force majeure clauses are common in commercial construction contracts to protect the parties if part of the contract cannot be performed as a result of causes that are outside the control of the parties and could not have been avoided by the exercise of due care. Black's Law Dictionary. In Government contracting, the clauses granting the Government the right to terminate for default (see TERMINATION FOR DEFAULT) generally contain EXCUSABLE DELAY provisions that are in the nature of force majeure clauses.

FOREIGN CARRIER See CARRIER (TELECOMMUNICATIONS).

FOREIGN END PRODUCT An article, material, or supply that, pursuant to the BUY AMERICAN ACT and its related statutes and regulations, is not a DOMESTIC END PRODUCT. FAR 25.101.

FOREIGN MILITARY SALES (FMS) Government-to-government sales of U.S. defense items, as authorized under the Foreign Assistance Act of 1961 and the ARMS EXPORT CONTROL ACT (AECA). In the normal situation, FMS transactions involve DoD contracts with U.S. contractors for the furnishing of military equipment to a foreign government. Although recipient governments generally pay cash for the full costs associated with such sales, some programs involve loans or other arrangements to permit the purchase. A MEMORANDUM OF UNDERSTANDING (MOU) may be used. The process typically entails a letter of request from the foreign country and a letter of offer and acceptance, DD Form 1513, DFARS 253.303-1513, which may require congressional approval. The Arms Export Control Act requires that FMS activities be conducted at no cost to the U.S. Government, that all costs be collected from the recipient government, and that payments be made in advance of delivery. FMS are considered a component of the U.S. Security Assistance Program, which provides defense articles, defense services, and military training to U.S. allies and friendly foreign nations. See DFARS Subpart 225.73; DoD Manual 5105.38-M, *Security Assistance Management*, and DoD Manual 7290.3-M, *Foreign Military Sales Financial Management*; DSMC, Program Manager's Notebook; Reuter, *The ABCs of FMS*, 30 Cont. Mgmt. 29 (Oct. 1990); Grossman, *Foreign Military Sales*, 87-12 Briefing Papers (Nov. 1987).

FOREIGN OFFER   An offered price for a FOREIGN END PRODUCT, including transportation to destination and duty (whether or not a duty-free entry certificate is issued). FAR 25.101.

FOREIGN OWNERSHIP, CONTROL, OR INFLUENCE (FOCI) Situation in which the degree of ownership, control, or influence over an offeror, bidder, contractor, or subcontractor by a foreign interest (government, organization, or individual) is such that a reasonable basis exists for concluding that CLASSIFIED INFORMATION or special nuclear material might be compromised. DoE has procedures that require certain offerors, bidders, contractors, or subcontractors to submit information that helps in determining whether award of a contract, or continued performance of a contract, may pose an undue risk to the common defense and security because of FOCI. DEAR 904.70; DEAR 952.204-74.

FORFEITURE   The loss of benefits received under a contract as a result of illegal conduct. For example, in one case of BRIBERY and CONFLICT OF INTEREST, the contractor was required to forfeit the entire contract price after completion of the work. *K & R Eng'g Co. v. United States*, 222 Ct. Cl. 340, 616 F.2d 469 (1980). 28 U.S.C. 2514 also requires forfeiture of any CLAIM filed in the courts that is tainted with FRAUD.

FORMAL ADVERTISING   The term used, before the COMPETITION IN CONTRACTING ACT (CICA) of 1984, to describe the procurement technique now referred to as SEALED BIDDING. Under the statutes and regulations preceding passage of CICA, there was an expressed preference for formal advertising. Formal advertising, like sealed bidding, entailed drafting and publicizing an INVITATION FOR BIDS (IFB), holding a public BID OPENING, and awarding the contract to the lowest responsive and responsible bidder (see

RESPONSIVENESS and RESPONSIBILITY). Formal advertising was aimed at securing the most advantageous contract for the Government by maximizing free and open competition; preventing favoritism, collusion, and fraud; and giving all interested parties an opportunity to compete. Nash and Cibinic, I Federal Procurement Law 222.

FORMAL SOURCE SELECTION A SOURCE SELECTION process where a specific evaluation group structure is established to evaluate proposals and select a source for contract award. FAR 15.612. This approach is generally used in high-dollar-value acquisitions. The source selection organization typically consists of a SOURCE SELECTION BOARD (SSB), a SOURCE SELECTION ADVISORY COUNCIL (SSAC), and a designated SOURCE SELECTION AUTHORITY (SSA) at a management level above the contracting officer. When using this process, the HEAD OF THE AGENCY or a designee ensures that (1) the official responsible for the source selection is formally designated as the source selection authority and (2) such authority formally establishes an evaluation group structure and, before conducting any PRESOLICITATION CONFERENCE, approves a SOURCE SELECTION PLAN. The source selection authority must consider rankings, ratings, and recommendations prepared by evaluation and advisory groups and must use the EVALUATION FACTORS established in the solicitation to make the source selection decision.

FORM, FIT, AND FUNCTION DATA Data that relate to items, components, or processes and are sufficient to enable physical and functional interchangeability, as well as data identifying source, size, configuration, mating and attachment characteristics, functional characteristics, and performance requirements. For COMPUTER SOFTWARE, the term means data identifying source, functional characteristics, and performance requirements but specifically excluding the source code, algorithm, process, formulae, and flow charts of the software. FAR 27.401. The term has a slightly different meaning in DFARS 227.401. Pursuant to 10 U.S.C. 2320, the Rights in Technical Data and Computer Software clause in DFARS 252.227-7013 provides that the Government acquires UNLIMITED RIGHTS in form, fit, and function data prepared in the performance of a contract. Under the Rights in Data—General clause at FAR 52.227-14, such data are furnished with unlimited rights and the contractor may protect qualifying LIMITED RIGHTS DATA and RESTRICTED RIGHTS computer software by withholding them from delivery to the Government and delivering form, fit, and function data instead. FAR 27.404.

FORMS Government documents used in the procurement process and governed by the policies in FAR Part 53. This Part gives rules for using forms, prescribes STANDARD FORMS (SFs), references OPTIONAL FORMS (OFs) and agency-prescribed forms used in acquisition, and illustrates all these forms (SFs in 53.301, OFs in 53.302, and selected agency forms in 53.303, in numerical order). Forms may be copied from the FAR. Executive agencies obtain forms (both SFs and OFs) from GSA; contractors and other parties can obtain them from the U.S. Government Printing Office, Washington, DC 20402. Agency forms can be obtained from the prescribing agency. FAR 53.107. See also Ferguson and Moss, *FAR Part 53—It's a Matter of Forms*, 24 Cont. Mgmt. 8 (Apr. 1984).

FORWARD PRICING RATE AGREEMENT (FPRA) A pricing arrangement that constitutes a written understanding negotiated between a contractor and the Government before costs have been incurred. The purpose is to make certain rates (including labor, indirect cost, material obsolescence and usage, spare parts provisioning, and material handling) available during a specified period for use in pricing contracts or contract modifications. These rates represent reasonable projections of specific costs that are not easily estimated for, identified with, or generated by a specific contract, contract end item, or task. FAR 15.801. In determining whether or not to establish such an agreement, the administrative contracting officer should consider whether the benefits to be derived from it are commensurate with the effort of establishing and monitoring it. FAR 15.809.

FRAGMENTATION OF REMEDIES A requirement that a contractor obtain remedies from different administrative agencies or courts for events that have occurred on a single transaction. One of the major difficulties that led to the passage of the CONTRACT DISPUTES ACT (CDA) OF 1978 was the complaint that disputes "ARISING UNDER THE CONTRACT" had to be appealed to the BOARDs OF CONTRACT APPEALS (BCAs), while claims for Government BREACH OF CONTRACT could be taken only to the Court of Claims. This problem was resolved in the Contract Disputes Act by permitting contractors to elect to take all claims

"RELATING TO THE CONTRACT" to either the BCA or the CLAIMS COURT (Cl. Ct.). Fragmentation of remedies still exists with regard to some claims of contractors involving both contract breach and tortious conduct (see TORT) by the Government. In such cases, contract claims must be processed under the Contract Disputes Act while tort claims must be taken to a U.S. District Court pursuant to the FEDERAL TORT CLAIMS ACT (FTCA).

FRAUD   An intentional perversion of truth for the purpose of inducing someone to rely upon it and part with something of value or surrender a legal right. The three necessary elements of a cause of action for fraud are (1) false representation of a present or past fact on the part of the defendant, (2) a plaintiff's action in reliance upon that misrepresentation, and (3) damage resulting to the plaintiff from the action that was based on the misrepresentation. A fraudulent representation is a false statement as to a material fact that another party believes and relies upon, and that induces that other party to act to his or her injury. The speaker must know the statement to be false or must make the statement with utter disregard for its truth or falsity and must intend that the other party will rely upon the statement. Fraud and corruption offenses, typically characterized as white-collar crimes, fall into two main areas: (1) fraud and false statement offenses, which involve deceptive conduct (see FALSE CLAIMS ACT and FALSE STATEMENTS ACT) and (2) public corruption offenses, which involve bribery or illegal gratuities (see GRATUITY). See Seyfarth et al., The Government Contract Compliance Handbook 1-4 through 1-6. See Cibinic and Elmer, *Government Contract Fraud*, 16 Pub. Cont. L.J. 331 (1986); Smith, *Statutes Countering Contract Administration Fraud*, 87-5 Briefing Papers (April 1987).

FREE ON BOARD   See F.O.B.

FREEDOM OF INFORMATION ACT (FOIA)   An act, 5 U.S.C. 552, part of the Administrative Procedure Act passed in 1966, that provides a mechanism for members of the public (including contractors) to gain access to AGENCY RECORDs maintained by the Government. The act requires public disclosure unless records fall within one of nine exemptions listed in the act. The exemption most relevant to information submitted by contractors is Exemption 4 covering "trade secrets and commercial or financial information obtained from a person and privileged or confidential." Even if information falls within this exemption, an agency may release it unless such release would constitute an abuse of discretion. However, an abuse of discretion would normally be found if the information fell within the scope of the TRADE SECRETS ACT. Executive Order 12600, 23 June 1987, requires agencies to notify persons that have submitted information to the Government when a FOIA request for that information is received. See Alder, Litigation under the Federal Freedom of Information Act and Privacy Act. And see the Department of Justice *Freedom of Information Case List*, which includes the Justice Department Guide to the FOIA and is available from the U.S. Government Printing Office, Washington, DC 20402. The FAR's limited treatment of FOIA is in Subpart 24.2. DoD and NASA, however, provide expanded FOIA coverage. See DoD Directive 5400.7, *DoD Freedom of Information Act Program*, 13 May 1988, and NFS 18-24.202.

FRONT-END LOADING The inclusion in a BID or PROPOSAL of inflated prices on items to be delivered early in the performance of the contract and unduly low prices on later items. Front-end loading, or front loading, is a form of unbalanced bidding (see UNBALANCED BID) that is aimed at enabling the bidder to recover money in advance of the performance of the work. Front-end loading may be permissible so long as the bid will clearly result in the lowest overall cost to the Government. But it will cause a bid to be found nonresponsive (see RESPONSIVENESS) if it cannot be justified on the basis of substantial mobilization or equipment costs or when it is so egregious as to amount, substantively, to an ADVANCE PAYMENT. See Cibinic and Nash, Formation of Government Contracts 442; Shnitzer, Government Contract Bidding 11–21.

FRUSTRATION OF PURPOSE A legal doctrine that excuses a party to a contract from performing its contractual obligations in situations when the objectives of the contract have been utterly defeated by circumstances arising after the contract was formed. In such situations, performance is excused even though there is no impediment to actual performance. Black's Law Dictionary. This doctrine is rarely used in Government contracting.

FULFORD DOCTRINE A legal rule that permits a contractor's APPEAL FROM A CONTRACTING OFFICER'S DECISION assessing EXCESS COSTS OF REPROCUREMENT following a TERMINATION FOR DEFAULT to "revive" the issue of the propriety of the default termination itself, even though the contractor failed to appeal the default termination in timely fashion. The name is derived from the decision of the ARMED SERVICES BOARD OF CONTRACT APPEALS (ASBCA) in *Fulford Manufacturing Co.*, ASBCA No. 2144 (20 May 1955). One result of the rule is that, upon default of a contract, a contractor may choose not to litigate the issue of whether the Government properly terminated the contract. But if the Government later charges the contractor for the excess costs of reprocurement, the contractor may appeal that cost assessment and simultaneously challenge the Government's termination action. See Williamson and Medill-Jones, *Government Damages for Default*, 89-7 Briefing Papers 9 (June 1989); Cibinic, *Another Attack on the Fulford Doctrine: So Much for Judicial Economy*, 2 N&CR ¶ 1 (Jan. 1988).

FULL AND OPEN COMPETITION   A procurement in which all responsible sources (see RESPONSIBILITY) are permitted to compete for a contract. FAR 6.003. Under 10 U.S.C. 2304(a) and 41 U.S.C. 253(a), full and open competition is the established norm in Government contracting. However, 10 U.S.C. 2304(c) and 41 U.S.C. 253(c) provide for seven circumstances permitting other than full and open competition: (1) only one responsible source (see RESPONSIBILITY); (2) UNUSUAL AND COMPELLING URGENCY; (3) INDUSTRIAL MOBILIZATION, or the need to maintain engineering, developmental, or research capability; (4) international agreement; (5) statutory authorization or requirement; (6) risk of compromising the national security; and (7) protecting the public interest. See FAR 6.302 for additional guidance on these exceptions to the full and open competition rule. The statutes and regulations also provide substantial guidance on the type of COMPETITIVE PROCEDURES that meet the requirement for full and open competition. See FAR 6.102. FAR Subpart 6.1 prescribes the policy and procedures to be used to promote and provide for full and open competition. FAR Subpart 6.2 describes limited exceptions for full and open competition after exclusion of sources. FAR 6.303 provides guidance on the preparation of justifications and on obtaining approvals (see JUSTIFICATION AND APPROVAL) when full and open competition is not obtained. See Cibinic and Nash, Formation of Government Contracts 288–318.

FULL COST   All significant expenses incurred in operating a data processing facility. FIRMR 201-4.001. This term is used in conjunction with the procedures set forth in OMB Circular No.

A-130, *Management of Federal Information Resources*, 12 Dec. 1985. The term includes the following cost elements: (1) personnel—salaries, overtime, fringe benefits, training, and travel; (2) equipment—depreciation, leased costs, and direct expenses; (3) software; (4) supplies; (5) contracted services—consulting, maintenance, and data entry; (6) space occupancy—rentals, depreciation, furniture, equipment, heating and air conditioning, utilities, security, and custodial services; (7) intra-agency services and overhead, whether billed or allocated; and (8) interagency services, whether reimbursed or estimated.

FULL-SCALE DEVELOPMENT The final development phase of a MAJOR SYSTEM. This is the term in the FAR that is synonymous with the DoD term FULL-SCALE ENGINEERING DEVELOPMENT (FSED). FAR 34.005-5 provides that, whenever practicable, full-scale development contracts should require contractors to submit priced proposals for production that are based on the latest quantity, schedule, and LOGISTICS requirements and other considerations that will be used in making the production decision.

FULL-SCALE ENGINEERING DEVELOPMENT (FSED) The third phase in the DoD MAJOR SYSTEM ACQUISITION process, in which the SYSTEM and the principal items necessary for its support are fully developed, engineered, designed, fabricated, tested, and evaluated. Systems in this phase must be approved before entering the production phase. DFARS 235.001. This phase is also known as the engineering and manufacturing development phase. Its objectives are to (1) translate a promising design approach into a stable, producible, and cost-effective system design; (2) validate the manufacturing or production process; and (3) demonstrate through testing that the system will meet stated requirements. DoD Directive 5000.2, *Defense Acquisition Management Policies and Procedures*, 23 Feb. 1991, part 3.

FUNCTIONAL SPECIFICATIONS Specifications that describe work to be performed in terms of end purpose, or the Government's ultimate objective, rather than in terms of the way in which the work is to be performed. Functional specifications are broader descriptions of the work than PERFORMANCE SPECIFICATIONS and are aimed at permitting more open competition on the ways of accomplishing the Government's purpose. A functional specification may include a statement of the qualitative nature of the product and, when necessary, will contain the minimum essential characteristics the product must exhibit in order to satisfy its intended use. See Cibinic and Nash, Formation of Government Contracts 344–45.

FUNDED PENSION COST The portion of PENSION PLAN costs for a current or prior COST ACCOUNTING PERIOD that has been paid to a funding agency. FAR 31.001. FAR 31.205-6 provides detailed guidance on the allowability of pension costs and generally requires that such costs be funded.

FUTURE CONTRACT SAVINGS Saving resulting from a VALUE ENGINEERING CHANGE PROPOSAL (VECP) on future contract units scheduled for delivery during the 3-year period following acceptance of the first unit incorporating the VECP. FAR 48.104-1 contains guidance on Government–contractor sharing arrangements for such savings. The calculation of these savings is based on an estimate made by the CONTRACTING OFFICER (CO) as prescribed in paragraph (g) of the Value Engineering clause in FAR 52.248-1. If the INSTANT CONTRACT is a multiyear contract (see MULTIYEAR CONTRACTING), future contract savings include savings on quantities funded after VECP acceptance. See Cibinic and Nash, Administration of Government Contracts 309–10.

G

GATEWAY AIRPORT An airport used by a traveler at the beginning or end of a trip. "Gateway airport abroad" means the airport from which the traveler last embarks en route to the United States or at which the traveler first debarks in travel from the United States. "Gateway airport in the United States" means the last U.S. airport from which the traveler's flight departs or the first U.S. airport at which the traveler's flight arrives. FAR 47.401. These terms are used in the FAR Subpart 47.4 implementation of the FLY AMERICA ACT, which requires that Federal employees and their dependents, consultants, contractors, grantees, and others use U.S.-flag air carriers for U.S. Government-financed international air travel and transportation of their property or personal effects, to the extent that service by these carriers is available.

GENERAL ACCOUNTING OFFICE (GAO) A Government agency that is part of the legislative branch and that investigates matters relating to the receipt, disbursement, and application of public funds. Headed by the COMPTROLLER GENERAL (COMP. GEN.), GAO evaluates the performance of Government programs (and typically issues reports when the assessment is negative), and issues decisions concerning PROTESTs against award. See FAR Subpart 33.1. GAO has broad powers to audit contractors under the EXAMINATION OF RECORDS clause and occasionally investigates contractors in the course of auditing Government programs. GAO maintains a network of 14 regional and field offices and has 7 divisions, including 4 program divisions (General Government, Human Resources, National Security and International Affairs, and Resources, Community, and Economic Development) and 3 technical divisions (Financial Management, Information Management and Technology, and Program Evaluation and Methodology). See Hordell, *Everyone Has Heard of the United States General Accounting Office—But What Does It Do?* 36 Fed. B.

News & J. 328 (1989); Schnitzer, *GAO Bid Protests*, 86-12 Briefing Papers (Nov. 1986).

GENERAL AND ADMINISTRATIVE (G&A) EXPENSE Any management, financial, or other expense incurred by or allocated to a business unit for the general management and administration of the business unit as a whole. FAR 31.001. G&A expenses do not include those management expenses whose beneficial or causal relationship to COST OBJECTIVEs can be more directly measured by a base other than a cost input base representing the total activity of a business unit during a COST ACCOUNTING PERIOD. G&A expenses include certain indirect expenses, including a company's general and executive offices; executive compensation; the cost of staff services such as legal, accounting, public relations, financial, and similar expenses; and other miscellaneous expenses related to the overall business. Armed Services Pricing Manual (ASPM) vol. 1, app. B. Cost Accounting Standard 410, FAR 30.410, deals with the allocation of business unit G&A expenses to final cost objectives. See also ALLOCATION OF COST.

GENERAL APPROPRIATION See APPROPRIATION.

GENERAL CONTRACTOR A contractor with the entire responsibility for performing a contract for CONSTRUCTION. This term is used in the construction industry to designate the contractor that bids for a construction contract and bears the entire risk if the contract cannot be performed at the contract price. See Nash, chap. 1, Construction Contracting 3–5.

GENERALLY ACCEPTED ACCOUNTING PRINCIPLES (GAAP) Accounting principles that are generally accepted by commercial organizations doing business in the United States. Under FAR 31.201-2, such principles are a factor to be considered in determining whether a cost is an ALLOWABLE COST, if none of the COST ACCOUNTING STANDARDS (CAS) apply. In such cases, unless the FAR's selected COST PRINCIPLES applying to commercial contractors in FAR 31.205 specifically deal with an accounting issue, the GAAP will be likely to prevail. Thus, pronouncements of the FINANCIAL ACCOUNTING STANDARDS BOARD (FASB) and the extensive body of uncodified GAAP found in general practice or individual industry practice are automatically incorporated into Government contracts. See Apostolou and Crubley, Handbook of Governmental Accounting and Finance 3–63.

GENERAL PROVISIONS The standard clauses that are used by Government agencies in various types of contracts. Most of these clauses are set forth in FAR Part 52, and guidance on their use is set forth in the PROVISION AND CLAUSE MATRIX in FAR Part 52.301. The term also includes clauses specified in FAR Supplements for agency-wide use. FAR 52.102-1 provides that general provisions will be incorporated by reference to the regulations "to the maximum practical extent" rather than by placing the full text of the clauses in the contract document.

GENERAL SCOPE See SCOPE OF THE CONTRACT.

GENERAL SERVICES ADMINISTRATION (GSA) An agency in the executive branch with the function of procuring supplies and services (including construction) that are used in common by many agencies. GSA procures (1) common-use supplies and services under direct contracts and in conjunction with the FEDERAL SUPPLY SCHEDULES (FSS), (2) office buildings, (3) FEDERAL INFORMATION PROCESSING (FIP) RESOURCES pursuant to the BROOKS ACT (AUTOMATIC DATA PROCESSING PROCUREMENTS), and (4) TELECOMMUNICATIONS SERVICES. With DoD and NASA, GSA has responsibility for the promulgation of the FEDERAL ACQUISITION REGULATION (FAR). GSA also supports the FAR Secretariat, the focal point for managing the FAR. GSA also has responsibility for issuing the FEDERAL INFORMATION RESOURCES MANAGEMENT REGULATION (FIRMR). See the U.S. Government Manual.

GENERAL SERVICES ADMINISTRATION BOARD OF CONTRACT APPEALS (GSBCA) The BOARD OF CONTRACT APPEALS (BCA) for the GENERAL SERVICES ADMINISTRATION (GSA) and certain other Federal agencies. As the second largest board, the GSBCA has 12 ADMINISTRATIVE JUDGEs. The GSBCA resolves disputes involving GSA as well as the Departments of the Treasury, Commerce, and Education; the Federal Communications Commission (FCC) and Nuclear Regulatory Commission (NRC); and the SMALL BUSINESS ADMINISTRATION (SBA). It also has jurisdiction to rule on PROTESTs involving any agency that is procuring FEDERAL INFORMATION PROCESSING (FIP) RESOURCES under the BROOKS ACT (AUTOMATIC DATA PROCESSING PROCURE-

MENTS). See Tolle and Duffey, *GSBCA Bid Protests*, 87-4 Briefing Papers (Mar. 1987).

GLOBAL SETTLEMENT A settlement between a contractor and the Government resolving criminal, civil, and administrative disputes with the Government through simultaneous, coordinated, comprehensive agreements. The term is generally used to describe the settlement of administrative proceedings involving a SUSPENSION or DEBARMENT as well as the settlement of any criminal charges arising out of a contractor's actions. See D'Aloisio, *Accusations of Criminal Conduct by Government Contractors: The Remedies, Problems, and Solutions*, 17 Pub. Cont. L.J. 265, 300 (1987); Bennett and Kriegel, *Negotiating Global Settlements of Procurement Fraud Cases*, 16 Pub. Cont. L.J. 30 (1986).

GOALS AND TIMETABLES A series of annual goals by labor category that a contractor establishes in an attempt to increase its minority employment as part of its AFFIRMATIVE ACTION commitment to the Government. These goals and timetables are not a firm contractual commitment but are an agreement to use best efforts to meet them. See FAR Subpart 22.8; 41 CFR 60-1 and 60-2.

GOOD FAITH AND FAIR DEALING See DUTY OF GOOD FAITH AND FAIR DEALING.

GOODS All things (including specially manufactured goods) that are movable at the time of identification to the contractor for sale, other than the money in which the price is to be paid, investment securities, and things in action. U.C.C. 2-105. Article 2 of the UNIFORM COMMERCIAL CODE (U.C.C.) governs contracts for the sale of goods throughout the United States, except in Louisiana. Government contracts for goods are called "supply contracts" and generally are not subject to Article 2 of the U.C.C. See SUPPLIES.

GOODWILL An intangible ASSET resulting when the price paid by an acquiring company exceeds the sum of the identifiable individual assets acquired less liabilities assumed, based upon their fair values. FAR 31.205-49 specifies that costs resulting from such goodwill are UNALLOWABLE COSTs.

GOVERNMENT BILL OF LADING (GBL) See BILL OF LADING.

GOVERNMENT CONTRACTOR DEFENSE A legal defense to a product liability claim (brought by or on behalf of a person injured by the product) that is available to Government contractors under certain scenarios. The defense permits the contractor to enjoy the Government's SOVEREIGN IMMUNITY from liability for the injury. The contractor escapes liability if (1) the U.S. Government approved reasonably precise specifications for the contractor, (2) the contractor's equipment conformed to those specifications, and (3) the supplier warned the Government about the dangers in the use of the equipment that were known to the supplier but not to the Government. See Michaels, *The Government Contractor Defense: The Limits of Immunity after Boyle*, 33 A.F. L. Rev. 147 (1990); Dempsey and Barsy, *Government Contractor Liability for Design Defects after Boyle*, 19 Pub. Cont. L.J. 405 (1990); Haizlip, *The Government Contractor Defense in Tort Liability: A Continuing Genesis*, 19 Pub. Cont. L.J. 116 (1989); Vacketta et al., *The "Government Contractor Defense" in Environmental Actions*, 89-13 Briefing Papers (Dec. 1989).

GOVERNMENT DELAY OF WORK See COMPENSABLE DELAY.

GOVERNMENT-FURNISHED MATERIAL (GFM) Property furnished to a contractor by the Government that may be incorporated into or attached to a deliverable end item or that may be consumed or expended in performing a contract. Material includes assemblies, components, parts, raw and processed materials, and small tools and supplies that may be consumed in normal use in performing a contract. FAR 45.301. The material in the possession of or directly acquired by the Government and subsequently made available to the contractor constitutes Government-furnished material. See also GOVERNMENT-FURNISHED PROPERTY (GFP).

GOVERNMENT-FURNISHED PROPERTY (GFP) Property in the possession of or directly acquired by the Government that is subsequently made available to the contractor. FAR 45.101. GFP is included in the broad term GOVERNMENT PROPERTY, which is subject to the policies and procedures of FAR Part 45.

GOVERNMENT-OWNED, CONTRACTOR-OPERATED PLANT (GOCO) An industrial or R&D facility that is owned by the Government but operated by a contractor. The procedures used in contracting for the operation of GOCOs are set forth in

FAR Subpart 17.6 dealing with MANAGEMENT AND OPERATING (M&O) CONTRACTs.

GOVERNMENT PRINTING   Printing, binding, and blankbook work for the use of an executive department, independent agency, or establishment of the Government. FAR 8.801. 44 U.S.C. 501 *et seq.* requires that such printing be done by the U.S. Government Printing Office (GPO) with specified exceptions. See FAR 8.802.

GOVERNMENT PRODUCTION AND RESEARCH PROPERTY   Government-owned FACILITIES, Government-owned SPECIAL TEST EQUIPMENT, and special Blank Sidetooling to which the Government has title or the right to acquire title. FAR 45.301. The CONTRACTING OFFICER (CO) must, "to the maximum practical extent," eliminate COMPETITIVE ADVANTAGE accruing to a contractor possessing such property under the procedures in FAR Subpart 45.2. Contractors are authorized to use such property under the procedures in FAR Subpart 45.4.

GOVERNMENT PROPERTY   All property owned by or leased to the Government or acquired by the Government under the terms of the contract. FAR 45.101. It includes both GOVERNMENT-FURNISHED PROPERTY (GFP) and CONTRACTOR-ACQUIRED PROPER-TY. FAR Part 45 contains detailed guidance on the policies and procedures relating to Government property.   FAR 45.103 provides that contractors are responsible and liable for Government property in their possession unless the contract provides otherwise. FAR Subpart 45.5 contains dctailcd guidance on the management of Government property in the possession of contractors.   See Cleary, *Government-Furnished Property: Government-Furnished Problems,* 22 NCMJ 1 (1989); Rindner, *For Beginners Only: Button, Button, Who Owns the Button?* 29 Cont. Mgmt. 16 (Aug. 1989).

GOVERNMENT-PURPOSE LICENSE RIGHTS (GPLR)   The right to use, duplicate, and disclose data, in whole or in part and in any manner, for Government purposes only, and to have or permit others to do so for Government purposes only. DFARS 227.401.   Government purposes include procurement under COMPETITIVE PROCEDURES, but do not include the right to have or permit others to use TECHNICAL DATA for commercial purposes. DFARS 227.402-72(a)(2) provides that, to encourage commercial utilization of technologies developed under Government contracts, the Government—instead of insisting on UNLIMITED RIGHTS—may agree to accept technical data subject to GPLR for a limited period of time. After that period, the Government is entitled to unlimited rights. DoD policy is that the Government should not agree to accept GPLR when technical data are likely to be needed to permit competitive procurement involving large numbers of potential competitors (for items such as spares) or when technical data must be published. GPLR can also be used when the technical data pertains to items, components, or processes developed with mixed funding. See DFARS 227.472-72(c). Contractors are required to notify the Government if they desire to negotiate agreements calling for GPLR. See the procedures in DFARS 227.403-70.

GOVERNMENT VERSUS CONTRACTOR PERFORMANCE See A-76 POLICY.

GOVERNMENT VESSEL A vessel owned by the U.S. Government and operated directly by the Government or for the Government by an agent or contractor, including a privately owned U.S.-flag vessel under bareboat charter to the Government. FAR 47.501. Such a vessel is included in the definition of U.S.-FLAG VESSEL for the purpose of the cargo preference regulations in FAR Subpart 47.5.

GRANT A legal instrument for transferring money, property, or services to the recipient in order to accomplish a public purpose of support or stimulation where there will be no substantial involvement between the Federal agency and the recipient during performance. Federal Grant and Cooperative Agreement Act of 1977, 31 U.S.C. 6304. This act distinguishes Federal assistance relationships, or grants and COOPERATIVE AGREEMENTs, from procurement relationships, or contracts. Unlike a contract, which is a legal instrument for acquiring supplies or services for the direct benefit of or use by the Federal Government, a grant—like a cooperative agreement—has, as its main purpose, support or stimulation. A grant differs from a cooperative agreement in that, under a cooperative agreement, there is substantial involvement between the Federal agency and the recipient during performance of the contemplated activity, whereas under a grant there is not. Cappalli, I Federal Grants and Cooperative Agreements 1-136 and 1-137. Grants are not subject to the FEDERAL ACQUISITION REGULATION (FAR). The term "grant" is an ambiguous term in that it is used to refer to agreements with private organizations (such as research grants) as well as arrangements where the Federal Government provides funds to State and local governments. With regard to the latter usage, there are three general types of grants: (1) categorical grants, (2) block grants, and (3) revenue sharing grants (currently not in use). See Riley, III Federal Contracts, Grants and Assistance 85–86.

GRATUITY Something acquired without bargain or inducement; something given freely or voluntarily in return for a favor or a service. Black's Law Dictionary. The Illegal Gratuities statute, 18 U.S.C. 201, applies to offers and solicitations of gifts, as well as acceptance of gifts, and, for practical purposes, prevents all gifts to public officials made to influence or appear to influence acts. The statute requires only a showing of wrongful purpose in offering or accepting a thing of value for or because of an official act. FAR Subparts 3.1 and 3.2 spell out the Government's policy on gratuities offered to or solicited by contracting personnel. Gratuities are also prohibited by the PROCUREMENT INTEGRITY rules. See Seyfarth et al., The Government Contract Compliance Handbook 1-23; Kenney and Sweeney, *Gratuities*, 90-3 Briefing Papers (Feb. 1990).

GROSS MISTAKE AMOUNTING TO FRAUD A major mistake so serious or uncalled for as not to be reasonably expected, or justifiable, in the case of a responsible contractor, or a mistake that cannot be reconciled in good faith. *Catalytic Eng'g & Manufacturing Corp.*, ASBCA 15257, 72-1 BCA ¶ 9342. This type of mistake overcomes the finality of ACCEPTANCE OF WORK in the Inspection of Supplies—Fixed-Price clause, FAR 52.246-2, and the Inspection of Construction clause, FAR 52.246-12.

GSA See GENERAL SERVICES ADMINISTRATION (GSA).

GSA SCHEDULE See FEDERAL SUPPLY SCHEDULES (FSS).

GUARANTEED LOAN A loan, revolving credit fund, or other financial arrangement made pursuant to Regulation V of the Federal Reserve Board (sometimes called a "V loan") under which funds are distributed, collected, and administered by the lending institution and the Federal guaranteeing agency is obligated, on demand of the lender, to purchase a stated percentage of the loan and to share any losses in the amount of the guaranteed percentage. FAR 32.301. Government funds are not involved except for the purchase of the guaranteed portion of the loan for the settlement of losses. Armed Services Pricing Manual (ASPM) vol. 1, app. B. Section 301 of the Defense Production Act of 1950, 50 U.S.C. app. 2061 *et seq.*, authorizes loan guarantees for contract performance or other operations related to the national defense, subject to amounts annually authorized by Congress. FAR 32.106 states that guaranteed loans are a preferred form of FINANCING over UNUSUAL PROGRESS PAYMENTs and ADVANCE PAYMENTs.

GUIDELINES FOR THE ACQUISITION OF INVESTIGA-TIONS See ANNOUNCEMENT OF OPPORTUNITY (AO).

H

HAMILTON STIPULATION A stipulation, relating to an uncertified CLAIM before a BOARD OF CONTRACT APPEALS (BCA), that the contracting officer was aware of the claim, considered it, and would have denied it formally had it been properly certified at the time of submission. The CONTRACT DISPUTES ACT (CDA) OF 1978 states that a contractor's demand or assertion seeking payment of a sum exceeding $50,000 does not become a claim until certified. However, in *United States v. Hamilton Enterprises*, 711 F.2d 1038 (Fed. Cir. 1983), the COURT OF APPEALS FOR THE FEDERAL CIRCUIT (CAFC or Fed. Cir.) held that "there was substantial compliance with the certification requirements" of the CDA, even though the contractor had not certified and therefore had not formally asserted its claim until it appealed the contracting officer's denial. Thus, the stipulation generates a sufficient basis for jurisdiction by a BCA to overcome the untimely certification and the lack of a final DECISION OF THE CONTRACTING OFFICER. Now referred to as a "Hamilton stipulation," this option is periodically suggested by BCAs. See also CERTIFICATION OF CLAIM.

HEAD OF THE AGENCY The Secretary, Attorney General, Administrator, Governor, Chairperson, or other chief official of an executive agency, including any deputy or assistant chief official of the executive agency and, in DoD, the Under Secretary and any Assistant Secretary of the Departments of the Army, Navy, and Air Force and the Director and Deputy Director of the Defense agencies. The term "authorized representative" means any person (other than the contracting officer), persons, or board authorized to act for the head of the agency or Secretary. FAR 2.101. DFARS 202.101 provides a more specific, detailed listing for DoD. FAR DEVIATIONs must be approved by heads of an agency. FAR 1.403, 1.404.

HEAD OF THE CONTRACTING ACTIVITY (HCA) The official with overall responsibility for managing the CONTRACTING ACTIVITY. FAR 2.101. Examples of contracting activities are the Naval Sea Systems Command, the Air Force Logistics Command, NASA's Goddard Space Flight Center, and GSA's Federal Supply Service. Some actions in the procurement process may be taken only by the HCA (not a contracting office).

HIGH-VALUE ITEM A contract end item that (1) has a high unit cost (normally exceeding $100,000 per unit), such as an aircraft, an aircraft engine, a communication system, a computer system, a missile, or a ship, and (2) is designated by the contracting officer as a high-value item. FAR 46.802. FAR 46.803 states the Government policy to relieve the contractor of liability for loss of or damage to such items. This is done by including in the contract the Limitation of Liability—High Value Item clause in FAR 52.246-24.

HISTORICAL COST The ACTUAL COST incurred by a contractor in performing the work. In *Bruce Constr. Corp. v. United States*, 163 Ct. Cl. 97, 324 F.2d 516 (1963), it was held that the measure for determining the amount of an EQUITABLE ADJUSTMENT is reasonable cost (see REASONABLENESS OF COST) plus an allowance for profit, and that historical cost, rather than FAIR MARKET VALUE, was presumed to be the proper measure of reasonable cost. This rule gives greater weight to a particular contractor's actual cost than to the determination of what the cost would have been to other contractors in general. 10 U.S.C. 2324(j) seeks to overcome the presumption of validity of historical costs with regard to indirect cost rulings by providing that contractors have the burden of proof of reasonableness when litigating such costs. FAR 31.201-3(a) carries this logic further by stating that contractors have the burden of proof when any cost is challenged as unreasonable.

HISTORICALLY BLACK COLLEGES AND UNIVERSITIES (HBCUs) Institutions that the Secretary of Education has determined meet the requirements of 34 CFR 608.2. In furtherance of the Government policy of placing a fair proportion of its acquisitions with HBCUs, MINORITY INSTITUTIONs (MIs), and SMALL DISADVANTAGED BUSINESS CONCERNs (SDBCs), section 1207 of Pub. L. 99-661 (10 U.S.C. 2301), section 806 of Pub. L. 100-180 (10 U.S.C. 2301), and section 831 of Pub. L. 101-189 (10

U.S.C. 2301) established an objective for DoD of awarding a combined total of 5 percent of its total contract dollars during each fiscal year 1987–1993 to HBCUs, MIs, and SDBs and of maximizing the number of such entities participating in Defense prime contracts and subcontracts. See DFARS 226.7003; Lambert and Shillito, *DOD Implements Congressional Mandate to Meet a Five Percent Contract Goal for Minorities*, 27 Cont. Mgmt. 16 (Oct. 1987). And see *An Inventory of the Capabilities of the Historically Black Colleges and Universities and Other Minority Institutions (HBCUs/MIs): A NAFEO/DoD Survey* (1989), available from the National Association for Equal Opportunity in Higher Education, 2243 Wisconsin Ave., N.W., Washington, DC 20007; 202/543-9111.

HOME OFFICE   An office responsible for directing or managing two or more, but not necessarily all, SEGMENTs of an organization. FAR 31.001. A home office typically establishes policy for, and provides guidance to, the segments in their operations. It usually performs management, supervisory, or administrative functions and may also perform support service functions. An organization that has intermediate levels, such as groups, may have several home offices reporting to a common home office. An intermediate organization may be both a segment and a home office. To the maximum extent practicable, home office expenses must be allocated directly to segments on the basis of the beneficial or causal relationship between supporting and receiving activities. See Cost Accounting Standard 403, FAR 30.403; Wingfield, *Contractor's Right To Recover Extended Home Office Overhead: The Capital Elective Case*, 19 Pub. Cont. Newsl. 3 (Summer 1984).

HOTLINE   A mechanism by which employees may report suspected instances of improper conduct. DoD operates a hotline and requires that contractors performing contracts expected to exceed $5 million display DoD Hotline Posters prominently in common work areas (or, alternatively, that they establish a comparable internal mechanism and encourage employee reporting). DFARS Subpart 203.70; 252.203-7002. See Whitlock, *How to Establish a Hot Line Reporting System That Works*, 29 Cont. Mgmt. 48 (Nov. 1989); Nadler, *Corporate Ethics: Guidelines for an Effective Hot Line Program*, 29 Cont. Mgmt. 4 (Aug. 1989); Seyfarth et al., The Government Contract Compliance Handbook, chap. 2.

I

IDENTICAL BIDS Bids for the same LINE ITEM that are determined to be identical in unit price or total line item amount, with or without the application of evaluation factors (such as, discounts or transportation cost). FAR 3.302. FAR 3.303(d) requires the reporting of such bids as possible ANTITRUST VIOLATIONS when there is some reason to suspect collusion between the bidders.

IDLE CAPACITY The unused capacity of partially used facilities. FAR 31.205-17. It is the difference between (1) what a facility could achieve under 100 percent operating time on a one-shift basis (or, in some cases, a multiple-shift basis) less operating interruptions resulting from time for repairs, setups, unsatisfactory materials, and other normal delays, and (2) the extent to which the facility was actually used to meet demands during the COST ACCOUNTING PERIOD. Costs of idle capacity are costs of doing business and are a factor in the normal fluctuations of use or overhead rates from period to period. Such costs are ALLOWABLE COSTs, provided the capacity is necessary or was originally reasonable and is not subject to reduction or elimination by subletting, renting, or sale, in accordance with sound business, economic, or security practices.

IDLE FACILITIES Completely unused facilities that are excess to the contractor's current needs. FAR 31.205-17. The costs of idle facilities are UNALLOWABLE COSTs unless the facilities (1) are necessary to meet fluctuations in workload or (2) were necessary when acquired and are now idle because of changes in requirements, production economies, reorganization, termination, or other causes that could not reasonably have been foreseen.

IMMEDIATE-GAIN ACTUARIAL COST METHOD Any of several ACTUARIAL COST METHODs under which actuarial gains and losses are included as part of the unfunded ACTUARIAL LIABILITY of a PENSION PLAN, rather than as part of the normal cost of the plan. FAR 31.001. Actuarial gains and losses under a pension plan whose costs are measured by this actuarial cost method must be amortized over a 15-year period in equal annual installments, beginning with the date of the actuarial valuation. FAR 30.413-50(a)(2).

IMPLIED AUTHORITY CONTRACTING OFFICER (CO) authority that is implied from the facts of the transaction rather than delegated in writing in accordance with FAR Subpart 1.6. Implied authority is found by the courts and boards when they determine that the Government should be bound by the acts of agency employees who do not have formal contracting officer authority. It generally flows from acts that a contracting officer was, or should have been, aware of. See Cibinic and Nash, Administration of Government Contracts 31–33; Reifel and Bastianelli, *Contracting Officer Authority*, 86-4 Briefing Papers (Mar. 1986).

IMPLIED CONTRACT A contract not created or evidenced by an explicit agreement of the parties but inferred, as a matter of reason and justice, from the parties' acts or conduct; in other words, the circumstances surrounding the transaction making it reasonable or even necessary to assume that a contract existed between the parties by tacit understanding. Implied contracts are sometimes divided into (1) those implied in fact, which derive from the above definition, and (2) those implied in law, often referred to as "quasi-contracts," which derive from obligations imposed upon a person by the law, not pursuant to the person's intention and agreement, either expressed or implied, but even against the person's will and design, because the circumstances between the parties are such as to render it just that one party should have a right, and the other party a corresponding liability, similar to those that would arise from a contract between them. Black's Law Dictionary. The CLAIMS COURT (Cl. Ct.) has jurisdiction over contracts implied in fact but not over contracts implied in law. 28 U.S.C. 1491(a)(1). See Cibinic and Nash, Formation of Government Contracts 179–85.

IMPLIED DUTY See IMPLIED PROMISE.

IMPLIED PROMISE A promise of a contracting party that is implied from the facts of the transaction. There are a number of implied promises that attach to most contracts, such as the implied DUTY OF GOOD FAITH AND FAIR DEALING and the implied DUTY TO COOPERATE. The Government is also held to an IMPLIED WARRANTY OF SPECIFICATIONS when it furnishes design specifications to a contractor and to an implied duty to disclose information (see SUPERIOR KNOWLEDGE) when it has vital information needed by a contractor to permit successful performance..

IMPLIED WARRANTY OF SPECIFICATIONS The warranty of the Government that its design SPECIFICATIONs can be successfully used to perform a contract. When a contractor fails to perform because of defective specifications, it can assert a CONSTRUCTIVE CHANGE claim in order to obtain an EQUITABLE ADJUSTMENT in the contract price. See Cibinic and Nash, Administration of Government Contracts 199–221; Harrington et al., *The Owner's Warranty of the Plans and Specifications for a Construction Project*, 14 Pub. Cont. L. J. 240 (1984).

IMPOSSIBILITY OF PERFORMANCE A legal doctrine deriving from the concept that an implied condition exists under which the parties to a contract intended to dissolve their contractual obligations upon an individual's death or incapacity or upon the destruction or loss of vital and irreplaceable materials. Thus, a party encountering impossibility of performance will have a defense against a suit for BREACH OF CONTRACT. Discussion of impossibility of performance typically references concepts of IMPRACTICABILITY OF PERFORMANCE and FRUSTRATION OF PURPOSE. "Impossibility" generally means technical or physical impossibility—that is, on the basis of all human experience, a thing clearly cannot be done; "impracticability of performance" typically includes unforeseen cost increases, extreme financial difficulty, illegality, or other situations in which a court may excuse lack of performance. Schooner, *Impossibility of Performance in Public Contracts: An Economic Analysis*, 16 Pub. Cont. L.J. 229 (1986). "Existing impossibility" refers to an impossibility of performance existing when the contract was entered into, so that the contract was to do something that was impossible from the outset; "supervening impossibility" refers to impossibility that developed after the inception of the contract. Ballentine's Law Dictionary. If a party has assumed the risk of impossibility, it will be denied the use of the defense and will be held liable for breach of contract. Very few experienced contractors have been able to prove that they did not assume the risk of impossibility. See

Martell and Meagher, *Impossibility of Performance/Edition III*, 88-7 Briefing Papers (June 1988); Vogel, *Impossibility of Performance—A Closer Look*, 9 Pub. Cont. L.J. 110 (1977).

IMPRACTICABILITY OF PERFORMANCE   Extreme and unreasonable difficulty, expense, injury, or loss to a contracting party. Restatement (Second) of Contracts § 261, comment d. See also U.C.C. 2-615. The Restatement gives as examples severe shortages of raw materials or supplies due to war, embargo, local crop failure, or unforeseen shutdown of major sources of supply, all of which cause a marked increase in costs. It warns, however, that a mere change in the degree of difficulty due to such causes as increased wages, prices of raw materials, or costs of construction, unless well beyond the normal range, does not amount to impracticability. The term derives from the legal concept of IMPOSSIBILITY OF PERFORMANCE and has the same legal effect: it excuses a party from performing a contract unless that party has assumed the risk of the event. In Government contracting, impracticability has also been treated as a type of CONSTRUCTIVE CHANGE giving a contractor that has incurred extra costs an EQUITABLE ADJUSTMENT. See Nash, Government Contract Changes 13-36 through 13-51; Cibinic and Nash, Administration of Government Contracts 225–33; Schooner, *Impossibility of Performance in Public Contracts: An Economic Analysis*, 16 Pub. Cont. L.J. 229 (1986).

IMPREST FUND   A cash fund (also known as "petty cash") of a fixed amount established by an advance of funds, without charge to an APPROPRIATION, from an agency finance or disbursing officer to a duly appointed cashier, for distribution as needed from time to time in making payment in cash for relatively small purchases. FAR 13.401. Imprest funds may be used for SMALL PURCHASEs when (1) the transaction does not exceed $500 or another limit approved by the HEAD OF THE AGENCY, (2) the use of imprest funds is considered to be advantageous to the Government, and (3) the use of imprest funds complies with any additional conditions established by agencies and certain Department of the Treasury and General Accounting Office manuals. FAR 13.402, 13.404. See also DFARS Subpart 213.4; DoD Instruction 7360.10, *Disbursing Policies*, 17 Jan. 1989; and NFS Subpart 18-13.4.

IMPROPER BUSINESS PRACTICES A broad range of activities forbidden or limited by FAR Part 3 with regard to the award and performance of Government contracts. The prohibitions and guidelines are based on the premise that Government business must be conducted in a manner above reproach and, except as otherwise authorized by statute or regulation, with complete impartiality and preferential treatment for none. Transactions relating to the expenditure of public funds should merit the highest degree of public trust and reflect an impeccable standard of conduct. FAR 3.101-1. The FAR discusses the following improper or potentially improper business practices: contractor gratuities (see GRATUITY) to Government personnel (Subpart 3.2); ANTITRUST VIOLATIONs (Subpart 3.3); CONTINGENT FEEs (Subpart 3.4); BUYING IN (3.501); KICKBACKs (3.502); unreasonable restrictions on subcontractor sales (3.503); and contracts with Government employees or organizations owned or controlled by them (Subpart 3.6). It also discusses the voiding and rescinding of contracts in relation to which improper business practices have been found (Subpart 3.7) and addresses PROCUREMENT INTEGRITY (FAR 3.104). FAR Part 3, while containing some specific guidance, is incomplete in terms of total coverage of improper business practices. See STANDARDS OF CONDUCT for other applicable coverage. And see Brunsman, *Standards of Conduct and Business Ethics for Buyers*, 27 Cont. Mgmt. 18 (June 1987).

IMPROVEMENT CURVE See LEARNING CURVE.

IMPUTED KNOWLEDGE Knowledge possessed by a Government employee that is ascribed to a CONTRACTING OFFICER (CO) by virtue of the relationship presumed to exist between the employee and the contracting officer. The principle of imputed knowledge is based on the common law concept that a principal is charged with knowledge that an agent has a duty to deliver to the principal. Courts and boards of contract appeals frequently assume that responsible Government employees will convey their knowledge to the contracting officer. The imputed knowledge issue arises, for example, in cases in which a contractor has failed to give formal notice of an event as required by one of the contract's adjustment clauses (such as the CHANGEs, DIFFERING SITE CONDITIONS, or SUSPENSION OF WORK clauses) but has made a Government employee aware of the event. In such a case, the courts and Boards frequently refuse to deny, solely on grounds that formal notice was not given to the contracting officer, contractor CLAIMs for price adjustment. See Cibinic and Nash, Administration of Government Contracts 40–44.

INCENTIVE COMPENSATION   Compensation paid to an employee to motivate good performance. FAR 31.205-6(f) specifies when the cost of such compensation by a contractor may be treated as an ALLOWABLE COST.

INCENTIVE CONTRACT   A negotiated pricing arrangement that gives the contractor higher profits for better performance and/or lower profits for worse performance in prescribed areas (cost, delivery, or technical performance). The standard types of incentive contract are prescribed in FAR Subpart 16.4. These include (1) contracts where the profit adjustment is made in accordance with a preestablished formula, such as FIXED-PRICE INCENTIVE (FPI) CONTRACTs (with firm or successive targets) and COST-PLUS-INCENTIVE FEE (CPIF) CONTRACTs; and (2) contracts where the profit adjustment is made by unilateral determination of an officer of the Government, such as COST-PLUS-AWARD FEE (CPAF) CONTRACTs. Additional guidance on incentive contracts is contained in Armed Services Pricing Manual (ASPM) vol. 1, chap. 1. Incentive contracts are designed to achieve specific acquisition objectives by (1) establishing reasonable and attainable targets that are clearly communicated to the contractor and (2) including appropriate incentive arrangements designed to (a) motivate contractor efforts and (b) discourage contractor inefficiency and waste. FAR 16.401. See Cibinic and Nash, Formation of Government Contracts 745–90; Fisher, *Risk Management for Incentive Contracts*, 29 Cont. Mgmt. 23 (Jan. 1989).

INCURRED COST   A cost identified through the use of the accrual method of accounting and reporting, or otherwise actually paid. Although a commercial definition of incurred costs would include all costs actually paid or properly accrued, the Government guidance may limit the definition to include only allowable costs. Thus, Armed Services Pricing Manual (ASPM) vol. 1, chap. 3, states that incurred costs include the costs of direct LABOR, direct materials, and direct services identified with and necessary for the performance of a contract, plus all properly allocable and allowable indirect costs as shown by the contractor's books. See ALLOCABLE COST and ALLOWABLE COST. Compare DCAA Contract Audit Manual (CAM) 6-102, which, in discussing audit objectives for and approaches to incurred costs, explains that the auditor's objective is to examine the contractor's cost representations, in whatever form they may be presented, and express an opinion whether the incurred costs (1) are reasonable, applicable to the contract, and determined according to GENERALLY ACCEPTED ACCOUNTING PRINCIPLES (GAAP) and COST ACCOUNTING STANDARDS (CAS) applicable in the circumstances; and (2) are not prohibited by the contract, by Government statute or regulation, or by previous agreement with, or decision of, a Government contracting officer.

INDEFINITE-DELIVERY CONTRACT   A type of contract in which the time of delivery is unspecified in the original contract but established by the contracting officer during performance. FAR Subpart 16.5 contains guidance on three types of indefinite-delivery contract: (1) DEFINITE-QUANTITY CONTRACTs, (2) REQUIREMENTS CONTRACTs, and (3) INDEFINITE-QUANTITY CONTRACTs.   FAR 16.501 states that the appropriate type of indefinite-delivery contract may be used when the exact times and/or quantities of future deliveries are not known at the time of contract award. Indefinite-delivery contracts permit maintenance of Government stocks at minimum levels and direct shipment to users.   Indefinite-delivery contracts may be FIRM-FIXED-PRICE (FFP) CONTRACTs, FIXED-PRICE CONTRACTs WITH ECONOMIC PRICE ADJUSTMENT, or FIXED-PRICE REDETERMINATION—PROSPECTIVE (FPRP) CONTRACTs, and their prices may be based on ESTABLISHED CATALOG OR MARKET PRICES. DoD notes that for items with a shelf life of less than 6 months, consideration should be given to use of these contracts along with simplified purchasing requirements. DFARS 216.501.

INDEFINITE-QUANTITY CONTRACT A contract providing for an indefinite quantity, within stated maximum or minimum limits, of specific supplies or services to be furnished during a fixed period, with deliveries to be scheduled by placing orders with the contractor. FAR 16.504(a). The contractor is legally bound to such a contract because the Government promises to procure, as CONSIDERATION, a minimum quantity that is more than a nominal quantity. The contract requires the Government to order at least the quantity designated as the minimum, and requires the contractor to furnish, when ordered, supplies or services up to and including the quantity designated as the maximum. The contract may also specify maximum or minimum quantities that the

Government may order under each delivery order and the maximum that it may order during a specific period of time. An indefinite-quantity contract should be used only when a recurring need is anticipated. Funds for other than the stated minimum quantity are obligated by each delivery order, not by the contract itself. See Cibinic and Nash, Formation of Government Contracts 854–59.

INDEMNIFICATION The agreement of a contracting party to hold the other party harmless, to secure the other party against loss or damage, or to give security for the reimbursement of the other party in case of an anticipated loss. Black's Law Dictionary. The Government does not generally require contractors to indemnify the Government, or protect the Government from liability, but a similar result is achieved in those cases where the Government requires the contractor to purchase INSURANCE or protect itself through SELF-INSURANCE.   See, for example, the Insurance—Liability to Third Persons clause in FAR 52.228-7. FAR 31.205-19 contains the cost principle on insurance and indemnification. The Government indemnifies contractors against losses only in unusual circumstances. See Nash and Cibinic, II Federal Procurement Law 1937–39, for a discussion of statutes that have permitted such indemnification. FAR Subpart 50.4 and the Indemnification under Public Law 85-804 clause at FAR 52.250-1 contain guidance on indemnifying contractors against unusually hazardous or nuclear risks. NASA, however, has its own indemnification clause, which is more specific than the FAR clause regarding the conditions under which the Government will indemnify or will not be held liable. NFS Subpart 18-50.4 and 18-52.250-70. NASA also has a special clause for unusually hazardous risks associated with space activity.   NFS 18-52.250-72.

INDEPENDENT RESEARCH AND DEVELOPMENT (IR&D)
A contractor's R&D effort that is not sponsored by, or required in performance of, a contract or grant and that consists of projects falling within the following areas: (1) BASIC RESEARCH, (2) APPLIED RESEARCH, (3) DEVELOPMENT, and (4) systems and other concept formulation studies. FAR 31.205-18(a). IR&D does not include (1) technical effort expended in developing and preparing TECHNICAL DATA specifically to support submission of an offer or (2) manufacturing engineering effort to develop or improve manufacturing or production materials, systems, processes,

methods, equipment, tools, and techniques not intended for sale. IR&D costs, together with BID AND PROPOSAL (B&P) COSTS, are generally ALLOWABLE COSTs under FAR 31.205-18, subject to negotiated cost ceilings contained in mandatory ADVANCE AGREEMENTs for major companies and proper allocation under Cost Accounting Standard 420, FAR 30.420. Additional limitations may be placed by the contracting officer on IR&D allocated to DoD contracts. DFARS 231.205-18. See Victorino and Briggerman, *The IR&D/B&P/Selling Costs Dilemma*, 87-10 Briefing Papers (Sep. 1987).

INDIAN PREFERENCE A policy established in 1975 by section 7(b) of the Indian Self-Determination and Education Assistance Act, 25 U.S.C. 450-450n, 455-458e, for contracts and subcontracts entered into under the act, as well as other contracts or subcontracts with Indian organizations or for the benefit of Indians. The policy requires that (1) preference and training/education opportunities in contract administration be given to Indians and (b) preference in SUBCONTRACTing be given to Indian organizations and Indian-owned economic enterprises. The Indian Preference Program is used primarily by the Bureau of Indian Affairs and the Indian Health Service but may be used by other contracting activities. See also BUY INDIAN ACT.

INDIAN TRIBE Any Indian tribe, band, nation, or other organized group or community of Indians, including any Alaska Native Corporation as defined in 13 CFR 124.100, which is recognized as eligible for the special programs and services provided by the United States to Indians because of their status as Indians, or which is recognized as such by the State in which the tribe, band, nation, group, or community resides. FAR 19.001. See also NATIVE AMERICANS.

INDIRECT COST Any cost not directly identified with a single final COST OBJECTIVE but identified with two or more final cost objectives, or with at least one intermediate cost objective. FAR 31.203. Also referred to as "overhead" or "burden." After direct costs have been determined and charged directly to the contract or other work, indirect costs are those remaining to be allocated to the several cost objectives. An indirect cost must not be allocated to a final cost objective if other costs incurred for the same purpose in like circumstances have been included as a direct cost of that or any other final cost objective. FAR Subpart 42.7 deals with establishing an indirect cost rate (see OVERHEAD RATE): the percentage or dollar factor that expresses the ratio of the indirect expense incurred in a given period to the direct labor cost, manufacturing cost, or other appropriate base for the same period. Procedures are prescribed to ensure that a single agency is responsible for negotiating BILLING RATEs and FINAL INDIRECT COST RATEs for each business unit of a contractor. See Shirk and Thompson, *Allowability of Unsettled Overhead and Accounting System Review Costs*, 91-9 CP&AR 3 (Sep. 1991).

INDIRECT COST POOL A grouping of INCURRED COSTs identified with two or more COST OBJECTIVEs but not specifically identified with any final cost objective. FAR 31.001. FAR 31.203 requires that indirect costs be accumulated by logical cost groupings, with due consideration of the reasons for incurring those costs. Each grouping should be determined to permit distribution of the grouping on the basis of the benefits accruing to the several cost objectives. In most circumstances, manufacturing overhead, selling expenses, and GENERAL AND ADMINISTRATIVE (G&A) COSTS are separately grouped. The contractor must select a distribution base common to all cost objectives to which the grouping is to be allocated. The contractor's method of allocating indirect costs must comply with Cost Accounting Standard 418, FAR 30.418, if applicable, or GENERALLY ACCEPTED ACCOUNTING PRINCIPLES (GAAP). See also ALLOCABLE COST.

INDIVIDUAL EXPERTS AND CONSULTANTS   Persons possessing special current knowledge or skill that may be combined with extensive operational experience. FAR 37.203(a). This background enables them to provide information, opinions, advice, or recommendations to enhance understanding of complex issues or to improve the quality and timeliness of policy development or decision making. Individual expert and consultant services fall within the realm of ADVISORY AND ASSISTANCE SERVICES, which support or improve agency policy development, decision making, management, administration, or management system operation. FAR 37.201. FAR Subpart 37.2 and DFARS 237.104 contain guidance on contracting for such services. See Pushkar and Stoughton, *Restrictions on Consultant Services*, 90-6 Briefing Papers (May 1990).

INDUSTRIAL BASE The manufacturing industry that produces consumer products, including components and parts, and that represents the basic capability available in the United States in the event of an INDUSTRIAL MOBILIZATION during a national emergency. The "mobilization base" consists of those companies that have entered into agreements with the Government to produce specific defense items in the event the Government declares a state of national emergency or war and the economy is mobilized for war. The industrial base supports the mobilization-base planned producers and, more important, must expand its capability to meet the large demands DoD would make in order to defend the country. See DoD Directive 5000.1, *Defense Acquisition*, 23 Feb. 1991, which implements OMB Circular No. A-109, *Major System Acquisitions*, 5 Apr. 1976, and requires industrial preparedness planning considerations in MAJOR SYSTEM ACQUISITIONs; DoD Directive 5000.2, *Defense Acquisition Management Policies and Procedures*, 23 Feb. 1991, part 5E, which further addresses industrial base considerations as part of the defense ACQUISITION PLANNING process; Nickolas, *The Industrial Base under Siege*, 27 Cont. Mgmt. 8 (July 1987).

INDUSTRIAL ENGINEERING The process of determining the utilization of personnel, equipment, and materials, as well as the coordination of activities and events, that will attain a desired quantity of output at a specified time and at an optimum cost. Industrial engineering may include gathering, analyzing, and acting upon facts pertaining to buildings and facilities, layouts, personnel organization, operating procedures, methods, processes, schedules, time standards, wage rates, wage payment plans, costs, and systems for controlling the quality and quantity of goods and services. Jones, Glossary: Defense Acquisition Acronyms and Terms. The techniques of industrial engineering are used when the Government makes a SHOULD-COST ANALYSIS of a contractor's proposed cost of performance.

INDUSTRIAL MOBILIZATION The use of American industry to produce supplies and services in the event of a national emergency. 10 U.S.C. 2304(c)(3) and 41 U.S.C. 253(c)(3) permit the awarding of contracts without FULL AND OPEN COMPETITION when it is necessary to maintain sources in order to achieve such mobilization. See FAR 6.302-3. See INDUSTRIAL BASE.

INDUSTRIAL MODERNIZATION INCENTIVES PROGRAM (IMIP) A program aimed at motivating contractors, through Government-provided incentives, to invest their own funds in facility improvements that should result in reduced acquisition costs and improved productivity. DFARS 215.870. An IMIP motivates contractors to (1) invest in facilities modernization and related productivity improvement efforts that they would not otherwise undertake or (2) invest in such efforts earlier than they otherwise would. Although DoD profit and competition policies are intended to provide adequate incentives to a contractor for capital investment and productivity, the Government recognizes that individual cases may require additional incentives to enhance productivity, reduce acquisition and other life-cycle costs, and improve quality and reliability. DoD policy permits industrial modernization incentives to be negotiated and included in contracts for research, development, and production of weapon systems, major components, or materials. The incentives may be in the form of productivity savings rewards (PSRs), contractor investment protection, or other appropriate form. See DoD Directive 5000.44, *Industrial Modernization Incentive Program*, 16 Apr. 1986.

INDUSTRIAL PLANT EQUIPMENT (IPE) See PLANT EQUIP-MENT.

INELIGIBILITY Exclusion from the award of contracts pursuant to statute, executive order, or regulatory authority other than for DEBARMENT or SUSPENSION. FAR 9.403. Common grounds for ineligibility are violations of the DAVIS-BACON ACT, the SERVICE CONTRACT ACT (SCA) OF 1965, the EQUAL EMPLOYMENT OPPORTUNITY (EEO) regulations, and the WALSH-HEALEY PUBLIC CONTRACTS ACT.

INFORMATION RESOURCES MANAGEMENT (IRM) The planning, budgeting, organizing, directing, training, promoting, controlling, and managing activities associated with the collection, creation, use, and dissemination of information by agencies. IRM includes the management of FEDERAL INFORMATION PROCESSING (FIP) RESOURCES. FIRMR 201-4.001. The FEDERAL INFORMATION RESOURCES MANAGEMENT REGULATION (FIRMR) is the primary Government-wide IRM regulation.

INFORMATION RESOURCES MANAGEMENT (IRM) NON-MANDATORY ADP SCHEDULES Nonmandatory, indefinite-quantity, multiple-award instruments used to purchase, rent, and maintain FEDERAL INFORMATION PROCESSING (FIP) RESOURCES.

These schedules are part of Federal Supply Class Group 70. They are often referred to as the "GSA Schedules," since the GENERAL SERVICES ADMINISTRATION (GSA) negotiates them with vendors on behalf of executive agencies to help cut procurement costs and time.

INFORMATION RESOURCES PROCUREMENT AND MAN-AGEMENT REVIEW (IRPMR) Periodic review of agency acquisitions of FEDERAL INFORMATION PROCESSING (FIP) RESOURCES by the GENERAL SERVICES ADMINISTRATION (GSA) under its BROOKS ACT (AUTOMATIC DATA PROCESSING PROCUREMENTS) authority. These reviews (1) verify agency compliance with regulations and DELEGATION OF PROCUREMENT AUTHORITY (DPA) conditions or limitations, (2) assess GSA procurement policies and directions given to agencies, and (3) assess agency use of delegated authority in acquiring, using, and managing FIP resources. FIRMR 201-11.003, 201-22.2.

INFORMATION SYSTEMS SECURITY (INFOSEC) A composite of factors necessary to (1) protect Federal information processing (FIP) systems (see FEDERAL INFORMATION PROCESSING (FIP) RESOURCES) and the information they process, from exploitation through interception, unauthorized electronic access, or intelligence disclosure threats, and (2) ensure authenticity. This protection results from the application of security measures to systems that generate, store, process, transfer, or communicate information of possible use to an adversary. It also includes the physical protection of sensitive material and sensitive technical security. FIRMR 201-4.001. GSA offers worldwide INFOSEC services in support of agencies' sensitive and classified information requirements, including installation, maintenance, key distribution, design, engineering, and consulting. Agencies must consider using these services to meet their requirements. FIRMR 201-24.203-2; FIRMR Bulletin C-19, *Information System Security (INFOSEC)*.

INFORMATION TECHNOLOGY FUND (ITF) Established by the PAPERWORK REDUCTION REAUTHORIZATION ACT OF 1986, the Information Technology Fund is the result of the merger of two former funds: the ADP Fund established by the BROOKS ACT (AUTOMATIC DATA PROCESSING PROCUREMENTS) and the Federal Telecommunications Fund. Agencies may use the ITF for financing expenses, including personal services and other costs;

for a FIP resources procurement by lease, purchase transfer, or otherwise; and for the efficient management, coordination, operation, and utilization of such resources. Although the FIRMR is silent on the ITF, Federal agencies are not precluded from petitioning the GENERAL SERVICES ADMINISTRATION (GSA) to use the fund.

IN-KIND CONTRIBUTIONS Non-cash contributions provided by a performing contractor or a non-Federal third party who is participating with the DEPARTMENT OF ENERGY (DoE) in a cosponsored project or contract. In-kind contributions may be in the form of personal property (equipment and supplies), real property (land and buildings), or services. Such contributions must be directly beneficial, specifically identifiable, and necessary to performance of the project or program. They must (1) be verifiable from the performer's books and records; (2) not be included as contributions to any other Federal program; (3) be necessary to effective and efficient accomplishment of profit objectives; (4) provide for types of charges that would otherwise be allowable under applicable Federal cost principles appropriate to the contractor's organization; and (5) not be paid for by the Federal Government under any contract, agreement, or grant, unless specifically authorized by legislation. DEAR 917.7007.

INSPECTION Examining and testing supplies or services (including, when appropriate, raw materials, components, and intermediate assemblies) to determine whether they conform to contract requirements. FAR 46.101. TESTING is the part of inspection that determines the properties or elements, including the functional operation, of supplies or their components, by the application of established scientific principles and procedures. Although contracts generally make contractors responsible for performing inspection before tendering supplies to the Government, there are situations in which contracts will provide for specialized inspection to be performed solely by the Government. FAR 46.201. The standard inspection clauses in FAR 52.246 require the contractor to (1) provide and maintain an inspection system that is acceptable to the Government, (2) give the Government the right to make inspections and tests while work is in progress, and (3) keep complete records of its inspection work and make them available to the Government. Regulatory guidance on inspection is contained in FAR Part 46 covering QUALITY ASSURANCE (QA). See Cibinic and Nash, Administration of Government Contracts

568–601; Bednar, chap. 10, Construction Contracting 786–815; Victorino and Ivey, *The "Inspection" Clause*, 88-10 Briefing Papers (Sep. 1988).

INSPECTOR GENERAL (IG)   An officer of the United States, appointed by the President and confirmed by the Senate, to serve in each major department of the Government to independently audit and investigate the activities of that department. The Inspector General Act of 1978, 5 U.S.C. app. 2, created Inspector General offices for Government agencies in order to establish independent and objective units to (1) conduct and supervise audits and investigations relating to the programs and operations of the agencies and organizations; (2) provide leadership and coordination and recommend policies for activities designed to promote administrative economy, efficiency, and effectiveness, and prevent and detect fraud and abuse; and (3) provide a means for keeping the head of the agency or organization and the Congress informed about administrative problems and deficiencies and about the necessity for, and progress of, corrective action. IGs are authorized to (1) have access to records, reports, and audits; (2) make investigations and reports; (3) request information and assistance from Federal, State, and local governments; (4) require production of documents by subpoena; (5) administer oaths; (6) have direct access to the head of the agency or organization; (7) select employees as necessary; (8) obtain services; and (9) enter into contracts and other arrangements for audits, studies, and analyses with public agencies and private persons. 5 U.S.C. app. 2, 6.

INSTANT CONTRACT   The contract, in the context of VALUE ENGINEERING (VE), under which a VALUE ENGINEERING CHANGE PROPOSAL (VECP) is submitted. FAR 48.001. It does not include increases in quantities made to the contract after acceptance of the VECP that are due to contract modification, exercise of options, or additional orders. If the contract is a multiyear contract (see MULTIYEAR CONTRACTING), the term does not include quantities funded after VECP acceptance. In a FIXED-PRICE REDETERMI-NATION-PROSPECTIVE (FPRP) CONTRACT, the term refers to quantities to be manufactured in the period for which firm prices have been established.

INSTANT CONTRACT SAVINGS   The net cost reductions on the contract under which a VALUE ENGINEERING CHANGE PROPOSAL

(VECP) is submitted and accepted. These reductions are equal to the instant unit cost reduction multiplied by the number of instant contract units affected by the VECP, less the contractor's allowable development and implementation costs. FAR 48.104-1 contains guidance on such savings; their calculation is prescribed in paragraph (g) of the Value Engineering clause in FAR 52.248-1. See also NEGATIVE INSTANT CONTRACT SAVINGS. And see Cibinic and Nash, Administration of Government Contracts 308.

INSTANT UNIT COST REDUCTION The amount of the decrease in unit cost of performance (without deducting any contractor's development or implementation costs) resulting from using a VALUE ENGINEERING CHANGE PROPOSAL (VECP) on the INSTANT CONTRACT. FAR 48.001. In service contracts, the instant unit cost reduction is normally equal to the number of hours per line-item task saved by using the VECP on the instant contract, multiplied by the appropriate contract labor rate. The concept of instant unit cost reduction is contrasted with that of future unit cost reduction, just as instant contract savings are contrasted with future contract savings.

INSURANCE Protection against a risk of loss or harm. Such protection may be obtained by purchasing an insurance policy from another party or by SELF-INSURANCE. FAR 31.205-19 specifies that most normal costs of insurance incurred by a contractor are ALLOWABLE COSTs. Cost Accounting Standard 416, FAR 30.416, governs the accounting techniques that are to be used by contractors for insurance costs and permits self-insurance in lieu of the purchase of insurance policies. FAR Subpart 28.3 sets forth the policies of the Government in dealing with insurance by contractors. See Patin, chap. 18, Construction Contracting 1439–1520.

INTANGIBLE CAPITAL ASSET An asset that has no physical substance, has more than minimal value, and is expected to be held by an enterprise for continued use or possession beyond the current accounting period for the benefits it yields. FAR 31.001. The value of such assets lies in the use that can be made of them, although they cannot be seen. Examples are GOODWILL and patented rights. Rosenberg, Dictionary of Banking and Finance. Intangible capital assets figure in the computation of COST OF CAPITAL COMMITTED TO FACILITIES.

INTEGRITY See PROCUREMENT INTEGRITY.

INTERAGENCY ACQUISITION A procedure by which one Government agency needing supplies or services (the requesting agency) obtains them from or through another (the servicing agency). FAR 17.501. Under the Economy Act, 31 U.S.C. 1535, an agency may place orders with any other agency for supplies or services that the servicing agency may be better able to supply, render, or obtain by contract, if it is determined by the head of the requesting agency, or by a designee, that it is in the Government's interest to do so. FAR 17.502. The agency head or the designee must determine that (1) legal authority for the acquisition exists, (2) the action does not conflict with any other agency's authority or responsibility, and (3) if the acquisition involves use of a commercial or industrial activity operated by the servicing agency, the acquisition conforms to the FAR requirements regarding contractor versus Government performance.   FAR 17.503. Agencies are forbidden to use interagency acquisition as a means of avoiding the requirement to obtain FULL AND OPEN COMPETITION. FAR 6.002.

INTERAGENCY MOTOR POOL VEHICLES AND SERVICES A pool of vehicles and service facilities maintained by GSA for the use of Federal agencies in a given area. FAR 51.201 provides that if it is in the Government's interest, the contracting officer may authorize the contractor under a COST-REIMBURSEMENT CONTRACT to obtain, for official purposes only, interagency motor pool vehicles and related services, including (1) fuel and lubricants, (2) vehicle inspection, maintenance, and repair, (3) vehicle storage, and (4) commercially rented vehicles for short-term use. Complete rebuilding of major components of contractor-owned or contractor-leased vehicle requires the approval of the contracting officer. The contractor must, among other things, (1) obtain vehicle liability insurance covering bodily injury and property damage protecting the contractor and the Government against third-party claims, and (2) establish and enforce penalties for its employees who use or authorize the use of Government vehicles for other than performance of Government contracts. When a contractor is authorized to follow these procedures, the solicitation and the contract will contain the Interagency Motor Pool Vehicles and Related Services clause in FAR 52.251-2. See also 41 CFR 101-39.

INTERDIVISIONAL WORK AUTHORIZATION (IWA)   See INTERORGANIZATIONAL TRANSFER.

INTERDIVISIONAL WORK ORDER (IWO)   See INTERORGANIZATIONAL TRANSFER.

INTEREST   An amount paid for the use of money. Interest on borrowings by a contractor (however represented) is not an ALLOWABLE COST under a contract. FAR 31.205-20. However, interest imputed to the cost of facilities is allowable. See COST OF CAPITAL COMMITTED TO FACILITIES. The PROMPT PAYMENT ACT (PPA) requires payment of an interest penalty for late Government payment of contractor invoices. FAR 32.903; OMB Circular No. A-125, *Prompt Payment*, 18 Aug. 1982. FAR 32.407 requires that the contracting officer charge interest on the daily unliquidated balance of ADVANCE PAYMENTs made to the contractor. The Interest clause at FAR 52.232-17 requires that all amounts payable by the contractor to the Government bear simple interest from the date due unless paid within 30 days of becoming due. The CONTRACT DISPUTES ACT (CDA) OF 1978, at 41 U.S.C. 611, provides for the payment of interest on the amount found due and unpaid on contractor claims, running from the date the contracting officer receives the CLAIM (or the due date, if later) until the date the Government pays the contractor. When interest is paid under these provisions, it is paid at the TREASURY INTEREST RATE. See Nash and Cibinic, *Interest Rates: Heads I Win, Tails You Lose*, 5 N&CR ¶ 13 (March 1991); Booth, Interest and Federal Contracts: A Perspective.

INTERESTED PARTY   An actual or prospective offeror whose direct economic interest could be affected by the award of a contract or by the failure to award a contract. FAR 33.101. Interested parties are parties entitled to bring PROTESTs—either to the awarding agency directly, before the GENERAL ACCOUNTING OFFICE (GAO) or, if the acquisition concerns FEDERAL INFORMATION PROCESSING (FIP) RESOURCES, before the GENERAL SERVICES ADMINISTRATION BOARD OF CONTRACT APPEALS (GSBCA). FAR 33.102. To determine whether a protester is an interested party, many factors are considered, including the protester's status in relation to the procurement (prospective offeror, offeror eligible for award, nonofferor, etc.), the nature of the issues raised, and the direct or indirect benefit or relief sought by the protester. See Tolle, *A Review of the First Year of ADP Bid*

Protests and the GSBCA, 16 Pub. Cont. L.J. 120, 131 (1986); Hopkins, *The Universe of Remedies for Unsuccessful Offerors on Federal Contracts*, 15 Pub. Cont. L.J. 364, 380 (1985).

INTEREST RATE See TREASURY INTEREST RATE.

INTERIM RATE See BILLING RATE.

INTEROPERABILITY The ability of FEDERAL INFORMATION PROCESSING (FIP) RESOURCES to provide services to and accept services from other FIP resources and to use the services so exchanged to enable them to operate effectively together. FIRMR 201-4.001.

INTERORGANIZATIONAL TRANSFER A transaction between a contractor and a sister division, an affiliate (see AFFILIATES), or a subsidiary. As a general rule, transactions between a prime contractor (the contracting division) and its affiliated subcontractor (the transferring division) must take place on the basis of cost incurred, without profit. Interorganizational transfers may be proposed at price (including profit), rather than cost, only where the transfer meets the FAR tests for ADEQUATE PRICE COMPETITION or a COMMERCIAL PRODUCT sale, and the transfer does not exceed the transferring division's MOST FAVORED CUSTOMER price. FAR 31.205-26(e); FAR Table 15-2. The Defense Contract Audit Agency (DCAA) instructs its auditors to give "careful consideration" to transactions between affiliated concerns. DCAA Contract Audit Manual (CAM) 6-313.1. See Nibley et al., *Applying TINA to Interorganizational Transfers*, 90-11 CP&AR 3 (Nov. 1990).

INTERPRETATION See CONTRACT INTERPRETATION.

INTERVENOR A person who voluntarily interposes in an action or other proceeding with the permission of the forum or court. Intervention is a procedure by which a third person, not originally a party to a suit but claiming an interest in the subject matter, comes into the dispute in order to protect its own right or interpose its own claim. Black's Law Dictionary. In proceedings before the GENERAL SERVICES ADMINISTRATION BOARD OF CONTRACT APPEALS (GSBCA), an intervenor of right is an INTERESTED PARTY that meets certain procedural prerequisites, whereas a permissive intervenor is any entity that is an interested party and has proceeded with a PROTEST of the same procurement at the GENERAL ACCOUNTING OFFICE (GAO). See GSBCA Rule 5; Tolle, *A Review of the First Year of ADP Bid Protests and the GSBCA*, 16 Pub. Cont. L.J. 120, 132 (1986). See also UNIFORM RULES.

INVENTORY A detailed list of articles of property or goods held for sale or lease or furnished under service contracts, or raw materials or work in process or materials used or consumed in a business. Black's Law Dictionary. "Contractor inventory" has a special meaning under FAR Subpart 45.6, which sets forth procedures for the reporting, redistribution, and disposal of contractor inventory. There it means (1) property acquired by, and in the possession of, a contractor or subcontractor under a contract, for which TITLE is vested in the Government and which exceeds the amounts needed to complete performance under the contract; (2) property that the Government is obligated or has the option to take over as a result of (a) changes in the contract's specifications or plans or (b) termination of the contract for the convenience of the Government (see TERMINATION INVENTORY); and (3) GOVERNMENT-FURNISHED PROPERTY (GFP) that exceeds the amounts needed to complete contract performance. FAR 45.601.

INVITATION FOR BIDS (IFB) The solicitation document used in SEALED BIDDING procurements. IFBs must describe the Government's requirements clearly, accurately, and completely, FAR 14.101, and must use the UNIFORM CONTRACT FORMAT to the maximum extent practicable, FAR 14.201-1. The IFB includes all documents needed by prospective bidders for the purpose of bidding and ensures that all bidders will submit bids on the same basis so that award can be made solely on the basis of PRICE and PRICE-RELATED FACTORS. IFBs must be publicized through distribution to prospective bidders, posting in public places, publication of a SYNOPSIS in the COMMERCE BUSINESS DAILY (CBD), and such other means as may be appropriate. FAR 14.203. They must not include unnecessarily RESTRICTIVE SPECIFICATIONS or requirements that might unduly limit the number of bidders. Publicizing must occur a sufficient time before bid opening to enable prospective bidders to prepare and submit bids.

INVOICE A written account or itemized statement, addressed to the purchaser, of merchandise shipped or services performed, together with the quantity and the prices and charges. An invoice is the contractor's bill or written request for payment for work or services performed under the contract.   Under FAR 32.902 a "proper" invoice is a bill or written request for payment that meets the minimum standards of the Prompt Payment clauses (see PROMPT PAYMENT ACT (PPA)) in FAR 52.232-25 through 52.232-27.   Under the DISPUTEs clause in FAR 52.233-1, a VOUCHER, invoice, or other routine request for payment that is not in dispute when submitted is not a CLAIM, although it may be converted to a claim. See FAR 33.201.

INVOICE PAYMENT   A Government disbursement of monies, subject to the PROMPT PAYMENT ACT (PPA), to a contractor under a contract or other authorization for supplies or services that have been accepted by the Government.   The term encompasses payments for partial deliveries that have been accepted by the Government, and final cost or fee payments when amounts owed have been settled between the Government and the contractor. Under the PROMPT PAYMENT ACT (PPA), invoice payments also include all progress payments made under the Payments under Fixed-Price Construction Contracts clause at FAR 52.232-5, and the Payments under Fixed-Price Architect-Engineer Contracts clause at FAR 52.232-10.   Invoice payments do not include contract FINANCING PAYMENTs. FAR 32.902. The due date for a designated payment office to make an invoice payment is generally the 30th day after the designated billing office has received a proper invoice from the contractor, or the 30th day after the Government's acceptance of supplies delivered or services performed by the contractor, whichever is later. FAR 32.905. See OMB Circular No. A-125, *Prompt Payment*, 19 Aug. 1982; Cibinic and Nash, Administration of Government Contracts 880–81.

ISSUE IN CONTROVERSY A material disagreement between the Government and a contractor which relates to a CLAIM or which could result in a claim. FAR 33.201. Agencies are encouraged to use ALTERNATIVE DISPUTE RESOLUTION (ADR) procedures to settle issues in controversy. FAR 33.204.

J

JEWEL BEARING A piece of synthetic corundum (sapphire or ruby) of any shape, except a phonograph needle, that has one or more polished surfaces to provide supporting surfaces or low-friction contact areas for revolving, oscillating, or sliding parts in an instrument, mechanism, subassembly, or part. FAR 8.201. With certain exceptions, jewel bearings used in precision instruments and similar equipment acquired under a Government contract must be purchased by the contractor from the Government-owned, contractor-operated William Langer Plant, Rolla, North Dakota. FAR Subpart 8.2 and clauses at 52.208-1 and -2.

JOB ORDER An order issued by a contracting agency for work to be performed under the terms and conditions of a BASIC AGREEMENT, BASIC ORDERING AGREEMENT (BOA), or MASTER AGREEMENT FOR REPAIR AND ALTERATION OF VESSELS. Job orders are usually FIRM-FIXED-PRICE CONTRACTs for specific items of work.

JOINT VENTURE A legal entity in the nature of a partnership engaged in the joint prosecution of a particular transaction for mutual profit. It is a grouping of two or more persons that, unlike a partnership, does not entail a continuing relationship between the parties. Joint ventures require a community of interest in the performance of the contract or project, a right to direct and govern the policy in connection with the contract or project, and a duty, which may be altered by agreement, to share in both profit and losses. Black's Law Dictionary. FAR 9.603 provides that the Government will recognize the integrity and validity of joint ventures. However, they are infrequently used, except in construction contracting. See Ingrao, *Joint Ventures: Their Use in Federal Government Contracting*, 20 Pub. Cont. L.J. 399 (1991); Sherrer, *Joint Ventures on Government Contracts: A Walk*

Through a Rose Garden Planted over Land Mines, 19 Pub. Cont. L.J. 331 (1990).

JUDGMENT IN PRICING A subjective factor used to estimate the cost of future work by projecting from the FACTs at the time of the estimate to the period of performance of the prospective contract. When a contractor submits COST OR PRICING DATA as a part of a contract pricing proposal pursuant to the TRUTH IN NEGOTIATIONS ACT (TINA), FAR 15.804-6(b), paragraph 2 of Table 15-2, Instructions for Submission of a Contract Pricing Proposal, requires the submission of such judgments as part of the proposal. Thus, pricing proposals consist of facts (cost or pricing data) and judgments. In the application of TINA, it has proved to be very difficult to draw a firm line between facts and judgments. See Lovitky, *Cost and Pricing Data Defined: An Analysis of the Scope of Contractor Disclosure Requirements Pursuant to the Truth in Negotiations Act*, 20 NCMJ 79 (1987); Lovitky, *Understanding Causation and Determining the Price Adjustment in Defective Pricing Cases*, 17 Pub. Cont. L.J. 407 (1988).

JUDGMENT OF COURT A decision issued by a court (an individual judge, a panel of judges, or the court sitting *en banc*) that resolves, as far as that court is concerned, an issue in a given case.

JURY VERDICT METHOD A technique used by BOARDs OF CONTRACT APPEALS (BCAs) and courts to resolve conflicting evidence about the amount of a contractual adjustment, or to arrive at an amount of compensation when incomplete or conflicting evidence has been submitted. It is often viewed as a means of determining the amount in cases of conflicting testimony rather than a method of proof of quantum (see BIFURCATION OF ENTITLEMENT AND QUANTUM). The jury verdict represents a figure that, in the view of the trier of the facts, is fair in the light of all the facts of the case, or, put another way, is supported by consideration of the entire record. Some BCAs and courts have refused to use the technique when very little or no evidence has been submitted. See Cibinic and Nash, Administration of Government Contracts 519–22; Nash, *The "Jury Verdict" Approach: Equitable Technique or Contractor Bonanza?* 5 N&CR ¶ 65 (Dec. 1991).

JUSTIFICATION AND APPROVAL The Government document required by 10 U.S.C. 2304(f)(1) and 41 U.S.C. 253(f)(1) when an agency is going to award a contract without providing for FULL

AND OPEN COMPETITION. In such case, the contracting officer must justify the action in writing, certify the accuracy and completeness of the justification, and obtain the approval of appropriate individuals. FAR 6.303-1. (The justification may be prepared and approved following contract award in situations of UNUSUAL OR COMPELLING URGENCY if prior preparation and approval would unreasonably delay the acquisition. FAR 6.302-2 and 6.303-1(e).) Justifications must (1) identify the agency, the contracting activity, the action being approved, the supplies or services sought, and the statutory authority permitting the action; (2) demonstrate that the proposed contractor's unique qualifications or the nature of the acquisition require the action; (3) describe efforts made to ensure that offers were solicited from as many potential sources as practicable; (4) determine that the anticipated cost will be fair and reasonable; (5) describe market surveys conducted; (6) list sources interested in the acquisition; and (7) cite actions being taken to provide for competition in future acquisitions. FAR 6.303-2. Depending on the size and nature of the contract, justifications must be approved in writing by an official at a level above the contracting officer, by the COMPETITION ADVOCATE for the procuring activity, or by the SENIOR PROCUREMENT EXECUTIVE of the Government agency conducting the acquisition. FAR 6.304. Justifications will be made available for public inspection as required by 10 U.S.C. 2304(f)(4) and 41 U.S.C. 303(f)(4). FAR 6.305. See Cibinic and Nash, Formation of Government Contracts 309–10.

K

KEY PERSONNEL Contractor personnel that are required to be used in the performance of a contract by a Key Personnel clause. See, for example, NFS 18-52.235-71. A CONTRACTING ACTIVITY uses such clauses to ensure that in performing the contract the winning contractor will not use personnel less qualified than those described and evaluated in the winning proposal. Such clauses generally permit substitution of personnel with the approval of the CONTRACTING OFFICER (CO).

KICKBACK Any money, fee, commission, credit, gift, GRATUITY, thing of value, or compensation of any kind provided, directly or indirectly, to any PRIME CONTRACTOR, prime contractor employee, SUBCONTRACTOR, or subcontractor employee for the purpose of improperly obtaining or rewarding favorable treatment in connection with a contract or subcontract. FAR 3.502-1. Kickbacks have been prohibited by statute for many years, but new legislation was enacted in the ANTI-KICKBACK ACT OF 1986. See Arnavas, *The New Anti-Kickback Act*, 87-9 Briefing Papers 2-3 (Aug. 1987). Kickbacks by construction workers to contractors and subcontractors are prohibited by the COPELAND ANTI-KICKBACK ACT.

L

LABOR Effort expended by people in exchange for wages or salary. DIRECT LABOR is one of the principal breakdowns used in costing, pricing, and profit determination. Indirect labor is an element of INDIRECT COST. FAR Part 22 sets forth the policies of the Government regarding the application of labor laws to the acquisition process. The FAR contains considerable guidance on the implementation of various labor laws and policies in contracts. Subjects treated include convict labor (Subpart 22.2); the CONTRACT WORK HOURS AND SAFETY STANDARDS ACT (CWHSSA) (Subpart 22.3); the DAVIS-BACON ACT (22.403-1, 22.404); the COPELAND ANTI-KICKBACK ACT (22.403-2); the WALSH-HEALEY PUBLIC CONTRACTS ACT (Subpart 22.6); EQUAL EMPLOYMENT OPPORTUNITY (EEO) (Subpart 22.8); the SERVICE CONTRACT ACT (SCA) OF 1965 (Subpart 22.10); and employment of the handicapped (Subpart 22.14).

LABORERS OR MECHANICS Employees of construction contractors or subcontractors at any tier composed of (1) those workers whose duties are manual or physical in nature (including workers who use tools or who are performing the work of a trade) rather than mental or managerial; (2) apprentices, trainees, helpers, and, in contracts subject to the CONTRACT WORK HOURS AND SAFETY STANDARDS ACT (CWHSSA), watchmen and guards; (3) working foremen who devote more than 20 percent of their time during a work week to performing the duties of a laborer or mechanic; and (4) any other person who performs the duties of a laborer or mechanic, regardless of any contractual relationship alleged to exist between the contractor and that individual. FAR 22.401. The DAVIS-BACON ACT requires that construction contractors and subcontractors pay this class of workers the prevailing wage in the locality. See Stephenson, chap. 3, Construction Contracting 225–27.

LABOR-HOUR (L-H) CONTRACT A type of contract under which the Government pays a fixed amount for each hour of work performed by specified classes of labor. FAR 16.602 limits the use of this type of contract and requires that the Government maintain "appropriate surveillance" to ensure that the contractor is using efficient methods of performance. See Cibinic and Nash, Formation of Government Contracts 790–95.

LABOR RELATIONS The process of dealing with employees. FAR 31.205-21 states that the costs incurred by a contractor in conducting labor relations are ALLOWABLE COSTs. FAR 22.101-1 establishes the basic policy of procuring agencies to remain impartial concerning any dispute between labor and contractor management. It also states that Government agencies should maintain sound relations with industry and labor to keep abreast of events that might adversely affect the Government acquisition process and to ensure that the Government obtains needed supplies and services without delay. See Stephenson, chap. 3, Construction Contracting.

LABOR SURPLUS AREA (LSA) A geographical area identified by the Department of Labor in accordance with 20 CFR 654, Subpart A, as an area of concentrated unemployment or underemployment. FAR 20.101. Lists of these areas are published by the Department of Labor periodically *(Area Trends in Employment and Unemployment)* and annually in the FEDERAL REGISTER.

LABOR SURPLUS AREA (LSA) CONCERN A business concern that, together with its first-tier subcontractors, will perform all work in a given procurement substantially in a LABOR SURPLUS AREA (LSA). FAR 20.101. Performance is considered substantially in LSAs if the cost incurred under the contract in those areas exceeds 50 percent of the contract price. FAR Part 20 states that it is the Government's policy to make awards to LSA concerns and to encourage contractors to place subcontracts with them, subject to the small business and small disadvantaged business order-of-preference provisions found at FAR 19.504. Agencies other than DoD make SET-ASIDEs to LSA concerns in accordance with FAR Subpart 20.2. In contracts of $500,000 or less, but more than the small purchase limitation, contractors are required to use their best efforts to subcontract with LSA concerns; in contracts exceeding $500,000, contractors are required to take affirmative action to subcontract with LSA concerns (see LABOR SURPLUS

AREA (LSA) SUBCONTRACTING PROGRAM). FAR 20.301. See
Cibinic and Nash, Formation of Government Contracts 964–68.

**LABOR SURPLUS AREA (LSA) SUBCONTRACTING PRO-
GRAM** Requirement that, in contracts that may exceed $500,000,
contractors take affirmative action to subcontract with LABOR
SURPLUS AREA (LSA) CONCERNs. Contractors are not required (as
they are with SUBCONTRACTING PLANs for SMALL BUSINESS
CONCERNs and SMALL DISADVANTAGED BUSINESS CONCERNs
(SDBCs)) to develop goals for subcontracting with LSA concerns.
FAR 20.301.

LATE BID A bid received in the office designated in the INVITATION
FOR BIDS (IFB) after the exact time for opening. FAR 14.304-1. A
late bid, late modification of a bid, or late withdrawal of a bid will
not be considered unless it is received before contract award, and
then only if the bid was sent (1) by registered or certified mail not
later than 5 calendar days before the bid receipt date specified, (2)
by regular mail (or telegram or FACSIMILE (FAX) if authorized by
the SOLICITATION) and the Government determines that the late
receipt was caused solely by the Government's mishandling after
receipt at the Government installation, or (3) by U.S. Postal
Service Express Mail Next-Day Service not later than 2 working
days before the bid receipt date specified. The only acceptable
evidence of mailing is a U.S. or Canadian Postal Service postmark. The only acceptable evidence to establish time of receipt at
the Government installation is the installation's time/date stamp.
The term "postmark" means a printed, stamped, or other impression (other than a postage meter machine impression) that is
readily identifiable without further action as having been supplied
and affixed on the date of mailing by an employee of the Postal
Service. Bidders should therefore request the postal clerk to place
a hand cancellation bull's-eye postmark on both the receipt and
the envelope or wrapper. See Cibinic and Nash, Formation of
Government Contracts 377–82.

LATENT Not readily discoverable by observation on inspection;
hidden or concealed. "Latent" can refer to a type of deficiency
potentially found in solicitations or contracts (a latent AMBIGUITY)
or in contract performance (LATENT DEFECT). "Latent" is an
antonym of the adjective PATENT.

LATENT AMBIGUITY See AMBIGUITY.

LATENT DEFECT   A defect in the contract work that is not discoverable by the Government by the use of reasonable inspection methods. A latent defect overcomes the finality of acceptance in the Inspection of Supplies—Fixed-Price clause, FAR 52.246-2, and the Inspection of Construction clause, FAR 52.246-12. See Cibinic and Nash, Administration of Government Contracts 632–36; Victorino and Ivey, *The "Inspection" Clause*, 88-10 Briefing Papers 8 (Sep. 1988).

LEADER-COMPANY CONTRACTING An acquisition technique used to establish a second source for a product that is being or has been developed by a single contractor. It is often called "leader/follower" procurement. FAR 17.401 states that leader-company contracting is an extraordinary acquisition technique used only in special circumstances. Under this technique, a developer or sole producer of a product or system is designated to be the leader company and to furnish assistance and know-how to one or more designated follower companies, which subsequently become sources of supply. Leader-company contracting is intended to do one or more of the following: (1) reduce delivery time; (2) achieve geographic dispersion of suppliers; (3) maximize use of scarce tooling and equipment; (4) ensure uniformity and reliability in equipment, compatibility or standardization of components, and interchangeability of parts; (5) eliminate problems in use of proprietary data; and (6) facilitate the transition from development to production to subsequent competitive acquisition of end items or major components. FAR 17.401. Leader-company contracting should be used only when (1) the leader company has the necessary production know-how, (2) no other source can meet the Government's requirements without assistance from a leader company, and (3) the assistance is limited to that which is essential to produce the item. FAR 17.402. This technique is unpopular with leader companies because it requires them to foster their own competition. DoD encourages the use of SMALL DISADVANTAGED BUSINESS CONCERNs (SDBCs) as follower companies. DFARS 217.401. NASA does not use leader-company contracting. NFS Subpart 18-17.4.

LEADER/FOLLOWER   See LEADER-COMPANY CONTRACTING.

LEARNING CURVE   A technique for projecting the amount of direct labor or material that will be used to manufacture a product on a repetitive basis. The learning curve concept originated in the observation that organizations performing repetitive tasks tend to exhibit a rate of improvement due to increased manual dexterity and improved manufacturing methodology. (Thus, it is more aptly called an "improvement curve.") Learning or improvement curve theories include the "Boeing" or "unit curve" theory and the "Northrop" or "cumulative average" theory. The Boeing theory holds that as the total quantity of units produced doubles, the cost per unit decreases by some constant percentage (the rate of learning). The Northrop, or "cumulative average," theory holds that as the total quantity of units produced doubles, the *average* cost per unit decreases by some constant percentage (the rate of learning). See Armed Services Pricing Manual (ASPM) vol. 1, app. B.

LEASE A contract with the owner of real or personal property to permit another party to use that property for a specified period of time. Leases are contracts subject the CONTRACT DISPUTES ACT (CDA) OF 1978. 41 U.S.C. 602. FAR Subpart 7.4 provides guidance on the decision of a CONTRACTING OFFICER (CO) whether to lease rather than purchase equipment. FAR Subpart 8.11 provides guidance on leasing of motor vehicles. See RENTAL COSTS for the treatment of the costs incurred by a contractor for leases. And see Day and Keogh, *A Risk Analysis of Financing Federal Government Equipment Leases*, 18 Pub. Cont. L.J. 544 (1989).

LEGAL FEES The amount paid to a lawyer for professional services. FAR 31.205-47 sets forth detailed rules governing whether such fees paid by contractors are ALLOWABLE COSTs. Generally, such fees are allowable when incurred in performing normal functions required for the performance or termination of a contract, but are unallowable in the PROSECUTION OF CLAIMS and in the defense of a number of specified claims. See Connelly and Schooner, *Recovery of Costs for Defense Against the Government's Charge of Illegality*, 16 Pub. Cont. L.J. 94 (1986).

LETTER CONTRACT A written preliminary contractual instrument authorizing the immediate commencement of activity under its terms and conditions, pending DEFINITIZATION of a pricing arrangement for the work to be done. FAR 16.603-1. Letter contracts are a means of permitting contractors to commence work immediately after a requirement is identified. They are strongly disfavored (see 10 U.S.C. 2326 placing restrictions on their use) and may not be used unless the HEAD OF THE CONTRACTING

ACTIVITY (HCA) determines in writing that no other instrument is suitable. FAR 16.603-3. A letter contract must specify the maximum liability of the Government and must be superseded by a definitive contract within a specified time. Letter contracts contain a negotiated definitization schedule including (1) dates for submission of the contractor's price proposal and related information, (2) a date for the start of negotiations, and (3) a target date for definitization, which should be either within 180 days after the date of the letter contract or before completion of 40 percent of the work to be performed, whichever occurs first. FAR 16.603-2. See the Contract Definitization clause in FAR 52.216-25.

LETTER OF CREDIT An instrument, issued by a bank or other financing institution, permitting the Government to withdraw funds up to a specified amount if a contractor does not meet its obligations under a contract. OFPP Policy Letter 91-4, *Use of Letters of Credit*, requires contracting officers to permit contractors to meet MILLER ACT obligations by providing irrevocable letters of credit in lieu of PERFORMANCE BONDs and PAYMENT BONDs.

LETTER OF INTENT A letter customarily employed to reduce to writing a preliminary understanding of parties that intend to enter into a contract. Black's Law Dictionary. In Government procurement, such instruments take the form of LETTER CONTRACTs (LCs) in almost all cases.

LETTER OF OFFER AND ACCEPTANCE (LOA) The instrument that creates a contractual relationship between the U.S. Government and a foreign purchaser in a FOREIGN MILITARY SALES (FMS) transaction. The LOA lists supplies or services to be purchased, estimated costs, terms and conditions of the transaction, and payment schedules. The purchaser, an authorized representative of the foreign government, must sign, date, and return the LOA before its expiration date. See Reuter, *The ABCs of FMS*, 30 Cont. Mgmt. 29 (Oct. 1990).

LETTER OF REQUEST (LOR) The instrument used as the first step in initiating a FOREIGN MILITARY SALES (FMS) transaction. The LOR is used to request defense articles and services, as well as planning and review data, price and availability data, or an actual LETTER OF OFFER AND ACCEPTANCE (LOA). It includes a statement of what is desired, with sufficient detail to enable DoD or another agency to provide a firm basis for a price estimate. The foreign state forwards the LOR through the U.S. Embassy, the designated Security Assistance Office, or the state's in-country representative in the United States. See Reuter, *The ABCs of FMS*, 30 Cont. Mgmt. 29 (Oct. 1990).

LEVEL-OF-EFFORT CONTRACT A type of contract stating the work in terms of an amount of effort (usually man-hours or man-years) to be performed by specified classes of employees over a given period of time. There are four types of level-of-effort contracts: the FIXED-PRICE LEVEL-OF-EFFORT CONTRACT, the TIME-AND-MATERIALS (T&M) CONTRACT, the LABOR-HOUR (L-H) CONTRACT, and the TERM CONTRACT. See Cibinic and Nash, Formation of Government Contracts 790–97.

LICENSE A legal instrument granting permission to do a particular thing, to exercise a certain privilege, to carry on a particular business, or to pursue a certain occupation. When granted by an appropriate government body, licenses are permits allowing a person, firm, or corporation to pursue some occupation or business, subject to regulation. Black's Law Dictionary. Under the Permits and Responsibilities clause in FAR 52.236-7, construction contractors bear the responsibility for obtaining necessary licenses and permits and complying with any Federal, State, and municipal laws, codes, and regulations applicable to the performance of the work on fixed-price construction or dismantling, demolition, or removal-of-improvements contracts. FAR 36.507.

LICENSE RIGHTS See GOVERNMENT-PURPOSE LICENSE RIGHTS (GPLR) and DIRECT LICENSE.

LICENSE TO USE INVENTION See PATENT LICENSE.

LIFE-CYCLE COST The TOTAL COST to the Government of acquiring, operating, supporting, and (if applicable) disposing of the items being acquired. FAR 7.101. Procuring agencies are expected to consider the life-cycle cost of a product in the ACQUISITION PLANNING process. FAR 7.105. However, the FAR contains no guidance on the use of life-cycle costs to improve the procurement process. Life-cycle COST ANALYSIS is the structured study of estimates and elements to identify cost drivers, total cost to the Government, cost-risk items, and cost-effective changes; it is a SYSTEM ENGINEERING tool with application to all elements of the system. DoD policy establishes life-cycle cost as a parameter equal in importance to technical requirements and schedules. DSMC, Program Manager's Notebook; Part 6 of DoD Instruction 5000.2, *Defense Acquisition Management Policies and Procedures*, 23 Feb. 1991. The only area in which life-cycle costs must be used as EVALUATION FACTORS is FEDERAL INFORMATION PROCESSING (FIP) RESOURCES procurement.   FIRMR 201-39.1701-1 requires comparative cost analysis to determine the methods of acquisition representing the lowest overall cost over the SYSTEM LIFE. See Cibinic and Nash, Formation of Government Contracts 544–46.

LIMITATION OF COST (LOC) CLAUSE A key clause used in COST-REIMBURSEMENT CONTRACTs to obligate the contractor to use its best efforts to perform the work specified and all obligations under the contract within the ESTIMATED COST. The clause meets the requirements of the ANTI-DEFICIENCY ACT by limiting the obligation of the Government to an amount no greater than the contract's estimated cost plus any required FEE, unless the contract is modified to state a greater amount. The clause requires the contractor to notify the contracting officer, in writing, whenever the contractor has reason to believe that (1) the costs the contractor expects to incur under the contract within a specified period (usually 1 to 3 months), when added to all costs previously incurred, will exceed a specified percentage (usually 75 to 85 percent) of the estimated cost, or (2) the total cost for the performance of the contract, exclusive of fee, will be either greater or substantially less than had been previously estimated. In the absence of the specified notice, the Government is not obligated to reimburse the contractor for any costs in excess of the estimated cost. The basic clause is set forth in FAR 52.232-20. See Cibinic and Nash, Cost Reimbursement Contracting 101–4; Madden and Walsh, *The Limitation of Cost & Funds Clauses*, 85-11 Briefing Papers (Nov. 1985).

LIMITATION OF FUNDS (LOF) CLAUSE   A clause, FAR 52.232-22, that must be included in all incrementally funded COST-REIMBURSEMENT CONTRACTs. It specifies, as prescribed in FAR 32.705-2(c), that a contractor must notify the contracting officer in writing when it appears that additional funds must be allotted to the contract to complete performance. The LOF clause and the LIMITATION OF COST (LOC) CLAUSE, FAR 52.232.20, are the basis for the contractor's freedom from performance risks. Even if the contract contains a completion-type statement of work, with definitive performance requirements and fixed performance dates, these clauses operate to relieve the contractor from any legal obligation to complete the work. The contractor agrees to perform the work as long as the Government continues to provide funds. Once the funds have been exhausted, the contractor's obligation is generally considered complete. See *Ball Brothers Research Corp.*, NASABCA 12277-6, 80-2 BCA ¶ 14,529; Cibinic and Nash, Cost Reimbursement Contracting 104–5; Madden and Walsh, *The Limitation of Cost & Funds Clauses*, 85-11 Briefing Papers (Nov. 1985).

LIMITED RIGHTS The right of the Government to reproduce and use data with the express limitation that they will not, without written permission of the contractor, be used for purposes of manufacture nor disclosed outside the Government (except for purposes listed in the contract). FAR 27.401. DFARS 227.401 contains a similar definition that is more detailed in coverage. In either regulation, limited rights are those rights which a contractor is entitled to assert in LIMITED RIGHTS DATA. The rights are basically designed to give the contractor protection against use of this type of data by competitors. Nash, *Removal of Limited Rights Legends from Technical Data: Playing Hardball*, 1 N&CR ¶ 85 (Nov. 1987).

LIMITED RIGHTS DATA   DATA (other than COMPUTER SOFT-WARE) that embody TRADE SECRETs or are commercial or financial and confidential or privileged, to the extent that such data pertain to items, components, or processes DEVELOPED AT PRIVATE EXPENSE, including minor modifications thereof. FAR 27.401. The FAR also contains an alternative, general definition that may be used in contracts for research work: data developed at private expense that embody trade secrets or are commercial or financial and confidential or privileged. FAR 27.404. Under the Rights in Data—General clause at FAR 52.227-14, the contractor may protect qualifying limited rights data and restricted computer software by withholding them from delivery to the Government and delivering FORM, FIT, AND FUNCTION DATA instead. Under the DFARS, "limited rights data" means unpublished TECHNICAL DATA pertaining to items, components, or processes DEVELOPED EXCLUSIVELY AT PRIVATE EXPENSE, provided the data are properly marked with the limited rights legend and provided they do not fall within a list of categories contained in the Rights in Technical Data and Computer Software clause at DFARS 252.227-7013.

LINE ITEM   An item of supply or service, specified in an INVITATION FOR BIDS (IFB), for which the bidder must bid a separate price. FAR 3.302. Line items are set forth in Section B of the UNIFORM CONTRACT FORMAT in both IFBs and REQUESTs FOR PROPOSALS (RFPs) whenever the contracting officer determines that separate prices should be obtained. Line item, as used in the FAR discussion of reporting, redistribution, and disposal of contractor inventory, means a single line entry on a reporting form that indicates a quantity of property having the same description and condition code from any one contract at any one reporting location. FAR 45.601. See DFARS Subpart 204.71, which discusses contract line items and subline items.

LIQUIDATED DAMAGES   An express provision in a contract stating a sum for which one of the parties will be liable upon BREACH OF CONTRACT or failure to perform. FAR Subpart 12.2 contains the policies and procedures governing the use of liquidated damages to cover late performance of Government contracts. FAR 12.202 states that liquidated damages clauses should be used only when both (1) the time of delivery or performance is such an important factor that the Government can reasonably expect to suffer damage if delivery or performance is delinquent, and (2) the extent or amount of damage would be difficult or impossible to ascertain or prove. The rate of liquidated damages used must be reasonable, since liquidated damages fixed without any reference to probable actual damages may be held to be a penalty, and therefore unenforceable. In construction contracts, liquidated damages should be assessed for each day of delay, and the rate should, as a minimum, cover (1) the estimated cost of inspection and superintendence for each day of delay in completion, and (2) specific losses due to the failure to complete the work, such as the cost of substitute facilities, rental costs, or continued payment of quarters allowance. FAR 12.203. 15 U.S.C. 637(d)(4)(F) allows a CONTRACTING OFFICER (CO) to assess liquidated damages when a contractor fails to make a good-faith effort (see DUTY OF GOOD FAITH AND FAIR DEALING) to comply with a subcontracting plan. FAR 19.705-7. See Cibinic and Nash, Administration of Government Contracts 799–816; Margulies, chap. 11, Construction Contracting 878–96; Witte, *Default, Liquidated Damages*

Changes, Excusable Delay and Contractor Fraud, 27 Cont. Mgmt. 36 (Oct. 1987).

LOAN GUARANTEE See GUARANTEED LOAN.

LOBBYING ACT See ANTI-LOBBYING ACT.

LOBBYING COSTS Costs incurred by a contractor to influence the outcome of legislation. Legislative lobbying costs are considered UNALLOWABLE COSTs if associated with any of the following: (1) attempts to influence the outcome of a Federal, State, or local election, referendum, initiative, or similar procedure, through contributions, endorsements, publicity, or similar activities; (2) establishing, administering, contributing to, or paying the expenses of a political party, political campaign, or political action committee; (3) any attempt to influence the introduction of Federal or State legislation, or the enactment or modification of any pending Federal or State legislation, through communication with a member or employee of the Congress or State legislature, or with a government official or employee in connection with a decision to sign or veto enrolled legislation, or by preparing, distributing or using publicity or propaganda, or by urging the public to contribute to or participate in a mass demonstration, march, rally, fund-raising drive, lobbying campaign, or letter-writing or telephone campaign; or (4) legislative liaison activities, gathering information regarding legislation, and analyzing the effect of legislation, when such activities are in support of or in knowing preparation for an effort to engage in unallowable activities. FAR 31.205-22. Lobbying costs are considered ALLOWABLE COSTs, however, if they involve (1) presentation of technical and factual information on a topic directly related to contract performance, (2) efforts to influence State legislation to directly reduce contract cost or avoid impairment of contract performance, and (3) any activity specifically authorized by statute to be funded under the contract. FAR 31.2-5-22(b).

LOGISTICS The science of planning, obtaining, maintaining, and transporting materials, personnel, and facilities. More specifically, logistics refers to those aspects of military operations that deal with (1) design and development, acquisition, storage, movement, distribution, maintenance, evacuation, and disposition of materials; (2) movement, evacuation, and hospitalization of personnel; (3) acquisition, maintenance, operation, and disposition of facilities; and (4) acquisition or furnishing of services. Jones, Glossary: Defense Acquisition Acronyms and Terms.

LOSS The failure to earn a profit on a contract because the costs of performance (both DIRECT COSTs and INDIRECT COSTs) have exceeded the amount paid to the contractor under the terms of a contract. FAR 31.205-23 states that losses on other contracts are UNALLOWABLE COSTs.

LOWEST OVERALL COST The least expenditure of funds over a system's or an item's life, with price and other factors considered. FIRMR 201-4.001. Agencies should use GSA's nonmandatory schedule contracts (see FEDERAL SUPPLY SCHEDULES (FSS)) for FIP resources when that would result in a lower overall cost than would other contracting methods. FIRMR 201-39.803-1. Lowest overall cost is calculated on the basis of purchase price, lease or rental prices, or service prices of the contract actions involved, as well as other identifiable and quantifiable costs directly related to the acquisition and use of the system/item (for example, personnel, maintenance and operation, site preparation, energy consumption, installation, conversion, system start-up, contractor support, and the PRESENT VALUE discount factor). The quantifiable cost of conducting the contracting action and other administrative costs directly related to the acquisition process are also included. FIRMR 201-39.201. The costs considered in deriving lowest overall cost for a telecommunication acquisition include such elements as personnel, purchase price or rentals, maintenance, site preparation and installation, programming, and training. See Gabig and Bean, *A Primer on Federal Information Systems Acquisitions: Part Two of a Two-Part Article*, 17 Pub. Cont. L.J. 553, 588 (1988).

LOWEST RESPONSIVE, RESPONSIBLE BIDDER The bidder in a sealed bid procurement (see SEALED BIDDING) that is entitled to award of the contract. 10 U.S.C. 2305(b)(3) and 41 U.S.C. 253b(c) require award to the responsible source (see RESPONSIBILITY) whose bid conforms to the solicitation (see RESPONSIVENESS) and is most advantageous to the Government, considering only price and other PRICE-RELATED FACTORS included in the solicitation. Detailed guidance is set forth in FAR Part 14.

M

MAILBOX RULE A common law rule providing that an ACCEP-
TANCE OF an OFFER becomes effective (creates a binding contract)
when it is transmitted rather than when it is received. Restatement
(Second) of Contracts § 63. However, there is some authority
holding that acceptance is not binding until the document is
received by the offeror. *Rhode Island Tool Co. v. United States*,
130 Ct. Cl. 698 (1955). See Cibinic and Nash, Formation of
Government Contracts 168–70.

MAINTENANCE AND OPERATING CONTRACT See MANAGE-
MENT AND OPERATING (M&O) CONTRACT.

MAJOR DEFENSE ACQUISITION PILOT PROGRAM The
program under which the Secretary of Defense may designate up
to six major defense acquisition programs and conduct those
programs in accordance with standard commercial industrial
practices in order to determine the potential for making the
acquisition process more efficient and effective. The program
permits the Secretary of Defense to waive or limit the applicability
of laws prescribing procurement procedures; source preference
requirements; contractor performance requirements; cost allowability, cost accounting, or auditing requirements; or management,
testing, evaluation, or reporting requirements. The program was
created by section 809 of the FY 91 Defense Authorization Act,
Pub. L. 101-510, 104 Stat. 1485, 10 U.S.C. 2430.

MAJOR DEFENSE ACQUISITION PROGRAM A program
designated as such by the Secretary of Defense or a program that
will exceed $200 million for research, development, test, and
evaluation or $1 billion for total procurement (calculated in FY
1980 constant dollars). 10 U.S.C. 2430. These programs are

subject to the detailed reporting and management requirements in chapter 144 of 10 U.S.C.

MAJOR SYSTEM A combination of elements that will function together to produce the capabilities required to fulfill a mission need, including hardware, equipment, software, or any combination of these, but excluding construction. A major system must meet one of the following guidelines: (1) DoD estimates that the costs of test, research, development, and evaluation will exceed $75 million; (2) DoD expects to spend more than $300 million on the acquisition; (3) a civilian agency estimates total expenditures exceeding $750,000; or (4) the agency head designates the system as such. 41 U.S.C. 403(9); FAR 34.001. Special procedures are generally used for the procurement of major systems. See MAJOR SYSTEM ACQUISITION.

MAJOR SYSTEM ACQUISITION The process used to acquire a MAJOR SYSTEM. Contracts formed as part of this process will be for one or more of the four phases of major system development: (1) concept exploration—relatively short contract periods of performance at low dollar levels; (2) demonstration—contractors submit priced proposals, funded by the Government, for full-scale system development; (3) full-scale development—contractors should be in a position to submit priced proposals for production based on the latest quantity, schedule, and LOGISTICS requirements as well as any other factor used in making the production decision; and (4) full production—production of successfully tested major systems selected from the full-scale development phase. FAR Part 34 reflects the guidelines in OMB Circular No. A-109, *Major Systems Acquisitions*, 5 Apr. 1976. See OFPP Pamphlet No. 1, Aug. 1976, A *Discussion of the Application of OMB Circular No. A-109*; NASA Management Instruction 7110.14, *Major Systems Acquisitions*; Kaeser, *Major Defense Acquisition Programs: A Study of Congressional Control over DoD Acquisitions*, 34 Fed. B. News & J. 430 (1987).

MAKE ITEM An item or work effort to be produced or performed by the prime contractor or its AFFILIATES, subsidiaries, or divisions. FAR 15.701. See also BUY ITEM. Such items are reviewed by the contracting officer when FAR 15.703 requires review of a contractor's MAKE-OR-BUY PROGRAM.

MAKE-OR-BUY PROGRAM   That part of a contractor's written plan for a contract identifying (1) those major items to be produced or work efforts to be performed in the prime contractor's facilities and (2) those to be subcontracted. FAR 15.701. The Government may reserve the right to review and agree on the contractor's make-or-buy program when necessary to ensure (1) negotiation of reasonable contract prices, (2) satisfactory performance, or (3) implementation of socioeconomic policies. Make-or-buy programs are required for negotiated acquisitions over $5 million, with certain exceptions. FAR 15.703.

MANAGEMENT AND OPERATING (M&O) CONTRACT   An agreement under which the Government contracts for the operation, maintenance, or support, on its behalf, of a Government-owned or Government-controlled research, development, special production, or testing establishment wholly or principally devoted to one or more major programs of the contracting Federal agency. FAR 17.601. An M&O contract is characterized both by its purpose and by the special relationship it creates between Government and contractor. Certain criteria generally apply: (1) the situation requires the use of Government facilities (in the interest of national defense or mobilization readiness, for example, or to perform the agency's mission adequately, or because private enterprise is unable or unwilling to use its own facilities for the work); (2) because of the nature of the work, or because it is to be performed in Government facilities, the Government must maintain a special, close relationship with the contractor and the contractor's personnel in such important areas as safety, security, cost control, and site conditions; (3) the conduct of the work is wholly or at least substantially separate from the contractor's other business, if any; and (4) the work is closely related to the agency's mission and is of a long-term or continuous nature, and there is a need (a) to ensure its continuity and (b) to have special protection covering the orderly transition of personnel and work in the event of a change in contractors. FAR 17.604. The FAR coverage on this subject, Subpart 17.6, was written principally with the needs of DoE in mind; the subpart's provisions do not apply to DoD. DFARS Subpart 217.6. See Madsen et al., *Management Contractors and Environmental Damage: Who Shall Pay?* 37 Fed. B. News & J. 601 (1990). See also GOVERNMENT-OWNED CONTRACTOR-OPERATED PLANT (GOCO).

MANUFACTURER A person who owns, operates, or maintains a factory or establishment that produces on the premises the materials, supplies, articles, or equipment that are required under the contract and are of the general character described by the specifications. FAR 22.601. Generally, all contracts subject to the WALSH-HEALEY PUBLIC CONTRACTS ACT for the manufacture or furnishing of materials in any amount exceeding $10,000 must (1) be made with manufacturers of or REGULAR DEALERs in the supplies manufactured or used in performing the contract, and (2) include or incorporate by reference the representation that the contractor is a manufacturer of or a regular dealer in the supplies offered. See FAR 22.602. FAR 22.606-1 provides different requirements for demonstrating whether an offeror qualifies as an established manufacturer or as a manufacturer newly entering into a manufacturing activity. An "established" manufacturer is one who offers the particular supplies of the general character sought and has the plant, equipment, and personnel needed to manufacture on the premises; whereas a manufacturer who is new to a particular area of industry must show that it has previously made binding arrangements for the facilities and personnel necessary to fulfill the contract, has not been set up solely to produce for the purposes of a single Government contract, and meets certain other criteria.

MANUFACTURING ENGINEERING Developing and deploying new or improved materials, systems, processes, methods, equipment, pilot production lines, tools, and techniques to be used in providing products or services. FAR 31.205-25 specifies that the costs of such work incurred by a contractor are ALLOWABLE COSTs. Such work is not a part of a contractor's INDEPENDENT RESEARCH AND DEVELOPMENT (IR&D) effort.

MANUFACTURING TECHNOLOGY Activities whose objectives are (1) to establish or improve, in a timely manner, the manufacturing processes, techniques, or equipment required to support current and projected programs and (2) to assure the ability to produce, reduce lead time, ensure economic availability of end items, reduce costs, increase efficiency, improve reliability, or enhance safety and anti-pollution measures. Postak, Glossary of Terms, in Subcontracts—Government and Industry Issues. DoD has established special programs to encourage contractors to develop and utilize better manufacturing technology. See DoD

Instruction 4200.15, *Manufacturing Technology Program*, 24 May 1985.

MARCH-IN The right of the Government under 35 U.S.C. 203 to require a contractor or subcontractor that has made a SUBJECT INVENTION to grant another party a license to use that invention if it is determined that the contractor has not achieved PRACTICAL APPLICATION of the invention or a license is needed for public purposes. The conditions for exercising this right are set forth in the Patent Rights clauses in FAR 52.227-11, -12, and -13. The march-in right has not been exercised in any reported instance, but its exercise is subject to appeal in the CLAIMS COURT (Cl. Ct.). 35 U.S.C. 203(2).

MARKET ANALYSIS The process of analyzing prices and trends in the competitive marketplace for the purpose of comparing product availability and offered prices with market alternatives, and establishing the reasonableness of offered prices. FAR 11.004. Armed Services Pricing Manual (ASPM) vol. 1, app. B. Market analysis is one of the elements of PRICE ANALYSIS that is undertaken by the contracting officer to ensure that the contract is being awarded at a FAIR AND REASONABLE PRICE. See also MARKET RESEARCH and MARKET SURVEY.

MARKETING CONSULTANT Any independent contractor that furnishes advice, information, direction, or assistance to an offeror or any other contractor in support of the preparation or submission of an OFFER for a Government contract. An independent contractor is *not* a marketing consultant when rendering the following: services excluded from the definition of ADVISORY AND ASSISTANCE SERVICES by FAR 37.2; routine engineering and technical services (such as installation, operation, or maintenance of systems, equipment, software, components, or facilities); routine legal, actuarial, auditing, and accounting services; or training services. FAR 9.501. FAR 9.507-1(b) requires the inclusion of the Organizational Conflicts of Interest Certificate—Marketing Consultants provision, FAR 52.209-7, in solicitations other than those for sealed bids when the contract amount is expected to exceed $200,000. The FAR coverage implements OFPP Policy Letter 89-1, *Conflict of Interest Policies Applicable to Consultants*.

MARKET PRICE See ESTABLISHED CATALOG OR MARKET PRICE.

MARKET RESEARCH The process used by the contracting officer to collect and analyze information about the entire market available to satisfy an agency's needs, so that the most suitable approach can be taken to acquiring, distributing, and supporting supplies and services. FAR 10.001. Market research is required by 10 U.S.C. 2305(a)(1)(A)(ii) and 41 U.S.C. 253a(a)(1)(B). It involves obtaining the following information: (1) the availability of products suitable for meeting a particular need; (2) the terms and conditions and warranty practices under which commercial sales of the products are made; (3) legal and regulatory requirements; (4) the number of sales and length of time over which they must occur to provide reasonable assurance that a particular product is reliable; (5) the distribution and support capabilities of potential suppliers; and (6) the potential cost of modifying commercial products to meet the Government's particular needs. FAR 11.004.

MARKET SURVEY An attempt by a contracting agency to ascertain whether there are unknown qualified sources capable of satisfying the Government's requirements. FAR 7.101. This testing of the marketplace may range from written or telephone contact with Federal and other experts regarding similar or duplicate requirements (and the results of any market test recently undertaken) to more formal "sources-sought" announcements in scientific journals or the COMMERCE BUSINESS DAILY (CBD) or SOLICITATIONs for information or planning purposes. When a solicitation is issued for information or planning purposes, the face of the solicitation must include a notice that no contract will be awarded under the solicitation. FAR 15.405. In such cases, the agency must include the Solicitation for Information for Planning Purposes provision in FAR 52.215-3.

MASTER AGREEMENT FOR REPAIR AND ALTERATION OF VESSELS A form of BASIC AGREEMENT used for the repair and alteration of ships. It is not a contract but, rather, a written instrument of understanding that establishes in advance the terms and conditions upon which a contractor will effect repairs, alterations, or additions to vessels, under the provisions of job orders awarded by contracting activities from time to time. Job orders (fixed-price contracts entered into with contractors that have previously executed master agreements) apply to specific acquisitions. They set forth the scope of work, price, delivery date, and additional matters peculiar to the acquisition, and they incorporate by reference or append the appropriate clauses from the master agreement. DFARS 217.7101.

MATERIAL Property that may be incorporated into or attached to a deliverable end item or that may be consumed or expended in the performance of a contract. FAR 45.301. The term includes assemblies, components, parts, raw and processed materials, and small tools and supplies that may be consumed in normal use in the performance of a contract. FAR 45.303-1 provides that contractors must ordinarily be required to furnish all material necessary to perform their contracts but that the Government should provide material when necessary to achieve significant economy, standardization, or expedited production. FAR 45.505-3 contains the requirements for contractor management and control of GOVERNMENT-FURNISHED MATERIAL (GFM), including material to which title has passed to the Government as the result of the payment provisions of the contract. Cost Accounting Standard 411, FAR 30.411, sets forth rules that govern accounting for costs of material.

MATERIAL INSPECTION AND RECEIVING REPORT (MIRR) A DoD form used to document the INSPECTION and acceptance (see ACCEPTANCE OF WORK) of supplies and services. DFARS Appendix F sets forth procedures and instructions for using, preparing, and distributing (1) the Material Inspection and Receiving Report (DD Forms 250 series) and (2) suppliers' commercial shipping/packing lists used as evidence of Government procurement QUALITY ASSURANCE (QA). MIRRs are used to document QA, acceptance of supplies and services, and shipments. They are used by receiving, status control, technical, contracting, inventory control, requisitioning, and paying activities. The procedures of Appendix F apply to supplies or services procured by DoD when the contract includes the Material Inspection and Receiving Report clause at DFARS 252.246-7000.

MATERIAL MANAGEMENT AND ACCOUNTING SYSTEM (MMAS) The contractor's system for planning, controlling, and accounting for the acquisition, use, and disposition of MATERIAL. Such systems may be manual or automated and may be integrated with planning, engineering, estimating, purchasing, inventory, accounting, and other systems, or they may be essentially stand-alone systems. DFARS 252.242-7004. DoD policy requires that all contractors have a system that reasonably forecasts material requirements, ensures that the costs of purchased and fabricated material charged or allocated to a contract are based on VALID TIME-PHASED REQUIREMENTS, and maintains a consistent, equitable, and unbiased logic for costing of material transactions. DFARS 242.7202. See Nash, *Material Management Accounting Systems: What Cost Perfect Knowledge?* 5 N&CR ¶ 36 (June 1991); Lemmer, *Material Management and Accounting*, 88-6 Briefing Papers (May 1988).

MATERIAL REQUIREMENTS PLANNING (MRP) SYSTEM Any form of computerized manufacturing management and scheduling system. The Defense Contract Audit Agency (DCAA) describes an MRP system as one that identifies, initiates procurement of, and maintains current and future materials necessary to support production operations. MRP is a method of inventory control, not inventory costing. DCAA identifies the following features as common to the various MRP design configurations: (1) highly automated systems with extensive use of data processing; (2) a master production schedule that maintains a balance between requirements and replenishments; (3) a netting process that involves a netting formula derived from requirements and replenishments; and (4) dynamic scheduling of items in the production process. DCAA Contract Audit Manual (CAM) 6-308. Concern that deficiencies in these systems, or in their use, caused overcharging led DoD to issue compliance guidelines and DCAA to publish extensive guidance on MRPs. See 48 Fed. Cont. Rep. 936 (14 Dec. 1987) and 49 Fed. Cont. Rep. 427, 482 (14 Mar. 1988). And see *House Panel Votes to Require Certification of MRP Systems*, 49 Fed. Cont. Rep. 579 (28 Mar. 1988); Fordham and Polakoff, *MRP and the DoD Solution*, 28 Cont. Mgmt. 16 (Oct. 1988); Holter, *MRP and Government Contract Costing: Are They Compatible?* 21 NCMJ 1 (1987).

MATRIX See PROVISION AND CLAUSE MATRIX.

MAXIMUM FEE Dollar amount negotiated at the inception of a COST-PLUS-INCENTIVE FEE (CPIF) CONTRACT as the maximum amount of PROFIT that the contractor is entitled to receive. After contract performance the FEE payable to the contractor is determined in accordance with a contract-specified fee-adjustment formula based on the relationship of total ALLOWABLE COST to total TARGET COST. When total allowable cost is *less* than the range of cost within which the fee-adjustment formula operates (see RANGE OF INCENTIVE EFFECTIVENESS), the contractor is paid the total allowable cost plus the maximum fee. FAR 16.404-1.

MEASUREMENT OF COST Accounting methods and techniques used in defining the components of cost, determining the basis for cost measurement, and establishing criteria for use of alternative cost measurement techniques. FAR 30.302-1. Such measurement is one type of COST ACCOUNTING PRACTICE. Examples of cost accounting practices that involve measurement of costs are (1) the use of HISTORICAL COST, MARKET VALUE, or PRESENT VALUE; (2) the use of STANDARD COST or ACTUAL COST; or (3) the designation of those items of cost that must be included in or excluded from TANGIBLE CAPITAL ASSET or PENSION PLAN costs.

MEMORANDUM OF UNDERSTANDING (MOU) An executive agreement with a foreign government. MOUs are used by DoD and NASA in situations in which it would be inconsistent with the public interest to apply the restrictions of the BUY AMERICAN ACT to acquisitions of certain supplies mined, produced, or manufactured in designated foreign countries. FAR 25.103. DoD policies for applying the domestic preference laws and programs to offers of products from "qualifying" foreign countries can be found at DFARS Subpart 225.872. Specific MOUs are negotiated with each country.

MENTOR FIRM See MENTOR–PROTÉGÉ PILOT PROGRAM.

MENTOR–PROTÉGÉ PILOT PROGRAM A test program that encourages major DoD contractors to act as "mentors" to SMALL DISADVANTAGED BUSINESS CONCERNs (SDBCs). The program seeks to increase the participation of SDBCs as subcontractors and suppliers under DoD contracts, other Federal Government contracts, and commercial contracts by furnishing them with assistance aimed at enhancing their performance. It provides mentor firms with incentives including reimbursement equal to the total amount of PROGRESS PAYMENTs made under the program to a protege firm, reimbursement for the costs of the assistance furnished, or recognition of costs as "credits" in lieu of subcontract awards towards subcontracting participation goals. The program was created by section 831 of the FY 91 Defense Authorization Act, Pub. L. 101-510, 104 Stat. 1485, 10 U.S.C. 2430, and is implemented by DFARS 219.71 (see DAC 91-1, 56 Fed. Reg. 67208, 30 Dec. 1991). A mentor firm must (1) have

DoD contracts of at least $100 million and (2) demonstrate the capability to assist in the development of protege firms, and (3) be approved by the Secretary of Defense. A protégé firm must be a small business concern owned and controlled by socially and economically disadvantaged individuals as defined by the Small Business Act. 15 U.S.C. 637(d)(3)(C).

MERGER See BUSINESS COMBINATION.

METHODS OF PROCUREMENT A broad term describing the way the Government procures supplies and services, including construction.   The Government uses two basic methods of procurement: SEALED BIDDING (see FAR Part 14) and NEGOTIA-TION (see FAR Part 15). Any contract awarded without using sealed bidding procedures is a negotiated contract. FAR 15.101. The simplified SMALL PURCHASE PROCEDURES of FAR Part 13 are a subset of negotiation.   Procurement methods can also be characterized as those meeting the statutory requirement for FULL AND OPEN COMPETITION and those not meeting this requirement. Those meeting the requirement are said to use COMPETITIVE PROCEDURES; those not meeting it include sole-source acquisition (see SOLE SOURCE), use of UNSOLICITED PROPOSALs, and various other processes.   FAR Part 17 discusses special contracting methods, including MULTIYEAR CONTRACTING (covering more than 1 year but not more than 5 years of requirements), OPTIONs (under which the Government has the unilateral right to increase the quantity or extend the term of the contract), LEADER-COMPANY CONTRACTING (under which a developer or sole proprietor furnishes assistance and know-how to another contractor so that the latter can become a source of supply), and INTERAGENCY ACQUISITION.

MILITARY DEPARTMENT See DEPARTMENT OF DEFENSE (DoD).

MILITARY SPECIFICATIONS (MIL-SPECs) AND STAN-DARDS (MIL-STDs) SPECIFICATIONs and STANDARDs, unique to DoD, that are prepared, maintained, and controlled by the Secretary of Defense. FAR 10.003(b). Unclassified MIL-SPECs and MIL-STDs, along with related standardization documents and VOLUNTARY STANDARDs adopted by DoD, are listed in the *Department of Defense Index of Specifications and Standards (DODISS)*. FAR 10.001. Military specifications and standards and voluntary standards listed in the DODISS are mandatory for use by Defense agencies, expect when any of the exceptions listed at FAR 10.006(a) apply. The DODISS is available from the U.S. Government Printing Office, Washington, DC 20402.

MILITARY STANDARD REQUISITIONING AND ISSUE PROCEDURE (MILSTRIP) A procedure used by the military departments to requisition material or place Government material under supply control. When authorized by the terms of a contract, contractors may also use MILSTRIP, which uses uniform codes and punch-card formats to standardize procedures for requisitioning, receiving, and returning material and permit the maximum utilization of automatic data processing equipment. MILSTRIP applies when DoD contractors requisition from GSA supply sources. The Defense Logistics Standard Systems Office (DLSSO) is responsible for MILSTRIP. See DoD Manual 4140.17-M, *Military Standards Requisitioning and Issue Procedures.*

MILLER ACT A 1935 act, 40 U.S.C. 270a-270f, requiring the execution of separate PERFORMANCE BONDs and PAYMENT BONDs as a prerequisite to award of CONSTRUCTION contracts exceeding $25,000. See FAR 28.102. See also DFARS 228.102-1 regarding waivers for cost-reimbursement-type construction contract bonding requirements. The act protects the Government by requiring the performance bond and gives some classes of persons furnishing labor and materials the right to recover under a payment bond. A performance bond SURETY under the Miller Act is liable for all monetary sums arising from the contract that the Government has with the contractor, not to exceed the bond's PENAL AMOUNT. Miller Act jurisdiction for laborers and material-men suing for compensation under the payment bond is limited to actions against the contractor or its sureties and grants no right of action against a subcontractor. Patin, chap. 17, Construction Contracting 1222–1334.

MINIMUM FEE Dollar amount negotiated at the inception of a COST-PLUS-INCENTIVE FEE (CPIF) CONTRACT as the minimum amount of PROFIT that the contractor is entitled to receive. After contract performance the FEE payable to the contractor is determined in accordance with a contract-specified fee-adjustment formula based on the relationship of total ALLOWABLE COST to total TARGET COST. When total allowable cost is *greater* than the range of cost within which the fee-adjustment formula operates (see RANGE OF INCENTIVE EFFECTIVENESS), the contractor is paid the total allowable cost plus the minimum fee. FAR 16.404-1. The minimum fee is usually a positive number (i.e., the contractor is guaranteed to make a profit). However, if a high MAXIMUM FEE is negotiated, the contract must also provide for a low minimum fee. This low minimum fee may be a zero fee (in which case the contractor would be paid total allowable cost only). In rare cases, it may be a negative fee (the contractor would be paid total allowable cost *minus* the minimum fee; in other words, its losses would be limited). FAR 16.404-1(b)(3).

MINIMUM NEEDS   A misnomer for the rule that contracting agencies may not use specifications or conditions that are unduly restrictive (see RESTRICTIVE SPECIFICATIONS). See FAR 10.004, which provides that plans, drawings, SPECIFICATIONs, STANDARDs, or PURCHASE DESCRIPTIONs must state only the Government's actual "minimum needs" and describe the supplies and/or services in a manner designed to promote FULL AND OPEN COMPETITION. The term is misleading because it suggests that Government agencies must buy supplies and services that are minimally effective. This clearly is not so because the determination of minimum needs is a technical and economic judgment properly left to the procuring agency. See Cibinic and Nash, Formation of Government Contracts 345–47.

MINITRIAL   A flexible, voluntary, and nonjudicial settlement procedure wherein members of top management (called "principals") hear a short presentation of the factual and legal positions of the parties and engage in nonbinding negotiations to resolve a CLAIM. In most cases they are aided by a NEUTRAL ADVISOR who acts as a mediator between the principals. This procedure permits either party to withdraw at any time without prejudicing the litigation process. Management officials of both parties meet to resolve the dispute rather than permit a third party—a judge or arbitrator—to control the process. This technique is expressly recognized by the ADMINISTRATIVE DISPUTE RESOLUTION ACT. Among the various ALTERNATIVE DISPUTE RESOLUTION (ADR) options, the minitrial process presently appears to be the most widely used in dealing with Government contract claims. See Page and Lees, *Roles of Participants in the Mini-Trial*, 18 Pub. Cont. L.J. 54 (1988) (includes the text of a minitrial agreement used by the Corps of Engineers); Crowell et al., *Applying Alternate Dispute Resolution to Contract Claims*, 1 Admin. L.J. 553

(1987) (issue devoted to a Colloquium on Improving Dispute Resolution: Options for the Federal Government).

MINOR INFORMALITIES OR IRREGULARITIES IN BIDS An immaterial defect or variation from the exact requirements of the INVITATION FOR BIDS (IFB) that can be corrected or waived without prejudice to other bidders. FAR 14.405. Such defects or variations are of so little import that they do not keep a bid from being responsive (see RESPONSIVENESS). A defect or variation is immaterial when the effect on price, quantity, quality, or delivery is negligible in comparison with the total cost or scope of the supplies or services being acquired. The contracting officer must give the bidder an opportunity to cure any deficiency resulting from a minor informality or irregularity, or must waive the deficiency, whichever is to the advantage of the Government. Examples of minor informalities or irregularities include failure of a bidder to return the number of copies of signed bids required by the IFB and failure to furnish required information concerning number of employees. See Cibinic and Nash, Formation of Government Contracts 408–37.

MINORITY INSTITUTION (MI) An institution meeting the requirements prescribed by the Secretary of Education at 34 CFR 607.2. The term also includes any nonprofit research institution that was an integral part of a HISTORICALLY BLACK COLLEGE OR UNIVERSITY (HBCU) before 14 Nov. 1986. DFARS 252.226-7000. In furtherance of the Government policy of placing a fair proportion of its acquisitions with MIs, HBCUs, and small disadvantaged business concerns (SDBCs), section 1207 of Pub. L. 99-661 (10 U.S.C. 2301), section 806 of Pub. L. 100-180 (10 U.S.C. 2301), and section 844 of Pub. L. 100-456 (10 U.S.C. 2301) established the DoD objectives of (1) awarding a combined total of 5 percent of its total contract dollars during each of the fiscal years 1987 through 1993 to MIs and HBCUs, and (2) maximizing the number of such entities participating in DoD prime contracts and subcontracts. See DFARS 226.7000; An Inventory of the Capabilities of the Historically Black Colleges and Universities and Other Minority Institutions (HBCUs/MIs): A NAFEO/DoD Survey; Lambert and Shillito, *DoD Implements Congressional Mandate to Meet a Five Percent Contract Goal for Minorities*, 27 Cont. Mgmt. 16 (Oct. 1987).

MISCHARGING The improper charging of a cost to a Government contract. FAR 31.205-15 makes such costs incurred by contractors—including the cost of identification, measurement and correction—UNALLOWABLE COSTs. Mischarging can arise through improper ALLOCATION OF COSTs or through charging of EXPRESSLY UNALLOWABLE COSTs to a contract. It constitutes criminal conduct under the FALSE CLAIMS ACT. See Graham, *Mischarging: A Contract Dispute or a Criminal Fraud?* 15 Pub. Cont. L.J. 208 (1985).

MISREPRESENTATION Any verbal or other communication made by one person to another that, under the circumstances, amounts to an assertion that does not accord with the facts. Misrepresentations include untrue statements of fact and intentional false statements. A misrepresentation entails either a false statement of a substantive fact or any conduct that intentionally deceives or misleads another person so that, with respect to a substantive fact material to proper understanding of the matter at hand, the other person believes what is not true. Black's Law Dictionary. See Cibinic and Nash, Administration of Government Contracts 99–100. The remedies for misrepresentation are DISQUALIFICATION before contract award or RESCISSION after contract award. See also FALSE STATEMENTS ACT.

MISTAKE A belief that is not in accord with the existing facts (but not an error in business judgment). Mistakes made by contractors may be discovered either before or after contract award. Before award, the contracting officer has a duty to notify the offeror of any suspected mistake and to request verification that no mistake was made (see DUTY OF VERIFICATION). In SEALED BIDDING procurements, mistakes discovered before award entitle the contractor either to withdraw the bid or to correct the bid, in very limited circumstances, in accordance with the guidance in FAR 14.406. In negotiated procurements (see NEGOTIATION), mistakes are generally corrected in the course of written or oral DISCUSSIONs in accordance with the procedures in FAR 15.607. If a mistake is discovered after award, the contractor may receive REFORMATION if there was a MUTUAL MISTAKE or a UNILATERAL MISTAKE that the contracting officer was, or should have been, on notice of. See Cibinic and Nash, Administration of Government Contracts 233–52; Arnavas and Ganther, *Preventive Preaward Actions*, 90-9 Briefing Papers (Aug. 1990); Gammon and Allen,

Postaward Relief for Mistakes in Bids, 88-11 Briefing Papers (Oct. 1988).

MOBILIZATION   See INDUSTRIAL MOBILIZATION.

MODEL PROCUREMENT CODE (MPC)   A model code containing basic rules for contracting by State and local governments that was adopted by the American Bar Association (ABA) in 1979. The MPC provides (1) the statutory principles and policy guidance for managing and controlling the procurement of supplies, services, and construction for public purposes; (2) administrative and judicial remedies for the resolution of controversies relating to public contracts; and (3) a set of ethical standards governing public and private participants in the procurement process. The MPC, which is based on established principles of State and Federal law, is currently adopted by 14 States and a large number of municipalities. Copies of the Model Procurement Code for State and Local Governments, Annotations to the Model Procurement Code, Recommended Regulations, and Ordinance for Local Governments may all be purchased from the American Bar Association (ABA), 750 North Lake Shore Drive, Chicago, IL 60611.

MODIFICATION   Any written change in the terms of a contract. FAR 43.101. any unilateral or bilateral written change in the specifications, delivery point, rate of delivery, contract period, price, quantity, or other provision of an existing contract, accomplished in accordance with a contract clause. Examples are change orders, notices of termination, supplemental agreements, and exercises of contract options. Armed Services Pricing Manual (ASPM) vol. 1, app. B. FAR 43.103 distinguishes bilateral modifications and unilateral modifications. A *bilateral* modification (supplemental agreement) is a contract modification that is signed by the contractor and the contracting officer. Bilateral modifications are used to (1) make negotiated equitable adjustments resulting from the issuance of a change order, (2) definitize letter contracts, and (3) reflect other agreements of the parties modifying the terms of the contract. A *unilateral* modification is a contract modification that is signed only by the contracting officer. Unilateral modifications are used, for example, to (1) make administrative changes, (2) issue change orders, (3) make changes authorized by clauses other than a Changes clause, and (4) issue termination notices. Most Government contracts contain a Changes clause permitting the contracting officer to make unilateral changes in designated areas, within the general scope of the contract. FAR 43.201. See also CHANGE and EQUITABLE ADJUSTMENT.

MOST ADVANTAGEOUS ALTERNATIVE The alternative that provides the greatest value to the Government over the SYSTEM LIFE in terms of price or cost, quality, performance, and any other relevant factors. FIRMR 201-4.001. The FIRMR requires agencies to determine whether using FEDERAL INFORMATION PROCESSING (FIP) RESOURCES available for reassignment or transfer is the most advantageous alternative for satisfying their requirements (although it does not give such use a higher priority than use of other alternatives such as commercial services). FIRMR 201-23.002. Agencies must use GSA's mandatory-for-consideration programs, such as the FEDERAL SOFTWARE EXCHANGE PROGRAM (FSEP), when such use represents the most advantageous alternative for meeting their needs. FIRMR 201-24.001. They must determine whether using purchase of telephones and services (POTS) contracts established by GSA is the most advantageous alternative when such use is not mandatory. FIRMR 201-39.802-1.

MOST FAVORED CUSTOMER   The hypothetical customer receiving the largest discount given to any entity with which the contractor does business. The Government expects contractors on the FEDERAL SUPPLY SCHEDULES (FSS) to sell supplies to the Government at prices not exceeding those given to a contractor's most favored customer. See 47 Fed. Reg. 50242 (5 Nov. 1982); 50 Fed. Reg. 11910 (26 Mar. 1985); 50 Fed. Reg. 50502 (10 Dec. 1985). However, some hold that the Government should receive this treatment only if it is in fact the contractor's largest and best customer, on the basis of past experience or reasonable projection. See Kaufman, *The Myth of the Most Favored Customer*, 18 Pub. Cont. L.J. 29 (1988); Goodrich and Mann, *Avoiding Disaster in Federal Supply Schedule Contracts*, 15 Pub. Cont. L.J. 1 (1984). MULTIPLE-AWARD SCHEDULE (MAS) contracts contain a price reduction clause under which the Government is entitled to receive a reduction in price (or an increase in discount) if a contractor lowers the price (or increases the discount) offered to an "identified" customer after the MAS contract is awarded. Note also that, when an agency orders an item from an MAS contractor at a price lower than the schedule price, the ordering office must notify the schedule contracting office within 10 days. FAR 8.405-1(d). In addition, FAR 15.813 (based on 41 U.S.C. 253(e)) states that, unless certain exceptions apply, the Government should not pay any more for supplies sold to the public than the contractor's lower price. Accordingly, unless exempt, offerors are required to certify that the prices offered are no higher than their lowest commercial prices, unless the difference can be justified. This requirement is implemented by use of the Certification of Commercial Pricing clause in FAR 52.215-32. See Kenney and Kirby, *"Most Favored Customer" Provisions*, 86-3 Briefing Papers (Feb. 1986).

MOVING AVERAGE COST An inventory costing method under which an average unit cost is computed after each acquisition by adding the cost of the newly acquired units to the cost of the units of inventory on hand and dividing this figure by the new total number of units. FAR 31.001.

MULTIPLE-AWARD SCHEDULE (MAS) A schedule in the FEDERAL SUPPLY SCHEDULES (FSS) system that contains prices for comparable supplies or services being offered by more than one supplier. These contracts cover items at either the same or different prices for delivery to a single geographic area. FAR 38.102-2. An MAS permits the Government to use industry distribution facilities effectively and to select among comparable supplies and services when there are no prescribed standards or specifications. Because agencies may select from among several contractors, contractors do not know what volume of sales to expect; consequently, although the agencies benefit by selecting, the sources suffer because of the possibility that few, if any, orders might be placed with them. MAS contracts differ from most Government contracts in that (1) items procured through them are not designed or manufactured to Government specifications, nor are they produced exclusively or principally for Government use, and (2) the Government makes no commitment to purchase any items covered by them. The contractor must sell to any authorized user of the MAS at the prices, and on the terms and conditions, provided in the contract. See MOST FAVORED CUSTOMER. The Government, however, incurs no obligation to buy anything. See Cibinic and Nash, Formation of Government Contracts 688–95; Kaufman, *What GSA Is Entitled to Know about an MAS Contractor's Commercial Discounts*, 15 Pub. Cont. L.J. 224 (1985).

MULTIYEAR APPROPRIATION See APPROPRIATION.

MULTIYEAR CONTRACTING A special contracting method covering more than 1 year but not more than 5 years of requirements, even though the total funds to be obligated are not available at the time of contract award. FAR 17.101, 17.102-2. FAR 17.102-3 states that these contracts are intended to achieve—by permitting early planning and economies of scale—lower costs, standardization, administrative simplicity, and stability, among other things. Multiyear contracts may not cover more than 5 years of requirements unless authorized by statute. Each program year is annually budgeted and funded, and at the time of award funds need only have been appropriated for the first year. The contractor is protected against loss resulting from cancellation by contract provisions that allow reimbursement of costs included in a CANCELLATION CEILING. If funds do not become available to support requirements for the succeeding years, the agency must cancel the contract. See FAR Subpart 17.1. DoD multiyear contracts are subject to the restrictions contained in 10 U.S.C. 2306(h). See Cibinic and Nash, Formation of Government Contracts 820–27.

MUTUAL MISTAKE A MISTAKE common to both parties to a contract. Mutual mistakes can occur when the parties include terms in the contract that do not conform to or express their actual intent or agreement (called mistakes in integration) or when the parties labor under the same misconception about a fundamental fact on which the contract is based (called mistakes in basic assumption). Both types of mutual mistake have led to contract REFORMATION by the courts or through EXTRAORDINARY CONTRACTUAL ACTIONs. FAR 33.205 states that such mistakes should now be dealt with under the DISPUTEs procedures. See Cibinic and Nash, Administration of Government Contracts 233–39.

N

NASA   See NATIONAL AERONAUTICS AND SPACE ADMINISTRATION (NASA).

NASA–DEFENSE PURCHASE REQUEST NASA Form 523, used by NASA contracting offices for requesting procurement of supplies or services from all DEPARTMENT OF DEFENSE (DoD) components. NFS 18-17.7002, 18-53.303-523.

NASA DOMESTIC PREFERENCE A NASA policy that provides that when the use of COMPETITIVE PROCEDURES results in the apparent award of a contract to a foreign firm, the contract will instead be awarded to a domestic firm offering a domestic product—if the domestic offer does not exceed the foreign offer by more than 6 percent. This NASA-unique provision has been placed in NASA's Authorizations Acts each year since FY 89. Pub. L. 100-685, section 209. It rarely applies because the implementing regulation, NFS Subpart 18-25.71, contains a number of exceptions for international agreements and related policies. The implementing regulation contains its own definitions for "domestic product," "domestic firm," and "foreign firm."

NASA FAR SUPPLEMENT (NFS) The NASA acquisition regulation that establishes agency-wide policies and procedures for implementing and supplementing the FEDERAL ACQUISITION REGULATION (FAR). NFS 18-1.101. All agency-wide policies and procedures that govern the contracting process, control contracting relationships, or require publication in the Federal Register for public comment are included in the NFS. NFS 18-1.301. The NFS is normally amended quarterly by NASA FAR Supplement Directives (NFSDs), which are analogous to FEDERAL ACQUISITION CIRCULARS (FACs). Amending the NFS by inserting pages transmitted by a NFSD produces a new version of the NFS. The

Version Number appears on the cover. NFS 18-1.104-2(c). A Procurement Notice (PN) may be used to make urgent amendments between NFSD issuances. NFS 18-1.270-2. PNs are distributed only within NASA, but any regulatory changes dealing with matters other than internal administrative matters are published in the Federal Register simultaneously with PN distribution. PNs are usually incorporated in the NFS within 3 to 4 months of issuance (i.e., when the next NFSD is published). The numbering schemes used in the NFS and in its formally published CFR version are slightly different. The NFS omits the CFR title number and inserts a hyphen after the CFR chapter; for example, 48 CFR 1801.102 is the same as NFS 18-1.102, and 48 CFR 1815.405-2 is the same as NFS 18-15.405-2. The NFS cites or incorporates provisions of some of NASA's nonprocurement documents and handbooks (NHBs). See also NASA MANAGEMENT INSTRUCTION (NMI). The NFS can be purchased as part of the looseleaf-bound subscription edition of the FEDERAL ACQUISITION REGULATIONS (FAR) SYSTEM available from the U.S. Government Printing Office, Washington DC 20402.

NASA MANAGEMENT INSTRUCTION (NMI) A formal document that governs some aspect of NASA operations. Some NMIs establish regulations that apply to all personnel, including procurement personnel. Under such circumstances, the NMI may be referenced in the NASA FAR SUPPLEMENT (NFS); for example, NMI 1210.2, NASA Competition Advocacy Program, is referenced at NFS Subpart 18-6.5. Instructions for obtaining NMIs and a related document series, NASA Handbooks (NHBs), are available from the NASA Information Center, Code DB-4, Washington, DC 20546; (202) 453-1000.

NASA PROCUREMENT REGULATION (NPR) The original regulation issued under the ARMED SERVICES PROCUREMENT ACT (ASPA) to govern NASA procurement practices. It was based on, and very similar to, the ARMED SERVICES PROCUREMENT REGULATION (ASPR) and was in effect from the inception of NASA until 1 Apr. 1984, the beginning of the FEDERAL ACQUISITION REGULATIONS (FAR) SYSTEM. The NPR still applies to any NASA contracts written before Apr. 1984 and not subsequently rewritten to meet FAR requirements. The looseleaf NPR published by NASA as NHB 5100.2 is out of print. However, it still appears in the 1 July 1984 printing of 41 CFR Chapter 18. See the current 41

CFR Subtitle A for more details on the public availability of pre-FAR procurement regulations.

NASA RESEARCH ANNOUNCEMENT (NRA)   A BROAD AGENCY ANNOUNCEMENT (BAA) used to announce NASA research interests and solicit proposals reflecting those interests. The NRA process is oriented to those research procurements for which it would be impossible to draft a sufficiently detailed RFP without constraining the technical responses. Special preparation and evaluation procedures apply. NFS 18-35.016-70, NFS Subpart 18-70.2.

NATIONAL AERONAUTICS AND SPACE ADMINISTRATION (NASA) An independent civilian agency of the U.S. Government, established by the National Aeronautics and Space Act of 1958, 42 U.S.C. 2452. Its basic mission is to conduct aeronautical and space activities for peaceful purposes in conjunction with the scientific and engineering communities and to widely disseminate information on the results of those efforts. NASA consists of a Headquarters in Washington, D.C., and a number of research and engineering field installations throughout the country. NASA contracts fall under the coverage of the FEDERAL ACQUISITION REGULATION (FAR) and the NASA FAR SUPPLEMENT (NFS). There are no lower-level acquisition regulations of general applicability. Before the FAR and the NFS went into effect in Apr. 1984, NASA contracts were governed by the NASA PROCUREMENT REGULATION (NPR). See the U.S. Government Manual.

NATIONAL CONTRACT MANAGEMENT ASSOCIATION (NCMA) An organization composed of individuals who are engaged in public and commercial contracting through Government agencies and companies or are in related fields of endeavor. NCMA's mission is to increase the effectiveness of public contract management by (1) helping members improve their skills through educational programs and contact with knowledgeable persons in the field; (2) establishing a uniform code of ethics; (3) providing a forum for the interchange of ideas; (4) introducing new literature, ideas, and improvements; (5) encouraging a professional attitude toward contract management and procurement; and (6) enabling members to share in the range of experience and knowledge represented by the membership as a whole. NCMA publishes a semi-annual Journal as well as the monthly Contract Management magazine, and it administers a certification program for contract professionals. (NCMA, 1912 Woodford Road, Vienna, VA 22182; (703) 448-9231.)

NATIONAL DEFENSE Any activity related to programs for military or atomic energy production or construction, military assistance to any foreign nation, stockpiling, or space. See FAR 2.101, but note that the Space Act, 42 U.S.C. 2452, does not give the NATIONAL AERONAUTICS AND SPACE ADMINISTRATION (NASA) a military role in space.

NATIONAL INSTITUTE OF STANDARDS AND TECHNOLO-GY (NIST) The organization (formerly known as the Bureau of Standards) responsible for operating certain FEDERAL TECHNOLO-GY TRANSFER programs, such as the Regional Centers for the Transfer of Manufacturing Technology. These programs transfer know-how and technologies developed by NIST and other Federal organizations to small and mid-sized manufacturing companies. The organization's authority was extended to cover technology by the Omnibus Trade and Competitiveness Act of 1988, 7 U.S.C. 1421 *et seq.* See Duncombe, *Federal Technology Transfer: A Look at the Benefits and Pitfalls of One of the Country's Best Kept Secrets*, 37 Fed. B. News & J 608 (1990).

NATIONAL SECURITY INDUSTRIAL ASSOCIATION (NSIA) A not-for-profit, nonpolitical, nonlobbying association established in 1944 to foster a close working relationship and effective two-way communication between Government (primarily defense) and its supporting industry. Conceived by James Forrestal, the first Secretary of Defense, NSIA is an association of some 400 industrial, research, legal, and educational organizations of all sizes and representing all segments of industry interested in and related to national security. NSIA's province is the business and technical aspects of the relationship between Government and industry.   The areas covered include, among many others, Government policy and practice in procurement, R&D, and logistic support. (NSIA, 1025 Connecticut Avenue, N.W., Suite 300, Washington, DC 20036-5405; (202) 775-1440.)

NATIVE AMERICANS American Indians, Eskimos, Aleuts, and native Hawaiians. FAR 19.001. These persons are presumed to be socially and economically disadvantaged for the purposes of determining the ownership of a SMALL DISADVANTAGED BUSINESS CONCERN (SDBC). See FAR 52.219-2, 52.219-8.

NATIVE HAWAIIAN ORGANIZATION Any community service organization serving Native Hawaiians in, and chartered as a not-for-profit organization by, the State of Hawaii that is controlled by Native Hawaiians and whose business activities will principally benefit Native Hawaiians. FAR 19.001. Any SMALL BUSINESS CONCERN that is at least 51 percent owned and controlled by a Native Hawaiian Organization is a SMALL DISADVANTAGED BUSINESS CONCERN (SDBC).

NEAR-EXCESS FOREIGN CURRENCY See EXCESS FOREIGN CURRENCY.

NEGATIVE INSTANT CONTRACT SAVINGS The increase in the INSTANT CONTRACT cost or price when the acceptance of a VALUE ENGINEERING CHANGE PROPOSAL (VECP) results in an excess of the contractor's allowable development and implementation costs over the product of the INSTANT UNIT COST REDUCTION multiplied by the number of instant contract units affected. FAR 48.001. The Value Engineering clause in FAR 52.248-1 provides that the contract price will be increased when such negative savings (increased costs) occur.

NEGLIGENCE The failure to use such care as a reasonably prudent and careful person would use under similar circumstances. Generally, all persons, including contractors, are liable for personal injury or property damage that occurs because of the negligence of their employees. Similarly, the Government is liable for the negligence of its employees under the FEDERAL TORT CLAIMS ACT (FTCA). Most contractors protect against claims for negligence of their employees by INSURANCE, but FAR 28.308 permits SELF-INSURANCE under prescribed circumstances. The Government does not carry insurance but utilizes self-insurance for the negligence of its employees. See Braude, chap. 15, Construction Contracting.

NEGOTIATION A method of contracting that uses either competitive or other-than-competitive PROPOSALs and (usually) DISCUSSION. Any contract awarded without use of SEALED BIDDING procedures is a negotiated contract. FAR 15.101. Contracting by negotiation is a flexible process that includes the receipt of proposals from offerors, permits bargaining, and usually affords offerors an opportunity to revise their offers before award of a contract. Bargaining—in the sense of discussion, persuasion, alteration of initial assumptions and positions, and give-and-take—may apply to price, schedule, technical requirements, type of contract, or other terms of the proposed contract. FAR 15.102. In negotiation, award can be made on the basis of technical excellence, management capability, personnel qualifications, prior experience, past performance, and other factors bearing on quality, as well as cost; while in sealed bidding, only PRICE and PRICE-RELATED FACTORS are considered. Negotiation also permits the use of COST-REIMBURSEMENT CONTRACTs. Prior to the passage of the COMPETITION IN CONTRACTING ACT (CICA), negotiation had to be justified; now it is an equally acceptable method of contracting as long as FULL AND OPEN COMPETITION is achieved (in which case it is called the COMPETITIVE PROPOSALS method of contracting). See Nash, *Competitive Negotiation vs. Sealed Bidding: Some Limitations on Agency Discretion*, 5 N&CR ¶ 68 (Dec. 1991); Nash, *Evaluation of Risk in Competitive Negotiated Procurements: A Key Element in the Process*, 5 N&CR ¶ 22 (Apr. 1991).

NETWORK ANALYSIS SYSTEM   A recognized scheduling system, such as the CRITICAL PATH METHOD (CPM), that shows the duration, sequential relationship, and interdependence of various work activities. DFARS 236.1. The HEAD OF THE CONTRACTING ACTIVITY must approve both contractor-prepared and Government-prepared network analysis systems. DFARS 236.273.

NEUTRAL   See NEUTRAL ADVISOR.

NEUTRAL ADVISOR   An individual who functions specifically to aid parties in resolving a controversy. 5 U.S.C. 581(9). Neutral advisors have been used extensively in the conduct of MINITRIALs. The ADMINISTRATIVE DISPUTE RESOLUTION ACT, 5 U.S.C. 581-593, contains detailed provisions regarding the meaning of "neutral" at 5 U.S.C. 583. These require the Administrative Conference of the United States to establish standards for neutral advisors and to maintain a roster of neutral advisors. The act also permits agencies to enter into contracts with neutral advisors.

NOLO CONTENDERE (no-lo kon-ten'-de'-ray)   A Latin phrase meaning "I will not contest it." As a plea in a criminal proceeding, it has an effect similar to pleading guilty; however, in pleading *nolo contendere*, the defendant neither admits nor denies the charges, and the plea cannot be used against the defendant in a civil action based on the same acts. Black's Law Dictionary. A plea of *nolo contendere* is treated as a conviction for the commission of a crime and can be used as a cause for DEBARMENT. FAR 9.403. If legal proceedings for a contractor's violation of law or regulation result in a conviction entered upon a plea of *nolo contendere*, costs related to the proceedings are unallowable. FAR 31.205-47. See Connelly and Schooner, *Recovery of Costs for Defense Against the Government's Charge of Illegality*, 16 Pub. Cont. L.J. 94 (1986).

NONAPPROPRIATED FUNDS Monies derived from sources other than congressional APPROPRIATIONs. An example would be funds (1) derived from the sale of supplies and services to military and civilian personnel and their dependents and (2) used to support or provide recreational, religious, or educational programs or programs to improve welfare or morale. The U.S. Treasury's fiscal records do not account for nonappropriated funds. Jones, Glossary: Defense Acquisition Acronyms and Terms.

NONAPPROPRIATED FUNDS INSTRUMENTALITY (NAFI) An organization operated with NONAPPROPRIATED FUNDS. Such instrumentalities may include post or base exchanges, officers and noncommissioned officers clubs, theaters, bowling alleys, and similar facilities at military installations. They are not subject to the FEDERAL ACQUISITION REGULATION (FAR) but frequently follow procedures essentially the same as those set forth in that regulation.

NONCOMMON CARRIER See CARRIER (TELECOMMUNICATIONS).

NONCOMPENSABLE DELAY See DELAY.

NONDEVELOPMENTAL ITEM (NDI) An item needed by the Government that does not require DEVELOPMENT. Such items include (1) any item of supply available in the commercial marketplace, (2) any previously developed item of supply in use by a department or agency of the United States, a State or local government, or a foreign government with which the United States has a mutual defense cooperation agreement, (3) any item of supply described above that requires only minor modification in order to meet the requirements of the contracting agency, or (4) any item of supply currently being produced that does not meet the above requirements solely because it is not yet in use or is not yet available in the commercial marketplace. DFARS 210.001. 10 U.S.C. 2325 states a strong congressional preference for the use of such items by DoD. See DoD Directive 5000.2, *Defense Acquisition Management Policies and Procedures*, part 6L, 23 Feb. 1991. See also OFF-THE-SHELF ITEM.

NONPERSONAL SERVICES CONTRACT A contract under which the personnel rendering the services are not subject, either by the contract's terms or by the manner of its administration, to the supervision and control usually prevailing in relationships between the Government and its employees. FAR 37.101. Such contracts are not subject to the restrictions imposed on PERSONAL SERVICES CONTRACTS.

NONPROFIT ORGANIZATION A domestic university or other institution of higher education or an organization of the type described in section 501(c)(3) of the Internal Revenue code of 1954, 26 U.S.C. 501(c), and exempt from taxation under section 501(a) of the Internal Revenue Code, 26 U.S.C. 501(a). Also, any domestic nonprofit scientific or educational organization qualified under a State nonprofit organization statute. FAR 27.301. Such organizations are entitled to use a PATENT RIGHTS clause in their contracts which permits them to retain title to SUBJECT INVENTIONs (giving the Government a license) in accordance with 35 U.S.C. 200-212. See FAR Subpart 27.2. A different definition of the term is set forth in FAR 45.301, where the term means any corporation, foundation, trust, or institution operated for scientific, educational, or medical purposes, not organized for profit, and no part of the net earnings of which inures to the benefit of any private shareholder or individual. This definition determines when a nonprofit educational institution is entitled to be bound by a less stringent clause when accounting for FACILITIES. See FAR 45.302-7.

NONRECURRING COSTS Costs incurred by a contractor that are not expected to recur on future work. Nonrecurring research, development, test, and evaluation (RDT&E) costs are those costs funded by an RDT&E APPROPRIATION to develop or improve the product or technology under consideration. Nonrecurring production costs include one-time costs incurred in support of previous production of the model specified and costs specifically incurred in support of the total projected production run. DFARS 252.270-7000. In MULTIYEAR CONTRACTING nonrecurring production costs, including plant and equipment relocation, plant rearrangement, special tooling and special test equipment, preproduction engineering, initial spoilage and rework, and special workforce training, are recoverable upon CANCELLATION OF the MULTIYEAR CONTRACT. When the Government has paid nonrecurring costs, they may be recovered through RECOUPMENT, in accordance with agency procedures, from contractors that sell, lease, or license the resulting products or technology to buyers other than the Federal Government. See FAR 35.001 and 35.003. DoD's recoupment policy requires that when products are sold to a foreign government, international organization, foreign commercial firm, or domestic organization, or when technology relating to the manufacture of the products is sold or licensed to such an entity, DoD recovers a fair share of its investment in nonrecurring costs, a fair price for its contribution to the development of related technology, or both. DoD Directive 2140.2, *Recovery of Nonrecurring Costs*, 27 July 1987. A proposed rule at DFARS Subpart 215.70 revises the policies and procedures for recoupment from DoD contractors and their subcontractors of a fair share of DoD's investment, or of a foreign military sale customer's investment, in the nonrecurring costs of major defense equipment, major items, and related technology. 56 Fed. Reg. 55264 (25 Oct. 1991). See Victorino and McQuade, *Nonrecurring Costs Recoupment*, 90-10 Briefing Papers (Sep. 1990).

NONSEVERABLE PRODUCTION AND RESEARCH PROPERTY GOVERNMENT PRODUCTION AND RESEARCH PROPERTY that cannot be removed after erection or installation without substantial loss of value or damage to the property or to the premises where it is installed. FAR 45.301. FAR 45.309 states that the Government should not provide Government production and research property to contractors when it will be installed or constructed on land not owned by the Government in such a way that it becomes nonseverable. The FAR further suggests special legal arrangements that can be made when such property must be provided.

NO-SETOFF COMMITMENT A contractual agreement that, to the extent permitted by the Assignment of Claims Act, 31 U.S.C. 3727, payments by the Government to the assignee under an ASSIGNMENT OF CLAIMS will not be reduced to liquidate the contractor's indebtedness to the Government. FAR 32.801. The act authorizes such a commitment during a war or other national emergency by DoD, GSA, NASA, the Coast Guard, or any other agency designated by the President. When this commitment is made, Alternate I to the Assignment of Claims clause in FAR 52.232-23 is included in the contract.

NOT DOMINANT IN THE FIELD OF OPERATION Not exercising a controlling or major influence on a national basis in a kind of business activity in which a number of business concerns are primarily engaged. FAR 19.001. In determining whether dominance exists, consideration must be given to all appropriate factors, including volume of business, number of employees, financial resources, competitive status or position, ownership or control of materials, processes, patents, license agreements, facilities, sales territory, and nature of business activity. The determination of dominance is a key element in the determination of affiliation (see AFFILIATES).

NOTICE OF AWARD A method of ACCEPTANCE OF OFFER that the Government uses to make an immediate award of a contract. FAR 14.407, 15.1002. A notice of award is usually given by telegram or FACSIMILE (FAX), and FAR 14.407(c)(2) requires that it be followed as soon as possible by the formal award using Standard Form (SF) 33, Solicitation, Offer, and Award, FAR 53.301-33, or SF 26, Award/Contract, FAR 53.301-26. FAR 36.304 contains additional guidance on the use of notices of award in construction contracts.

NOTICE OF INTENTION TO MAKE A SERVICE CONTRACT A notice, submitted by contracting officers to the Wage and Hour Division of the Department of Labor, requesting a WAGE DETERMI- NATION under the SERVICE CONTRACT ACT (SCA) OF 1965. This notice is required to be submitted on all service contracts and modifications over $2,500. FAR 22.1007. It is prepared on Standard Form 98, FAR 53.301-98, in accordance with the instructions in FAR 22.1008.

NOTICE OF INTENT TO DISALLOW COSTS See DISALLOW- ANCE.

NOTICE TO PROCEED A Government notice that directs the contractor to proceed with the performance of the work called for by a contract. In a construction contract, the NOTICE OF AWARD must specify the date of commencement of work or advise that a notice to proceed will be issued. FAR 36.304.

NOVATION A novation agreement is a legal instrument executed by a contractor (transferor), a successor in interest (transferee), and the Government, by which the transferor guarantees performance of the contract, the transferee assumes all obligations under the contract, and the Government recognizes the transfer of the contract and related assets. FAR 42.1201. Under the common law, a novation is an agreement where a contracting party accepts a new party *in place of* the prior party (relieving the prior party of any further obligations). However, in Government contracting a novation is merely an ASSIGNMENT OF CONTRACT (with the prior party retaining all obligations in the event the new party fails to perform). Although the law (41 U.S.C. 15) prohibits assignment of Government contracts, the Government may, in its interest, recognize a third party as the successor in interest to a Government contract when the third party's interest in the contract arises out of the transfer of all the contractor's assets or the entire portion of the assets involved in performing the contract. FAR 42.1204. A format for novation agreements can be found at FAR 42.1204(e). See Cibinic, *Novation Agreements: Is You Is or Is You Ain't My Baby?* 4 N&CR ¶ 56 (Sep. 1990); Mullin, *Novation Agreements in Response to Merger and Consolidation in the Aerospace Industry*, 29 A.F. L. Rev. 69 (1988).

NO-YEAR APPROPRIATION See APPROPRIATION.

O

OBLIGATION A definite commitment by the Government to spend appropriated funds. Obligations may not be made prior to the enactment of an APPROPRIATION or other statutory authority. A binding contract is an obligation. See ANTI-DEFICIENCY ACT. And see Principles of Federal Appropriations Law (2d ed.), chap. 7.

OFFER A response to a SOLICITATION that, if accepted, would bind the offeror to perform the resultant contract. FAR 2.101. Responses to an invitation for bids (IFB), in SEALED BIDDING, are offers that are called BIDs or "sealed bids." Responses to a request for proposals (RFP), in NEGOTIATION, are offers that are called PROPOSALs. Responses to a request for quotations (RFQ), in negotiation, are called QUOTATIONs or "quotes" and are *not* offers, because they cannot be accepted by the Government to create a binding contract. FAR 15.402. An offer may also take the form of an UNSOLICITED PROPOSAL. Generally, the Government structures each procurement so that offers are made by prospective contractors and ACCEPTANCE OF an OFFER is made by the Government. However, in SMALL PURCHASE PROCEDURES the offer is generally made by the Government by sending the prospective contractor a PURCHASE ORDER (PO). See Cibinic and Nash, Formation of Government Contracts 153–62.

OFFEROR The party that makes an offer and looks for acceptance from the offeree. Black's Law Dictionary. In Government contracting offeror is the generic term for prospective contractors that submit BIDs, PROPOSALs, or QUOTATIONs.

OFFICE OF FEDERAL PROCUREMENT POLICY (OFPP) A Government organization, located in the Executive Office of the President (in the OFFICE OF MANAGEMENT AND BUDGET (OMB)), that is responsible for providing overall executive branch guidance

279

and direction of Government procurement policy and prescribes policies and regulations to be followed by executive agencies in acquiring goods, services, and facilities. 41 U.S.C. 405. The OFPP leadership role in the procurement process entails, among other things, chairing the FEDERAL ACQUISITION REGULATORY (FAR) COUNCIL, which prescribes Government-wide regulations (the FEDERAL ACQUISITION REGULATIONS (FAR) SYSTEM), providing for GSA's FEDERAL PROCUREMENT DATA SYSTEM (FPDS), providing for a FEDERAL ACQUISITION INSTITUTE (FAI) at GSA, consulting with agencies (including the SMALL BUSINESS ADMINISTRATION (SBA)), developing innovative procurement methods and procedures to be tested by selected executive agencies, issuing policy regarding conflict-of-interest standards for individuals providing consultant services, establishing and maintaining the COST ACCOUNTING STANDARDS (CAS) BOARD, and serving as advocate for the acquisition of COMMERCIAL PRODUCTs. See the U.S. Government Manual.

OFFICE OF FEDERAL PROCUREMENT POLICY (OFPP) POLICY LETTERS Policy guidance issued by the OFFICE OF FEDERAL PROCUREMENT POLICY (OFPP) to implement procurement policy. These letters are numbered sequentially by the year of issuance (thus, 91-2 would be the second policy letter issued in 1991). They are usually incorporated in a subsequent edition of the FEDERAL ACQUISITION REGULATION (FAR). OFPP publishes annually a pamphlet containing all letters still in effect. See OFPP Pamphlet No. 6, *Procurement Policy Letters* (Sep. 1991).

OFFICE OF GOVERNMENT ETHICS (OGE) An office of the executive branch of the Government with the responsibility for issuing uniform STANDARDS OF CONDUCT for all Government employees. Executive Order 12674, 12 Apr. 1989, as amended by Executive Order 12731, 17 Oct. 1990. See the U.S. Government Manual.

OFFICE OF MANAGEMENT AND BUDGET (OMB) A Government agency, in the Executive Office of the President, that serves as the President's principal arm for exercising the managerial functions of the presidency. 31 U.S.C. 501. OMB strives to improve Government organization, information, and management systems and devises programs for developing career executive talent throughout the Government. OMB assists the President in preparing the annual budget and in overseeing its execution. The

PAPERWORK REDUCTION ACT OF 1980 imposes a requirement on Federal agencies to obtain OMB's approval before collecting information from 10 or more members of the public. The information collection and recordkeeping requirements contained in the FAR have been approved by OMB. FAR 1.105. See the U.S. Government Manual.

OFFICE OF MANAGEMENT AND BUDGET (OMB) CIRCU-LARS Policy guidelines issued by the OFFICE OF MANAGEMENT AND BUDGET (OMB) to Federal agencies to promote efficiency and uniformity in Government activities. The Code of Federal Regulations contains an indexed list of these circulars at 5 CFR 1310. OMB Circulars can be obtained from the Office of Administration, Publications Unit, Room G-236, New Executive Office Building, Washington, DC 20503. The contents of OMB Circulars are frequently incorporated in the FAR but the documents continue to remain in effect as circulars. Relevant OMB Circulars and their FAR references include A-76, *Policies for Acquiring Commercial or Industrial Products and Services Needed by the Government*, FAR Subpart 7.3; A-109, *Major Systems Acquisitions*, FAR Part 34; and A-125, *Prompt Payment*, FAR Subpart 32.9.

OFFICE OF RESEARCH AND TECHNOLOGY APPLICATION (ORTA) An office within a Federal laboratory that serves as a Federal mechanism for FEDERAL TECHNOLOGY TRANSFER. ORTAs are responsible for identifying and assessing technologies, know-how, or ideas that may have commercial or other outside applications, as well as cooperating with State and local governments and other Federal organizations involved in technology transfer. Created by the Stevenson-Wydler Technology Innovation Act, 15 U.S.C. 3701–3714, these laboratories have annual budgets in excess of $20 million and are staffed by one or more full-time professionals. See Duncombe, *Federal Technology Transfer: A Look at the Benefits and Pitfalls of One of the Country's Best Kept Secrets*, 37 Fed. B. News & J. 608 (1990).

OFFICE OF TECHNICAL ASSISTANCE A GSA organization that assists Federal agencies, on a reimbursable basis, in designing, procuring, managing, and operating information systems and information technology. FIRMR 201-7.001(c).

OFFSET See SETOFF.

OFF-THE-SHELF ITEM An item produced and placed in stock by a contractor, or stocked by a distributor, before orders or contracts are received for its sale. The item may be commercial or may be produced to military or Federal specification or description. FAR 46.101. "Off-the-shelf" also refers to procurement of existing systems or equipment without a research, development, test, and evaluation program or with only minor development to make the system suitable for Government needs. The item may be a commercial system or commercial equipment, or something already in the Government's inventory. Off-the-shelf items are also known as NONDEVELOPMENTAL ITEMs (NDIs). Use of such items reduces R&D costs and speeds the acquisition process. The PACKARD COMMISSION's 1986 report on defense management states: "Rather than relying on excessively rigid military specifications, DoD should make much greater use of components, systems, and services available 'off the shelf.' It should develop new or custom-made items only when it has been established that those readily available are clearly inadequate to meet military requirements."

OPERATING REVENUE Amounts accrued or charged to customers, clients, and tenants for the sale of products manufactured or purchased for resale, services, and rental of property held primarily for leasing to others. FAR 30.301. This term is used in connection with the COST ACCOUNTING STANDARDS (CAS) in FAR Part 30. Operating revenue includes both reimbursable costs and fees under COST-REIMBURSEMENT CONTRACTs and percentage-of-completion sales accruals, except that it includes only the fee for those management contracts under which the contractor acts essentially as an agent of the Government in erecting or operating Government-owned facilities. Operating revenue excludes incidental interest, dividends, royalties, rental income, and proceeds from the sale of assets used in the business.

OPTION A unilateral right in a contract by which, within a specified period, the Government may elect to purchase additional supplies or services called for by the contract, or may elect to extend the contract. FAR 17.201. Options are common in commercial as well as Government contracting, and they are a useful means of preventing BUYING-IN. When exercising an option, the contracting officer must provide the contractor written notice within the time period specified in the contract. The contracting officer may exercise an option only after determining that (1) funds are available, (2) the requirement covered by the option fulfills an existing Government need, and (3) exercise of the option is the most advantageous method of fulfilling the Government's need, price and other factors considered. FAR 17.207. See the contract clauses at FAR 52.217-3 through -9, which deal with evaluation exclusive of options, evaluation of options, options for increased quantity, and options to extend services or the term of the contract. And see Cibinic and Nash, Formation of Government Contracts 835–54; Nash, *Options: They Seem to Be Many-Splendored Things*, 4 N&CR ¶ 60 (Oct. 1990); Vacketta and Frulla, *"Option" Clauses*, 88-13 Briefing Papers (Dec. 1988).

OPTIONAL FORMS (OFs) Forms used in the procurement process that may be altered at the option of the agency. FAR 53.302 illustrates those few optional forms relevant to procurement, of which the most commonly used is OF 347, Order for Supplies and Services. OFs are distinguished from STANDARD FORMS (SFs) by the fact that the latter cannot be altered or substituted for without receipt, in advance, of an exception (an approved departure from the established design, content, printing specifications, or conditions for use). FAR 53.103. Agencies may computer-generate OFs without exception approval, provided that there is no change to the name, content, or sequence of the data elements and that the form carries the OF number and edition date. FAR 53.105. Holders of the looseleaf edition of the FAR may photocopy the sample OFs from FAR 53.302. Executive agencies obtain OFs through the GSA Supply Catalog (Office Products). Contractors may obtain them from the U.S. Government Printing Office, Washington, DC 20402. See Ferguson and Moss, *FAR Part 53—It's a Matter of Forms*, 24 Cont. Mgmt. 8 (Apr. 1984).

ORDER See JOB ORDER.

ORDER OF PRECEDENCE The hierarchy of various parts of the contract in the CONTRACT INTERPRETATION process. In the absence of a specific contract clause stating an order of precedence, the general rule of common law is that, when contracts contain inconsistencies, specific provisions will prevail over general provisions and that written or typed provisions will prevail over general provisions. This general rule does not apply, however, when a specific provision conflicts with a standard Government contract clause required by statute or regulation. Cibinic and Nash, Administration of Government Contracts

116–18. The Order of Precedence clauses in FAR 52.214-29 and 52.215-33 state that inconsistencies in the solicitation or contract are to be resolved by giving precedence in the following order: (1) the Schedule (excluding the specifications); (2) representations and other instructions; (3) contract clauses; (4) other documents, exhibits, and attachments; and (5) the specifications. See UNIFORM CONTRACT FORMAT. And see Cibinic, *Order of Precedence: Resolving the Battle of the Documents*, 4 N&CR ¶ 23 (Apr. 1990).

"OR EQUAL" See BRAND-NAME-OR-EQUAL DESCRIPTION.

ORGANIZATIONAL CONFLICT OF INTEREST (OCI) A conflict of interest of a Government contractor that arises or might arise because the nature of the work to be performed may, absent some restriction on future activities, result in an UNFAIR COMPETITIVE ADVANTAGE to the contractor, impair the contractor's objectivity in performing the contract work, or make the contractor unable or potentially unable to render impartial assistance or advice to the Government. FAR 9.501. The contracting officer is responsible for resolving any significant potential conflicts before the award is made. FAR 9.504 and 9.507. The FAR coverage on OCI also implements OFPP Policy Letter 89-1, *Conflict of Interest Policies Applicable to Consultants*. In addition, some agencies have unique or additional statutory OCI requirements. For instance, DoE's OCI regulations implement 42 U.S.C. 5918. According to these regulations, an OCI exists when an offeror or a contractor has past, present, or currently planned interests that (1) either directly or indirectly, through a client relationship, relate to the work to be performed under a DoE contract and (2) may diminish the offeror's or contractor's capacity to give impartial, technically sound assistance and advice or may give the offeror or contractor an unfair competitive advantage. Offerors and contractors include chief executives and directors who will or do become involved in the contract performance and proposed consultants or subcontractors who may perform services similar to the services provided by the prime. DEAR 909.570-3. See Woodruff, *Organizational Conflicts of Interest: Not What It's Said to Be*, 16 Pub. Cont. L.J. 213 (1986); Taylor, *Organizational Conflicts of Interest in Department of Defense Contracting*, 14 Pub. Cont. L.J. 158 (1983); Taylor, *Organizational Conflicts of Interest/Ed. II*, 84-8 Briefing Papers (Aug. 1984).

ORGANIZATION COSTS Costs of organization or reorganization of a business, including but not limited to incorporation fees and costs of attorneys, accountants, brokers, promoters, organizers, management consultants, and investment counselors, whether or not employees of the contractor. FAR 31.205-27. Organization costs in connection with the following are UNALLOWABLE COSTs: (1) planning or executing the organization or reorganization of the corporate structure of a business, including mergers and acquisitions, (2) resisting or planning to resist the reorganization of the corporate structure of a business or a change in the controlling interest in the ownership of a business, and (3) raising capital (net worth plus long-term liabilities). Also unallowable are certain "reorganization" costs, including the cost of any change in the contractor's financial structure (except the administrative costs of short-term borrowings for working capital) resulting in alterations in the rights and interests of security holders, whether or not additional capital is raised.

ORIGINAL COMPLEMENT OF LOW-COST EQUIPMENT A group of items acquired for the initial outfitting of a TANGIBLE CAPITAL ASSET or an operational unit, or as a new addition to either. FAR 31.001. The items in the group individually cost less than the minimum amount established by the contractor for CAPITALIZATION of the classes of assets acquired, but in the aggregate they represent a material investment. Under the COST PRINCIPLES in FAR Part 31, the group, as a complement, is expected to be held for continued service beyond the current accounting period. Initial outfitting is completed when the unit is ready and available for normal operations.

OUTDATED FEDERAL INFORMATION PROCESSING (FIP) EQUIPMENT Any Federal information processing equipment (see FEDERAL INFORMATION PROCESSING (FIP) RESOURCES) that is over 8 years old, based on the initial commercial installation date of the model, and that is no longer in current production. FIRMR 201-4.001. Agencies must determine strategies for avoiding outdated FIP resources. FIRMR 201-20.203. Outdated FIP equipment should not be reused within the Federal Government unless an analysis in accordance with FIRMR 201-20.203 shows that reuse will be the lowest cost alternative for satisfying a FIP requirement. See FIRMR Bulletin C-27, *Reuse of Outdated Federal Information Processing (FIP) Equipment*, which lists outdated FIP equipment and provides guidelines for determining whether FIP equipment is obsolescent.

OVERHEAD See INDIRECT COST.

OVERHEAD RATE A percentage rate that is derived by dividing a contractor's INDIRECT COST POOL for an accounting period by the allocation base used to allocate INDIRECT COSTs to contracts performed during the period (see ALLOCATION OF COST). Cost Accounting Standard 418, FAR 30.418, provides guidance on the selection of allocation bases that equitably allocate indirect costs.

OVERRUN An amount representing the actual cost of performance that is greater than the amount estimated by the parties when the contract was entered into. The procedures for dealing with COST OVERRUNs on COST-REIMBURSEMENT CONTRACTs are set forth in the LIMITATION OF COST (LOC) CLAUSE.

OVERTIME Time worked by a contractor's employee in excess of the employee's normal workweek or workday. FAR 22.103-1. "Normal workweek" means, generally, a workweek of 40 hours. FAR 22.103-2 provides that contractors must perform Government contracts, so far as is practicable, without using overtime, particularly as a regular employment practice, except when lower overall costs to the Government will result or when overtime is necessary to meet urgent program needs. Any approved overtime, extra-pay shifts, and multishifts should be scheduled to achieve these objectives. FAR 22.103-2. The contracting officer must review any contractor requests for overtime. FAR 22.103-4. The CONTRACT WORK HOURS AND SAFETY STANDARDS ACT (CWHSSA) requires that LABORERS OR MECHANICS employed by construction contractors be paid premium wages (not less than 1-1/2 times the basic rate) for overtime hours. See FAR Subpart 22.3. This requirement is implemented by including the Contract Work Hours and Safety Standards Act—Overtime Compensation clause in FAR 52.222-4 in such contracts. See Bauder, *Uncompensated Overtime: Is It in the Government's Best Interest?* 29 Cont. Mgmt. 10 (July 1989); Cibinic, *Uncompensated Overtime: White Collar Sweatshops?* 3 N&CR ¶ 21 (Mar. 1989).

P

PACKARD COMMISSION The popular name of the President's Blue Ribbon Commission on Defense Management, which published its final report, *A Quest for Excellence*, in June 1986. Chaired by David Packard, the Commission made a number of significant recommendations on reorganizing the Joint Chiefs of Staff, the defense command structure, and the defense acquisition process, including creating the position of Under Secretary of Defense for Acquisition. The Commission's Acquisition Task Force suggested (1) streamlining acquisition organization and procedures, (2) using technology to reduce costs, (3) balancing cost and performance, (4) stabilizing programs, (5) expanding the use of COMMERCIAL PRODUCTs, and (6) enhancing the quality of acquisition personnel. The Commission's preliminary report was called *A Formula for Action: A Report to the President on Defense Acquisition* (Apr. 1986). See Cavanaugh and Kalkowski, *The Packard Commission: A Blueprint for Change*, 26 Cont. Mgmt. 14 (Apr. 1986).

PAPERWORK REDUCTION ACT OF 1980 An act, 44 U.S.C. 3501 et seq., that, among other objectives, seeks to "ensure that automatic data processing and telecommunications technologies are acquired and used by the Federal Government in a manner which improves service delivery and program management." The act created the Office of Information and Regulatory Affairs in the OFFICE OF MANAGEMENT AND BUDGET (OMB) to "implement policies and oversee, review, and approve the acquisition and use of automatic data processing telecommunications and other technology for managing information." It directed each executive agency to designate a senior official (see DESIGNATED SENIOR OFFICIAL) to ensure that all automatic data processing and telecommunications acquisitions are conducted properly.

PAPERWORK REDUCTION REAUTHORIZATION ACT OF 1986 An act, 44 U.S.C. 101 and 3503, that defined AUTOMATIC DATA PROCESSING EQUIPMENT (ADPE) for purposes of the BROOKS ACT (AUTOMATIC DATA PROCESSING PROCUREMENTS); defined the term INFORMATION RESOURCES MANAGEMENT (IRM); required agencies, through the OFFICE OF MANAGEMENT AND BUDGET (OMB), to develop/revise 5-year automatic data processing plans each year; and created the INFORMATION TECHNOLOGY FUND.

PARALLEL PROCEEDING A simultaneous proceeding, whether administrative, civil, or criminal, brought by the Government in another forum against a contractor litigating a contract CLAIM before a BOARD OF CONTRACT APPEALS (BCA). This situation raises complex strategic decisions for both the Government and the contractor. For example, when the contractor is litigating an affirmative claim before a BCA, Government counsel may move to stay the BCA action pending the outcome of a criminal action. See the President's Council on Integrity and Efficiency booklet *Guidelines for Civil Fraud Remedies and Parallel Proceedings* (27 Sep. 1985); McCastlain and Schooner, *To Stay or Not to Stay: Difficult Decisions for Boards of Contract Appeals Confronted with Parallel Proceedings*, 16 Pub. Cont. L.J. 418 (1987) (which concludes with an analytical guide stressing four considerations: BCA jurisdiction, commonality of issues, prejudice to the parties, and whether the equities favor one party over the other); Barletta and Pollack, *Civil Litigation of Allegations of Fraud in Connection with Government Contract Claims*, 18 Pub. Cont. L.J. 235 (1988).

PARENT COMPANY A company that, for the purposes of bidding, owns or controls the activities and basic business policies of the bidder. To own the bidder, the company must own more than 50 percent of the voting rights in the bidder's company. To control the bidder without owning it, the company must be able to formulate, determine, or veto basic policy decisions of the bidder through the use of dominant minority voting rights, use of proxy voting, or otherwise. All INVITATIONs FOR BIDS (IFBs) for work other than construction not exceeding $10,000 must contain the Parent Company and Identifying Data solicitation provision in FAR 52.214-8. This requires bidders to identify a parent company that owns them.

PARTIAL PAYMENT A payment made, as authorized by the contract, upon delivery and Government acceptance of one or more complete units (or one or more distinct items of service) as called for by the Government under the contract, even though other quantities remain to be delivered. Although partial payments are not generally considered FINANCING PAYMENTs, they can help contractors participate in Government contracts without, or with only minimal, contract financing. FAR 32.102(d). A payment made against a termination claim before final settlement of the total termination claim is also called a "partial payment." Under contracts authorizing partial payments on termination SETTLEMENT PROPOSALs before settlement, contractors may request partial payment at any time after submission of interim or final settlement proposals. FAR 49.112-1. FAR 49.602-4 prescribes use of Standard Form 1440, Application for Partial Payment, in FAR 53.301-1440. See also TERMINATION FOR CONVENIENCE.

PARTIAL SET-ASIDE See SET-ASIDE (n).

"PARTICIPATED PERSONALLY AND SUBSTANTIALLY" A key term, under the PROCUREMENT INTEGRITY provisions of the FAR, that refers to an individual's active and significant involvement in activities directly related to the procurement. 41 U.S.C. 423; FAR 3.104-4(g). Such individuals are subject to the procurement integrity rules. To participate "personally" means to be involved directly and includes the participation of a subordinate when the subordinate was directed by the supervisor in the matter. To participate "substantially" means to be involved in a significant way. Substantial participation requires more than official responsibility or knowledge, perfunctory involvement, or involvement on an administrative or peripheral issue. A finding of substantiality should be based not only on the effort devoted to a matter, but also on the importance of the effort. While a series of peripheral involvements may be insubstantial, the single act of approving or participating in a critical step may be substantial. An employee whose responsibility is to review a procurement solely for compliance with administrative procedures or budgetary considerations and who reviews a document involved in the procurement for such a purpose should not be regarded as having participated substantially in the procurement. See also PROCUREMENT OFFICIAL.

PARTIES EXCLUDED FROM PROCUREMENT PROGRAMS
A list (formerly referred to as the Consolidated List of Debarred, Suspended and Ineligible Contractors) compiled, maintained, and distributed by the GENERAL SERVICES ADMINISTRATION (GSA), in accordance with FAR 9.404, containing the names of contractors proposed for DEBARMENT, debarred, or suspended (see SUSPENSION) by agencies, as well as contractors declared ineligible under other statutory or regulatory authority. FAR 9.403. This list is supplemented monthly and distributed quarterly. Agencies may not solicit offers from, award contracts to, or consent to subcontracts with contractors on the list unless the HEAD OF THE AGENCY determines that there is compelling reason to do so. FAR 9.405. Contractors may not award subcontracts of $25,000 or more to a firm on the list without compelling reason and written notice to the Government. FAR 9.405-2(b).

PARTNERING   A procedure, adopted at the beginning of performance of a contract, to encourage the employees of the contractor and the Government to work together to achieve the contract objectives. Partnering involves the development of a cooperative management team, representing both the Government and the contractor, that seeks to identify common goals and objectives. Both sides work to bring about a "mutual win" situation and discourage an "us against them" attitude. The goal is to avoid litigation, which involves unnecessary expense, delay, and disruption. See Nash, *Partnering: A New Corps of Engineering Effort to Avoid Disputes*, 5 N&CR ¶ 32 (June 1991).

PATENT (adj)   Readily discoverable by observation or inspection. The adjective "patent" can refer to the type of deficiency potentially found in solicitations or contracts (patent AMBIGUITY) or in contract performance (PATENT DEFECT). Patent means "open or manifest" and is an antonym of the adjective LATENT.

PATENT (n)   A grant of some privilege, property, or authority made by the Government to one or more individuals. A patent is the instrument by which the Government grants or conveys to an inventor the exclusive right to make, use, and sell an invention for 17 years. Black's Law Dictionary. The Government honors rights in patents and complies with the stipulations of law in using or acquiring such rights. FAR 27.104. 28 U.S.C. 1498(a) provides that the Government will pay reasonable compensation if it, or its contractors with AUTHORIZATION AND CONSENT, infringe a patent.

FAR Subpart 27.2 prescribes policy with respect to PATENT RIGHTS in inventions made during the performance of Government contracts, the granting of authorization and consent to infringe patents, patent infringement liability of contractors through PATENT INDEMNIFICATION, royalties payable in connection with performing Government contracts, and security requirements covering patent applications containing classified subject matter filed by contractors. FAR 31.205-30 makes the costs of obtaining patents that are required by a contract ALLOWABLE COSTs.

PATENT AMBIGUITY See AMBIGUITY.

PATENT DEFECT A defect in the contract work that is discoverable by the Government by the use of reasonable inspection methods. In accordance with the Inspection of Supplies—Fixed-Price clause in FAR 52.246-2 and the Inspection of Construction—Fixed-Price clause in FAR 52.246-12, Government ACCEPTANCE OF WORK containing patent defects is conclusive on the Government—with the result that the Government cannot require the contractor to correct such defective work at the contractor's own expense. The fact that the Government did not inspect the work is not relevant to the determination of whether a defect was patent. The issue is whether the defect *could have been discovered* had the Government conducted a reasonable inspection. A patent defect is the opposite of a LATENT DEFECT. See Cibinic and Nash, Administration of Government Contracts 630–48; Victorino and Ivey, *The "Inspection" Clause*, 88-10 Briefing Papers 8 (Sep. 1988).

PATENT INDEMNIFICATION The promise of a contractor to reimburse the Government for any amount it is required to pay an owner of a PATENT for use of that patent during performance of the contract. FAR 27.203 states the policy of the Government to obtain patent indemnification from all contractors (including construction contractors) furnishing supplies or services that normally are or have been sold or offered for sale to the public in the commercial open market or are the same as such supplies or services except for minor modifications. Such indemnification is necessary because the Government is primarily liable for paying compensation to the owner of a patent under 28 U.S.C. 1498(a). See AUTHORIZATION AND CONSENT. The Government obtains patent indemnification by using the Patent Indemnification clauses in FAR 52.227-3 and -4. If the contract work contains some commercial supplies and services and some work made to the design of the Government, the FAR requires the contracting officer to segregate the commercial work and to provide for indemnification for that work only.

PATENT INFRINGEMENT Selling, making, or using a patented invention without the consent of the owner of the PATENT. Under the patents laws, the owner of a patent can usually obtain an injunction against patent infringement or damages for infringement. Such injunctions are not permitted against the Government because the only remedy for infringement by the Government or its contractors with AUTHORIZATION AND CONSENT is reasonable compensation under the provisions of 28 U.S.C. 1498(a). See Nash and Rawicz, Patents and Technical Data, chap. 5.

PATENT LICENSE An agreement of the owner of a PATENT to permit another to make, use, or sell an invention to the extent the owner has such a right. The Government obtains a license in all SUBJECT INVENTIONs under its policy on PATENT RIGHTS. In addition, 10 U.S.C. 2386 gives the DoD the right to acquire patent licenses. FAR 31.205-37 makes the costs incurred by contractors for licenses ALLOWABLE COSTs unless the Government has license rights.

PATENT RIGHTS The rights of the Government in PATENTs resulting from inventions made during the course of performance of Government contracts (see SUBJECT INVENTIONs). 35 U.S.C. 202 requires the Government to permit all SMALL BUSINESS CONCERNs and NONPROFIT ORGANIZATIONs to take "title" to all subject inventions and provides that the Government will have, at a minimum, a nonexclusive, nontransferable, irrevocable, paid-up license to practice the invention on its own behalf. This, in effect, divides the rights in a patent—giving the contractor commercial rights to it and the Government the right to use it for Government purposes. Executive Order 12591, 10 Apr. 1987, requires that this policy be followed with regard to large contractors to the extent authorized by law. This policy is implemented in FAR Subpart 27.3. The major agencies that are precluded by law from directly following this policy are NASA and DoE. See Nash, *Patent Rights: Parallel Development Projects*, 1 N&CR (Apr. 1987).

PAY-AS-YOU-GO COST METHOD A method of recognizing PENSION PLAN costs only when benefits are paid to retired employees or their beneficiaries. FAR 31.001. For pay-as-you-go pension plans, the entire cost assignable to a COST ACCOUNTING PERIOD may be assigned to the COST OBJECTIVEs of that period only if the payment of benefits can be compelled. Otherwise, the assignable cost is limited to the amount of benefits actually paid. FAR 30.412-40(c).

PAYMENT The satisfaction of the Government's obligation to compensate the contractor in accordance with the terms of a contract. The Government's payment obligation is not dealt with in any single part of the FAR but is scattered through various parts. Most of the clauses setting forth the requirement for payment are contained in the FAR 52.216 or 52.232 series of clauses. See, for example, the standard Allowable Cost and Payment clause in FAR 52.216-7, which is used in cost-reimbursement contracts; the Payments clause in FAR 52.232-1, which is used in fixed-price supply contracts; and the Payments under Fixed-Price Construction Contracts clause in FAR 52.232-5. Payment may be made in the form of PROGRESS PAYMENTs, PARTIAL PAYMENTs, and FINAL PAYMENTs. The PROMPT PAYMENT ACT (PPA) uses the terms INVOICE PAYMENTs and FINANCING PAYMENTs. See Nash, chap. 12, Construction Contracting 897–927.

PAYMENT BOND A promise of a SURETY assuring payment to all persons supplying labor or materials in the work provided for in a contract. FAR 28.001. This bond is purchased by a prospective contractor in accordance with the requirement of the Government. The MILLER ACT requires such bonds for construction contracts exceeding $25,000, and they may occasionally be required for other contracts as well. FAR 28.102-1, 28.103. The PENAL AMOUNT of Miller Act payment bonds must be (1) 50 percent of the contract price if that price does not exceed $1 million, (2) 40 percent of the contract price if that price is more than $1 million but not more than $5 million, or (3) $2.5 million if the contract price is more than $5 million. FAR 28.102. The bond is furnished on Standard Form 25-A, FAR 53.301-25-A. LETTERs OF CREDIT may be used in lieu of payment bonds. See Patin, chap. 17, Construction Contracting 1222–1309.

PENAL AMOUNT The amount of money specified in a BOND (or a percentage of the bid price in a BID BOND) as the maximum payment for which the SURETY is obligated. FAR 28.001. For example, on construction contracts, the penal amount of performance bonds must normally be 100 percent of the original contract price. The penal amount of payment bonds must equal (1) 50 percent of the contract price if that price is not more than $1 million, (2) 40 percent if the contract price is between $1 million and $5 million, or (3) $2.5 million if the contract price exceeds $5 million. FAR 28.102-2.

PENAL SUM See PENAL AMOUNT.

PENSION PLAN A deferred compensation plan established and maintained by one or more employers to provide systematically for the payment of benefits to plan participants after their retirements, provided that the benefits are paid for life or are payable for life at the option of the employee. FAR 31.001. Additional benefits, such as permanent and total disability payments, death payments, and survivorship payments to beneficiaries of deceased employees, may be an integral part of a pension plan. Pension plans are generally either the insured type (insured under a contract with a life insurance company) or the trustee type (self-insured under a formal trust agreement with a trustee). The allowability of costs (see ALLOWABLE COST) incurred by a contractor to fund pension plans is governed by FAR 31.205-6. The allocability of such costs (see ALLOCABLE COST) is covered in Cost Accounting Standards 412 and 413, FAR 30.412 and 30.413. See DCAA Contract Audit Manual (CAM) 7-600.

PERFORMANCE BOND A promise of a SURETY, sometimes referred to as a "completion bond," assuring the Government that once the contract is awarded, the contractor will perform its obligations under the contract. FAR 28.001. This bond is purchased by a prospective contractor in accordance with the requirements of the Government. The MILLER ACT generally requires performance bonds for construction contracts exceeding $25,000, and they may occasionally be required for other contracts as well. FAR 28.102-1, 28.103. The penal amount of a Miller Act performance bond must be 100 percent of the original contract price, unless the contracting officer determines that a smaller amount will adequately protect the Government. FAR 28.102-2. LETTERs OF CREDIT may be used in lieu of performance bonds. See Patin, chap. 17, Construction Contracting 1310–34.

PERFORMANCE EVALUATION The periodic evaluation of the performance of a contractor in carrying out its obligations on Government contracts. Contracting activities evaluate the performance of construction contractors by preparing Standard Form 1420, Performance Evaluation—Construction Contracts in FAR 53.301-1420, for contracts of (1) $500,000 or more; (2) $100,000 or more, if any element of performance was either unsatisfactory or exceptionally good; (3) $100,000 or more if the contract was terminated for the convenience of the Government; or (4) more than $10,000, if the contract was terminated for default. Before making determinations of RESPONSIBILITY, contracting officers may consider these performance evaluations in accordance with agency instructions. FAR 36.201. In DoD, information from the standard forms is inputted to a computerized system maintained by the Office of the Chief of Engineers. In addition, a Construction Contractor Appraisal Support System (CCASS) is maintained by the Army Corps of Engineers' North Pacific Division in Portland, Oregon. DFARS 236.201. See Yasenchak, *A CM Report: System Provides Contractor Performance Histories*, 28 Cont. Mgmt. 50 (Nov. 1988). Performance evaluation systems are also being used by NASA and the Air Force Systems Command. See Nash, *Evaluation of Risk in Competitive Negotiated Procurements: A Key Element in the Process*, 5 N&CR ¶ 22 (Apr. 1991).

PERFORMANCE SCHEDULE See DELIVERY OR PERFORMANCE SCHEDULE.

PERFORMANCE SPECIFICATIONS Technical requirements that set forth the operational characteristics desired for an item. They tell the contractor what the final product must be capable of accomplishing rather than describing how the product is to be built or what its measurements, tolerances, or other design characteristics must be. When the contract contains performance specifications, the contractor accepts general responsibility for product design and engineering and for achievement of the stated performance requirements. See Cibinic and Nash, Formation of Government Contracts 341. Performance specifications and FUNCTIONAL SPECIFICATIONS are generally to be preferred over DESIGN SPECIFICATIONS. FAR 10.002.

PERFORMANCE VALIDATION Technical verification of the ability of a proposed FEDERAL INFORMATION PROCESSING (FIP)

RESOURCES system configuration or replacement component to handle Government agency workload volumes within predetermined performance time constraints. Examples of performance validation techniques include (1) timed execution of the existing agency programs, transactions, and data files on the proposed configuration; (2) execution with synthetically generated workloads; (3) remote terminal emulation with simulated on-line workloads; (4) acceptance testing with present operational software, data files, and workloads; (5) stress testing with exaggerated workload volumes; (6) modeling of the interaction of the new information processing system and its workload; (7) benchmarking; and (8) simulation modelling of FIP system performance. FIRMR 201-4.001, 201-20.304. See also BENCH-MARK and CAPABILITY VALIDATION.

PERSONAL CONFLICT OF INTEREST   One of a number of types of personal conduct proscribed by law and regulation, on grounds that the conduct would compromise, or appear to compromise, the complete impartiality of the procurement process. Prohibitions apply to Government employees, contractors competing for Government business, former Government employees, and members of Congress. As a rule, no Government employee may solicit or accept a GRATUITY (18 U.S.C. 201, FAR 3.101-2) or offer or accept a bribe (see BRIBERY) (10 U.S.C. 2207, 5 U.S.C. 7353, FAR 3.104-1). Nor, as a rule, may a procurement official discuss future employment or business opportunities with a contractor seeking a Government contract (41 U.S.C. 423, FAR 3.104); knowingly disclose PROPRIETARY INFORMATION or SOURCE SELECTION INFORMATION to an unauthorized person (41 U.S.C., FAR 3.104); or knowingly award a contract to a Government employee or to a business substantially owned or controlled by a Government employee (18 U.S.C. 202, FAR 3.601). During the conduct of a procurement, no competing contractor may, as a rule, discuss future business or employment opportunities with a procurement official (41 U.S.C. 423, FAR 3.104) or offer or give a gratuity to a Government employee (18 U.S.C. 201, FAR 3.202). Per post-employment restrictions, no procurement official who leaves the Government during the conduct of a procurement may disclose proprietary or source selection information, participate in a competing contractor's negotiations for contract award or modification, or participate directly or significantly in the successful contractor's performance of the contract (41 U.S.C. 423, FAR 3.104-7). As a rule, no member of Congress may be awarded a Government contract or personally benefit from award of a contract (41 U.S.C. 22, FAR 3.102-1). See DFARS Part 203 and DoD Directive 5500.7, *Standards of Conduct*, 6 May 1987; ABA, Personal Conflicts of Interest in Government Contracting; Darley, *Personal Conflicts of Interest Digest*, 20 Pub. Cont. L.J. 302 (1991). OFPP Policy Letter 89-1, *Conflict of Interest Policies Applicable to Consultants*, provides guidelines concerning the conditions or circumstances wherein a person is unable, or potentially unable, to render impartial ADVISORY AND ASSISTANCE SERVICES to the Government because of other activities or relationships with other persons, or wherein a person has an unfair competitive advantage. See also PROCUREMENT INTEGRITY.

PERSONAL PROPERTY Property of any kind, or interest in it, with the exception of REAL PROPERTY, RECORDS of the Federal Government, and naval battleships, cruisers, aircraft carriers, destroyers, and submarines. FAR 45.601. More generally, all property other than real property; everything that is the subject of ownership, not coming under the denomination of real estate. Black's Law Dictionary. Instructions on contractor reporting of excess personal property are set forth in FAR 45.608-8. Such reports, when required by the contract, are submitted on Standard Form 120, Report of Excess Personal Property, FAR 53.301-120.

PERSONAL SERVICES CONTRACT A contract that, by its express terms or as administered, makes the contractor personnel appear to be, in effect, Government employees. FAR 37.101. Government agencies may not award personal services contracts unless specifically authorized by statute to do so, since such contracts tend to circumvent the civil service laws requiring the Government to obtain its employees by direct hire using established competitive procedures. FAR 37.104(b). FAR 37.104(c) provides that the key indicator of a personal services contract is "relatively continuous supervision and control" of contractor employees by Government officials. FAR 37.104(d) provides a list of other elements that may indicate that a personal services contract exists.

PETTY CASH See IMPREST FUND.

PILOT ACQUISITION PROGRAM See MAJOR DEFENSE ACQUISITION PILOT PROGRAM.

PILOT MENTOR–PROTÉGÉ PROGRAM   See MENTOR–PROTÉGÉ PILOT PROGRAM.

PLAINTIFF The party bringing suit in a court. In the U.S. CLAIMS COURT (Cl. Ct.) the contractor is always the plaintiff even though the suit may be based on a Government CLAIM under the CONTRACT DISPUTES ACT (CDA) OF 1978. In such cases, the Government is referred to as the DEFENDANT. (If such a case were appealed to a BOARD OF CONTRACT APPEALS (BCA), the contractor would be referred to as the appellant and the Government would be called the respondent.)

PLANT CLEARANCE All actions relating to the screening, redistribution, and disposal of contractor INVENTORY from a contractor's plant or work site. The term "contractor's plant" includes any GOVERNMENT-OWNED, CONTRACTOR-OPERATED PLANT (GOCO). FAR 45.601. FAR Subpart 45.6 contains guidance on the procedures to be followed in the plant clearance process. For this function, Government agencies normally appoint a plant clearance officer to act as the authorized representative of the contracting officer. The plant clearance period is the period beginning on the effective date of contract completion or termination and ending 90 days (or later, if agreed to) after the contracting officer receives acceptable inventory schedules for each property classification.

PLANT EQUIPMENT Personal property of a capital nature (including equipment, machine tools, test equipment, furniture, vehicles, and accessory and auxiliary items) for use in manufacturing supplies, in performing services, or for any administrative or general plant purpose. It does not include SPECIAL TEST EQUIPMENT or SPECIAL TOOLING. FAR 45.101. The contracting officer must approve in advance any contractor use of active plant equipment, and such approval may be granted only when in the Government's interest. FAR 45.407. The DFARS categorizes plant equipment as "industrial plant equipment (IPE)" or "other plant equipment (OPE)." IPE means plant equipment in Federal stock group 34 with an acquisition cost of $15,000 or more used for cutting, abrading, grinding, shaping, forming, joining, heating, treating, or otherwise altering the physical properties of materials, components, or end items entailed in manufacturing, maintenance, supply, processing, assembly, or R&D operations. OPE excludes items categorized as IPE. It is that part of plant equipment, regardless of dollar value, that is used in, or in conjunction with, the manufacture of components or end items for maintenance, supply, processing, assembly, or R&D operations. DFARS 245.301. Before acquiring IPE, DoD contracting offices must notify the Defense Industrial Plant Equipment Center (DIPEC), which will determine whether existing, reallocable Government-owned equipment can fill the requirement. DFARS 245.302-1.

POOL OF CONTRACTORS See DEFENSE PRODUCTION POOL and DEFENSE RESEARCH & DEVELOPMENT POOL.

POOL OF COSTS See INDIRECT COST POOL.

PRACTICAL APPLICATION The manufacture (in the case of a composition or product), the practice (in the case of a process or method), or the operation (in the case of a machine or system) of an invention, under conditions establishing that the invention is being utilized and that its benefits are, to the extent permitted by law or Government regulations, available to the public on reasonable terms. FAR 27.301. The Patent Rights clauses in FAR 52.227-11, -12, and -13 provide that the Government may require the contractor to license others to use the invention in the United States if it does not bring the invention to the point of practical application. See MARCH-IN.

PREAWARD SURVEY An evaluation, usually conducted by the cognizant CONTRACT ADMINISTRATION OFFICE, of a prospective contractor's capability to perform a proposed contract. FAR 9.101. A preaward survey is normally required when the information on hand or readily available to the contracting officer is not sufficient to make a determination regarding RESPONSIBILITY. The surveying activity begins by checking whether the prospective contractor is debarred, suspended, or ineligible (see PARTIES EXCLUDED FROM PROCUREMENT PROGRAMS), in which case the surveying activity notifies the contracting officer and does not proceed with the preaward survey. FAR 9.106-1. The following standard forms (SFs) are used for preaward surveys: SF 1403 (General), SF 1404 (Technical), SF 1405 (Production), SF 1406 (Quality Assurance), SF 1407 (Financial Capability), and SF 1408 (Accounting System). FAR 53.301-1403 through 1408. In NASA, a preaward survey board reviews the preaward survey report before action is taken by the contracting officer. NFS

18-9.106-70. See Cibinic and Nash, *Formation of Government Contracts* 238–41.

PRE-BID CONFERENCE A meeting of the contracting officer with prospective bidders during the SOLICITATION period of a SEALED BIDDING procurement. FAR 14.207 provides that such conferences may be used, usually in complex acquisitions, as a means of briefing prospective bidders and explaining complicated specifications and requirements to them as early as possible after the invitation for bids (IFB) has been issued and before bids are submitted. They are not to be used, however, as a substitute for amending a defective or ambiguous IFB. Notice of the conference must be provided to all prospective bidders. See Cibinic and Nash, *Formation of Government Contracts* 373–76.

PRECIOUS METALS Uncommon and highly valuable metals characterized by their superior resistance to corrosion and oxidation. FAR 45.601. Included are silver, gold, and the platinum group metals—latinum, palladium, iridium, osmium, rhodium, and ruthenium. FAR Subpart 45.6 prescribes special procedures to be used for such metals when contractors dispose of unused inventory and SCRAP at the end of contract performance.

PRECONTRACT COSTS Costs incurred by a contractor before the effective date of the contract. FAR 31.205-32 specifies that such costs are ALLOWABLE COSTs if they would have been allowable after the date of the contract and if they were incurred in anticipation of contract award and were necessary to comply with the contract schedule. See Wiener, *The Allowability of Precontract Costs*, 91-11 CP&AR 3 (Nov. 1991); Hordell, *The Precontract Cost Principle (FAR 31.205-32)*, 89-1 CP&AR 13 (Jan. 1989); Cibinic, *Precontract Costs: A Risky Business*, 1 N&CR ¶ 29 (Apr. 1987).

PRELIMINARY DESIGN REVIEW (PDR) A review, conducted during SYSTEMs acquisition, of each configuration item to (1) evaluate the progress, technical adequacy, and risk resolution of the selected design approach; (2) determine the item's compatibility with the performance and engineering requirements of the development SPECIFICATION; and (3) establish the existence and compatibility of the physical and functional interfaces among the item and other items of equipment, facilities, computer programs, and personnel. Part 15 of DoD Directive 5000.2, *Defense*

Acquisition Management Policies and Procedures, 23 Feb. 1991. PDRs are a required step in the process of developing systems for DoD. See MIL-STD-1521, *Technical Reviews and Audits for Systems, Equipment, and Computer Programs.*

PREPRODUCTION TEST   A test of design-qualified hardware using production tooling and processes that will be used to produce the operational hardware. The Government should not accept production hardware before satisfactory completion of this test, whose objectives include instilling confidence that the hardware will work, will prove reliable, can be maintained and supported by the agency, and is not overdesigned. Jones, Glossary: Defense Acquisition Acronyms and Terms. Preproduction tests are more commonly called first article tests (see FIRST ARTICLE TESTING).

PREPROPOSAL CONFERENCE   A meeting of the contracting officer with prospective offerors during the SOLICITATION period of a procurement by NEGOTIATION. FAR 15.409 provides that such conferences may be held, generally in complex acquisitions, to brief prospective offerors and to explain or clarify complicated specifications and requirements. Adequate notice of the conference must be given to all prospective offerors. FAR 15.409(b) suggests that technical and legal personnel should be invited to attend and prospective offerors should be invited to submit questions in advance. See Cibinic and Nash, Formation of Government Contracts 373–76. See also PRESOLICITATION CONFERENCE.

PREQUALIFICATION   Determination of the RESPONSIBILITY of an OFFEROR prior to SOLICITATION; in other words, determination of an offeror's eligibility to *compete* for a Government contract. Prequalification has generally been held to be an undue restriction on FULL AND OPEN COMPETITION and therefore rejected as a means of easing the administrative burden of evaluating large numbers of offerors. FAR Subpart 9.2, which implements 41 U.S.C. 253c and 10 U.S.C. 2319, sets forth conditions that agencies must meet in establishing a prequalification system. For a discussion of situations in which the use of a prequalification system has been upheld or rejected by the Comptroller General, see Cibinic and Nash, Formation of Government Contracts 250–51. And see Jackson, *Prequalification and Qualification: Discouragement of New Competitors,* 19 Pub. Cont. L.J. 702 (1990).

PRESENT VALUE The value in current dollars of work to be performed in the future. This value is determined by discounting the price of work to be paid for in the future by a rate commensurate with the interest rate on the funds for the period before payment is required. Making a determination of present value is a beneficial way of comparing competing offers that call for payment by the Government at varying times. Thus, it is a way of dealing with UNBALANCED BIDs. FIRMR 201-39.1402-1 and 201-39.1501-1 require the use of this technique when the timing of payments is expected to vary among the alternatives being considered. FIRMR 201-20.203-2 requires its use during the analysis-of-alternatives phase for FEDERAL INFORMATION PROCESSING (FIP) RESOURCES. OMB Circular A-104 (revised), *Comparative Cost Analysis for Decisions To Lease or Purchase General-Purpose Real Property*, 1 June 1986, provides guidance on present value calculations in another context.

PRESIDENT'S BLUE RIBBON COMMISSION ON DEFENSE MANAGEMENT See PACKARD COMMISSION.

PRESOLICITATION CONFERENCE A meeting held by the contracting officer with prospective offerors as a preliminary step in negotiated acquisitions (see NEGOTIATION) in order to develop or identify interested sources, request preliminary information based on a general description of the supplies or services involved, explain complicated specifications and requirements, and aid prospective contractors in preparing proposals without undue expenditure of effort, time, and money. Such a conference may be used only when approved at a level higher than the contracting officer and must not be used to prequalify offerors. FAR 15.404(c). See Cibinic and Nash, Formation of Government Contracts 360–62.

PRESOLICITATION NOTICE A notice sent by the contracting officer to business concerns on the SOLICITATION MAILING LIST and published by SYNOPSIS. Such notice must in many procurement situations be given 15 days before issuance of a solicitation. 15 U.S.C. 637(a), 41 U.S.C. 416(a). The requirement for a presolicitation synopsis is implemented in FAR Subpart 5.2. In SEALED BIDDING, the notice (1) briefly describes the requirement and furnishes other essential information to enable concerns to determine whether they have an interest in the invitation for bids (IFB); (2) specifies the final date for requesting a complete bid set;

and (3) notifies concerns that, if no bid is to be submitted, they should advise the issuing office in writing if they want to receive future IFBs for similar supplies or services. Drawings, plans, and specifications normally will not be furnished with the notice. This procedure is particularly suitable when the solicitation mailing list, the IFB, or both are lengthy. FAR 14.205-4(c). In negotiated procurements (see NEGOTIATION), a presolicitation notice may also be used to develop or identify interested sources, request preliminary information based on a general description of the requirement, explain complicated specifications and requirements, and aid prospective contractors in subsequent proposal preparation. FAR 15.404. The notice states whether a PRESOLICITATION CONFERENCE is contemplated and requests an expression of interest in the planned acquisition by a specific date. In a complex acquisition, the notice may request information on management, engineering, and production capabilities.   See FAR 36.302 regarding the use of presolicitation notices in construction contracting. And see Cibinic and Nash, Formation of Government Contracts 356–62.

PREVAILING PARTY A party who succeeds on any significant issue in litigation and thereby achieves some of the benefit sought by the individual or corporation bringing the suit.   Under the EQUAL ACCESS TO JUSTICE ACT (EAJA), courts and agencies award fees and other expenses to small businesses that are prevailing parties in adversary adjudications. A party may be deemed to have prevailed if that party obtains a settlement of the dispute; victory following a trial on the merits is not a prerequisite. A party is also deemed a prevailing party if it has established entitlement to relief on the merits, and a court remands the dispute to an agency for further proceedings consistent with the court's opinion. Prevailing parties must meet the size eligibility requirements of the EAJA. See Kinlin, *Equal Access to Justice Act*, 16 Pub. Cont. L.J. 266 (1986); 28 U.S.C. 2412, 5 U.S.C. 504.

PRICE A monetary amount paid, received, or asked in exchange for supplies or services, expressed in terms of a single item of, or unit of measure for, the supplies or services. Armed Services Pricing Manual (ASPM) vol. 1, app. B.   The term "price" is usually associated with a FIXED-PRICE CONTRACT, which calls for the payment of a negotiated amount, established at the outset or by redetermination, for satisfactorily completed work—rather than a

COST-REIMBURSEMENT CONTRACT, which calls for payment of the contractor's ALLOWABLE COSTs plus any negotiated FEE.

PRICE ADJUSTMENT An adjustment to the price that is called for by the terms of a contract. Most price adjustments are EQUITABLE ADJUSTMENTs that contain an adjustment of PROFIT as well as an amount commensurate with the change in costs that has occurred. However, the Suspension of Work clause in FAR 52.212-12 and the Government Delay of Work clause in FAR 52.212-15 call for price adjustments that exclude profit and reflect only the costs incurred by the contractor during the time the contracting officer unreasonably delayed performance.   See Cibinic and Nash, Administration of Government Contracts, chap. 7.

PRICE ANALYSIS The process of examining and evaluating a prospective PRICE without performing COST ANALYSIS; that is, evaluating the separate cost elements and PROFIT of the offeror of that price. FAR 15.801. Price analysis may be accomplished by (1) comparing offers with one another, (2) comparing offers with current market prices or with current or previous contract prices for the same or similar items, (3) using yardsticks (dollars per pound or per horsepower, or other units) to highlight significant inconsistencies that warrant additional inquiry, or (4) comparing proposed prices with independently developed Government estimates. FAR 15.805-2. The contracting officer is responsible for selecting and using whatever price analysis techniques will ensure a FAIR AND REASONABLE PRICE.   See Armed Services Pricing Manual (ASPM) vol. 2; Cibinic and Nash, Formation of Government Contracts 882–88.

PRICE COMPETITION The competition that is achieved on a Government procurement when offers are solicited and received from at least two responsible offerors (see RESPONSIBILITY) capable of satisfying the Government's requirements wholly or partially. See FAR 15.804-3. COST OR PRICING DATA is generally not required to be submitted by contractors when there is ADEQUATE PRICE COMPETITION. See Cibinic and Nash, Formation of Government Contracts 883–85.

PRICE NEGOTIATION MEMORANDUM (PNM) A Government document that summarizes the process of negotiating a contract's price and the outcome of that process, and serves as a record of the decisions made in determining a price to be fair and reasonable.

FAR 15.808 requires the Government's contracting officer to promptly prepare a PNM at the conclusion of each negotiation of an initial or revised PRICE. The memorandum, which is included in the contract file, must document the purpose of the negotiation; describe the acquisition; give information on participants in the negotiation and the status of the contractor's purchasing system; contain a statement about reliance on or exemption from COST OR PRICING DATA; summarize the contractor's proposal and any FIELD PRICING SUPPORT recommendations; discuss the prenegotiation price objective vis-á-vis the negotiated price; and state the basis for determining PROFIT. See Cibinic and Nash, Formation of Government Contracts 939–41.

PRICE REASONABLENESS See FAIR AND REASONABLE PRICE.

PRICE REDETERMINABLE CONTRACT See FIXED-PRICE REDETERMINATION—PROSPECTIVE (FPRP) CONTRACT and FIXED-PRICE REDETERMINATION—RETROACTIVE (FPRR) CONTRACT.

PRICE REDUCTION The amount by which the Government is entitled to adjust a contract formed by NEGOTIATION if CERTIFIED COST OR PRICING DATA required under the TRUTH IN NEGOTIA-TIONS ACT (TINA) are found not to be ACCURATE, COMPLETE, AND CURRENT. This adjustment consists of any significant amount by which the negotiated price, including PROFIT or FEE, was increased because of the DEFECTIVE COST OR PRICING data. In arriving at this price reduction, the contracting officer is to consider the time when the cost or pricing data became reasonably available to the contractor and the extent to which the Government relied on the defective data. FAR 15.804-7(b). Offsets against the amount of the reduction are required for understated cost or pricing data up to (but not exceeding) the amount of the reduction. FAR 15.804-7(b)(4). See Lovitky, *Understanding Causation and Determining Price Adjustments in Defective Pricing Cases*, 17 Pub. Cont. L.J. 407 (1988); Vacketta et al., *The "Price Reductions" Clause*, 85-12 Briefing Papers (Dec. 1985).

PRICE-RELATED FACTORS Evaluation factors other than price that affect a contract's overall cost to the Government; the term is used mainly in the context of SEALED BIDDING procurements, which must be awarded solely on the basis of price and the price-related factors included in the SOLICITATION. FAR 14.101. Examples of price-related factors that may be applicable in evaluating bids are (1) foreseeable costs or delays to the Government resulting from such factors as differences in inspection procedure, locations of supplies, and transportation costs; (2) changes made or requested by a bidder in any of the provisions of the invitation for bids, if the changes do not constitute grounds for rejection; (3) advantages or disadvantages to the Government that might result from making more than one award ($250 is assumed to be the administrative cost to the Government for issuing and administering each contract awarded under a solicitation); (4) the applicability of Federal, State, and local taxes; and (5) the origin of supplies and, if foreign, the application of the BUY AMERICAN ACT or any other factor affecting foreign purchases. FAR 14.201-8. See Cibinic and Nash, Formation of Government Contracts 449–54.

PRICING See CONTRACT PRICING.

PRICING ARRANGEMENT A basis agreed to by contractual parties for the payment of amounts for specified performance. Such an arrangement usually takes the form of a specific TYPE OF CONTRACT, either cost-reimbursement or fixed-price. Armed Services Pricing Manual (ASPM) vol. 1, app. B.

PRIME CONTRACT A contract entered into directly between the Government and a contractor (the PRIME CONTRACTOR). The term "prime" is used to distinguish that contract from any SUBCONTRACT entered into between the prime contractor and a supplier or vendor called a subcontractor, or between such a subcontractor and another, lower-level subcontractor. FAR 3.502-1 and 44.101. There is PRIVITY OF CONTRACT between the Government and prime contractors, but not between the Government and subcontractors.

PRIME CONTRACTOR A person or organization entering into a contract directly with the United States. FAR 3.502-1. This term is synonymous with CONTRACTOR.

PRIOR COURSE OF DEALING The dealings between the contracting parties on transactions prior to the current contract. Under U.C.C. 1-205(1), "prior course of dealing" or "course of dealing" refers to a sequence of interactions between the parties to a particular transaction that may fairly be regarded as establishing a basis for interpreting their statements and other conduct. The concept is similar to, yet more specific than, "course of business," which refers to what is usually and normally done in the management of trade or business. Black's Law Dictionary. When the parties to a contract interpretation dispute have interpreted the provisions of a similar, previously performed contract, the courts and boards of contract appeals presume that the parties intended the same meaning for the provisions in the disputed contract. See Cibinic and Nash, Administration of Government Contracts 146–56.

PRISON INDUSTRIES See FEDERAL PRISON INDUSTRIES, INC.

PRIVATELY OWNED U.S.-FLAG COMMERCIAL VESSEL A vessel that is (1) registered and operated under the laws of the United States, (2) used in commercial trade of the United States, and (3) owned and operated by U.S. citizens, including a vessel under voyage or time charter to the Government; or a Government-owned vessel under bareboat charter to, and operated by, U.S. citizens. FAR 47.501. Such vessels are included in the definition of U.S.-FLAG VESSELs for purposes of the cargo preference regulations in FAR Subpart 47.5.

PRIVITY OF CONTRACT The legal relationship and responsibilities between parties to the same contract. The Government has privity of contract with the PRIME CONTRACTOR; the prime contractor has privity of contract with the first-tier SUBCONTRACTOR. The result is that CLAIMs of subcontractors against the Government under the CONTRACT DISPUTES ACT (CDA) OF 1978 must be asserted by the prime contractor or in the name of the prime contractor. This proves problematic because the act requires prime contractors to certify claims of more than $50,000 submitted by their subcontractors. Thus, under this "sponsorship" system, contract disputes are certified by the prime contractor, even though it may take a passive role in litigating the dispute. See Pachter, *Certification of Subcontractor Claims*, 19 Pub. Cont. Newsl. 3 (Fall 1983).

PROCUREMENT All stages of the process of acquiring supplies or services, beginning with determination of a need for the supplies or services and ending with contract completion and closeout. 41 U.S.C. 403. "Procurement" also means the acquisition (and directly related matters), from non-Federal sources, of personal property and nonpersonal services (including construction) by such means as purchasing, renting, leasing (including the leasing of real property), contracting, or bartering, but not by seizure, condemnation, donation, or requisition. The synonymous term ACQUISITION is usually used in the FEDERAL ACQUISITION REGULATIONS (FAR) SYSTEM, whereas "procurement" is used in the United States Code. Contracting is a subset of procurement.

PROCUREMENT AUTOMATED SOURCE SYSTEM (PASS) A system, initiated by the SMALL BUSINESS ADMINISTRATION (SBA) in 1977, to provide a single automated database of small, women-owned, and minority firms. The system helps Federal agency procurement offices, prime contractors, and major subcontractors meet their respective small business procurement goals. At the end of 1991, the PASS database contained more than 233,000 firms, of which 39,000 were minority-owned, 51,000 were women-owned, and 70,000 were veteran-owned. The user fee for PASS in 1991 was $24 per hour. Questions about PASS, and company profiles intended for inclusion in the PASS database, should be directed to regional or district SBA offices.

PROCUREMENT EXECUTIVE   See SENIOR PROCUREMENT EXECUTIVE.

PROCUREMENT INSTRUMENT IDENTIFICATION (PII) NUMBERS A system of identifying numbers that are assigned to DoD contracts and related instruments. DFARS 204.7000. The basic PII number remains unchanged throughout the life of the instrument; it consists of 13 alphanumeric characters. The first 6 positions begin with the capital letters assigned to the Department preparing the instrument (e.g., "DA" for Department of the Army, "F" for Air Force) and identify the activity preparing the instrument. The 7th and 8th positions contain the last 2 digits of the fiscal year in which the PII number is assigned. The 9th position contains a capital letter indicating the type of instrument code (e.g., "A" for blanket purchase agreement, "B" for invitation for bids). Finally, the 10th through the 13th positions represent the serial number of the instrument. DFARS 204.7003. NASA has a similar system, called ACQUISITION INSTRUMENT IDENTIFICATION.

PROCUREMENT INTEGRITY A set of rules of conduct, contained in the 1989 amendments to the Office of Federal Procurement Policy Act, 41 U.S.C. 423, that were formalized for the purpose of upholding the integrity of the Government procurement process. The rules, implemented by FAR 3.104, are as follows: During the conduct of any Federal agency procurement, no competing contractor may knowingly (1) offer or discuss a future business or employment opportunity with an agency PROCURE-MENT OFFICIAL, (2) offer or give anything of value to a procurement official, or (3) solicit or obtain, before contract award, proprietary information or SOURCE SELECTION INFORMATION about the procurement. No procurement official may knowingly discuss future business or employment opportunities, receive gratuities (see GRATUITY), or disclose proprietary or source selection information. No person with access to proprietary or source selection information about a procurement may disclose that information improperly. In addition, the employment and post-employment activities of Government officials, civilian and military, are further restricted. FAR 3.104-3. The procurement integrity provisions require CERTIFICATION by competing contractors and the contracting officer. FAR 3.104-9. They have been applied intermittently since the enactment of the statute in 1989. See FAR 3.104-2 for explicit guidance on the periods in which various parts of the statute have been applicable. And see Gerich et al., The Revised Procurement Integrity Rule; Arnavas and Marsh, *The Procurement Integrity Act*, 91-9 Briefing Papers (Aug. 1991).

PROCUREMENT OFFICIAL   Any civilian or military official or employee of an agency who, as defined under the PROCUREMENT INTEGRITY prohibitions of the Office of Federal Procurement Policy Act, 41 U.S.C. 423, has "PARTICIPATED PERSONALLY AND SUBSTANTIALLY" in the conduct of the relevant agency procurement, including all officials and employees responsible for reviewing or approving the procurement. The term includes participation in the following activities: (1) developing acquisition plans; (2) developing specifications, statements of work, purchase descriptions, or purchase requests; (3) developing solicitation or contract provisions; (4) evaluating or selecting a contractor; and (5) negotiating or awarding a contract or a modification to a contract. FAR 3.104-4. NASA regulations provide a more detailed list of potential procurement officials, including DoD personnel, who participate in preaward surveys or technical evaluations. NFS 18-3.104-5.

PROCUREMENT SYSTEM The integration of the PROCUREMENT process, the professional development of procurement personnel, and the management structure for carrying out the procurement function. 41 U.S.C. 403.

PROCURING CONTRACTING OFFICER (PCO) A CONTRACTING OFFICER (CO) in the Government's buying office who enters into contracts and signs them on behalf of the Government. This term is used by DoD and other major agencies. In such agencies, after contract execution, an ADMINISTRATIVE CONTRACTING OFFICER (ACO) typically assumes responsibility for contract administration. Generally, a PCO is responsible for creating and publicizing the solicitation, selecting the source, negotiating and executing the contract, negotiating and executing certain contract modifications, determining whether exceptions to requirements for submission of certified cost or pricing data apply, and settling certain defective pricing issues. A PCO will not normally be involved in a contract termination (usually handled by a TERMINATION CONTRACTING OFFICER (TCO)). In many agencies, particularly those with decentralized contracting offices, all of the contracting officer functions are handled by the same person.

PRODUCTION ENGINEERING See MANUFACTURING ENGINEERING.

PRODUCTION READINESS A SYSTEM's readiness to proceed into production. A system is ready for production when the production design and the managerial and physical preparations necessary for a viable production effort have progressed to the point where a production commitment can be made without incurring unacceptable schedule, performance, cost, or other risks. A production readiness review is performed during the development phase (see ACQUISITION PROCESS) to determine whether the design is ready for production and whether the producer has planned adequately for the production phase. DoD Directive 5000.2, *Defense Acquisition Management Policies and Procedures*, parts 6O and 15, 23 Feb. 1991.

PRODUCTION SURVEILLANCE A function of CONTRACT ADMINISTRATION used to determine contractor progress and to identify any factors that may delay performance. Production surveillance involves Government review and analysis of (1) the contractor's performance plans, schedules, controls, and industrial processes and (2) the contractor's actual performance under them. FAR 42.1101. Although the contractor is responsible for timely contract performance, the Government maintains surveillance as necessary to protect its interests. FAR 42.1103. The office administering the contract determines the extent of surveillance on the basis of (1) the criticality (degree of importance to the Government) of the supplies or services; (2) the contract reporting requirements, schedule, and production plans; and (3) the contractor's performance history, experience, and financial capability.

PRODUCT SUBSTITUTION Delivery to the Government of a product that does not meet the contract requirements. Such substitution can occur by mismarking products, deviation from specifications, and other types of conduct that indicate an intention to deceive the Government in the performance of the contract. Such conduct subjects contractors to criminal sanctions under the FALSE CLAIMS ACT. See Seyfarth et al., The Government Contract Compliance Handbook, chap. 18; *Review of Significant Product Substitution Cases Within DoD*, 7050.1-R Inspector Gen. Rep. (Sep. 1987).

PROFESSIONAL AND CONSULTANT SERVICES Services by members of a recognized profession, such as the legal, accounting, and engineering professions. FAR 31.205-33 specifies that the costs of contracting for such services incurred by contractors are generally ALLOWABLE COSTs subject to specified conditions. When the Government enters into contracts for such services, they may be subject to the rules governing PERSONAL SERVICES CONTRACTS. See OFPP, Study of Professional Services Contracting. 10 U.S.C. 2331 states a preference that DoD contracts for professional services be for stated tasks rather than for hours of services provided. This provision is implemented by DFARS 237.104.

PROFESSIONAL EMPLOYEE Any person meeting the definition of "employee employed in a bona fide . . . professional capacity" given in 29 CFR 541. The term embraces members of the professions that have a recognized status based upon professional knowledge acquired by prolonged study. These professions include, among others, accountancy, actuarial computation, architecture, dentistry, engineering, law, medicine, nursing, pharmacy, the sciences (for example, biology, chemistry, and physics), and teaching. To be a professional employee, a person must not only be a professional but must also be involved essentially in discharging professional duties. FAR 22.1102. When the amount of a SERVICE CONTRACT formed by NEGOTIA- TION is expected to exceed $250,000 and the contract work will require meaningful numbers of professional employees, offerors must submit for evaluation a total compensation plan for those employees. FAR 22.1103.

PROFIT   The amount realized by a contractor after the costs of performance (both direct and indirect) are deducted from the amount to be paid under the terms of the contract. On an annual basis, profit is computed by subtracting total costs of a contractor from the total amount received from sales. In procurements by NEGOTIATION where there is COST ANALYSIS, the Government negotiates a projected amount of profit in accordance with FAR Subpart 15.9. FAR 15.901 states that it is in the Government's interest to offer contractors opportunities for financial rewards sufficient to (1) stimulate efficient contract performance, (2) attract the most capable and qualified contractors, and (3) maintain a viable industrial base. Just as actual costs may differ from estimated costs, the contractor's actually realized profit may differ from the negotiated profit because of such factors as efficiency of performance and incurrence of costs not allowed by the Govern- ment (see ALLOWABLE COST and TYPE OF CONTRACT). In COST- REIMBURSEMENT CONTRACTs, the amount of projected profit included in the contract by negotiation is called FEE. FAR 15.903(d) imposes limitations on negotiated FIXED FEEs on COST- PLUS-FIXED FEE (CPFF) CONTRACTs. See Cibinic and Nash, Formation of Government Contracts 911–41.

PROFIT CENTER   The smallest organizationally independent SEGMENT of a company charged by management with profit and loss responsibilities. FAR 31.001. INDIRECT COSTS are normally accumulated and reported for each profit center.

PROFIT OBJECTIVE   The amount that the contracting officer, in preparing to negotiate PRICE based on COST ANALYSIS, concludes is the appropriate negotiated PROFIT or FEE for the procurement at hand. FAR Subpart 15.9 provides overall guidance to agencies in establishing profit objectives and FAR 15.902(a) requires each agency making noncompetitive awards totaling $50 million or more a year to have a structured approach to establishing such objectives. See the WEIGHTED GUIDELINES APPROACH used by

DoD. When cost analysis is undertaken, a profit objective should be developed after (1) thorough review of the proposed contract work and all available knowledge about an offer, (2) analysis of the offeror's cost estimate, and (3) comparison of the cost estimate with the Government's estimate or projection of cost. Armed Services Pricing Manual (ASPM) vol. 1, app. B. In establishing a profit objective for a prospective contract award, the contracting officer must consider all pertinent information (including audit data) available before negotiation. The profit objective need not be computed using precise mathematical calculations, however, particularly with respect to sub-elements of the major profit factors. DCAA Contract Audit Manual (CAM) 9-902.

PROGRAM EXECUTIVE OFFICER (PEO) The Government official in DoD with immediate supervisory authority over PROGRAM MANAGERs.   PEOs report directly to the SENIOR PROCUREMENT EXECUTIVE of the procuring agency. 10 U.S.C. 1622 requires that there be no more than three levels of authority in the management of a MAJOR WEAPON SYSTEM.

PROGRAM FRAUD CIVIL REMEDIES ACT A 1986 act, 31 U.S.C. 3801 *et seq.*, that allows Federal agencies to adjudicate small-dollar cases, arising out of false claims and statements made to the Government, that previously would have required court litigation. Agencies may assess civil penalties of up to $5,000 per false claim or false statement, as well as double damages for those claims that the Government has paid. Liability for false claims requires the establishment of four elements: (1) there must be a claim, (2) the claim must be made to an authority, (3) the claim must be false, and (4) the defendant must know or have reason to know that the claim is false. 31 U.S.C. 3802(a)(1). There is a ceiling of $150,000 on claims that can be prosecuted under the act. See Brown and Boyd, *The Program Fraud Civil Remedies Act: The Administrative Adjudication of Fraud Against the Government*, 50 Fed. Cont. Rep. 691 (24 Oct. 1988); Bellman, *The Program Fraud Civil Remedies Act*, 88-4 Briefing Papers (Mar. 1988). See also FALSE CLAIMS ACT.

PROGRAM MANAGER (PM) The individual tasked with managing a system acquisition (typically a MAJOR SYSTEM ACQUISITION) program. PMs are tasked with developing acquisition strategies, promoting full and open competition, and sustaining effective competition between alternative major system concepts and sources (as long as it is economically beneficial and practicable to do so). FAR 34.004. In DoD the PM is responsible to the PROGRAM EXECUTIVE OFFICER (PEO) and reports directly to the PEO on all program matters.

PROGRAM OPPORTUNITY NOTICE (PON) A type of BROAD AGENCY ANNOUNCEMENT (BAA) used by DoE to inform potential offerors of scientific and technological areas in which DoE wants to accelerate demonstration of the technical, operational, economic, and commercial feasibility and environmental acceptability of potentially beneficial non-nuclear energy technologies, systems, subsystems, and components. As a result of response to a PON, a contract, grant, or cooperative agreement may be executed. DEAR 917.72. DoE may accept—for award or support—all, none, or any number or part of the proposals submitted. DEAR 917.7204.

PROGRAM POLICY FACTORS Factors that, while not appropriate indicators of a proposal's individual merit (technical excellence, offeror's ability, cost, etc.), are essential to the process of choosing which of the proposals received will best achieve the program objectives. All program policy factors should be specified in the PROGRAM OPPORTUNITY NOTICE (PON) or PROGRAM RESEARCH AND DEVELOPMENT ANNOUNCEMENT (PRDA) to notify offerors that factors essentially beyond their control will affect the selection process. Program policy factors may reflect the desirability of selecting concerns based on geographic distribution, diverse types and sizes of organizations, or duplicative or complementary efforts. DEAR 917.7203(d).

PROGRAM RESEARCH AND DEVELOPMENT ANNOUNCEMENT (PRDA) A type of BROAD AGENCY ANNOUNCEMENT (BAA) used by DoE to inform potential offerors of DoE's interest in entering into arrangements for research, development, and related activities in the energy field. As a result of response to a PRDA, a contract, grant, or cooperative agreement may be executed. A PRDA is used only when (1) RESEARCH AND DEVELOPMENT (R&D) is required within a broadly defined area of interest to support program goals, but it is difficult, if not impossible, to describe in any reasonable degree of detail the nature of the work contemplated; (2) it is anticipated that choices will have to be made among dissimilar concepts, ideas, or approaches; and (3) a broad range of organizations exist that would be capable of contributing towards the overall R&D goals of the program. DEAR 917.73. DoE may accept—for award or support—all, none, or any number or part of the proposals submitted. DEAR 917.7304.

PROGRESS PAYMENT A payment made as costs are incurred by the contractor as work progresses under a contract, or on the basis of percentage of completion or achievement of a particular stage of completion. Progress payments made on the basis of percentage of completion to construction contractors and architect-engineers are considered to be INVOICE PAYMENTs for purposes of the PROMPT PAYMENT ACT (PPA). All other progress payments are considered to be FINANCING PAYMENTs, which are not subject to the Prompt Payment Act. FAR Subpart 32.5 sets forth the policy and procedures for making progress payments based on costs. The payments are made under FAR guidelines using the CUSTOMARY PROGRESS PAYMENT rate, the cost base and frequency of payment established in the contract's Progress Payments clause, and either the ordinary liquidation method (see FAR 32.503-8) or the alternate method (see FAR 32.503-9). Any other progress payments based on costs are considered UNUSUAL PROGRESS PAYMENTs and may be used only when authorized in exceptional cases. FAR 32.501-1 and -2. The Progress Payments Not Included clause at FAR 52.232-15 is used to warn offerors that no progress payments will be included in the contract. See also FINANCING. And see Cibinic and Nash, Administration of Government Contracts 887–94.

PROJECTED AVERAGE LOSS The estimated long-term average loss per period for periods of comparable exposure to risk of loss. FAR 31.001. When a contractor has a SELF-INSURANCE program, costs of actual losses are not ALLOWABLE COSTs if they exceed projected average losses. FAR 31.205-19. See Cost Accounting Standard 416, Accounting for Insurance Costs, FAR 30.416.

PROJECT MANAGER (PM) An official responsible for planning and controlling assigned projects to achieve program goals. Typical duties that relate to the Government procurement process include establishing program objectives; developing requirements, including PURCHASE REQUESTs containing SPECIFICATIONs and STATEMENTS OF WORK (SOWs); obtaining required approvals; scheduling, estimating, budgeting, and controlling projects; coordinating project planning with the CONTRACTING OFFICER

(CO); and functioning as the CONTRACTING OFFICER REPRESENTA-TIVE (COR) or CONTRACTING OFFICER TECHNICAL REPRESENTATIVE (COTR). See also PROGRAM MANAGER (PM).

PROMISSORY ESTOPPEL A legal doctrine binding a person to a promise when another party has relied on the promise to its detriment and the person making the promise could have reasonably foreseen the reliance. Restatement (Second) of Contracts § 90. The court usually gives damages for breach of the promise commensurate with the costs incurred in reliance on the promise. The CLAIMS COURT (Cl. Ct.) has ruled that it has no jurisdiction over claims of BREACH OF CONTRACT based on promissory estoppel. See Nash, *Promissory Estoppel: A Theory Without a Home in Government Contracts*, 3 N&CR ¶ 52 (July 1989).

PROMPT PAYMENT ACT (PPA) A 1982 act, 31 U.S.C. 3901 *et seq.*, requiring solicitations and contracts to specify payment procedures, payment due dates, and INTEREST penalties for late INVOICE PAYMENTs. The act is implemented by FAR Subpart 32.9 and OMB Circular No. A-125, *Prompt Payment*, 19 Aug. 1982. The Government must make invoice payments and contract FINANCING PAYMENTs as close as possible to, but not later than, the due dates specified in the contract (generally 30 days after receipt of a proper invoice; 14 days for construction contract progress payments). The detailed procedures followed are set forth in the Prompt Payment clause in FAR 52.232-25, the Prompt Payment for Fixed-Price Architect-Engineer Contracts clause in FAR 52.232-26, and the Prompt Payment for Construction Contracts clause in FAR 52.232-27. Payment is based on receipt of a proper invoice or contract financing request and satisfactory contract performance. Checks are mailed and electronic funds transfers are made on or about the same day the payment action is dated. Agencies pay an interest penalty for late invoice payments or improperly taken discounts for prompt payment. See Rosen et al., *Prompt Payment Act Amendments of 1988*, 90-4 Briefing Papers (1990); Cibinic, *Payment Due Dates: Complexity as an Art Form*, 3 N&CR ¶ 59 (Aug. 1989); Cibinic, *Prompt Payment Act Amendments of 1988; Construction Subcontract Coverage and More*, 3 N&CR ¶ 12 (Feb. 1989); Nash, chap. 12, Construction Contracting 912–14.

PROPERTY Tangible things of value. In FAR Part 45, providing guidance on GOVERNMENT PROPERTY, property is defined as all property, both real and personal. FAR 45.101. It includes FACILITIES, MATERIAL, SPECIAL TOOLING, SPECIAL TEST EQUIPMENT, and AGENCY-PECULIAR PROPERTY.

PROPERTY ADMINISTRATOR An AUTHORIZED REPRESENTATIVE of the CONTRACTING OFFICER (CO) assigned to administer contract requirements and obligations relating to GOVERNMENT PROPERTY. FAR 45.501.

PROPOSAL An OFFER submitted to the Government to enter into a contract, contract MODIFICATION, or termination settlement (see TERMINATION FOR CONVENIENCE). FAR 31.001. Proposals for new contracts are submitted in response to a REQUEST FOR PROPOSALS (RFP) or a BROAD AGENCY ANNOUNCEMENT (BAA). When they are submitted without prior request from a Government agency they are called UNSOLICITED PROPOSALs. Proposals for contract modifications or termination settlements are submitted pursuant to clauses of the contract.

PROPOSAL EVALUATION In contracting by NEGOTIATION, the process by which the Government assesses both an offeror's PROPOSAL and the offeror's ability to successfully accomplish a prospective contract. The Government conducts both a cost or price evaluation (using COST ANALYSIS or PRICE ANALYSIS) and a TECHNICAL EVALUATION. FAR 15.608. 10 U.S.C. 2305(b)(1) and 41 U.S.C. 253b(a) require agencies to evaluate competitive proposals solely on the basis of factors specified in the SOLICITATION. They require that the solicitation describe the SOURCE SELECTION system to be used by listing all significant EVALUATION FACTORS and stating their relative importance. This statutory language essentially leaves procuring agencies free to use any proposal evaluation system they choose, and a wide variety of systems have been adopted. The agency manuals, handbooks, and documents that provide instructions on proposal evaluation demonstrate that there is no consensus on the procedures to be followed. For example, some call for numerical scoring on all evaluation factors, including cost or price, whereas others require comparison of raw data on cost or price and narrative analysis of quality factors such as technical merit and management ability. See Cibinic and Nash, Formation of Government Contracts 569–84; Nash, *Source Selection: A Variety of Agency Guidance*, 3 N&CR ¶ 60 (Aug. 1989); Nash, *Source Selection: The "Solicitation-Evaluation-Decision" Linkage*, 1 N&CR ¶ 56 (July 1987).

PROPRIETARY DATA   TECHNICAL DATA submitted to the Government under a contract and subject to protection by the contractor. Under FAR Subpart 27.4 and DFARS Subpart 227.4 such data are subject to LIMITED RIGHTS if they are DEVELOPED AT PRIVATE EXPENSE or DEVELOPED EXCLUSIVELY AT PRIVATE EXPENSE, respectively. Under the DFARS the data can also be delivered subject to GOVERNMENT-PURPOSE LICENSE RIGHTS (GPLR). See Witte, *Safeguards of Proprietary Data*, 26 Cont. Mgmt. 37 (June 1986). Restrictions on disclosure of proprietary data by Government employees are set forth in the PROCUREMENT INTEGRITY provisions and the TRADE SECRETS ACT.

PROPRIETARY INFORMATION   Information contained in a bid or proposal, COST OR PRICING DATA, or any other information submitted to the Government by a contractor and designated as proprietary. FAR 15.413 permits offerors to mark all pages of their proposals as proprietary information. NASA defines "proprietary information," as used at FAR 5.202(a)(8), as "information (data) that constitutes a trade secret and/or information that is commercial or financial and confidential or privileged." NFS 18-5.202(d). Proprietary information is subject to the PROCUREMENT INTEGRITY provisions of the Office of Federal Procurement Policy Act, 41 U.S.C. 423, but FAR 3.104-4 provides that proprietary information does *not* include (1) information otherwise available without restriction to the Government, to a competing contractor, or to the public; (2) information contained in bid documents following bid opening; (3) information that the contracting officer determines to release as not subject to protection; or (4) information not marked on each page as proprietary information. This information is also subject to release of protection in accordance with the FREEDOM OF INFORMATION ACT (FOIA).

PROSECUTION OF CLAIMS   The assertion by a contractor of a CLAIM for additional compensation or other benefit from the Government in a court or Board of Contract Appeals (BCA). The cost of this effort is barred from being included in a judgment by 28 U.S.C. 2412. FAR 31.205-47(f) provides that costs of legal, accounting, and consulting services and directly associated costs incurred by contractors for such efforts are UNALLOWABLE COSTs. See Cibinic, *Costs Associated with Claims by or Against the Government: Reshuffling the Deck*, 4 N&CR ¶ 33 (May 1990).

See also EQUAL ACCESS TO JUSTICE ACT (EAJA) and PROFESSIONAL AND CONSULTANT SERVICES.

PROSPECTIVE PRICING Pricing of a contract before the work is begun. It is the policy of the Government to use prospective pricing whenever possible. See LETTER CONTRACT.

PROTÉGÉ FIRM See MENTOR–PROTÉGÉ PILOT PROGRAM.

PROTEST A written objection, submitted by an INTERESTED PARTY, to an agency solicitation for offers or to the award or proposed award of a contract. FAR 33.101. Protests are also known as "bid protests" or "protests against award." Possible actions are (1) protests to the procuring agency, before or after award (FAR 33.103); (2) protests to the GENERAL ACCOUNTING OFFICE (GAO), before or after award (FAR 33.104 and DFARS 233.104); (3) protests to the GENERAL SERVICES ADMINISTRATION BOARD OF CONTRACT APPEALS (GSBCA) relating to AUTOMATIC DATA PROCESSING EQUIPMENT (ADPE) procurements (FAR 33.105); (4) protests to the U.S. CLAIMS COURT (Cl. Ct.), before award; and (5) protests to the U.S. District Court, after award (see SCANWELL ACTION). See FAR 52.233-2 and -3; Cibinic and Nash, Formation of Government Contracts 1005–34; ABA, The Protest Experience under the Competition in Contracting Act; Shnitzer, *Bid Protest: GSA vs. GSBCA*, 89-12 Briefing Papers (Nov. 1989); Stamps, *Subcontractor GAO Protests*, 89-5 Briefing Papers (Apr. 1989); Webber, *Bid Protests and Agency Discretion: Where and Why do the GSBCA and GAO Part Company?* 18 Pub. Cont. L.J. 1 (1988).

PROTEST FILE See APPEAL FILE.

PROVISION A written term or condition used only in SOLICITATIONs and applying only before contract award. Solicitation provisions are distinguished from CLAUSEs, which are terms and conditions in contracts. FAR Subpart 52.2 sets forth the text of all FAR provisions and clauses (as do DFARS Subpart 252.2 and NFS Subpart 18-52.2 for DFARS and NASA provisions and clauses, respectively), each in its own separate subsection. The subpart is arranged by subject matter in the same order as, and keyed to, the parts of the FAR. All FAR provision numbers begin with "52.2." The next two digits correspond with the number of the FAR subject part in which the provision is prescribed. The number is completed by a hyphen and a sequential number assigned within each section of FAR Subpart 52.2. For example, FAR 52.223-1 contains the Clean Air and Water Certification provision prescribed at FAR 23.105(a), whereas FAR 52.223-2 contains the Clean Air and Water provision prescribed at FAR 23.105(b). The FAR provision number will be followed by the provision's title and, in solicitations, its effective date. FAR Subpart 52.1 contains instructions for using provisions, and FAR Subpart 52.3 contains an extensive PROVISION AND CLAUSE MATRIX.

PROVISIONAL PAYMENT An interim payment made by the Government to a contractor to provide compensation during the negotiation and settlement of CLAIMs or EQUITABLE ADJUSTMENT proposals. The FAR contains no guidance on such payments, but they are used by agencies to provide financing to contractors that have incurred substantial costs in performing work not covered by contract clauses. Provisional payments are made pursuant to MODIFICATIONs that generally limit such payments to an amount commensurate with the Government's evaluation of the value of the claim or proposal. See Nash, *Provisional Payments: Another Technique*, 3 N&CR ¶ 18 (Feb. 1989); Nash, *Provisional Payments: A Well Kept Secret*, 2 N&CR ¶ 67 (Nov. 1988).

PROVISION AND CLAUSE MATRIX A comprehensive chart in FAR Subpart 52.3 that provides menus of the solicitation PROVISIONs and contract CLAUSEs suitable for contracts of various types and purposes. The matrix (1) lists all FAR-prescribed provisions and clauses by number and title; (2) tells users where in the FAR each provision or clause is prescribed; (3) distinguishes provisions from clauses; (4) codes all the provisions and clauses to indicate whether they can be incorporated by reference or must be set forth in full text; (5) designates the section of the UNIFORM CONTRACT FORMAT in which each provision or clause should appear; and (6) categorizes the provisions and clauses as *required*, *required when applicable*, or *optional* in terms of each applicable type/purpose of contract.

PUBLIC INTEREST In the interest of the United States. This term is frequently used when broad authority is granted to an officer of the Government. For example, 10 U.S.C. 2304(c)(7) and 41 U.S.C. 253(c)(7) permit award of contracts without FULL AND OPEN COMPETITION when the HEAD OF THE AGENCY determines that such action would be in the public interest. Further, FAR

14.209 instructs that solicitations should not be cancelled unless cancellation is clearly in the public interest, and FAR 25.102 explains that the BUY AMERICAN ACT requires purchase of domestic end products except where the agency head determines that domestic preference would be inconsistent with the public interest.

PUBLICIZING CONTRACT ACTIONS See COMMERCE BUSINESS DAILY (CBD).

PUBLIC LAW 85-804 See EXTRAORDINARY CONTRACTUAL ACTION.

PUBLIC RELATIONS All functions and activities dedicated to (1) maintaining, protecting, and enhancing the image of a concern or its products, or (2) maintaining or promoting reciprocal understanding and favorable relations with the public. FAR 31.205-1. Public relations costs are ALLOWABLE COSTs only in specified circumstances. See also ADVERTISEMENT.

PURCHASE DESCRIPTION   A description of the essential physical characteristics and functions required to meet the Government's requirements. FAR 10.001. When used in a general sense, the term embraces SPECIFICATIONs, STANDARDs, and other means of describing the Government's requirements; it can be used more narrowly, however, to denote a description developed for a given procurement when no existing specification is appropriate. Purchase descriptions must describe the supplies or services to be acquired in a manner designed to permit FULL AND OPEN COMPETITION. They must not be written to specify a product, or a particular feature of a product, peculiar to one manufacturer, thereby precluding consideration of a product manufactured by another company, unless the particular product or feature is essential to the Government's requirements and other companies' similar products lacking the particular feature would not meet the Government's MINIMUM NEEDS. The minimum acceptable purchase description, therefore, is generally one that identifies a requirement by the use of a brand name followed by the words "or equal." FAR 10.004. See BRAND-NAME-OR-EQUAL DESCRIPTION.

PURCHASE ORDER (PO) An OFFER by the Government to buy certain supplies or nonpersonal services or construction from commercial sources, upon specified terms and conditions, the aggregate amount of which does not exceed the SMALL PURCHASE limit of $25,000. A binding contract may be formed upon either (1) written acceptance of the purchase order by the contractor or (2) the contractor's undertaking performance of the work. FAR 13.503. Optional Form 347, Order for Supplies or Services, FAR 53.302-347, is designed for use as a purchase order. FAR 13.101. Purchase orders are issued on a FIRM-FIXED-PRICE CONTRACT basis; they do not provide for economic price adjustment or price redetermination. They do, however, reflect any trade or prompt payment discounts that are offered. FAR 13.501. DoD purchase orders may be modified. DFARS 213.503.

PURCHASE REQUEST A document that, when submitted to a contracting office, officially initiates a particular procurement action; sometimes called a requisition or request for contract. Purchase requests provide the official basis for deciding how a procurement will be conducted and how a contract will be awarded. They contain a description of the requirement, required authorizations, and necessary administrative details that enable the contracting officer to prepare and issue a SOLICITATION and develop a contract document. The heart of the procurement request is the SPECIFICATION, STATEMENT OF WORK (SOW), or PURCHASE DESCRIPTION, which tells what must be delivered or accomplished.

Q

QUALIFICATION REQUIREMENT See PREQUALIFICATION.

QUALIFIED BIDDERS LIST (QBL) A list of bidders who have had their products examined and tested and who have satisfied all applicable qualification requirements for that product or have otherwise satisfied all applicable qualification requirements. FAR 9.201. See also PREQUALIFICATION.

QUALIFIED MANUFACTURERS LIST (QML) A list of manufacturers who have had their products examined and tested and who have satisfied all applicable qualification requirements for that product. FAR 9.201. See also PREQUALIFICATION.

QUALIFIED PRODUCTS LIST (QPL) A list of products that have been examined, tested, and have satisfied all applicable qualification requirements. FAR 9.201. See also PREQUALIFICATION.

QUALITY ASSURANCE (QA) Tasks performed by persons *outside* an organization to monitor or improve the quality of the organization's output. In Government contracting, QA refers to the various functions, including INSPECTION, performed by the Government to determine whether a contractor has fulfilled its contract obligations pertaining to quality and quantity. FAR 46.101. Government contracting QA may also be defined as a planned, systematic pattern of actions taken to provide adequate confidence that sufficient technical requirements are established, that products and services conform to those requirements, and that satisfactory performance is achieved. DFARS 246.101. The term QUALITY CONTROL (QC) is sometimes used interchangeably with quality assurance (QA); for example, GSA has a Quality Control Division in each of its 10 regions that ensures the quality of the products and services GSA procures.

323

QUALITY CONTROL (QC) Tasks performed by persons *within* an organization to improve the quality of the organization's output. The INSPECTION requirements of most Government contracts call for the contractor to provide a QC system that ensures that the work meets contract requirements. QC can be seen as consisting of four steps: (1) setting cost, performance, safety, and reliability standards (or noting the standards that apply to a given contract); (2) comparing the offered product or service with those standards; (3) taking corrective action when necessary; and (4) planning for improvements. Feigenbaum, Total Quality Control 10.

QUANTUM See BIFURCATION OF ENTITLEMENT AND QUANTUM.

QUASI-CONTRACT See IMPLIED CONTRACT.

QUI TAM (kwee tam) PROCEEDINGS A legal procedure named for a Latin phrase meaning (in its entirety) "who sues for the king as well as for himself in the matter." Under the 1986 amendments to the FALSE CLAIMS ACT, any person may bring a civil action under the act "for the person and for the United States," and the action is brought in the name of the United States." 31 U.S.C. 3730b. The qui tam plaintiff files a civil complaint, typically against an employer/contractor. If the Department of Justice intervenes, it bears primary responsibility for prosecuting the action. Qui tam plaintiffs are given a share of the Government's monetary recovery against the contractor and are granted WHISTLEBLOWER protection. See Brady, *Recent Developments in the Area of "Qui Tam" Lawsuits: A New Weapon for Challenging Those Who May Be Submitting False Claims*, 37 Fed. B. News & J. 592 (1990); Victorino et al., *"Qui Tam" Lawsuits*, 89-10 Briefing Papers (Sep. 1989); Waldman, *The 1986 Amendments to the False Claims Act: Retroactive or Prospective?* 18 Pub Cont. L.J. 469 (1989); Graham, *The Qui Tam Amendments: Privatizing the Civil Prosecution Function*, 49 Fed. Cont. Rep. 659 (4 Apr. 1988).

QUOTATION A statement of current prices for items being procured under SMALL PURCHASE PROCEDURES, made for informational purposes in response to Standard Form 18, Request for Quotations (RFQ), FAR 53.301-18, or to an oral request for quotations. FAR 13.108. Quotations are also solicited, on occasion, on major procurements when competition is not contemplated. A quotation does not constitute a binding OFFER;

therefore, issuance by the Government of an order in response to a supplier's quotation does not establish a contract.

R

**RACKETEER INFLUENCED AND CORRUPT ORGANIZA-
TIONS (RICO) ACT** An act, 18 U.S.C. 1961–1968, that does
not penalize on the basis of a specific crime, but imposes additional criminal and civil penalties on persons who engage in a pattern
of racketeering activity, defined as the violation of 2 or more of
over 30 specified Federal and State statutes during a 10-year
period. Crimes that can serve as predicates for a RICO violation
include BRIBERY, the furnishing of an illegal GRATUITY, and mail
and wire FRAUD, but not false claims or false statements (see
FALSE CLAIMS ACT and FALSE STATEMENTS ACT. To establish a
RICO criminal violation, the Government must prove the
existence of an enterprise that affected interstate or foreign
commerce and employed an individual who knowingly and
willfully participated, directly or indirectly, in the affairs of the
enterprise through a pattern of racketeering activity. See Seyfarth
et al., The Government Contract Compliance Handbook 1-42 and
1-43.

RANGE OF INCENTIVE EFFECTIVENESS (RIE) Under a
COST-PLUS-INCENTIVE FEE (CPIF) CONTRACT, the dollar range of
possible cost outcomes under which the contractor has an
incentive to control costs through sound management. This range
is bounded by the contract's specified MAXIMUM FEE at one end
and its MINIMUM FEE at the other. It is a function of the contractual formula or ratio that governs how the Government and the
contractor will share in any difference between the contract's total
TARGET COST and actual total ALLOWABLE COST. See Armed
Services Pricing Manual (ASPM) vol. 1, chap. 1, 22-24; Cibinic
and Nash, Formation of Government Contracts 754–58.

RATED ORDER A PRIME CONTRACT or resulting SUBCONTRACT or
PURCHASE ORDER (PO) for products, services, or materials

(including CONTROLLED MATERIALS) that is placed by a delegate agency (one authorized by delegation from the Department of Commerce) under the provisions of the DEFENSE PRIORITIES AND ALLOCATIONS SYSTEM (DPAS) in support of an authorized program (one approved by the Federal Emergency Management Agency (FEMA)). Such orders receive preferential treatment. FAR 12.301; 50 U.S.C. app. 2061 *et seq.* Rated orders receive ratings of DX and DO; DX ratings have priority. Contractors and suppliers may be directed to accept rated orders, rearrange production or delivery schedules to accommodate them, or improve shipments against them. See FAR 12.303.

RATIFICATION The act, by an official who has the authority to do so, of approving an unauthorized commitment. FAR 1.602-3(a). An unauthorized commitment is an agreement that is not binding solely because the Government representative who made it lacked the authority to enter into that agreement on behalf of the Government. The HEAD OF THE CONTRACTING ACTIVITY (HCA), unless a higher-level official is designated by the agency, may ratify any unauthorized commitment if (1) supplies or services have been provided to and accepted by the Government, (2) the official could have entered into a HCA or higher-level contractual commitment at the time it was made and still has the authority to do so, (3) the contract would have been proper if made by an appropriate contracting officer, (4) the contracting officer reviewing the unauthorized commitment determines the price to be fair and reasonable, (5) the contracting officer recommends payment and legal counsel concurs, (6) funds are available and were available at the time the unauthorized commitment was made, and (7) the ratification is in accordance with any other limitations prescribed under agency procedures. FAR 1.602-3. Courts and boards of contract appeals also find that ratification has occurred in the course of contract performance. See Cibinic and Nash, Formation of Government Contracts 73–82.

REAL PROPERTY Land and rights in land, ground improvements, utility distribution systems, and buildings and other structures. FAR 45.101. Real property does not include foundations and other work necessary for installing SPECIAL TOOLING, SPECIAL TEST EQUIPMENT, or PLANT EQUIPMENT. Real property purchases are not covered by the CONTRACT DISPUTES ACT (CDA) OF 1978.

REASONABLENESS, REASONABLE PRICE   See FAIR AND
REASONABLE PRICE.

REASONABLENESS OF COST   One of the elements in the
determination of whether a cost is an ALLOWABLE COST. A cost
is reasonable if, in its nature and amount, it does not exceed that
which would be incurred by a prudent person in the conduct of
competitive business. The Government attaches no presumption
of reasonableness to the incurrence of costs by a contractor; if an
initial review of the facts results in the challenge of a specific cost
by the contracting officer or the contracting officer's representative, the burden of proof is on the contractor. What is reasonable
depends upon a variety of considerations and circumstances,
including (1) the type of cost generally recognized as ordinary and
necessary for the conduct of the contractor's business or the
performance of the contract; (2) generally accepted sound business
practices, arm's length bargaining, and Federal and State laws and
regulations; (3) the contractor's responsibilities to the Government, other customers, the owners of the business, employees, and
the public at large; and (4) any significant deviations from the
contractor's established practices. FAR 31.201-3. See Cibinic
and Nash, Cost Reimbursement Contracting, chap. 5.

RECORD   Under the Privacy Act of 1974, 5 U.S.C. 552a, any item,
collection, or grouping of information about an individual that is
maintained by an agency, including the individual's education,
financial transactions, medical history, and criminal or employment history, and that contains the name, identifying number,
symbol, or other identifying particular assigned to the individual,
such as a fingerprint, voice print, or photograph. FAR 24.101.
"Records" also means all books, papers, maps, photographs,
machine-readable materials, or other documentary materials,
regardless of physical form or characteristic, made or received by
an agency of the U.S. Government under Federal law or in
connection with the transaction of public business, and preserved
or appropriate for preservation by that agency or its legitimate
successor either as evidence of the organization, functions,
policies, decisions, procedures, operations, or other activities of
the Government or because of the informational value of the data
in them. Library and museum material made or acquired and
preserved solely for reference or exhibition purposes, extra copies
of documents preserved only for convenience of reference, and
stocks of publications and of processed documents are not in-

cluded. 44 U.S.C. 3301; FIRMR 201-4.001, 201-6.1, 201-22, 201-45. The term AGENCY RECORDS is used in conjunction with the FREEDOM OF INFORMATION ACT (FOIA). See FAR Subpart 4.7 regarding contractor records. And see West and Kassel, *Access to Contractor Records*, 88-5 Briefing Papers (Apr. 1986).

RECORD DRAWINGS Drawings submitted by a contractor or subcontractor at any tier to show the CONSTRUCTION of a particular structure or work as actually completed under the contract. FAR 36.102. When these drawings are required to be prepared, FAR 36.521 requires the use of alternate versions of the Specifications and Drawings for Construction clause in FAR 52.236-21. Record drawings are often used, in conjunction with AS-PLANNED DRAWINGS, to prove DELAY.

RECORDS DISPOSITION Any disposal by destruction or donation of temporary RECORDs no longer necessary for the conduct of business; transfer of records to Federal agency storage facilities or records centers; transfer to the National Archives of the United States of records determined to have sufficient historical or other value to warrant continued preservation; or transfer of records from one Federal agency to any other Federal agency. FIRMR 201-4.001. Electronic records may be destroyed only in accordance with a records disposition schedule approved by the Archivist of the United States. FIRMR Bulletin B-1, *Electronic Records Management*.

RECORDS MAINTENANCE AND USE Any activity involving location of RECORDs of a Federal agency; storage, retrieval, and handling of records kept at office file locations by or for a Federal agency; processing of mail by a Federal agency; or selection and use of equipment and supplies associated with records and copying. FIRMR 201-4.001.

RECORDS MANAGEMENT The planning, controlling, directing, organizing, training, promoting, and other managerial activities involved in RECORDs creation, RECORDS MAINTENANCE AND USE, and RECORDS DISPOSITION in order to achieve (1) adequate and proper documentation of the policies and transactions of the Federal Government and (2) effective and economical management of agency operations. 44 U.S.C. 2901(2). The HEAD OF THE AGENCY is responsible for complying with the records management policies and guidance provided by the Administrator of GSA and the Archivist of the United States for all media (paper, electronic, or other). 44 U.S.C. 2901(2) and FIRMR 201-9.001.

RECOUPMENT The recovery by the Government, pursuant to contract provisions, of Government-funded NONRECURRING COSTS from contractors that sell, lease, or license the resulting products or technology to buyers other than the Federal Government. FAR 35.001. DoD recoupment policy requires that non-Government purchasers (including foreign governments, international organizations, foreign commercial firms, domestic organizations, and parties purchasing items sold commercially) pay a fair price for the value of DoD nonrecurring investment in technology developed through R&D contracting. See DFARS Part 270 and DoD Directive 2140.2, *Recoupment of Nonrecurring Costs on Sales of U.S. Products and Technology*, 5 Aug. 1985.

RECOVERED MATERIALS Materials that have been collected or recovered from solid waste. FAR 23.402. FAR Subpart 23.4 sets forth the Government policy to encourage contractors to use such materials in the performance of their contracts. See RESOURCE CONSERVATION AND RECOVERY ACT (RCRA).

RECRUITMENT COSTS The costs of locating and hiring new employees necessary for the performance of the contractor's work. FAR 31.205-34 specifies that such costs, typically including help-wanted advertising, operating costs of an employment office, aptitude and testing programs, recruiter and prospective employee travel costs, and fees paid to employment agencies, are ALLOW-ABLE COSTs, with certain specified limitations.

RECURRING COSTS Production costs, such as labor and materials, that vary with the quantity being produced. FAR 17.101. Such costs are distinguished from NONRECURRING COSTS.

REDETERMINABLE CONTRACT See FIXED-PRICE REDETER-MINATION—PROSPECTIVE (FPRP) CONTRACT and FIXED-PRICE REDETERMINATION—RETROACTIVE (FPRR) CONTRACT.

REFORMATION An equitable remedy used to reframe written contracts to reflect accurately the real agreement between the contracting parties when, either through (1) MUTUAL MISTAKE or (2) unilateral mistake coupled with actual or equitable FRAUD by the other party, the writing fails to represent the contract the parties actually made. If the writing does not conform to the parties' agreement, by mistake of fact as to the writing's contents or by mistake of law with regard to the writing's legal effect, the writing can be reformed to accord with the agreement. Black's Law Dictionary. Usually a court will not grant reformation unless it can determine from the conduct of the parties the terms of the agreement that they would have agreed to but for the mistake. See, however, *National Presto Industries, Inc. v. United States,* 167 Ct. Cl. 749, 338 F.2d 99 (1964), where the court granted reformation in the contract price without clear evidence of the price that would have been agreed to. And see Cibinic and Nash, Administration of Government Contracts 249–51; Nash, *Contract Reformation: A Means of Getting Rid of Nasty Clauses*, 4 N&CR ¶ 58 (Oct. 1990).

REGULAR DEALER A person who owns, operates, or maintains a store, warehouse, or other establishment in which the materials, supplies, articles, or equipment of the general character described by specifications and required under a contract are bought, kept in stock, and sold to the public in the usual course of business. FAR 22.601. To qualify as a regular dealer, an offeror must (1) have an establishment or leased or assigned space in which it maintains a stock of the items; (2) maintain the stock as a true inventory from which sales are made; (3) stock items of the same general character as those to be supplied under the contract; (4) regularly make sales from stock; (5) make regular sales to the public in the usual course of business; and (6) have a business that is an established and going concern. FAR 22.606-2. Generally, all contracts subject to the WALSH-HEALEY PUBLIC CONTRACTS ACT for the manufacture or furnishing of materials in any amount exceeding $10,000 must (1) be with manufacturers or regular dealers in the supplies manufactured or used in performing the contract and (2) include or incorporate by reference the representation that the contractor is a MANUFACTURER or a regular dealer of the supplies offered. FAR 22.602.

REJECTION OF BID The determination by the contracting officer that a bid does not conform to the essential requirements of an INVITATION FOR BIDS (IFB). Such bids must be rejected because they are not responsive (see RESPONSIVENESS). FAR 14.404-2. All bids may be rejected, and the invitations for bids cancelled before award but after bid opening, for reasons including, but not limited to, the following: (1) cancellation is in the public interest,

(2) bids were collusive or submitted in bad faith, (3) the supplies or services being procured are no longer needed, or (4) the specifications have been revised. FAR 14.404-1.

REJECTION OF WORK The refusal of the Government to accept work because it does not conform to the requirements of a contract. The right of rejection is the initial right granted to the Government in the standard INSPECTION clauses used in Government contracts. FAR 46.407 states that contracting officers should reject supplies or services not conforming in all respects to contract requirements, but contractors ordinarily should be given an opportunity to correct or replace nonconforming supplies or services when correction or replacement can be accomplished within the required delivery schedule. FAR 46.407(d) permits contracting officers to decide not to reject work when the nonconformance is minor, but FAR 46.407(f) requires that an EQUITABLE ADJUSTMENT reducing the price or other CONSIDERATION be obtained when this is done. See Cibinic and Nash, Administration of Government Contracts 601–21.

"RELATING TO THE CONTRACT" A term of art used in the CONTRACT DISPUTES ACT (CDA) OF 1978 to broaden the scope of the DISPUTEs process by bringing all CLAIMs of contractors and the Government within its scope. The narrower term is "ARISING UNDER THE CONTRACT." The effect of this broadened scope is to make the current Disputes clause in FAR 52.233-1 an ALL-DISPUTES CLAUSE. FAR 33.205 emphasizes the all-encompassing scope of the current clause by stating that MISTAKEs should be corrected through the disputes procedures.

RELEASE An agreement of a contracting party that the other party will not be liable if CLAIMs are asserted in the future. An unconditional general release by a contractor operates to bar all existing contractor claims, including pending claims as well as known and unknown claims. The contractor, however, may preserve its rights to specific claims by expressly excepting those claims when the release is executed. The contract may require the contractor to give a release of claims and liabilities before the Government makes final payment. FAR 43.204(c)(2) states that contracting officers should insert releases in SUPPLEMENTAL AGREEMENTs settling claims. The language of releases is subject to interpretation to ensure that they are not too broad in their coverage. See Cibinic and Nash, Administration of Government Contracts 933–35.

RELOCATION COSTS The costs incident to the permanent change of duty or assignment of an existing employee or upon recruitment of a new employee. FAR 31.205-35 specifies that such costs incurred by contractors are ALLOWABLE COSTs if the assignment is for a period of not less than 12 months and if specified limitations are met. Allowable relocation costs include travel and transportation costs, cost of finding a new home, closing costs, mortgage interest differential payments, rental differential payments, and the cost of canceling an unexpired lease.

REMEDY The right of a contracting party when the other party does not fulfill its contractual obligations. In general, contracting parties have remedies for BREACH OF CONTRACT by the other party. However, in Government contracts most of the remedies available to the parties are spelled out in contract clauses. Thus, the Government has remedies for nonperformance under the TERMINATION FOR DEFAULT clause and for defective performance under the INSPECTION clause of the contract. The contractor's remedies are generally for EQUITABLE ADJUSTMENT or PRICE ADJUSTMENT under a variety of clauses. Prospective contractors also have remedies against the Government through the PROTEST procedures. See Taylor, *Subcontractor Remedies*, 86-8 Briefing Papers (July 1986).

REMEDY COORDINATION OFFICIAL (RCO) A person or entity that coordinates within an agency the administration of criminal, civil, administrative, and contractual remedies (see REMEDY) resulting from investigations of FRAUD or corruption related to procurement activities. The term was created by section 836(a) of the FY 91 Defense Authorization Act, Pub. L. 101-510, 10 U.S.C. 2307(e). If an agency RCO finds substantial evidence that a contractor's request for advance, partial, or progress payment under a contract is based on fraud, the RCO must recommend that the head of the agency reduce or suspend further payments to that contractor. 10 U.S.C. 2307(e)(1). See Knight and Ochs, *Withholding Payments under the FY 1991 DOD Authorization Act*, 90-12 CP&AR 3 (Dec. 1990).

REMOTE TERMINAL EMULATION (RTE) A technique for validating the performance of FEDERAL INFORMATION PROCESSING

(FIP) RESOURCES equipment and teleprocessing systems when it is not practical to conduct BENCHMARKs with the total proposed network of computers, terminal devices, and data communications facilities. RTE was originally developed in the 1960s by computer hardware manufacturers to test the functions and performance of their interactive systems. RTE, as originally formulated, emulated a set of dumb terminals attached to a large host processor. GSA subsequently developed standards for RTE, which it published in a 1979 (out of print) handbook, *Use and Specification of Remote-Terminal Emulation in ADP System Acquisition*. The material is somewhat dated and no longer mandatory, but it still provides useful information and guidance on RTE. The disadvantages of using RTE are the same as for any other benchmark test and are compounded by the fact that the procedure is much more complex.

RENEGOTIATION   The recovery from a contractor of an amount determined to reflect "excessive profits" made in the performance of defense contracts. 50 U.S.C. 1213 *et seq.* Renegotiation began in 1942 and ended in 1976 and was carried out by an independent Government agency known as the Renegotiation Board. Essentially covering defense and space-related contracts, renegotiation considered a contractor's business in a single, composite assessment each fiscal year. In most cases, the most difficult and complex part of renegotiation was determining the extent to which the contractor's profits were excessive. Contractors were entitled, under the statute, to DE NOVO review of the Renegotiation Board's decision in the Court of Claims. See Cibinic and Nash, II Federal Procurement Law 1996–2026.

RENTAL COSTS   The costs paid to the owner of real or personal property for the use of that property. FAR 31.205-36 sets forth the rules on when such costs incurred by a contractor are ALLOWABLE COSTs. The cost principle focuses on the reasonableness of the rental costs, considering the following factors: (1) rental costs of similar property, (2) market conditions in the area, (3) type, estimated life, and value of the property, (4) alternatives to the leased asset, and (5) the provisions of the lease. The allowability of rental costs of AUTOMATIC DATA PROCESSING EQUIPMENT (ADPE) is discussed in FAR 31.205-2.

RENTAL EQUIVALENT   An evaluation factor, equivalent to the amount of rent that would normally be charged, that is added to a competitor's offered price to overcome the UNFAIR COMPETITIVE ADVANTAGE gained from the rent-free use of GOVERNMENT PRODUCTION OR RESEARCH PROPERTY. FAR 45.202-1. This amount is computed in accordance with the Use and Charges clause in FAR 52.245-9. The rental equivalent is generally calculated by the contracting officer issuing the supply contract on which the property will be used. In the alternative, rent can be charged by the contracting officer having cognizance over the FACILITIES CONTRACT governing the property. FAR 45.202.

REPAIRS AND MAINTENANCE The total endeavor to obtain the expected service during the life of TANGIBLE CAPITAL ASSETs. FAR 30.301. Maintenance is the regularly recurring activity of keeping assets in normal or expected operating condition. Repair is the activity of putting them back into normal or expected operating condition. Under Cost Accounting Standard 409, FAR 30.409, the costs of repairs and maintenance must be taken into account in estimating the service life of a TANGIBLE CAPITAL ASSET and determining appropriate DEPRECIATION charges. FAR 30.409-50(a).

REPUDIATION Rejection, disclaimer, or renunciation. Repudiation of a contract is the refusal to perform a duty or obligation owed to the other party. It may consist of words or actions. Repudiation of a contract before the performance is due serves as an anticipatory BREACH OF CONTRACT but does not constitute a breach unless the other party elects to treat it as such. Black's Law Dictionary. If the contractor, at any time, repudiates the contract, the Government can terminate the contract for default (see TERMINATION FOR DEFAULT). *Fairfield Scientific Corp.*, ASBCA 21151, 78-1 BCA ¶ 13,082, *aff'd*, 78-2 BCA ¶ 13,429. Repudiations may be withdrawn, however, if the withdrawal occurs before the termination action. U.C.C. 2-611. See Cibinic and Nash, Administration of Government Contracts 717–24. See also ANTICIPATORY REPUDIATION.

REPURCHASE AGAINST CONTRACTOR'S ACCOUNT See EXCESS COSTS OF REPROCUREMENT.

REQUEST FOR EQUITABLE ADJUSTMENT (REA) A request by one of the contracting parties for an EQUITABLE ADJUSTMENT under a contract clause providing for such adjustment. Most REAs are submitted by contractors under the CHANGEs clause of the contract, which generally requires that such requests be submitted within 30 days of receipt of a CHANGE ORDER. However, this time limitation is enforced only when the Government has been prejudiced by late submission of the request. See Cibinic and Nash, Administration of Government Contracts 357–67. The Government can also submit an REA to a contractor when the CONTRACTING OFFICER (CO) determines that a downward adjustment in the price is warranted.

REQUEST FOR CONTRACT   See PURCHASE REQUEST.

REQUEST FOR PROPOSALS (RFP)   A SOLICITATION document used in other-than-sealed-bid procurements. RFPs are used in negotiated procurements (see NEGOTIATION) to communicate Government requirements to prospective contractors and to solicit proposals (in the form of OFFERs) from them. RFPs are prepared using the UNIFORM CONTRACT FORMAT shown at FAR 15.406-1. They must contain the information necessary to enable prospective contractors to prepare proposals properly. FAR 15.402. When an RFP so states, the Government reserves the right to award a contract on the basis of initial offers received, without any written or oral discussion with offerors. An RFP can be compared with a REQUEST FOR QUOTATIONS (RFQ), the other type of solicitation document used in negotiated procurement. An RFP is intended to result in a contracting action, whereas an RFQ solicits information rather than binding offers. Compare Standard Form (SF) 33, Solicitation, Offer and Award, FAR 53.301-33, with SF 18, Request for Quotations, FAR 53.301-18.

REQUEST FOR QUOTATIONS (RFQ)   A SOLICITATION document (usually Standard Form 18, FAR 53.301-18) used in other-than-sealed-bid procurements. As it is merely a request for information, quotes submitted in response to it are not OFFERs, and consequently may not be accepted by the Government to form a binding contract. (A contract comes into being only when the supplier accepts the Government's order in response to its quotation or the parties mutually agree to a subsequent contract.) An RFQ may be used when the Government does not intend to award a contract on the basis of the solicitation but wishes to obtain price, delivery, or other market information for planning purposes. FAR 15.402(e). For SMALL PURCHASEs, quotations may be solicited orally rather than in writing whenever economical and practical. FAR 13.106. Written requests for quotations should be prepared using the UNIFORM CONTRACT FORMAT shown at FAR 15.406-1.

REQUEST FOR TECHNICAL PROPOSALS (RFTP) A solicitation document used in the first step of TWO-STEP SEALED BIDDING. FAR 14.503-1 requires that RFTPs include, at a minimum, the following: (1) a description of the supplies or services required; (2) a statement of intent to use the two-step method; (3) the requirements of the proposal; (4) the evaluation factors; (5) a statement that proposals are not to include prices or pricing information; (6) the time by which proposals must be received; (7) a statement that, in the second step, only bids based upon proposals determined to be acceptable, either initially or as a result of discussions, will be considered for award, and that each bid in the second step must be based on the bidder's own proposal; (8) a statement that offerors should submit proposals acceptable without additional explanation, and that proposals may be evaluated as submitted or after discussion; (9) a statement that a notice of unacceptability will be forwarded to unsuccessful offerors following proposal evaluation; and (10) a statement about whether multiple proposals may be submitted. Requests for technical proposals are also used in negotiated procurements (see NEGOTIATION) when ALTERNATIVE SOURCE SELECTION PROCEDURES are used. DFARS 215.613.

REQUIRED SOURCES OF SUPPLIES AND SERVICES Mandatory sources from which the Government must (frequently in accordance with statutory requirements) buy specific products or services. Such sources are designated in FAR Part 8. Agencies must satisfy requirements for supplies and services from or through the following sources, listed in descending order of priority. *Supplies*: from (1) agency inventories; (2) EXCESS PERSONAL PROPERTY from other agencies; (3) FEDERAL PRISON INDUSTRIES, INC.; (4) procurement lists of products available from the Committee for Purchase from the BLIND AND OTHER SEVERELY HANDICAPPED; (5) wholesale supply sources, such as stock programs of GSA, the Defense Logistics Agency, the Department of Veterans Affairs, and military inventory control points; (6) mandatory FEDERAL SUPPLY SCHEDULES (FSS); (7) optional Federal Supply Schedules; and (8) commercial sources. *Services*: from (1) procurement lists of services available from the Committee for Purchase from the Blind and Other Severely Handicapped; (2) mandatory Federal Supply Schedules; (3) optional Federal Supply

Schedules; (4) Federal Prison Industries, Inc.; and (5) commercial sources. FAR 8.001.

REQUIREMENTS CONTRACT   A contract that provides for filling all actual purchase requirements of designated Government activities for specific supplies or services during a specified contract period, with deliveries to be scheduled as orders are placed. FAR 16.503. The contractor is legally bound to such a contract because the Government's promise to buy its requirements constitutes CONSIDERATION. A requirements contract may be used when the Government anticipates recurring requirements but cannot predetermine the precise quantities of supplies or services that designated Government activities will need. Generally, a requirements contract is appropriate for items or services that are COMMERCIAL PRODUCTs or COMMERCIAL-TYPE PRODUCTs. Funds are obligated by each DELIVERY ORDER, not by the contract itself. FAR 16.503. Requirements contracts are a type of INDEFINITE-DELIVERY CONTRACT. They may permit faster deliveries than the other two types—DEFINITE-QUANTITY CONTRACTs and INDEFINITE-QUANTITY CONTRACTs—when production lead time is involved, because a contractor is usually willing to maintain limited stocks when the Government will obtain all of its actual purchase requirements from the contractor. Requirement contracts have been used to purchase all supplies and services in excess of those that can be provided by a Government activity or to purchase a stated percentage of the activity's requirements. See Cibinic and Nash, Formation of Government Contracts 799–820.

REQUISITION   See PURCHASE REQUEST.

RESCISSION   The relieving of a party from all obligations under a contract. Rescission is a remedy for MUTUAL MISTAKE when REFORMATION is not possible and for other defects in contract formation such as DURESS, FRAUD, MISREPRESENTATION, and UNCONSCIONABILITY. AVOIDANCE is used to mean rescission when the party to the contract exercises the right on its own initiative. See Cibinic and Nash, Administration of Government Contracts 251–52.

RESEARCH   Effort directed toward increasing knowledge by study and experimentation. Research is generally divided into BASIC RESEARCH and APPLIED RESEARCH. See FAR Part 35 for guidance on contracting for research. Research is also supported by GRANTs and COOPERATIVE AGREEMENTs.   DFARS 235.001 does not distinguish between basic and applied research but defines "research" as all scientific study and experimentation directed toward increasing knowledge and understanding in the fields of the physical, engineering, environmental, and life sciences that are related to long-term national security needs. Research, according to the DFARS, provides fundamental knowledge required for the solution of military problems.   It forms part of the base for subsequent exploratory and advanced developments in defense-related technologies and for new or improved military functional capabilities in areas such as communications, detection, tracking, surveillance, propulsion, mobility, guidance and control, navigation, energy conversion, materials and structures, and personnel support.   NASA defines "basic research" as including all scientific effort and experimentation directed toward increasing knowledge in those fields of the physical, engineering, environmental, social, and life sciences related to long-term national needs.   "Applied research" is defined as including all efforts directed toward the solution of specific problems, short of major development projects.   NFS 18-4.671-4(x)(2).   See also RESEARCH AND DEVELOPMENT (R&D).

RESEARCH AND DEVELOPMENT (R&D) Effort that constitutes either RESEARCH or DEVELOPMENT, or both.   FAR Part 35 prescribes policies and procedures that apply Government-wide to R&D contracting.   R&D contracts are to be used only to acquire supplies or services for the direct benefit or use of the Federal Government; if the goal is to stimulate or support R&D for some other public purpose, GRANTs or COOPERATIVE AGREEMENTs are appropriate.   Further, it is important to distinguish R&D contracting from INDEPENDENT RESEARCH AND DEVELOPMENT (IR&D), which is defined and discussed at FAR 31.205-18.   In many agencies, the funds to support R&D are contained in a separate APPROPRIATION (such as the Research, Development, Test, and Engineering appropriation for DoD).

RESEARCH, DEVELOPMENT, TEST AND EVALUATION (RDT&E) See RESEARCH AND DEVELOPMENT (R&D) and TEST AND EVALUATION (T&E).

RESEARCH OPPORTUNITY ANNOUNCEMENT (ROA) DoE's term for BROAD AGENCY ANNOUNCEMENT (BAA).   ROAs are a form of competitive SOLICITATION under which DoE's broad missions and program-level research objectives are defined and proposals are requested from all offerors capable of satisfying DoE's needs. The proposals are evaluated by scientific or peer review against stated evaluation criteria. Selection for award is based on that evaluation, on the importance of the research to program objectives, and on the funds available. DEAR 934.016-1.

RESIDUAL VALUE The proceeds, less removal and disposal costs, if any, realized upon disposition of a TANGIBLE CAPITAL ASSET. FAR 31.001. Residual value usually is measured by the net proceeds from the sale or other disposition of the asset, or its fair value if the asset is traded in on another asset. The estimated residual value is a current forecast of the residual value. Cost Accounting Standard 409, FAR 30.409, requires that DEPRECIA-TION be computed on the acquisition cost of an asset, less its estimated residual value.

RESOURCE CONSERVATION AND RECOVERY ACT (RCRA) A 1976 act, 42 U.S.C. 6901 *et seq.*, that requires agencies responsible for drafting or reviewing specifications to ensure that Government SPECIFICATIONs and STANDARDs (1) do not exclude the use of recovered materials, (2) do not require the item to be manufactured from virgin materials, and (3) require the use of recovered materials to the maximum extent possible without jeopardizing the intended end use of the item. FAR 23.401. Recovered materials are materials that have been collected or recovered from solid waste. FAR 23.402. The Government's policy is to acquire items composed of the highest percentage of recovered materials practicable, consistent with maintaining a satisfactory level of competition, without adversely affecting performance requirements or exposing suppliers' employees to undue hazards from the recovered materials. FAR 23.403. See *A CM Report: Recycled Materials: Procurement Guidelines for Government Agencies*, 29 Cont. Mgmt. 36 (May 1989); Hall and Davis, *Environmental Compliance at Federal Facilities*, 88-9 Briefing Papers (Aug. 1988).

RESPONDENT In a contract DISPUTE, the party that must file an ANSWER to a COMPLAINT presented by an APPELLANT BEFORE A BOARD OF CONTRACT APPEALS. The respondent is normally the Government because the contractor is generally the appellant.

RESPONSIBILITY   The status of a prospective contractor that makes it eligible for award of a contract. 10 U.S.C. 2305(b) and 41 U.S.C. 253b require that contracts be awarded to responsible contractors only. FAR 9.103(b) implements this requirement by requiring contracting officers to make an "affirmative determination" of responsibility before making an award. To be considered responsible, a prospective contractor must (1) have or be able to obtain adequate financial resources to perform the contract; (2) be able to comply with the required or proposed delivery or performance schedule, taking into consideration all existing commercial and government business commitments; (3) have a satisfactory performance record; (4) have a satisfactory record of integrity and business ethics; (5) have or be able to obtain the necessary organization, experience, accounting and operational controls, and technical skills; (6) have or be able to obtain the necessary production, construction, and technical equipment and facilities; and (7) be otherwise qualified and eligible to receive an award under applicable laws and regulations. FAR 9.104-1. The contracting officer's signature on a contract constitutes a determination that the prospective contractor is responsible with respect to that contract. FAR 9.105-2. A PREAWARD SURVEY is normally undertaken when the information available is insufficient to permit the contracting officer to make a determination regarding responsibility. In almost all procurements, if the prospective contractor is a SMALL BUSINESS CONCERN, the SMALL BUSINESS ADMINISTRATION (SBA) can issue a CERTIFICATE OF COMPETENCY (COC) overriding a determination of nonresponsibility; see FAR Subpart 19.6. See Cibinic and Nash, Formation of Government Contracts 206–51; Ginsburg and Patin, chap. 2, Construction Contracting 60–87.

RESPONSIBLE OFFICIAL   The CONTRACTING OFFICER (CO) or other official designated under agency procedures to administer the collection of contract debts and applicable interest. FAR 32.601. In most contracting agencies, the responsible official is not the contracting officer but a fiscal officer.

RESPONSIVENESS   An objective, nondiscretionary determination by the contracting officer, at the time of opening of sealed bids (see SEALED BIDDING), that a bid conforms to the INVITATION FOR BIDS (IFB). 10 U.S.C. 2305(b)(3) and 41 U.S.C. 253b(c) require a bid to conform in all material respects to the IFB in order to be considered for award. Any bid that fails to conform to the IFB's essential requirements must be rejected. FAR 14.404-2. This requirement for compliance ensures that all bidders stand on an equal footing and maintains the integrity of the sealed-bidding system. Bids should be filled out, executed, and submitted in accordance with the IFB's instructions. If a bidder uses its own bid form or a letter to submit a bid, the bid may be considered only if (1) the bidder accepts all the terms and conditions of the IFB and (2) award on the bid would result in a binding contract with terms and conditions that do not vary from the terms and conditions of the IFB. FAR 14.301. Bids are not nonresponsive if they contain minor informalities (see MINOR INFORMALITIES OR IRREGULARITIES IN BIDS). The concept of responsiveness does not apply to procurements by NEGOTIATION. See Cibinic and Nash, Formation of Government Contracts 394–437; Ginsburg and Patin, chap. 2, Construction Contracting 88–127.

RESTATEMENT OF THE LAW OF CONTRACTS A methodical summary of the common law of contracts, prepared and adopted by the American Law Institute. The first Restatement was adopted in 1932, the second in 1981. The Restatement is composed of statements of each legal rule, followed by comments and factual examples. It attempts to state the current legal rules being applied by the courts of the various States. The Restatement is frequently cited by the courts and either followed or distinguished.

RESTRICTED COMPUTER SOFTWARE COMPUTER SOFTWARE that was DEVELOPED AT PRIVATE EXPENSE and that employs a TRADE SECRET; is commercial or financial and confidential or privileged; or is published, copyrighted computer software, including minor modifications of such software. FAR 27.401. Under the Rights in Data—General clause in FAR 52.227-14, the contractor is entitled to assert RESTRICTED RIGHTS in such software.

RESTRICTED DATA Defined in section 2 of the Atomic Energy Act of 1954, 42 U.S.C. 2014(y), as all data concerning (1) the design, manufacture, or utilization of atomic weapons, (2) the production of special nuclear material, or (3) the use of special nuclear material in the production of energy, except for data declassified or removed from the Restricted Data category pursuant to section 142. DEAR 904.401.

RESTRICTED RIGHTS   Rights that the Government has in COMPUTER SOFTWARE in accordance with the Rights in Data—General clause in FAR 52.227-14 and the Rights in Technical Data and Computer Software (Foreign) clause in DFARS 252.227-7032. (The comparable term relating to TECHNICAL DATA is LIMITED RIGHTS). DFARS 227.471 provides that restricted rights include, at a minimum, the right to (1) use computer software with the computer for which or with which it was acquired, including use at any Government installation to which the computer may be transferred by the Government; (2) use computer software with a backup computer if the computer for which or with which it was acquired is inoperative; (3) copy computer programs for safekeeping (archiving) or backup purposes; and (4) modify computer software or combine it with other software, subject to the provision that those portions of the derivative software incorporating restricted rights software are subject to the same restricted rights. In addition, restricted rights include any other specific rights not inconsistent with the minimum rights in (1) through (4) above that are listed or described in a contract or described in a licensing agreement made a part of a contract. The DoD clause provides a somewhat different set of restricted rights when the software is "commercial computer software." The FAR clause also contains a slightly different set of restricted rights in accordance with the policy in Subpart 27.4. NASA, however, uses the clause at FAR 52.227-14 but requires contractors (except educational institutions) to obtain permission to establish claim to a copyright, and publish or release to others computer software first produced in performance of the contract. NFS 18-27.404(e). NASA also provides modified versions of the FAR requirements for "commercial computer software" and a substitute clause for FAR 52.227-19, which may be less restrictive regarding use of the vendor's or contractor's standard commercial software license. NFS 18-27.405. See Taylor and Burgett, *Government Rights in Data and Software*, 88-3 Briefing Papers (Feb. 1988).

RESTRICTIVE LEGENDS   Markings on TECHNICAL DATA or COMPUTER SOFTWARE that restrict the rights of the Government to use such data or software. Under the policy in FAR Subpart 27.4 the contractor may use either a LIMITED RIGHTS legend or a RESTRICTED RIGHTS legend in appropriate circumstances. Under the DoD policy in DFARS Subpart 227.4 the legends may be limited rights, restricted rights, or GOVERNMENT-PURPOSE LICENSE

RIGHTS (GPLR). If any data delivered under the contract are marked with these notices and use of the notices is not authorized by the contract, or if the data bear any other restrictive or limiting markings not authorized by the contract, the contracting officer may, at any time, either return the data to the contractor or cancel and ignore the markings subject to the VALIDATION procedures in 10 U.S.C. 2321 and 41 U.S.C. 253d. See FAR 27.404(h); DFARS 227.473-3; Nash, *Removal of Limited Rights Legends from Technical Data: Playing Hardball*, 1 N&CR ¶ 85 (Nov. 1987).

RESTRICTIVE SPECIFICATIONS   SPECIFICATIONs that unnecessarily exclude a potential contractor from competing for a procurement.   10 U.S.C. 2305(a)(1)(B)(ii) and 41 U.S.C. 253a(a)(2)(B) permit restrictive provisions or conditions only to the extent necessary to satisfy the needs of the agency (often described as meeting the Government's MINIMUM NEEDS). Thus, the specifications must describe the supplies or services in a manner designed to promote FULL AND OPEN COMPETITION. FAR 10.004. PERFORMANCE SPECIFICATIONS containing unnecessary design requirements, specifications including arbitrary requirements not related to the Government's needs, and specifications written around a specific product are examples of restrictive specifications. See Cibinic and Nash, Formation of Government Contracts 345–51.

RETAINAGE A percentage of the PROGRESS PAYMENT due under a CONSTRUCTION contract that is retained either routinely or because the contractor has failed to make satisfactory progress. Such retainage is permitted by paragraph (e) of the Payments under Fixed-Price Construction Contracts clause in FAR 52.232-5. FAR 32.103 provides that retainage should not be used as a substitute for good contract management, and the contracting officer should not withhold funds without cause. Determinations of whether and how much to retain are made on a case-by-case basis and are based on the contracting officer's assessment of past performance and of the likelihood that such performance will continue. The amount of retainage withheld will not normally exceed 10 percent of the amount due in accordance with the terms of the contract and may be adjusted as the contract approaches completion to recognize better-than-expected performance, the ability to rely on alternative safeguards, and other factors. Upon completion of all contract requirements, retained amounts must be paid promptly. See Nash, chap. 12, Construction Contracting, 898–906.

RETENTION OF RECORDS Retention by contractors of documents connected with Government contracts. Such retention is required by various contract clauses, including the EXAMINATION OF RECORDS CLAUSE. FAR Subpart 4.7 gives guidance on the requirements for records retention and the methods that may be used to satisfy these requirements. See Skupsky, Records Retention Procedures: Your Guide to Determining How Long to Keep Your Records and How to Safely Destroy Them.

REVERSE ENGINEERING The process of developing DESIGN SPECIFICATIONS by inspection and analysis of a product. The TRADE SECRETS ACT provides that reverse engineering is a proper means of obtaining a person's TRADE SECRETs. See Nash and Rawicz, Patents and Technical Data 388–89. DFARS 217.503(d) provides that reverse engineering by the Government is the least desirable means of obtaining competition in the face of PROPRIETARY DATA. See Nash, *Reverse Engineering: The Government Is Using It To Work Around Proprietary Data*, 4 N&CR ¶ 26 (Apr. 1990); Nash, *Postscript: Reverse Engineering*, 5 N&CR ¶ 16 (Mar. 1991).

REVOLVING DOOR The process of Government employees leaving Government service to join private industry. Restrictions on such employment are contained in 18 U.S.C. 207 (civilian employees) and 37 U.S.C. 801 (military employees). These provisions are amplified and interpreted by regulations issued by the OFFICE OF GOVERNMENT ETHICS (OGE) at 5 CFR 2637 and 2641. Additional restrictions are contained in the PROCUREMENT INTEGRITY rules. Special statutory provisions governing post-Government employment with defense contractors are contained in 10 U.S.C. 2397 *et seq.* The revolving door problem is especially serious when it involves the employment of former Government personnel by contractors seeking the individual's contacts or expertise in order to bolster their business relationship with the Government. See Darley, *New "Revolving Door" Issues for Federal Officials under the OFPP Policy Act Amendments of 1988: A Quick Overview*, 18 Pub. Cont. L.J. 432 (1989); Darley, *Conflict of Interest Restrictions Applicable to Separating and Former Department of Defense Personnel*, 17 Pub. Cont. L.J. 388 (1988); Cohen, *The Revolving Door: A Job Hunting Primer*, 29 A.F. L. Rev. 157 (1988); Brown, *The Current State of the Federal Law on Post Government Employment Restrictions*, 35 Feb. B. News & J. 434 (1988).

RIGHTS IN TECHNICAL DATA   The Government's rights to make various uses of TECHNICAL DATA. Very broadly speaking, if the Government has funded or will fund development of an item, component, or process, the Government may gain entitlement to UNLIMITED RIGHTS in the technical data. If, in contrast, a contractor or subcontractor developed the item, component, or process at private expense, the Government may be entitled only to LIMITED RIGHTS in the technical data. The distinction is important, since data delivered with unlimited rights may be disclosed to competing contractors, whereas LIMITED RIGHTS DATA are considered proprietary and must be protected. See Jones, Glossary: Defense Acquisition Acronyms and Terms. The DoD may also agree to accept technical data subject to GOVERN-MENT-PURPOSE LICENSE RIGHTS (GPLR). DFARS 227.472-3. See Nash, *Government Rights in Technical Data: Recent Court Decisions*, 3 N&CR ¶ 83 (Dec. 1989); Taylor and Burgett, *Government Rights in Data and Software*, 88-3 Briefing Papers (Feb. 1988); Nash, *Proprietary Rights in the Competitive Era*, Gov't Executive 51 (Apr. 1987).

RISK   The assumption of possible monetary loss or gain in view of the job or work to be done. FAR 16.104 requires that risk be one of the elements to be considered in negotiating a FAIR AND REASONABLE PRICE, as well as in determining the TYPE OF CONTRACT under which performance will occur. See Armed Services Pricing Manual (ASPM) vol. 1, app. B. The contractor's assumption of greater cost risks should result in a proportionate increase in compensation. The contractor assumes the greatest cost risk in a FIRM-FIXED-PRICE (FFP) CONTRACT, in which the contractor has full responsibility for the performance costs and the resulting profit or loss. Under a COST-PLUS-FIXED FEE (CPFF) CONTRACT, the contractor bears minimal responsibility for the performance costs, and the negotiated FEE is fixed. FAR 15.905-1(b) requires that this risk also be assessed in negotiating the contractor's PROFIT. Complex requirements, particularly those unique to the Government, usually lead to the Government's assuming greater risk. FAR 16.104. See Cibinic, chap. 5, Construction Contracting 406–99; Nash, *Evaluation of Risk in Competitive Negotiated Contracts: A Key Element in the Process*, 5 N&CR ¶ 22 (Apr. 1991).

ROYALTY   Compensation for the use of property. In Government procurement, royalties are generally paid by contractors for the use of PATENTs or COPYRIGHTs. FAR 31.205-37 provides that patent royalties are ALLOWABLE COSTs if they are arrived at through arm's length bargaining, unless the Government has a license in the patent. In order to ascertain whether a contractor has licensed a patent to which the Government has rights, FAR 27.204 requires the reporting of royalties on most contracts. See the Royalty Information clause in FAR 52.227-6. There are no similar provisions with regard to contractor payment of royalties for the use of copyrights. The Government also assesses royalties against contractors as part of its RECOUPMENT policy. See Nash, *Royalties for Successful Development: A New Form of Profit!* 1 N&CR ¶ 62 (Aug. 1987).

RULE 4 FILE See APPEAL FILE.

RULE OF TWO A judgmental rule that requires a small business SET-ASIDE when the contracting officer determines that there is a reasonable expectation that (1) offers will be obtained from at least two responsible (see RESPONSIBILITY) small business concerns offering the products of different small business concerns and (2) award will be made at FAIR MARKET PRICEs. FAR 19.502-2(a). This rule is based on the assumption that two competing concerns will provide sufficient competition to ensure a FAIR AND REASONABLE PRICE. The rule generates considerable controversy in the acquisition community. Critics have asserted that it is unfair to reserve a contract or all contracts in a given category for small business whenever only two small business offerors express an interest, with no regard to whether the contract could be awarded at a lower price to a large firm or to the effect on the overall percentage of the contracts set aside in a particular industry.

RULE 12 PROCEDURES See EXPEDITED PROCEDURES.

S

SALIENT CHARACTERISTICS Those qualities of an item that are essential to ensure that the intended use of the item can be satisfactorily realized. The term is mainly used in connection with a BRAND-NAME-OR-EQUAL DESCRIPTION, which should set forth those salient physical, functional, or other characteristics of the referenced product that an equal product must have in order to meet the Government's needs. FAR 10.004(b) contains a list of characteristics that are frequently used.

SALVAGE Property that, because of its worn, damaged, deteriorated, or incomplete condition or specialized nature, has no reasonable prospect of sale or use as serviceable property without major repairs, but has some value in excess of its SCRAP value. FAR 45.501. FAR 45.505-8 requires contractors to maintain records of all salvage generated from GOVERNMENT PROPERTY.

SCANWELL ACTION A PROTEST filed in a U.S. District Court after the award of a contract (or before award in a few circuits). The case *Scanwell Laboratories, Inc. v. Shaffer*, 424 F.2d 859 (D.C. Cir. 1970), established that an unsuccessful offeror may challenge the award of a Government contract on the grounds of arbitrary or capricious action not in compliance with the Administrative Procedure Act, 5 U.S.C. 552. The courts and congressional committee reports acknowledge the Scanwell doctrine as a judicial REMEDY; it is a settled feature of Government contracting. See Pachter, *The Need for a Comprehensive Judicial Remedy for Bid Protests*, 16 Pub. Cont. L.J. 47 (1986); Hopkins, *The Universe of Remedies for Unsuccessful Offerors on Federal Contracts*, 15 Pub. Cont. L.J. 365 (1985).

SCHEDULE CONTRACT, SCHEDULES See FEDERAL SUPPLY SCHEDULES (FSS).

SCIENTIFIC AND TECHNICAL REPORTS Reports documenting the work accomplished under a RESEARCH AND DEVELOPMENT (R&D) contract. FAR 35.010 provides that such reports must be required in order to make a permanent record of the work accomplished. Agencies are encouraged to make R&D contract results available to other Government activities and to the private sector, and R&D contracts should require that contractors send copies of scientific and technical reports to the Defense Technical Information Center (DTIC) or the National Technical Information Service (NTIS); these activities provide a central service for the interchange of scientific and technical information. Scientific and Technical Information Reports (STARs) announcing current publications that address aeronautics, space, and supporting disciplines are available from NASA. NFS 18-35.003-70. The DTIC provides DoD information to qualified requestors. DFARS 235.010.

SCOPE OF THE CONTRACT All work that was fairly and reasonably within the contemplation of the parties at the time the contract was made. Nearly all Government contracts contain a Changes clause that permits the contracting officer to make unilateral changes, in designated areas, within the general scope of the contract. FAR 43.201. Changes beyond the scope of the contract are CARDINAL CHANGEs. The determination of whether changes lie beyond the contract's general scope typically entails comparing the total work performed by the contractor with the work called for by the original contract. If the function of the work as changed is generally the same as the work originally called for, the changes fall within the contract's general scope. See Nash, Government Contract Changes, chap. 4; Willmeth, *Determining Whether Modifications are Within the Scope of the Contract*, 29 A.F. L. Rev. 93 (1988).

SCRAP Personal property that has no value except for its basic material content. FAR 45.501. FAR 45.505-8 requires contractors to maintain records of scrap generated from GOVERNMENT PROPERTY. See also FAR 45.607, which discusses sorting and disposal of scrap and recovery of PRECIOUS METALS.

SEALED BIDDING A method of contracting that, through an INVITATION FOR BIDS (IFB), solicits the submission of competitive bids, followed by a public opening of the bids and a contract award to the responsive and responsible bidder (see RESPONSIVE-

NESS and RESPONSIBILITY) whose bid is most advantageous to the Government, considering price and PRICE-RELATED FACTORS. FAR 14.103-2. Prior to the COMPETITION IN CONTRACTING ACT (CICA) it was called "formal advertising" and was the preferred method of contracting. Under CICA it is merely one of the COMPETITIVE PROCEDURES that meets the requirement to obtain FULL AND OPEN COMPETITION. See Cibinic and Nash, Formation of Government Contracts, chap. 5; Nash, *Competitive Negotiation vs. Sealed Bidding: Some Limitations on Agency Discretion*, 5 N&CR ¶ 68 (Dec. 1991).

SECOND SOURCE An alternative source for a supply or service, obtained to foster competition. When quantities of work are sufficient to permit economical performance by two sources, it is the Government's policy to obtain second sources. See DUAL SOURCE. See Kirshner, *Second Sourcing in the Department of Defense* (thesis for The George Washington University National Law Center's Government Contracts Program, 1982).

SECRETARY The head of an agency with cabinet status. Exceptions are the Department of Justice, whose head is called the Attorney General, and DoD, where there is a Secretary of Defense and Secretaries of the Departments of the Army, Navy, and Air Force. The term is similar to the broader term HEAD OF THE AGENCY. It is used primarily in statutes governing the activities of a single cabinet-level department. Some decisions are only permitted to be made by the Secretary or at the "secretarial level." When handling extraordinary contractual actions to facilitate the national defense, "secretarial level" means a level at or above the level of a deputy assistant agency head, or a contract adjustment board. FAR 50.001, DFARS 250.001. Acquisitions conducted without providing for FULL AND OPEN COMPETITION because it is not in the public interest, under the authority of 10 U.S.C. 2304(c)(7) or 41 U.S.C. 253(c)(7), require a written determination by the Secretary of Defense, the Secretary of the Army, the Secretary of the Navy, the Secretary of the Air Force, the Secretary of Transportation for the Coast Guard, the Administrator of NASA, or the head of any other executive agency. This authority may not be delegated. FAR 6.302-7.

SECTION 8(a) See 8(a) PROGRAM.

SEGMENT   One of two or more divisions, product departments, plants, or other subdivisions of an organization reporting directly to a HOME OFFICE, usually identified with responsibility for profit and/or production. FAR 31.001. The term includes GOVERN-MENT-OWNED, CONTRACTOR-OPERATED PLANTs (GOCOs) as well as JOINT VENTUREs and subsidiaries (domestic and foreign) in which the organization has a majority ownership. The term also includes those joint ventures and subsidiaries (domestic and foreign) in which the organization has less than a majority of ownership, but over which it exercises control. A contractor's cost accounting system must, to the maximum extent practicable, allocate HOME OFFICE expenses directly to segments, based on the relationship between the expenses and the segments that incur them or benefit from them. See Cost Accounting Standard 403, FAR 30.403.

SELECTED ACQUISITION REPORTS (SARs)   Standard, comprehensive summary status reports on selected DoD acquisition programs, required by 10 U.S.C. 2432 to be submitted by DoD to Congress. SARs provide key cost, schedule, and technical information in a concise, summary form, generally limited to 20 pages or less. They are required for MAJOR DEFENSE ACQUISITION PROGRAMs in which the eventual expenditure for research, development, test, and evaluation will exceed $200 million or the total expenditure will exceed $1 billion. (Both thresholds are calculated in FY 80 constant dollars.) In addition to an initial filing, programs may require submission of SARs quarterly or annually. See DoD Instruction 5000.2-M, *Defense Acquisition Management Documentation and Reports*, 23 Feb. 1991, part 17.

SELECTED COSTS   A type of cost, incurred by a contractor, that is dealt with specifically in the FAR COST PRINCIPLES. FAR 31.205 discusses the allowability (see ALLOWABLE COST) or unallowability (see UNALLOWABLE COST) of 51 selected costs: PUBLIC RELATIONS and ADVERTISEMENT costs; AUTOMATIC DATA PROCESSING EQUIPMENT (ADPE) leasing costs; BAD DEBTS; BONDING COSTS; CIVIL DEFENSE COSTS; compensation for personal services (see PERSONAL SERVICES CONTRACT); contingencies (see CONTINGENCY); contributions or DONATIONs; cost of money (see COST OF MONEY FACTORS (CMF)); DEPRECIATION; ECONOMIC PLANNING COSTS; employee morale, health, welfare, food service, and dormitory costs and credits; ENTERTAINMENT costs; FINEs, penalties, and mischarging costs; gains and losses on disposition of depreciable property or other capital ASSETs; IDLE CAPACITY

and IDLE FACILITIES costs; INDEPENDENT RESEARCH AND DEVEL-
OPMENT (IR&D) costs and BID AND PROPOSAL (B&P) COSTS;
INSURANCE and INDEMNIFICATION; INTEREST and other financial
costs; LABOR RELATIONS costs; legislative LOBBYING COSTS;
LOSSes on other contracts; REPAIRS AND MAINTENANCE costs;
manufacturing and production engineering costs (see MANUFAC-
TURING ENGINEERING); MATERIAL costs; ORGANIZATION COSTS;
other business expenses; plant protection costs; PATENT costs;
plant reconversion costs; PRECONTRACT COSTS; PROFESSIONAL
AND CONSULTANT SERVICES costs; RECRUITMENT COSTS; RELOCA-
TION COSTS; RENTAL COSTS; ROYALTY and other costs for use of
patents; SELLING costs; service and WARRANTY costs; SPECIAL
TOOLING and SPECIAL TEST EQUIPMENT costs; TAXES; termination
costs (see TERMINATION FOR CONVENIENCE and TERMINATION FOR
DEFAULT); TRADE, BUSINESS, TECHNICAL, AND PROFESSIONAL
ACTIVITY COSTS; TRAINING COSTS; EDUCATION COSTS; TRANSPOR-
TATION costs; TRAVEL COSTS; costs related to legal and other
proceedings (see LEGAL FEES); deferred RESEARCH AND DEVELOP-
MENT (R&D) costs; GOODWILL; executive lobbying costs; costs of
alcoholic beverages; and asset valuations resulting from BUSINESS
COMBINATIONs.

SELECTIVE APPLICATION See TAILORING.

SELF-CERTIFICATION The certification by a firm that it qualifies
as a SMALL BUSINESS CONCERN. This is the initial step in determining whether a contractor is a small business, and the contracting officer is bound to accept the self-certification unless another
bidder or interested party challenges the contractor's small
business representation in a SIZE PROTEST, or the contracting
officer has reason to question the representation. FAR 19.301(b).
See SIZE STATUS.

SELF-COMPLIANCE See SELF-GOVERNANCE.

SELF-GOVERNANCE A program adopted by contractors, with the
encouragement of DoD, to ensure that they fulfill their responsibility to avoid improper business practices. Contractors should
have STANDARDS OF CONDUCT and internal control systems
designed to (1) promote those standards, (2) facilitate the timely
discovery and disclosure of improper conduct in connection with
Government contracts, and (3) ensure that corrective measures are
promptly carried out. DFARS 203.7000. A self-governance

program is an ongoing, internally created and managed effort designed to ensure that the contractor complies with both corporate and contractual requirements. Self-governance programs typically include a CODE OF ETHICS, an education and training program, and systematic reviews of existing practices and procedures. Programs may also include screening of employees for drug or alcohol abuse, review of the records of new employees for evidence of prior misconduct, audits, hotlines, and disciplinary actions. See also CONTRACTOR RISK ASSESSMENT GUIDE (CRAG). And see Seyfarth et al., The Government Contract Compliance Handbook 2-1 and 2-2; Mur, *Ethics in Government Contracting: Putting Your House in Order*, 20 NCMJ 15 (1987); Victorino and Kadue, *Compliance Programs*, 86-11 Briefing Papers (Oct. 1986).

SELF-INSURANCE Assumption or retention of the risk of loss by the contractor, whether voluntarily or involuntarily. FAR 31.001. Cost Accounting Standard 416, FAR 30.416, which contains rules governing the accounting for insurance costs, provides that self-insurance costs will generally be measured on an actuarial basis rather than an actual-loss basis. Under the FAR cost principles, self-insurance includes the deductible portion of purchased insurance. FAR 31.001. FAR 28.308 requires that the contractor submit information on any proposed self-insurance program to the administrative contracting officer and obtain approval of the program when it is anticipated that (1) 50 percent or more of the self-insurance costs to be incurred at a SEGMENT of a contractor's business will be allocable (see ALLOCABLE COST) to negotiated Government contracts and (2) self-insurance costs at the segment for the fiscal year will be $200,000 or more. To qualify for a self-insurance program, a contractor must demonstrate its ability to sustain the potential losses involved. See also INSURANCE.

SELLING All efforts to market a contractor's products or services. FAR 31.205-38. Selling costs are generally UNALLOWABLE COSTS under FAR 31.205-38 unless they constitute "direct selling costs" or are made allowable by other COST PRINCIPLES of FAR 31.205. The principal activities that fall within the generic term "selling" include (1) PUBLIC RELATIONS and advertising (see ADVERTISE-MENT) (FAR 31.205-1); (2) preparing, submitting, and supporting bids and proposals for potential contracts (FAR 31.205-18); (3) ENTERTAINMENT (FAR 321.205-14); and (4) MARKET RESEARCH and analysis concerned with development of the contractor's business (FAR 31.205-12).

SENIOR PROCUREMENT EXECUTIVE An individual appointed pursuant to section 16 of the Office of Federal Procurement Policy Act, 41 U.S.C. 414, who is responsible for managing the direction of the acquisition system of an executive agency, including implementation of the agency's unique acquisition policies, regulations, and standards. FAR 2.101. Each agency must appoint a senior procurement executive to ensure that there is clear authority for carrying out efficient and effective procurement policies.

SENSITIVE INFORMATION Any information which, in the event of loss, misuse, or unauthorized access or modification, could adversely affect the national interest, the conduct of Federal programs, or the privacy to which individuals are entitled under the Privacy Act, 5 U.S.C. 552a, but which has not been specifically authorized, under criteria established by an executive order or an act of Congress, to be kept secret in the interest of national defense or foreign policy. DFARS 252.39-7016. Contractors must agree to secure such information during telecommunications. DFARS 239.7402(b).

SERVICEABLE OR USEABLE PROPERTY Property that has a reasonable prospect of use or sale either in its existing form or after minor repairs or alterations. FAR 45.601 provides policies and procedures for reporting, redistribution, and disposal of this property.

SERVICE CONTRACT A contract that directly engages the time and effort of a contractor to perform an identifiable task rather than to furnish an end item of supply. FAR 37.101. Guidance on service contracting is contained in FAR Part 37. A service contract may be either a PERSONAL SERVICES CONTRACT or a NONPERSONAL SERVICES CONTRACT and can cover services performed by either professional or nonprofessional personnel on either an individual or an organizational basis. Service contracts include those for (1) maintenance, overhaul, repair, servicing, rehabilitation, salvage, modernization, or modification of supplies, systems, or equipment; (2) routine recurring maintenance of real property; (3) housekeeping and base services; (4) advisory and assistance services; (5) operation of Government-owned equipment, facilities, and systems; (6) communications services; (7) architect-engineer services; and (8) transportation and related services. NFS 18-37.000 explicitly states that construction is not considered to be a service. See also SERVICE CONTRACT ACT (SCA) OF 1965.

SERVICE CONTRACT ACT (SCA) OF 1965 An act, 41 U.S.C. 351–357, requiring that contractors pay not less than prevailing wages and fringe benefits and provide safe conditions of work under contracts for the performance of services in the United States through the use of SERVICE EMPLOYEEs. Prevailing wage rates are established by the Department of Labor upon receipt of a Standard Form 98 from a contracting officer. FAR 22.1007, 22.1008. Examples of services subject to the act include (1) motor pool operation, parking, taxicab, and ambulance services; (2) packing, crating, and storage; (3) custodial, janitorial, housekeeping, and guard services; (4) food service and lodging; (5) laundry, dry cleaning, linen supply, clothing alteration, and repair services; (6) snow, trash, and garbage removal; (7) aerial spraying and aerial reconnaissance for fire detection; (8) some support services at installations, including grounds maintenance and landscaping; (9) certain specialized services requiring specific skills, such as drafting, illustrating, graphic arts, stenographic reporting, or mortuary services; (10) electronic equipment maintenance and operation and engineering support services; (11) maintenance and repair of all types of equipment, such as aircraft, engines, electrical motors, vehicles, and electronic, telecommunication, office and related business and construction equipment; (12) operation, maintenance, or logistics support of a Federal facility; and (13) data collection, processing, and analysis services. FAR 22.1003-5. Service contracts over $2,500 must contain provisions regarding minimum wages and fringe benefits, safe and sanitary working conditions, notification to employees of the minimum allowable compensation, and equivalent Federal employee classifications and wage rates. FAR Subpart 22.10. See Cibinic and Nash, Formation of Government Contracts 995–1004; Ginsburg et al., *The Service Contract Act*, 90-7 Briefing Papers (June 1990).

SERVICE EMPLOYEE Any person engaged in the performance of a service contract other than any person employed in a bona fide executive, administrative, or professional capacity. FAR 22.1001. Service employees are those employees given the protection of the SERVICE CONTRACT ACT (SCA) OF 1965.

SERVICES See SERVICE CONTRACT.

SET-ASIDE (n) An acquisition exclusively or partially reserved for the participation of SMALL BUSINESS CONCERNs pursuant to the Small Business Act, 15 U.S.C. 644. A set-aside restricts the competition to small business concerns that qualify under the applicable standards. A total set-aside restricts the entire procurement, whereas a partial set-aside restricts only a stated portion of it. The contracting officer makes the initial determination of whether an acquisition should be set aside and must document why a set-aside is inappropriate when the procurement is not set aside. FAR 19.501(c). FAR 19.502-5 provides that the following, in and of themselves, do not make a set-aside inappropriate: (1) a large percentage of previous contracts for the required items have been with small business concerns; (2) the item is on the QUALIFIED PRODUCTS LIST (QPL); (3) the contract is classified; and (4) small businesses are already receiving a fair portion of the agency's contracts. On the basis of various preference programs, the Government may also set aside contracts for LABOR SURPLUS AREA (LSA) CONCERNs or other categories of businesses. Section 133 of Pub. L. 100-590, 15 U.S.C. 644(c), authorizes public and private organizations for the handicapped to participate for fiscal years 1989 through 1993 in acquisitions set aside for small business concerns. FAR 19.501(k). See SET-ASIDE PROGRAM ORDER OF PRECEDENCE. See also Black, *An Evaluation of Federal Contract Set-Aside Goals in Reducing Socioeconomic Discrimination*, 20 NCMJ 87 (1987).

SET ASIDE (v) To reserve an acquisition exclusively or partially for the participation of a special class of contractors. The Small Business Act, at 15 U.S.C. 644, authorizes procuring agencies to set aside procurements or portions of procurements for the exclusive participation of SMALL BUSINESS CONCERNs. See also SET-ASIDE (n).

SET-ASIDE PROGRAM ORDER OF PRECEDENCE The sequence of classes of contractors that will be considered for award when an acquisition is SET ASIDE. In carrying out small business set-aside programs, contracting officers of agencies other than DoD must award contracts and encourage placement of subcontracts in the following order of precedence: (1) total set-aside for small business concerns located in LABOR SURPLUS AREAs (LSAs), (2) total set-aside for SMALL BUSINESS CONCERNs, (3) partial set-aside for small business concerns located in labor surplus areas, (4) partial set-aside for small business concerns, and

(5) total set-aside for labor surplus area concerns that are not small businesses. 15 U.S.C. 644(e)(f); FAR 19.504. The following order of precedence applies to DoD contracts: (1) total SMALL DISADVANTAGED BUSINESS CONCERN (SDBC) set-aside, (2) combined small business/labor surplus area set-aside, (3) partial set-aside for labor surplus area firms, (4) total set-aside for small business firms, (5) partial set-aside for small business firms with preferential consideration for small disadvantaged businesses, and (6) partial set-aside for small business. DFARS 219.504.

SETOFF The reduction of contract payments by the amount of a contractor's indebtedness to the Government. The Government's right of setoff applies to debts arising from unrelated as well as related transactions and to noncontractual as well as contractual debts. There is no requirement that the Government's claim be judged by a court before setoff may be used. See Principles of Federal Appropriations Law (2d ed.), chap. 13; FAR 32.611 and 32.612. However, it has been held that setoff (but not WITHHOLD-ING) can only be made in accordance with the procedures of the DEBT COLLECTION ACT and the CONTRACT DISPUTES ACT (CDA) OF 1978. See Nash, chap. 12, Construction Contracting 907–11; Cibinic and Nash, *Debt Collection by Offset: What's Wrong?* 1 N&CR ¶ 5 (Jan. 1987); Cibinic, *Postscript II: Debt Collection by Offset*, 3 N&CR ¶ 80 (Nov. 1989). See also NO-SETOFF COMMIT-MENT.

SETTLEMENT AUTHORITY The authority to settle contractual DISPUTEs by agreement. FAR 33.210 provides that the contracting officer has the authority to settle all CLAIMs arising under or related to the contract that are subject to the CONTRACT DISPUTES ACT (CDA) OF 1978. Exceptions are (1) claims involving penalties or forfeitures prescribed by statute or regulation that another Federal agency is specifically authorized to administer, settle, or determine and (2) claims involving FRAUD. If a contracting officer is unable to settle a claim but renders a decision, the settlement authority varies thereafter. If the DECISION OF THE CONTRACTING OFFICER on a claim is the subject of an appeal to an agency BOARD OF CONTRACT APPEALS (BCA), the contracting officer retains settlement authority and may not delegate that authority to a Government trial attorney. If the decision of the contracting officer is appealed to the CLAIMS COURT (Cl. Ct.) or the decision of a BCA is appealed to the COURT OF APPEALS FOR THE FEDERAL CIRCUIT (CAFC or Fed. Cir.), settlement authority resides with the Attorney General and is normally delegated to Department of Justice attorneys. See Latham, Government Contract Disputes 5-23 and 5-24.

SETTLEMENT PROPOSAL A proposal for effecting settlement of a contract terminated by the Government in whole or in part, submitted by a contractor or subcontractor in the form, and supported by the data, required by FAR Part 49. A settlement proposal is included within the generic meaning of the word CLAIM under the FALSE CLAIMS ACT. FAR 49.001. Settlement proposals are submitted by contractors in TERMINATIONs FOR CONVENIENCE, as well as by cost-reimbursement contractors in TERMINATIONs FOR DEFAULT. In the case of a termination for default, however, the costs of preparing the proposal are not ALLOWABLE COSTs. FAR 49.403.

SEVERANCE PAY A payment in addition to regular salaries and wages by contractors to workers whose employment is being involuntarily terminated. To be an ALLOWABLE COST, severance pay, or dismissal wages, must meet the requirements of FAR 31.205-6(g). The FAR distinguishes between normal turnover severance pay, which is allowable, and mass severance pay, which is unallowable.

SEVERELY HANDICAPPED See BLIND AND OTHER SEVERELY HANDICAPPED.

SEVERIN DOCTRINE A legal rule preventing contractors from recovering damages on behalf of subcontractors for BREACH OF CONTRACT by the Government if the contractor has no liability to the subcontractor. The rule originated with the case of *Severin v. United States*, 99 Ct. Cl. 435 (1943), which held that a clause in a subcontract completely exculpating the contractor from liability barred any CLAIM on behalf of the subcontractor against the Government because the contractor could not prove that it (rather than the subcontractor) had suffered any damages. The rule does not apply to claims for compensation under contract clauses. See Cibinic and Nash, Administration of Government Contracts 495–96; Nash, *The Severin Doctrine: It's Still Barely Alive and Well*, 4 N&CR ¶ 63 (Nov. 1990).

"SHALL" The imperative term used in the FEDERAL ACQUISITION REGULATIONS (FAR) SYSTEM. FAR 2.101. When a regulation uses the term "shall," it denotes that the regulation is mandatory and must be followed unless the contracting officer has obtained a DEVIATION. If a mandatory clause is omitted from the contract without a deviation, it is included in the contract by operation of the CHRISTIAN DOCTRINE.

SHARING BASE The number of affected end items on contracts of the contracting office accepting a VALUE ENGINEERING CHANGE PROPOSAL (VECP). FAR 48.001. The sharing base is one of the elements in the computation of ACQUISITION SAVINGS.

SHARING PERIOD The period beginning with acceptance of the first unit incorporating the VALUE ENGINEERING CHANGE PROPOS-AL (VECP) and ending at the later of (1) 3 years after the first unit affected by the VECP is accepted or (2) the last scheduled delivery date of an item affected by the VECP under the contract delivery schedule in effect at the time the VECP is accepted. FAR 48.001. The sharing period is one of the elements in the computation of FUTURE CONTRACT SAVINGS.

SHORT FORM RESEARCH CONTRACT (SFRC) A form of contract used by DoD to purchase RESEARCH on a cost-reimbursement basis (see COST-REIMBURSEMENT CONTRACT) from educational institutions or domestic nonprofit organizations. DFARS 235.015-71. SFRCs need not follow the UNIFORM CONTRACT FORMAT but must include certain FAR and DFARS clauses. DFARS 235.015-71 (h) and (i). Contractors must use DD Form 2222-2, Short Form Research Contract—Research Proposal, DFARS 253.303-2222-2, when submitting research proposals for SFRC awards. DFARS 235.015-71(d). The contracting officer may award an SFRC on the basis of FULL AND OPEN COMPETITION if the contract is based on a BROAD AGENCY ANNOUNCEMENT (BAA); the contracting officer may award the contract on the basis of other than full and open competition if it is based on an UNSOLICITED PROPOSAL for research work or if it is necessary to award the contract to establish or maintain an essential engineering research or development capability. DFARS 235.015-71(e).

SHOULD-COST ANALYSIS A technique aimed at establishing a PRICE on the basis of what it *should* cost the contractor to produce, assuming reasonable economy and efficiency of operation. It is a specialized form of COST ANALYSIS that is used to evaluate the cost of major production programs by analyzing and challenging a contractor's management and operation systems. FAR 15.810. A should-cost analysis is performed at the contractor's plant, employing an integrated SHOULD-COST TEAM. The objective is to promote both short- and long-range improvements by identifying uneconomical or inefficient practices in the contractor's existing workforce, methods, materials, facilities, or management and operating systems; quantifying the findings in terms of their impact on cost; and developing a realistic price objective for negotiation. Use of a should-cost analysis is typically considered for MAJOR SYSTEM ACQUISITIONs when some production has taken place; the contract will be SOLE SOURCE; there will be future requirements for production, perhaps substantial, of like items; the work is sufficiently defined to permit an effective analysis (i.e., major changes are unlikely); and the items being acquired have a history of increasing costs. FAR 15.810(b). DoD requires a should-cost analysis for major system contracts over $100 million in situations where all but the last of the above criteria have been met. DFARS 215.810. See Cibinic and Nash, Formation of Government Contracts 907.

SHOULD-COST TEAM   An integrated team of Government procurement, contract administration, pricing, audit, and engineering representatives formed to conduct a coordinated, in-depth SHOULD-COST ANALYSIS at the contractor's plant. The team normally consists of a team leader, a deputy team leader, a DEFENSE CONTRACT AUDIT AGENCY (DCAA) representative, an operations and administration officer, and three sub-teams—technical, management, and pricing. FAR 15.810. See DCAA Contract Audit Manual (CAM) 9-1303 and 9-1304.

SHOW CAUSE NOTICE A preliminary written notice given to the contractor by the contracting officer when TERMINATION FOR DEFAULT appears to be appropriate. FAR 49.402-3(e)(1). It (1) notifies the contractor of the possibility of termination, (2) points out the contractual liabilities of default termination, and (3) asks the contractor to show cause why the contract should not be terminated for default. The notice may state that failure of the contractor to show cause may be taken as admission that there is no valid cause. The notice may also invite the contractor to discuss the matter at a meeting or conference. A suggested format for a show cause notice is set forth in FAR 49.607. See Cibinic and Nash, Administration of Government Contracts, 755–58. See also CURE NOTICE.

SIGNIFICANT REVISION A revision to the FAR or one of its agency supplements that alters the meaning of any coverage having a significant cost or administrative impact on contractors or offerors, or a significant effect beyond the internal operating procedures of the issuing agency. Significant revisions do not include editorial, stylistic, or other revisions that have no impact on the basic meaning of the coverage being revised. FAR 1.501-1. Public comments on a revision need not be solicited when the proposed coverage does not constitute a significant revision. FAR 1.501-3.

SIMPLIFIED CONTRACT FORMAT A standardized format used in lieu of the UNIFORM CONTRACT FORMAT when obtaining supplies or services using a FIRM-FIXED-PRICE (FFP) CONTRACT or a FIXED-PRICE WITH ECONOMIC PRICE ADJUSTMENT (EPA) CONTRACT. The recommended format is the Solicitation/Contract form (Standard Form 1447), followed by the contract schedule, clauses, a list of documents and attachments (if necessary), and representations and instructions. The contracting officer, however, has flexibility in organizing and preparing the documentation. See FAR 14.201-9 and 15.416.

SINGLE-AWARD SCHEDULE A schedule in the FEDERAL SUPPLY SCHEDULES (FSS) series for which there is only one contract made with a supplier for any given item at a stated price, for delivery to points within a geographic area as defined in the schedule. FAR 8.403-1. Award of a single-award schedule contract is appropriate if there are adequate commercial descriptions or specifications to permit competitive offers. FAR 38.102-1. The procedures to be followed in ordering from these schedules are set forth in FAR Subpart 8.4.

SINGLE SOURCE See SOLE SOURCE.

SITE OF WORK The physical place or places where construction called for in the contract will remain when work is completed, and nearby property used by the contractor or subcontractor during construction that is so close that it can reasonably be included in the site. FAR 22.401. Fabrication plants, mobile factories, batch plants, borrow pits, job headquarters, tool yards, and the like are parts of the site of work, provided they are dedicated exclusively, or nearly so, to performance of the contract or project, and are close enough to the actual construction location that it would be reasonable to include them. The site of work does not include permanent home offices, branch plant establishments, fabrication plants, or tool yards of a contractor or subcontractor whose locations and continuance in operation are determined wholly without regard to a particular Federal contract or project. The DAVIS-BACON ACT is applicable only to LABORERS OR MECHANICS employed directly on the site of work.

SIZE APPEAL See SIZE PROTEST.

SIZE PROTEST The protest by an offeror or interested party challenging an offeror's representation of itself as a SMALL BUSINESS CONCERN. Such protests must be filed within 5 days after bid opening or receipt of notice of an apparent successful offeror. FAR 19.302(d)(1). Size protests are referred to the SMALL BUSINESS ADMINISTRATION (SBA) regional office where the principal office of the challenged offeror is located. FAR 19.303(c). Once the contracting officer receives a protest, he or she may not award the contract until (1) SBA makes a size determination or (2) 10 business days transpire after SBA's receipt of the protest, whichever occurs first. When the contracting officer determines in writing that award must be made to protect the public interest, the award need not be stayed, although the contracting officer must notify the SBA. FAR 19.302(h). The contracting officer may stay the award longer than 10 days, until SBA's determination is received, unless the delay would prove disadvantageous to the Government. Appeals from adverse size determinations by the SBA must be filed with the SBA Office of Hearings and Appeals in Washington, D.C. FAR 19.302(i). See Patin, chap. 4, Construction Contracting 335–43. See also SIZE STATUS.

SIZE STANDARDS See SMALL BUSINESS CONCERN.

SIZE STATUS The characteristics of a firm that qualify it to obtain the benefits of being a SMALL BUSINESS CONCERN. The size status of a concern is determined, in the first instance, by SELF-CERTIFI-CATION that the firm meets size standards established by the SMALL BUSINESS ADMINISTRATION (SBA) and set forth at FAR 19.102. If the status is challenged, the size is determined through the SIZE PROTEST procedures.

SMALL AND DISADVANTAGED BUSINESS UTILIZATION SPECIALIST (SADBUS) A Government employee with the responsibility of ensuring the utilization of SMALL BUSINESS CONCERNs and SMALL DISADVANTAGED BUSINESS CONCERNs (SDBCs) in accordance with agency regulations. FAR 19.201. Agencies frequently use titles such as Small Business Specialist or Small Business/Disadvantaged Business Specialist in lieu of SADBUS. See, for example, NFS 18-19.201(c). The duties assigned to this function vary from agency to agency. Within DoD, DFARS 219.201(d) specifies that the SADBUS must (1) make sure that programs affecting small business concerns, HISTORICALLY BLACK COLLEGES AND UNIVERSITIES (HBCUs), MINORITY INSTITUTIONs (MIs), and LABOR SURPLUS AREA (LSA) CONCERNs are implemented; (2) advise contracting, program, and requirements personnel on all matters affecting small businesses, HBCUs, MIs, and LSA concerns; (3) advise and inform small businesses, SDBCs, HBCUs, MIs, and LSA concerns about acquisition procedures and proposed acquisitions, and instruct them in preparing proposals and interpreting solicitation provisions and contract clauses; (4) maintain outreach programs designed to locate small businesses, SDBCs, HBCUs, and MIs, and to develop information on their technical competence; (5) ensure that small business concerns are offered financial assistance available under existing regulations and that they obtain payment under their contracts; (6) help contracting officers determine when subcontracting plans are needed, whether they are acceptable, and whether they are being complied with; and (7) monitor performance against small and disadvantaged business program goals and recommend action to correct deficiencies. NASA prescribes slightly different duties. NFS 18-19.201(c). For a list of Offices of Small and Disadvantaged Business Utilization, see Swain and Weiss, *The Contribution of Small Business to the Federal Prompt Payment Law and Similar State Laws*, 29 Cont. Mgmt. 12 (May 1989).

SMALL BUSINESS ACT An act, 15 U.S.C. 631 *et seq.*, that in 1963 created the SMALL BUSINESS ADMINISTRATION (SBA). The SBA is jointly responsible with the Federal procuring agencies for promoting policies and taking actions to ensure that SMALL BUSINESS CONCERNs and SMALL DISADVANTAGED BUSINESS CONCERNs (SDBCs) obtain their fair share of Government procurements. The 1978 amendments gave added emphasis to the 8(a) PROGRAM by providing for business development assistance, establishing new eligibility standards, and requiring prime contractors to submit formal plans for subcontracting to small businesses and 8(a) firms.

SMALL BUSINESS ADMINISTRATION (SBA) A Government agency that counsels SMALL BUSINESS CONCERNs and helps contracting personnel ensure that a fair proportion of contracts for supplies and services is placed with small business. FAR 19.201(a). The SBA is authorized to (1) define specific small business size standards; (2) make loans; (3) enter into contracts with the Government and arrange for performance by subcontracting to small business (see 8(a) PROGRAM); (4) engage in determinations that certain interests would be served by awarding all or part of a contract to small business; (5) determine the SIZE STATUS of small business concerns; (6) certify the competency, including capacity and credit, of small businesses to perform particular contracts (see CERTIFICATE OF COMPETENCY (COC)); and (7) assist and encourage small business to undertake joint R&D programs (see SMALL BUSINESS INNOVATIVE RESEARCH (SBIR) CONTRACT). FAR Part 19. SBA regulations are at 13 CFR Parts 101–140. See the U.S. Government Manual; Lambert and Shillito, *New Developments in Small Business*, 29 Cont. Mgmt. 24 (Mar. 1989).

SMALL BUSINESS COMPETITIVENESS DEMONSTRATION PROGRAM A program to improve the small business policies of the Government, enacted by the Business Opportunity Development Reform Act of 1988, 15 U.S.C. 644. The program is in effect during a 4-year period covering calendar years 1989 through 1992 and is intended to (1) show the competitive capabilities of small business on unrestricted Government contracts and (2) target for expansion small business SET-ASIDEs in industries that historically demonstrate low small business involvement. As long as selected agencies maintain a level of at least 40 percent small business awards for selected industries—construction, refuse systems, architect-engineer services, and non-nuclear ship repair—the agency will use FULL AND OPEN COMPETITION rather than set-asides. However, the agencies must designate industries with which they have had low small business involvement for special efforts to increase the percentage of work performed by small business. This program calls for participation by the following agencies: the Departments of Agriculture, Defense, Energy, Health and Human Services, Transportation, and Veterans Affairs; the Environmental Protection Agency; and the General

Services and National Aeronautics and Space Administrations. The program creates a new category of small business concern known as EMERGING SMALL BUSINESS. FAR Subpart 19.10. See Nash, *Small Business: The Machinery Gets a Major Retuning*, 3 N&CR ¶ 44 (June 1989).

SMALL BUSINESS CONCERN   A concern, under the Small Business Act, 15 U.S.C. 632, that is independently owned and operated and not dominant in its field of operation. The SMALL BUSINESS ADMINISTRATION (SBA) is responsible for further definition of the term and does this through its Small Business Size Standards Regulations, 13 CFR Part 121, incorporated in FAR 19.102. The definition of a small business varies by industry. To qualify, a contractor must fall within the size standard applicable to the industry under the Standard Industrial Classification (SIC), which divides industries into 89 major groups and then into subgroups. Depending on the industry in question, the standard applied is based on either dollar volume (average annual receipts for the preceding 3 fiscal years) or number of employees. See Lambert and Shillito, *New Developments in Small Business*, 29 Cont. Mgmt. 24 (Mar. 1989); Kennedy and Trilling, *Pathways and Pitfalls for Small Business: Federal Procurement Socioeconomic Programs*, 22 NCMJ 55 (1988); Seidman, *An Overview of Small and Disadvantaged Business Contracting*, 19 NCMJ 5 (1985). See also SIZE STATUS and SIZE PROTEST.

SMALL BUSINESS INNOVATIVE RESEARCH (SBIR) CON-TRACT   A contract issued pursuant to the Small Business Innovation Development Act of 1982, 15 U.S.C. 638. This act requires agencies with a budget for "extramural" research and development of more than $10 million to expend 1.25 percent of their budget with small businesses on SBIR contracts. These contracts are issued in two phases: Phase I for $50,000 to demonstrate the feasibility of the innovation and Phase II for $500,000 for development of the innovation. Procedures for these contracts are contained in 13 CFR 121. The Rights in Data—SBIR Program clause at FAR 52.227-20 is used in the contracts to give SBIR contractors special rights in the TECHNICAL DATA developed under them. See Cibinic and Nash, Formation of Government Contracts 696–701.

SMALL BUSINESS SET-ASIDE See SET-ASIDE (n) and SET-ASIDE PROGRAM ORDER OF PRECEDENCE.

SMALL CLAIMS PROCEDURES See EXPEDITED PROCEDURES.

SMALL DISADVANTAGED BUSINESS CONCERN (SDBC) A SMALL BUSINESS CONCERN that is at least 51 percent unconditionally owned by one or more individuals who are both socially and economically disadvantaged (see SOCIALLY DISADVANTAGED INDIVIDUALS and ECONOMICALLY DISADVANTAGED INDIVIDUALS), or a publicly owned business with at least 51 percent of its stock unconditionally owned by, and its management and daily business controlled by, one or more socially and economically disadvantaged individuals. FAR 19.001. This term also means a small business concern that is at least 51 percent unconditionally owned by an economically disadvantaged INDIAN TRIBE or NATIVE HAWAIIAN ORGANIZATION, or a publicly owned business with at least 51 percent of its stock unconditionally owned by one of these entities, its management and daily business controlled by members of an economically disadvantaged Indian tribe or Native Hawaiian Organization, and that meets the requirements of 13 CFR Part 124. Individuals must certify that they are members of named groups that are considered socially and economically disadvantaged— Black Americans, Hispanic Americans, NATIVE AMERICANS, ASIAN-PACIFIC AMERICANS, and SUBCONTINENT-ASIAN AMERICANS—in order to qualify for SDBC benefits and other minority aid programs. The defense authorization or appropriation acts of 1987 and the following years have established the goal that 5 percent of all DoD procurements be awarded to SDBCs and have authorized less than FULL AND OPEN COMPETITION and premiums not to exceed 10 percent of the FAIR MARKET PRICE. In DoD procurements, SDBCs include HISTORICALLY BLACK COLLEGES AND UNIVERSITIES (HBUCs) and other MINORITY INSTITUTIONS (MIs). See DFARS 226.7003; Lambert and Shillito, *DoD Implements Congressional Mandate to Meet a Five Percent Contract Goal for Minorities*, 27 Cont. Mgmt. 16 (Oct. 1987).

SMALL PURCHASE An acquisition of supplies, nonpersonal services, or construction in the amount of $25,000 or less using the procedures prescribed in FAR Part 13. These simplified procedures are intended to (1) reduce administrative costs and (2) improve opportunities for SMALL BUSINESS CONCERNs and SMALL DISADVANTAGED BUSINESS CONCERNs (SDBCs) to obtain Government contracts. FAR 13.102. See Cibinic and Nash, Formation of Government Contracts 164–70.

SMALL PURCHASE PROCEDURES The prescribed methods for making SMALL PURCHASEs using IMPREST FUNDs (Subpart FAR 13.4), PURCHASE ORDERs (POs) (FAR Subpart 13.5), and BLANKET PURCHASE AGREEMENTs (BPAs) (FAR Subpart 13.2). These procedures must be used to the maximum extent practicable for all purchases not exceeding the small purchase limitation ($25,000), unless requirements can be met by using required sources of supply. FAR 13.103. The contracting officer is required to SET ASIDE all small purchases, except foreign purchases, for small business. FAR 13.105.

SOCIALLY DISADVANTAGED INDIVIDUALS Individuals who have been subjected to racial or ethnic prejudice or cultural bias because of their identity as a member of a group without regard to their qualities as individuals. FAR 19.001. Businesses owned by such individuals who are also ECONOMICALLY DISADVANTAGED INDIVIDUALS are given special preferences in Government procurement; see SMALL DISADVANTAGED BUSINESS CONCERN (SDBC).

SOCIOECONOMIC PROGRAMS Programs that are incorporated into the procurement process to foster the achievement of national goals. Although Federal procurement policy endeavors to obtain supplies and services economically, efficiently, and in a timely manner, the Government also utilizes its purchasing power as a means of promoting public policies. Government contracts attempt to further such national goals as fostering small business, overcoming regional unemployment, assisting minority workers, giving preference to domestic and other special sources, ensuring fair treatment of employees, maintaining integrity and fair competitive practices, and protecting the environment. See FAR Parts 19, Small Business and Small Disadvantaged Business Concerns; 20, Labor Surplus Area Concerns; 22, Application of Labor Laws to Government Acquisitions; 23, Environment, Conservation, Occupational Safety, and Drug-Free Workplace; 24, Protection of Privacy and Freedom of Information; and 25, Foreign Acquisition. See Black, *Socioeconomic Contract Goal Setting Within the Department of Defense: Promises Still Unfulfilled*, 22 NCMJ 67 (1989); Horowitz and Wickersty,

Socio-Economic Procurement Requirements, 85-3 Briefing Papers (Mar. 1985).

"SOLD IN SUBSTANTIAL QUANTITIES TO THE GENERAL PUBLIC" See COMMERCIALITY.

SOFTWARE See COMPUTER SOFTWARE.

SOFTWARE DOCUMENTATION See COMPUTER SOFTWARE DOCUMENTATION.

SOLE SOURCE The only source known to be able to perform a contract, or the one source among others that, for justifiable reason, is found to be most advantageous for the purpose of contract award. A sole source acquisition means a contract for the purchase of supplies or services that is entered into, or proposed to be entered into, by an agency after soliciting and negotiating with only one source. FAR 6.003. Such an acquisition is normally justified only when there is just one responsible source (see RESPONSIBILITY) and no other supplies or services will satisfy agency requirements. FAR 6.302-1. Justifying a procurement without obtaining FULL AND OPEN COMPETITION does not automatically permit contracting with a sole source because FAR 6.301(d) requires contracting officers to solicit offers from as many potential sources as is practicable in these circumstances. See Cibinic and Nash, Formation of Government Contracts 299–307.

SOLICITATION A document, sent to prospective contractors by a Government agency, requesting the submission of OFFERs or of information. This generic term includes INVITATIONs FOR BIDS (IFBs), REQUESTs FOR PROPOSALS (RFPs), and REQUESTs FOR QUOTATIONS (RFQs). The term is also used to denote the process of issuing such documents and obtaining responses. See Cibinic and Nash, Formation of Government Contracts 362–76; Nagle, How to Review a Federal Contract and Research Federal Contract Law 14–47.

SOLICITATION MAILING LIST A list of known or potential sources for each type of supplies or services, including construction, that an agency acquires. Each CONTRACTING ACTIVITY must maintain such lists. FAR 14.205-1 and 15.403. An application (Standard Form 129, FAR 53.301-129) to be placed on a solicitation mailing list (sometimes called a bidders mailing list) must be signed by the actual supplier, dealer, or manufacturer, and not by an agent. Contracting activities should notify prospective contractors when they are placed on the mailing list or if they fail to meet the criteria for inclusion on the list. FAR 14.205-1(b). If solicitation mailing lists become excessively long, the Government may reduce the number of concerns on the list, rotate or use different portions of the list for separate acquisitions, or send PRESOLICITATION NOTICEs rather than complete bid sets. FAR 14.205-4. Concerns failing to submit an offer, respond to a presolicitation notice, or otherwise respond to a solicitation may be removed from the mailing list without notice. FAR 14.205-2. See *CM Update: GSA Replacing System Used to Maintain Centralized Bidder's Mailing List*, 28 Cont. Mgmt. 33 (Jan. 1988).

SOLICITATION PROVISION See PROVISION.

SOURCE SELECTION The process of selecting a contractor through competitive NEGOTIATION. Source selection procedures are designed to (1) maximize competition; (2) minimize the complexity of the solicitation, evaluation, and selection process; (3) ensure the impartial and comprehensive evaluation of proposals; and (4) ensure selection of the source whose proposal is most advantageous and realistic and whose performance is expected to best meet stated Government requirements. FAR 15.603. Agency heads or their designees (see HEAD OF THE AGENCY) are responsible for source selection. The contracting officer is responsible for selecting the source unless another official is designated as the source selection authority. FAR 15.604. Source selection typically entails determining EVALUATION FACTORS, developing REQUESTs FOR PROPOSALS (RFPs), evaluating proposals, determining the COMPETITIVE RANGE, conducting written or oral DISCUSSIONs, requesting BEST AND FINAL OFFERs (BAFOs), selecting the source, and awarding the contract. NASA source selection is unique because it limits discussions with offerors. In particular, NASA does not advise offerors of deficiencies in their proposals. NFS 18-15.610. NASA's formal source selection regulations appear in NFS Subpart 18-70.3 and NHB 5103.6, NASA Source Evaluation Handbook. Almost all other major agencies have source selection directives or manuals, outside of the FEDERAL ACQUISITION REGULATIONS (FAR) SYSTEM, which contain detailed guidance on the procedures followed in FORMAL SOURCE SELECTIONs. See Cibinic et al., Source Selection; Cibinic and Nash, Formation of Government Contracts 528–672.

SOURCE SELECTION ADVISORY COUNCIL (SSAC) A panel of senior Government personnel appointed by a SOURCE SELECTION AUTHORITY (SSA) to advise on the conduct of the source selection process and prepare a comparative analysis of the evaluation results on a competitively negotiated procurement (see NEGOTIATION). SSACs are used on major procurements under agency policies, which are generally promulgated by handbooks or regulations outside of the FAR system.

SOURCE SELECTION AUTHORITY (SSA) The Government official in charge of selecting a source or sources in a competitive negotiated acquisition (see NEGOTIATION). The title is most often used in the FORMAL SOURCE SELECTION process, when the official is someone other than the contracting officer. FAR 15.601. The agency head or a designee formally designates the source selection authority, who (1) establishes an evaluation group structure, (2) approves a SOURCE SELECTION PLAN, and (3) considers the recommendations of evaluation and advisory groups in making the source selection decision. FAR 15.612. See Cibinic et al., Source Selection.

SOURCE SELECTION BOARD (SSB) A panel of agency officials that oversees the evaluation of PROPOSALs submitted on competitively negotiated procurements. SSBs are generally responsible for ensuring that the evaluations submitted to the SOURCE SELECTION AUTHORITY (SSA) are consistent and represent a fair evaluation of the proposals submitted. SSBs are used most frequently on major procurements, and the procedures that they follow vary in accordance with agency procedures, which are generally found in handbooks or regulations outside the FAR system.

SOURCE SELECTION EVALUATION BOARD (SSEB) A synonym for SOURCE SELECTION BOARD (SSB).

SOURCE SELECTION INFORMATION Information (including information stored in electronic, magnetic, audio, or video formats) that is prepared or developed for use by the Government to conduct a particular procurement and (1) the disclosure of which to a competing contractor would jeopardize the integrity or successful completion of the procurement concerned and (2) is required by statute, regulation, or order to be secured in a source selection file or other facility to prevent disclosure. FAR 3.104-4(k). This information is subject to the PROCUREMENT INTEGRITY provisions of the Office of Federal Procurement Policy Act, 41 U.S.C. 423. FAR 3.104-4(k) further provides that this information is limited to bid prices in SEALED BIDDING; proposed costs or prices on negotiated procurements (see NEGOTIATION); SOURCE SELECTION PLANs; TECHNICAL EVALUATION plans; technical evaluations of proposals; cost or price evaluations of proposals; COMPETITIVE RANGE determinations; rankings of BIDs, PROPOSALs, or competitors; SOURCE SELECTION reports and evaluations, and SOURCE SELECTION ADVISORY COUNCIL (SSAC) recommendations; and other information marked with the legend "Source Selection Information—See FAR 3.104." The HEAD OF THE AGENCY, his or her designee, or the CONTRACTING OFFICER (CO) determines on a case-by-case basis whether the information meets the standards requiring nondisclosure. Such information must be secured, since its disclosure to a competing offeror would jeopardize the integrity or successful completion of the procurement. FAR 3.104-5. See Arnavas and Marsh, *The Procurement Integrity Act*, 91-9 Briefing Papers (Aug. 1991).

SOURCE SELECTION OFFICIAL (SSO) A synonym for SOURCE SELECTION AUTHORITY (SSA).

SOURCE SELECTION PLAN A plan formulated by an agency to specify the key elements of a proposed SOURCE SELECTION. When FORMAL SOURCE SELECTION procedures are used in high-dollar-value and other significant acquisitions, a written source selection plan is required. The plan must include (1) a description of the source selection organization structure, (2) proposed presolicitation activities, (3) a summary of the ACQUISITION STRATEGY, (4) a statement of the proposed EVALUATION FACTORS and their relative importance, (5) a description of the evaluation process, methodology, and techniques to be used, and (6) a schedule of significant milestones. FAR 15.612(c). See Cibinic et al., Source Selection, chap. IV; Cibinic and Nash, Formation of Government Contracts 532–62.

SOVEREIGN IMMUNITY A legal doctrine that precludes a litigant from asserting an otherwise meritorious cause of action against a sovereign or a party with sovereign attributes unless the sovereign consents to suit. Sovereignty is the supreme, absolute, and uncontrollable power by which any independent state is governed. Sovereignty entails the power to make laws, regulate, collect taxes, and make war or peace. Historically, governments (whether

Federal, State, city, or other) are immune from TORT (injury to person or property) liability arising from activities that were governmental in nature. Black's Law Dictionary. The Government has waived its sovereign immunity to permit certain types of actions against the Government through a wide variety of statutes, such as the FEDERAL TORT CLAIMS ACT (FTCA) (tort actions), the TUCKER ACT (actions based on the Constitution, statutes, regulations or contracts, express or implied in fact), the CONTRACT DISPUTES ACT (CDA) OF 1978 (disputes concerning claims arising under or relating to contracts), 28 U.S.C. 1498 (use of patents and copyrights), and the EQUAL ACCESS TO JUSTICE ACT (EAJA) (recovery of attorney's fees).

SPARES ACQUISITION INTEGRATED WITH PRODUCTION (SAIP)   A technique used to acquire spare and repair parts combined with procurement of identical items produced for the primary system, subsystem, or equipment. DFARS 217.7502. SAIP minimizes the cost of spares by avoiding the charges normally associated with separate material orders and manufacturing actions. SAIP is appropriate where economies of scale achieved by combining spares orders with installation orders substantially exceed any added administrative costs. Part 7 of DoD Instruction 5000.2, *Defense Acquisition Management Policies and Procedures*, 23 Feb. 1991, explains the criteria to be considered by DoD managers in selecting items for SAIP applications.

SPECIAL DRAWING RIGHTS (SDRs)   An international reserve asset that serves as the International Monetary Fund's official unit of account. "Drawing right" means a grant of credit from one nation to another that is a condition for the granting of funds or credit to the first nation from a third and is intended to stimulate and facilitate international trade. The SDR is, in effect, a universal currency. Janik, *A U.S. Perspective on the GATT Agreement on Government Procurement*, 20 Geo. Wash. J. Int'l L. & Econ. 491, 494 n. 31 (1987). SDRs are an element in determining the threshold amount to which the TRADE AGREEMENTS ACT OF 1979, an exception to the BUY AMERICAN ACT, applies. The Trade Agreements Act excluded from its coverage contracting actions involving less than 150,000 SDRs (typically between $150,000 and $200,000), a figure set by the U.S. Trade Representative and published in the Federal Register. See FAR 25.402.

SPECIAL RESEARCH CONTRACT (SRC) A contract for BASIC RESEARCH entered into between DoE and an educational or other nonprofit institution. The DEAR policies for SRCs are also followed for certain contracts for APPLIED RESEARCH with educational institutions and for educational and training activities with educational or other nonprofit institutions. DEAR 917.71. Under the Atomic Energy Act of 1954, 42 U.S.C. 2051, DoE is directed to exercise its powers in a manner that ensures the continued conduct of research and training activities, and to assist in the acquisition of an ever-expanding fund of theoretical and practical knowledge in fields including (1) nuclear processes; (2) theory and production of atomic energy; (3) utilization of special nuclear material and radioactive material for medical, biological, agricultural, health, or military purposes; (4) utilization of special nuclear material and radioactive material for other purposes; (5) protection of health and promotion of safety during research and production activities; and (6) preservation and enhancement of viable environment. DEAR 917.7103.

SPECIAL TEST EQUIPMENT Single or multipurpose integrated test units engineered, designed, fabricated, or modified to accomplish special-purpose testing in performing a contract. FAR 45.101. Special test equipment consists of items or assemblies of equipment, including standard or general-purpose items or components, that are so interconnected and interdependent that they become a new functional entity for special testing purposes. It does not include MATERIAL, SPECIAL TOOLING, FACILITIES, or PLANT EQUIPMENT used for general plant testing purposes. FAR 45.307 permits agencies to provide existing special test equipment to contractors. It has traditionally been the policy of the Government to permit contractors to include the full cost of special test equipment needed for a specific contract in the price of that contract. FAR 31.205-40 specifies that such costs incurred by a contractor are ALLOWABLE COSTs. However, 10 U.S.C. 2329 limits this policy when special tooling and special test equipment with a value of over $1 million are acquired by a contractor. See DFARS 215.871 for regulations implementing this policy. And see Hill, *The Special Tooling and Test Equipment Cost Principle (FAR 31.205-40)*, 89-7 CP&AR 14 (July 1989).

SPECIAL TOOLING Jigs, dies, fixtures, molds, patterns, taps, gauges, other equipment and manufacturing aids, and all components and replacements of these items that are of such a specialized nature that, without substantial modification or alteration, their use is limited to the development or production of particular supplies or parts thereof or to the performance of particular services. FAR 45.101. It does not include MATERIAL, SPECIAL TEST EQUIPMENT, FACILITIES (except foundations and similar improvements necessary for installing special tooling), general or special machine tools, or similar capital items. FAR 45.306 permits agencies to provide existing special tooling to contractors and provides guidance on when contractors should be permitted to retain title to special tooling required for contract performance. When existing Government tooling is not available, it has traditionally been the policy of the Government to include the full cost of special tooling in the contract price. FAR 31.205-40 specifies that such costs incurred by a contractor are ALLOWABLE COSTs. However, 10 U.S.C. 2329 limits this policy when special tooling and special test equipment with a value of over $1 million are acquired by a contractor. See DFARS 215.871 for regulations implementing this policy. And see Hill, *The Special Tooling and Special Test Equipment Cost Principle (FAR 31.205-40)* 89-7 . CP&AR 14 (1989).

SPECIFIC APPROPRIATION See APPROPRIATION.

SPECIFICATION A document intended primarily for use in procurement that clearly and accurately describes the essential technical requirements for items, materials, or services, including the criteria for determining that the requirements have been met. FAR 10.001. Specifications may be prepared to cover a group of products, services, or materials, or a single product, service, or material. Specifications should not be restrictive (see RESTRIC-TIVE SPECIFICATIONS) and should be designed to promote FULL AND OPEN COMPETITION, with due regard to the nature of the supplies or services to be acquired. FAR 10.001. For some purposes, specifications are classified as FUNCTIONAL SPECIFI-CATIONS, DESIGN SPECIFICATIONS, and PERFORMANCE SPECIFICA-TIONS. Generally, specifications listed in the GSA Index of Federal Specifications, Standards, and Commercial Item Descrip-tions are mandatory for use by agencies. FAR 10.006. See NCMA, Specifications and Standards; Allen and Villet, *Implied Warranty of Specifications*, 91-8 Briefing Papers (July 1991); Beran, *Specifications: The Duty Trilogy, Government and Contractor Responsibilities*, 27 Cont. Mgmt. 4 (Aug. 1987), 12 (Sep. 1987), and 11 (Oct. 1987). See also SPECIFICATION,

STANDARD, MILITARY SPECIFICATIONS (MIL-SPECs) AND STANDARDS (MIL-STDs), and SPECIFIC MAKE AND MODEL SPECIFICATION.

SPECIFIC MAKE AND MODEL SPECIFICATION A description of a Government requirement that is expressed in a form so restrictive that only the specified make and model will satisfy the Government's needs, regardless of the number of suppliers that may be able to furnish the specific make and model. FIRMR 201-4.001. Use of this type of specification requires a JUSTIFICATION AND APPROVAL in accordance with FAR 6.303. See Gabig, *A Primer on Federal Information Systems Acquisitions: First Part of a Two-Part Article*, 17 Pub. Cont. L.J. 31, 56–66 (1987).

SPONSORSHIP OF SUBCONTRACTOR CLAIMS A process of permitting SUBCONTRACTORs to appeal adverse DECISIONs OF THE CONTRACTING OFFICER wherein the prime contractor permits the subcontractor to use the prime's name or agrees to appeal for the benefit of the subcontractor. The sponsorship system is a means of preserving the technical concept of PRIVITY OF CONTRACT by permitting appeals and suits to be brought by or in the name of the prime contractor even though the prime has no real interest in the matter and plays a passive role. Sponsorship means that the subcontractor may have its attorney prosecute the appeal, but the paperwork must be done in the name of the prime contractor and the prime contractor must certify the claim as required by the CONTRACT DISPUTES ACT (CDA) OF 1978. See *United States v. Johnson Controls, Inc.*, 713 F.2d 1541 (Fed. Cir. 1983); Pachter, *Certification of Subcontractor Claims*, 19 Pub. Cont. Newsl. 3 (Fall 1983). If sponsorship occurs in a claim for BREACH OF CONTRACT, the SEVERIN DOCTRINE will bar the claim if the contractor is totally absolved of liability to the subcontractor.

SPREAD-GAIN ACTUARIAL COST METHOD Any of several projected benefit actuarial cost methods under which actuarial gains and losses are included as part of the current and future normal costs of a PENSION PLAN. Actuarial gains and losses under a pension plan whose costs are measured by this actuarial cost method must be included as part of current and future normal cost and spread over the remaining average working lives of the work force. FAR 30.413-50(a)(2).

STANDARD A document that establishes engineering and technical limitations and applications of items, materials, processes, methods, designs, and engineering practices. FAR 10.001. It includes any related criteria deemed essential to achieve the highest practical degree of uniformity in materials or products, or interchangeability of parts used in those products. Standards may be used in SPECIFICATIONs, INVITATIONs FOR BIDS (IFBs), REQUESTs FOR PROPOSALS (RFPs), and contracts. A voluntary standard is a standard established by a private sector body and available for public use. The term does not include private standards of individual firms. See OMB Circular No. A-119 (revised), *Federal Participation in the Development and Use of Voluntary Standards*, 26 Oct. 1982. Generally, standards listed in the GSA Index of Federal Specifications, Standards, and Commercial Item Descriptions are mandatory for use by agencies. FAR 10.006.

STANDARD COST Any cost computed with the use of preestablished measures. FAR 31.001. A standard cost is a goal or baseline cost that is used to expedite the costing of transactions; it is determined from historical experience or derived from the best information available. Except for costs attributable to precise and highly predictable operations, ACTUAL COSTs will almost always vary from standard costs due to factors that affect performance, such as employee fatigue, unforeseen interruptions, and other delays (called VARIANCEs). Armed Services Pricing Manual (ASPM) vol. 1, app. B. Guidance on the use of standard costs for estimating, accumulating, and reporting costs of direct material and direct labor is contained in Cost Accounting Standard 407 at FAR 30.407.

STANDARD FORMS (SFs) Forms prescribed by the FAR for use throughout the Government in the contracting process. FAR Part 53 illustrates SFs for Government procurement prescribed elsewhere in the FAR, and it contains requirements and information generally applicable to SFs, OPTIONAL FORMS (OFs), and agency-prescribed forms. Agencies may not alter an SF prescribed by the FAR, or use for the same purpose any form other than the SF prescribed by the FAR, without receiving, in advance, an exception (an approved departure from the form's established design, content, printing specifications, or conditions for use). Executive agencies obtain SFs through the GSA Supply Catalog (Office Products). Contractors may obtain them from the U.S. Government Printing Office, Washington, DC 20402. See Ferguson and Moss, *FAR Part 53—It's a Matter of Forms*, 24 Cont. Mgmt. 8 (Apr. 1984).

STANDARD INDUSTRIAL CLASSIFICATION (SIC) A classification system dividing industries into 89 major groups, each with subgroups. The Government's SIC Manual classifies and defines the entire field of economic activities by these industry categories. It is the source used by the SMALL BUSINESS ADMINISTRATION (SBA) in defining size standards for the purpose of small business qualification.

STANDARDIZATION The adoption of a single product or group of products to be used by different organizations or all parts of one organization. Standardization is the process by which an organization such as DoD or the North Atlantic Treaty Organization (NATO) (1) achieves the closest practicable cooperation among forces; (2) facilitates the most efficient use of research, development, and production resources; and (3) agrees to adopt on the broadest possible basis the use of (a) common or compatible operational, administrative, and logistic procedures and criteria, (b) common or compatible technical procedures and criteria, (c) common, compatible, or interchangeable supplies, components, weapons, or equipment, and (d) common or compatible tactical doctrines with corresponding organizational compatibility. Jones, Glossary: Defense Acquisition Acronyms and Terms.

STANDARDS OF CONDUCT The rules applicable to Government employees and individuals dealing with the Government. The primary standards set forth in 18 U.S.C. 201–218 as follows: 201, Bribery and Gratuities; 202, Definitions; 203, Compensation of Members of Congress and Government Officers; 204, Practice in U.S. Claims Court and Court of Appeals for the Federal Circuit by Members of Congress; 205, Activities of Officers and Employees in Claims Against and Other Matters Affecting Government; 206, Exemption of Retired Officers of the Uniformed Services; 207, Post-Employment Restrictions (see REVOLVING DOOR); 208, Acts Affecting a Personal Financial Interest (see PERSONAL CONFLICT OF INTEREST); 209, Supplementation of Salary of Government Employees; 210, Offer to Procure Appointive Public Office; 211, Acceptance or Solicitation to Obtain Appointive Public Office; 212, Offer of Loan or Gratuity to Bank Examiner; 213, Acceptance of Loan or Gratuity by Bank Examiner; 214, Offer for Procurement of Federal Reserve Bank Loan and Discount of Commercial Paper; 215, Receipt of Commissions or Gifts for Procuring Loans; 216, Penalties and Injunctions; 217, Acceptance of Consideration for Adjustments of Farm Indebtedness; and 218,

Voiding Contracts Violating These Criminal Provisions. Other standards are set forth in other parts of the criminal code (see, particularly, the FALSE CLAIMS ACT and the FALSE STATEMENTS ACT). Guidance on these standards is set forth in the regulations of the Office of Government Ethics, 5 CFR 2600 *et seq.* See Brunsman, *Standards of Conduct and Business Ethics for Buyers*, 27 Cont. Mgmt. 18 (June 1987). See also PROCUREMENT INTEGRITY.

STATE AND LOCAL TAXES TAXES imposed by a State or local government. Such taxes include income taxes, sales and use taxes, franchise taxes, EXCISE TAXes, and property taxes. FAR 31.205-41 specifies the rules governing whether such taxes paid by contractors are ALLOWABLE COSTs. Contractors are frequently not subject to such taxes when working on Federal contracts. See FAR Subpart 29.3. Contractors normally bear the risk of determining what taxes of this nature apply to their contracts but are given price adjustments for changes in such taxes under the Federal, State, and Local Taxes clause in FAR 52.229-3. See Weckstein and Kempler, *Tax Considerations in Government Contracting*, 85-10 Briefing Papers (Oct. 1985); Cavin, *Federal Immunity of Government Contractors From State and Local Taxation: A Survey of Recent Decisions and Their Impact on Government Procurement Policies*, 61 Denver L.J. 797 (1984).

STATEMENT OF WORK (SOW) That portion of a contract which describes the actual work to be done by the contractor by means of (1) SPECIFICATIONs or other minimum requirements, (2) quantities, (3) performance dates, (4) time and place of performance of services, and (5) quality requirements. Jones, Glossary: Defense Acquisition Acronyms and Terms. The SOW is set forth in Section C of the UNIFORM CONTRACT FORMAT. It plays a key role in the solicitation because it serves as the basis for the contractor's response. It also serves as a baseline against which progress and subsequent contractual changes are measured during contract performance. The FAR uses the term WORK STATEMENT in referring to the SOW for an R&D contract.

STATUTE OF LIMITATIONS A law prescribing limitations to the right of action on certain described causes of action, declaring that no suit may be maintained on such causes of action unless brought within a specified period of time after the right accrued. Black's Law Dictionary. Under 28 U.S.C. 2501, the limitation period for

CLAIMs against the Government in the CLAIMS COURT (Cl. Ct.) is 6 years after the right of action accrues. Under 28 U.S.C. 2415(a), the limitation period for claims filed by the Government is 6 years after the right of action accrues, or 1 year after the final decision in any applicable administrative proceeding required by contract or law, whichever is later. Neither of these acts is applicable to claims filed under the CONTRACT DISPUTES ACT (CDA) OF 1978. See Principles of Federal Appropriations Law (2d ed.), chap. 13; Nash, *Application of Statutes of Limitations to the Contract Disputes Act: Does Unequal Treatment Yield a Fair Result?* 3 N&CR ¶ 86 (Dec. 1989); Nash, *Postscript: Application of Statutes of Limitation to the Contract Disputes Act,* 6 N&CR ¶ 6 (Jan. 1992).

STEVEDORING Loading cargo from a point of rest on a pier or lighter and storing it aboard a vessel, or breaking out and discharging cargo from any space in a vessel to a point of rest dockside or in a lighter. DFARS 247.270-2. Normally, stevedoring services will be contracted for by means of an INDEFINITE-QUANTITY CONTRACT. DFARS 247.270-4. Since conditions vary at different ports and sometimes within the same port, standard technical provisions covering all phases of stevedoring operations are impractical. If car loading and unloading or other dock and terminal work will be performed under a stevedoring contract, technical provisions appropriate for that work should be added to the contract as separate items of work. DFARS 247.270-5.

STOCK OPTION An option to buy stock in a corporation. FAR 31.205-6(i) provides that the costs of such options, when given by contractors to employees as compensation, are ALLOWABLE COSTs only when they meet the rules governing DEFERRED COMPENSATION.

STOCK RECORD A perpetual inventory record that shows by nomenclature the quantities of each item received and issued and the balance on hand. FAR 45.501. FAR 45.505-3 requires that contractors maintain such records for MATERIAL that is furnished by the Government or to which the Government has title.

STOP-WORK ORDER A unilateral order of the contracting officer requiring the contractor to stop all or any part of the work called for under the contract. Stop-work orders may be issued if the contract contains the Suspension of Work clause in FAR 52.212-15 (mandatory in fixed-price construction and architect-engineer contracts) or the Stop-Work Order clause in FAR 52.212-13 (optional in contracts for supplies, services, or R&D). These clauses give the contractor an adjustment in the price to compensate for costs incurred because of the order (plus profit under the Stop-Work Order clause). FAR 12.503 provides that stop-work orders may be used in negotiated, fixed-price or cost-reimbursement supply, R&D, or service contracts if work stoppage is required for reasons such as advancements in the state-of-the-art, production or engineering breakthroughs, or realignment of programs. Generally, a stop-work order will be issued only if it is advisable to suspend work pending a decision by the Government but a supplemental agreement providing for the suspension is not feasible. Issuance of a stop-work order must be approved at a level higher than the contracting officer. A stop-work order may not be used in place of a termination notice after a decision to proceed with a TERMINATION FOR DEFAULT has been made. See Cibinic and Nash, Administration of Government Contracts 452–54.

SUBCONTINENT-ASIAN AMERICANS   U.S. citizens whose origins are in India, Pakistan, Bangladesh, Sri Lanka, Bhutan, or Nepal. FAR 19.001. These persons are presumed to be socially and economically disadvantaged for the purpose of determining the ownership of a SMALL DISADVANTAGED BUSINESS CONCERN (SDBC). See FAR 52.219-2 and 52.219-8.

SUBCONTRACT   A contract or contractual action entered into by a PRIME CONTRACTOR or SUBCONTRACTOR for the purpose of obtaining supplies, materials, equipment, or services under a PRIME CONTRACT. FAR 3.502-1. Subcontracts include purchase orders as well as changes and modifications to purchase orders. The FAR addresses situations in which the Government must consent to a prime contractor's subcontract (FAR Subpart 44.2) and CONTRACTOR PURCHASING SYSTEM REVIEW (CPSR) (FAR Subpart 44.3). Consent to subcontract is required when subcontract work is complex, the dollar value is substantial, or the Government's interest is not adequately protected by competition and the type of prime contract or subcontract. FAR 44.102. 10 U.S.C. 2306(e) and 41 U.S.C. 254(b) require contractors to give notice (but not to obtain consent) on COST CONTRACTs and COST-PLUS-FIXED FEE (CPFF) CONTRACTs for (1) all cost-plus-fixed fee subcontracts and (2) all fixed-price subcontracts over $25,000 or 5 percent of the estimated cost of the prime contract. Successful offerors in both negotiated and sealed bidding acquisitions that exceed or are expected to exceed $500,000 (or $1 million for construction contracts), and that have substantial subcontracting possibilities, must provide formal SUBCONTRACTING PLANs for Government review. 15 U.S.C. 637(d); FAR 19.704. Although a subcontractor lacks PRIVITY OF CONTRACT with the Federal Government, prime contractors pass on significant Government requirements to subcontractors, such as the requirements for submission of COST OR PRICING DATA and the TERMINATION FOR CONVENIENCE clause.   See Brechtel and Marks, Subcontracts—Government and Industry Issues; Patin and Ginsburg, chap. 16, Construction Contracting 1111–1207.

SUBCONTRACTING PLAN   A plan, adopted by a contractor, to further the Government's program under the SMALL BUSINESS ACT by subcontracting parts of the contract work. Successful offerors under both negotiated and sealed bidding acquisitions that are expected to exceed $500,000 (or $1 million for construction), and that have subcontracting possibilities, must provide formal subcontracting plans. 15 U.S.C. 637(d). FAR 19.704 provides that the subcontracting plans must include: (1) percentage goals for using SMALL BUSINESS CONCERNs and SMALL DISADVANTAGED BUSINESS CONCERNs (SDBCs) as subcontractors; (2) the name of an individual who will administer the offeror's subcontracting program; (3) a description of the efforts the offeror will make to ensure that small business has an equitable opportunity to compete for subcontracts; (4) assurances that the offeror will include the clause at FAR 52.219-8, Utilization of Small Business Concerns and Small Disadvantaged Business Concerns, in all subcontracts; (5) assurances that the offeror will (a) cooperate in studies or surveys, (b) submit periodic reports to allow the Government to determine the extent of the offeror's compliance, and (c) submit Standard Form (SF) 294, Subcontracting Report for Individual Contracts, and SF 295, Summary Subcontract Report, at FAR 53.301-294 and -295; and (6) a recitation of the records the offeror will maintain to demonstrate procedures adopted to comply with the plan. DoE contractors and subcontractors are not required to submit the SF 295 quarterly report because DoE is able to extract this information from the SF 294. In order to do this, DoE requires submittal of the SF 194 on a quarterly basis rather than semiannually. DEAR 919.708(b). DFARS 219.705-2 states that subcontracting plans will be an evaluation factor in source selection for RESEARCH AND DEVELOPMENT (R&D), MAJOR SYSTEM

ACQUISITIONs, and other complex or sensitive acquisitions. FAR 19.702(c) provides that any contractor or subcontractor failing to comply in good faith with the requirements of a subcontracting plan is in material BREACH OF CONTRACT. Further, 15 U.S.C. 637(d)(4)(F) directs that a contractor's failure to make a good faith effort to comply with the requirements of the subcontracting plan must result in the imposition of LIQUIDATED DAMAGES. See FAR 19.705-7.

SUBCONTRACTOR Any supplier, distributor, vendor, or firm that furnishes supplies or services to a prime contractor or another subcontractor. FAR 44.101. For the purposes of the ANTI-KICK-BACK ACT OF 1986, it means any person, other than a PRIME CONTRACTOR, who offers to furnish or furnishes supplies, materials, equipment, or services of any kind under a prime contract or a subcontract entered into in connection with a prime contract, and includes any person who offers to furnish or furnishes general supplies to the prime contractor or a higher-tier subcontractor. FAR 3.502-1. The term "first-tier subcontractor" means a subcontractor holding a subcontract with a prime contractor. FAR 22.801. Second or third-tier subcontractors hold a subcontract with a subcontractor.

SUBCONTRACTOR CLAIMS See SPONSORSHIP OF SUBCON-TRACTOR CLAIMS.

SUBJECT INVENTION Any invention of a contractor conceived or first actually reduced to practice in the performance of work under a Government contract. 35 U.S.C. 201(e); FAR 27.301. Under its PATENT RIGHTS policy, the Government obtains a license to use such inventions. The determination of whether an invention is a subject invention is not dependent on the relative financial contributions of the parties in funding the work that led to the invention; rather, it depends on whether either of two events—conception or first actual reduction to practice—occurred during contract performance. See Nash and Rawicz, Patents and Technical Data 163–206.

SUBSTANTIAL COMPLETION A term used in construction contracting to mean SUBSTANTIAL PERFORMANCE of contract requirements, though not complete performance. Substantial completion is often found when the contractor completes construction of the structure but fails to complete punch list items, install ornamental features, finish site cleanup, etc. The doctrine of substantial completion bars the Government from assessing LIQUIDATED DAMAGES or terminating the contract without providing a reasonable period of time to correct the deficiencies. The doctrine does not bar the Government, however, from insisting upon strict compliance and full completion of the work, or from obtaining an EQUITABLE ADJUSTMENT in the contract price if strict compliance is not attained. The term has also been used to decide DISPUTEs under service contracts for services. See Cibinic and Nash, Administration of Government Contracts 685–91, 808–10.

SUBSTANTIAL COMPLIANCE A term used in supply contracts to mean that a contractor may not be subject to a TERMINATION FOR DEFAULT for failure to timely deliver strictly conforming goods if the contractor delivers, on time, supplies that substantially meet the contract's requirements. In order to avoid termination, (1) the contractor must demonstrate that it had reasonable grounds to believe that the delivery would conform to the contract requirements and (2) the defects must be minor in nature and extent and susceptible to correction within a reasonable time. Other relevant considerations include the usability of the items, the nature of the product, and the urgency of the Government's requirement. See Cibinic and Nash, Administration of Government Contracts 680–85; Venema, *Substantial Compliance in Fixed-Price Supply Contracts: A Call for Commercial Reasonableness*, 17 Pub. Cont. L.J. 187 (1987).

SUBSTANTIALLY JUSTIFIED A position of the Government regarding a DISPUTE that is clearly reasonable. Under the EQUAL ACCESS TO JUSTICE ACT (EAJA), a court or an agency must award attorney's fees and other expenses to individuals with net worth of no more than $2 million, profit-making small businesses with no more than $7 million net worth or 500 employees, and tax-exempt organizations that prevail in adversary adjudications in which the Government's position during settlement negotiations and litigation was not substantially justified. If the Government, during litigation concerning the recovery of attorney's fees and expenses, can demonstrate that its prior position was substantially justified, the prevailing party cannot recover under the EAJA. In determining substantial justification, the courts and boards of contract appeals evaluate the issue of reasonableness of the Government's position based on what support in law and fact the

Government offers in defending its case. See Nash, *Equal Access to Justice Act: A Statute That Is Working Well*, 2 N&CR ¶ 20 (Apr. 1988); Kinlin, *Equal Access to Justice Act*, 16 Pub. Cont. L.J. 266, 273 (1986).

SUBSTANTIAL PERFORMANCE   Performance short of full performance but nevertheless performance in good faith and in compliance with the contract, except perhaps for minor and relatively unimportant deviations. Ballentine's Law Dictionary. Substantial performance is a synonym for SUBSTANTIAL COMPLETION.

SUCCESSOR IN INTEREST   See NOVATION.

SUM CERTAIN   The monetary amount being claimed by a contractor under the CONTRACT DISPUTES ACT (CDA) OF 1978. Under this act a CLAIM entails, among other things, a written demand for the payment of money in a "sum certain." FAR 33.201. When the recovery of money is the essence of the contractor's request for relief, the contracting officer need not issue a final decision (see DECISION OF THE CONTRACTING OFFICER) unless the contractor's claim specifies an amount of recovery sought—a sum certain—in a finite amount not subject to qualification or conditions. The reasoning behind this rule is that the contracting officer cannot determine whether the act's requirement for certification of claims of $50,000 or more applies to the contractor's claim unless the claim is made in a specific dollar amount. See Nash, *The Contract Disputes Act: No Claim, No Jurisdiction*, 5 N&CR ¶ 66 (Dec. 1991).

SUPERIOR KNOWLEDGE   A legal rule providing that a contracting party has an obligation to disclose vital information to the other party. Generally, the Government must disclose to offerors or contractors information it possesses that (1) is relevant to contradictory information in the solicitation or contract, and should be disclosed to keep the offeror or contractor from being misled; (2) may materially affect an offer, and the offeror lacks the information or is relying on erroneous assumptions; or (3) it knows the contractor does not know. Failure to disclose such information may result in the Government's assuming responsibility for the contractor's increased costs through the CONSTRUCTIVE CHANGE doctrine. To establish that the Government breached its duty to disclose superior knowledge, the contractor must prove that the Government possessed such knowledge, that the knowledge was vital to contract performance, that the information was unknown and not reasonably available to the contractor, and that the contractor was misled by the nondisclosure. See Nash, Government Contract Changes, chap. 14; Beran, *Specifications: The Duty Trilogy—Government and Contractor Responsibilities, Part Two: The Duty to Disclose Superior Knowledge*, 27 Cont. Mgmt. 12 (Sep. 1987).

SUPPLEMENTAL AGREEMENT A contract MODIFICATION that is accomplished by the mutual action of the parties. FAR 43.101.

SUPPLIES All property except land or interest in land. Supplies include, but are not limited to, public works, buildings, and facilities; ships, floating equipment, and vessels of every character, type, and description, together with parts and accessories; aircraft and aircraft parts, accessories, and equipment; machine tools; and the alteration or installation of any of the foregoing. FAR 2.101. Supplies also include raw materials, components, intermediate assemblies, and end products.   FAR 52.246-3. Supplies do not include data, except when the contract includes the clause at FAR 52.246-19, Warranty of Systems and Equipment under Performance Specifications or Design Criteria. The term "supplies" is a term used primarily in Government contracting; the synonymous term in commercial contracting is GOODS.

SURETY The individual or corporation that has agreed to be legally liable for the debt, default, or failure of a principal to satisfy a contractual obligation. FAR 28.001. Contractors purchase BONDs from sureties when such bonds are specified by the Government to be a condition of award. The types of sureties referred to in the FAR include (1) an individual surety—one person who is liable for the entire PENAL AMOUNT of the bond; (2) a corporate surety that is licensed under various insurance laws and that, under its charter, has legal power to act as surety for others; and (3) a cosurety—one of two or more sureties that are jointly liable for the penal amount of the bond. FAR 28.201 requires agencies to obtain adequate security for bonds (including coinsurance and reinsurance agreements) required or used with a contract for supplies or services (including construction). The FAR discusses corporate sureties (28.202-1), individual sureties (28.202-2), and options in lieu of sureties (28.203). See Standard Form (SF) 28, Affidavit of Individual Surety, FAR 53.301-28; SF 1414, Consent of Surety, FAR 53.301-1414; and SF 1415, Consent of Surety and Increase of Penalty, FAR 53.301-1415. See Nash, *Sureties' Obligations: The Duty To Deal in Good Faith*, 3 N&CR ¶ 55 (Aug. 1989); Cibinic, *In Defense of Corporate Surety Bonds*, 2 N&CR ¶ 75 (Dec. 1988); Nash, *Rights of Sureties: They're Growing*, 2 N&CR ¶ 42 (July 1988); Nash, *Dealing with Performance Bond Sureties*, 1 N&CR ¶ 35 (Apr. 1987); Patin, chap. 17, Construction Contracting.

SURPLUS PROPERTY Contractor inventory not required by any Federal agency. FAR 45.601. FAR 45.610 sets forth the procedures to be followed in disposing of surplus property resulting from Government contracts.

SUSPENSION An action taken by the HEAD OF AN AGENCY, or a designee authorized by the agency head, to disqualify a contractor temporarily from Government contracting and Government-approved subcontracting; a contractor so disqualified is "suspended." FAR 9.403. Causes for suspension include adequate evidence of or indictment for (1) commission of a fraud or criminal offense related to obtaining or performing a public contract; (2) violation of antitrust statutes; (3) commission of embezzlement, theft, forgery, making false statements, and the like; (4) violation of the Drug-Free Workplace Act of 1988, 41 U.S.C. 701 *et seq.*; (5) commission of any other offense indicating a lack of business integrity or business honesty that seriously and directly affects the present responsibility of a Government contractor or subcontractor. FAR 9.407-2. Suspension can occur without prior notice to the contractor, but notice must be given after the decision to suspend has been made. FAR 9.407-3. No suspension can exceed 18 months unless legal proceedings are initiated. FAR 9.407-4. See Toomey et al., *Debarment & Suspension/Edition III*, 89-4 Briefing Papers (Mar. 1989); Nadler, *Suspension and Debarment of Government Contractors: The Current Climate*, 22 NCMJ 9 (1989); Norton, *The Questionable Constitutionality of the Suspension and Debarment Provisions of the Federal Acquisition Regulations: What Does Due Process Require?* 18 Pub. Cont. L.J. 633 (1989).

SUSPENSION OF WORK Government delay, either by order or constructively, of the work of a construction contractor or an architect-engineer. The Suspension of Work clause in FAR 52.212-12 is required to be included in fixed-price construction and architect-engineer contracts. FAR 12.505. It permits the contracting officer to order the contractor, in writing, to suspend, delay, or interrupt performance of all or any part of the work for the period of time that the contracting officer determines appropriate for the convenience of the Government. If performance is suspended, delayed, or interrupted for an unreasonable period of time by (1) an act of the contracting officer in the administration of the contract or (2) the contracting officer's failure to act within the time specified in the contract, a PRICE ADJUSTMENT is required to be made for any increase in the cost of performance of the contract (excluding profit) that necessarily results, and the contract is modified in writing accordingly. See Cibinic and Nash, Administration of Government Contracts 450–78; Margulies, chap. 8, Construction Contracting, 634–47.

SYNOPSIS A notice of contract awards and proposed contract actions published in the COMMERCE BUSINESS DAILY (CBD) as required by 15 U.S.C. 637(e) and 41 U.S.C. 416. Guidance on synopsis requirements is contained in FAR Subparts 5.2 and 5.3. When a synopsis of a proposed contract action is required, it must be published 15 days before issuance of the SOLICITATION. The format for the synopsis of proposed contract actions is contained in FAR 5.207. FAR 5.206 also encourages contractors to place synopses of subcontract opportunities in the Commerce Business Daily.

SYSTEM A composite of equipment, skills, and techniques capable of performing or supporting an operational role. A complete system includes the facilities, equipment, material, services, software, technical data, and personnel required for its operation and support. MIL-STD-499A, Engineering Management, app. 1.

SYSTEM ENGINEERING A logical sequence of activities and decisions that transforms an operational need into a description of SYSTEM performance parameters and a preferred system configuration. MIL-STD-499A, Engineering Management, app. 1. System engineering is a disciplined approach to coordinating all aspects of a system, ensuring that its individual parts will function as intended in the operational environment and meet contract requirements. It is a process for identifying and assessing each technical and other variable involved in total system design. A contractor that performs system engineering is barred from contracting for manufacturing work on that system by the

ORGANIZATIONAL CONFLICT OF INTEREST (OCI) rules. See DoD Directive 5000.2, *Defense Acquisition Management Policies and Procedures*, part 6A, 23 Feb. 1991.

SYSTEM LIFE A forecast or projection of the period of time that begins with installation of a SYSTEM or item and ends when the Government no longer needs that system or item. System life is established by the initial acquiring agency on the basis of its requirement and predicted reuse. System life is not necessarily synonymous with technological life (utility before becoming obsolete), physical life (utility before wearing out), or application life (utility in a given function). FIRMR 201-20.103-2 requires that agencies establish a system life as a part of the requirement analysis for FEDERAL INFORMATION PROCESSING (FIP) RESOURCES. FIRMR 201-39.1701-1 requires that agencies evaluate costs over the system life. See LIFE-CYCLE COST.

SYSTEM OF RECORDS A group of any records under the control of any agency from which information is retrieved by the name of an individual or by some number, symbol, or other identifying particular assigned to the individual. FAR 24.101. The Privacy Act of 1974, 5 U.S.C. 552a, requires that contracts for the maintenance of such systems must comply with its provisions. FAR Subpart 24.1 provides guidance on the implementation of this requirement. NFS 18-24.103 provides examples of systems of records to which the Privacy Act applies or does not apply.

T

TAILORING The process by which individual sections, paragraphs, or sentences of the SPECIFICATIONs, STANDARDs, and related documents selected for use in a procurement are reviewed and modified so that each one that is selected contains an accurate statement of the Government's needs and is not unduly restrictive (see RESTRICTIVE SPECIFICATIONS). FAR 10.004. FAR 10.002 requires specifications and standards to be selectively applied and tailored in their application. Selective application is the process of reviewing and choosing from the many available specifications, standards, and related documents only those relevant to a particular acquisition. Such tailoring need not be made a part of the basic specification or standard but will vary with each application, depending upon the nature of the acquisition.

TAKEOVER AGREEMENT An agreement between the Government and the SURETY that has furnished a PERFORMANCE BOND that the surety will complete the performance of a contract that has been terminated for default (see TERMINATION FOR DEFAULT). Guidance on entering into such agreement is contained in FAR 49.404. Since the surety is liable to the Government for the consequences of the contractor's default, it is not required to enter into a takeover agreement. However, FAR 49.404(c) provides that the contracting officer will normally enter into such an agreement if the surety offers to complete the contract. If a surety enters into a takeover agreement, it gives up any financial protection that it has pursuant to the ceiling amount in the bond (see PENAL AMOUNT) but it gains access to the CLAIMS COURT (Cl. Ct.) and the BOARDs OF CONTRACT APPEALS (BCAs) to pursue CLAIMs against the Government. See Nash, *Dealing with Performance Bond Sureties*, 1 N&CR ¶ 35 (Apr. 1987).

TANGIBLE CAPITAL ASSET   An ASSET that has physical substance and more than minimal value, and is expected to be held by an enterprise for continued use or possession beyond the current accounting period for the services it yields. FAR 31.001. Such assets may take the form, for example, of cash, land, or buildings. Rosenberg, Dictionary of Banking and Finance. Cost Accounting Standard 404, FAR 30.404, sets forth criteria that contractor policies on the CAPITALIZATION of tangible assets must meet.   Cost Accounting Standard 409, FAR 30.409, provides guidance on the DEPRECIATION of tangible capital assets.

TANKER   A vessel used primarily for the carriage of bulk liquid cargoes such as liquid petroleum products, vegetable oils, and molasses.   FAR 47.501.   Under the Preference for Privately Owned U.S.-Flag Commercial Vessels clause in FAR 52.247-64, contractors must compute shipments in these vessels separately in determining whether they have met the requirement that at least 50 percent of the gross tonnage shipped be in U.S.-FLAG VESSELs.

TARGET COST   The negotiated amount of cost included in INCENTIVE CONTRACTs.   See FAR Subpart 16.4.   The target cost serves as a benchmark for adjusting the contractor's TARGET PROFIT (in FIXED-PRICE INCENTIVE (FPI) CONTRACTs) or TARGET FEE (in COST-PLUS-INCENTIVE FEE (CPIF) CONTRACTs).   In these types of contracts the initially negotiated profit or fee will be adjusted, upon completion of the contract, by a formula based on the relationship of total ALLOWABLE COSTs to total target costs. The formula provides, within limits, for increases in profit or fee when total allowable costs are less than target costs, and decreases in fee when total allowable costs exceed target costs. The increase or decrease is intended to provide an incentive for the contractor to manage the contract effectively. FAR 16.401(a)(2). Before this adjustment is made, the parties must adjust the target cost to reflect all EQUITABLE ADJUSTMENTs and PRICE ADJUSTMENTs called for by the contract.

TARGET FEE   The amount of FEE the contractor will receive if its total ALLOWABLE COSTs equal total TARGET COSTs in a COST-PLUS-INCENTIVE FEE (CPIF) CONTRACT.   In the CPIF contract, under the contract sharing arrangement, the target fee is adjusted downward if actual costs exceed the target costs, and the fee increases if actual costs prove less than target costs.   This adjustment is limited, however, by the RANGE OF INCENTIVE EFFECTIVENESS

(RIE) resulting from the MINIMUM FEE and MAXIMUM FEE contained in the contract. FAR 16.404-1.

TARGET PRICE The sum of the TARGET COST and the TARGET PROFIT in a FIXED-PRICE INCENTIVE (FPI) CONTRACT.

TARGET PROFIT The amount of PROFIT the contractor will receive if its total ALLOWABLE COSTs equal total TARGET COSTs in a FIXED-PRICE INCENTIVE (FPI) CONTRACT. In FPI contracts with a firm target, the parties work with a target cost and CEILING PRICE. The target profit is adjusted in accordance with the contract sharing arrangement until costs reach the ceiling, at which point (the "point of total cost assumption") the contractor absorbs all additional costs. FAR 16.403-1. In fixed-price incentive contracts with successive targets, the parties negotiate at the outset the production point at which a firm target cost and target profit will be negotiated. FAR 16.403-2. The profit formula is based on a profit formula substantially the same as the WEIGHTED GUIDELINES METHOD, which determines negotiated profit primarily on the basis of RISK and contractor effort.

TAXES Mandatory amounts paid to governments to support their operation. Guidance on taxes is contained in FAR Part 29. See EXCISE TAXes and STATE AND LOCAL TAXES. See Weckstein and Kempler, *Tax Considerations in Government Contracting*, 85-10 Briefing Papers (Oct. 1985); the MAC Group, *The Impact on Defense Industrial Capability of Changes in Procurement and Tax Policy, 1984–1987*, 22 NCMJ 37 (1989).

TEAM ARRANGEMENT An arrangement in which (1) two or more companies form a partnership or JOINT VENTURE to act as a potential PRIME CONTRACTOR or (2) a potential prime contractor agrees with one or more other companies to have them act as SUBCONTRACTORs under a specified Government contract or acquisition program. FAR 9.601. Team arrangements enable the companies involved to complement each other's capabilities and offer the Government the best combination of performance, cost, and delivery for the system or product being acquired. The arrangements prove particularly appropriate in complex RESEARCH AND DEVELOPMENT (R&D) acquisitions. Companies normally form a team arrangement before the offer is submitted. FAR 9.602. See Eger, *Contractor Team Arrangements under the Antitrust Laws*, 17 Pub. Cont. L.J. 595 (1988).

TECHNICAL ANALYSIS The examination and evaluation—by personnel having specialized knowledge, skills, experience, or capability in engineering, science, or management—of proposed quantities and kinds of materials, labor, processes, special tooling, facilities, and associated factors set forth in a PROPOSAL, in order to determine and report on the need for and reasonableness of the proposed resources, assuming reasonable economy and efficiency. FAR 15.801. FAR 15.805-4 explains that, when COST OR PRICING DATA are required, the contracting officer should generally request a technical analysis of proposals, asking that requirements, logistics, or other qualified personnel review and assess, at a minimum, (1) the quantities and kinds of materials proposed, (2) the need for the number and kinds of labor hours and the labor mix, (3) the special tooling and facilities proposed, (4) the reasonableness of proposed scrap and spoilage factors, and (5) any other data that may be pertinent to the COST ANALYSIS or PRICE ANALYSIS.

TECHNICAL DATA DATA (other than COMPUTER SOFTWARE) of a scientific or technical nature. FAR 27.401. Under DFARS 227.401 the term "technical data" is more fully described as follows: "Recorded information, regardless of the form or method of the recording, of a scientific or technical nature (including COMPUTER SOFTWARE DOCUMENTATION). The term does not include COMPUTER SOFTWARE or data incidental to contract administration, such as financial or management information." The only significant difference between the definitions is that the DFARS definition includes computer software documentation. The Government obtains LIMITED RIGHTS, UNLIMITED RIGHTS, or GOVERNMENT-PURPOSE LICENSE RIGHTS (GPLR) in technical data in accordance with the clauses used. See Victorino and McQuade, *Enforcing Data Rights*, 91-10 Briefing Papers (Sep. 1991); Nash, *Removal of Limited Rights Legends from Technical Data: Playing Hardball*, 1 N&CR ¶ 85 (Nov. 1987); Vacketta and Holmes, *Government Rights in Technical Data*, 84-12 Briefing Papers (Nov. 1984).

TECHNICAL DIRECTION Government guidance of a contractor's effort toward certain areas of endeavor or lines of inquiry that fall within the contract STATEMENT OF WORK (SOW). Technical direction is generally provided in writing by the CONTRACTING OFFICER TECHNICAL REPRESENTATIVE (COTR), with a copy to the contracting officer. The COTR coordinates such direction with the contractor to ensure that it does not impose work over and above what the contract requires. The FAR contains no standard technical direction clause, but a number of agencies have adopted agency clauses.

TECHNICAL EVALUATION   The evaluation of the technical aspects of a PROPOSAL submitted in a COMPETITIVE PROPOSALS procurement or a TWO-STEP SEALED BIDDING procurement. Such evaluation is conducted by Government employees (or occasionally by contractor employees) skilled in the fields of technology addressed in the proposal. FAR 15.608(a)(2) contains guidance on evaluation of proposals in competitive negotiations. FAR 14.503-1(e) discusses evaluation of technical proposals in two-step procurements. Evaluation must be done against the criteria contained in the solicitation. See Cibinic and Nash, Formation of Government Contracts 569–84.

TECHNICAL LEVELING   An unfair practice of coaching or helping an offeror to bring its PROPOSAL up to the level of other proposals through successive rounds of DISCUSSION, such as by pointing out weaknesses resulting from the offeror's lack of diligence, competence, or inventiveness in preparing the proposal. FAR 15.610(d). This FAR provision prohibits the contracting officer and other Government procurement personnel from engaging in technical leveling. See Nash, *Technical Leveling: Confusion and Clarification*, 1 N&CR ¶ 2 (Jan. 1987), for a critique of this definition suggesting that technical leveling should be defined as "helping an offeror to bring its proposal up to the level of other proposals by coaching or providing solutions or approaches desired by the agency." See also Nash, *Postscript: Understanding the Meaning of "Technical Leveling,"* 4 N&CR ¶ 62 (Nov. 1990). To prevail in a protest involving technical leveling (1) the protester must be an interested party; (2) the Government, rather than another source, must have provided the assistance; (3) the assistance must have raised the quality of the proposal; (4) the assistance must have come during successive rounds of discussion; and (5) the weakness pointed out must have stemmed from the offeror's lack of diligence, competence, or inventiveness. See Feldman, *Traversing the Tightrope Between Meaningful Discussions and Improper Practices in Negotiated Federal Acquisitions: Technical Transfusion, Technical Leveling, and Auction Techniques*, 17 Pub. Cont. L.J. 211, 238 (1987). See also AUCTION, SOURCE SELECTION, and TECHNICAL TRANSFUSION.

TECHNICAL TRANSFUSION Government disclosure of technical information pertaining to a PROPOSAL that results in improvement of a competing proposal. FAR 15.610(e)(1). The FAR forbids the contracting officer and other Government procurement personnel from engaging in technical transfusion. To prevail in a PROTEST asserting technical transfusion, (1) the protester must be an interested party, (2) the disclosure must come from the Government rather than another source, (3) the disclosure must be technical information, (4) the disclosed information must be derived from another offeror's proposal, (5) the recipient of the information must be selected for award, and (6) the protester must show a correlation between the disclosure and an improvement in the successful offeror's proposal. See Feldman, *Traversing the Tightrope Between Meaningful Discussions and Improper Practices in Negotiated Federal Acquisitions: Technical Transfusion, Technical Leveling, and Auction Techniques*, 17 Pub. Cont. L.J. 211, 227 (1987). See also SOURCE SELECTION.

TECHNOLOGY TRANSFER See FEDERAL TECHNOLOGY TRANSFER.

TELECOMMUNICATIONS FACILITIES Equipment used for such modes of transmission as telephone, data, facsimile, video, radio, and audio, and such corollary items as switches, wire, cable, access arrangements, and communications security facilities. FIRMR 201-4.001. Executive agencies are authorized to enter into multiyear contracts for telecommunications resources, including facilities, subject to certain conditions. FIRMR 201-20.306.

TELECOMMUNICATIONS SERVICES The transmission, emission, or reception of signals, signs, writing, images, sounds, or intelligence of any nature, by wire, cable, satellite, fiber optics, laser, radio, or any other electronic, electric, electromagnetic, or acoustically coupled means. FIRMR 201-4.001. The term includes the telecommunications facilities and equipment necessary to provide such services. DFARS 239.7401. GSA provides both local and long distance telecommunications service for Federal agencies, including service at locations where consolidation can bring better prices or where meeting a common need (for example, national security) cannot be cost justified by individual agencies. The objective is to have a single telecommunications service to meet the needs of all agencies at a location. FIRMR

Bulletin C-15, *Mandatory Local Telecommunications Service*. DoD's policy is to acquire telecommunications services from both common and noncommon carriers (see CARRIER (TRANSPORTA-TION)), normally on a competitive basis. DFARS 239.7402. See Galloway and Schloth, *Telecommunications Procurement*, 86-10 Briefing Papers (Sep. 1986).

TERM CONTRACT   A type of COST-PLUS-FIXED FEE (CPFF) CONTRACT in which the scope of work is described in general terms and the contractor's obligation is stated in terms of a specified level of effort for a stated period of time.   FAR 16.306(d)(2).   This is contrasted to a completion-form CPFF contract in which the scope of work is stated as a definite goal or target with a specified end product.   In the term-type contract, the contractor earns the fixed fee when the level of effort has been completed—without regard to the work accomplished.   In the completion form contract, the fixed fee is not earned until the end result is accomplished.   See Cibinic and Nash, Cost Reimbursement Contracting, chap. 2.

TERMINATION CONTRACTING OFFICER (TCO)   A CONTRACTING OFFICER (CO) who settles terminated contracts.   FAR 49.001.   After the CO issues a notice of TERMINATION FOR CONVENIENCE, the TCO is responsible for negotiating any settlement with the contractor, including a no-cost settlement if appropriate.   FAR 49.101.   In accordance with the termination clause and the notice of termination, the TCO (1) directs the action required of the prime contractor; (2) examines the SETTLEMENT PROPOSAL of the prime contractor, and, when appropriate, the settlement proposals of the subcontractors; (3) promptly negotiates settlement with the contractor and enters into a settlement agreement; and (4) if a complete settlement cannot be negotiated, promptly settles the contractor's settlement proposal by determination for the elements that cannot be agreed on. FAR 49.105. In DoD, TCOs are frequently specialists with no other responsibilities.   In other agencies, the TCO functions are usually handled by the contracting officer that was responsible for initiation of the procurement.

TERMINATION FOR CONVENIENCE   The right of the Government to terminate or cancel performance of work under a contract, in whole or in part, if the contracting officer determines that termination is in the Government's interest. FAR 49.101.   This right is made a part of almost all Government contracts by the inclusion of standard Termination for the Convenience of the Government clauses in FAR 52.249-1 through -5. See FAR 49.502 for guidance on the use of these clauses. Procedures for administering terminations for convenience are set forth in FAR Subparts 49.1, 49.2, and 49.3. The parties may settle contracts terminated for the convenience of the Government by negotiated agreement, by determination of the TERMINATION CONTRACTING OFFICER (TCO) (only when settlement cannot be reached by agreement), by costing out (in cost-reimbursement contracts), or by a combination of these methods. FAR 49.103. If the parties are unable to agree on a settlement, the Government must pay the contractor the costs incurred in performing the terminated work, the costs of settling and paying SETTLEMENT PROPOSALs under terminated subcontracts, and a fair and reasonable profit on work performed (but not on terminated work). See Cibinic and Nash, Administration of Government Contracts 817–72; Martell and Featherstun, *Convenience Termination: More Selected Problems*, 91-13 Briefing Papers (Dec. 1991); Pettit and Vacketta, *Convenience Termination: Selected Problems*, 90-12 Briefing Papers (Nov. 1990).

TERMINATION FOR DEFAULT The right of the Government to completely or partially terminate a contract because of the contractor's actual or anticipated failure to perform its contractual obligations (also called "default termination"). FAR 49.401. This right is included in almost all Government contracts by the inclusion of the standard Default clauses in FAR 52.249-8 through -10. See FAR 49.504 for guidance on the use of these clauses. Procedures for administering default terminations are set forth in FAR Subparts 49.1 and 49.4. Under fixed-price supply and service contracts, the Government has the right, subject to the notice requirements required in certain situations, to terminate the contract if the contractor fails to (1) deliver the supplies or perform the services within the time specified, (2) perform any other provision of the contract, or (3) make sufficient progress, if that failure endangers performance of the contract. FAR 49.402. The contractor is liable to the Government for any excess costs incurred in acquiring supplies or services similar to those terminated for default and for any other damages, whether or not repurchase is effected; see EXCESS COSTS OF REPROCUREMENT. FAR 49.402-2, 49.402-6, 49.402-7. If the contractor can establish, or it is otherwise determined, that the contractor was not in default or that the failure to perform is excusable, the default clauses provide that a termination for default will be considered to have been a TERMINATION FOR CONVENIENCE, and the rights and obligations of the parties will be governed accordingly. FAR 49.401. See Cibinic and Nash, Administration of Government Contracts 667–760; Pettit et al., Government Contract Default Termination; Margulies, chap. 11, Construction Contracting 837–77.

TERMINATION INVENTORY   Any property (1) purchased, supplied, manufactured, furnished, or otherwise acquired for the performance of a contract subsequently terminated and (2) properly allocable to the terminated portion of the contract. FAR 45.601. Termination inventory includes GOVERNMENT-FURNISHED PROPERTY (GFP) in the possession of or directly acquired by the Government and subsequently made available to the contractor but does not include any facilities, material, or items of SPECIAL TEST EQUIPMENT or SPECIAL TOOLING that are subject to a separate contract or to a special contract requirement governing their use or disposition. After termination the contractor prepares schedules of all termination inventory in accordance with FAR Subpart 45.6, the contracting officer decides on the disposition of the inventory (FAR 49.105(6)(4)), and the contractor disposes of the inventory as directed by the contracting officer (FAR 48.104(i)).

TERMINATION LIABILITY   The maximum cost the Government would incur if a contract is terminated. FAR 17.101. When a multiyear contract (see MULTIYEAR CONTRACTING) is terminated before completion of the work on the current year, the amount includes the current year termination charges plus the cancellation charges for the unfunded years.

TERMINATION NOTICE   A notice from the contracting officer to the contractor stating that the contract is partially or completely terminated, under either a TERMINATION FOR CONVENIENCE or a TERMINATION FOR DEFAULT. FAR 49.601 provides recommended formats for notices of termination for convenience and suggests that a telegraphic notice be used. FAR 49.402-3 contains guidance on the issuance of notices of termination for default. In such cases, DELINQUENCY NOTICEs may be required or desirable prior to the issuance of the termination notice. The default termination notice is a final DECISION OF THE CONTRACTING OFFICER, which is subject to immediate appeal under the CONTRACT DISPUTES ACT

(CDA) OF 1978.   FAR 49.402-3(g)(7).   See Cibinic and Nash, Administration of Government Contracts 758–60, 826.

TERMS AND CONDITIONS All the provisions of a contract. FAR 14.201-1 and 15.406-1 require that the terms and conditions follow the UNIFORM CONTRACT FORMAT.   See also GENERAL PROVISIONS.

TEST AND EVALUATION (T&E) A process by which a SYSTEM or components are compared with requirements and specifications through testing. The Government evaluates the results to assess the progress of design, performance, supportability, and the like. During the ACQUISITION PROCESS, T&E can be of three kinds: developmental (DT&E), which assists the engineering design and development phase and verifies attainment of technical performance specifications and objectives; operational (OT&E), which estimates a system's operational effectiveness and suitability, identifies needed modifications, and provides information on tactical, organizational, and personnel requirements; and production acceptance (PAT&E), which demonstrates that the items meet the requirements and specifications of the contract.   Jones, Glossary: Defense Acquisition Acronyms and Terms. 10 U.S.C. 2399 requires DoD to conduct OT&E on all MAJOR DEFENSE ACQUISITION PROGRAMs.

TESTING That element of INSPECTION that determines the properties or elements, including functional operation, of supplies or their components, by the application of established scientific principles and procedures. FAR 46.101. Testing is part of the QUALITY CONTROL (QC) and the QUALITY ASSURANCE (QA) processes. It is done by both the contractor (and its subcontractors) and the Government to ensure that supplies meet contract requirements.

TIME-AND-MATERIALS (T&M) CONTRACT   A type of contract providing for the acquisition of supplies or services on the basis of (1) direct labor hours at specified fixed hourly rates that include wages, overhead, GENERAL AND ADMINISTRATIVE (G&A) EXPENSEs, and PROFIT, and (2) materials at cost including, if appropriate, material handling costs. FAR 16.601. A time-and-materials contract may be used only (1) when it is not possible at the time of placing the contract to estimate accurately the extent or duration of the work or to anticipate costs with any reasonable degree of confidence; (2) after the contracting officer executes a

DETERMINATION AND FINDINGS (D&F) concluding that no other contract type is suitable; and (3) if the contract includes a CEILING PRICE that the contractor exceeds at its own risk. A time-and-materials contract provides no positive profit incentive to the contractor for cost control or labor efficiency. See Cibinic and Nash, Formation of Government Contracts 791–94.

TITLE The paramount right to property. The Government claims title to all property bought by the contractor during the performance of a contract when the PROGRESS PAYMENTs clause in FAR 52.232-16 is included in the contract. However, *Marine Midland Bank v. United States*, 231 Ct. Cl. 496, 687 F.2d 395 (1982), holds that the Government right is not title but rather a lien with priority over all other claims against the property. See also FAR 32.503-15, which gives the contractor considerable control over the property during performance of the contract.

TITLE I, TITLE II, TITLE III SERVICES Categories of ARCHITECT-ENGINEER (A-E) SERVICES used by DoE. Title I requires the A-E to provide necessary topographical and other field surveys, test borings, and other subsurface investigation; prepare preliminary studies, sketches, layout plans, and outline specifications; and prepare reports including cost estimates for the proposed project and all related structures, utilities, and appurtenances. Title II requires the A-E to provide complete design services, including all required preliminary and final working drawings, specifications, estimates, and contract documents; to assist in securing, analyzing, and evaluating bids or proposals for construction; and to consult with DoE on all questions arising in connection with the A-E's services. Title III requires the A-E to provide complete A-E supervision and inspection of construction, to check shop drawings, and to furnish drawings to show that construction has actually been accomplished. DEAR 936.6.5(c). See also CONCEPTUAL DESIGN.

TORT Injury to a person by negligence or through committing an act that is proscribed by community standards. Tort is one of the common causes of action that can be used to recover damages. The FEDERAL TORT CLAIMS ACT (FTCA) permits persons injured by negligent conduct of the Government to sue for damages in U.S. District Courts.

TOTAL COST The sum of the allowable direct and indirect cost allocable to the contract, incurred or to be incurred, less any allocable credits, plus any allocable cost of money. FAR 31.201-1. See ALLOWABLE COST, ALLOCABLE COST, and COST OF MONEY FACTORS. This is the amount that is reimbursable by the Government under COST-REIMBURSEMENT CONTRACTs or is accepted in pricing of FIXED-PRICE CONTRACTs. FAR Subpart 31.2 contains detailed guidance on the computation of total costs.

TOTAL COST METHOD A method of establishing the amount of DAMAGES or EQUITABLE ADJUSTMENT which results in the contractor's being compensated for the difference between its actual expenses and its bid or estimated costs. The courts and boards of contract appeals look upon this method of proving damages with disfavor, tolerating its use only when no other method of calculating damages is available. Acceptability of the method requires a demonstration that (1) the nature of the particular losses makes it impossible or highly impracticable to determine them with a reasonable degree of accuracy, (2) the contractor's bid or estimate was realistic, (3) the actual costs expended were reasonable, and (4) the contractor was not responsible for the added expenses. See Cibinic and Nash, Administration of Government Contracts 514–19; Nash, Government Contract Changes, chap. 19.

TOTAL QUALITY MANAGEMENT (TQM) A philosophy and set of guiding principles that are intended to be the foundation of a continuously improving organization by encouraging employees to focus their attention on means of improving efficiency and effectiveness. TQM has been adopted by DoD to improve quality. It is the application of human resources and quantitative methods to improve (1) the materials and services supplied to an organization, (2) all the processes within an organization, and (3) the degree to which the needs of the customer are met, now and in the future. TQM integrates fundamental management techniques, existing improvement efforts, and technical tools within a disciplined approach focused on continuous process improvement. See Yurcisin, *The Way to Quality*, 29 Cont. Mgmt. 4 (Nov. 1989).

TOTAL SET-ASIDE See SET-ASIDE (n).

TRADE AGREEMENTS ACT OF 1979 An act, 19 U.S.C. 2501–2582, requiring agencies to evaluate offers from contractors from designated countries without regard to the restrictions of the BUY AMERICAN ACT. The exemption applies only to procurements at or over the dollar equivalent of 150,000 SPECIAL DRAWING RIGHTS (SDRs) units. FAR 25.401 lists the 45 designated countries eligible for exemption and the 22 additional countries eligible under the CARIBBEAN BASIN ECONOMIC RECOVERY ACT. The U.S. Trade Representative has determined that these countries provide appropriate reciprocal competitive government procurement opportunities for American products and suppliers. See Kenney and Duberstein, *Domestic Preference Provisions*, 89-3 Briefing Papers (Feb. 1989); Rothlein and Schooner, *The Trade Agreements Act: Installation Procurement and International Government Acquisition Law*, Army Law. 1 (Sep. 1983). Exceptions to the Trade Agreements Act, under which the Buy American Act does apply, are found at FAR 25.403.

TRADE, BUSINESS, TECHNICAL, AND PROFESSIONAL ACTIVITY COSTS Costs incurred by a contractor as a result of membership in trade, business, technical, and professional organizations. FAR 31.205-43 makes the following costs allowable: membership costs; subscriptions to trade, business, professional, or other technical periodicals; and costs associated with meetings, conferences, symposia, or seminars, as specified below, when their principal purpose is the dissemination of trade, business, technical, or professional information or the stimulation of production or improved productivity. Allowable meeting costs are the costs of organizing, setting up, and sponsoring the meetings, symposia, etc., including rental of meeting facilities, transportation, subsistence, and incidental costs; the costs of attendance by contractor employees, including travel costs; and the costs of attendance by individuals who are not employees of the contractor, provided such costs are not also reimbursed to the individual by the employing company or organization and provided the individual's attendance is essential in achieving the purpose of the conference, meeting, symposium, etc. See also ALLOWABLE COST.

TRADE SECRET Information—including a formula, pattern, compilation, program, device, method, technique, or process—that is the subject of reasonable efforts to maintain its secrecy and that derives independent economic value, actual or potential, as a result of not being generally known to and not being readily ascertainable by proper means. See Nash and Rawicz, Patents and

Technical Data 52–64. When the Government obtains trade secrets it is generally barred from disclosing them under the TRADE SECRETS ACT and the FREEDOM OF INFORMATION ACT (FOIA).

TRADE SECRETS ACT An act, 18 U.S.C. 1905, making it a crime for an employee of the United States to publish or disclose trade secrets and other confidential information obtained as a result of Government employment. The act has not led to any significant amount of criminal prosecution, but it is important in establishing a standard barring disclosure of information under the FREEDOM OF INFORMATION ACT (FOIA). See Nash, *The Trade Secrets Act: An Enigma*, 4 N&CR ¶ 57 (Oct. 1990).

TRAIL BOSS PROGRAM An alternative approach for managing the Government's major information technology acquisitions in the 1990s, initiated by the GENERAL SERVICES ADMINISTRATION (GSA). The Trail Boss Program focuses on a single manager for an acquisition and emphasizes individuals, cooperation, and accomplishment over process and procedure. See FIRMR Bulletin C-7, *Trail Boss Program.*

TRAINING COSTS Costs of providing vocational training intended to increase the skills of a contractor's employees. FAR 31.205-44 specifies that such costs are ALLOWABLE COSTs, with some limitations.

TRANSPORTATION The shipment of material, parts, components, or end items in the procurement of supplies. FAR Part 47 deals with policies and procedures for applying transportation and traffic management considerations in the acquisition of transportation or transportation-related services by contract methods other than bills of lading, transportation requests, transportation warrants, and similar transportation forms. The preferred method of transporting supplies for the Government is by commercial carrier (see CARRIER (TRANSPORTATION)). However, Government-owned, -leased, or -chartered vehicles, aircraft, and vessels may be used if they are available and not fully utilized, if their use will result in substantial economies, and if their use is in accordance with all applicable statutes, policies, and regulations. FAR 47.101.

TRANSPORTATION TERM CONTRACTS   REQUIREMENTS CONTRACTs for transportation or transportation-related services. FAR 47.203. Such contracts are generally used for the transportation of household goods, office furniture, and other general freight. FAR Subpart 47.2 provides guidance on the use of such contracts. See also INDEFINITE-DELIVERY CONTRACT.

TRAVEL COSTS   The cost of transportation, lodging, subsistence, and incidental expenses. FAR 31.205-46 specifies that such costs incurred by a contractor are ALLOWABLE COSTs, with some limitations, if they are incurred on official company business.

TREASURY INTEREST RATE   The interest rate, set by the Secretary of the Treasury, for each 6-month period on a calendar year basis. The rate is published in the Federal Register and is used to calculate the amount of INTEREST payable under Government contracts. The interest rates for the past decade have been the following:

Year	Jan.–June	July–Dec.
1980	12 1/4%	10 1/2%
1981	14 5/8%	14 7/8%
1982	14 3/4%	15 1/2%
1983	11 1/4%	11 1/2%
1984	12 3/8%	14 3/8%
1985	12 1/8%	10 3/8%
1986	9 3/4%	8 1/2%
1987	7 5/8%	8 7/8%
1988	9 3/8%	9 1/4%
1989	9 3/4%	9 1/8%
1990	8 1/2%	9%
1991	8 3/8%	8 1/2%

TRUTH IN NEGOTIATIONS ACT (TINA)   An act, 10 U.S.C. 2306a, 41 U.S.C. 254(d), that was added to the ARMED SERVICES PROCUREMENT ACT (ASPA) in 1963 to enhance the Government's ability to negotiate fair prices by ensuring that the contracting officer has the same factual information that is available to the contractor. TINA established the requirement for the submission of COST OR PRICING DATA and certification of their accuracy, completeness, and currency for the award of any negotiated contract expected to exceed $100,000 (or $500,000 for DoD, NASA, and Coast Guard contracts awarded after 5 Dec. 1990), subject to exemptions when ADEQUATE PRICE COMPETITION or other conditions reflecting a competitive marketplace exist, as discussed at FAR 15.804-3; (see CERTIFIED COST OR PRICING DATA). It also provided for contract price adjustment as a result of submission of DEFECTIVE COST OR PRICING DATA. In 1984 the COMPETITION IN CONTRACTING ACT (CICA) added these requirements to the FEDERAL PROPERTY AND ADMINISTRATIVE SERVICES ACT (FPASA) OF 1949 at 41 U.S.C. 254(d). Subsequently, in 1986, TINA was greatly expanded and codified at 10 U.S.C. 2306a. TINA is not the only remedy available to the Government for defective data; a contractor may be found liable for civil fraud under the FALSE CLAIMS ACT, 31 U.S.C. 231–233, for knowingly submitting defective data. Certification under the act is accomplished by the Certificate of Current Cost or Pricing Data in FAR 15.804-4. The act is implemented by the Price Reduction for Defective Cost or Pricing Data clauses at FAR 52.215-22 and -23. The data are submitted as a part of Standard Form (SF) 1411, Contract Pricing Proposal Cover Sheet, FAR 53.301-1411. Exemptions are claimed using SF 1412, Claim for Exemption from Submission of Certified Cost or Pricing Data, FAR 53.301-1412. See Kipps and Rice, Living with TINA: A Practical Guide to the Truth in Negotiations Act; Morrison and Ebert, *Truth in Negotiations/Edition III*, 89-11 Briefing Papers (Oct. 1989); Feldman, *The Truth in Negotiations Act: A Primer*, 21 NCMJ 67 (1988).

TUCKER ACT   An act, 28 U.S.C. 1346(a) and 1491, that waives SOVEREIGN IMMUNITY from suit for all CLAIMs founded upon any contract, express or implied, with the U.S. Government. Originally passed in 1855 and enacted in its present form in 1887, the Tucker Act made the Court of Claims the major court resolving Government contract DISPUTEs. The CONTRACT DISPUTES ACT (CDA) OF 1978 (1) repealed the part of the Tucker Act that gave the Federal District Courts jurisdiction over claims up to $10,000 and (2) gave contractors direct access to the Court of Claims to challenge contracting officer decisions on contract disputes. See Nash and Cibinic, II Federal Procurement Law 2140. The FEDERAL COURTS IMPROVEMENT ACT (FCIA) further altered the process by creating the CLAIMS COURT (Cl. Ct.) and the COURT OF APPEALS FOR THE FEDERAL CIRCUIT (CAFC or Fed. Cir.) out of the former Court of Claims. See Nash, *Tucker Act Jurisdiction: It's Narrower than You Think*, 4 N&CR ¶ 28 (May 1990).

TURNKEY See DESIGN/BUILD.

TWENTY-NINE-CENT INJUNCTION See AUTOMATIC STAY.

TWO-STEP SEALED BIDDING A method of procurement that combines competitive procedures in order to obtain the benefits of SEALED BIDDING when adequate SPECIFICATIONs are not available. FAR 14.501. One objective of this process is to permit the development of a sufficiently descriptive and not unduly restrictive statement of the Government's requirements, including an adequate TECHNICAL DATA package, so that subsequent acquisitions can be made by conventional sealed bidding. This method is especially useful in acquisitions requiring technical proposals, particularly those for complex items. Step One consists of the request for, and submission, evaluation, and discussion of, technical proposals; no pricing is involved. Step Two involves the submission of sealed bids by offerors that submitted acceptable technical proposals in Step One. See Cibinic and Nash, Formation of Government Contracts 506–21.

TYPE OF CONTRACT Categories of contracts that are differentiated according to the time the price is arrived at and the firmness of the price. FAR Part 16 describes and states the policies governing the various types of contract. Contracts are of two basic types: FIXED-PRICE CONTRACTs and COST-REIMBURSEMENT CONTRACTs. Within these two basic families are a sizeable number of specific types, such as FIRM-FIXED-PRICE (FFP) CONTRACTs, FIXED-PRICE INCENTIVE (FPI) CONTRACTs, COST-PLUS-INCENTIVE FEE (CPIF) CONTRACTs, and COST-PLUS-FIXED FEE (CPFF) CONTRACTs. Under a fixed-price contract, the contractor agrees to perform the work called for by the contract for the firm-fixed-price stated in the contract or, if the price is tentative and subject to later adjustment, for some amount under a specified price ceiling. Under a cost-reimbursement contract, the Government agrees to reimburse the contractor for the costs it incurs in performing the contract and usually to pay a fee representing the contractor's profit for performing the contract. Under a fixed-price contract, the contractor must complete the contract for the agreed-upon price. If costs are less than anticipated, the contractor will increase its profits. But if costs are greater than anticipated, the contractor will incur a loss, or at least not realize the profit contemplated. Whatever the situation, the responsibility is entirely the contractor's, and the contractor must deliver for the specified price regardless of how badly it may have miscalculated. Under a cost-reimbursement contract, on the other hand, the contractor agrees to use its best efforts to complete contract requirements within a TOTAL COST previously estimated and agreed upon. The contractor must notify the Government if and when it believes that the contract will not be completed within that estimate, giving a revised estimate of the cost of performance. The contractor is not obliged to continue performance or incur additional costs beyond the original estimate—if it does, it does so at its own risk—unless and until notified that the contract funding and estimate have been increased. The major test applied in the selection of contract type is the degree of uncertainty involved: solid bases for pricing lead to fixed-price arrangements, whereas uncertainties lead to cost-reimbursement arrangements.   Special contract types include INDEFINITE-DELIVERY CONTRACTs, TIME-AND-MATERIALS (T&M) CONTRACTs, LABOR-HOUR CONTRACTs, and LETTER CONTRACTs. For discussion of the various contract types, see Armed Services Pricing Manual (ASPM) vol. 1 and Cibinic and Nash, Formation of Government Contracts, chap. 7.

U

UNABSORBED OVERHEAD Overhead (see INDIRECT COST) that cannot be charged to a contract as originally anticipated because the direct costs of performance have been stopped due to a delay. During periods of Government delay in, or suspension of, a particular contract, there is a marked decrease in or cessation of DIRECT COSTs incurred for that contract. Consequently, the HOME OFFICE costs that would otherwise have been charged to that contract by means of applying the home office overhead rate to direct costs cannot be "absorbed" by that contract and must be borne by the contractor's other work. The term "unabsorbed overhead" has its roots in manufacturing accounting and is often used to describe this additional overhead burden. The EICHLEAY FORMULA is the prevalent method for calculating unabsorbed and extended overhead. See Cibinic and Braude, chap. 9, Construction Contracting 751–64.

UNALLOWABLE COST A cost incurred by a contractor that is not chargeable to Government contracts. Unallowable costs must be identified and excluded from any billing, claim, or proposal applicable to a Government contract. FAR 31.201-6. Cost Accounting Standard 405, FAR 30.405, provides guidance in accounting for such costs. 10 U.S.C. 2324 calls for severe sanctions for claiming costs that are unallowable pursuant to statute or regulation. See also ALLOWABLE COST and EXPRESSLY UNALLOWABLE COST.

UNAUTHORIZED COMMITMENT See RATIFICATION.

UNBALANCED BID A bid that states nominal or low prices for some work and enhanced prices for other work. For the bid to be deemed nonresponsive (see RESPONSIVENESS), it must be both mathematically unbalanced and materially unbalanced. A determination of mathematical unbalance asks whether each bid item carries its share of the cost of the work plus profit or whether the bid is based on nominal or low prices for some work and enhanced prices for other work. A determination of material unbalance asks whether there is reasonable doubt that award to the bidder submitting the mathematically unbalanced bid ultimately will result in the lowest cost. See Cibinic, *Unbalanced Bids and Proposals: Trying to Beat the System*, 5 N&CR ¶ 21 (Apr. 1991); Preston, *Evaluating Bids Against Cost Limitations*, 15 Pub. Cont. L.J. 463, 476–85 (1985).

UNCONSCIONABILITY An unconscionable bargain or contract is one that no person in possession of his or her senses—that is to say, not under a delusion—would make and that no fair and honest person would accept. The basic test of unconscionability is whether, under circumstances existing when the contract was made and in light of general commercial background and commercial needs of the particular trade or case, the contract clauses are so one-sided as to oppress or unfairly surprise a party. Unconscionability generally implies an absence of meaningful choice on the part of one of the parties. Moreover, the one-sidedness often obtains when the imbalance is buried in small print or couched in language unintelligible even to a person of moderate education. Black's Law Dictionary. Unconscionability is grounds for contract AVOIDANCE. U.C.C. 2-302. See Cibinic and Nash, Administration of Government Contracts 247–49.

UNDEFINITIZED CONTRACTUAL ACTION A contract in which the parties have not fully agreed on all the TERMS AND CONDITIONS. In most cases in Government procurement, such contracts are called LETTER CONTRACTs. 10 U.S.C. 2326 precludes agencies from entering into undefinitized contractual actions without proper justification and provides that DEFINITIZATION should occur within 180 days of the contractor's proposal to definitize and before the expenditure of more than 50 percent of the funds to be used. Procedures for complying with this statute are contained in DFARS Subpart 217.74.

UNFAIR COMPETITIVE ADVANTAGE An advantage of one competitor over another competitor that is derived from improper Government action or is created by the Government. An unfair competitive advantage exists when a contractor competing for the award of any Federal contract possesses (1) PROPRIETARY

INFORMATION that was obtained from a Government official without proper authorization or (2) SOURCE SELECTION INFORMATION that is relevant to the contract but is not available to all competitors, and such information would assist that contractor in obtaining the contract. The underlying concept is that no competitor should benefit from exclusive access to information. OFPP Policy Letter 89-1, *Conflict of Interest Policies Applicable to Consultants*. See also FAR Subpart 9.5. An unfair competitive advantage also exists when a contractor is permitted to use GOVERNMENT PRODUCTION AND RESEARCH PROPERTY in a competitive procurement without payment of rent or addition of a RENTAL EQUIVALENT. FAR 45.201. FAR Subpart 45.2 sets forth the procedures for overcoming this type of unfair advantage by charging rent or adjusting bid prices.

UNICOR   See FEDERAL PRISON INDUSTRIES, INC.

UNIFORM COMMERCIAL CODE (U.C.C.)   A uniform law governing commercial transactions such as sales of GOODS, commercial paper, bank deposits and collections, LETTERs OF CREDIT, bulk transfers, warehouse receipts, BILLs OF LADING, investment securities, and secured transactions. All States except Louisiana have adopted the U.C.C. The U.C.C. is one of the Uniform Laws drafted by the National Conference of Commissioners on Uniform State Laws. Black's Law Dictionary. The U.C.C.'s underlying purposes and policies are to simplify, clarify, and modernize the law governing commercial transactions; permit the continued expansion of commercial practices through custom, usage, and agreement of the parties; and make the law uniform throughout the various jurisdictions. U.C.C. 1-102. The U.C.C. is not directly applicable to Government contracting, but it is used by analogy and for guidance when the terms of a contract or the regulations do not deal directly with a subject. See Nash and Cibinic, I Federal Procurement Law 796–98.

UNIFORM CONTRACT FORMAT   A standardized format for structuring Government SOLICITATIONs and CONTRACTs. Its use facilitates preparation of the solicitation and contract as well as reference to, and use of, the documents in the solicitation and contract. FAR 14.201-1 and 15.406-1. Found on Standard Form (SF) 26, Award/Contract, and SF 33, Solicitation, Offer and Award, the UCF is simply a table of contents for organizing contractual documents into 4 parts and 13 sections. In negotiated acquisitions, Part I, the Schedule, includes sections A, Solicitation/contract form; B, Supplies or services and prices/costs; C, Description/specifications/work statement; D, Packaging and marking; E, Inspection and acceptance; F, Deliveries or performance; G, Contract administration data; and H, Special contract requirements. Part II, Contract Clauses, consists of a single section I, Contract clauses. Part III, List of Documents, Exhibits, and Other Attachments, consists of a single section J, List of attachments. Part IV, Representations and Instructions, contains sections K, Representations, certifications, and other statements of offerors or quoters; L, Instructions, conditions, and notices to offerors or quoters; and M, Evaluation factors for award. In sealed bidding, the format is the same, with minor differences in language.

UNIFORM RULES A standardized set of rules of procedure for the various agency BOARDs OF CONTRACT APPEALS (BCAs). The CONTRACT DISPUTES ACT (CDA) OF 1978 requires that the Administrator of the Office of Federal Procurement Policy (OFPP) issue guidelines with respect to the establishment, functions, and procedures of the agency BCAs. 41 U.S.C. 607(h). OFPP issued "Uniform Rules of Procedure for Boards of Contract Appeals" in 1979. See 44 Fed. Reg. 12519 (7 Mar. 1979); 44 Fed. Reg. 34227 (14 June 1979). The rules resemble the uniform rules drafted by the National Conference of Boards of Contract Appeals Members (now called the Board of Contract Appeals Judges Association), with sections added to implement the Contract Disputes Act's small claims and subpoena provisions. OFPP intended that the various BCAs would adopt the Uniform Rules in place of their individual rules, except when a BCA's size or the nature of its docket justified a variance. Each BCA's "customized" version of the rules can be found in the looseleaf advance sheet section of the *Board of Contract Appeals Decisions* available from Commerce Clearing House, Inc., 4025 West Peterson Avenue, Chicago, IL 60646.

UNILATERAL CHANGE A CHANGE ORDER issued by a contracting officer under a Changes clause. Most Government contracts contain a Changes clause permitting the contracting officer to make unilateral changes in designated areas, within the general SCOPE OF THE CONTRACT. FAR 43.201. It is the policy of the Government to avoid issuing unilateral changes by attempting instead to price changes before they are issued and then issue a bilateral modification. FAR 43.102(b). When this cannot be done, it is the policy of the Government to negotiate a maximum price in the change order. See Nash, Government Contract Changes, chap. 7. Unilateral changes are issued on Standard Form 30, Amendment of Solicitation/Modification of Contract, FAR 53.301-30. FAR 43.201(a). See also UNILATERAL MODIFICATION.

UNILATERAL MISTAKE   A MISTAKE of only one party—generally the contractor. Relief for such mistakes may be given if they are alleged by the offeror before award, provided they are not mistakes in business judgment. See FAR 14.406, 15.610. No relief is given for such mistakes alleged by a contractor after award unless the contracting officer had notice of the mistake before award or failed to ask for verification (see DUTY OF VERIFICATION). See FAR 14.406-4; Cibinic and Nash, Administration of Government Contracts 239–47.

UNILATERAL MODIFICATION   A MODIFICATION to a contract that is signed only by the contracting officer. Unilateral modifications are generally used to make administrative changes, issue CHANGE ORDERs (COs), make changes authorized by clauses other than a Changes clause, and issue TERMINATION NOTICEs. FAR 43.103. The alternative to a unilateral modification is a bilateral modification.

UNILATERAL PRICE DETERMINATION   A Government-directed MODIFICATION to the contract that sets forth a presumptively fair price for the supplies or services that are at issue. This presumption is rebuttable upon a contractor showing that the unilaterally determined price is either not fair or not reasonable, or both, based on certain facts, cost or price principles or assumptions, or legal theories. If a contractor does not sign the unilateral price determination but fails to object in a timely manner, the modification may have the force and effect of a bilateral agreement and not be susceptible to subsequent legal challenge. See Jeroslow, *Avoiding Negotiation Deadlock: The Use and Care of Unilateral Price Determinations*, 86-1 Caveat Emptor 1, cited in Henson, *The Legality of the UPD*, 30 Cont. Mgmt. 9 (Aug. 1990). See also UNILATERAL CHANGE.

UNIQUE AND INNOVATIVE CONCEPT   A concept that, in the opinion and the best knowledge of the Government evaluator, is the product of original thinking submitted in confidence by one source; contains novel or changed concepts, approaches, or methods; was not submitted previously by another; and is not otherwise available within the Federal Government. FAR 6.003. In this context, the term does not mean that the source has the sole capability of performing the research. When such a concept is included in an UNSOLICITED PROPOSAL, a contracting agency may award a contract to the offeror without obtaining FULL AND OPEN COMPETITION. See FAR 6.302-1(a)(2)(i); Cibinic and Nash, Formation of Government Contracts 304–05.

UNIT COST REDUCTION See INSTANT UNIT COST REDUCTION.

UNITED STATES CODE (U.S.C.) A consolidation and codification of all the general and permanent laws of the United States. The code provides an organized system for finding Federal laws by title (50 headings, primarily alphabetical) and section. For example, Title 41, Public Contracts, contains many of the basic laws governing the procurement process. Within Title 41, sections 151–260 contain the procurement parts of the FEDERAL PROPERTY AND ADMINISTRATIVE SERVICES ACT (FPASA) OF 1949, sections 401–424 contain the OFFICE OF FEDERAL PROCUREMENT POLICY (OFPP) Act, and sections 601–613 contain the CONTRACT DISPUTES ACT (CDA) OF 1978. Note, however, that the ARMED SERVICES PROCUREMENT ACT (ASPA) is codified in Title 10, Armed Forces. Whereas bills passed by Congress are sequentially numbered as public laws or statutes, the code organizes the laws by subject matter, often placing portions of new statutes in multiple U.S.C. titles. As officially published, the code is generally updated and reissued every 6 years; however, current versions of the code are published by commercial vendors such as West Publishing Company (United States Code Annotated or U.S.C.A.) or the Lawyer's Co-operative Publishing Company (United States Code Service or U.S.C.S.).

UNLIMITED RIGHTS The rights of the Government, with respect to rights in DATA and COPYRIGHTS, to use, disclose, reproduce, prepare derivative works, distribute copies to the public, and perform publicly and display publicly, in any manner and for any purpose, and have others do so or permit them to do so. FAR 27.401. A different definition, referring only to TECHNICAL DATA and omitting all references to copyrights, is contained in DFARS 227.401. Under the Rights in Data—General clause in FAR 52.227-14, the Government acquires unlimited rights in (1) data first produced in the performance of a contract; (2) FORM, FIT, AND FUNCTION DATA delivered under contract; (3) data that constitute manuals or instructional and training material for installation, operation, or routine maintenance and repair of items, components, or processes delivered or furnished for use under a contract; and (4) all other data delivered under a contract, other than LIMITED RIGHTS DATA or restricted COMPUTER SOFTWARE. FAR 27.404. Under the Rights in Technical Data and Computer Software clause in DFARS 252.227-7013, the Government acquires unlimited rights in a broader set of situations. See Nash, *Department of Defense Technical Data Policy: The New Interim Rule*, 3 N&CR ¶ 1 (Jan. 1989).

UNPRICED PURCHASE ORDER   An order for supplies or services whose PRICE is not established at the time the order is issued. FAR 13.502. An unpriced PURCHASE ORDER may be used only when (1) the transaction is not expected to exceed the SMALL PURCHASE limit, (2) it is impractical to obtain pricing before issuing the purchase order, and (3) the purchase is for (a) repairs to equipment requiring disassembly to determine the nature and extent of repairs, (b) material that is available from only one source and for which the cost cannot be readily established, or (c) supplies or services for which prices are known to be competitive but exact prices are not known (for example, miscellaneous repair parts or maintenance services).

UNSOLICITED PROPOSAL   A written proposal that (1) is submitted to a Government agency on the initiative of the submitter for the purpose of obtaining a contract with the Government and (2) is not in response to a formal or informal request (other than an agency request constituting a publicized general statement of need). FAR 15.501. Unsolicited proposals are a valuable means for Government agencies to obtain approaches to accomplishing their missions from sources outside the Government. FAR 15.503. 10 U.S.C. 2304(d)(1) and 41 U.S.C. 253(d)(10) provide that agencies may enter into contracts based on unsolicited RESEARCH proposals without obtaining FULL AND OPEN COMPETITION. See FAR 15.507 providing that a valid unsolicited proposal must contain a UNIQUE AND INNOVATIVE CONCEPT; must be independently originated and developed, prepared without Government supervision, and sufficiently detailed for Government review; and must not be an advance proposal for a known agency requirement. Agencies are to encourage potential offerors to make preliminary contacts with appropriate agency personnel before the offerors expend extensive effort on detailed unsolicited proposals or submit proprietary data to the Government. Potential offerors' preliminary contacts should include inquiries into the general need for the type of effort contemplated and discussions with agency technical personnel for the limited purpose of obtaining an understanding of the agency's mission and responsibilities in relation to the contemplated effort. FAR 15.504. FAR 15.509 permits proprietary legends on unsolicited proposals and directs Government personnel to attempt to protect data in such proposals even if proprietary legends are not applied. See Cibinic and Nash, Formation of Government Contracts 304–05.

UNUSUAL AND COMPELLING URGENCY An urgent need that will lead to serious injury if not addressed. 10 U.S.C. 2304(c)(2) and 41 U.S.C. 253(c)(2) permit the award of a contract without FULL AND OPEN COMPETITION when such urgency exists. However, 10 U.S.C. 2304(f)(5)(A) and 41 U.S.C. 253(f)(5)(A) preclude the avoidance of COMPETITION if the urgency is created by lack of ACQUISITION PLANNING or concerns over the amount of funds available for the procurement. Examples of unusual and compelling urgencies are provided in DFARS 206.302-2. See FAR 6.302-2; Cibinic and Nash, Formation of Government Contracts 307–09.

UNUSUAL PROGRESS PAYMENT Any PROGRESS PAYMENT based on cost that provides payment in a higher amount than would a CUSTOMARY PROGRESS PAYMENT. FAR 32.501. The contracting officer may provide unusual progress payments only if (1) the contract necessitates predelivery expenditures that are large in relation to contract price and in relation to the contractor's working capital and credit, (2) the contractor fully documents an actual need to supplement any private financing available, including GUARANTEED LOANs, and (3) the contractor's request is approved by the HEAD OF THE CONTRACTING ACTIVITY (HCA) or a designee. FAR 32.501-2. The excess of the unusual progress payment rate approved over the customary progress payment rate should be the lowest amount possible under the circumstances. PROGRESS PAYMENTs are not considered unusual merely because they are on LETTER CONTRACTs or the definitive contracts that supersede letter contracts.

URGENCY See UNUSUAL AND COMPELLING URGENCY.

U.S.-FLAG VESSEL Either a GOVERNMENT VESSEL or a PRIVATELY OWNED U.S.-FLAG COMMERCIAL VESSEL. FAR 47.501. FAR 47.503 requires that contractors and subcontractors give preference to the use of such vessels in the performance of their contracts under the terms of the Preference for Privately Owned U.S.-Flag Commercial Vessels clause in FAR 52.247-64, which implements the policies of the CARGO PREFERENCE ACTS and the Merchant Marine Act of 1936, 46 U.S.C. 1101.

UTILITY DISTRIBUTION SYSTEM Distribution and transmission lines, substations, or installed equipment forming an integral part of the system by which gas, water, steam, electricity, sewerage, or other utility services are transmitted between the outside building or structure in which the services are used and the point of origin, disposal, or connection with some other system but excluding TELECOMMUNICATION SERVICES. FAR 45.501. This term is used in FAR Subpart 45.5 with regard to management of GOVERNMENT PROPERTY in the possession of contractors.

UTILITY SERVICE A service, such as the furnishing of electricity, gas, water, steam, and sewerage, that is available to the general public and performed by government entities or private companies. FAR 8.301. Utility services are ordinarily subject to government regulation. The term also includes services, such as snow removal and removal of garbage, rubbish, and trash, that are performed on a contractual basis and may or may not be subject to government or public regulation. The term "utility service" generally does not include telecommunication services. FAR Subpart 8.3 sets forth policies and procedures for the procurement of utility services.

V

VALIDATION The checking of all TECHNICAL DATA submitted by a contractor with RESTRICTIVE LEGENDS to ensure that such legends are properly applied. Validation procedures are prescribed by 10 U.S.C. 2321 and 41 U.S.C. 253d for contracts for MAJOR SYSTEMs; they are implemented by FAR 27.406(d) and DFARS 227.403-73. A contractor may appeal any challenges of a legend through the DISPUTEs procedure.

VALID TIME-PHASED REQUIREMENTS A part of a contractor's plan for accounting for MATERIAL that ensures that such material is (1) needed to fulfill a production plan, including reasonable quantities for scrap, shrinkage, yield, etc. and (2) charged or billed to contracts or other COST OBJECTIVEs in a manner consistent with the need to fulfill the plan. DFARS 242.7202. DoD policy requires contractors to have a MATERIAL MANAGEMENT AND ACCOUNTING SYSTEM (MMAS) that reasonably forecasts material requirements, ensures that the costs of purchased and fabricated material charged or allocated to a contract are based on valid time-phased requirements, and maintains a consistent, equitable, and unbiased logic for the costing of material transactions. DFARS 242.7203.

VALUE ENGINEERING (VE) A formal technique by which contractors may (1) voluntarily suggest methods for performing more economically and may share in any resulting savings or (2) be required to establish a program or identify and submit to the Government methods for performing more economically. FAR 48.101(a). VE attempts to eliminate, without impairing essential functions or characteristics, anything that increases acquisition, operation, or support costs. FAR Part 48 contains guidance on VE. The Government encourages VE by including one of the Value Engineering clauses in FAR 52.248-1 through -3 in almost

416

all Government contracts. These clauses contain one of two approaches to submission of VALUE ENGINEERING CHANGE PROPOSALs (VECPs): an incentive or voluntary approach or a mandatory program in which the Government pays for a specific VE effort. In either case, the contractor is motivated to submit VECPs by being paid for INSTANT CONTRACT SAVINGS, CONCURRENT CONTRACT SAVINGS, FUTURE CONTRACT SAVINGS, and COLLATERAL SAVINGS in accordance with the provisions of the specific clause used in the contract. FAR 48.104. See Nash, Government Contract Changes, chap. 9; Rozanski, *The Capital Gain Controversy over VECP Payments in Government Contracts*, 16 Pub. Cont. L.J. 321 (1987).

VALUE ENGINEERING CHANGE PROPOSAL (VECP) A change proposal that (1) requires a change to the INSTANT CONTRACT to implement and (2) results in reducing the overall projected cost to the agency without impairing essential functions or characteristics. FAR 48.001. Not qualifying as VECPs are proposals for changes in quantities of deliverable end items only, proposals for changes in R&D items or test quantities based solely on the results of previous testing, or proposals for changes to contract type only. See Nash, Government Contract Changes, chap. 9.

VARIABLE COSTS Costs of an organization that vary with the amount of work performed. Variable costs are usually contrasted with FIXED COSTS in analyzing a contractor's INDIRECT COSTs. If variable costs are a large percentage of a contractor's indirect costs, the contractor's OVERHEAD RATEs can be expected to decrease more sharply with a decrease in volume of work than would be the case if fixed costs were a large percentage of the contractor's indirect costs.

VARIANCE The amount that a contractor's ACTUAL COSTs deviate from its STANDARD COSTs. See FAR 31.100. Variances are normally recorded for each unit of a contractor's manufacturing operation and are used to compute actual costs and to estimate future costs. They must be allocated at least annually and may be included in INDIRECT COST POOLs if they are immaterial. See Cost Accounting Standard 407, FAR 30.407.

VARIATION IN QUANTITY A variation in the quantity of supplies or services ordered or estimated to be required in the performance of a contract. FAR 12.401 requires the use of the Variation in Quantity clause in FAR 52.212-9 in supply contracts. This clause provides for specified variations in quantity when such variation will meet the needs of the Government. FAR 12.402 requires the use of the Variation in Estimated Quantity clause in FAR 52.212-11 in construction contracts calling for the furnishing of work to be paid for by unit prices. This clause provides for price adjustments if the quantity of actual work varies from the estimated quantity by more than 15 percent. See Cibinic and Nash, Administration of Government Contracts 403–08.

VENDOR A seller of goods. In Government contracting the term vendor is generally used to refer to persons and organizations selling goods to contractors. However, the terms can also mean the person or organization selling to the Government under SMALL PURCHASE PROCEDURES.

VERIFICATION See DUTY OF VERIFICATION.

V-LOAN See GUARANTEED LOAN.

VOLUNTARY DISCLOSURE Agreed-upon contractor identification of improper and illegal practices. Under an agreement between the contractor and the DoD Inspector General, contractors obligate themselves to self-govern by monitoring compliance with Federal procurement laws, adopting procedures for disclosing violations of those laws, and taking corrective action. See ABA, The Department of Defense Voluntary Disclosure Program: A Description of the Process; Kluber, *The Department of Defense Voluntary Disclosure Program*, 19 Pub. Cont. L.J. 504 (Spring 1990); McVey and Lemmer, *Voluntary Disclosure*, 87-6 Briefing Papers (May 1987).

VOLUNTARY REFUND A payment or credit, not required by any contractual or other legal obligation, made to the Government by a contractor or subcontractor either as a payment or as an adjustment under one or more contracts or subcontracts. DFARS 242.7100. It may be unsolicited, or it may be made in response to a request by the Government. In most cases, voluntary refunds are requested after it has been determined that no contractual REMEDY is readily available for the Government to obtain the amount sought from the contractor. Acceptance of a voluntary refund does not prejudice remedies otherwise available to the Government. The refund should generally be used as a SETOFF against a future debt owed to the Government by the contractor, provided the contracting officer determines that the refund relates directly to that debt and the setoff is not prohibited by law or regulation.

VOLUNTARY STANDARD A STANDARD established by a private sector body and available for public use. The term does not include private standards of individual firms. FAR 10.001. See OMB Circular No. A-119 (revised), *Federal Participation in the Development and Use of Voluntary Standards*, 26 Oct. 1982. Such standards may be used to describe supplies or services being procured by the Government.

VOUCHER A document recording a business transaction, such as an expense voucher that records expenses incurred by an employee or in relation to a certain transaction. FAR 4.705-1 requires that financial and cost accounting records such as vouchers be retained by contractors for 4 years.

W

WAGE DETERMINATION A determination of the Department of Labor that a certain scale of WAGES is the prevailing wage in a locality. Wage determinations are issued under the DAVIS-BACON ACT and the SERVICE CONTRACT ACT (SCA) OF 1965 and establish the minimum wages that Government contractors may pay their employees. Under the Davis-Bacon Act, wage determinations are either "general wage determinations"—issued periodically with no expiration date—or "project wage determinations"—issued for a specific project at the request of the procuring agency and expiring in 180 days. Under the Service Contract Act, wage determinations are all issued for specific projects. These wage determinations are requested by use of a NOTICE OF INTENTION TO MAKE A SERVICE CONTRACT, Standard Form 98, FAR 53.301-98.

WAGES Compensation to employees for work. As used in regard to the DAVIS-BACON ACT, wages are the total compensation paid to employees of construction contractors, including the following: basic hourly rate of pay; any contribution irrevocably made by a contractor or subcontractor to a trustee or to a third person pursuant to a bona fide fringe benefit fund, plan, or program; and the rate of costs to the contractor or subcontractor that may be reasonably anticipated in providing bona fide fringe benefits to laborers and mechanics pursuant to an enforceable commitment to carry out a financially responsible plan or program that has been communicated in writing to the affected LABORERS OR MECHAN-ICS. FAR 22.401. These are the elements of the compensation that must meet the minimum wage requirement of the Davis-Bacon Act. The fringe benefits enumerated in the act include medical or hospital care, pensions on retirement or death, compensation for injuries or illness resulting from occupational activity, or insurance to provide any of the foregoing; unemployment benefits; life insurance, disability insurance, sickness insurance, or accident insurance; vacation or holiday pay; costs to defray the expense of apprenticeship or other similar programs; or other bona fide fringe benefits.

WAIVER   The intentional or voluntary relinquishment of a known right, or conduct that warrants an inference that the right has been relinquished.   Waiver entails the renunciation, repudiation, abandonment, or surrender of some claim, right, or privilege, or of the opportunity to take advantage of some defect, irregularity, or wrong. Black's Law Dictionary. If for example, the Government fails within a reasonable period to issue a TERMINATION FOR DEFAULT based on late delivery of supplies, and the contractor relies on the failure to terminate the contract and continues performance, the Government has waived its right to terminate the contract for the contractor's failure to meet the delivery date. See Cibinic and Nash, Administration of Government Contracts 724–38. Waiver of a specification entails written authorization to accept an item that departs from specified requirements but is nevertheless considered suitable either "as is" or after rework by an approved method.   Jones, Glossary: Defense Acquisition Acronyms and Terms.   The parties may also waive contract requirements, such as delivery dates, testing requirements, and performance standards, or may waive potential rights regarding future claims, interest on claims, attorney's fees, appeal, and so forth. See Carberry and Johnstone, *Waiver of the Government's Right to Terminate for Default in Government Defense Contracts*, 17 Pub. Cont. L.J. 470 (1988).

WALSH-HEALEY PUBLIC CONTRACTS ACT A 1936 act, 41 U.S.C. 35–45, requiring that contracts over $10,000 for the manufacture or furnishing of materials, supplies, articles, or equipment (1) be with MANUFACTURERs of or REGULAR DEALERs in (as defined in FAR 22.606) the supplies manufactured or used in performing the contract, and (2) include or incorporate by reference (a) the representation that the contractor is a manufacturer of or a regular dealer in the supplies offered and (b) the stipulations required by the act pertaining to such matters as minimum wages, maximum hours, child labor, convict labor, and safe and sanitary working conditions. FAR 22.602. The Department of Labor does not issue WAGE DETERMINATIONS under this act; all contractors subject to the act must pay the minimum wages specified in the FAIR LABOR STANDARDS ACT (FLSA). The act is implemented by using the Walsh-Healey Public Contracts Act

Representation solicitation provision in FAR 52.222-19 and the Walsh-Healey Public Contracts Act clause in FAR 52.222-20. When a contract subject to the act is awarded, the contracting officer must furnish to the contractor Department of Labor Publication WH-1313, *Notice to Employees Working on Government Contracts*. FAR 22.608-5.

WARNER AMENDMENT A provision, 40 U.S.C. 759(a)(3)(C), incorporated into the BROOKS ACT (AUTOMATIC DATA PROCESSING PROCUREMENTS) at 40 U.S.C. 759(a)(3)(c) by the PAPERWORK REDUCTION REAUTHORIZATION ACT OF 1986. The Warner Amendment makes the Brooks Act inapplicable to DoD procurements of FEDERAL INFORMATION PROCESSING (FIP) RESOURCES or services if (1) the function, operation, or use of the equipment or services involves intelligence activities, cryptologic activities related to national security, command and control of military forces, or equipment that is an integral part of a weapon or weapons system, or if (2) the equipment or service is critical to the direct fulfillment of military or intelligence missions (unless it is used for routine administrative and business applications, such as payroll, finance, logistics, and personnel management).

WARRANT The CONTRACTING OFFICER's (CO's) certificate of authority to enter into, administer, or terminate contracts and make related determinations and findings. COs may bind the Government only to the extent of the authority delegated to them. Information about the limits of the contracting officer's authority must be readily available to the public and to agency personnel. FAR 1.602-1. COs are appointed in writing on a Certificate of Appointment, Standard Form 1402, FAR 53.301-1402, which states any limitation on the scope of authority to be exercised other than limitations contained in applicable laws or regulations. Appointing officials must maintain files containing copies of all Certificates of Appointment that have not been terminated. FAR 1.603-3. See Cibinic and Nash, Formation of Government Contracts 66–69; Bednar and Jones, The DoD Contracting Officer.

WARRANTY A promise or affirmation made by a contractor to the Government regarding the nature, usefulness, or condition of the supplies or services furnished under the contract. FAR 46.701. The principal purpose of a warranty in a Government contract is to relieve the Government of the conclusiveness of ACCEPTANCE OF WORK, which would otherwise preclude it from imposing the liability for PATENT DEFECTs on the contractor. Other purposes of warranties are to delineate the rights and obligations of the contractor and the Government for defective items and services and to foster quality performance. Generally, a warranty should provide a contractual right to correction of defects, notwithstanding any other contract requirement pertaining to Government acceptance of the supplies or services. It should also specifically state the period of time after acceptance during which the Government may assert its right to have defects corrected. The benefits to be derived from a warranty must be commensurate with the cost of the warranty to the Government. FAR 46.702. In determining whether a warranty is appropriate for a specific acquisition, the contracting officer considers (1) the nature and use of the supplies or services, (2) warranty cost, (3) the feasibility of administration and enforcement, (4) whether warranty is customary in the trade, and (5) whether warranty costs can be offset by reduced QUALITY ASSURANCE (QA) requirements. FAR 46.703. In DoD, the chief of the contracting office must approve the use of a warranty, with certain exceptions. See DFARS 246.704. Standard warranty clauses are included in FAR 52.246-17 through -21. See Cibinic and Nash, Administration of Government Contracts 649–66; Kopf, *Warranties and Commercial Supply Contracts: A Need for Definitive Rules*, 17 Pub. Cont. L.J. 534 (1988).

WEIGHTED GUIDELINES METHOD DoD's structured technique for establishing the contracting officer's negotiating position on PROFIT. See DFARS Subpart 215.9. The technique is also used as a basis for documenting and explaining the final pricing agreement reached between buyer and seller. The weighted guidelines method ensures consideration of the relative value of appropriate profit factors, including the contractor's degree of performance risk, the risk imposed on the contractor by the type of contract, facilities investment, and working capital. DFARS 215.971-1. The contracting officer uses DD Form 1547, Record of Weighted Guidelines Application, DFARS 253.303-1547, in computing profit. See DFARS 215.970. FAR 15.902 requires other agencies to have a structured system similar to the weighted guidelines method, including the profit factors discussed in FAR 15.905 (which are somewhat different from the DoD factors). DoE provides extensive guidance on its weighted guidelines at DEAR 915.970-2. See Brunsman, *Subcontracting Made Easy: Coping with the New Weighted Guidelines*, 25 Cont. Mgmt. 36

(May 1988); Nash, *Adverse Effects of New DoD Profit Policy*, 1 N&CR ¶ 3 (Jan. 1987).

WHISTLEBLOWER An employee who discloses to an outside person or entity an activity by his or her employer that the employee characterizes as illegal, immoral, or otherwise improper. The Defense Acquisition Improvement Act of 1986 provides that no one may be discharged, demoted, or otherwise discriminated against as a reprisal for disclosing to a member of Congress, or to an authorized DoD or Department of Justice official, information about a substantial violation of law related to a defense contract. 10 U.S.C. 2409. Other statutes permit a whistleblower who has been discharged, demoted, or otherwise discriminated against as a reprisal for such disclosure to seek reinstatement, an award of twice the applicable back pay plus interest, and compensation for special damages, including litigation costs and attorney's fees. See Seyfarth et al., The Government Contract Compliance Handbook 3-7.

WITHHOLDING The nonpayment of contract amounts by the contracting officer because the contractor failed to carry out some obligation under the contract. This term is sometimes used more broadly to denote SETOFF: the nonpayment of contract amounts because of debts of the contractor outside of the contract. Withholding is permitted by a number of contract clauses such as the Withholding of Funds clause in FAR 52.222-7, under which the Government may withhold funds necessary to pay contractor employees the full amount of wages required by the contract. However, withholding is a general right of the Government, even without such a clause. The amount withheld should be commensurate with the anticipated amount of damage the Government will suffer as a result of the nonperformance. See Nash, *Government Withholding of Payment: Handle with Care*, 3 N&CR ¶ 51 (July 1989).

WOMEN-OWNED SMALL BUSINESSES SMALL BUSINESS CONCERNs that are at least 51 percent owned by women who are U.S. citizens and who also control and operate the business. FAR 52.219-13. FAR 19.901 states that, in response to the need to aid and stimulate women's business enterprises, Executive Order 12138, 18 May 1979, directs agencies to take appropriate action to facilitate, preserve, and strengthen women's business enterprises and to ensure full participation by women in the free enterprise system. Appropriate action includes the award of subcontracts under Federal PRIME CONTRACTs. Contracting officers must insert in most contracts the Utilization of Women-Owned Small Businesses clause in FAR 52.219-13. Contractors must use their "best efforts" to provide women-owned small businesses the maximum opportunity to participate in SUBCONTRACTs. The Women's Business Ownership Act of 1988, 15 U.S.C. 631(h), makes an affirmative finding of discrimination in entrepreneurial endeavors based on gender and establishes a National Women's Business Council. The Council will make annual recommendations to Congress and the President.

WORK BREAKDOWN STRUCTURE (WBS) A graphic display of a contract's STATEMENT OF WORK (SOW) or an organizational chart depicting the necessary hardware, software, and services required in contract performance, and their relationship to each other. A WBS subdivides the work to be performed under a contract into logical segments in order to help track progress and performance cost. MIL-STD-881A, paragraph 3.4, defines a WBS as a product-oriented family tree (composed of hardware, services, and data) that results from project engineering efforts during the development and production of a defense material item and completely defines the project or program. A WBS displays and defines the products to be developed or produced under the contract and relates the elements of work to be accomplished to each other and to the end product. WBSs are required as a part of a COST/SCHEDULE CONTROL SYSTEM used to manage major contracts. See DFARS 234.005-70 and Part 6B of DoD Instruction 5000.2, *Defense Acquisition Management Policies and Procedures*, 23 Feb. 1991. And see Grskovich, *What is C/SCSC?—In English, Please!* 23 NCMJ 25 (1990); Dominic, *Understanding the C/SSR*, 30 Cont. Mgmt. 8 (Nov. 1990).

WORKERS ADJUSTMENT AND RETRAINING NOTIFICATION (WARN) ACT An act, 29 U.S.C. 2101 *et seq.*, that provides that employers must give employees advance warning of plant closings or mass layoffs. Implementation of the act requires no action by Government contracting activities; however, the act might apply to some contracts (such as on-site support service contracts), and some of the costs of a contractor's noncompliance with the act could be subject to reimbursement by the Government. NFS 18-22.101-72.

WORK-IN-PROCESS Material that has been released to manufacturing, engineering, design, or other services under the contract and includes undelivered manufactured parts, assemblies, and products, either complete or incomplete. FAR 45.501. FAR 45.505-3 requires contractors to keep records of such material.

WORKSHOP FOR THE BLIND OR OTHER SEVERELY HANDICAPPED A qualified nonprofit agency for the BLIND AND OTHER SEVERELY HANDICAPPED approved by the Committee for the Purchase from the Blind and Other Severely Handicapped, an independent Government activity with members appointed by the President, to produce a commodity for or provide a service to the Government under the act. FAR 8.701. Such workshops are given preference for some procurements in accordance with the procedures in FAR Subpart 8.7.

WORK STATEMENT The part of a RESEARCH AND DEVELOPMENT (R&D) contract that describes the work to be performed by the contractor. FAR 35.005 provides that in such contracts, a clear and complete work statement concerning the area of exploration (for BASIC RESEARCH) or the end objectives (for DEVELOPMENT and APPLIED RESEARCH) is essential. The work statement should allow contractors to be innovative and creative; it must be individually tailored by technical and contracting personnel for this purpose. In basic research, the emphasis is on achieving specified objectives and knowledge rather than achieving predetermined end results prescribed in a statement of specific performance characteristics. In reviewing work statements, contracting officers should ensure that language suitable for a level-of-effort approach is not intermingled with language suitable for a task-completion approach. A level-of-effort approach requires the furnishing of technical effort and a report on the results; a task-completion approach often requires the development of a tangible end item designed to achieve specific performance characteristics. The wording of the work statement should also be consistent with the type and form of contract to be negotiated. See also STATEMENT OF WORK (SOW).

WRITTEN OR ORAL DISCUSSIONS See DISCUSSION.

WUNDERLICH ACT A 1954 act, 41 U.S.C. 321–322, that precluded contract clauses from preventing judicial review of agency decisions on DISPUTEs. The act codified the "arbitrary and capricious" standard of review for administrative decisions and permitted the courts to overrule administrative decisions that were not supported by "substantial evidence." The act also provided that contractors could bargain away their right to full-scale judicial review of administrative decisions on questions of law. The purpose of the legislation was to overcome the effect of the Supreme Court decision in the case of *United States v. Wunderlich*, 342 U.S. 98 (1951), under which the decisions of Government officers rendered pursuant to the Disputes clause were held to be final in the absence of fraud on the part of the Government officers. The act has been subsumed by the CONTRACT DISPUTES ACT (CDA) OF 1978, which incorporates judicial review of agency decisions in the DISPUTEs process. See Gantt and Roberts, *Wunderlich Act Review in the Court of Claims under Bianchi, Utah, and Grace*, 3 Pub. Cont. L.J. 1 (1970).

Acronyms and Abbreviations Used in This Reference Book

The acronyms and abbreviations in this listing are alphabetized using the letter-by-letter method described in *How to Use This Reference Book* on page xi. This method ignores spaces and punctuation marks. *D.C. Cir.*, for example, is read *DCCIR*; as such, it follows *DCAS* and precedes *DCMC* in the listing. Numbers within acronyms and abbreviations are spelled out; thus, *A-76* is alphabetized as *ASEVENTYSIX*, following *ASCE* and preceding *ASPA*.

ABA	American Bar Association
ACO	Administrative Contracting Officer
ACRN	Accounting Classification Reference Number
ACWP	Actual Cost of Work Performed
ADP	Automatic Data Processing
ADPE	Automatic Data Processing Equipment
ADPE/DS	Automatic Data Processing Equipment/Data System
ADR	Alternative Dispute Resolution
A-E	Architect-Engineer
AECA	Arms Export Control Act
AGC	Associated General Contractors of America
AIA	Aerospace Industries Association of America
AIA	American Institute of Architects
AO	Announcement of Opportunity

APR	Agency Procurement Request
ASA	American Subcontractors Association
ASBCA	Armed Services Board of Contract Appeals
ASCE	American Society of Civil Engineers
A-76	OMB Circular No. A-76
ASPA	Armed Services Procurement Act
ASPM	Armed Services Pricing Manual
ASPR	Armed Services Procurement Regulation
BAA	Broad Agency Announcement
BAFO	Best and Final Offer
BCA	Board of Contract Appeals
BCWP	Budgeted Cost of Work Performed
BCWS	Budgeted Cost of Work Scheduled
BOA	Basic Ordering Agreement
B&P	Bid and Proposal
BPA	Blanket Purchase Agreement
BPCR	Breakout Procurement Center Representative
CAAC	Civilian Agency Acquisition Council
CAAS	Contracted Advisory and Assistance Services
CACO	Corporate Administrative Contracting Officer
CAFC	Court of Appeals for the Federal Circuit
CAM	Contract Audit Manual
CAS	Cost Accounting Standards
CBD	Commerce Business Daily
CCASS	Construction Contractor Appraisal Support System
CCDR	Contractor Cost Data Reporting
CDA	Contract Disputes Act of 1978
CDRL	Contract Data Requirements List
CFR	Code of Federal Regulations
CICA	Competition in Contracting Act

CID	Commercial Item Description
CIPR	Contract Insurance/Pension Review
Cl. Ct.	Claims Court
CLIN	Contract Line Item Number
CMAA	Construction Management Association of America
CMF	Cost of Money Factors
CO	Contracting Officer
COC	Certificate of Competency
COGP	Commission on Government Procurement
Comp. Gen.	Comptroller General
COMSEC	Communications Security
COR	Contracting Officer Representative
COTR	Contracting Officer Technical Representative
CPAF	Cost-Plus-Award Fee
CPCM	Certified Professional Contracts Manager
CPFF	Cost-Plus-Fixed Fee
CPIF	Cost-Plus-Incentive Fee
CPM	Critical Path Method
CPPC	Cost-Plus-a-Percentage-of-Cost
CPSR	Contractor Purchasing System Review
CRADA	Cooperative Research and Development Agreement
CRAG	Contractor Risk Assessment Guide
C/SCSC	Cost/Schedule Control Systems Criteria
C/SSR	Cost/Schedule Status Report
Ct. Cl.	Court of Claims
CWAS	Contractor Weighted Average Share
CWHSSA	Contract Work Hours and Safety Standards Act
DAB	Defense Acquisition Board
DAC	Defense Acquisition Circular
DAE	Defense Acquisition Executive

DAR	Defense Acquisition Regulation
DAR Council	Defense Acquisition Regulatory Council
DCAA	Defense Contract Audit Agency
DCAM	Defense Contract Audit Manual
DCAS	Defense Contract Administration Service
D.C. Cir.	Court of Appeals for the District of Columbia Circuit
DCMC	Defense Contract Management Command
DEAR	Department of Energy Acquisition Regulation
D&F	Determination and Findings
DFARS	Department of Defense FAR Supplement
DID	Data Item Description
DIPEC	Defense Industrial Plant Equipment Center
DLA	Defense Logistics Agency
DLSSO	Defense Logistics Standard Systems Office
DO	Disbursing Officer
DoD	Department of Defense
DoDD	DoD Directive
DODISS	Department of Defense Index of Specifications and Standards
DoE	Department of Energy
DPA	Delegation of Procurement Authority
DPAS	Defense Priorities and Allocations System
DSMC	Defense Systems Management College
DT&E	Developmental Test and Evaluation
DTIC	Defense Technical Information Center
EAJA	Equal Access to Justice Act
ECP	Engineering Change Proposal
EEO	Equal Employment Opportunity
EIA	Electronics Industries Association
EOQ	Economic Order Quantity
EPA	Economic Price Adjustment

ESOP	Employee Stock Ownership Plan
FAC	Federal Acquisition Circular
FAI	Federal Acquisition Institute
FAR	Federal Acquisition Regulation
FASB	Financial Accounting Standards Board
FAX	Facsimile
FCC	Federal Communications Commission
FCCM	Facilities Capital Cost of Money
FCIA	Federal Courts Improvement Act
FDPC	Federal Data Processing Center
Fed. Cir.	Court of Appeals for the Federal Circuit
FED-STDS	Federal Telecommunications Standards
FEMA	Federal Emergency Management Agency
FFP	Firm Fixed Price
FFRDC	Federally Funded Research and Development Center
FIP	Federal Information Processing
FIPS PUBS	Federal Information Processing Standards Publications
FIRMR	Federal Information Resources Management Regulation
FLC	Federal Laboratory Consortium for Technology Transfer
FLSA	Fair Labor Standards Act
FMS	Foreign Military Sales
FOCI	Foreign Ownership, Control, or Influence
FOIA	Freedom of Information Act
FPASA	Federal Property and Administrative Services Act of 1949
FPDC	Federal Procurement Data Center
FPDS	Federal Procurement Data System
FPI	Fixed-Price Incentive
FPMR	Federal Property Management Regulation

FPR	Federal Procurement Regulations
FPRA	Forward Pricing Rate Agreement
FPRP	Fixed-Price Redetermination—Prospective
FPRR	Fixed-Price Redetermination—Retroactive
FSC	Federal Supply Class
FSEC	Federal Software Exchange Center
F.2d	Federal Reporter Second Series (e.g., 614 F.2d 740)
FSED	Full-Scale Engineering Development
FSEP	Federal Software Exchange Program
FSS	Federal Supply Schedule
FTCA	Federal Tort Claims Act
FTS	Federal Telecommunications System
FY	Fiscal Year
G&A	General and Administrative
GAAP	Generally Accepted Accounting Principles
GAO	General Accounting Office
GBL	Government Bill of Lading
GFM	Government-Furnished Material
GFP	Government-Furnished Property
GOCO	Government-Owned, Contractor-Operated Plant
GPLR	Government-Purpose License Rights
GPO	Government Printing Office
GSA	General Services Administration
GSBCA	General Services Administration Board of Contract Appeals
HBCU	Historically Black College or University
HCA	Head of the Contracting Activity
IFB	Invitation for Bids
IG	Inspector General
IMIP	Industrial Modernization Incentives Program
INFOSEC	Information Systems Security

IPE	Industrial Plant Equipment
IR&D	Independent Research and Development
IRM	Information Resources Management
ITF	Information Technology Fund
IWA	Interdivisional Work Authorization
IWO	Interdivisional Work Order
L-H	Labor-Hour
LOA	Letter of Offer and Acceptance
LOC	Limitation of Cost
LOF	Limitation of Funds
LOR	Letter of Request
LSA	Labor Surplus Area
LTD	Live Test Demonstration
MAS	Multiple-Award Schedule
MI	Minority Institution
MIL-SPEC	Military Specification
MIL-STD	Military Standard
MILSTRIP	Military Standard Requisitioning and Issue Procedure
MIRR	Material Inspection and Receiving Report
MMAS	Material Management and Accounting System
M&O	Management and Operating
MOU	Memorandum of Understanding
MPC	Model Procurement Code
MRP	Material Requirements Planning
NAFI	Nonappropriated Funds Instrumentality
NASA	National Aeronautics and Space Administration
NASABCA	National Aeronautics and Space Administration Board of Contract Appeals
NCMA	National Contract Management Association
NDI	Nondevelopmental Item
NFS	NASA FAR Supplement

NFSD	NASA FAR Supplement Directive
NHB	NASA Handbook
NIST	National Institute of Standards and Technology
NMI	NASA Management Instruction
NPR	NASA Procurement Regulation
NRA	NASA Research Announcement
NRC	Nuclear Regulatory Commission
NSF	National Science Foundation
NSIA	National Security Industrial Association
NTIS	National Technical Information Service
OCD	Operational Capability Demonstration
OCI	Organizational Conflict of Interest
OF	Optional Form
OFPP	Office of Federal Procurement Policy
OGE	Office of Government Ethics
OIRA	Office of Industrial Resource Administration
OMB	Office of Management and Budget
OPE	Other Plant Equipment
OPM	Office of Personnel Management
ORTA	Office of Research and Technology Application
OSD	Office of the Secretary of Defense
OT&E	Operational Test and Evaluation
PASS	Procurement Automated Source System
PAT&E	Production Acceptance Test and Evaluation
PCO	Procuring Contracting Officer
PCR	Procurement Center Representative
PEO	Program Executive Officer
PII	Procurement Instrument Identification
PM	Program Manager, Project Manager
PN	Procurement Notice
PO	Purchase Order

PON	Program Opportunity Notice
PPA	Prompt Payment Act
PRDA	Program Research and Development Announcement
PSR	Productivity Savings Reward
QA	Quality Assurance
QBL	Qualified Bidders List
QC	Quality Control
QML	Qualified Manufacturers List
QPL	Qualified Products List
RCO	Remedy Coordination Official
RCRA	Resource Conservation and Recovery Act
R&D	Research and Development
RDT&E	Research, Development, Test, and Evaluation
REA	Request for Equitable Adjustment
RFP	Request for Proposals
RFQ	Request for Quotations
RFTP	Request for Technical Proposals
RICO	Racketeer Influenced and Corrupt Organization
RIE	Range of Incentive Effectiveness
ROA	Research Opportunity Announcement
RTE	Remote Terminal Emulation
SADBUS	Small and Disadvantaged Business Utilization Specialist
SAIP	Spares Acquisition Integrated with Production
SAR	Selected Acquisition Report
SBA	Small Business Administration
SCA	Service Contract Act of 1965
SDBC	Small Disadvantaged Business Concern
SDR	Special Drawing Right
SF	Standard Form
SFRC	Short Form Research Contract

SIC	Standard Industrial Classification
SOW	Statement of Work
SPICE	Simplified Procurement in a Competitive Environment
SRC	Special Research Contract
SSA	Source Selection Authority
SSAC	Source Selection Advisory Council
SSB	Source Selection Board
SSEB	Source Selection Evaluation Board
SSO	Source Selection Official
TCO	Termination Contracting Officer
T&E	Test and Evaluation
TINA	Truth in Negotiations Act
TQM	Total Quality Management
U.C.C.	Uniform Commercial Code
U.S.	United States (Supreme Court) Reports (e.g., 450 U.S. 785)
U.S.C.	United States Code
U.S.C.A.	United States Code Annotated
U.S.C.S.	United States Code Service
VE	Value Engineering
VECP	Value Engineering Change Proposal
WBS	Work Breakdown Structure

Texts Cited in This Reference Book

Administration of Government Contracts. 2d ed. John Cibinic, Jr., and Ralph C. Nash, Jr. Washington, D.C.: The George Washington University Government Contracts Program, 1985.

The Antitrust Government Contracts Handbook. William Kovacic. Chicago: American Bar Association, Section of Antitrust Law, 1990.

Armed Services Pricing Manual (ASPM). Vol. 1: Contract Pricing. Vol. 2: Price Analysis. Department of Defense. Chicago: Commerce Clearing House, Inc., 1986 (vol. 1) and 1987 (vol. 2).

Ballentine's Law Dictionary. 3d ed. Rochester, New York: The Lawyers Cooperative Publishing Company, 1969.

Barron's Finance and Investment Handbook. 2d ed. John Downes and Jordan Elliott Goodman. New York: Barron's Educational Series, Inc., 1987.

Black's Law Dictionary. 6th ed. St. Paul, Minnesota: West Publishing Co., 1990.

Construction Contracting. Richard J. Bednar (chapters 10 and 13), Herman M. Braude (chapters 7, 9, and 15), John Cibinic, Jr. (chapters 5 and 9), Gilbert J. Ginsburg (chapters 2 and 16), J. Richard Margulies (chapters 8, 11, and 14), Ralph C. Nash, Jr. (chapters 1, 6, and 12), Douglas L. Patin (chapters 2, 4, 16, 17, and 18), and Andrew W. Stephenson (chapter 3). Washington, D.C.: The George Washington University Government Contracts Program, 1991.

Cost Reimbursement Contracting. 2d ed. John Cibinic, Jr., and Ralph C. Nash, Jr. Washington, D.C.: The George Washington University Government Contracts Program, 1981. (New edition to be available Summer 1992.)

440

A Current Guide to Cost Recovery under the Equal Access to Justice Act. Donald J. Kinlin. Chicago: American Bar Association, Section of Public Contract Law, 1989.

DCAA Contract Audit Manual (CAM). 2 vols. Defense Contract Audit Agency. Washington, D.C.: U.S. Government Printing Office, 1992.

The Department of Defense Voluntary Disclosure Program: A Description of the Process. Department of Defense Inspector General. Chicago: American Bar Association, Section of Public Contract Law, 1988.

Dictionary of Banking and Finance. Jerry M. Rosenberg. New York: John Wiley & Sons, 1982.

The DoD Contracting Officer. Richard J. Bednar and John T. Jones, Jr. Chicago: American Bar Association, Section of Public Contract Law, 1987.

The Dollars and Sense of Government Contract Funding. William Alton Hill, Jr. Chicago: American Bar Association, Section of Public Contract Law, 1988.

Federal Contracts, Grants and Assistance. 3 vols. Dennis J. Riley. Colorado Springs, Colorado: Shephard's/McGraw-Hill, 1983.

Federal Grants and Cooperative Agreements. Vol. I. Richard B. Cappalli. Wilmette, Illinois: Callaghan & Company, 1982 (as supplemented).

Federal Procurement Law. 3d ed. Vol. I: Contract Formation. Vol. II: Contract Performance. Ralph C. Nash, Jr., and John Cibinic, Jr. Washington, D.C.: The George Washington University Government Contracts Program, 1977 (vol. I) and 1980 (vol. II).

Formation of Government Contracts. 2d ed. John Cibinic, Jr. and Ralph C. Nash, Jr. Washington, D.C.: The George Washington University Government Contracts Program, 1986.

Glossary: Defense Acquisition Acronyms and Terms. 2d ed. Wilbur D. Jones, Jr. Fort Belvoir, Virginia: Defense Systems Management College, 1987.

Government Contract Bidding. 3d ed. Paul Shnitzer. Washington, D.C.: Federal Publications Inc., 1987 (1991 supplement).

Government Contract Changes. 2d ed. Ralph C. Nash, Jr. Washington, D.C.: Federal Publications Inc., 1989 (1991 supplement).

The Government Contract Compliance Handbook. Seyfarth, Shaw, Fairweather, and Geraldson (Government Contracts Group). Washington, D.C.: Federal Publications Inc., 1988.

Government Contract Default Termination. Walter F. Pettit, Carl L. Vacketta, and David V. Anthony. Washington, D.C.: Federal Publications Inc., 1991.

Government Contract Disputes. 2d ed. Peter S. Latham. Washington, D.C.: Federal Publications Inc., 1986 (1991 supplement).

Government Contracts under the Federal Acquisition Regulation. W. Noel Keyes. St. Paul, Minnesota: West Publishing Co., 1986.

Handbook of Governmental Accounting and Finance. Nicholas G. Apostolou and D. Larry Crumbley. New York: J. Wiley & Sons, 1988.

How to Review a Federal Contract and Research Federal Contract Law. James F. Nagle. Chicago: American Bar Association, Section of General Practice, 1990.

Interest and Federal Contracts: A Perspective. James W. Booth. Chicago: Arthur Anderson, 1982.

Litigation under the Federal Freedom of Information and Privacy Act. 15th ed. Allen Adler, editor. Washington, D.C.: American Civil Liberties Union, 1990.

Living with TINA: A Practical Guide to the Truth in Negotiations Act. Clarence T. Kipps, Jr., and John Lloyd Rice. Washington, D.C.: Washington Legal Foundation, 1988.

Manual for Practice Before the Boards of Contract Appeals. Washington, D.C.: Federal Bar Association (Boards of Contract Appeals Committee), 1981.

Murray on Contracts. 3d ed. John Edward Murray, Jr. Charlottesville, Virginia: Michie Co., 1990 (as supplemented).

Patents and Technical Data. Ralph C. Nash, Jr., and Leonard Rawicz. Washington, D.C.: The George Washington University Government Contracts Program, 1983.

Personal Conflicts of Interest in Government Contracting. L. James D'Agostino, James R. Humphries, and James W. Taylor. Chicago: American Bar Association, Section of Public Contract Law, 1988.

Principles of Federal Appropriations Law. 2d ed. 4 vols. U.S. General Accounting Office. Washington, D.C.: Government Printing Office, 1991. *(Editor's note: At press time, this second edition was still being prepared for publication. Citations in this book are therefore to chapters rather than to specific pages. See also the first (1982) edition.)*

Program Manager's Notebook. 2d ed. Fort Belvoir, Virginia: Defense Systems Management College, 1989.

The Protest Experience under the Competition in Contracting Act. Chicago: American Bar Association, Section of Public Contract Law, 1989.

Records Retention Procedures: Your Guide to Determining How Long to Keep Your Records and How to Safely Destroy Them. Donald S. Skupsky. Denver, Colorado: Information Requirements Clearinghouse, 1990.

Restatement (Second) of Contracts. 3 vols. St. Paul, Minnesota: American Law Institute, 1981 (as supplemented).

The Revised Procurement Integrity Statute and Regulations. Michael D. Gerich, Stephen M. Ryan, and James W. Taylor. Vienna, Virginia: National Contract Management Association, 1990.

Sourcebook: Federal Agency Use of Alternative Means of Dispute Resolution. Marguerite S. Millhauser. Washington, D.C.: Administrative Conference of the United States (Office of the Chairman), 1987.

Source Selection. John Cibinic, Jr., Ralph C. Nash, Jr., Steven Schooner, and Richard J. Bednar. Vienna, Virginia: National Contract Management Association, 1988.

Specifications and Standards: Training Manual. Vienna, Virginia: National Contract Management Association, 1984.

Study of Professional Services Contracting. Washington, D.C.: Office of Federal Procurement Policy, 1985.

Subcontracts—Government and Industry Issues. Donald L. Brechtel and H. Philip Marks. Vienna, Virginia: National Contract Management Association, 1989.

Total Quality Control. 3d ed. Armand V. Feigenbaum. New York: McGraw-Hill, 1991.

United States Government Manual. Washington, D.C.: Government Printing Office, 1991–1992.

Williston on Contracts. 3d ed. Rochester: The Lawyers Cooperative Publishing Company, 1970 (as supplemented).

Periodicals Cited in This Reference Book

Admin. L.J.

Administrative Law Journal. Published three times a year by The American University, 4400 Massachusetts Avenue, N.W., Washington, DC 20016. (202) 885-3412.

A.F. L. Rev.

The Air Force Law Review. Published semi-annually by the Air Force Judge Advocate General School (CPD/JAL), Maxwell Air Force Base, AL 36112-5712. Available for purchase from the U.S. Government Printing Office, Washington, DC 20402. (202) 783-3238.

Antitrust Bull.

Antitrust Bulletin. Published quarterly by Federal Legal Publications Inc., 157 Charles Street, New York, NY 10007. (212) 619-4949.

Army Law.

Army Lawyer. Published monthly by the Judge Advocate General's School, United States Army, Charlottesville, VA 22903-1781. (804) 972-6306.

Briefing Papers

Briefing Papers. Published monthly (except January—twice monthly) by Federal Publications Inc., 1120 20th Street, N.W., Washington, DC 20036. (202) 337-7000.

Caveat Emptor

Caveat Emptor Consumer Report. Published monthly (except October) by Consumer Education Research Group, Consumer Center, 350 Scotland Road, Orange, NJ 07050. (201) 676-6663.

Constr. Briefings	*Construction Briefings*. Published monthly (except January—twice monthly) by Federal Publications Inc., 1120 20th Street, N.W., Washington, DC 20036. (202) 337-7000.
Constr. Law.	*Construction Lawyer*. Published quarterly by the American Bar Association, 750 North Lake Shore Drive, Chicago, IL 60611. (312) 988-5580.
Cont. Mgmt.	*Contract Management*. Published monthly by the National Contract Management Association, 1912 Woodford Road, Vienna, VA 22182. (703) 448-9231.
CP&AR	*Government Contract Costs, Pricing & Accounting Report*. Published monthly by Federal Publications Inc., 1120 20th Street, N.W., Washington, DC 20036. 202 337-7000.
Denver L.J.	*Denver University Law Journal* (now *Denver University Law Review*). Published quarterly by the University of Denver College of Law, 1900 Olive Street, Denver, CO 80220. (303) 871-6172.
Duq. L. Rev.	*Duquesne Law Review*. Published quarterly by the Duquesne University Law School, 132 Edward J. Hanley Hall, Pittsburgh, PA 15282. (412) 434-6300.
Employee Rel. L.J.	*Employee Relations Law Journal*. Published quarterly by Executive Enterprises Publishing Co. Inc., 22 West 21st Street, 10th floor, New York, NY 10010-6904. 1-800-332-8804; (212) 645-7880, ext. 208.
Fed. B. News & J.	*Federal Bar News & Journal*. Published 10 times a year by the Federal Bar Association, 1815 H Street, N.W., Suite 408, Washington, DC 20006-3697. (202) 638-0252.
Fed. Cont. Rep.	*Federal Contracts Report*. Published weekly by The Bureau of National Affairs, Inc., 1231 25th Street, N.W., Washington, DC 20037. (202) 452-4383.

Geo. Mason U. L. Rev.	*George Mason University Law Review.* Published 3 times a year by the George Mason University School of Law, 3401 North Fairfax Drive, Arlington, VA 22201. (703) 993-8148.
Geo. Wash. J. Int'l L. & Econ.	*George Washington University Journal of International Law and Economics.* Published 3 times a year by The George Washington University, National Law Center, 716 20th Street, N.W., Washington, DC 20052. (202) 994-7161.
Gov't Executive	*Government Executive.* Published monthly by National Journal, Inc., 1730 M Street, N.W., 11th floor, Washington, DC 20036. (202) 857-1400.
Inspector Gen. Rep.	*Inspector General Reports.* Issued by the Office of Inspector General, Department of Defense, 400 Army-Navy Drive, Arlington, VA 22202. (703) 693-0340.
N&CR	*The Nash & Cibinic Report.* Published monthly by Keiser Enterprises Inc., Room 309, 2828 Pennsylvania Avenue, N.W., Washington, DC 20007. (202) 337-1000.
NCMJ	*National Contract Management Journal.* Published semiannually by the National Contract Management Association, 1912 Woodford Road, Vienna, VA 22182. (703) 448-9231.
Pub. Cont. L.J.	*Public Contract Law Journal.* Published quarterly by the Section of Public Contract Law, American Bar Association, 750 North Lake Shore Drive, Chicago, IL 60611. (312) 988-5555.
Pub. Cont. Newsl.	*Public Contract Newsletter.* Published quarterly by the Section of Public Contract Law, American Bar Association, 750 North Lake Shore Drive, Chicago, IL 60611. (312) 988-5555.
Rutgers Computer Tech. L.J.	*Rutgers Computer Technology Law Journal.* Published semiannually by the Rutgers University Law School, 15 Washington Street, Newark, NJ 07102. (201) 648-5549.

A Note to Our Readers

*Dictionaries are like watches; the worst is better than
none, and the best cannot be expected to go quite true.*
—Samuel Johnson

We suspect that the old lexicographer knew what he was talking
about. In this dictionary-style reference book, we've aimed to give
you the best—currency, accuracy, consistency, astuteness, lucidity.
But constant change in the Government contracting arena has made
ours a moving target. And, given the range of subjects and disciplines
treated, some entries may have fallen short of the mark.

We welcome your suggestions of terms to be included in the next,
expanded edition—and any other suggestions you may have. Address
your comments to:

Joan Phillips, Editor in Chief
GW—Government Contracts Program
2100 Pennsylvania Avenue, N.W., Suite 250
Washington, DC 20037-3202

Or fax them to the Government Contracts Program at (202) 223-1387.

Publications

Government Contracts Program
National Law Center
The George Washington University

Formation of Government Contracts (2d ed., 1986). *John Cibinic, Jr., and Ralph C. Nash, Jr.* Reference edition: Hardbound with tables, xxiv + 1,171 pp. Student edition: Softcover without tables, xxiv + 1,046 pp.

> Acclaimed as a classic, this indispensable text provides a comprehensive overview of the principles and procedures governing the formation of government contracts. Chapters cover the legal rules of contracting, types of Federal contracts, responsibility determinations, suspension and debarment, sealed bidding procedures, two-step sealed bidding, competitive negotiation policies and practices, competition in contracting, pricing techniques, socioeconomic policies, and protests and mistakes.

Administration of Government Contracts (2d ed., 1985). *John Cibinic, Jr., and Ralph C. Nash, Jr.* Reference edition: Hardbound with tables, xxvi + 1,184 pp. Student edition: Softcover without tables, xxvi + 1,025 pp.

> This companion volume to *Formation of Government Contracts* covers the substantive issues that arise most frequently between the parties during performance of government contracts. Topics include the role of the contracting officer; rules and principles of contract interpretation; risk allocation principles and rights of parties to the contract; the government's implied warranties and duties; impracticability of performance and mutual mistake—doctrines and defenses; pricing of equitable adjustments; interpretations of major clauses—Changes, Differing Site Conditions, Suspension of Work, Default, Inspection, and Termination for Convenience; payment problems; and disputes resolution—the Contract Disputes Act of 1978.

Cost Reimbursement Contracting (2d ed., available Summer 1992). *John Cibinic, Jr., and Ralph C. Nash, Jr.*

> This authoritative text, first published in 1981, is undergoing a major revision to update and expand its coverage of the special issues surrounding the formation and administration of cost-reimbursement contracts. Topics will include the power to contract, authority of government agents, principles governing the use of cost-type contracts, types of cost-reimbursement contracts, negotiating and awarding cost-type contracts, cost accounting and allowability of costs, and administration of cost-type contracts.

Construction Contracting (1991). *Richard J. Bednar, et al.* Hardbound in two volumes, vli + 1,773 pp.

> This timely text fills a dramatic void in the reference literature on construction contract law, for contracting professionals and legal practitioners alike. Prepared by eight leading authorities in the field, the book presents definitive treatments of all major areas of the construction contracting process, including award controversies; subcontract formation; differing site conditions; labor relations; architect-engineer liability; changes and claims; disputes; cost recovery principles; bonds, liens, and insurance; and alternative dispute resolution. Not limited in scope to Federal contracting, *Construction Contracting* gives equal attention to contracting with state and local governments and to contracts between private parties. A detailed subject index allows readers to quickly locate particular topics. Citation indexes provide easy access to relevant discussions of pertinent statutes, regulations, case law, Comptroller General decisions, and board opinions.

Suspension and Debarment (1992). *Alan M. Grayson.* 85 pp.

> This text provides an indispensable, step-by-step review of Federal suspension and debarment procedures, from initiation through decision and judicial review. A detailed discussion of the regulations governing bases for debarment, the burden of proof, the opportunity to be heard, and the exact effect of the decision to debar is augmented by practical evaluation of the various legal themes and strategies that contractors employ to contest these actions.

Patents and Technical Data (1983). *Ralph C. Nash, Jr., and Leonard Rawicz.* xviii + 672 pp.

This text is a comprehensive guide to the rights that the government obtains to patents and technical data (including computer software) in the course of Federal procurement. Topics include the uses the government makes of such patents and data; litigation issues that arise in resolving disputes over rights; principles of patent law, copyright law, and trade secret law as they apply to litigation; and application of the Freedom of Information Act. Of special value is the detailed discussion of Federal contract clauses and regulations pertinent to rights in patents and technical data.

Patents and Technical Data—Regulations Supplement (1992). *Leonard Rawicz,* Editor. 600 pp.

This companion course manual to *Patents and Technical Data* includes the most current information available on legal and regulatory developments, Federal policies, and court and board decisions affecting patents and data rights.

Federal Procurement Law *John Cibinic, Jr., and Ralph C. Nash, Jr.* Volume I: Contract Formation (3d ed., 1977, viii + 938 pp.). Volume II: Contract Performance (3d ed., 1980, viii + 1,479 pp.).

This two-volume casebook provides a definitive account of the evolution of the body of law governing Federal contract formation and performance. Each volume is divided into sections on major topics in the field, with explanatory introductory comments, tightly edited leading cases, and extensive notes on key legal issues. Each volume also contains a comprehensive topical index and case, statute, and regulation tables. A vital reference book for all contract attorneys.

A History of Government Contracting: 1754–1980 **(1992).** *James F. Nagle.* xvi + 575 pp.

In this far-ranging chronicle, noted procurement write and scholar James F. Nagle traces the evolution of Government contracting over two centuries, from the French and Indian Wars to the creation of the Office of Federal Procurement Policy. His spirited recounting lends insight into perennial issues at the heart of procurement: the make-or-buy dilemma, the search for a contract that will yield an "ideal" business relationship, and the American public's love–hate relationship with the military–industrial complex. The narrative also reveals the origins of government contracting conventions such as sealed bidding, fixed-price contracting, and the use of standard forms. Readers already familiar with military contracting will particularly value Nagle's account of the fascinating but less well-known history of civilian contracting, as told here in accounts of activities of the Post Office, the Treasury Department, the Bureau of Reclamation, and the National Aeronautics and Space Administration.

Monographs

Monograph No. 4—*Contract Interpretation and Defective Specifications* (2d ed., 1975)

Monograph No. 11—*Labor Standards and Equal Employment* (1971)

Monograph No. 12—*Two Step Formal Advertising* (1979)

Monograph No. 13—*Specifications in Government Contracts* (1980)

For more information contact:

GW–Government Contracts Program
2100 Pennsylvania Avenue, N.W., Suite 250
Washington, DC 20037-3202
(202) 223–2770